THE SEX OFFENDER

THEORETICAL ADVANCES, TREATING SPECIAL POPULATIONS AND LEGAL DEVELOPMENTS

VOLUME III

Edited by
Barbara K. Schwartz, Ph.D.

 **Civic Research Institute**
4490 U.S. Route 27 • P.O. Box 585 • Kingston, NJ 08528

Printed in the United States of America

Library of Congress Cataloging in Publication Data
The sex offender: Volume III: Theoretical advances, treating special poplulations, and legal developments/Barbara K. Schwartz

ISBN 1-887554-11-4

Library of Congress Catalog Card Number 95-70893

To the Survivors—especially Sarah

Preface

The preceding volumes of *The Sex Offender* have been well received by the sex offender treatment and supervisory community. It has been the intent of the authors and editors to provide practical information that can inform the work of those dealing with this challenging population. Models presented in these works have been used around the world to develop treatment programs and assist judges and probation and parole officers in making their difficult decisions. It is hoped that this volume will further enhance that base of knowledge. A number of chapters in this volume have been chosen because they present controversial opinions. These are meant to challenge the reader to look at new approaches or reaffirm their traditional way of operating after consideration of alternative ways. Therefore, although some of these chapters do not reflect the opinion of the editors, they are set forth here as food for thought.

Many individuals have contributed to production of this work. The editor thanks the many authors who have contributed chapters. Associate Publisher Deborah Launer and line editor Lori Jacobs have had to wade their way through this volume coping with all the details of putting separate articles into a unified, grammatically correct book. Publisher Art Rosenfeld's interest in criminal justice has enhanced the amount of research and information available to the professional working with the offender population. The Association for the Treatment of Sexual Abusers through its annual conference has provided the primary motivation for much of this research. I would also like to thank colleagues Henry R. Cellini, Ph.D., Roger Smith, D.Cr., Rob Freeman-Longo, Nancy Steele, John Bergman, Anita Schlank, Ph.D., and Fran Henry, for their continued efforts to improve the management of this population. To Susan Wayne, M.S.W., Greg Canfield, M.S.W., and John Cusack, Ph.D. of Justice Resource Institute go my thanks for their moral support. To Robert, Randy, Debra, Bill, Tim, Nancy, Mike, and their teams along with David, Dennis, and Mary goes my appreciation for their hard work. To those in Corrections Departments throughout the country who have supported sex offender treatment, especially Tim App of Massachusetts, goes my admiration for their perseverence. To the staff and boys of Cliff House goes my appreciation for teaching me about adolescent sex offenders. Finally, thanks to my family and especially my husband, Ed, for support and patience, and to Thomas, my cotherapist.

Barbara K. Schwartz
January 1999

About the Authors

Barry Anechiarico, L.I.C.S.W.

Barry Anechiarico, M.S.W., L.I.C.S.W. is the Clinical Director of the Counseling and Psychotherapy Center in Needham, Massacusetts. The center has been in operation since 1989 and is a community-based sex offender and domestic violence treatment program providing services throughout New England and California. Mr Anechiarico previously treated sex offenders at the Massachusetts Treatment Center for Sexually Dangerous Persons.

D. Anderson, M.A.

Dana Anderson earned her B.A. (Hons.) at the University of Waterloo and her M.A. at Queen's University in Kingston, Ontario. She is working on her Ph.D. under the supervision of William Marshall, Ph.D. She is currently the Director of the Sexual Offenders' Treatment Program at Kingston Penitentiary (a maximum-security federal penitentiary). She has treated sexual offenders of all security levels within the Canadian federal prison system. She has made several conference presentations and has published articles in refereed journals, books, and one coauthored book on the treatment of sex offenders.

Jocelyn Aubut, M.D.

Jocelyn Aubut is a psychiatrist. He is Associate Professor at the Medical School of the University of Montreal. During the last twenty years he worked in clinical practice with sexual aggressors at the Institut Philippe Pinel de Montreal.

Carol Ball, Ph.D.

Carol Ball received her Ph.D. in counseling psychology from Indiana State University. She is one of the founding partners of New England Forensic Associates. Dr. Ball has many years of experience working with victims of physical and sexual abuse, as well as with offenders. In 1977, in Fort Wayne, Indiana, she developed and founded the first Shelter for Woman Victims of Violence and was its Executive Director for four years. Her interest in this area of community concern has continued. She provides treatment for women in abusive relationships, and she has testified as an expert in cases that have raised the issue of the Battered Woman's Syndrome. In addition, she has also worked extensively with offender populations and has consulted to correctional systems at both the state and federal level. Dr. Ball has been at the forefront of developing innovative approaches to the comprehensive treatment and management of sexual compulsive disorders and is on the national Board of Directors of the Association for the Treatment of Sexual Abusers (ATSA). She currently is an Attending Psychologist at McLean Hospital and holds a faculty appointment in the Department of Psychiatry, Harvard University Medical School.

Jon M. Barnes, M.A.

Jon M. Barnes received his M.A. from the University of Louisville in 1994, where he is presently completing his doctorate in clinical psychology. He has worked with sex offenders in the Kentucky Department of Corrections' Sex Offender Treatment Program since 1994 and has served as supervisor of the Kentucky State Reformatory program site since 1995. He also works with female offenders at the Kentucky Correctional Institute for Women, and with juvenile offenders and families affected by incest at the Family Place in Louisville. Mr. Barnes is a part-time instructor at the University of Louisville. He has presented at a number of state and national conferences and has coauthored several articles and book chapters.

Scott Blankenship, M.S.W.

Scott Blankenship is a licensed clinical social worker in the states of New York and New Jersey. He is the author of *Figuring It Out Fast: The Family's Best Approach to Nursing Homes* (1997). He received his B.S. in psychology from Louisiana State University and an M.S.W. degree from Southern University of New Orleans. He has treated sex offenders at the Justice Resource Institute at the Massachusetts Treatment Center and is currently specializing in operating a therapeutic community for sex offenders at the Adult Diagnostic and Treatment Center in Avenel, New Jersey.

Julie Brown, L.I.C.S.W.

Julie Brown received her B.A. from Roger Williams University and her M.S.W. from Boston University. She has worked with developmentally disabled students at Swansea Woods School, a program of the Justice Resource Institute. She recently launched an initiative to bring specialized support services to programs dealing with developmentally disabled sex offenders in Rhode Island. She is currently Director of Integrated Clinical Services, a Justice Resource Institute program for outpatient adult developmentally disabled sex offenders. She has authored articles, book chapters, and conference presentations on this population.

Kurt Bumby, Ph.D.

Kurt Bumby is a forensic clinical psychologist specializing in the assessment and treatment of sexual offenders. He is currently employed by the Missouri Division of Youth Services and also serves as the Director of Sexual Offender Services at Behavioral Health Concepts in Columbia, Missouri. Dr Bumby is a Clinical Assistant Professor of Psychiatry at the University of Missouri-Columbia School of Medicine. His clinical experiences have included state and federal correctional systems, forensic hospitals, and juvenile justice agencies. He has published journal articles and book chapters and presented at national and international conferences on sexual offenders and other forensice topics. Dr Bumby is a clinical member of the Association for the Treatment of Sexual Abusers, where he serves as Missouri's public policy representative. Beyond sexual offender management, his professional interests include child maltreatment, patricide and juvenile delinquency.

Henry R. Cellini, Ph.D.

Henry R. Cellini received his doctorate in counseling psychology from Southern Illinois University. He is the president of TriCorps, a consulting company specializing in providing training and treatment materials related to corrections, drugs, gangs, violence, and sexual assault. He has co-edited Volumes I and II of *The Sex Offender* and authored *Alcohol, Tobacco and Other Drugs of Abuse,* along with numerous articles and book chapters. He has consulted with programs throughout the country and most recently with the Illinois Sexually Violent Predator Program.

Terry D. Childers, L.I.C.S.W.

Terry D. Childers is a Senior United States Probation Officer in Chicago, Illinois. He specializes in the investigation, supervision, and management of mentally ill offenders and sex offenders. He has been active in developing mental health training and policy for the Federal Judicial Center and the Adminstrative Office of the United States courts. A licensed clinical social worker, Mr. Childers currently serves on several federal task forces focusing on treatment and registration of sex offenders. Prior to his appointment as a U.S.Probation Officer, he was a Japanese linguist with the U.S. Army Security Agency. He received his B.A. and M.S.W. from the University of Illinois. He has presented papers at numerous professional meetings and has taught criminal profiling with the FBI. Along with numerous professional papers, he has written a novel and a sceenplay about the U.S. Probation System. Mr. Childers is Adjunct Professor of Criminal Justice at Loyola University.

Collette L. Corcoran, M.Ed.

Collette L. Corcoran is the family treatment coordinator for High Point in Cooper City, Florida. She also works in the area of substance abuse. Currently, in addition to her clinical work, she is pursuing a law degree with the ultimate goal of doing research in forensic psychology. She has done numerous presentations on juvenile and adult sex offenders. Her research interests include sexual assault, psychology resilience, and the law.

Lisa L. Coston, M.S.

Lisa L. Coston graduated from Indiana State University with dual M.S. degrees in Criminology and Agency Counseling. She has worked extensively as a therapist with both perpetrators and survivors of sexual abuse. She has presented nationally on the topic of sexual abuse. For five years she worked at the Gibault School for Boys in the ISIS Unit for adolescent sex offenders. Currently she is employed as a Specialist for the Sexual Abuse Family Treatment and Intervention Program. She coordinates and co-facilitates the intensive outpatient program for adolescent and adult sexual offenders.

David P. Fago, Ph.D.

David P. Fago is Co-Director of the Maryland Institute for Individual and Family Therapy and is a faculty member in the Department of Psychology at the University of Maryland, College Park. His research interests include the neuropsychology of learning, the developmental trajectory of psychopathology, and the uses and misuses of forensic assessment. He is an active clinician and evangelist for relevant research conducted in clinical settings. He was educated at Boston College and the University of Maryland.

Y. M. Fernandez, M.A.

Y. M. Fernandez received her B.A. (Hons.) and her M.A. from Queen's University in Kingston, Ontario. She is currently in her third year of a Ph.D. program in Clinical

Forensic Psychology at Queen's University under the supervision of William Marshall, Ph.D. In addition to her studies, she is a therapist in the Sex Offender Program at Bath Institution (a medium-security federal penitentiary). She is an active researcher who currently has several presentations at international conferences and fifteen publications, including one coauthored book and one co-edited book.

Brian M. Flaherty, M.L.S.

Brian M. Flaherty, M.L.S., received his undergraduate degree from Tufts University in 1989 and his Master's of Library Science from Simmons College in 1995. He has worked on several Civic Research Institute projects, including *Sex Offender Registration and Community Notification: A "Megan's Law" Sourcebook*, and contributes reviews of recent literature to *Correctional Law Reporter* and *Offender Programs Report*.

Billy Franklin, B.S.

Billy Franklin received a B.S. degree from the University of San Diego and completed a three-year Law Reader Program. He is a graduate of the National Training Center of Lie Detection. He is a licensed polygrapher and a licensed private investigator in both Virginia and North Carolina. He is also a licensed attorney in Virginia. He is a former Special Agent for the U.S. Army Counter Intelligence Corps and has been elected a Distinguished Fellow by the Academy of Certified Polygraphers. Currently he is president of Franklin Security Systems and Director of the Virginia School of Polygraph.

Pryor Green, B.S.

Pryor Green received his B.S. from Virginia Commonwealth University. He has been a probation officer since 1984 and has specialized in sex offender supervision since 1993. He coordinates sex offender evaluations and serves as a therapist with the Newport News Sex Offender Community Protection Program. In 1996 he served as the Co-Chairman of the Assessment and Treatment Subcommittee for the Virginia Megan's Law Task Force. He is a consultant for the Sex Offender Evaluation and Treatment Training Program, which is designed to satisfy the educational requirements for the Virginia Sex Offender Treatment Providers' Certification.

Donald R. Hands, Ph.D.

Donald R. Hands is a psychologist with six years of experience treating sex offenders with the Wisconsin Department of Corrections. For the previous six years he directed an inpatient center for impaired religious professionals and worked with more than 400 clergy. He is a graduate of Columbia University and the State University of New York at Buffalo.

R. Karl Hanson, Ph.D.

R. Karl Hanson received his Ph.D. in clinical psychology from the University of Waterloo (Ontario) in 1986. He conducted clinical work with sex offenders for the Ontario Ministry of Correctional Services and the Clarke Institute of Psychiatry before starting his current position as Senior Research Officer with the Department of the Solicitor General Canada in 1991. Dr. Hanson is also an Adjunct Research

Professor in the Psychology Department of Carleton University. His research has focused on the prediction of sexual offender recidivism and the development of new assessment measures for sexual offenders and male batterers.

Andrew J. R. Harris, M.Sc.

Andrew J. R. Harris is a Senior Policy Analyst, Corrections Directorate, Solicitor General Canada. He specializes in managing large field-team research projects such as the Survey of Mentally Disordered Offenders (1992), the Dangerous Offender Review Project (1996), and the Dynamic Predictors of Sexual Reoffense Project (1998). Mr. Harris's Ph.D. thesis explores the intersection of Hare's (1995) conception of psychopathy and measures of sexual deviance. Mr. Harris lectures on prison history and design, the assessment of sexual preference and managing the developmentally delayed sex offender.

Laura Heinz, B.A.

Laura Heinz received her B.A. degree from Lakehead University and has recently begun her doctoral studies at the University of Saskatchewan in the Applied Social Psychology program. Her current research activities include the evaluation of young offender services and developing community programs for high-risk youths.

Brian J. Holmgren, J.D.

Brian J. Holmgren joined the staff of the American Prosecutors Research Institute National Center for Prosecution of Child Abuse as a Senior Attorney in November, 1995. Prior to that he was an Assistant District Attorney in Kenosha County, Wisconsin, for ten years where he directed their sensitive crimes unit. As an Assistant District Attorney Mr. Holmgren tried more than 160 jury trials, including 125 felonies and handled hundreds of child abuse cases. He was a board member of the Wisconsin chapter of the American Professional Society on the Abuse of Children and a frequent lecturer at statewide and national conferences. Mr. Holmgren received his undergraduate degree from the University of Chicago in 1981 and his law degree from Vanderbilt University in 1985. Mr. Holmgren's duties at the Center include providing training and assistance to prosecutors and other professionals across the country concerning the investigation and prosecution of child maltreatment cases. He is also actively involved in research and writing on various topics involving child abuse prosecution. The Center also provides technical assistance and research on the current issues facing professionals in responding to child abuse.

Scott A. Johnson, M.A., L.P.

Scott A. Johnson is a licensed psychologist who has worked with physical and sexual abusers for many years. He is currently employed with the Minnesota Department of Corrections as a Sex Offender Assessor and Civil Commitment Review Coordinator. Mr. Johnson is the first person to use the Abel Assessment in the State of Minnesota, as well as in a correctional setting. His work experience includes working with sex offenders at Alpha Services Industries, in Minneapolis, Minnesota and at Project Pathfinder in St. Paul, Minnesota. Mr. Johnson has spoken at national and international conferences on the issues of sexual and physical assault. He is the author of *When "I Love You" Turns Violent* (New Horizon Press,

1993) and *Man to Man: When Your Partner Says No* (Safer Society Press, 1992). His current research includes "The Overlooked Force in Sexual Assault," which identified the types of psychological and physical force sex offenders used in the commission of their offenses, which will be published in an upcoming issue of *The Journal of Offender Rehabilitation*. He is also currently working on research comparing the Abel Assessment with Plethysmography. Mr. Johnson authored a chapter included in Volume II of *The Sex Offender* (Civic Research Institute, 1997). His upcoming book is titled *A Handbook for Mental Health and Law Enforcement Personnel Working With Sex Offenders*. He is on the editorial board for the journal *Acta Sexologica*.

David Kalal, M.A.

David Kalal received his B.A. in psychology from the University of California at Santa Barbara. He began work on his Ph.D. at Hahnemann University in Philidaphia. He has worked at Project STOP (Sex Offender Treatment with Persons with Mental Retardation) and completed his master's thesis on cognitive distortions in mentally retarded sex offenders. Currently he is completing his dissertation on impulsivity in pedophiles and is doing his predoctoral internship at Eastern Pennsylvania Psychiatric Institute.

Joyce F. Lakey, M.A.

Joyce F. Lakey received her A.B. degree in journalism from Indiana University and her M.A. in agency counseling from Indiana State University. She worked with adolescent male sex offenders for eleven years at the Gibault School for Boys. She has authored numerous publications in the field. She recently retired and is currently working on an anecdotal account of her experiences as a therapist with this population.

Calvin Langton, M.A.

Calvin Langton received his M.A. in psychology from the University of Edinburgh, Scotland. He is currently a research associate with the Sexual Behaviors Clinic, Forensic Program, Clarke Division, Centre for Addiction and Mental Health. He is a doctoral candidate in medical science at the University of Toronto, Ontario. His research interests include information processing approaches to sexually assaultive behavior, cognition and affect in sexual offenders, and the development and evaluation of treatment interventions.

Alan Listiak, Ph.D., L.I.C.S.W.

Alan Listiak received his doctorate in sociology from the University of Toronto in 1981. Through a research interest in sexual health he became involved in work with sexual abusers. He developed an interest in therapeutic work with this population and obtained licensure as an independent clinical social worker. He has worked with sexual offenders since 1982 in outpatient, residential, and correctional settings. He has also consulted with local agencies, counties, and state agencies regarding developmentally delayed offenders, educational evaluation, and prevention programming. Since 1992, Dr. Listiak has worked for the Minnesota Department of Corrections in the Sex Offender/Chemical Dependency Services Unit. He recently developed legislatively mandated standards for the residential treatment of sex offenders in Minnesota that take effect in 1998. He will monitor the implementation of the standards and their impact on treatment services in Minnesota. His current research interest is the role of sexual motivation in sexual offending and exploring the differences between sex offenders and non-sex offenders.

Jan Looman, M.A.

Jan Looman received his M.A. in psychology from Queen's University in Kingston, Ontario, Canada and is currently working on completing his Ph.D. He has worked in the assessment and treatment of sex offenders since 1987 and is currently the program director of the Sexual Offender Treatment Program at the Regional Treatment Centre in Kingston, Ontario. His research interests include psychopathy, sexual deviance, and fantasies.

W. L. Marshall, Ph.D.

William L. Marshall received his B. Psych. from the University of Western Australia, an M.A. from the University of London, and his Ph.D. from Queen's University. He is currently a Professor in Psychology, a Professor in Psychiatry, and an Associate Professor in Urology at Queen's University in Ontario, Canada and Director of Sex Offender Programs at Bath Institute (a medium-security federal penitentiary). He has been instrumental in establishing several prison and community treatment programs for sexual offenders in Canada and in six other countries. He has written 190 publications, including more than 40 book chapters. He is or has been on the editorial board of fourteen international scientific journals. He is a recipient of the Lifetime Achievement Award of the Association for the Treatment of Sexual Abusers and is that organization's President-Elect.

Patrick McGuffin, Ph.D.

Patrick McGuffin received his doctorate in 1987 from Temple University. He is currently Professor and Director of the Master's Degree Program in the Department of Clinical and Health Psychology at MCP Hahneman University. He is also Co-Director of Project STOP, an assessment and treatment program for persons with mental retardation who display inappropriate sexual behaviors as well as Co-Director of Project Challenge, an assessment and therapy program for children and adults with mental retardation.

Andre McKibben, M.Sc.

Andre McKibben has an M.Sc. in sexology. During the past twenty years, he has been involved in both research and clinical practice with sexual aggressors at the Institut Philippe Pinel de Montreal.

Alexis O. Miranda, Ph.D.

Alexis O. Miranda is Assistant Professor in the Department of Counselor Education at the Florida Atlantic University specializing in adult and juvenile sex offenders. He has done numerous presentations and published widely on this population. He also consults with private agencies on sex offenders and their evaluation and treatment as well as on treatment efficacy.

Arthur M. Nezu, Ph.D.

Arthur Nezu is currently a Professor of Clinical and Health Psychology, Medicine and Public Health at MCP Hahnemann University, where he also serves as Senior Associate Dean for Research and Associate Director of the Center of Mind/Body Studies. He is a fellow of the American Psychological Association, the American Psychological Society, the American Association of Applied and Preventive Psychology, and the Society of Behavioral Medicine. He serves on the editorial boards of numerous journals including the *Journal of Consulting and Clinical Psychology* and is the past editor of the *Behavior Therapist.* He has more than 100 publications on a variety of health and mental health topics, and his work has been translated into Japanese, Dutch, Spanish, French, and Italian. He is the President-elect of the Association of Behavior Therapy and is the codirector of Project STOP, a sex offender treatment program.

Christine Maguth Nezu, Ph.D.

Christine Maguth Nezu is currently Associate Professor of Clinical and Health Psychology and Medicine as well as the Director of the Center for Mind/Body Studies at MCP Hahneman University. She has authored or coauthored more than fifty publications concerning aggressive and violent behavior, behavioral medicine, clinical decision-making, psychopathology, and developmental disabilities. She has served as the principal investigator for Project STOP, a clinical demonstration outpatient program for intellectually disabled sex offenders, since 1991. She is currently an associate editor for the *Behavior Therapist*, serves on the editorial boards of *Cognitive and Behavioral Practice* and *Holistic Health* and is a grant reviewer for the National Institutes of Health.

William F. Northey Jr., Ph.D.

William F. Northey Jr. is an Assistant Professor in Human Development and Family Studies in the School of Family and Consumer Sciences at Bowling Green State University. Formerly he was the Co-Project Director of the Juvenile Sex Offender Project at Kansas State University. He has also directed a program for juvenile delinquents and an adolescent emergency unit in Baltimore, Maryland. He received his B.A. from the University of Delaware in Individual and Family Studies and his M.S. in Marriage and Family Therapy from the University of Maryland-College Park. He has presented at numerous conferences and has published journal articles and book chapters.

Marc Ouimet, Ph.D.

Marc Ouimet has a Ph.D. in criminology. He is Associate Professor at the School of Criminology at the University of Montreal. During the past fifteen years, he has published a number of papers on the subjects of comparative criminal statistics and criminal careers

Rebecca Palmer, M.S.

Rebecca Palmer is currently the Director of Programs and Administration at the Center for Contextual Change, Ltd. She did her postgraduate training in marriage and family therapy at the Institute for Juvenile Research at the University of Illinois where she currently serves as adjunct faculty in the Family Systems Program. She is also adjunct faculty at the Illinois School for Professional Psychology where she teaches sex offender treatment and couples and family therapy. She has trained nationally in the area of sex offender treatment and assessment and working with sexually reactive children as well as sexually assaultive clergy.

Yves Paradis, M.Sc.

Yves Paradis has a M.Sc. in sexology. His main clinical activities include phallometric assessment and outpatient treatment of sexual aggressors.

Bruno Pellerin, M.Sc.

Bruno Pellerin has an M.Sc. in criminology. His main clinical activities include phallometric assessment and outpatient treatment of sexual aggressors.

Katherine D. Peterson, Psy.D.

Katherine D. Peterson received her degrees from the University of Alaska and Spalding University. She is a licensed psychologist who has specialized in offender treatment in three state correctional systems. Since 1988, she has been administrator of the Kentucky Justice Cabinet's Sex Offender Treatment Program. Dr. Peterson is a part-time instructor at the University of Louisville. She maintains a private practice and has consulted nationally with correctional systems and training institutes.

Andy Pond, L.I.C.S.W.

Andy Pond began working with developmentally disabled adolescents in 1986 as residential director of Justice Resource Institute's Swansea Woods School. A graduate of the Boston University School of Social Work, he has specialized in working with developmentally disabled sex offenders. He is currently a Division Director for the Justice Resource Institute, overseeing programs for adults and children with a variety of problems.

Steven G. Price, M.A.

Steven G. Price received his M.A. from the University of Massachusetts. He studied pastoral counseling at the Worcester Pastoral Counseling Center. Currently he is Clinical Director of Lake Grove School, a residential treatment program for adolescent sex offenders. He has also worked with adult sex offenders at the Massachusetts Treatment Center. He has consulted on the issues of program development for juvenile offenders and has presented at national and international conferences on the treatment of seriously conduct-disordered juvenile sex offenders.

Jean Proulx, Ph.D.

Jean Proulx has a Ph.D. in psychology. He is Associate Professor at the School of Criminology at the University of Montreal. He has been involved during the last fifteen years in both research and clinical practice with sexual aggressors incarcerated in the Institut Philippe Pinel de Montreal and the Regional Reception Center of the Correctional Services of Canada. He has published more than fifty papers and book chapters in French and English on the subject of sexual aggression.

Steven P. Sawyer, M.S.S.W.

Steven P. Sawyer received his M.S.S.W. from the University of Wisconsin-Madison. He is a Clinical Social Worker and Certified Group Psychotherapist. He has provided evaluation and treatment services to adult sex offenders for sixteen years. He is a founding board member and Executive Director of Project Pathfinder, Inc. in St. Paul, Minnesota. He has presented locally, nationally, and internationally on the treatment of sex offenders, treatment outcome, and original research on men who use prostitutes.

Anita Schlank, Ph.D.

Anita Schlank received her doctorate in clinical psychology with a specialty in forensic psychology from the University of Nebraska at Lincoln. She has treated sex offenders in Nebraska, Florida, and Vermont and is currently the Clinical Director of the Minnesota Sexual Psychopathic Personality Treatment Center.

Fred Schmidt, Ph.D.

Fred Schmidt is a clinical psychologist who has been actively involved in both individual and group work with adolescent sex offenders since 1990. His clinical and research interests also include young offenders, children with disruptive behavior disorders, and treatment outcome evaluation of mental health programs. He currently works at the Lakehead Regional Family Centre and holds an adjunct faculty position in the psychology department at Lakehead University in Thunder Bay, Ontario.

Barbara K. Schwartz, Ph.D.

Barbara K. Schwartz received her degrees from the University of New Mexico and the New School for Social Research in New York City. She has been treating sex offenders since 1971 and has directed statewide sex offender treatment programs for Departments of Correction in New Mexico, Washington State, and Massachusetts. She is currently the Clinical Director of Justice Programs for Justice Resource Institute of Boston and in that capacity directs programs for involuntarily committed Sexually Dangerous Persons as well as incarcerated offenders throughout Massachusetts. She is the clinical consultant to Cliff House School, a residential program for adolescent sex offenders. She has consulted throughout the country for the National Institute of Corrections and the Center for Sex Offender Management as well as in Canada and Israel. She has authored, edited, and co-edited five major books in the field of sex offender treatment, as well as numerous articles and conference presentations.

Richard K. Seely, L.I.C.S.W.

Richard K. Seely is the Director of Community Relations at the Leo A. Hoffman Center, a residential treatment program for adolescent male sex offenders and adolescent girls. He began his career as the Educational Director at the Youth Vocational Center, a Department of Corrections Camp for delinquent youths. He became the Educational Director at the Minnesota Security Hospital in 1970 and subsequently served as Staff Coordinator of two special projects related to treating sex offenders. He was founder and director of the Intensive Treatment Program for Sexual Aggressives from 1975 through 1991. He was the Curriculum Coordinator for the new Sex Offender Program at the Minnesota Security Hospital from 1991 to 1996. He has consulted widely on the treatment of sex offenders, appearing on national television and presenting at numerous conferences. He has served on the Minnesota Attorney General's Task Force on Violence Against Women. He is on the adjunct faculty at Gustavus Adolphus College.

Theoharis K. Seghorn, L.P.

Theo Seghorn, a licensed psychologist with more than thirty-five years of experience in forensic psychology, has been qualified as an expert in numerous civil and criminal court jurisdictions through New England and in the federal district court. Trained in both adult and child psychology, he has extensive experience in the assessment of disabilities and in the emotional and psychological consequences of trauma, injury, and disability. During twenty years as a consultant to the Social Security Disability Administration, he evaluated more than 2,000 neurological and psychiatric disability cases. Dr. Seghorn formerly was clinical director of a major, statewide treatment program for sexually dangerous offenders. Since cofounding New England Forensic Associates in 1985, he has specialized in diagnostic evaluations and case consultation in civil, probate, and criminal forensic cases and in the treatment of sexually acting-out persons and impaired professionals. He has presented at national conferences. He has taught on the subjects of rapists and child molesters, profiling, and assessment and treatment of sex offenders. He formerly served on the U.S. Surgeon General's Task Force on Violence in America. He also serves on the Board of Directors of the Massachusetts Association for the Treatment of Sex Abusers (MATSA) and formerly edited the *ATSA Forum,* the international organization's quarterly newsletter.

Jim Shevich, B.A.

Jim Shevich received his B.A.in psychology from the University of Minnesota-Duluth. He has worked with the Minnesota Department of Corrections for eleven years. In this time he has worked both as an Assistant Group Supervisor and a Corrections Program Therapist in two separate programs serving all types of offenders. In 1994 he was instrumental in the development/design and implementation of a program track (Alternatives) for intellectually disabled/socially inadequate sex offenders. He is currently a therapist working with this population at the Sex Offender Program at the Minnesota Correctional Facility-Willow River/Moose Lake.

Nancy Stacken, M.A., L.P.

Nancy Stacken received her undergraduate degree from the University of St. Thomas and her master's from Antioch College. She has been involved in the development and implementation of sex offender programs in the Minnesota Department of Corrections and the Minnesota Department of Human Services and was involved in the early development of the program for Minnesota's Sexual Psychopathic Personality Treatment Center. Currently she is the director of the Sex Offender Program at the Minnesota Correctional Facility-Willow River/Moose Lake.

Ben D. Taylor, M.A.

Ben D. Taylor has ten years of experience working with adolescent and adult sex offenders in both forensic and outpatient settings. He currently has a private practice in West Palm Beach, Florida. He is particularly interested in the dynamics of the families of sex offenders. He consults widely with the courts on the dynamics of sexual abuse.

Kathleen W. Tenukas-Steblea, L.I.C.S.W.

Kathleen W. Tenukas-Steblea is a licensed social worker with a private practice in West Palm Beach, Florida specializing in the treatment of adult and adolescent sex

offenders. She has consulted with the courts on this population and has designed and
implemented programs for juvenile sex offenders and their families.

Nancy H. Walbek, Ph.D, L.P.

Nancy H. Walbek is a research psychologist at the St. Peter Regional Treatment
Center. She was raised in New York, attended Antioch College in Ohio, and earned
M.A. and Ph.D. degrees in the Psychology Department of Northwestern University.
After several years of teaching psychology at Union College, she completed a post-
doctoral internship with Schenectady County Child Guidance Center and Eleanor
Roosevelt Developmental Services in upstate New York. She has worked at Minnesota
Security Hospital since 1977, with primary responsibilities in the areas of program
development, evaluation, and research. Initially, she worked with the Intensive
Treatment Program for Sexual Aggressives which dealt with over 1,000 offenders during these years. The program received a Significant Achievement Award for its innovative treatment from the American Psychiatric Association in 1980. Beginning in
1992, she was centrally involved in the development of the new Minnesota Sex
Offender Program designed to treat individuals committed as sexually dangerous persons and sexual psychopathic personalities. Since that program was moved to north-
ern Minnesota in 1996, most of her energy has been devoted to program development
and evaluation within the general forensic program at Minnesota Security Hospital.
During these years Dr. Walbek has also taught at Gustavus Adolphus College and been
involved in private consulting and clinical work. She has published several articles and
presented at national meetings addressing sex offender evaluation and treatment.

Elizabeth Rahmberg Walsh, J.D., M.L.S.

Elizabeth Rahmberg Walsh is a 1985 graduate of the University of Wyoming
College of Law. She is admitted to practice law in Wyoming and Massachusetts and
has practiced as a prosecuting attorney and as a criminal defense attorney. She is currently a Ph.D. candidate in the School of Criminal Justice at the State University of
New York at Albany. She works as a legal consultant, is editor of *Community
Corrections Report*, is a contributing editor to *Criminal Law Bulletin*, and is an assistant professor of criminal justice and program coordinator of the Undergraduate
Criminal Justice Track at Fitchburg State College in Fitchburg, Massachusetts. She is
married to Jim Walsh and lives in Fitchburg, Massachusetts.

Tony Ward, Ph.D.

Tony Ward currently coordinates the forensic psychology program in the
Department of Criminology at the University of Melbourne, Australia. He was for-
merly Director of Clinical Training at the University of Canterbury, Christchurch,
New Zealand and a research consultant to the Kia Marama Sex Offender Treatment
Program at Rolleston Prison. He has written widely in the area of attachment theory
and relapse prevention with sex offenders.

Sharon M. Williams, Ph.D., C. Psych.

Sharon M. Williams received her B.A. from McGill University and her Ph.D. from
Queens University in Kingston, Ontario. She is the special advisor on sex offender
programs for the Correctional Service of Canada. She is also an Assistant Professor

in the Department of Psychiatry at Queens University. Dr. Williams and her husband, Bill Isaacs, have been training staff on how to survive forcible confinement since 1984. Dr. Williams has recently been involved in the production of "Forcible Confinement: A Survivor's Story," an award-winning staff training video.

James M. Yokley, Ph.D.

James M. Yokley is a clinical psychologist, a member of the medical staff in the Department of Psychiatry at MetroHealth Medical Center, Cleveland, Ohio, and an Assistant Professor at Case Western University School of Medicine. He has expertise in the use of therapeutic community learning experiences and behavior therapy with abusive, addictive (self-reinforcing), criminal problems that are a danger to self or others. Dr. Yokley designed the Treatment for Appropriate Social Control (TASC) program in 1988. The TASC program employs therapeutic community learning experiences in a social responsibility therapy to develop appropriate social behavior control in multiple abusers (i.e., offenders referred for sexual abuse along with other types of abuse such as physical abuse, property abuse, substance abuse, and trust abuse). He is the consulting psychologist at Quest Recovery Services, a drug and alcohol treatment agency that operates two therapeutic communities in the state prison system.

Joan Zorza, J.D.

Joan Zorza is a graduate of Boston University and Boston College School of Law and a member of the bars in New York, Massachusetts, and the District of Columbia. She is the editor of *Sexual Assault Report* and *Domestic Violence Report* and has represented more than 2,000 women and children, often in cases involving child sexual assault allegations. She has been a consultant on family violence to both the American Medical Association and the Family Violence Project of the National Council of Juvenile and Family Court Judges and is a liaison to the Domestic Violence Commission of the American Bar Association. She sits on the board of the National Coalition Against Domestic Violence and is President of the New York Coalition Against Domestic Violence.

Introduction

This is the third volume in a series devoted to bringing the latest research and techniques for working with sex offenders to treatment specialists, prison officials, probation and parole officers, judges, police, and those who work with victims. Since 1992 the authors and editors have studied and written about those they work with in an increasingly repressive environment. At this writing all but one of the states have passed public notification laws. In some states seven year old children could have their pictures posted on buses or on the Internet and be required to register for twenty years. In some states mandatory overrides automatically place the least dangerous offenders on the highest level of notification while overlooking the truly dangerous. Involuntary commitment, low parole rates, and a lack of transitional programs for this population make dealing with these clients increasingly frustrating and dangerous.

Yet within this highly punitive atmosphere, sex offender treatment continues to expand. The Association for the Treatment of Sexual Abusers (ATSA) continues to grow and now has members from around the world. The United States Department of Justice has officially made a commitment to enhance the supervision and treatment of sex offenders. Through funding to the Center for Effective Public Policy, the Center for Sex Offender Management (CSOM) has been established and funded to assist states in pursuing effective management of this population. CSOM has identified mentor sites that can serve as models and training sites. They routinely bring together teams of experts to work on enhancing these models.

STOP IT NOW is a model of an innovative approach to sex offenders. This program which is based in Massachusetts but has operated primarily in Vermont seeks to reach out to individuals who may have offended or thought of offending but have not yet been caught. This approach targets some of the 84% of all sex offenses that are never reported. According to their November, 1998 newsletter, the project began working with media to increase the amount of responsible information on sexual assault. They pursued this through the following approaches:

- Distributed monthly radio public service announcements
- Convinced Vermont major television stations to devote more in-depth coverage to this issue, resulting in thirty-three news programs with an average of five-minute length rather than the former forty-eight seconds.
- Published fifty-nine articles in Vermont newspapers
- Released five op-ed articles to major newspapers
- Increased the complexity of the stories done by Vermont reporters on STOP IT NOW

A helpline was established, targeting adults with sexual behavior problems, families and friends of these individuals and parents of sexually abusing youth. A process was developed by which an anonymous abuser could obtain a confidential assessment. This person would then be referred to an appropriate treatment provider. If an assault had already occurred but could be defined as not presenting a threat to the community, the abuser would be referred to the District Attorney to self-report his or her crime, and hopefully receive a deferred sentence or probation.

STOP IT NOW has conducted an evaluation of its program and has found that individuals who are concerned about their behavior will call the helpline. Ten adults and twenty-nine adolescents have voluntarily sought out treatment. STOP IT NOW has also significantly increased the awareness of sexual abuse in Vermont.

Politicians and public policy directors have long maintained that the public neither supports nor believes in the efficacy of treating sex offenders. However, STOP IT NOW's research has shown that 62% of Vermonters agree that abusers can stop their behavior with appropriate treatment.

More types of sex offenders have emerged as professionals who work with the mentally ill and developmentally disabled recognize these individuals in their populations. Sex offender treatment originated in mental hospitals that housed the early Mentally Disordered Sex Offender Programs. Later a few prisons began to develop programs. In many cases staff members who had worked in these environments opened community-based programs. The first subgroup of sex offenders to be recognized were juveniles who were convicted of sex crimes. There are a growing number of programs, community-based and residential, that specialize in working with youth. Yet many states do not offer specialized sex offender treatment to their incarcerated juvenile sex offenders.

Next therapists began to realize that many of their patients had cognitive deficits that required special approaches. Oregon State Hospital established a highly innovative program for developmentally disabled sex offenders. There are now a number of programs for this population throughout the country.

The vast majority of sex offenders in treatment programs have been men. The public in the past has been reluctant to acknowledge that women can also be sexual abusers although this is a very real fact to all the victims who have experienced molestation by a female. Women are such a minority in correctional institutions that their treatment needs are often overlooked. While a few individual clinicians working in women's prisons have staunchly persisted in treating these sex offenders, there have been few formally organized treatment programs. Yet more resources are now being developed for both adult and juvenile female sex offenders.

Psychiatric hospitals have always housed sexual abusers. One group of sexual abusers in these institutions are those individuals who have been charged with a sex offense but found incompetent to stand trial. Another group has been found not guilty by reason of insanity. Yet another group are mental patients who sexually accost staff and fellow patients but are never charged. With the continuing move to shut down large facilities, administrators are realizing that they have a population of sexually dangerous individuals who rarely have had any offense-specific treatment. Often these individuals could be released to the community if they could learn to control their sexual impulses. Thus programs are having to come to grips with the choice of treating these individuals or continuing to house them indefinitely.

Furthermore programs for emotionally disturbed children of all ages are realizing that they too must cope with sexually aggressive individuals. Children as young as three and four who have been sexually abused may respond by repeating that behavior on others. These sexually reactive youngsters need special treatment as well.

Consequently the field of sex offender treatment is continuing to grow and diversify. Professionals in the field of mental health, mental retardation, child development and those dealing with disabled populations such as the deaf, blind, or orthopedically handicapped are realizing that in their populations there may be individuals who need treatment for sexually inappropriate behavior. Special programs are being developed, and therapists are beginning to specialize in subpopulations.

As mentioned previously, although the field is rapidly expanding to respond to treatment and supervisory needs, public policies are making it increasingly difficult to respond to sex offenders so that public safety is enhanced. Megan's Laws have indeed resulted in increased vigilantism. Sex offenders and their perfectly innocent neighbors have had their homes burned. Families and victims of sex offenders have been held up to public ridicule. Sex offenders have killed themselves and in certain cases reoffended in response to the loss of jobs, homes, and support. Probation and parole officers as well as therapists attempt to help these individuals deal with overwhelming stress. While specialized supervision units have developed significant expertise in overseeing sexual abusers, they are struggling against communities that by and large are actively rejecting these individuals. Some communities including towns in Washington State are attempting to deal proactively with sex offenders living in the community by helping them to find housing and jobs but these examples are few.

Given the trepidation that the general public feels in regard to sex offenders, parole boards may be reluctant to release these individuals on supervision. However, this is often the most dangerous policy that can be pursued. To allow a sex offender to finish his or her sentence means that these individuals will leave prison with no external controls. Pedophiles may move into homes with children. Rapists may immediately begin to drink or take drugs. Relapse Preventions Plans cannot be enforced. States need to either support the decisions of parole boards rather than frighten them into inaction or develop sentence structures that mandate periods of post-release supervision.

Many states have also eliminated sex offenders from pre-release or work release programs. Given public notification laws sex offenders have by far the most difficult time acquiring jobs and housing compared to other types of offenders. Programs which afforded sex offenders the opportunity to get that first job and save enough money to find appropriate housing significantly eased the stress of release. Dumping these individuals unemployed, homeless, and pennyless on the streets can do nothing but increase their desperation. Some of these individuals decide that the only place they can survive is back in prison, and they know exactly how to get back there.

Even agencies dedicated to helping ex-offenders often close their doors to this population. Certainly it is difficult enough to locate a halfway house for ex-offenders within any neighborhood. Additionally public notification laws may quickly let neighbors know if a sex offender is in residence. However, communities must recognize that these individuals are citizens who must live somewhere. Residing in homeless shelters that do not provide a place for the sex offender to find refuge during the day forces these individuals to wander the streets. Hopefully they are looking for work. However, they also may be hanging around playgrounds or stalking women. Citizens are not made safer by creating outcasts who continue to reside in their home towns. However, given the low reoffense rate of the majority of sex offenders (see Chapter 8, in Part 2), these individuals are not doomed to commitment new sex crimes. Given support or at least decreasing harrassment these persons can become contributing citizens.

In another poorly conceived public policy, as of this writing twelve states have adopted involuntary commitment laws that also have questionable impact on public safety. Aside from the civil rights issues raised by these laws, the expense of these programs is overwhelming. The typical treatment program for these individuals costs over $100,000 per year exclusive of the costs associated with the trials to determine whether these individuals are and remain "sexual predators." Furthermore these individuals are highly litigious. In several states including Washington, consent decrees have been ordered by the courts along with the appointment of Special Masters. Inmates in Washington have already been awarded cash settlements. Identifying "sexual predators" is no easy matter and treating this population is a real challenge given their degree of anger and resistance engendered by the commitment process.

Each year more and more sex offenders are receiving treatment, and more criminal justice systems are developing systems for responsibly supervising sex offenders. However, over the past eight years more and more irresponsible public policies have been enacted which are not based in any research or factual basis and may well diminish public safety. Community education such as the type organized by STOP IT NOW may well be one of the few ways that this tide can be redirected.

Table of Contents

PART 1: NEW THEORETICAL ADVANCES

Chapter 1: Social Reconciliation Theory—Developing a New Foundation for Community-Based Responses to Sex Offenders

Chapter 2: A Closer Look at Sex Offender Character Pathology and Relapse Prevention—An Integrative Approach

Chapter 3: Mood, Conflict, and Deviant Sexual Fantasies

Chapter 4: The Relationship Among Empathy, Cognitive Distortions, and Self-Esteem in Sex Offenders

Chapter 5: A Theoretical Model of the Influences of Shame and Guilt on Sexual Offending

Chapter 6: A Self-Regulation Model of the Relapse Process in Sexual Offenders

PART 2: ADMINISTRATION

Chapter 7: Proactivity in the Public Domain—Legislative Advocacy and Dealing With the Media

Chapter 8: Sex Offender Recidivism and Risk Factors in the Involuntary Commitment Process

Chapter 9: Dynamic Predictors of Sex Offense Recidivism—New Data From Community Supervision Officers

Chapter 10: Total Quality Management Implications for Sex Offender Program Planning, Implementation, and Evaluation

Chapter 11: Forcible Confinements and Sexual Assault of Staff in a Correctional Environment

Chapter 12: The Grand Alliance—Probation Officer and Therapist

PART 3: ADOLESCENT SEX OFFENDERS

Chapter 16: Comorbidity of Attention-Deficit/Hyperactivity Disorder in Sexually Aggressive Children and Adolescents

Chapter 17: Inclusion of the Family in the Treatment of Juvenile Sexual Abuse Perpetrators

Chapter 18: Treatment Success of a Community-Based Program for Young Adolescent Sex Offenders

Chapter 19: Using Therapeutic Community Learning Experiences With Youth Sex Offenders

PART 4: DEVELOPMENTALLY DISABLED OFFENDERS

Chapter 20: Creative Therapy With Intellectually Disabled Male Adolescent Sex Offenders

Chapter 21: "They Just Don't Get It"—Essentials of Cognitive-Behavioral Treatment for Intellectually Disabled Sexual Abusers

Chapter 22: Working With the Intellectually Disabled/Socially Inadequate Sex Offender in a Prison Setting

Chapter 23: Therapeutic Community Learning Experiences: Appplication to Mentally Retarded/Developmentally Disabled Sexual Abusers

PART 5: TREATING THE ADULT SEX OFFENDER

Chapter 24: Measuring Treatment Efficacy Through Long-Term Follow-up

Chapter 25: The Application of Therapeutic Community Learning Experiences to Adult Abusers

Chapter 26: The Measurement of Sexual Preference—A Preliminary Comparison of Phallometry and the Abel Assessment

Chapter 27: Sex Education and Sexually Explicit Media in Residential Treatment Programs for Sex Offenders

Chapter 28: Diagnosis and Treatment of Exhibitionism and Other Sexual Compulsive Disorders

Chapter 29: Beyond the Cloister— Shamed Sexuality in the Formation of Sex-Offending Clergy

PART 6: DIFFERENT VIEWS ON DENIAL

Chapter 30: Issues in the Assessment of Sexual Offenders' Cognitive Distortions

Chapter 31: Cognitive Distortions in Sexual Offenders With Intellectual Deficits

Chapter 32: The Politics of Denial—A Postmodern Critique

Chapter 33: Why Courts Are Reluctant to Believe and Respond to Allegations of Incest

PART 7: LEGAL ISSUES

Chapter 34: Civil Commitment of Sexually Violent Predators

Chapter 35: Update on Megan's Law

Chapter 36: Non-*Hendricks*-Related Constitutional Challenges to Sexually Violent Predator Statutes

Chapter 37: Forging New Alliances—Proposals for Change in Managing Sex Offenders Within the Criminal Justice System

Part 1

New Theoretical Advances

Public notification, involuntary commitments, abolishment of transitional programs: "three" or "two" or "one strikes, you're out." These are the current responses to sexual assault. As opposed to the chapters in this section, these responses are not based on well-thought-out, theoretical approaches. They are based on a need for retribution, ignorance, and politics. Public officials can look "tough on crime" by punishing sex offenders. And what is the outcome of these measures? Increased costs, vigilante responses frequently aimed at innocent victims, and desperation among offenders leading to increased risk of recidivism.

Is the public truly interested in reducing the rate of sexual assault? Communities may be forced to grapple with the reality that public notification has prevented sex offenders from gaining housing and employment and brought humiliation to innocent families and friends, including in many cases, the victims. They may have to recognize that sexual predator laws cost incredible sums of money and often are directed at the wrong individuals. They may have to cope with the fact that long, harsh sentences often discourage reporting.

Steven Price, in his chapter on social reconciliation theory, urges communities to take an alternative approach. Casting offenders out may be a temporary cure, but in most cases they come back. Will they come back as "the stranger"—shunned by neighbors, employers, churches? If these individuals cannot join the mainstream community, they will turn against that community.

Sex offenders are particularly sensitive to community rejection. A number of authors in this section echo a common theme. They all discuss how feelings of shame, loneliness, rejection, and low self-esteem create high-risk situations for sex offenders.

Ironically, these sex offenders, who do such terrible damage to others, are desperate for human connection. Only people who want to be accepted respond with the anger of the rapist or turn to children as the only individuals to whom they can relate. Regardless of the type of sex offender, an underlying theme is the demand that someone, somehow, will be there to meet their needs. Different styles of attachment produce different relations to others.

Barry Anechiarico, in his chapter "A Closer Look at Sex Offender Character Pathology and Relapse Prevention: An Integrative Approach," discusses the need to understand the roots of high-risk situations. He discusses the absolutely vital role of self-esteem; far from merely making one "feel better" about one's self, Anechiarico maintains that self-esteem forms the core of the sense of self and allows for the regulation of energy. Impairment of this function leads to shame, which leads to violence. Therapy must then assist the sex offender in restoring self-esteem and establishing interpersonal connections. The sex offender must learn to recognize when his self-esteem is threatened and incorporate interventions into a relapse prevention plan.

Jan Looman's chapter, "Mood, Conflict and Deviant Sexual Fantasies," also discusses how deviant sexual fantasies have their roots in negative mood states, which may be related to attachment styles. The research discussed in Looman's chapter presents interesting patterns which may surprise some therapists who believe that all sex offenders engage in deviant sexual fantasies. Clearly this has direct implications for treatment.

Y. M. Fernandez, D. Anderson, and W. L. Marshall, in their chapter, "The Relationship Among Empathy, Cognitive Distortions, and Self-Esteem in Sex Offenders, " challenge another basic assumption of sex offender treatment. Most therapists and certainly the general public believe that sex offenders are devoid of empathy for others. However, these authors take a very different perspective. Their research shows that sex offenders are no less empathetic than their normal control group. However, they do show a lack of empathy toward their victims. This finding has led these authors to conclude that the apparent lack of empathy is produced by cognitive distortions which are created to protect self-esteem. This fragile self-esteem is produced by insecure attachment styles. These authors urge therapists to incorporate into sex offender treatment self-esteem enhancement and supportive challenges to the sex offenders' views of their victims.

Kurt M. Bumby, W. L. Marshall, and Calvin M. Langton investigate the degree to which guilt or shame contribute to sexual assault. They suggest that the offender's guilt over specific transgressions should be the focus of treatment.

The final chapter in this section summarizes Tony Ward's alternative relapse prevention model, stating that traditionally relapse prevention has focused on skill deficits. However, sex offenders offend for many reasons. True, some have poor social and stress management skills. However, other sex offenders have excellent social skills but truly believe that it is proper to have sex with children. Others are incredibly impulsive. Still others may choose avoidance strategies, which increase rather than decrease their ability to control their behavior. Ward presents a new relapse prevention cycle based on these assumptions.

The approach to treating sex offenders is being challenged at fundamental levels. Research is suggesting that therapists should consider moving away from highly confrontive styles to more supportive approaches. Basic beliefs about the incompatibility of psychodynamic and cognitive-behavioral approaches, the role of sexually deviant fantasies, and empathy are being challenged. Theorists and therapists need to maintain an open mind and strive to be flexible enough to respond as new ideas and findings remold our field.

Chapter 1

Social Reconciliation Theory—Developing a New Foundation for Community-Based Responses to Sex Offenders

by Steven G. Price, M.A.

Overview

Today public policy appears to respond to the sex offender as some alien species, a group not even entitled to the most basic human rights. This chapter urges an outlook that refuses to dehumanize any individual and encourages a restorative justice approach to this problem.

Introduction

Criminology and other theoretical disciplines involved with issues of criminal justice stand at a crossroads brought on by the movement from "modernity" to "postmodernity." Old styles of thinking about and approaches to the tasks of correction and rehabilitation have been called into serious question. Some have been discarded out-right. Even the usually optimistic Braithwaite (1992) has pointed to these difficulties and where they have brought us:

> The grand 19th century utilitarian doctrines—deterrence, incapacitation, rehabilitation—are manifest failures. The return to classicism in criminolo-gy—the just deserts movement—has been worse than a failure. It has been a disastrous step backward. . . . With rehabilitation and preventive measures having failed, the future of criminology will be to come up with strategies of penal control in increasingly divided societies. (p. 1)

In the face of the failure of utilitarian approaches to rehabilitation and the resul-tant backlash, expressed in the "just deserts" movement, criminology will be, he fears, reduced to a militaristic exercise in control theory. Whether one believes that rehabil-itation theory(s) were ever given a fair trial in American culture is a moot point. The governing public view is that they were, and that they failed; and, further, that their failure is, in part, responsible for the perceived rise in criminal activity—particularly violent crime—in our society. It is this judgment of the failure of "liberal" and "per-missive" approaches to dealing with crime that has provided fuel for the just deserts approach to criminal justice. Nowhere has this thinking been so clearly voiced as in the area of society's response to sex offenders.

The Need for a New Paradigm

The heat generated by highly publicized crimes has only added to the assumptions made by persons in state legislatures as well as the general population that a more rigid approach is needed to resolve these issues. But there are also deep-rooted philo-sophical reasons for this movement. Old values and old structures of all kinds have been challenged by the emergence of a technological society with its resultant para-digmatic "shaking of the foundations. . . . Without systems which impose meaning upon existence humans experience life as 'senselessness' wherein no meaning can be given to innocent suffering, chance events, death and the elements of randomness in the distribution of wealth, power and status" (Morrison, 1994, p. 137).

Technology and social change have run far ahead of the philosophical and theo-logical underpinnings that were once foundational to the structure of society, not just in their response to crime but in their response to other traumas to the social structure as well, such as Vietnam and the AIDS crisis. These have shown that "little in our pre-vious structures of thought has prepared us for life in societies which do not have over reaching master narratives" (Morrison, 1994, p. 150). Theories of criminology need to be placed within an articulated vision of the social order, and for many observers of present-day culture there is none. There is no governing myth, no guiding metaphor, no story of which we may see ourselves as a part. This cynicism is not limited to the field of criminology but is also shared by many struggling with these issues from the perspective of philosophy, psychology, theology, and even the more "concrete" sci-ences. But in that common plight may also lie some hope: "Criminology has the same theoretical ambitions as the disciplines that constitute it and are constituted by it. It is therefore no surprise that important theoretical breakthroughs occur in conjunction with other disciplines" (Ericson & Carriere, 1994, p. 95).

Other disciplines from quantum physics to theology have returned to take a second look at the concept of "interdependence." The notion that all of creation, and from a social standpoint particularly all of humanity, live out lives of interrelatedness is finding new proponents. Exploring this interdependence, philosophers and theologians are discovering new ways to look at the ancient myths and master narratives that provide new foundations for the life and work of those engaged in a variety of endeavors including psychology, public policy, medicine, and scientific research. What would it look like if criminology were to draw from the wisdom of this approach as well?

Master Narrative and Social Imagination

We might start from any number of places in exploring this approach. One of the most fruitful is to return to the issue of master narrative or governing myth. Even here we could move in a number of directions depending on our own cultural bias or history. The Navaho concept of "walking in beauty" and the Eastern understanding of "being in the Tao" could both be pursued toward an understanding of the interrelated nature of the human condition. But as I am a male Anglo-Saxon, raised in and committed to a Judeo-Christian heritage, I offer three brief images: two from scripture and one from Greek mythology, as indicative of the kind of governing narrative that might be explored in support of the type of criminological theory I later seek to propose and apply. The first of these is an Old Testament eschatological vision found in *Isaiah* 43:5-7

> Fear not, for I am with you;
>   I will bring your offspring from
>   the east,
> and from the west I will gather
>   you;
> I will say to the north, Give up,
>   and to the south, Do not withhold;
> bring my sons from afar
>   and my daughters from the end of
>   the earth,
>   every one who is called by my name,
> whom I created for my glory,
> whom I formed and made.

The image is one of restoration, of the gathering of those scattered by calamity and warfare. It is also an image of *family*. Those being brought home are brother and sister to one another, and though the family has been tossed to the four corners of the earth, it will be reunited. The second eschatological image comes from the New Testament book of *Revelation* 22:1-3. It is a description of the New Jerusalem, a city described as one where the gates are never shut, where the emphasis is on welcome rather than on defense. In the New Jerusalem the only reason for not entering would be that one had made a decision for one's self not to do so. "Then he showed me the river of the water of life, bright as crystal flowing from the throne of God and of the Lamb through the middle of the street of the city; also, on either side of the river, the tree of life with its twelve kinds of fruit, yielding its fruit each month; and the leaves of the tree were for the healing of the nations." To speak of the New Jerusalem is to talk about social imagination. It is to imagine a social structure open to anyone, where the symbols for the availability of healing and restoration are also equally available because they are located in the center of the city. No one who desires them is denied accessibility.

To claim these, or any other, eschatological images, as foundational is to state that this is the vision we have of what the future should look like, and the vision of what our work will strive to imitate. To claim these two particular images for the work of criminological theory is to put forth a theory that sees as its goal the gathering in of those who are wounded and scattered by crime's disruptive influence and the making available to all with equity the possibility for healing and restoration.

Finally, we come to a story from Greek mythology which may help us to understand the importance of such care for the life of our society. It is the story of a Greek hero named Philoctetes. Philoctetes' father, Poe'as, lit the funeral pyre of Hercules when no one else would do so—even though Hercules pleaded with them to do so. And, as a gift in response to this act, Hercules gave Poe'as his bow and arrows. Poe'as, in turn, gave them to his son.

Now Philoctetes was part of the expedition that was to attempt to conquer the city of Troy. On the way to Troy, the fleet stopped at Tenedos. Here Philoctetes was bitten on the foot by a serpent. Philoctetes began to cry out with the great pain of this poisonous bite and a severe infection set in which had a foul odor.

Because Philoctetes' cries were so loud, and because the odor of his wound was so offensive to those who sailed with him, they carried Philoctetes to the island of Lemnos where they left him to his fate. And there he stayed, his wound unhealed, suffering in abject misery.

Meanwhile, the Greeks were unable to take the city of Troy, and many were lost in the effort. Finally they captured a Trojan seer named Helenus and found out from him that there were three conditions without which the city could not be taken— one of them was the arrows of Hercules. These arrows were on Lemnos with Philoctetes.

Suddenly everybody became concerned about Philoctetes. He carried with him part of the secret for their victory over this great enemy. So Ulysses and Diaomedes were sent to Lemnos to bring back Philoctetes (and, of course, the bow and arrows of Hercules), and Philoctetes was healed by Macha'on, son of the renowned healer Aesculapius. Now with Hercules' arrows, Philoctetes killed Paris, and with the other two conditions met, and the use of the fabled "Trojan Horse," the city of Troy was taken.

The message of this ancient myth is clear. Those whom we abandon or cast away because of the "stink" they raise may well hold the secrets to our victory. Both victims of crime and perpetrators of crime tend to be rejected by our society. We do not want to be reminded of our own vulnerabilities nor of our own shadow-side potentials for violence and other acts which society deems unfit. And so it is easier to put these folks off somewhere, both literally and figuratively. In doing so we rob ourselves of the gifts they carry—gifts such as an understanding of what causes someone to choose crime, how the experience of victimization affects those choices, and what can we do for one another that will bring healing to the torn fabric of our society.

These are radically different governing narratives than those that have traditionally guided the enterprise of criminology and criminological theory. But perhaps it is time for a radical departure. For the model out of which we work will affect the results we get. If we see offenders as enemies, we will create subcultures of violence among both police and offenders as is consistent with a warfare/siege mentality. However, if we see the offender as "alienated kinfolk" we will get a different result, one less damaging to victims and those tasked with responding to crime along the criminal justice spectrum as well as to offenders.

Application of the New Paradigm

We know that crime tears the fabric of our social structures and the life of our communities. Viewed from the perspective of these guiding images the purpose of criminology is not the creation of strategies of control; rather, from this perspective *criminology has as its primary task the mediation of social reconciliation for the purpose of the restoration of community*. This implies that the task of the criminologist is to seek to discover *why* and *how* the community has been broken and to search for the best means of *restoration*. In doing so, it may join forces with, and draw wisdom from, other disciplines and enterprises that are also engaged in the work of restoration and reconciliation.

Zehr (1990) speaks of the impact of such a paradigm shift in clear and forceful terms. Because of the strength of his presentation, I quote from him at length here:

> Restitution represents recovery of losses, but its real importance is symbolic. Restitution implies an acknowledgment of the wrong and a statement of responsibility. Making right is itself a form of vindication, a form which may promote healing better than retribution. Retribution often leaves a legacy of hatred. Perhaps it is more satisfying as an experience of justice than no justice at all, but it does little to address hostilities. Such hostilities can impede healing. That is the beauty of forgiveness. By addressing hostilities, it allows both the victim and the offender to take control of their own lives. Like reconciliation, however, forgiveness is not easy and cannot be forced. For many an experience of justice is a necessary precondition for forgiveness to occur. For some, forgiveness will not seem possible. . . . Most of us assume that retribution is high on victims' agenda. Most surveys of victims, however, suggest a different picture. Victims are often open to nonincarcerative, reparative sentences—more frequently, in fact, than is the public. Moreover, they often rank rehabilitation for the offender as an important value. Help for the offender, after all, is one way of addressing the problem of safety and the prevention of future wrongs. Victims also need to be empowered. Justice cannot simply be done to and for them. They must feel needed and listened to in the process. Since one dimension of the wrong was that they were robbed of power, one dimension of justice is to return power to them. At minimum, this means they must be a key in determining what their needs are, how they should be met, and when they should be addressed. But victims should have some role in the overall process. (p. 193)

To operate from such a viewpoint is to step out beyond merely seeking to "rehabilitate" or even "reintegrate" individual offenders and to include in the purview of criminology the restoration of victims and others affected by the far-reaching effects of criminal behavior (including family members of both victim and offender as well as members of the larger community). Such a concern with reconciliation and restoration is to openly claim and acknowledge the value to the life of the community of each of these persons. And such a viewpoint involves major changes in the way that both the community and the criminal justice system approach victims and offenders. A radical shift of paradigm is required: "it will treat victims and offenders and citizens rather than as legal subjects, empower communities at the expense of judges. . . . It involves a shift from a liberal to a civic republican frame" (Braithwaite & Daly, 1994, p. 192). It means reclaiming a sense of connectedness and mutual responsibility. It means that communities need to take responsibility for dealing with crime within the social structure as opposed to removing it to the distanced and distancing locale of the courtroom, where the criminal act becomes an issue belonging to the state as opposed to a breach in the social relationship between the offender and the community.

Family Group Conferencing

In their article quoted previously, Braithwaite and Daly (1994) explore how New Zealanders have since 1989 adapted the concept of family group conferences in dealing with juvenile crime. In particular they explore how this model is used with adolescent sex offenders. It is a model adapted from the Maori culture where for centuries it has been used to respond to a variety of offenses including sexual offenses and family violence. In the Maori culture the purpose of such a gathering is to promote the "healing" of social relationships. It is noteworthy that in the effort to deal with one of the most difficult of juvenile justice issues—sexual aggression and misconduct— white New Zealanders (or *Pakeha*) have turned to an ancient governing narrative of a primitive peoples to discover a model for coping with this criminal justice issue. Because the family group conference (FGC), both in its literal expression and in its underlying paradigm, is expressive of much of the thesis of this chapter, I quote from Braithwaite and Daly's description of it at some length:

> After an offense is detected by the state, a youth justice coordinator convenes a conference. Those invited are the offender (let us assume here a male), the boy's family members (often extending to aunts, grandparents, cousins), other citizens who are key supports in the boy's life (perhaps a football coach he particularly respects), the police, the victim, victim supporters, and in some instances, a youth justice advocate. . . . The theory of the FGC is that discussion of the harm and distress caused to the victim and the offender's family will communicate shame to the offender. The assembling of people who care about and respect the offender fosters reintegration (or healing in Maori terms) of social relationships. In a successful conference, the offender is brought to experience remorse for the effects of the crime; *to understand that he or she can count on the continuing support, love and respect of family and friends* [emphasis added]; and to agree on a plan of action to prevent further harm. All conference participants are given the opportunity to explain how the offense affected them and to put forward proposals for the plan of action. *The offender and his or her family members then propose a plan* [emphasis added], which is discussed and modified until it is agreeable to all FGC participants including the police. (p. 193)

This approach defines the crime as a community issue, a wound or a break in the social bond in need of healing. The presence and participation of the youth's friends and family members, especially the assurance of their continuing care, make it possible for him to experience the empathic flood of shame and remorse brought on by understanding the impact of his crime. (Although it is imperative that our society explore the issue of female sexual offenders, that is beyond the scope of this chapter and I refer to offenders as "he" in recognition that most of the offenders who find their way into the criminal justice system are male.) It also moves to destroy the quality of secrecy which is so necessary for sexual deviance in particular to grow. In addition, it is far better to propose the plan of action to the youth and his family, which makes it clear that it is the youth who is responsible for making amends and seeking solutions, and to bring the youth into the positive aspects of promoting the healing of the community instead of casting the youth as a bystander in a drama in which the state will decide needs to be done and what his fate will be. The fact that this plan must be acceptable to all the other FGC participants guarantees a level of quality to that plan.

How different this approach is to the difficulties expressed by the following writers as they discuss the social factors that make psychopathy and delinquency possible within the historical social structures of our time: "Delinquency and delinquent recidivism may be viewed as a consequence of the failure of primary groups to provide the child with appropriate non-delinquent social roles and to exercise social control over the child so these roles are accepted or submitted to in accord with need" (Reiss, 1951, p. 198), whereas the FGC may be viewed as an attempt to provide a "corrective social role model" based on shared community values.

What is proposed is that when a crime is committed, the movement of the community needs to be *toward* rather than away from the victim, the offender, and the rift created in the life of the community by the crime. Such a response affects more than just those directly involved in the FGC. It communicates to the larger, extended community a particular viewpoint about the nature of the community's life together. It communicates this lesson clearly to the peers of the youths involved, defining expectations for behavior and life in the community and outlining publicly and graphically the consequences of failing in that responsibility. As such, it becomes a part of education for life in the community.

> An education for public life would teach us to be supportive of and accountable to one another; to deal creatively with conflicting interests; to understand that we are all in this together, and together we sink or swim. It would do so not by preachment and exhortation but through lived experience. . . . In the process, truth would be served, for truth is a very large matter and we have a better chance of embracing it together than alone. (Palmer, 1986, p. 79)

A criminological theory of social reconciliation takes seriously the message that its application conveys to those who observe it as well as to those who are involved. It is keenly aware of the impact of its application on the social structure of the community and its life together.

On Cape Cod a 13-year-old girl was assaulted and digitally raped by a gang of four boys ranging from 12 to 14 years of age. Though the incident happened off school property during the weekend, two of the boys were immediately suspended from school. Parents held their children at home and expressed their concern about the school's ability to provide for their safety. Somewhere down the road there will be a juvenile hearing and a judge will make decisions about what needs to happen with these adolescent males. In the meantime, their peers gossip, their peer's parents gossip, and the social fabric of this Cape community continues to be torn. Compare this scenario to Braithwaite and Daly's description of a similar incident:

> Another recent Wagga Wagga conference concerned the sexual assault of a 14-year-old girl in a swimming pool by a 14-year-old boy. The victim was most upset by the way the boy had been bragging to his mates, within the victim's hearing, that he had "got one finger in her." The victim was not only re-victimized by this humiliation, but was labeled as a "dobber" (a tattletale) by boys at her school after she reported the incident. Gossip among her classmates was that she "deserved what she got." Dialogue at the conference clarified that this was not the case. It also made it impossible for the offender's father to believe, as he had before the conference, that his son had been singled out unfairly for a bit of "horseplay." Participants at the conference affirmed her "courage" for coming forward in the face of such social pressures. The offender not only apologized to the victim in a meaningful way, but undertook, with five other classmates (one male, four female) who attended the conference, to spread the word among their peers that her conduct was blameless in every respect. In this conference, an exploitative masculinity of 14-year-old boys and an excusing "boys will be boys" fatherly masculinity was confronted by six teenagers and the parents of the victim. Our hypothesis is that this is a better way to confront a misogynist culture than a criminal trial ten years later. (Braithwaite & Daly, 1994, pp. 203–204)

This is not just "early intervention" but an intervention in the life of the culture and the community as well. It is an intervention that moves not just toward community restoration but toward social transformation as well. It utilizes an understanding of the individual's accountability to the larger community as well as specific individuals with whom they may interact. Such an accountability is different from a punishment mentality which reduces compliance with societal norms to a cost-benefit calculation. This approach represents social disappointment that the offender should engage in behavior contrary to a morality which representatives of that society expect him to hold and expresses satisfaction and restorative welcome when the offender has moved to make amends for his criminal conduct.

> The distinction is between shaming that leads to stigmatization—to outcasting, to confirmation of a deviant master status—versus shaming that is reintegrative, that shames while maintaining bonds of respect or love, that sharply terminates disapproval with forgiveness, instead of amplifying deviance by progressively casting the deviant out. Reintegrative shaming controls crime; stigmatization pushes offenders toward criminal subcultures. (Braithwaite, 1989, p. 13)

It is also an approach that gives greater voice to those injured by criminal activity. One of the major complaints of those who work with victims of sexual abuse has long been that the victims emerge from the criminal justice system and the process of a trial further victimized. The process often leaves the victims feeling more afraid, less in control, and sensing that their reputation has suffered more damage possibly than even the offender's. By comparison, the community conference model, if managed well, can give victims a voice, can confront and neutralize the cognitive distortions often used by offenders to justify their behavior, and can return control to the victim in her right to veto any plan of action proposed by the offender until one is reached that is satisfactory. In fact, "in some Maori tribes an accused male abuser would have no right to speak at the conference. Any statements in his defense would have to be made through someone moved to speak on his behalf" (Braithwaite & Daly, 1994, p. 194). The needs of the offender are also addressed in that this process calls forth and empowers "communities of concern" (Braithwaite & Daly 1994) that will involve themselves in not only care for the victim but care for the offender resulting in ritual termination of shame once the standards of response to his crime have been met. Such a response to the offender will not necessarily guarantee a successful outcome to this attempt to intervene in this destructive behavioral pattern, but it is clear that one is more likely to respond when an opportunity to change is offered than when one is not. Nor is this an image of community response that is limited to reaction to juvenile crime. Imagine how such an opportunity might look in terms of the response of a faith community to one of the community's members, a clergyperson, who has been tried and convicted of child molestation:

> *It is visiting day and two of the members of the church have been asked to represent the church as they visit with their former pastor. The three of them sit in the visiting room of the maximum security prison at one of the small tables along the wall. Joe, the offender, is surprised that they have come and almost did not come up for this visit. He expects a torrent of anger and hatred from them . He figures that this is all that he deserves and that it will be a fitting ending as he has plans to take his own life this evening after final count. There is a razor blade hidden in his mattress. Fred, one of the deacons who has come to visit, begins to speak, "Joe, we've been doing a lot of talking and a lot of praying about what happened. To be honest, we haven't worked through nearly all of our anger or shock or sadness. That's going to be an ongoing job for our church for a long time. But we've also been asking ourselves what our responsibility to you is. We've had some lengthy conversations with the Bishop and with the denomination's attorneys and with some folks who do sex offender treatment who we called in to consult with us. We've spit, cussed, and cried over the decision that we want to share with you and we want you to know that it's a decision that has cost a lot in terms of struggle and prayer and change." John, a clergyperson involved in ministry outside the parish, and a member of the congregation, takes over, "what we'd like to do is commit ourselves to continuing to be your faith community while you are incarcerated. A small group of us—myself, Fred, Annie, and Pete—want to be added to your visiting list and one of us will come out each week to visit. You can write to us at any time that you want and we will keep the church up-to-date on how you're doing. What we expect from you is that you will begin immediately to make amends for*

your crime by getting into the Sex Offender Treatment Program here. We've been told that this will be a difficult move for you, but we're letting you know that this is what the church is asking you to do; not just for yourself, but for the health and life of our church as well. We'd like for you to sign a release of information so that the four of us can talk with your therapist and can become part of your community support team when that time comes in your treatment and you get ready to be released in 6 or 8 years from now. We're committed to sticking by you over the long haul if you will do what you need to be doing to move toward healing these broken places in your life. We were told by our consultant that you might choose to separate from us rather than meet these expectations. I want to tell you, on behalf of the church that any time you choose to connect with us and to engage in treatment—we'll be here. And the four of us will continue to visit anyway as long as you want us to. But no communication will be shared with the church community until you are in treatment. Now if you complete treatment and get into therapy on the outside, we are prepared to help you there as well. We had a major fight with the Bishop over this, but we feel that when you are in recovery you still have major gifts to offer to ministry. While our consultant made it clear that you should never again be in a position that would give you the opportunity to offend against a child, there are places where your gifts at administration and organization could be utilized without placing you at risk to reoffend. The door is open. You will need to make some ongoing decisions as to what you are willing to do. Two other things that I'd like for you to know; first of all is that the church has gathered today at Annie's house to pray while we came here to visit. The second is that one of the families whose child you offended against has chosen to remain a part of the church. They feel that their son's healing will be faster if they respond to this as your 'illness' that he was hurt by rather than having Billy feel like he is being punished by losing his church. We're giving them all the space they need to be angry and to grieve your betrayal of them and your call as a pastor and we have assigned a support team to them as well. It is not our desire to turn our back on anyone. We've put this all in writing for you so that you'll have it as you work out your decision."

Fantasy? Maybe, but maybe not. In this imaginary scenario one can see acceptance, the addressing of shame, and the invitation to reconciliation all at work. Clearly such an approach represents a greater opportunity for community healing as well as maintaining the integrity of the faith community which is attempting to respond to its wounds.

The Role of Shame

There are, however, some specific difficulties with adopting a social reconciliation theory of criminology, particularly as it applies to sexual offenders. One of them is to be found in the limits of Braithwaite's concept of shame; one is structural; and the third has to do with addressing and managing the escalating nature of sexually assaultive behavior. I attempt to address each of them in turn and suggest possible solutions to the described difficulties. For Braithwaite, the focus is on shame which is the result of external response to deviant behaviors. Such a definition is too limiting and fails to address one of the primary causes of sexually assaultive behaviors—namely, the past victimization of offenders and the resultant internalization of shame as a part of their characterological make-up.

> A basic thesis . . . is that shame originates interpersonally, primarily in significant relationships, but later can become internalized so that the self is able to activate shame without an inducing interpersonal event. Interpersonally induced shame develops into interpersonally induced shame. . . . Our identity is that vital sense of who we are as individuals, embracing our worth, our adequacy, and our very dignity as human beings. All these can be obliterated through protracted shame, leaving us feeling naked, defeated as persons and intolerably alone. (Kaufman, 1985, p. 7)

The sexual offender, even the juvenile offender, most likely comes to whatever type of confrontation of his sexual misconduct with a hefty dose of unhealthy shame. This shame is the result of multiple kinds of abuse, and the offending behavior itself may be an attempt to gain mastery over the shaming event(s). Nicholas Groth's (1979) presentation of the research done by clinicians at the Massachusetts Treatment Center—particularly that of Murray Cohen—points to this reality:

> Evidence of some form of such sexual trauma was found in the life histories of about one-third of the offenders we worked with. (p. 98)

> The offender's adult crimes may be in part a repetition and an acting out of a sexual offense he was subjected to as a child, a maladaptive effort to solve an unresolved early sexual trauma. It can be observed, especially with reference to the child molester, that his later offenses often appear to duplicate the aspects of his own victimization, that is, age of victim, type of acts performed, and the like. (p. 102)

What needs to be understood is that sexual victimization, particularly of males, is itself a cause of internalized shame. Boys in our culture are given the message that being victimized is *their fault*, that it is a sign of their weakness and lack of manhood. In one respect this is true: a 6-year-old boy is not a man, and he is definitely weaker, emotionally and physically, than, for example, his cub scout master or his mother—either of whom might conceivably assault him sexually. What happens then is that he turns the shame on himself because this is what he has been taught to do. "Boys need to be told that it is acceptable and proper to report their molestation without being labeled, rejected and ostracized. Without programs of this type, the 'merry-go-round of sexual abuse will continue perpetually" (Pendergast, 1991, p. 198).

Without such guidance and assurance, the sexual abuse victim's internal experience looks much like what Braithwaite (1989) refers to as "stigmatization": "Stigmatization, in contrast, is disintegrative shaming in which no effort is made to reconcile the offender with the community. Offenders are outcasts; their deviance is allowed to become a *master status trait* [emphasis added]; degradation ceremonies are not followed by ceremonies to decertify deviance" (p. 341).

Difficulties With the New Paradigm

When we realize that child molesters frequently tell their victims that the offending behavior is their fault, that they were seductive, that they wanted it, that they liked it, and (in many ways both true and most damaging) that others will reject and make fun of them if they tell, we can begin to see how, even in the life of a child or adolescent, shame and deviance can be allowed to become a master status trait. "To live with shame is to feel alienated and defeated, never quite good enough to belong and secretly we feel to blame.The deficiency lies within ourselves alone. Shame is without parallel a sickness of the soul" (Kaufman, 1985, p 11).

The victimization, with its resultant sense of shame and self-doubt, often creates in victims what Merton (1968) referred to as a self-fulfilling prophesy: "The self fulfilling prophesy is, in the beginning, a *false* definition of the situation evoking a new behavior which makes the originally false conception come *true*" (p. 477).

What this means is that, particularly in attempting early intervention with child or adolescent sexual offenders, we need to tread carefully as we attempt to navigate the differences between healthy shame engendered by the behaviors for which we are, rightly, holding them accountable, and the highly likely presence of internalized shame created by their own victimization. Otherwise the worst predictions of labeling theory may well come true despite the best of our intentions. "Thus, in the face of repeated designation as criminals, offenders are likely to forfeit their self-concept as conformists or 'normal' persons and internalize increasingly their public definition as deviants" (Lilly, Cullen, & Ball, 1995, p. 119)

Restoration to the Community

In the case of young offenders this may point us to the need to ritualize not only restoration to the community but also, in some symbolic way, that their decision to make amends for their assaultive behavior and to take responsibility for their own lives in this way marks their freedom from being tied to, and controlled by, their own sexual victimization.

These concerns need not, however, deter us from seeking to engage in new, reconciliatory forms of dealing with young offenders. In fact, research into why some men who were victimized as children become offenders and some do not reveals some interesting patterns:

The main personality difference in these men when compared to sex offenders, was that they did not put the blame or guilt on themselves, but on the offender, where it belongs [further,]

- Their self esteem was strong and positive
- There was an important adult in their lives with whom they could discuss anything without fear of repercussion
- Their religious education was along positive and forgiving pathways
- They had several real friends in their peer group with whom they could discuss anything
- They were successful in school, sports or some other area that produced pride, both for their parents and themselves. (Pendergast, 1991, p. 135)

These patterns show a marked similarity to situations and relationships either evident in or engendered by the family group conference when appropriately convened. Thus we are able to point to an intentional shift toward this model of response as holding great possibility for intervening in the destructive potential of both the victim and the offender.

Which brings us to the second structural difficulty in adopting a social reconciliation model. If we allow for the possibility that many of the young offenders whose behavior may be addressed in an FGC (or some similar process) have been sexually victimized themselves, we need to also allow for the possibility that their victimizer may well be part of the group gathered there with them. Fathers, mothers, coaches, older brothers or sisters—in some cases entire families of victim/victimizers may be uncovered by this process. The structures created to deal with these individual cases of criminal misconduct need to engage the systemic problems that may emerge as a result of their successful encounter with the young offender. The fact that such an occurrence is possible is also an expression of the underlying belief that crime, and especially sexually assaultive crime, affects the whole of the community's life. Those who would approach dealing with sexual offenders, particularly young offenders, from this perspective need to be prepared for the possibility that such an event might occur. And they need to be prepared to respond to the adult offender in a way that is consistent with what they have been telling the youthful offender about himself.

This brings us to the final difficulty mentioned earlier, namely, the management within a social reconciliation theory of the escalating nature of sexually assaultive behavior. Work with sexual offenders has taught us that, for many of them, this behavior escalates if left unchecked (Prentky, Lee, Knight, & Cerce, 1995). Further, we know that for many, by the time they reach adulthood, their sexually acting out has taken on a compulsive quality which calls for interventions and limits beyond those heretofore mentioned. Braithwaite and Daly (1994) suggest an "enforcement pyramid" model of response (p. 197) with increased levels of intervention, resulting finally in imprisonment. Such a response is indicative of both the strength and the weakness of their model. The weakness lies in the fact that as one moves up the pyramid toward imprisonment, there is an implied move further and further from the "communities of concern," which they hold to be so important for reintegrative shaming to be possible. In fact, built into their model is a process of disintegrative shaming.

Reconciling With the Community of Concern

However, inherent in this pyramid is also the possibility for creating communities of concern at each level—even as the community is forced to escalate its intervention in the interest of public safety. If the commitment is truly there on the part of the community, it will be possible to maintain the options for change even if the offender needs to be incarcerated. For example, different levels might be applied to a juvenile offender.

- *Level 1:* First community conference. Contracts for no contact with victim. Contributes to therapy fees for victim. Required to attend sex offender therapy. Probation.

- *Level 2:* Second community conference. Placed under house arrest with electronic monitor. Continues in sex offender therapy. Increased level of monitoring by probation officer (i.e., phone checks) and/or other members of community of concern.
- *Level 3:* Probation is violated and offender is imprisoned. Condition of parole is completion of sex offender intensive treatment program (in Massachusetts Department of Corrections this is a therapeutic community housed in a medium-security facility. This functions as a community of concern for the incarcerated offender). This level responds to the reality that currently in Massachusetts, adolescents who commit serious sexual offenses can be tried as adults.
- *Level 4:* Offender is terminated form the intensive treatment program and returned to general prison population. Conditions are defined for return to the program; failure to meet them means that sentence will be done in its entirety within an medium- or maximum-security facility. (Sentence structures will need to be long enough to provide incentive to not wait out the sentence.) At each of these levels there is the possibility available for the young offender to engage in treatment and social reconciliation.

At each of these levels a community of concern is present or available that will both hold the offender accountable for his behavior and offer him the opportunity for restoration to the social community. At each of these levels, however, the response will be based on his willingness and ability to engage in accepting responsibility for his behavior and endeavoring to make amends in some reasonable form for the harm caused both to his victim and to the larger life of the community. This set of responses is consistent with the understanding of deviant behavior put forth in the work of Gusfield (1981) who divided deviants (in the case of his study, problem drinkers) into four major categories:

- *"Sick deviants"*: persons with no control who are truly abnormal;
- *"Repentant deviants"*: persons engaged in recovery, treatment, and reparative service to others;
- *"Cynical deviants"*: persons who know they are doing wrong but exhibit no remorse; and
- *"Enemy deviants"*: persons who blame society and see nothing wrong with their behaviors.In the case of child molesters, members of NAMBLA (the North American Man Boy Love Association) would fall into this category.

Such a standard allows the community's response to be based not simply on the severity of the crime (which is important) but on the willingness of the offender to work toward restoration and reconciliation with the community. It also allows for the offender to move from one category to another. This standard presupposes, of course, a community willing to be reconciled to the offender. Therein lies another major difficulty. But it is a difficulty that may have its solution in the very discussion with which this chapter opened. Transforming cultural response to crime—particularly such emotion-laden crimes as sexual offenses—will require that criminologists not only rediscover for themselves the new meanings in the old governing myths but that they reach out to those in the community who are the guardians of these stories—clergy of all denominations, identified community "keepers of story"—and even to those who create media events and write film scripts. Imagine an HBO "After School Special" about a juvenile sex offender *who got help,* or an NBC "Monday Night Movie" about a sex offender's confrontation within a community forum (like the one described earlier) and subsequent treatment (complete with flashbacks to his own childhood and highlighted portrayal of his attempt to find work, friends, relationships, and to live a life of "recovery" in the face of cultural hostility). There is more than enough drama here (the film *Rage* is an excellent example) to produce a quality story if treated in a quality fashion. Culture's understanding of disturbing issues such as alcoholism, Alzheimer's disease, and incest have all been challenged and transformed because concerned persons got involved in educating the larger culture and community on a multitude of levels. This work made it possible for persons with these problems to come forward for help with less stigmatization and gradually moved the culture toward attitudes which both held persons responsible for their behavior and offered the possibility for acceptance and restoration to community. Another possibility is involvement in the creation of "communities of concern" to meet the juvenile offender at each of the levels mentioned previously. An example of this involvement would be a local church working with a regional director of a social service agency to create a program aimed at juveniles returning to the community from residential treatment settings and to develop a model for a support/recovery maintainance group for the youths and a multifamily support group for their families. The goal is to provide a responsive, supportive, place of welcome for these youth and their families upon the return of the youth to the community.

Conclusion

If those of us involved in the treatment of sex offenders are going to be involved in transforming the cultural response to these offenders in ways that promote public safety and lower recidivism rates by calling offenders into responsible reconciliation with the community, we will have to step out, to see ourselves as agents of change, reaching out to other disciplines, to community structures, and to persons at all levels of the criminal justice system. Finally, as active agents of change in these settings and as active participants in the work of the various systems in which these goals are pursued, we will find ourselves involved not only in the transformation of the justice system but in the transformation of the culture at large.

References

Braithwaite, J. (1989). *Crime, shame and reintegration.* Melbourne, Australia: Osford University Press.

Braithwaite, J. (1992). Reducing the crime problem: A not so dismal criminology. *Australian and New Zealand Journal of Criminology, 25.*

Braithwaite, J., & Daly, K. (1994). Masculinities, violence and communitarian control. In T. Newburn & E. Starks (Eds.), *Just boys doing business?* London: Routledge.

Ericson, R., & Carriere, K. (1994). The fragmentation of criminology. In D. Nelson (Ed.), *The futures of criminology.* Thousand Oaks, CA: Sage.

Groth, N. (1979). *Men who rape.* New York: Plenum Press.

Gusfield, J. (1981). *The culture of public problems: Drinking, driving and the symbolic order.* Chicago: University of Chicago Press.

Kaufman, G. (1985). *Shame: The power of caring* (rev. ed.). Cambridge, MA Schenkman Books.

Lilly, J., Cullen, F., & Ball, R. (1995). *Criminological theory.* Thousand Oaks, CA: Sage .

Merton, R. (1968). *Social theory and social structure.* New York: Free Press.

Morrison, W. (1994). Criminology, modernity, and the "truths" of the human condition: Reflections on the melancholy of postmodernism. In D. Nelson (Ed.), *The futures of criminology*. Thousand Oaks, CA: Sage.

Palmer, P. (1986). *The company of strangers.* New York: Cross Road.

Pendergast, W. (1991). *Treating sex offenders in correctional institutions and outpatient clinics.* New York: Hawthorn Press.

Prentky, R. A., Lee, A. F. S., Knight, R. A., & Cerce, D. (1995). Predictive validity of lifestyle impulsivity for rapists. *Criminal Justice and Behavior, 32*(2), 106–128.

Reiss, A. (1951). Delinquency as the failure of personal and social controls. *American Sociological Review, 16*, 196–207.

Zehr, H. (1990). *Changes lenses.* Scottsdale, AZ: Herald Press.

Chapter 2

A Closer Look at Sex Offender Character Pathology and Relapse Prevention—An Integrative Approach

by Barry Anechiarico, L.I.C.S.W.

Overview

In discussions of techniques for treating sex offenders, psychoanalytical theory is usually contrasted to cognitive behavioral approaches, particularly relapse prevention. However, research on sex offenders that identifies the critical role of self-esteem has awakened new interest in the analytical approach. This chapter discusses the integration of these approaches.

Introduction

The inability of sex offenders to cope with a strong negative emotional state is considered a high-risk factor and a significant precursor to relapse (Hanson, 1996; Ward & Hudson, 1996). Understanding the nature of both strong negative emotions and the particular kind of stress that activates these negative emotions adds a needed third dimension—the interpersonal dimension—to the two dimensions of relapse prevention, the internal and external, as formulated by Pithers (1990). Viewing relapse prevention from the perspective of this new dimension helps offenders to understand that fragile and unstable self-esteem is their underlying vulnerability (risk factor), setting up a high-risk situation for offending. This understanding brings into sharper focus the strategies necessary to manage strong negative emotions and thereby avert relapse.

The Character Disorder in Sex Offenders

The concept of a character disorder was originally a psychoanalytical construct. Until recently, the treatment of the character disorder underlying the sex offender's behavior has been ineffective in reducing relapse, due to limitations in the theoretical models and treatment strategies available. Psychoanalysis was designed to treat the anxiety and guilt of neurotic disorders by engaging the observing ego of the patient to form an analyzable neurotic transference (Fenichel, 1945). However, sexually exploitative behavior is a symptom of character pathology rather than neurosis. Patients who exhibit such exploitative behavior form a narcissistic transference where the fundamental experience of deprivation, neglect, and entitlement overpowers an observing ego and renders the primary analytical method of transference analysis ineffective (Kohut, 1987).

The failure of psychoanalysis to adequately treat sexually deviant behavior has led to the bulk of research and practice in the field over the last thirty years of sex offender treatment being focused on cognitive, behavioral, and psychopharmacological interventions and relapse prevention.

The Relational View Offers New Approach

Understanding and treating the character pathology in sex offenders have been challenges for researchers and practitioners in the field for many years. However, in the past 40 years new concepts of how attachment shapes character have evolved. From Fairbain's early ideas of the development of object relations, ranging from absolute dependence to mature dependence, to Mahler's understanding of the process of separation and individuation to Kohut's theory of the evolution of a cohesive self, new research and theories about the earliest years of life (referred to analytically as the pre-Oedipal period) have emerged These theories incorporate discoveries not found in Freud's seminal work. These advancements in developmental psychology and object relations theory offer an alternative relational model to the drive conflict model in understanding character development and character disorders. Specifically, the study of the interpersonal realm of experience in development brings a new understanding to sexual deviancy by examining the nature of attachment and the development of self-esteem.

In a study by Prentky and Knight (1989), the inconsistency in attachments to significant others throughout the lives of sex offenders was found to be significantly linked to sexual aggression. The character defect in sex offenders that arises out of this kind of failure in early attachments is best formulated in the study of the narcissistic character disorder. This perspective suggests that traumatic disruptions in early formative attachment to significant others is a contributor to sex offending and plays a key role in the motivation of the offense. Thus, sex offending is not only a behavior disorder but a relational disorder as well. It is an extortion of intimacy in an attempt to restore damaged self-esteem and establish an interpersonal connection.

The Role of Attachment in the Development of Self-Esteem

Self-esteem, as it is understood in this context, means more than just feeling good about oneself. It is our very sense of self—the energy that drives volition, initiative, and motivation. The ability to regulate the flow of this energy from high to low and recover from narcissistic injuries constitutes the health and resiliency of our self-esteem.

Experiencing attachment and accomplishment provides the foundation of our sense of self and affirms our self-worth. When experiencing an assault to our sense of self, those of us with resilient self-esteem turn to the people and things we love for reassurance and a sense of connection (Spencer, Josephs, & Steele, 1993). The consistency and quality of those attachments profoundly affect our sense of self and our ability to form future self-enhancing attachments. To say that offenders have low self-esteem is incomplete. It is more accurate to say that their self-esteem is fragile and unstable—a sense of self that is vulnerable to assault and feelings of shame without adequate resources to make repairs when damaged. This deficiency can manifest itself as chronic low self-esteem or an unstable high self-esteem. The latter is commonly considered narcissism. However, in narcissistic disorders the defect lies in the fragility of one's sense of self as well as the difficulty in regulating self-esteem. This is more fundamental than whether self-esteem is high or low (Kernis, 1993).

This state of diminished sense of self is experienced as shame. Recent research on violence has found the emotion of shame to be the primary psychological motivation in violent behavior (Gilligan, 1996). The inability to build effective strategies to restore self-esteem and recover from shame leads to reactions ranging from despair to rage (Steffenhagen, 1990). The lack of experience and confidence in need-fulfilling relationships with others and the lack of internalized feelings of connection and affirmation from others sets the stage for the formation of narcissistic behavioral patterns for compensatory strategies.

The Extortion of Intimacy

A brief look at the structure of the self as outlined by Kohut (1987) is useful in understanding the two basic motivations of sexually exploitative behavior. Kohut hypothesizes that the basic striving in human development is toward attachment to others and that there is no self without another. He suggests that this pursuit of attachment is more fundamental in human motivation than are sexual and aggressive drives. He adds that there are two basic interpersonal strivings (representing two "poles" of the self) that must be addressed to establish healthy self-esteem:

1. Exhibitionistic/grandiose strivings (mirroring/affirming)—the need to have consistent mirroring and affirming responses in the earliest attachments of life to build strong resilient self-esteem, complete with ambition, pride, and feelings of self-worth.
2. Voyeuristic strivings (idealizing)—the need to have available an idealized role model toward whom one can look for guidance, protection, and identification, which creates a feeling of belonging and the ability to self-soothe and moderate assaults to self-esteem.

When this natural process breaks down or is traumatically thwarted, character deficiencies develop. These deficiencies become most evident in the way one sustains and repairs self-esteem. The deficient self is vulnerable to rejection, disappointment, and loss of purpose. In this weakened state the self becomes fragmented, splitting into its component parts of primitive sexual and aggressive impulses, desperately substituting the pursuit of sensually gratifying, isolated, sexual and aggressive behavior for unavailable self-enhancing relationships. Specifically, primitive voyeuristic and exhibitionistic preoccupations, depending on which pole of the self is most deficient, takes the place of relationships. The nature of the deficiencies in the self is evident in the two general types of sexual offending: exhibitionistic sexual acts and voyeuristic sexual acts.

Primitive exhibitionistic sexual acts are demonstrations of sexual power and control over others (e.g., rape), through rageful protest against feeling diminished and shamed by others, as well as narcissistic sexual acts performed for the affirmation by others (e.g., flashing and obscene phone calls). Primitive voyeuristic sexual acts are acts of sexually "peeping" and/or touching others in search of unconditional/idealized love (e.g., pedophilia and fondling). Voyeuristic sexual pleasure, derived from the idealization of others, appeals to the need to feel secure and safe in an emotionally non-threatening intimacy. Rather than power and control, the aim of these sexual acts is to attain idealized love.

The Interpersonal Dimension of Relapse Prevention

The interpersonal dimension adds to the internal and external dimensions of relapse prevention. As noted earlier, this dimension helps the offender to learn that a fragile and unstable self-esteem is a high-risk factor and that interpersonal conflicts can create overwhelming emotional instability, thereby triggering relapse. This understanding brings into sharper focus the strategies necessary to manage this risk factor and avert relapse. The following are functions of this dimension:

- To teach offenders about the high-risk factor of fragile self-esteem and enable them to identify the stressful events that trigger overwhelming narcissistic injuries;
- To teach offenders that their sexually exploitative behavior is an extortion of intimacy to restore self-esteem through primitive sexualized exhibitionistic and/or voyeuristic acts;
- To teach new strategies to build and sustain self-esteem through healthy reciprocal relationships with others who are informed of the offender's cycle;
- To develop skills and talents from which a sense of accomplishment can be derived; and
- To experience the enhancement of self-esteem through meaningful connections to others and a sense of accomplishment through work and recreation.

Pithers's antecedent model of relapse prevention suggests that the offender's inability to deal effectively with a change in his emotional state, which is triggered by external factors, leads to fantasies of sexual aggression. Distorted thinking justifies the offender's behavior and minimizes his feeling of responsibility. He then forms a to actualize the fantasy. The next step is acting out the fantasy through an offense (Pithers, 1990).

The interpersonal dimension builds on this basic construct by suggesting that internal factors (fragile and unstable self-esteem) along with external factors (injuries to self-esteem) create an unmanageable change in the offender's emotional state. The offender's inability to deal effectively with these negative emotions is due to the fragility and instability of his sense of self. Thus, in the chain of behaviors described in relapse prevention, the fantasies, distorted thinking or entitlement, and ensuing plans and actions of the offender can be seen as primitive and perverse attempts to restore self-esteem to a more tolerable equilibrium, following the stress of an unmanageable emotional assault.

$$\text{Stress} \longrightarrow \text{Fantasy} \longrightarrow \text{Entitlement} \longrightarrow \text{Plan} \longrightarrow \text{Action}$$

The stress of an unmanageable emotional assault leads to isolation and disconnection from others, thus triggering the relapse cycle. In this desperate and alienated state, deviant sexual fantasies and delusions of love and attachment are formed. These deviant sexual fantasies are powerful images designed to restore energy to a depleted self-esteem. The fantasy of violent sexual aggression can temporarily alleviate a feeling of powerlessness and inadequacy, and a fantasy of kissing or holding a sexualized and idealized child can provide a strong, albeit temporary, surge of well-being. The power of these fantasies becomes compelling, and the offender justifies his actions with a sense of entitlement derived from his deep feelings of deprivation and emotional isolation. Because these attempts to restore self-esteem are not sustaining, a plan forms o act out the fantasies. The plan is what makes the offense possible.

In an effort to find the earliest point of intervention in the relapse cycle, Pithers notes that there are "seemingly unimportant decisions" the offender makes that put him in high-risk situations. In his construct, Pithers suggests that such decisions are an early sign of a lapse and are precursors to relapse.

However, the interpersonal dimension suggests that because of the offender's character defect—his unstable and vulnerable sense of self—the offender is always at risk and becomes high risk whenever he is triggered by an unmanageable injury to his self-esteem. Deviant sexual fantasies are then activated as an attempt to revitalize his self-esteem. Therefore, it is this severely diminished sense of self—this state of shame, following an unmanageable injury to self-esteem—that is the earliest point of intervention in the cycle. It is at this moment that new healthy strategies, designed to bolster a damaged self-esteem, need to be activated, before the actual lapse occurs with a reactivation of the deviant sexual fantasies.

Recovery: The Restoration of Self-Esteem

To develop the capacity for intimacy, that is, the ability to bring the needs of the self into a mutual relational experience, requires not only learning about the nature of the narcissism but also experiencing a revitalization of the self through mutual attachments. The experience of being listened to and feeling understood in group therapy is often the beginning of an offender's first intimate attachment. In a group that works to develop an awareness of intimacy needs, offenders begin to recognize how they had all but given up hope of feeling connected and attached to others, often resulting in emotional isolation, loneliness, anger, and despair.

Two recent studies found that improvement in the fragile self-esteem of sex offenders was significantly correlated to a reduction in sexual deviant indices demonstrated in phallometric assessments (Marshall, 1996). Building a more resilient sense of self that is better able to manage inevitable assaults requires gradually bringing the needs of the self into the context of a mutual relationship and thereby changing the interpersonal emotional experience. The restoration of self-esteem through the experience of affirming intimate connections with others abrogates the need to restore self-esteem through narcissistic sexually exploitative behavior and can make a significant contribution in reducing recidivism in sex offenders.

References

Fenichel, D. (1945). *The psychoanalytic theory of neurosis.* New York: Norton.

Gilligan, J. (1996). *Violence: Our deadly epidemic and its causes.* New York: G.P. Putnam's Sons.

Hanson, R. K. (1996). Evaluating the contribution of relapse prevention theory to the treatment of sexual offenders. *Sexual Abuse: A Journal of Research and Treatment, 8*(3), 201–208.

Kernis, M. (1993). The roles of stability and level of self-esteem in psychological functioning. In R. F. Baumeister, *Self-esteem: The puzzle of low self-regard* (pp. 76–85). New York: Plenum Press.

Kohut, H. (1987). *The restoration of the self.* New York: International Universities Press.

Marshall, W. L. (1996). The sexual offender: Monster, victim, or everyman. *Sexual Abuse: A Journal of Research and Treatment, 8,* 317–335.

Pithers, W. D. (1990). Relapse prevention with sexual aggressors. In W. L. Marshall, D. R. Laws, & H. E. Barbaree (Eds.), *Handbook of sexual assault* (pp. 343–361). New York: Plenum Press.

Prentky, R. A., Knight, R. A., Sims-Knight, J. E., Strauss, H., Rokous, F., & Cerce, D. (1989). Developmental antecedents of sexual aggression. *Development and Psychopathology, 1,* 153–169.

Spencer, K., Josephs, S., & Steele, M. (1993). Low self-esteem: The uphill struggle for self-integrity. In R. F. Baumeister (Ed.), *Self-esteem: The puzzle of low self-regard* (pp. 21–36). New York: Plenum Press.

Steffenhagen, R. A. (1990). *Self-esteem therapy.* New York: Praeger.

Ward, T., & Hudson, S. M. (1996). Relapse prevention: A critical analysis. *Sexual Abuse: A Journal of Research and Treatment, 8*(3), 171–200.

Chapter 3

Mood, Conflict, and Deviant Sexual Fantasies

by Jan Looman, M.A.

Overview

Most sex offenders are generally thought to have deviant sexual fantasies. Most relapse prevention programs use models that show high-risk situations generating negative emotional states, which in turn produce deviant fantasies. This model is used for all sex offenders. However, as suggested by this research even groups of child molesters differ significantly in the role their deviant fantasies play.

Introduction

It is well-known that at least some sexual offenders fantasize about their offenses prior to committing them, and that the type of deviant fantasy is related to the type of offense (Marshall, Barbaree, & Eccles, 1991). However, to date, the research concerning sexual offenders' fantasies has focused primarily on the content of the fantasies; little has been done to explore why they may be thinking that way. An important question to ask, which goes beyond the immediate content of a sexual offender's deviant sexual fantasy, is: What function does that fantasy serve for the offender?

Role of General Fantasies

Freud (1962) expressed the belief that most people fantasize at least occasionally, and that fantasies are typically based on some sort of wish: "a happy person never phantasies, only an unsatisfied one" (p. 146). Freud hypothesized that every fantasy is therefore a correction of unsatisfying reality. He added that fantasies fall into two forms—ambitious and erotic—although the two often coincide.

Singer (1978) summarized the research on the functions of fantasies up to that time and concluded that fantasy serves a definite cognitive function. His conclusion was that fantasies reflect unfinished business facing the person. They involve looking to the future and planning.

Zelin and his colleagues (1983) wrote about sustaining fantasies—fantasies which a person uses during times of intense negative affect (e.g., anger). They tend to be consistent, familiar, and repetitive and produce a sense of satisfaction or decreased frustration through the creation of a more ideal situation in fantasy. Thus, both Singer and Zelin support Freud's notion of wish fulfillment in the sense that they see fantasies as serving a function of meeting unmet needs.

Prevalence of Sexual Fantasies

Turning now to sexual fantasies, a large body of research has emerged over the past few decades detailing people's sexual fantasies. Kinsey (1948) demonstrated that sexual fantasies played an important role in the imaginal lives of both men and women. Since that time, research has further explored this phenomenon, mostly in the college student population.

For example, Knafo and Jaffe (1984) administered questionnaires to thirty men and thirty women to examine the frequency of sexual fantasies during masturbation, intercourse, and nonsexual activities. Some 80% of men and 70% of women reported fantasizing sexually outside of sexual activity, whereas 90% of males and 76.6% of females reported fantasizing during masturbation and 60% of males and 56.7% of females reported fantasizing during intercourse. They also found that the tendency to engage in nonsexual deydreaming was correlated with the tendency to engage in sexual fantasies.

Studies such as these have explored the prevalence of fantasies, but studies have also been conducted that explore the nature of the fantasies in which people engage. For example, Crepault and Courture (1980) reported that the most popular fantasy of the men in his sample was being with a woman other than their partner. Other common fantasies involved various sexual activities, such as fellatio or cunnilingus, group sex, and so on.

Wilson and Lang (1981) examined the fantasies of forty-five men and forty-five women, contrasting their content. For both sexes it was found that "intimate" (typical heterosexual foreplay and intercourse) themes were the most common, followed by "exploratory" (group sex, homosexuality, unusual settings) themes. "Impersonal" (fetishistic, voyeuristic) and sadomasochistic themes were least common for both sexes, although men reported a higher number of such fantasies than did women.

Deviant Fantasies Among "Normals." Researchers have examined the prevalence of inappropriate fantasies in normal populations. For example, Rokach's (1990) content analysis study of college student's fantasies revealed that 2.6% of men and 1.2% of women reported a fantasy about children. Similarly, Briere and Runtz (1989) had 193 college males fill out a questionnaire containing questions related to sexual interest in children. Questions related to sexual attraction ("Little children sometimes attract me sexually"), frequency of fantasies (how often do subjects have fantasies about "having sex with a child"?), masturbation to these fantasies, and the likelihood of having sex with children if they knew they would not be caught. All questions required subjects to respond on a scale that ranged from "never" or "completely false" to "always" or "completely true." An answer that did not ntotally reject the statement was considered a positive response. These researchers report that 21% of the men reported some sexual attraction to children; 9% reported some fantasies and 5% had masturbated to these fantasies. In response to the question regarding the likelihood of having sex with children, 7% reported at least some likelihood of engaging in such behavior. However, there is some difficulty with this type of question. The way in which the questions are framed (e.g., How likely are you to . . . ?) may encourage a positive response from those who will "try anything."

Even when not looking specifically for deviant fantasies, some research has revealed evidence of fantasies which could be considered to be of a deviant nature among nonoffender populations. For example, Crepault and Couture (1980) found that among other fantasies, 61.7% of his subjects fantasized about sexually initiating a young girl, 39% fantasized about tying a woman up, and 33% about raping a woman.

Wilson and Lang (1981) found in their study of the contents of the fantasies of a normal sample that the frequency of all fantasy themes (described earlier) was correlated with the self-reported strength of libido for both males and females. Satisfaction with sex life was positively correlated with intimate fantasies of both men and women, but impersonal, sadomasochistic and exploratory fantasies were negatively correlated with satisfaction for men. The frequency of "deviant" fantasies increased as well.

Sexual Offenders' Fantasies. A number of authors have examined the nature and content of sexual offender's fantasies, and found that some sexual offender's fantasies are concerned with themes related to their offenses. For example, Marshall et al. (1991) reported that 52.7% of their sample of child molesters treated in a community setting admitted to fantasies about children, and 21.7% indicated that these fantasies preceded their first offense.

MacCulloch, Snowden, Wood, and Mill (1983) examined the fantasies of 16 sadistic sexual offenders and found that in the case of 13 of these men, the fantasies leading to their index offense(s) could be seen as rehearsal for the crimes. The men in the study had long histories of failure in social relationships, feelings of inadequacy, and lack of assertiveness. Their sadistic fantasies also were seen as providing a relief from this constant sense of failure.

Moods Related to Content of Fantasies. The relapse prevention model (Laws, 1989) suggests that inappropriate behavior serves as a maladaptive coping mechanism. For example, Pithers, Beal, Armstrong, and Petty (1989) report that sexual reoffenses were often preceded by negative emotional states or conflicts with significant others. These data are based on post-reoffense interviews with a sample of offenders. This suggests that deviant fantasies serve as an inappropriate strategy for coping with unpleasant events and the feelings that accompany them. The present study explored this hypothesis.

Most studies completed to date have been based on interviews with offenders and rely on anecdotal, retrospective accounts or the researcher's impressions to conclude that the deviant fantasies are related to feelings of betrayal, frustration, and lack of control (e.g., Abel & Blanchard, 1974; Burgess, Hartman, Ressler, Douglas, & McCormack, 1986). A recent example is a study completed by Looman (1995). In this study, incarcerated sexual offenders were interviewed regarding their sexual fantasies in the period preceding their offenses. It was found that child molesters reported that their fantasies regarding children were more likely to occur when they were feeling depressed or had been rejected by an adult female. Adult fantasies were more likely to occur when feeling happy or when having a "good day." The conclusion drawn was that the deviant sexual fantasies serve as an inappropriate coping mechanism. Also of interest in this study was the finding that deviant fantasies were followed by negative emotional states (i.e., the abstinence violation effect), suggesting that a cycle of using deviant fantasies to cope with negative emotional states leads to further negative emotional states, which leads to further fantasies.

To date, two articles based on one ongoing study by McKibben and his colleagues (McKibben, Proulx, & Lusignan, 1994; Proulx, McKibben, & Lusignan, 1996) have been published which look specifically at the relationship between moods and deviant sexual fantasies. These studies have included sequel offenders who admitted to deviant fantasies. Every two days the subjects went to a lab and answered questions on a computer indicating the frequency of both deviant and nondeviant sexual fantasies. They also reported on a number of affective states and on the presence or absence of conflict with others. It was found that, for all subjects, deviant fantasies were associated with negative affective states and the presence of conflict. Masturbatory fantasies were related to negative affect for the heterosexual pedophiles and rapists but not for the homosexual pedophiles.

However, as with other studies these two studies relied on retrospective recall, although for no more than two days, and they used only offenders who reported deviant fantasies. The purpose of the present study was to examine the relationships between emotional states, conflict, and deviant sexual fantasies in a group of sexual offenders to test the hypothesis that deviant fantasies serve as a means of coping with negative experiences and emotional states. This study attempted the use of a real-time fantasy and mood-monitoring procedure to record the data, in order to reduce the influence of retrospective recording. In addition, the study explored relationships between reported fantasies and office characteristics.

Offenders Monitor Mood and Fantasies

Thirty-two sex offenders (thirteen rapists, fourteen extrafamilial child molesters, and five incest offenders) completed fantasy- and mood-monitoring forms for up to four weeks. The monitoring sheets had two parts: a fantasy-monitoring form and a mood-monitoring form. These forms were adapted from the research of McKibben et al. (1994) and Jones and Barlow (1990). These authors report that similar data collection techniques were successful with college students (Jones & Barlow, 1990) and sexual offenders in treatment (McKibben et al., 1994). Each fantasy-monitoring sheet is divided into seven blocks, corresponding to the days of the week. Each block is also divided into two periods (A.M. and P.M.). On the sheet the subject is asked to record whether he masturbated (without fantasy) or experienced a fantasy, an urge, or a masturbatory fantasy for each of the periods. Definitions of the various terms are provided on the sheet, as well as instructions for completion.

To reduce the influence of delayed recalling of fantasy material, subjects were requested to complete the form as soon as possible after experiencing the fantasy or urge. The suggestion was made that if circumstance prevented immediate completion of the form, it could be completed at noon, dinner, or just before going to bed at the end of the day. These times are typical "count" times in institutions, in which inmates are required to be in their cells to be counted.

The mood sheet is also divided into seven blocks for each day of the week. Several emotions are listed on the sheet, taken from the research of McKibben et al. (1994). The emotions listed (anger, depression, anxiety, rejection, humiliation, inadequacy, and loneliness) have been identified in previous research as being common precursors to actual sexual offenses (Pithers et al., 1989). The subject was instructed to place a checkmark in the column below each of the emotional states he experienced over the course of the day. He was also requested to record whether or not he experienced the emotional state as a result of conflict with another person. As well, subjects were asked to rate their general mood for each day on a scale from 1 (much better than unusual) to 5 (much worse than usual). Once again, instructions for the completion of the sheet were provided.

Subjects were requested to complete both forms for a period of four weeks (i.e., twenty-eight consecutive days). For purposes of analysis, only the first three weeks (twenty-one days) of data were used due to a declining number of completed forms. Ten of the subjects did not complete twenty-eight days of fantasy monitoring, leading to a greatly reduced sample at the end of the period. This attrition rate of almost one third was due to the intrusive and rather tedious nature of the task.

In addition, data regarding a number of offense characteristics were collected. This information included the subjects' index and past offenses, the length of their sentence, and their age. For the sexual offenders, information regarding the age, gender, number of victims, and relationship to the victim was recorded. An index of the degree of coercion used in the commission of the current offense, rated by the author, was also employed (1 = no force or coercion to 4 = victim injury). Intrusiveness of the offense (1 = fondling over clothes to 9 = anal intercourse) was recorded, using the most intrusive of the behaviors. That is, if a victim was both fondled and vaginally penetrated the vaginal penetration was the act recorded. Finally, the degree of victim injury was also rated (1 = none to 7 = post-death mutilation). For these latter three ratings, if there was more than one victim in the current offense, the most serious of the victims was rated.

Offenders Report Relation Between Fantasies and Mood. Eleven (61%) of the child molesters and one (7.7%) rapist reported deviant sexual urges or fantasies. Daily reports of fantasies were summarized by simply adding the number of fantasies

reported. The number of nonmasturbatory sexual fantasies, sexual urges, and masturbatory sexual fantasies reported were calculated (see Table 3.1). The child molesters
reported fantasies involving both prepubescent and pubescent children, as well as consensual fantasies of adult females. The one rapist reporting deviant fantasies and urges
reported both violent sexual thoughts of adult and pubescent females and thoughts
concerning pubescent females. All but one of the child molesters reporting deviant
fantasies offended exclusively against boys.

Fantasy and Emotional States. Reports or urges and fantasies were correlated with
reports related to emotional states and conflict. Analyses are reported for the child
molesters only (see Table 3.2) due to the rapists' failure to report deviant fantasies.
Loneliness was found to be related to both child and pubescent urges, whereas feelings of loneliness, inadequacy and depression were related to sexual fantasies of
children. No significant relationships were detected for reports of conflict and
deviant sexual fantasies. Adult sexual fantasies and masturbatory fantasies were
related to feelings of rejection, inadequacy, and depression, as well as reports of
conflicts.

Fantasies and Offense Characteristics. To examine the relationship between offending and deviant fantasies, the dichotomous variable representing the presence or
absence of sexual thoughts of children during the three-week period of the study was
cross-tabulated with a number of characteristics of the subject's offense history.

The presence of fantasies about children was related to the sex of the victim
$(x^2(1, n = 22) = 7.87, p < .005)$, with 83% of those with male victims and only 19%
of those with female victims reporting fantasies about children. Fantasies about children were also reported more often by men whose relationship with the victim was
one of friend. All but one of the men who reported deviant fantasies were classified
in this manner $(x^2(5, n = 22) = 12.40, p < .03)$, whereas those who did not report
fantasies of children were evenly distributed across the other categories.
Intrusiveness (ranging from fondling of clothes to anal intercourse) of the offense
was unrelated to the presence of deviant fantasies; however, the amount of the coercion was. Offenders who reported deviant fantasies were coded as using either no
coercion (62.5%) or "coercion with psychological restraints" (i.e., bribes, threats
only) (37.5%) whereas 53.9% of those who did not report deviant fantasies used
some sort of physical coercion $(x^2(3, \underline{n} = 21) = 9.52, p < .023)$. Similarly, none of
the victims of men with deviant fantasies were physically injured, whereas 53.8% of
other victims experienced some form of physical injury.

Correctional analyses were conducted using the age of the victim, the number of
victims in the index conviction, and total number of known victims, with the presence
or absence of deviant fantasies. When these analyses were conducted only of the child
molesters, the number of victims $(r = .64, p < .01)$ and the total number of victims $(r = .73, p < .002)$ were related to the presence of deviant sexual fantasies. When conducted of the total sample, the age of the victim was negatively related to the presence
of fantasies $(r = -.44, p < .045)$, whereas the relationship between fantasies and the
number of victims in the index offense and total number of known victims was
stronger than the previously observed relationship $(r = .70, p < .001$, and $r = .79, p < .001$, respectively).

Table 3.1
Descriptive Statistics for Fantasy Reports

	Adult Fantasies		Adult Urges		Adult Masturbatory Fantasies		Child Fantasies		Child Urges		Child Masturbatory Fantasies		Pubescent Urges		Pubescent Fantasies		Pubescent Masturbatory Fantasies	
	M	SD	M	SD	M	SD	M	SD	M	SD	M	SD	M	SD	M	SD	M	SD
Child molesters	4.0	4.7	7.9	9.0	3.6	4.1	0.5	1.1	1.0	2.5	0.3	0.9	1.9	3.2	1.7	3.4	1.5	2.7
Rapists	5.6	7.8	7.8	16.9	3.5	4.5	—	—	—	—	—	—	—	—	—	—	—	—

Note. For purposes of this table, one rapist who admitted to fantasies of children was omitted. M = mean; SD = standard deviation.

Deviant Fantasies Play a Variety of Roles. Thus child molesters" deviant fantasies show significant relationships with negative emotional states, especially loneliness. This result supports the research of McKibben and colleagues, and the hypothesis that deviant fantasies serve a sustaining function (i.e., coping with negative affect). Masturbatory fantasies for this sample of primarily homosexual pedophiles were not found to be related to negative moods, which is also similar to the finding reported by Proulx et al. (1996). They suggest that deviant fantasies for homosexual child molesters may be linked directly to sexual desire, independent of emotional state. (See Table 3.2.)

It is interesting to note that adult fantasies also appear to be related to the experience of negative emotions but are related more to conflict and feelings of rejection and inadequacy than to loneliness. McKibben et al. (1994) also found that deviant fantasies were not related to conflicts for homosexual pedophiles but were for rapists and heterosexual pedophiles. It may be that the relationship between conflict and adult fantasies is due to the influence of the heterosexual child molesters in the present sample. Unfortunately, the numbers are too small to perform analyses with the groups broken down further.

Fantasy Content Correlates With Offense Characteristics. The findings related to offense characteristics are interesting. Offenders who reported current deviant fantasies on the Fantasy Monitoring Form were primarily homosexual child molesters. Their offenses were less coercive, resulted in less injury to the victim, were somewhat less intrusive (i.e., less likely to have intercourse, more likely to engage in oral sex), and were more likely to establish a friendship with the victim before molesting her than were the men who did not report deviant fantasies. Deviant fantasies were also related to a larger number of victims in the current offense as well as a larger number of victims in total. This offense pattern is indicative of a lifestyle related to sexual offending (e.g., pedophilia), rather than a more situationally determined offense or an offense in which the victim serves as a substitute for an adult (e.g., incest offending).

Fantasies Most Associated With Loneliness and Depression. Ward, Hudson, Marshall, and Siegert (1995) proposed a model relating attachment theory and intimacy deficits to the sexual offender literature. They hypothesized that an anxious–ambivalent attachment style may characterize a man who sexually offends against children. They indicated that such an offender may be emotionally dependent on relationships with children as a result of his inability to satisfy intimacy needs in adult relationships. Furthermore, they suggested that the offender enjoys his involvement with the child and is concerned that the victim(s) enjoys the interaction. The results discussed previously fit with this hypothesis. The offenders who admitted to deviant sexual fantasies in the current research were more likely to experience these fantasies when feelingly lonely or depressed. They formed friendships with their victims, and they did not use coercion.

Conclusion

Unfortunately, only one rapist admitted to deviant fantasies, Thus the results obtained in this part only apply to child molesters. Deviant fantasies for child moles-

Table 3.2
Correlations Between Emotional States and Sexual Thoughts for Child Molesters Only

	Humiliation	Rejection	Inadequacy	Loneliness	Depression	Anxiety	Anger	Conflict
Child urges	-.19	-.07	-.02	.43*	.06	-.16	-.03	-.11
Child fantasies	.07	.31	.58**	.45*	.46*	.05	.33	.29
Child masturbatory fantasies	.01	.25	.19	-.03	.33	.08	-.17	.13
Pubescent urges	-.24	-.08	-.10	.51*	.09	-.29	.13	-.23
Pubescent fantasies	-.09	.14	-.06	.02	.19	-.10	.13	-.04
Pubescent masturbatory fantasies	.21	-.04	.01	.25	.32	-.07	.16	-.06
Adult urges	.22	.12	.28	-.10	.37	-.16	-.03	.18
Adult fantasies	.25	.63*	.46*	.23	.52*	.21	.34	.49*
Adult masturbatory fantasies	.29	.65**	.57**	.32	.78***	.31	.29	.51*

Note. n = 19.
* p < .05. ** p < .01. *** p < .001. n = 19.

ters appear to be related to feelings of loneliness and depression, whereas sexual fantasies of adults were found to be related to conflict and feelings of rejects. Thus, sexual fantasies, both about adults and about children, do appear to be used to cope with negative emotional states.

The relapse prevention model for the treatment of sexual offenders emphasizes the necessity of improving the coping skills of sexual offenders. This research supports the value of this approach. Previous research indicates that sexual offenders who report deviant fantasies are among those who are at highest risk for sexual reoffense. This study indicates that these men may use sexual fantasies to cope with stressful experiences, which may set them up for future problems. Clearly, teaching adaptive coping strategies, problem solving, and assertiveness will help to reduce the probability of reoffense. In addition, focusing on intimacy issues, especially the formation and maintenance of appropriate relationships, may also serve to reduce recidivism.

References

Abel, G. G., & Blanchard, E. B. (1974). The role of fantasy in the treatment of sexual deviations. *Archives of General Psychiatry, 30,* 467–475.

Briere, J., & Runtz, M. (1989). University males' sexual interest in children: Predicting potential indices of "pedophilia" in a non-forensic sample. *Child Abuse and Neglect, 13,* 65–75.

Burgess, A. W., Hartman, C. R., Ressler, R. K., Douglas, J. E., & McCormack, A. (1986). Sexual homicide: A motivational model. *Journal of Interpersonal Violence, 1*(3), 251–272.

Crepault, C., & Courture, M. (1980). Men's erotic fantasies. *Archives of Sexual Behavior, 9,* 565–582.

Freud, S. (1962). Creative writers and daydreaming. In J. Strachey (Ed.), *The standard edition of the complete works of Sigmund Freud* (Vol. 9). London: Hogarth Press.

Huba, G. J., Singer, J. L., Aneshensel, C. S., & Antrobus, J. S. (1984). *The short Imaginal Processes Inventory*. Port Huron, MI: Research Psychologists Press.

Jones, J. C., & Barlow, D. H. (1990). Self-reported frequency of sexual urges, fantasies, and masturbatory fantasies in heterosexual males and females. *Archives of Sexual Behavior, 19*(3), 269–279.

Kinsey, A. C. (1948). *Sexual behavior in the human male.* Philadelphia: Saunders.

Knafo, D., & Jaffe, Y. (1984). Sexual fantasizing in males and females. *Journal of Research in Personality, 18,* 451–462.

Laws, D. R. (1989). *Relapse prevention with sex offenders.* New York: Guilford Press.

Looman, J. (1995). Sexual fantasies of child molesters. *Canadian Journal of Behavioral Sciences, 27,* 321–332.

MacCulloch, M. J., Snowden, P. R., Wood, P. J. W., & Mill, H. E. (1983). Sadistic fantasy, sadistic behavior and offending. *British Journal of Psychiatry, 143,* 20–29.

Marshall, W. L., Barbaree, H. E., & Eccles, A. (1991). Early onset and deviant sexuality in child molesters. *Journal of Interpersonal Violence, 6,* 323–336.

McKibben, A. Proulx, J., & Lusignan, R. (1994). Relationships between conflict, affect and deviant sexual behaviors in rapists and pedophiles. *Behavior Research and Therapy, 32,* 571–575.

Pithers, W. D., Beal, L. S., Armstrong, J., & Petty, J. (1989). Identification of risk factors through clinical interviews and analysis of records. In D. R. Laws (Ed.), *Relapse prevention with sex offenders* (pp. 63–72). New York: Guilford Press.

Proulx, J., McKibben, A., & Lusignan, R. (1996). Relationships between affective components and sexual behaviors in sexual aggressors. *Sexual Abuse: A Journal of Research and Treatment, 8*(4), 279–290.

Rokach, A. (1990). Content analysis of sexual fantasies of males and females. *Journal of Psychology, 124*(4), 427–436.

Singer, J. L. (1975). *The inner world of daydreaming.* New York: Harper & Row.

Singer, J. L. (1978). Experimental studies of daydreaming and the stream of thought. In K. S. Pope & J. L. Singer (Eds.), *The stream of consciousness* (pp. 187–223). New York: Plenum Press.

Ward, T., Hudson, S. M., Marshall, W. L., & Siegert, R. (1995). Attachment style and intimacy deficits in sexual offenders: A theoretical framework. *Sexual Abuse: A Journal of Research and Treatment, 7,* 317–335.

Wilson, G. D., & Lang, R. J. (1981). Sex differences in sexual fantasy patterns. *Journal of Personality and Treatment, 7,* 317–335.

Zelin, M. L. Bernstein, S. B., Heijin, C., Jampel, R. M., Myerson, P. G., Adler, G., Buie, D. H., & Rizzuto, A. M. (1983). The Sustaining Fantasy Questionnaire: Measurement of sustaining functions of fantasies in psychiatric inpatients. *Journal of Personality Assessment, 47,* 427–439.

Chapter 4

The Relationship Among Empathy, Cognitive Distortions, and Self-Esteem in Sexual Offenders

**by Y. M. Fernandez, M.A., D. Anderson, M.A.,
and W. L. Marshall, Ph.D.**

Overview

Enhancing empathy is a standard sex offender treatment procedure. The assumption is that sex offenders lack the capacity to empathize with others. In this chapter the authors present research that suggests that sex offenders are no less empathetic toward others than are normals unless one is measuring attitudes toward victims similar to their own. Consequently, it is suggested that this apparent lack of empathy is a set of cognitive distortions designed to protest faltering self-esteem. Viewing empathy not as a character trait but as a self-protective defense has definite implications for treatment.

Introduction

In recent years there has been a burst of research in the area of empathy deficits and cognitive distortions in sexual offenders. Studies using measures of generalized empathy have been unable to discriminate between sexual offenders and men who have not committed sexual offenses (Rice, Chaplin, Harris, & Coutts, 1994; Seto 1992). However, studies using empathy measures that specifically target either victims of sexual assault or the offender's own victims have reported clear differences between nonoffenders and sexual offenders (Fernandez, Marshall, Lightbody, & O'Sullivan, 1996; Hanson & Scott, 1995; McGrath, Cann, & Konopasky, 1998; Scully, 1988). A consideration of these findings led us (Fernandez & Marshall, 1998) to suggest that deficits in empathy may reflect the use of cognitive distortions. That is, sexual offenders may deliberately distort their perceptions of their victims' distress in order to be able to continue offending without feeling guilt or remorse. Thus they will appear empathic toward their victims while displaying empathy toward others.

Cognitive Distortions May Protect Self-Esteem

Sexual offenders' use of cognitive distortions may also be related to their sense of self-esteem. Because people low in self-esteem are motivated to protect their sense of self-worth from further erosion, such individuals are most likely to engage in self-serving biases when interpreting events and their behavior (Baumeister, Tice, & Hutton, 1989; Wills, 1981). Thus, the probability that sexual offenders will engage in cognitive distortions to avoid recognizing their victims' distress (i.e., the degree to which they will appear empathic toward their victims) should be a function of the level of their self-esteem. In this chapter, we examine the link between cognitive distortions and empathy deficits and offer an interpretation for these processes in sexual offenders that is based on the literature of self-esteem.

Empathy Is Context Determined

Measures of generalized empathy such as Hogan's Empathy Scale (Hogan, 1969), the Emotional Empathy Scale (Mehrabian & Epstein, 1972), and the Interpersonal Reactivity Index (Davis, 1983) follow the standard "trait" approach to empathy reflected in most of the literature (for a review of the use of these scales in the assessment of sexual offenders see Hanson, in press). As a rule, empathy has been conceptualized as a fixed disposition that is demonstrated unvaryingly across time and place. However, this conceptualization implies that empathy should be demonstrated equally toward all people in all situations. Everyday experience seems to contradict this implication. Most, if not all, people seem to have no trouble withholding empathy toward some individuals while readily expressing compassion for others. Recently, sexual offender literature has shown a trend toward identifying situations in which people are more or less likely to show empathy. Marshall, Hudson, Jones, and Fernandez (1995) strongly endorsed context-specific research on empathy. They suggested that we should not expect general empathy deficits in sexual offenders anymore than we would in the population at large. Although some sexual offenders, such as those who score high on measures of psychopathy, might reasonably be expected to demonstrate little empathy toward anyone, the majority of sexual offenders can be expected to be quite empathic in a variety of non–sexual-offense-related situations.

A Multistage Model of Empathy

Before describing research that has attempted to examine more person-specific empathy among sexual offenders, it may be helpful to provide a framework for understanding the empathetic process. There are many views expressed in the general literature on the nature of empathy, but currently multicomponent models seem to be the most popular (Marshall et al., 1995). The model of Marshall and associates suggests that empathy is a multistage unfolding process. First, it is necessary to recognize the emotional state of the observed person before the empathy process is initiated. We can hardly feel sorry for another person unless we recognize their suffering. Next, our empathic response will be proportional to the degree to which we can see things from the perspective of the observed person. Once these two stages have been effectively engaged, our empathic response will depend on our capacity to emotionally respond to these cognitions. Finally, feeling genuine concern for the suffering person, we may or may not take actions to ameliorate their distress. Marshall et al. (1995) suggest that sexual offenders may have problems at any or all of these stages. Insofar as cognitive distortions play a part in inhibiting empathy, sexual offenders may distort their view of the victim's suffering or distort their perspective of the victim's position (i.e., they may believe the victim could terminate the abuse). Of course, some sexual offenders, as we noted, may be sufficiently psychopathic that they do not care about, or are not moved by, their victim's suffering. The evidence suggests that few sexual offenders are psychopathic (Serin, Malcolm, Khanna, & Barbaree, 1994). In addition, sadistic sexual offenders can be expected to accurately recognize distress but enjoy it rather than experience empathy. Again, however, sadists constitute a small portion of sexual offenders (Hucker, 1997).

Measure of Empathy

A number of measures have been developed that tackle this new approach to conceptualizing empathy. The Empathy for Women and Empathy for Children tests (Hanson & Scott, 1995) use written vignettes to assess perspective-taking deficits in sexual offenders. Fernandez et al. (1997) described a measure of empathy for child molesters that required subjects to identify their own feelings and the various emotions and problems experienced by three different children: an automobile accident victim who is permanently disfigured, a nonspecific victim of child sexual abuse, and the offender's own victim. The Empat Scale attempts to assess both general and specific empathy. It measures an individual's ability to show empathy for victims of sexual abuse, as well as empathy toward others across many common, nonsexual situations (McGrath et al., 1998). Other measures that have been developed to assess sexual offenders' empathy toward victims of sexual abuse include having rapists rate women's reactions in videotaped vignettes of dating situations (Lipton, McDonel, & McFall, 1987; Murphy, Coleman, & Haynes, 1986) and having child molesters respond to written descriptions of adult and child sexual interactions (Beckett, Beech, Fisher, & Fordham, 1994; Stermac & Segal, 1989).

Sex Offender's Deficits Appear to Be Victim Specific

Evidence has been generated that supports the conclusion that sexual offenders' empathy deficits are victim specific. Hudson, Marshall, Wales, McDonald, Bakker, and McLean (1993) found that sexual offenders and violent offenders had difficulty identifying surprise, fear, anger, and disgust in others. Of course, these emotions are just the types of responses we might expect a victim of sexual abuse to display. Unless the observer accurately identifies a person's distress, he will not manifest empathy. In a separate study these same authors found that child molesters performed more poorly than a group of community males at identifying the emotions of both adults and children (Hudson et al., 1993).

Fernandez et al. (1997) found that child molesters showed lower empathy scores, relative to a group of nonoffenders, toward a child who had been the victim of sexual abuse but showed no deficits in empathy toward a child who had been a victim of a car accident. In addition, the child molesters exhibited their greatest empathy deficits toward their own victim(s). In a subsequent study Fernandez and Marshall (1998) used a modified version of the Child Empathy measure to assess rapists. They reported that the rapists demonstrated more empathy as the nonsex offenders toward the sexual assault victim. Of particular interest, however, was that the rapist group revealed significant empathy deficits toward their own victim(s).

McGrath et al. (1998) determined that their sexual offender sample showed less empathy toward victims of sexual abuse than did either a community group of nonoffenders or nonsex offenders on the Empat scale. Even when the sexual offenders were instructed to "fake good," they still responded less empathetically toward victims of sexual abuse than did the other groups.

Rapists Unable to Identify Distress in Women

Lipton et al. (1987) reported that rapists had difficulty recognizing women's negative signals in videotaped vignettes of dating situations. Similarly, Murphy, Coleman, and Haynes (1986) found that difficulties identifying women's distress in videotapes was correlated with self-reported sexually coercive behavior while McDonel and McFall (1991) found that such difficulties were correlated with self-reported likelihood of raping. Once again the men studied by these researchers appeared to have specific problems identifying women's negative cues rather than general decoding deficits. Effective empathy, we note again, is dependent on first recognizing the emotional state of the other person.

Scully (1988) examined the perceptions of forty-seven rapists of their own responses and the victim's responses to their assault. Fifty-four percent of the sample was unable to describe any of their own emotions during the assault of their feelings toward the victim. If a person is unable to recognize his feelings, it seems unlikely that he will experience empathy or if he does feel compassion, he will not be able to identify it and report it as empathy. In a study by Deitz, Blackwell, Daley, and Bentley (1982), reseasrchers found that nonoffender subjects who demonstrated high empathy toward rape victims reported less desire to actually commit rape than did men who demonstrated lower empathy toward the victim. In a later study, Deitz and his colleagues reported that empathy toward both the victim and the offender predicted nonoffender male subjects' perception of the victim, the offender, and the offense (Deitz, Littman, & Bentley, 1984). Wiener, Wiener, and Grisso (1989) found that the scores of nonoffender males on the measure used in the studies (Deitz, Blackwell, et al., 1982; Dietz, Littman, & Bentley, 1984) influenced the subjects' processing of information given by witnesses in a rape trial.

Child Molesters Underestimate Child's Distress

Written vignettes of adult and child sexual interactions were used in a study by Stermac and Segal (1989). They found that in vignettes describing the child as show-ing few overt signs of resistance, the child molesters, as compared to rapists and nonoffenders, tended to underestimate the child's distress. Apparently the child moles-ters read the absence of signs of distress as indicating no distress whereas the other subjects seemed to assume that the act of molestation itself automatically induced dis-tress. Beckett et al. (1994) similarly found that child molesters, when asked to respond to written vignettes of adult and child sexual interactions, underestimated the harm-lessness of some types of sexual offenses. As with the Stermac and Segal (1989) study, the sexual offenders in the Beckett study were more likely to minimize the harmful-ness of sexual assaults that did not involve obvious force. In all cases, mistakes reflect-ed an inability to perceive distress.

On their Empathy for Women Test, Hanson and Scott (1995) reported clear group differences between the sexual offenders and comparison groups. Similar to the video-taped studies (Lipton et al., 1987; Murphy et al., 1986) the sexual offenders tend to underestimate the women's distress in the vignettes. The Child Empathy Test study found that the child molesters who were in treatment made fewer errors on the test than did untreated sexual offenders. In addition, incest offenders made more mistakes on the incest items than did other sexual offenders.

Empathy Deficits Product of Cognitive Distortion

The results of these studies strongly suggest that empathy deficits in sexual offenders are best examined in relation to particular people (i.e., victims of sexual abuse) or in particular circumstances (i.e., when victimization is occurring). The find-ings of the previous studies clearly suggest that the majority of sexual offenders have their primary problem in empathizing with their victims. That is, they suffer from vic-tim-specific empathy deficits. However, there may be another way to interpret these results. Perhaps the apparent empathy deficits demonstrated by sexual offenders are not necessarily evidence of a lack of empathy but, rather, another facet of the cogni-tive distortions that are so characteristically evident in sexual offenders. Sexual offenders appear to have general empathic skills that are equal to those of nonoffend-ers (i.e., they are just as empathic toward a disfigured accident victim, and on gener-al measures of empathy, they appear normal) but display little empathy toward their own victim. Thus it is tempting to construe the latter apparent deficit as either a delib-erate withholding of empathy or, more likely, a deliberate and successful attempt to deny having done any harm to the victim. This denial may result from both shutting out and distorting perceptions of the victim's distress during the assault and subse-quently ignoring or distorting post-assault signs of distress. Sexual offenders certainly do deny harming their victims (Abel et al., 1989), and this is usually considered to represent distorted perceptions.

Lack of Empathy Relieves Personal Distress

Sexual offenders, like most people, tend to perceive things in a self-surveying way. In their case, sexual offenders want to continue offending without feeling any personal distress, and the best way to achieve this is to see their victims as unharmed by the abuse. Unfortunately, persistently construing their victims in this way, which is often supported by the offender's family and friends, allows the sexual offender to convince himself that his offenses are exceptions to the general rule that sexual abuse causes damage to victims. In our model of empathy, emotional recognition is the necessary first step. Thus the denial of harm prevents the unfolding of the empathic process and results in an apparent victim-specific deficit in empathy. According to this view, most sexual offenders should appear appropriately empathic toward people distressed by events other than sexual abuse (e.g., a person injured in a motor vehicle accident). Some sexual offenders may adopt the conservative strategy of distorting their recognition of harm resulting from sexual offending in general, although most are likely to restrict their distortions to their own victim. Thus, a cognitive distortion analysis of apparent empathy deficits would suggest that the primary problem for sexual offenders is an apparent lack of empathy toward their own victim. Because some sexual offenders could be expected to adopt a somewhat more generalized strategy of denying harm to any victims of sexual assault, some will appear unempathic toward all such victims.

Other researchers have also pointed out that empathy deficits in sexual offenders are inextricably linked to cognitive distortions. Hilton (1993), for example, has suggested that lack of empathy could be "woven into the bed of cognitive distortions" promoting further minimizations and justifications of the offensive behavior. Likewise, Hanson (in press) points out that measures of cognitive distortions are an alternative route to identifying empathy deficits. It has been shown that treatment aimed at increasing empathy to sexual assault victims decreases cognitive distortions in sexual offenders (Bumby, 1994; Pithers, 1994; Schewe & O'Donohue, 1993). A look at many of the current victim-specific empathy questionnaires (Beckett et al., 1994; Fernandez et al., 1997; Hanson & Scott, 1995) reveals that these measures include many items that could readily be interpreted as revealing cognitive distortions (e.g., items that address minimization of harm to the victim). For example, sexual offenders claim that their victims are either not harmed from the experience or actually enjoy the interaction (Abel, Becker, & Cunningham-Rathner, 1984; Snowden, 1984).

Relevance of Self-Esteem

The supposition that sexual offenders are deficient in their ability to empathize with others, particularly with their victims or with women or children in general, has led treatment providers to target empathy enhancement as a goal of therapy. Similar deficiencies in empathic responses have been found among people with low self-esteem (Kalliopuska, 1987), and more recently, Marshall, Champagne, Brown, and Miller (1995) found that child molesters who had low self-esteem were more likely to demonstrate empathy deficits than were those whose self-esteem was higher.

Baumeister (1993) points out that people with low self-esteem experience considerable problems in their social relationships. Both clinical experience and research findings indicate that sexual offenders also have difficulty with their social and sexual relationships (Marshall, Barbaree, & Fernandez, 1995; Stermac, Segal, & Gillis, 1990). It has been proposed (Marshall, 1989) that these relationship difficulties stem from the lack of intimacy, and indeed sexual offenders have been found to have marked intimacy deficits (Seidman, Marshall, Hudson, & Robertson, 1994). The need for a feeling of closeness may be part of the underlying motivation to seek sexual interaction, even to the point of using force or involving children to gratify this need (Marshall, 1989).

It is possible that sexual offenders are not able to distinguish the need for intimacy from their desire for sex, and they may not have learned the necessary skills to fulfill intimacy needs. As noted, sexual offenders do indeed lack many of the skills that would help them with social and sexual interactions, and consequently satisfy their need for intimacy. Ward, McCormack, and Hudson (1997) found that sexual offenders are reluctant to express physical affection or to self-disclose, and they tend to have poor conflict resolution skills.

If sexual offenders do not possess these necessary relationship skills, they have either failed to learn them or someone has failed to teach them. Research tends to support the latter explanation. Theorists (Bowlby, 1969) and researchers (Bartholomew, 1993) indicate that the source of poor relationship styles in adults originates with insecure attachment styles resulting from troubled relationships with parents. Sexual offenders have been found to display such insecure attachment patterns, with child molesters having demonstrated increased sensitivity to rejection and a greater likelihood to be anxiously dependent (Ward, Hudson, & Marshall, 1996). It is understandable that an adult who is highly sensitive to rejection and incapable of forming secure attachments with other adults may feel more comfortable in a relationship with a child. A relationship with a child may feel less risky because there may be less perceived risk of being abandoned and, quite reasonably, less fear of being rejected. Similarly, sexual offenders confuse sex with intimacy; thus forcing a woman to have sex may also represent a nonthreatening route to intimacy in the view of the rapist.

It might be expected that if an inability to achieve intimacy is related to problematic attachment patterns, and difficulties in expressing empathy are associated with a lack of intimacy, there might be a relationship between attachment styles and the expression of empathy. Indeed, deficits in empathic expressions have been observed in people who experienced problematic relationships with parents. Corollary findings from Zahn-Waxler and Radke-Yarrow (1990) indicated that children who exhibited empathy and the ability to engage in prosocial behavior were more likely to display secure attachment patterns.

An associated link between self-esteem and the parent–child relationships has also been examined. Coopersmith (1967) found that boys who exhibited high self-esteem had a closer and more loving relationship with their parents than did boys with low self-esteem. He found that the boys with low self-esteem were more depressed, anxious, isolated, and destructive than those with high self-esteem. The male college students in a study by Child, Frank, and Storm (1956) evaluated themselves positively on traits their parents had rewarded and negatively on traits their parents had punished. Marshall and Mazzucco (1995) subsequently demonstrated that the degree of disruption in the relationships between offenders and their parents was inversely related to their adult self-esteem.

Space Relations Between Victim-Specific Empathy, Cognitive Distortions, and Self-Esteem

As Fernandez and Marshall (1995) have suggested, the apparent empathy deficits observed in sexual offenders may not be a problem with empathy but rather may reflect the use of cognitive distortions. The research reviewed in the previous section suggests that, to date, empathy research on sexual offenders has actually been examining a specific set of cognitive distortions (i.e., those related to harm caused to the victim). Fernandez and Marshall's theory would help explain the lack of evidence indicating generalized empathy deficits among sexual offenders. This view of empathy problems suggests links between empathy deficits in sexual offenders and both their uses of cognitive distortions and low self-esteem. For instance, people low in self-esteem have been found to pay little attention to others because they are so self-focused (Hutton, 1991). Being unable to attend to others would almost certainly cause a person to miss cues of distress in others. This would suggest a connection between a lack of empathy and low self-esteem, and we have already suggested that empathy and cognitive distortions are linked.

Sexual offenders' use of cognitive distortions may also be related to their sense of self-esteem. These cognitive distortions may reflect the offender's use of "self-serving biases," which are common in the cognitive processes of all people (Bradley, 1978; Miller & Ross, 1975; Zuckerman, 1979), although these processes are exaggerated in those low in self-esteem (Blaine & Crocker, 1993; Tennen & Herzberger, 1987). These cognitive processes allow individuals to make interpretations such that their views of themselves are preserved. However, others may have a different interpretation, and when they offer it, an individual may perceive the comments as negative feedback, especially if the individual attempting to preserve his sense of self-worth does not have a positive self-evaluation. Those with negative self-evaluations are more likely to use self-serving biases in their interpretations of negative events because of a greater need for security in their sense of self-worth (Wills, 1981). These individuals are thus able to maintain a weak grip on a mediocre, but tolerable, self-evaluation. These biases can be related to the victim-specific empathy deficits seen in the sexual offender as he attempts to block perceptions of harm to his victim in order not to feel guilt or shame. These biased interpretations of their own offense and its consequences prevent compassionate thoughts about their victims, which effectively precludes feelings of shame and guilt.

Researchers and clinicians agree that the cognitive distortions observed in sexual offenders are self-serving (e.g., Murphy, 1990; Segal & Stermac, 1990). For example, many offenders minimize the extent of violence or the amount of threats used during their offenses. Also, they tend to minimize the frequency and the intrusiveness of the assaults. Many offenders offer external attributions for their behaviors (e.g., they attribute their behavior to the use of drugs and alcohol), and some may even deny interaction with certain victims altogether. Prompts and challenges in treatment have been shown to lead some offenders to admit aspects of their offenses that they had previously denied or minimized (Barbaree, 1991; Marshall, 1989). These offenders have not suddenly recalled details but have merely altered their perceptions of the offense. These changes result in a different, more accurate, portrayal of their own behaviors and the behaviors of their victims. Such modifications suggest that many sexual offenders, not surprisingly, begin therapy with a strong motivation for self-protection (i.e., protection from negative feedback and consequent threats to their self-image).

Therapy is not the first time, however, that many offenders have felt the need to protect themselves from feeling the negative affect associated with a blow to their self-image. The vast majority of offenders know they are doing something wrong from the first time they commit an offense. Otherwise, we would expect them to discuss their offenses openly with others, but they do not. In order to integrate their abusive behavior with their self-image in a way that is self-protective, sexual offenders must engage in some form of distorted interpretations of the offenses.

Offenders With High Self-Esteem Rely Less on Cognitive Distortions

We would expect such a thought process to allow the offender to maintain his level of self-esteem (i.e., to prevent further decline) when he would otherwise be susceptible to self-disparaging thoughts and the accompanying negative emotional experience. Some of our own preliminary research supports this claim. In a sample of child molesters, we found differences between those with high self-esteem and those with low self-esteem in the patterns of relationships among empathy, cognitive distortions, and self-esteem (Anderson, Fernandez, & Marshall, 1997). The results suggest that offenders with high self-esteem might not need to engage in cognitive distortions related to their offenses to maintain their self-image. Rather, it is possible that these men are drawing on other attributes in the face of the threat to their self-worth that offending presents. Consequently, these high-self-esteem offenders are equipped to face this threat without using cognitive distortions, and they should, therefore, feel more empathic toward their victims. This is just what we (Anderson et al., 1997) found.

On the other hand, the offenders with low self-esteem in our study appeared to be using cognitive distortions to protect themselves from the damage of this threat to their already low self-esteem. Spencer, Josephs, and Steele (1993) indicated that people with low self-esteem are less capable of retrieving other positive self-attributes to build their self-worth and hence must focus on reducing the impact of immediate threats. In our preliminary study, then, it appears that the group of child molesters low in self-esteem, engaged in cognitive distortions and exhibited victim-specific empathy deficits in order to protect their self-esteem from further erosion.

Conclusion

Our own research suggests that components targeted in treatment (empathy and cognitive distortions) do not serve the same function for all sexual offenders (Anderson et al., 1997). It is important for clinicians to understand the function that clinging to cognitive distortions and resisting empathic responses may be serving for their clients. If self-esteem is threatened by sexual offending, then such offenders distort information from this victim to protect their self-esteem. Unless this is done, we can expect sexual offenders to respond to challenges by feeling threatened and by withdrawing from effective therapeutic interactions. It follows, then, that one goal during the treatment process should be to maintain or enhance the self-esteem of all group participants. This approach may help to break their grasp on the distorted thought processes among those sexual offenders who are motivated to protect themselves from threats to their self-esteem.

In addition, attempting to enhance the general capacity for empathy among sexual offenders in treatment not only may be ineffective (as they appear already to be generally empathic) but may discourage confidence in the therapists and may cause the offenders to see treatment as irrelevant to their real problems. If, as we have suggested, apparent empathy deficits are restricted to their own victim and result from distorting information about the offenses and its consequences, then these empathy deficits can be overcome by challenging the offenders' distortions rather then enhancing their capacity for empathy. Thus a combination of self-esteem enhancement and supportive challenges to the offender's view of victim harm may be the most effective treatment approach to deal with apparent empathy deficits in sexual offenders.

References

Abel, G. G., Becker, J. V., & Cunningham-Rathner, J. (1984). Complications, consent, and cognitions in sex between children and adults. *International Journal of Law and Psychiatry, 7,* 89–103.

Abel, G. G., Gore, D. K., Holland, C. L., Camp, N., Becker, J. V., & Rathner, J. (1989). The measurement of the cognitive distortions of child molesters. *Annals of Sex Research, 2,* 135–152.

Anderson, D., Fernandez, Y. M., & Marshall, W. L. (1997). *Integrating treatment components in sexual offender therapy: Toward a more cost-effective approach.* Paper presented at the meeting of the Association for the Treatment of Sexual Abusers, Arlington, VA.

Barbaree, H. E. (1991). Denial and minimization among sex offenders: Assessment and treatment outcome. *Forum on Corrections Research, 3,* 300–333.

Bartholomew, K. (1993). Understanding the inner nature of low self-esteem: Uncertain, fragile, protective, and conflicted. In R. F. Baumeister (Ed.), *Self-esteem: The puzzle of low self-regard* (pp. 201–218). New York: Plenum Press.

Baumeister, R. F. (1993). Understanding the inner nature of low self-esteem: Uncertain, fragile, protective, and conflicted. In R. Baumeister (Ed.), Self-esteem: The puzzle of low self-regard (pp. 201–218). New York: Plenum Press.

Baumeister, R. F., Tice, D., & Hutton, D. (1989). Self-presentational motivations and personality differences in self-esteem. *Journal of Personality, 57,* 547–579.

Beckett, R., Beech, A., Fisher, D., & Fordham, A. S. (1994). *Community-based treatment of sex offenders: An evaluation of seven treatment programmes.* Home Office Occasional Paper.. London: Home Office.

Blaine, B., & Crocker, J. (1993). Self-esteem and self-serving biases in reaction to positive and negative events: An integrative review. In R. F. Baumeister (Ed.), *Self-esteem: The puzzle of low self-regard* (pp. 55–58). New York: Plenum Press.

Bowlby, J. (1969). *Attachment and loss: Attachment* (Vol. 1). New York: Basic Books.

Bradley, G. W. (1978). Self-serving biases in the attribution processes: A re-examination of the fact or fiction question. *Journal of Personality and Social Psychology, 36,* 56–71.

Bumby, K. (1994, November). *Cognitive distortions of child molesters and rapists.* Paper presented at the Thirteenth Annual Research and Treatment Conference of the Association for the Treatment of Sexual Abusers, San Francisco.

Child, I. L., Frank, K. F., & Storm, T. (1956). Self-ratings and TAT; their relation to behavior. *Journal of Personality, 25,* 96–114.

Coopersmith, S. (1967). *The antecedents of self-esteem.* San Francisco: Freeman.

Davis, M. H. (1983). Measuring individual differences in empathy: Evidence for a multidimensional approach. *Journal of Consulting Psychology, 24,* 349–354.

Deitz, S. R., Blackwell, K. T., Daley, P. C., & Bentley, B. J. (1982). Measurement of empathy toward rape victims and rapists. *Journal of Personality and Social Psychology, 43,* 372–384.

Deitz, S. R. Littman, M., & Bentley, B. J., (1984). Attribution of responsibility for rape: The influence of observer empathy, victim resistance, and victim attractiveness, *Sex Roles, 10,* 261–280.

Fernandez, Y. M., & Marshall, W. L. (1995). *The Rapist Empathy Measure.* Manuscript submitted for publication.

Fernandez, Y. M., Marshall, W. L., O'Sullivan, C., & Lightbody, S. (1997). *The Child Molester Empathy Measure: Description and examination of its reliability and validity.* Manuscript submitted for publication.

Hanson, R. K. (in press). Assessing sexual offenders' capacity for empathy. *Psychology, Crime and Law.*

Hanson, R. K., & Scott, H. (1995). Assessing perspective taking among sexual offenders, nonsexual criminals and nonoffenders. *Sexual Abuse: A Journal of Research and Treatment, 7*(4), 259–277.

Hilton, Z. (1993). Childhood sexual victimization and lack of empathy in child molesters: Explanation or excuse? *International Journal of Offender Therapy and Comparative Criminology, 37*(4), 287–296.

Hogan, R. (1969). Development of an empathy scale. *Journal of Consulting and Clinical Psychology, 33,* 307–316.

Hucker, S. J. (1997) Sexual sadism: Psychopathology and theory. In D. R. Laws & W. O'Donohue (Eds.), *Sexual deviance: Theory, assessment and theory* (pp. 194–209) New York: Guilford Press.

Hudson, S. M., Marshall, W. L., Wales, D., McDonald, E., Bakker, L., & McLean, A. (1993). Emotional recognition in sex offenders. *Annals of Sex Research, 6,* 199–211.

Hutton, D. G. (1991). *Self-esteem and memory for social interaction.* Unpublished dissertation, Case Western Reserve University, Ohio.

Kalliopuska, M. (1987). Relation of empathy and self-esteem to active participation in Finnish baseball. *Perceptual and Motor Skills, 65,* 107–113.

Lipton, D. N., McDonel, E. C., & McFall, R. M. (1987). Heterosexual perception in rapists. *Journal of Consulting and Clinical Psychology, 55,* 17–21.

Marshall, W. L. (1989). Intimacy, loneliness, & sexual offenders. *Behavior Research and Therapy, 27,* 491–503.

Marshall, W. L., Barbaree, H. E., & Fernandex, Y. M. (1995). Some aspects of social competence in sexual offenders. *Sexual Abuse: A Journal of Research and Treatment, 7,* 113–127.

Marshall, W. L., Champagne, F., Brown, C., & Miller, S. (1995). *Empathy, intimacy, loneliness, and self-esteem in nonfamilial child molesters.* Unpublished manuscript.

Marshall, W. L., Hudson, S. L., Jones, R., & Fernandez, Y. M. (1995). Empathy in sex offenders. *Clinical Psychology Review, 15*(2), 99–113.

Marshall, W. L., & Mazzucco, A. (1995). Self-esteem and parental attachments in child molesters. *Sexual Abuse: A Journal of Research and Treatment, 7,* 279–285.

McDonel, E. C., & McFall, R. M. (1991). Construct validity of two heterosexual perception skill measures for assessing rape proclivity. *Violence and Victims, 6,* 17–30.

McGrath, M., Cann, S., & Konopasky, R. (1998). New measures of defensiveness, empathy and cognitive distortions for sexual offenders against children. *Sexual Abuse: A Journal of Research and Treatment, 10*(1), 25–36.

Mehrabian, A., & Epstein, N. (1972). A measure of emotional empathy. *Journal of Personality, 40,* 525-543.

Miller, D. T., & Ross, M. (1975). Self-serving biases in attribution of causality: Fact or fiction? *Psychological Bulletin, 82,* 213–225.

Murphy, W. D. (1990). Assessment and modification of cognitive distortions in sex offenders. In W. L. Marshall, D. R. Laws, & H. E. Barbaree (Eds.), *Handbook of sexual assault: Issues, theories, and treatment of the offender* (pp. 331–342). New York: Plenum Press.

Murphy, W. D., Coleman, E. M., & Haynes, M. R. (1986). Factors related to coercive sexual behavior in a nonclinical sample of males. *Violence and Victims, 1,* 255–278.

Pithers, W. D. (1994). Process evaluation of a group therapy component designed to enhance sex offenders' empathy for sexual abuse survivors. *Behavior Research and Therapy, 32,* 565–570.

Rice, M. E., Chaplin, T. E., Harris, G. E., & Coutts, J. (1994). Empathy for the victim and sexual arousal among rapists and nonrapists. *Journal of Interpersonal Violence, 9*(4), 435–449.

Schewe, P. A., & O'Donohue, W. (1993). Sexual abuse prevention with high-risk males: The roles of victim empathy and rape myths. *Violence and Victims, 8,* 339–351.

Scully, D. (1988). Convicted rapists' perceptions of self and victim: Role taking and emotions. *Gender and Society, 2,* 200–213.

Segal, Z. V., & Stermac, L. E. (1990). The role of cognition in sexual assaults. In W. L. Marshall, D. R. Laws, & H. E. Barbaree (Eds.), *Handbook of sexual assault: Issues, theories, and treatment of the offender* (pp. 161–174). New York: Plenum Press.

Seidman, B. T., Marshall, W. L., Hudson, S. M., & Robertson, P. J. (1994). An examination of intimacy and loneliness in sex offenders. *Journal of Interpersonal Violence, 9,* 3–11.

Serin, R. C., Malcolm, P. B., Khanna, A., & Barbaree, H. E. (1994). Psychopathy and deviant sexual arousal in incarcerated sexual offenders. *Journal of Interpersonal Violence, 9*(1), 3–11.

Seto, M. (1992). *Victim blame, empathy and disinhabition of sexual arousal to rape in community males and incarcerated rapists.* Unpublished master's thesis, Queen's University, Kingston, Ohio.

Snowdon, R. (1984). Working with incest offenders: Excuses, excuses, excuses. *Aegis, 35,* 56–63.

Spencer, S. J., Josephs, R. A., & Steele, C. M. (1993). Low self-esteem: The uphill struggle for self-integrity. In R. F. Baumeister (Ed.), *Self-esteem: The puzzle of low self-regard* (pp. 21–36). New York: Plenum Press.

Stermac, L. E., & Segal, Z. V. (1989). Adult sexual contact with children: An examination of cognitive factors. *Behavior Therapy, 20,* 573–584.

Stermac, L. E., Segal, Z. V,. & Gillis, R. (1990). Social and cultural factors in sexual assault. In W. L. Marshall, D. R. Laws, & H. E. Barbaree (Eds.), *Handbook of sexual assault: Issues, theories, and treatment of the offender* (pp. 143–159). New York: Plenum Press.

Tennen, H., & Herzberger, S. (1987). Depression, self-esteem, and the absence of self-protective attributional biases. *Journal of Personality and Social Psychology, 52,* 72–80.

Ward, T. Hudson, S. M., & Marshall, W. L. (1996). Attachment style in sex offenders: A preliminary study. *Journal of Sex Research, 33,* 17–26.

Ward, T., McCormack, J., & Hudson, S. M. (1997). Sexual offenders' perceptions of their intimate relationships. *Sexual Abuse: A Journal of Research and Treatment, 9,* 57–74.

Wiener, R. L., Wiener, A. T., & Grisso, T. (1989). Empathy and biased assimilation of testimonies in cases of alleged rape. *Law and Human Behavior, 13,* 343–355.

Wills, T. A. (1981). Downward comparison principles in social psychology. *Psychological Bulletin, 90,* 245–271.

Zahn-Waxler, C., & Radke-Yarrow, M. (1990). The origins of empathic concern. *Motivation and Emotion, 14,* 107–130.

Zuckerman, M. (1979). Attribution of success and failure revisited, or the motivational bias is alive and well in attribution theory. *Journal of Personality, 47,* 245–287.

Chapter 5

A Theoretical Model of the Influences of Shame and Guilt on Sexual Offending

by Kurt M. Bumby, Ph.D., W. L. Marshall, Ph.D., and Calvin M. Langton, M.A.

Overview

The authors of this chapter investigate the differences between guilt and shame and the degree to which each contributes to sexual assault. Treatment implications for dealing with each of these concepts are explored. It is suggested that shame, which is an emotion connected with a condemnation of the total person, should be avoided, whereas guilt over specific transgressions should be the focus of treatment.

Introduction

It has generally been accepted that negative affective states play a significant role at various points in the sexual offending cycle. Of particular importance is the recognition of the negative cognitive and affective responses used to cope with transgressions such as lapses or actual offenses, otherwise referred to as the abstinence violation effect (AVE) in terms of the relapse prevention model. Indeed, the AVE is believed to be critical in determining continued abstinence or, conversely, an increased likelihood for offending. To summarize, following a cognitive or behavioral lapse or the actual perpetration of a sexual offense, an attributional process occurs whereby the offender ascribes the transgression to either internal stable and global determinants or external unstable and specific elements. The particular attributions regarding the cause of the offense, combined with a variety of other factors (the nature of the violation, level of commitment to abstinence, use of cognitive distortions, prior successes or failures, self-esteem, etc.), determine the magnitude of the AVE as well as the intensity and type of negative affect experienced (Russell, Sturgeon, Miner, & Nelson, 1989).

A Theoretical Conceptualization of Negative Affect

Unfortunately, although negative affect has been clinically observed and speculated as being influential in the initiation and maintenance of sexually offending behavior, empirically it has been found to have little predictive value with respect to recidivism among sexual offenders (Hanson & Bussière, 1996). This lack of predictive utility may, in part, be the result of the absence of a clear theoretical framework within which to guide empirical investigations with respect to negative affect and sexual offending. In this chapter, therefore, we propose a theoretical conceptualization within which to consider the distinct negative affective experiences of shame and guilt in the context of sexually offending behavior. To be explicit, in our model we concentrate on the role of shame and guilt with respect to the AVE and subsequent risk of reoffense. To begin, we briefly review some of the more general psychological literature pertaining to shame and guilt (Tangney & Fischer, 1995), underscoring the similarities and differences between the two affective experiences and then applying them to sexual offending behaviors.

Similarities Between Shame and Guilt. Shame and guilt have been referred to as "social emotions": Both emotions are typically experienced within interpersonal contexts and social interactions (Barrett, 1995; Tangney, 1995). The social nature of shame and guilt is also underscored by the influential nature of socialization in the development of these emotions (see Barrett, 1995). Specifically, socialization processes are critical in the determination and significance of the rules, morals, and standards that often become goals for the individuals of a particular culture. Conversely, social emotions such as shame and guilt motivate individuals to follow these socially prescribed standards of behavior. Along this vein, shame and guilt have been classified as "moral emotions," due to their common role in regulating ethical and conscientious behavior while inhibiting transgressions (see Barrett, 1995; Tangney, 1995). Further, both shame and guilt are considered to be negatively valanced affective experiences that ensue following an individual's perception of a failure to adhere to an internal or external moral code (Tangney, 1995). Finally, as shame and guilt involve self-referential attributions of a negatively evaluative quality with regard to a specified standard for the self or one's behavior, these affective experiences have the connotation of being "self-conscious" emotions (Tangney, 1995; Lewis, 1991).

The similarities between shame guilt have been long recognized. To be sure, until Lewis (1971) offered a clear conceptualization of the distinct role these affective experiences play in symptom formation and interpersonal dynamics, many theorists failed to differentiate between the two emotions. However, a considerable and growing body of theoretical and empirical support for a distinction between shame and guilt, with many studies revealing differences among cognitive, affective, and motivational dimensions, now exists (Tangney, 1995). It is the discrimination between shame and guilt which is most relevant to our theoretical framework; hence, we contrast these negative affective experiences in Table 5.1.

Shame Reflects Global Assessment. Contemporary theorists generally agree that shame reflects a focus on the entire or global self and involves a negative, scrutinizing, self-appraisal (i.e., "bad self") (Barrett, 1995; Lewis, 1971, 1987; Tangney, 1995). This painful self-evaluation is associated with a subsequent sense of worthlessness, helplessness, and powerlessness, as well as with the perception and fear of negative evaluation by others, whether or not others are actually present. In turn, these concerns of disapproval prompt the individual to want to "shrink" or hide from others. Intense and painful evaluation of a person's global self poses a clear threat to the individual's sense of self-worth and self-efficacy. Consequently, this threat induces passivity and a crippling of adaptive coping responses, as the individual holds a consequent belief that only limited opportunities exist to change what he perceives to be global defect (Barrett, 1995; Tangney, 1995). Moreover, perceiving themselves as being wholly negative or defective (i.e., a bad person), shamed individuals will likely see little reason to expend effort toward change, as by definition they believe themselves to be unworthy and incapable.

Shame Fuels Anger. It is important to highlight the identified relationship between shame and anger. Initially following the transgression, anger may be directed toward the self. However, due to the projected image of negative evaluation from a disapproving other, the shamed individual directs hostility and anger toward others as a retaliatory response, in what Tangney (1995) refers to as "humiliated fury." This displaced anger, hostility, and externalization of blame temporarily ameliorate the painful experience of shame. These increased tendencies toward anger, hostility, and defensive externalization, coupled with the self-focused nature of the shame experience, have particularly significant implications for our model with respect to empathy. Again, as shame is self-focused (i.e., on the global self rather than on the specific behavior), emphasis is oriented away from the harm that was caused or with the pain experienced by the harmed person. Rather, the focus is on the negative characteristics of the self (e.g., "I am a bad person for having hurt someone"), which in turn leads to self-oriented distress rather than other-oriented empathy.

Clearly, what appears to be suggested is the negative and debilitating nature of the shame phenomenon. Indeed, this has been empirically supported, with numerous investigations revealing positive associations between shame and decreased self-esteem, dysfunctional interpersonal relationships, general psychological maladjustment, escapist and avoidance responses, externalization of blame, and an impaired

Table 5.1
Key Differences Between Shame and Guilt

Dimension	Shame	Guilt
Focus of evaluation	Global self	Spcific behavior
Attributions	Internal, global, stable	Internal, specific, less stable
Degree of distress	Overwhelming pain from global self-scrutiny	Less painful, as the behavior rather than the self is scrutinized
Focus of concern	Concern with how others will evaluate the person	Concern with the effect of the behavior on others
Impact on self	Core identity devalued	Self remains intact
Phenomenonological experience	Feeling small, exposed, powerless, worthless	Tension, anxiety, remorse regret
Counterfactual processes	Mentally undoing some aspect of the self (If only I weren't such a bad person	Mentally undoing some aspect of behavior (If only I hadn't done such a bad thing)
Coping responses	Crippled, feels opportunity for change is limited	Able to identify ways of changing or coping with the situation
Motivational features	Desire to hide or escape, or to blame and strike out at others	Desire to confess, apologize, repair, or make amends

capacity for empathy (Burggraf & Tangney, 1989; Tangney, 1991; Tangney, Wagner, Fletcher, & Gramzow, 1992). In addition, shame-prone individuals have been found to be more prone to defensive and retaliatory anger, anger in general, and the destructive utilization of anger (Tangney, 1995).

Guilt Focuses on Specific Transgressions. In contrast to the focus of shame on the entire self, theorists posit that guilt involves the negative assessment of either a specific behavior for which one is responsible or a specific failure to act (Barrett, 1995; Lewis, 1971, 1987; Tangney, 1995). Due to the recognition that the particular behavior was problematic or harmful, illustrative of the individual's understanding of social standards and the desire to follow such standards, anxiety, tension, and discomfort, similar to the experience of shame, result. However, in the guilt experience, this negative affect is typically less intense than would be encountered in the shame experience, as the focus does not surround one's core identity. The individual tends to become preoccupied with the transgression and its damage, which subsequently motivates the individual either to undo or to repair the damage caused by the transgression

(Barrett, 1995; Tangney, 1995). Moreover, when efforts at reparation are blocked, the discomfort is further intensified.

Particularly noteworthy with respect to guilt is the less self-focused nature of the experience, again due to the emphasis on a specific behavior rather than on the whole self. In turn, this allows for regret, remorse, and an other-oriented concern, which involves an examination of the effects of one's behavior on the affected others (Tangney, 1995). Put simply, empathic responsiveness is facilitated when the individual experiences guilt versus the self-oriented distress accompanying the shame experience. The guilt-experiencing individual, in contrast to the debilitated and crippled shame-focused individual, is therefore more able to identify potential coping responses such as apology, confession, or making amends (Tangney, 1995). Overall, this reflects an active self versus the passive and helpless self which has been incapacitated and paralyzed by shame (Barrett, 1995).

Offering support for these theorized phenomenological experiences of guilt, empirical studies have revealed positive associations between guilt and empathy, responsibility taking, and motivation for corrective or reparative actions (Tangney, 1990, 1991; Tangney et al., 1992). In addition, studies involving individuals' ratings of guilt and shame experiences along a variety of dimensions have revealed that in contrast to guilt experiences, shame experiences were more painful, leaving the shame-experiencing individuals feeling more inferior, powerless, exposed, and concerned regarding negative evaluations (Tangney, 1993). Taken together, this finding indicates that the experience of guilt is more adaptive. First, guilt can readily foster a sense of responsibility rather than a tendency to blame others. Second, as the focus is on behaviors rather than on the global self, the guilt experience is less threatening and therefore less likely to result in the invoking of defensive maneuvers. Third, as the individual justifiably tends to feel discomfort and remorse over the specific behavior, he is more likely to be empathic and concerned and subsequently will be motivated (and able) to make reparative or corrective actions.

Theories of Shame and Guilt Applied to Sex Offenders

Having highlighted some of the pertinent, more general literature on shame and guilt, we now incorporate the differential experiences of shame and guilt into our framework with respect to sexual offending behaviors. As indicated previously, our theoretical model centers primarily around the manner in which the individual responds to and copes with transgressions such as lapses or actual offenses at the point of the AVE. It is generally accepted that when an individual threatens or breaches his abstinence from offending, an attributional and evaluative process occurs which is generally followed by negative affect in the form of shame or guilt. However, as Ward, Hudson, and Siegert (1995) have argued, a positive affective experience (i.e., problem of immediate gratification) immediately follows the transgression or lapse and, in fact, precedes the AVE. Therefore, the negative affect accompanying the AVE is delayed by immediate gratification and positive affect, which may actually reinforce the offending behaviors. In other words, following the transgression and the subsequent immediate gratification and positive affective experience, the attributional and evaluative process occurs, often having a negative, self-referential bias. It is during this process that the experience of shame or guilt is likely to be manifested.

Using Cognitive Distortions to Deal With Negative Affect. Particularly relevant to our theoretical model are the cognitive processes believed to occur during the AVE. Specifically, it has been argued that to escape from or minimize the delayed negative affective experience following a transgression, the individual may engage in a form of intellectual maneuvering referred to by Baumeister (1989, 1990, 1991) as cognitive deconstruction. In this deconstructed state, awareness of both the immediate and long-term negative consequences of the behavior is minimized via a more concrete and superficial thought process. Through the use of cognitive distortions (e.g., justification, victim blaming minimization, and rationalization) and attention to selected, more positive features of the offensive behavior, the transgressing experience becomes absent of evaluations that might induce negative affect. The disinhibited individual avoids self-awareness and fails to attend to the concerns of others, which clearly implicates the increased likelihood of empathy deficits occurring in a cognitively deconsructed state. Indeed, as Marshall, Hudson, Jones, and Fernandez (1995) suggested, the demonstration of empathy may be affected by situational or temporal factors, whereby the extent of empathic responding may be affected by the perceived characteristics of the victim, which, in turn, may result from distorting processes aimed at protecting the offender from experiencing negative affect. The use of these self-serving cognitive distortions, and subsequently the manifestation of empathy deficits, may also be a function of the individual's sense of self-esteem. Because those low in self-esteem have a tendency to need to protect their self-esteem from further threat, such individuals are more likely to engage in those self-serving cognitive distortions when interpreting and evaluating the transgression. Therefore, denial, rationalization, minimization, justification, and externalization protect offenders from feelings of shame and guilt about their offending behavior.

Cognitive Deconstruction Helps Maintain Offense Behavior. Ward, Hudson, and Marshall (1995) have outlined the role of cognitive deconstruction in sexual offending. They emphasize the role of negative affective states in first inducing a cognitively deconstructed state, which facilitates the actual offense behavior, and then in coping with the consequent negative evaluations of the self, which prompt a desire to minimize the experience of negative affect (Ward Hudson, & Marshall, 1995; Ward, Hudson, & Siegert 1995). Given the identified evidence of the distinct cognitive, affective, and motivational dimensions of shame versus guilt, the consequences therefore have differing implications for the transgressing sexual offender with respect to the AVE and the potential for continued abstinence or reoffending.

Shame and Sexual Offending. When the offending individual attributes having committed a sexual offense to internal, stable, and characterological factors such as lack of ability (e.g., "No matter how hard I try, I can't stop myself"), the resulting affective experience is shame. Based on the general literature, and as outlined in our model (see Figure 5.1), painful and global self-scrutiny, self-consciousness, and perceptions of negative evaluation occur (e.g., "I am a terrible person, and others perceive me as a terrible person"). This is likely associated with decreased self-efficacy and feelings of worthlessness and powerlessness, which ultimately cripple the individual's ability to identify and utilize adaptive coping responses (e.g., "This is just how I am; I can't change—there is nothing I can do"). Under these conditions, feelings of self-oriented

Figure 5.1
The Shame Experience in Sexual Offenders

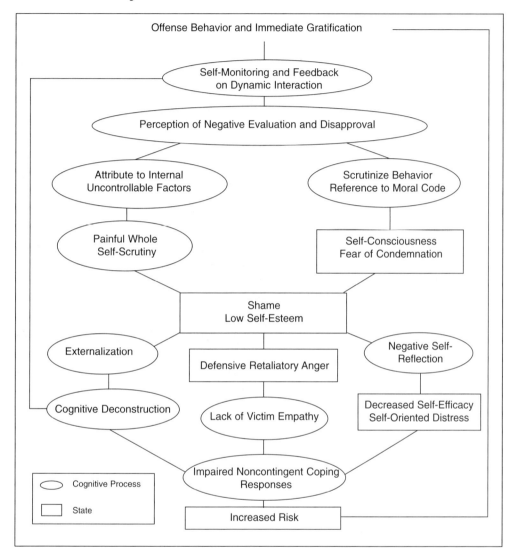

distress are likely to develop, and these feelings, as we have seen, are likely to impede progress in treatment.

At the same time, due to the perceived negative evaluation by others, the offender may develop a hostile, defensive, and retaliatory form of anger that is then directed outward. Consequently, the tendencies to externalize blame increase, serving to reduce culpability for the sexual offense (e.g., "It's not really my fault—it was hers"). To escape the negative self-evaluation and minimize the perceptions of negative evaluations by others, the offender may cognitively deconstruct at this point or at any number of stages during the offense cycle. Underlying and internal motivations which are self-referential and consequently shame evoking may not be consciously considered.

Rather, attention may be selectively focused on ambiguous features of the interaction (e.g., victim passivity) or on procedural factors to achieve immediate gratification (e.g., grooming or restraining the victim). This selective encoding or processing may consequently enable restricted recall and distorted evaluations of the offense behaviors (Johnston & Ward, 1996). Additional cognitive distortions about the offense (e.g., "S/he asked for it"; "It wasn't so bad"; "I was teaching her") in concert with the angry, defensive, and retaliatory response are clearly associated with an inability or unwillingness to empathize with the victim (i.e., victim-specific empathy deficits). Although designed to reduce the negative affective experience of shame, ultimately, this type of response actually sets up a negative emotional state with empathic deficits and dysfunctional cognitions, all of which increase the risk for reoffense.

Guilt and Sexual Offending. If the individual attributes the sexual offense to internal but controllable factors such as lack of effort (e.g., "I didn't try hard enough"; "I was careless"; "I didn't care in this instance"), the experience will be that of guilt. Scrutiny occurs regarding the behavior (e.g., "I did a terrible thing") rather than global self-devaluation. When evaluating the behavior versus the self as a whole, it becomes much easier for the offender to take responsibility for the offense, in part because it is less painful or threatening. The offender is then more apt to examine and recognize the effects of the offense on the victim. What is likely to follow (assuming the person is able to identify his own emotions and the emotional expressions of others) is an experience of discomfort and tension due to the recognition of the harm done to the victim (i.e., the display of victim-specific empathy). This discomfort and tension are likely to lead to feelings of remorse, which in turn motivate the offender to actively take reparative or corrective steps. The offender, recognizing that the offense was within his control, is better able to explore the potential options (e.g., "How can I fix this?" "What could I have done differently?") and identify adaptive coping responses (e.g., seek treatment and attempt to make amends). A sense of increased self-efficacy develops in concert with the identification of adaptive coping responses and commitment to recognizing the harmful and offensive nature of the behavior, which ultimately decreases the risk for reoffense (see Figure 5.2).

Treatment Implications

The therapeutic implications associated with this theoretical model of shame and guilt involve the manner in which treatment is delivered, such that shame and its accompanying negative responses can be overcome and guilt can be used in the treatment process. It has been suggested that the use of shame-inducing techniques may be effective in the management of sexual offending behaviors (Maletzky, 1991; Serber, 1970; Serber & Wolpe, 1972), but it is our position that the focus in treatment should be on guilt as a response to sexual offending. To achieve this, it is necessary to distinguish the offender as a person from his inappropriate behavior. We have elsewhere stressed the value of this distinction for enhancing sexual offenders' self-esteem (Marshall, Anderson, & Champagne, 1997; Marshall, Champagne, Sturgeon, & Bryce, 1997) and in a more general sense in facilitating behavior change (Marshall, 1996). Making behaviors the focus in treatment, rather than the person, should contribute to a reduction in feelings of shame and to an emphasis on feelings of guilt. We

Figure 5.2
The Guilt Experience in Sexual Offenders

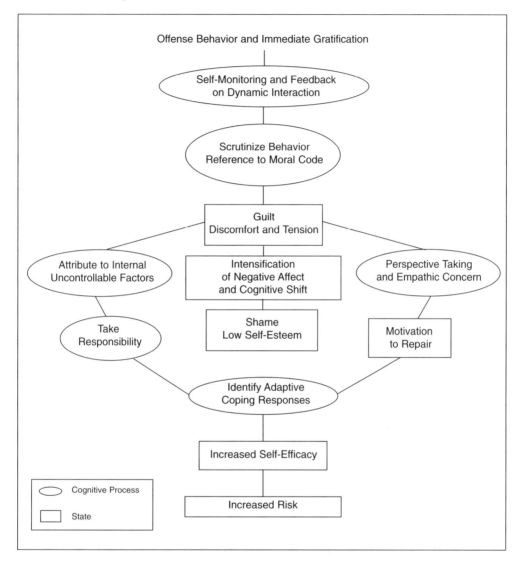

expect therefore that emphasizing guilt will initiate attempts to reduce the negative affective experience by addressing the full range of problematic issues in order to eliminate the offensive and guilt-inducing behaviors. Once offenders recognize that it is their behavior, not themselves as a whole, that is the problem, their optimism over the possibility of change should increase, and they should engage in treatment more enthusiastically.

Of course, it is also necessary to distinguish for clients the experiences of shame and guil and make clear the meaning of these two different experiences. That is, shame reflects a negative appraisal of the self that discourages taking responsibility for behavior, whereas guilt reflects distress over enacting particular behaviors and encourages taking responsibility and initiating change processes. Making the distinction between guilt and shame in this way should assist offenders in recognizing that feeling guilty over particular behaviors is helpful whereas feeling shame is not because it encourages despondency.

In an earlier work (Marshall, 1996), we also argued against the use of a confrontational approach in the treatment of sexual offenders. Although not explicitly discussed in that work, such an approach inevitably identifies the offender as a "bad person," thereby inducing shame which, according to the present thesis, should obstruct change. Similarly, our claim (Marshall et al., 1997) that enhancing the self-esteem of sexual offenders should encourage them to feel confident enough to effectively enter the treatment process fits well with the present view. For those who have committed an offense that brings the wrath and repugnance of society down on their heads, as is the case for sexual offenders, it is difficult to enhance their sense of self-worth unless they see themselves as potentially worthwhile and capable of change. For a clear presentation of how to treat sexual offenders in a respectful and supportive way, at the same time assisting them to take responsibility for their actions, readers are referred to Jenkins (1990, 1998). To date, these procedures have not been empirically evaluated, but we are in the process of examining their efficacy.

Research Implications

The obvious implication of this discussion is that our clients are more likely to feel shame than guilt as a consequence of being identified as a sexual offender, and as such they may be less likely to assume responsibility for their actions or to be concerned about the effects of their behaviors on others. We recently attempted to explore the relationship between these issues among a small sample of sexual offenders in an outpatient treatment program (Bumby, Levine, & Cunningham, 1996). The offenders completed measures of shame proneness, guilt proneness, externalization, empathy (i.e., perspective taking, empathic concern, and self-oriented personal distress), and self-consciousness. As hypothesized, a significant positive association was revealed between the shame-proneness measure and the measures of personal distress, self-consciousness, and externalization. In other words, as the sexual offenders' proneness to experience shame increased, so did the tendency to experience self-oriented personal distress, to feel self-conscious, and to externalize responsibility. Conversely, as the sexual offenders' proneness to experience guilt increased, so did their level of empathic concern and perspective-taking ability. A limitation to this study concerns the fact that what was evaluated was shame proneness and guilt proneness (i.e., measures of traits). Although these feelings are related to our model in an important way, for treatment purposes the offender's present state may be more relevant. For example, an offender who is not particularly prone to feeling shame over unacceptable behaviors but is typically more inclined to feel guilty may, as a result of the very negative reaction of society and his family, friends, and workmates, experience shame after his offenses become public. Research then should examine both the proneness to shame and guilt as well as the offenders' current feeling state of shame and guilt. Some offenders may typically experience shame over transgressions (i.e., be shame prone) whereas others may simply have shame induced by the social reactions to the transgressions (i.e., be in a state of shame). Procedures are available that evaluate proneness to shame and guilt (i.e., measures of traits) as well as measures of the person's current states of shame and guilt. In addition, we would expect strong moral beliefs to be more prominent in those offenders who are disposed to feel shame (i.e., who are shame prone) but to be either absent or more tenuously held in those who only experience a state of shame as a result of the processes of identification and prosecution. Future investigations should also include examinations of the relationships between shame and guilt and emotional recognition, victim-specific empathy, and cognitive distortions about sexual offending.

Finally, it is important to systematically evaluate the relationship between the mode/style of treatment delivery (i.e., therapist features which may either be shame inducing or guilt inducing), the treatment process, subsequent experiences of shame or guilt in the treatment process, and client responsivity (i.e., progress toward goals such as empathy, responsibility taking, and reductions of denial and minimization). We hypothesize that there is a positive relationship between challenging but supportive therapist style and the enhancement of self-esteem, increased self-efficacy, reduced denial and minimization, and greater displays of empathy among sexual offenders. At present, we have studies under way to address these propositions.

Conclusion

We hope our consideration of the possible relevance of shame and guilt will encourage other researchers and clinicians to address these issues. Our initial study has suggested that these may be important matters in understanding and managing sexual offenders, and our clinical work has offered similarly encouraging feedback. We look forward to the results of future studies.

References

Barrett, K. C. (1995). A functionalist approach to shame and guilt. In J. P. Tangney & K. W. Fischer (Eds.), *Self-conscious emotions: Shame, guilt, embarrassment, and pride* (pp. 25–63). New York: Guilford Press.

Baumeister, R. F. (1989). Masochism as escape from self. *Journal of Sex Research, 25,* 28–59.

Baumeister, R. F. (1990). Suicide as escape from self. *Psychological Review, 97,* 90–113.

Baumeister, R. F. (1991). *Escaping the self.* New York: Basic Books.

Bumby, K. M., & Hansen, D. J. (1997). Intimacy deficits, fear of intimacy, and emotional loneliness among sexual offenders. *Criminal Justice and Behavior, 24,* 315–331.

Bumby, K. M., Levine, H., & Cunningham, D. (1996). *Empathy deficits, shame, guilt, and self-conscious.* Paper presented at Fifteenth Annual Association for the Treatment of Sexual Abusers, Chicago.

Burggraf, S. A., & Tangney, J. P. (1989). *The Self-Conscious Affect and Attribution Inventory for Children (SCAAI-C).* Bryn Mawr, PA: Bryn Mawr.College.

Hanson, R. K., & Bussière, M. T. (1996). *Predictors of sexual offender recidivism: A meta-analysis* (User Report No. 1996-04). Ottawa: Corrections Branch, Ministry of the Solicitor General of Canada.

Jenkins, A. (1990). *Invitations to responsibility.* Adelaide, Australia: Dulwich Centre Publications.

Jenkins, A. (1998). Invitations to responsibility: Engaging adolescent and young men who have sexually abused. In W. L. Marshall, Y. M. Fernandez, S. M. Hudson, & T. Ward (Eds.), *Sourcebook of treatment programs for sexual offenders* (pp. 163–189). New York: Plenum Press.

Johnston, L., & Ward, T. (1996). Social cognition and sexual offending: A theoretical framework. *Sexual Abuse: A Journal of Research and Treatment, 8,* 55–80.

Lewis, H. B. (1971). *Shame and guilt in neurosis.* New York: International Universities Press.

Lewis, H. B. (1987). Shame and the narcissistic personality. In D. L. Nathanson (Ed.), *The many faces of shame* (pp. 93–132). New York: Guilford Press.

Lewis, H. B. (1991). Self-conscious emotions and the development of self. In T. Shapiro & R. Emde (Eds.), New perspectives on affect and emotion in psychoanalysis. *Journal of the American Psychoanalytic Association, 39*(Suppl.), 45–73.

Maletzky, B.M. (1991). Aversive respondent conditioning techniques. In B. M. Maletzky, *Treating the sexual offender* (pp. 67–95). Newbury Park, CA: Sage.

Marshall, W .L. (1996). The sexual offender: Monster, victim, or everyman? *Sexual Abuse: A Journal of Research and Treatment, 8,* 317–335.

Marshall, W. L., Anderson, D., & Champagne, F. (1997). Self-esteem and its relationship to sexual offending. *Psychology, Crime and Law, 3,* 161–186.

Marshall, W. L., Champagne, F., Sturgeon, C., & Bryce, P. (1997). Increasing the self-esteem of child molesters. *Sexual Abuse: A Journal of Research and Treatment, 9,* 321–333.

Marshall, W. L., Hudson, S. M., Jones, R., & Fernandez, Y. M. (1995). Empathy in sex offenders. *Clinical Psychology Review, 15,* 99–113.

Russell, K., Sturgeon, V. H., Miner, M. H., & Nelson, C. (1989). Determinants of the abstinence violation effect in sexual fantasies. In D. R. Laws (Ed.), *Relapse prevention with sex offenders* (pp. 63–72). New York: Guilford Press.

Serber, M. (1970). Shame aversion therapy. *Journal of Behavior Therapy and Experimental Psychiatry, 1,* 217–226.

Serber, M., & Wolpe, J. (1972). Behavior therapy techniques. In H. L. P. Resnick & M. E. Wolfgang (Eds.), *Sexual behaviors* (pp. 239–254). Boston: Little, Brown.

Tangney, J. P. (1990). Assessing individual differences in proneness to shame and guilt: Development of the Self-Conscious Affect and Attribution Inventory. *Journal of Personality and Social Psychology, 59,* 102–111.

Tangney, J.P. (1991). Moral affect: the good, the bad, and the ugly. Journal of Personality and Social Psychology, 61, 598–607.

Tangney, J. P. (1995). Shame and guilt in interpersonal relationships. In J. P. Tangney & K. W. Fischer (Eds.), *Self-conscious emotions: Shame, guilt, embarrassment, and pride* (pp. 114–139). New York: Guilford Press.

Tangney, J. P., & Fischer, K. W. (1995). *Self-conscious emotions: Shame, guilt, embarrassment, and pride.* New York: Guilford Press.

Tangney, J. P., Wagner, P. E., Fletcher, C., & Gramzow, R. (1992). Shamed into anger? The relation of shame and guilt to anger and self-reported aggression. *Journal of Personality and Social Psychology, 62,* 669–675.

Ward, T., Hudson, S. M., & Marshall, W. L. (1995). Cognitive distortions and affective deficits in sex offenders: A cognitive deconstructionist interpretation. *Sexual Abuse: A Journal of Research and Treatment, 7,* 67–83.

Ward, T., Hudson, S. M., & Siegert, R. J. (1995). A critical comment on Pithers's relapse prevention model. *Sexual Abuse: A Journal of Research and Treatment, 7,* 167–175.

Chapter 6

A Self-Regulation Model of the Relapse Process in Sexual Offenders

by Tony Ward, Ph.D.

Overview

The assumption that relapse constitutes a process or a chain of behavior occurring across time has revolutionized treatment for sex offenders and led to the adoption of relapse prevention as a treatment model. Pithers's influential relapse prevention model focuses on factors proximal to offending, describing the process as an affective/cognitive/behavioral chain that culminates in the recurrence of sexually aggressive behavior (Pithers, Marques, Gibat, & Marlatt, 1983).

Introduction

Despite its enormous value in guiding treatment and research, both Pithers's and Marlatt's (Marlatt & Gordon, 1985) original model suffer from a number of conceptual and empirical problems. Both were constructed from very different, and arguably incompatible, theoretical elements leading to conceptual confusion and redundancy. However, from a clinical perspective the most serious shortcoming of Pithers's framework is that it does not cover all the possibilities involved in reoffending. His model emphasizes skill deficits as the major mediators of relapse and fails to cover situations in which individuals consciously decide to use drugs or engage in sexually abusive behavior (for a systematic critique of both Marlatt's and Pithers's perspectives, see Ward & Hudson, 1996; Ward & Hudson, in press).

I suggest that a comprehensive model of the relapse process needs to contain a number of pathways, preferably taking into account different types of goals (e.g., approach vs. avoidance goals), varying emotional states (initial and ongoing), and different types of planning. Second, it should include an explicit temporal emphasis and be able to account for the dynamic nature of the offense process. Third, it needs to be able to account for the various phases, or milestones, of the offense process, at least as they are currently understood. This includes the influence of background factors, distal vulnerability factors, decisions that lead to high-risk situations, the initial lapse, the sexual offense, and the impact of the offense on subsequent offending. In addition, the psychological mechanisms that drive or inhibit the relapse process should be identified and described in a theoretically coherent way. In this chapter I present a self-regulation model of the relapse process that meets these criteria.

A Self-Regulation Model of the Relapse Process

Self-regulation consists of the internal and external processes that allow an individual to engage in goal-directed actions over time and in different contexts (Baumeister & Heatherton, 1996). Goals are psychological states or situations that individuals strive to achieve or to avoid, and as such they are important components of personality (Austin & Vancouver, 1996). Some goals can be directly activated by environmental factors and result in automatic goal-directed behavior without the need for conscious decision making (Austin & Vancouver, 1996). It is helpful to distinguish between acquisitional (approach) and inhibitory (avoidance) goals. Acquisitional goals concern the successful achievement of a particular state or situation, and they essentially involve approach behavior. Attention is focused on information indicating success, and therefore positive memories and thoughts are more likely to be experienced. By way of contrast, inhibitory goals are concerned with the reduction of a state or situation, and they involve avoidance behavior. Failure is usually construed in an all-or-nothing manner, and attention is focused on information signaling failure rather than success. Therefore, failure-related memories or thoughts are more commonly experienced by individuals whose behavior is guided by inhibitory goals.

There are three major types of problems that people can experience with self-regulation (Baumeister & Heatherton, 1996). First, individuals can fail to control their behavior or emotions, thus behaving in a disinhibited manner. Second, the use of ineffective strategies to achieve goals can backfire and ultimately result in a loss of control. The third pattern has been somewhat neglected and paradoxically involves effective self-regulation. The major problem resides in the choice of goals rather than a breakdown in the components of self-regulation. For example, the setting of goals and their subsequent planning and implementation by a preferential child molester may be impeccable. The difficulty resides in his initial goals and associated values and beliefs.

The self-regulatory model of the relapse process outlined here is based on our earlier descriptive model of the offense process (Ward, Louden, Hudson, & Marshall,

1995), theoretical and empirical research on self-regulation, and our ongoing research on the offense process in sexual offenders. Due to space limitations I can only describe the model in a general way in this chapter (for a full description, see Ward & Hudson, in press). The model consists of nine different steps, or, more accurately, phases, as the process is fluid and indeed may appear seamless to the individual. It is important to note that an offender can exit the relapse process at any time by implementing appropriate coping strategies.

Phase One: Life Event. In this first phase some kind of life event occurs and is appraised by an individual who is attempting to control his sexually abusive behavior. The event might be a major life transition (e.g., a divorce) or a daily hassle such as an argument. The initial appraisal of these life events is hypothesized to be relatively automatic and directly precipitated by external events. These life events are interpreted in light of preexisting beliefs, needs, and abstract goals and the interpersonal context in which they occur. For example, if a man with long-standing resentment and distrust of women argues with his partner, he may feel humiliated and angry. These feelings could lead to the activation of important goals and behavior designed to enhance his self-esteem, which may eventually involve a sexual assault.

Phase Two: Desire for Deviant Sex or Activity. The life event and its subsequent appraisal results in the emergence of a desire for offensive sex or maladaptive activities (e.g., to humiliate someone) and emotions associated with these desires. For example, an offender may desire to have sex with a woman or child, engage in peeping behavior, or to sexually expose himself to others. Alternatively, he might want to retaliate against someone and to engage in violent and intimidatory behavior. We suggest that the processes necessary to reach these goals may be mentally rehearsed, which in turn may lower an offender's inhibitions against indulging these fantasies. The accompanying emotional states might be happiness, curiosity, sexual arousal, anxiety, and anger.

These desires are hypothesized to be directly triggered by the person's associations to the event and may well be outside of his awareness. The activation of memories associated with past offending functions to increase the accessibility of core dysfunctional beliefs and attitudes. These knowledge structures are hypothesized to contain goals related to offending and trigger the desire to sexually offend, or to engage in some kind of aggressive action (Ward & Hudson, in press). It is likely that links between certain internal and external cues and the desire to offend reflect inappropriate learning experiences (e.g., sexual abuse as a child) and the belief that abusive actions can help the offender to achieve valued goals, for example, a sense of personal adequacy.

Phase Three: Offense-Related Goals Established. The desire to engage in deviant sex or a maladaptive activity results in the establishment of an offense-related goal. At this point, an offender considers the acceptability of his desire(s) and what, if anything, he should do about it. We suggest that there are two broad classes of relevant goals: avoidance and approach goals. The former is associated with the desire to avoid sexually reoffending, and it is essentially negative in nature. That is, the goal is to not offend. These types of goals are more effortful and difficult to implement as there are a number of ways a person can fail to prevent something from happening, whereas a positive goal may be associated with just one pathway (Wegner, 1994). The emotional state associated with this category of goals is likely to be negative; a person is fearful or anxious about the possibility of an unwanted event or action occurring and typically experiences higher levels of psychological distress than do individuals with approach goals (Austin & Vancouver, 1996).

In contrast, approach goals reflect the determination to sexually offend, whether in the service of other needs such as aggression, or as an end in itself, for example, believing that one is entitled to sex. This type of goal may be related to positive or negative emotional states depending on the actual aims of the offender. If the aim is to gratify a desire, it is likely to be positive (e.g., desire for sexual gratification). However, if the intention is to humiliate a person or to execute an aggressive behavior, strong negative emotions may also be involved.

Phase Four: Strategy Selected. The selection of strategies designed to achieve a goal occurs at this point. It is important to stress that this selection may not be a conscious decision. Goals and their accompanying strategies can be selected automatically as the result of the activation of behavioral scripts (i.e., action sequences for well-earned and habitual behaviors. There are four offense pathways (avoidant–passive, avoidant–active, approach–automatic, and approach–explicit) in the proposed self-regulation model that are related to the two broad classes of goals concerning sexual offending. There are two relapse pathways associated with avoidance or inhibitory goals where the aim is to not sexually offend. There are also two pathways associated with approach or acquisitional goals. Each of these relapse routes is distinguished by the use of distinct strategies in relation to sexually offensive contact, and each can be further divided into implicit and explicit subpathways. Because the implicit pathways are characterized by disinhibition, they may be traversed more quickly than the explicit ones.

The avoidance–passive pathway is characterized by both the desire to avoid sexual offending and the failure to actively attempt to prevent this from happening. It involves the inability to control sexually deviant intentions and is a underregulation or disinhibition pathway (it is similar to Pithers's relapse process). Powerful negative affective states may function as disinhibitors or else lead to behaviors that in turn result in a loss of control. Individuals who follow this relapse pathway are likely to lack coping skills, be more impulsive, have low efficacy expectations, and to utilize covert planning. The predominant emotional state is likely to be negative because of the anxiety associated with the possibility of relapse (i.e., sexual offending).

The avoidance–active or misregulation pathway involves an active attempt to avoid sexual offending. It represents a direct attempt to control deviant thoughts, fantasies, or affective states that threaten to lead to a loss of control. The major difference between this relapse route and the avoidant–passive one, is that there is an explicit attempt to deal with the threat to restraint. The problem is that the selected strategies are not appropriate and, paradoxically, increase the probability of an offense occurring. For example, an offender might mistakenly believe that the use of alcohol or drugs might suppress the desire for offensive sex. Such men may have high efficacy expectations; possess the ability to plan, monitor, and evaluate their behavior; but lack knowledge concerning the likely effectiveness of the coping response selected. Unfortunately, the use of alcohol can increase the risk of sexually offending by strengthening the desire for deviant sex and by decreasing self-control. The predominant emotional state is also likely to be negative.

There are two relapse pathways associated with approach or acquisitional goals. The third pathway, approach–automatic involves following overlearned behavioral scripts designed to lead to the commission of a sexual offence. Such behavior is relatively impulsive and only planned in a rudimentary way; it appears to occur "out of the blue" and often unfolds in a relatively short period of time. It is basically a mirror image of the passive–avoidance relapse process in that the goals and the associated strategies are unlikely to be under attentional control and are activated by situational features. It is essentially an underregulation or disinhibition pathway, but it differs from the avoidant–passive route to relapse by virtue of its association with an approach goal and appetitive processes. In a sense, it represents a planned impulsiveness (Pithers et al., 1983). These offenders may vary in their primary affective state, with some experiencing predominantly positive emotions and others predominantly negative.

Finally, the fourth pathway, approach–explicit, involves conscious, explicit planning and well-crafted strategies that result in a sexual offense. Thus, there is intact self-regulation but inappropriate, harmful goals as, for example, where there are inappropriate standards concerning sex with children or attitudes toward women. The notion of disinhibition does not apply to such individuals; they do not lose control and do not use sex to escape from or reduce powerful negative mood states. Rather, the reverse might very well be true; these offenders may have the goal of maintaining or heightening positive emotions through the offending act. The predominant affective state is likely to be positive or negative.

Phase Five: High-Risk Situation Entered. In the next stage contact with the victim comes about as a consequence of the earlier implicit or explicit planning or counterproductive strategies. Offenders who are following the avoidant–passive pathway will be struggling with conflicting goals at this point. The contact, or anticipated contact, with a victim will activate goals linked to offending behavior, and the individuals are likely to be experiencing increasing sexual arousal. Alternatively, those individuals who are using counterproductive strategies (avoidant–active) will also find it increasingly difficult to control their behavior. Ineffective control strategies, such as attempting to suppress unwanted cognitions through the use of drugs, may result in a dramatic increase in deviant sexual thoughts or feelings (Johnston, Ward, & Hudson, 1997). The emotional states of offenders with avoidant goals is likely to be predominantly negative, and their self-efficacy will be low with respect to restraint.

Offenders following the approach–automatic pathway will be responding to the situational cues in a rapid and automatic manner. They will be focused on the prospect of immediate gratification and be concerned about their chances of achieving sexual pleasure and/or related goals. Those offenders consciously planning to achieve their goal of sex with children or the assault of women (approach–explicit) are likely to experience increasingly positive emotions. They will be focused on proximal planning, for example, considering how to sexually seduce a child or subdue a woman. The sense of efficacy of both approach subtypes is expected to be high at this point. It is important to stress that, depending on the exact nature of their intentions, some men with approach goals may still be experiencing negative emotions.

Phase Six: Lapse. The next phase in the model concerns the immediate precursors to the sexual offense, involving behaviors such as getting into bed with a child. In relapse prevention terms, the offender has lapsed and is intending to engage in an offense. I suggest that at this point individuals following the avoidant–passive pathway replace their avoidance goals with an approach goal. They are hypothesized to give up attempting to control their behavior and become preoccupied with the prospect of sexual gratification. The tendency to focus on immediate gratification signals the dominance of appetitive processes (e.g.., the desire for sexual gratification) and lead up to a sexual offense. Similarly, the avoidant–active individual also judges the attempt to actively control his deviant sexual desires as a failure, and as a consequence, he adopts an approach or acquisitional goal.

Those offenders with approach goals continue to strive toward goal satisfaction. Offenders whose offending is driven by automatic processes may exhibit aggressive behavior reflecting their impulsivity. Their behavior is regulated by lower-level goals and associated habitual responses. As such, this behavior is more easily captured by situational cues and likely to be impulsive. Those individuals with explicit approach strategies should demonstrate careful planning and management of the situation and any potential obstacles. Any aggression should be a function of their explicit goals, for example, to inflict pain on a victim (sadism), rather than reflect impulsivity. Because of the impact of increased sexual arousal and/or pleasurable anticipation, the emotional state of all offenders is hypothesized to be primarily positive at this phase of the relapse process. The existence of high levels of arousal may cause offenders to reduce the victim to a functionary status; their purpose is serve as an outlet for the offenders sexual and aggressive needs.

Phase Seven: Sexual Offense. In this phase the offender sexually abuses a child or a woman. It is important to note that chronically accessible goals and interpersonal themes partly determine the manner in which offending is manifested and accomplished. For example, offenders with long-standing negative attitudes toward women are expected to relish the opportunity to express these feelings in their offending behavior. They may exhibit more violence than is necessary or intensify their efforts to humiliate and intimidate their victim. Reflecting the existence of approach goals, the affective state of all individuals is hypothesized to be primarily positive at this phase in the relapse process. However, men whose intention is to intimidate or inflict psychological distress on their victim might experience a combination of negative and positive emotional states.

Phase Eight: Post-Offense Evaluation. Following the sexual offense, an evaluative process is likely to occur. Offenders following the avoidant pathways are hypothesized to evaluate themselves negatively and feel guilt or shame (a classic abstinence violation effect; see Ward, Hudson, & Marshall, 1994). In this situation the comparison of current behavior with the goal of behavioral inhibition (abstinence) reveals a discrepancy and therefore results in the perception that the person has failed. Because an important goal has not been achieved the offender is likely to experience negative affect. Offenders who have approach goals should experience positive affect due to the fact they have achieved their goals.

Phase Nine: Attitude toward Future Offending. The final stage of the model concerns the impact of sexual offending on future intentions and expectations. Generally speaking, whatever offenders learn in a particular offense episode is hypothesized to be assimilated into their existing knowledge structures and to influence the way future salient life events are interpreted. We suggest that those men whose goals are inhibitory may resolve not to offend in the future and attempt to reassert control or return to the use of misregulation strategies. However, it is possible that they may reevaluate their goals and decide that they lack the ability to refrain from further sexual abuse and therefore continue offending. Alternatively, some individuals may be persuaded that sexual offending represents a positive option and may change their goals to approach or acquisitory ones.

Individuals characterized by the approach–automatic offense route are likely to have the behavioral scripts associated with their sexual offending reinforced and strengthened because of their "success." Relatedly, those men following the approach–explicit pathway should continue to refine and develop their abuse-related strategies; they are expected to learn from their experiences and to adjust their modus operandi accordingly. Because of the successful achievement of their approach goals, men following the two acquisitional relapse routes are expected to continue pursuing their goals of sexually assaulting women or children and unlikely to attempt future restraint.

Conclusion

A number of clinical implications follow from a self-regulation model of the offense process. The motivational properties of goals means that therapists should assess the kind of goals individuals possess, and whether or not they are acquisitory or inhibitory. For example, preferential child offenders are more likely to have distorted or maladaptive goals rather than marked problems with impulsivity. Relatedly, it is clinically useful to identify the particular kind of self-regulatory deficits offenders may have. The treatment needs of offenders who are characterized by undercontrol or misregulation are markedly different from those with intact self-regulation skills. For example, issues of impulse control, mood management, and dealing with an unexpected high-risk situation are likely to be common in offenders, generally characterized by self-regulatory deficiencies. However these issues are less likely to be central foci of interventions for a classic pedophile with entrenched beliefs about the rightness of adult–child sexual contact in the context of competent self-regulatory processes. The focus of therapy for this individual should be appreciating the harm done to victims and challenging the cognitive distortions that justify the deviant behavior.

In conclusion, a model of the relapse process attempts to describe the factors associated with sexual abuse as it unfolds over time. Historically, Pithers's relapse prevention model has provided clinicians with a conceptual map of the factors associated with offenders' sexually deviant behavior and guided clinical decision making. We suggest that our self-regulation model can provide a more comprehensive understanding of the factors associated with relapse and, consequently, help clinicians to tailor treatment to individual offenders.

References

Austin, J. T., & Vancouver, J. B. (1996). Goal constructs in psychology: Structure, process, and content. *Psychological Bulletin, 120,* 338–375.

Baumeister, R. F., & Heatherton, T. F. (1996). Self-regulation failure: An overview. *Psychological Inquiry, 7,* 1–15.

Johnston, L., Ward, T., & Hudson, S. M. (1997). Suppressing sex: Mental control and the treatment of sexual offenders. *Journal of Sex Research, 34,* 121–130.

Marlatt, G. A., & Gordon, J. R. (Eds.). (1985). *Relapse prevention: Maintenance strategies in the treatment of addictive behaviors.* New York: Guilford Press.

Pithers, W. D., Marques, J. K., Gibat, C. C., & Marlatt, G. A. (1983). Relapse prevention with sexual aggressives: A self-control model of treatment and maintenance of change. In J. G. Greer & I. R. Stuart (Eds.), *The sexual aggressor: Current perspectives on treatment* (pp. 214–234). New York: Van Nostrand Reinhold.

Ward, T., & Hudson, S. M. (1996). Relapse prevention: A critical analysis. S*exual Abuse: A Journal of Research and Treatment, 8,* 177–200.

Ward, T., & Hudson, S. M. (in press). A self-regulation model of relapse prevention. In D. R. Laws, S. M. Hudson, & T. Ward (Eds.), *Remaking relapse prevention with sex offenders: A Sourcebook* (2nd ed.). Thousand Oaks, CA: Sage.

Ward, T., Hudson, S. M., & Marshall, W. L. (1994). The abstinence violation effect in child molesters. *Behaviour Research and Therapy, 32,* 431–437.

Ward, T., Louden, K., Hudson, S. M., & Marshall, W. L. (1995). A descriptive model of the offense chain for child molesters. *Journal of Interpersonal Violence, 10,* 453–473.

Wegner, D. M. (1994). Ironic processes of mental control. *Psychological Bulletin, 101,* 34–52.

Part 2

Administration

The administration of a sex offender treatment program is a task for which one needs all the help and support that one can muster. This is an occupation that engenders constant conflict and controversy. Furthermore, everyone in the community has strong opinions about how the job should be done. The local bridge club has strong feelings about which sex offenders should be on work release. Newspaper columnists rant on about the efficacy of sex offender treatment. In addition, most sex offender programs operated by public entities are conducted in environments in which numerous conflicting forces seek to shape the program. Then the administration must cope with the constant changes dictated by politicians who influence the program directly through legislation and indirectly through political pressure.

It would be difficult enough if all that was required was that the administration of the program succeeded in running a top-notch program. However, in the realm of sex offender treatment one is constantly anticipating that sensational crime that will galvanize the community and particularly the policymakers into making ill-advised changes in treatment.

This section offers suggestions on improving the administration of programs and building cooperative networks that can decrease recidivism by cooperation between treatment and supervision. The section begins with a description by Katherine D. Peterson and Jon M. Barnes of how one program, the Kentucky Department of Corrections Sex Offender Treatment Program, withstood everyone's nightmare. The program was able to withstand a heinous crime by building coalitions with victim's groups and key legislators. This program made sure that it was keeping abreast of the latest trends and kept track of outcome data. The authors of this chapter also have a number of suggestions about dealing with the media. By taking a proactive approach, this program not only withstood public scrutiny and criticism but emerged stronger than ever.

One of the keys to a successful sex offender treatment program is a working knowledge of risk assessment data. Some programs are able to use this information to screen program applicants. Other programs are mandated to accept all inmates, but knowing who may be the most dangerous can help the therapist and probation or parole officer develop appropriate plans to deal with these high-risk offenders. Many therapists are also called on to advise courts in making sentencing decisions. Being aware of the risk assessment data is vital, even though the data are highly controversial. Barbara K. Schwartz and Henry R. Cellini present an overview of the research in this area. Andrew J. Harris and R. Karl Hanson present their research on dynamic factors that predict reoffense.

Scott Blankenship offers suggestions for adopting management strategies that are revolutionizing industry to sex offender treatment. Total quality management (TQM) presents a new paradigm for administering programs. This chapter offers a variety of techniques for analyzing and improving treatment. By instituting some of these reforms, staff burnout and countertransference issues can be effectively addressed.

Treating sex offenders is difficult work. Programs often have high staff turnover. However, even more important than staff morale is staff safety. With prisons becoming more punitive and communities more hostile, sex offenders are becoming more desperate. Attacks against staff are on the increase. Sex offenders often have different agendas than other prisoners who assault staff. Sharon M. Williams, of the Canadian system, has studied situations in which sex offenders take staff members hostage. Most corrections departments are not prepared to adapt their hostage policy to situations involving this type of offender. Most hostage procedures are designed to "buy time." However, in sexually motivated hostage situations the offender usually attacks immediately. A change in the response to this type of emergency should be considered.

An effective method of supervising sex offenders has been identified. Studying various approaches to dealing with sex offenders in the community, researchers found that successful programs tended to use a three-pronged approach incorporating treatment, supervision and polygraphy (see English, Pullen, & Jones, 1996). This method has been labeled the containment approach. Chapters in this section outline the ingredients of this paradigm. Rebecca Palmer and Terry Childers discuss the benefits of cooperation between the therapist and the probation officer at each phase of treatment. Pryor Green and Billie Franklin discuss how the polygraph can be effectively used in the monitoring of the sex offender.

Not only is tracking the progress of the sex offender both in and after treatment vital if professionals are to identify what works, but it can also be useful should the program come under criticism. Nancy H. Walbek presents a system for monitoring participation in an involuntary commitment program. In this type of setting, accurate documentation of progress in treatment is mandatory as the program participants routinely go to court in an attempt to lift their commitments. This Minnesota program has developed some useful tracking tools and correlated them to participant behavior.

Finally, the basic question that is raised for every sex offender treatment program is, "Does it work?" This question is usually related to the reoffense rate. There are multiple research problems related to answering that question. Jean Proulx and colleagues present a follow-up on a Canadian program that compares dropouts to treatment completers. This design has problems as it could be argued that these two populations are not comparable. The study has attempted to match subjects on a number of variables to overcome that problem. Interesting differences were found between child molesters and rapists and the type of program that was successful with each group.

The authors in this sections offer practical suggestions for managing programs, identifying risk, and monitoring and tracking these offenders. Ideally, consideration of the situations presented in this section will encourage administrators to proactively address concerns that have in the past been the undoing of some treatment programs.

References

English, K., Pullen, S., & Jones, L. (1996). *Managing adult sex offenders: A containment approach.* Colorado Division of Criminal Justice & American Probation and Parole Association.

Chapter 7

Proactivity in the Public Domain—Legislative Advocacy and Dealing with the Media

by Katherine D. Peterson, Psy.D., and Jon M. Barnes, M.A.

Overview

The administration of every sex offender program lives in terror that a sensational sex crime, most often the rape and murder of a child, will bring the wrath of public engendered by the media down on the treatment program. The Kentucky Sex Offender Treatment Program experienced just such a tragedy and lived through it. This chapter describes how to build public support for the sex offender treatment program proactively.

Introduction

The provision of mental health services to disturbed individuals in our country is a well-accepted practice that generally does not excite much public attention.

However, relative to other client populations and domains of clinical practice, sex offender treatment operates in an atmosphere of unusually high public and legislative scrutiny. People who perpetrate sex offenses are simultaneously behaviorally disordered clinical clients and criminals. Unlike treatment for substance abusers, another clinical population with significant involvement in the legal system, the efficacy of our treatment efforts and even the very morality of providing treatment for sex offenders is subject to often emotionally charged debate. This public discourse gets reenergized whenever a particularly gruesome sex crime is perpetrated. Sex offender treatment programs are likely at such tragic times to attract significant media attention.

Support for Sex Offender Treatment Programs Often Controversial

It is fair to say that we who work with men and women who commit sex offenses are likely at some point in our practice to find ourselves explaining and perhaps justifying what we do. Those of us in state-funded programs may be called by our legislators for testimony. More often, perhaps, members of the media may solicit us for various reasons. This chapter amplifies remarks originally made at the 1997 convention of the Association for the Treatment of Sexual Abusers (ATSA) on the issue of proactivity in the domains of legislation and dealing with the media. Our professional frame of reference is correctional: Dr. Peterson is the program administrator for both the community and institutional components of the Kentucky Department of Corrections (DOC) Sex Offender Treatment Program (SOTP); Mr. Barnes supervises an institutional program site. We hope our remarks find an audience and application for treatment professionals in all arenas of practice, private and public. Certainly we are all affected by the laws of our various states and by the messages disseminated by the media about sex offenders. Dr. Peterson has had a role in legislative advocacy for the last decade. In the very recent past, we have both had an abundance of interaction with the Kentucky legislature and with local and national media. We propose to share our processing of those experiences in an anecdotal manner and perhaps to derive some general meaning and guidance from them.

Legislative Advocacy

Since 1986, the Kentucky Justice Cabinet has operated a continually growing, well-funded SOTP. The program is so large that in 1998, 675 offenders receive treatment in five prisons and seven probation/parole districts around the state. In every session of the legislature since 1986, laws expanding services for victims and perpetrators have passed. Dynamic legislators have enjoyed the success that resulted from sponsoring these bills. Media attention, even after several well-publicized and particularly gruesome reoffenses, has been ultimately favorable for the program.

In contrast to the situation in some other states, the Kentucky SOTP has been most fortunate. Whenever we consult with other state programs or speak at national conferences, people are astonished at the relatively high level of support for offender treatment that exists in Kentucky. To what can we attribute this success?

Considerable responsibility rests with the efforts of the Kentucky Coalition against Rape and Sexual Assault (the Coalition). This broad-based grass-roots organization has been a strong advocate since the late 1970s for substantive changes in the laws pertaining to sex offenders and victims. Even more interesting is the fact that since 1986, all significant Kentucky legislation in this area has been drafted by the Coalition, then supported and pushed through the legislature by Coalition-chosen sponsors. Dr. Peterson has been a member of the Coalition since the inception of the SOTP, and all of our supervisory staff have since become members as well. The Coalition has consistently advocated for the SOTP on the grounds that we aid in preventing future crime and hence have an important role in the protection of victims. We have been able, through our participation, to aid the Coalition in being an informed advocate concerning treatment issues.

Building Broad-Based Community Support

The Coalition was founded in 1979 by a number of influential individuals with a shared concern about improving Kentucky's response to victims of rape and sexual assault. These individuals included county and local government officials, victim advocacy groups, directors of rape crisis centers, law enforcement, and Claude Turpin, the Department of Corrections clinician who was Kentucky's pioneer in sex offender treatment. The founders wisely placed the Coalition under the auspices of the Jefferson County Crime Commission. Louisville is located in this most populous of the state's counties. This important decision provided government funding for staff support. The funding of staff support continues to be a major factor in our success. Because we are not an organization that relies solely on volunteers, staff stability can be maintained over a long period of time. Another key factor underlying our success is that we are a nonpartisan group. Membership is voluntary and not based on political party affiliation, and the Coalition's bills have sponsored by both Democrats and Republicans. The Coalition also carefully avoids links to unrelated controversial bills, so that politicians perceive little risk in espousing our causes. The Coalition is sensitive to the public acknowledgment of its supporters. We arrange very public award ceremonies and receptions for state officials who sponsor our bills and have recently recognized the Governor of Kentucky and First Lady for their support.

As of 1998, the Coalition is chaired by the Jefferson County Judge Executive and continues to be staffed by the Jefferson County Crime Commission. Besides our ongoing SOTP representation, membership continues to include local government officials, rape crisis center leadership, law enforcement officials, and victims' advocates. Membership has also expanded to include an official from the Governor's Commission on Women, a governor's advisor on domestic violence and child abuse, and representatives of community and professional organizations statewide, as well as attorneys in private practice, victims, and concerned citizens.

Keeping Stakeholders Informed. With a mailing list of 500 individuals and organizations statewide, the Coalition has established a strong network for information sharing and advocacy. Relevant to our purposes, the Coalitions's quarterly newsletter, which we mail to all legislators, judges, prosecutors, trial attorneys, and Coalition members, informs interested parties about important issues and progress in the SOTP.

This has resulted in widespread recognition and enhanced support of the program by judges, victims' groups, and the media.

Keeping Informed of Latest Trends. Another of the Coalition's important activities involves research on national sex offender and victim legislative trends and key judicial decisions in these areas. This research aids in determining what is working in other states when it is time to craft Kentucky's legislation. The organization also conducts surveys statewide to monitor the impact of existing sex offender-related legislation, such as on sentencing practices and law enforcement recordkeeping. Kentucky's legislature meets biannually. In the interim year, the Coalition holds public forums to obtain citizens' input across the Commonwealth of Kentucky prior to the drafting of a bill.

Providing Political Support. Given the scope of the Coalition's activities, it is easy to see why the organization has been an unqualified boon for Kentucky's SOTP. Yet the Coalition has an additional major function: It acts as both a watchdog and a safety net for the Sex Offender Treatment Program. At least twice in the past 10 years, our program has faced challenges from the media and to some extent, from legislators, over major issues. In one instance, an aggressive reporter called for an official inquiry to explain the perceived low number of offenders who "successfully" completed the program, with the implication that the program was underserving the population. Coalition leadership responded by providing a realistic picture of the scope of the problem and clear explanations of the nature of sex offenders' motivation for treatment. At the same time, the Coalition encouraged the program to consult with the National Institution of Corrections (NIC) to critique the program and offer a model for program evaluation. We were then able to complete a rigorous and comprehensive five-year outcome study that answered the concerns of the media and public (discussed further later).

In January 1997, the Coalition's support was crucial after a heinous rape and murder by a sex offender who refused treatment in prison (discussed further later). In response to this tragedy, the combined forces of the Coalition, legislators from both the Kentucky House of Representatives and Senate and officials of the Kentucky Department of Corrections came together to propose statutory changes that would create an even greater incentive for treatment participation.

Creating Coalitions

Of course, an active coalition is ideal. So what can sex offender programs do in states in which no such coalition exists? Like many psychologists, we initially approached the idea of proactivity in politics with trepidation. Certainly our graduate training did nothing to prepare us to draft bills, meet legislators, or cope with the press. Graduate school did, however, train us to observe and assess people, motives, and situations, and these are the crucial skills to begin with. Remember also that as experts in sex offender treatment we have much to offer, but we must also educate ourselves about the impact of sexual offending across the board: victims, offenders, the public, law enforcement, corrections policy, the media, and the lawmakers in our state.

If no coalition presently exists in the state, why not start one? Our advice is to look around; survey the field. Most states have victims' rights groups, rape crisis centers, or crime commissions. Set up a series of meetings with a view to forming a coalition. Find one agency that can both sponsor the coalition and devote at least part of one key staff member's time to leadership of the group. Meet at least quarterly. Search the legislature for state representatives who have sponsored bills relating to victims, offenders, or correctional issues. Stay nonpartisan, avoid controversial and inflammatory issues. Consider the benefits to the legislator who will sponsor the bill. Recognize the legislator publicly and continue to nurture that relationship through subsequent legislative sessions.

When speaking to interested groups, the media, or state representatives, some basic rules should be followed:

- Be succinct
- Avoid psychological jargon.
- Be factual, have simple statistics.
- Don't alienate them with elaborate methodological explanations.
- Don't be afraid to debate an issue or to say when you need more input before reaching a conclusion.

Above all, be persistent. It is easy to be discouraged when a proposed bill that has been worked long and hard on is shot down in the legislature, or worse, never reaches the level of serious discussion. These outcomes are facts of legislative life. Accept that the time was not right, rework the bill, and go back at the very next opportunity, with a compromised position if necessary.

Being Prepared for the Media

For the previously mentioned NIC-funded evaluation of the SOTP, our consultants were William Murphy, immediate past president of ATSA, and Craig Nelson of Atascadero State Hospital in California and a principal investigator in California's SOTP. One of the NIC's many cogent recommendations was that we continue our networking with community groups such as the Coalition. As described earlier, we have certainly done so with gusto. Dr. Murphy and Dr. Nelson also recommended that we prepare and regularly update a brief report on the program and its effectiveness, with the specific end audience of the media in mind.

To this end, we undertook the previously referenced outcome study comparing recidivism rates for treated and untreated offenders. We broke our sample down along a number of dimensions: by offender type, nature of recidivism (sexual or nonsexual offenses), length of time in treatment, length of time at risk in community, and time to reoffense after release. Although it is beyond the scope of our immediate purposes to the present all our data, following are some of the key findings. In a sample of 147 untreated and 138 treated offenders with an average at-risk period of 30.4 months, we found that untreated offenders recidivated sexually at a rate almost three times higher than treated offenders. The bulk of this variance was captured by the rapists with adult victims; almost 18% of the untreated rapists reoffended sexually, whereas none the treated rapists did. In contrast, familial incest perpetrators reoffended at very low rates, independent of treatment status. (As these findings are unpublished elsewhere, please contact the authors for a full summary of the study.)

Our original intention was to prepare a limited, simple summary of our findings and incorporate them into a brief program overview that would also include a description of our program's history, the treatment model, and some data on utilization of services. We envisioned about ten pages of nontechnical text and bulleted lists. In January 1997, we had our data analyzed, our utilization statistics collected, and our history and program overview outlined. Wrestling this information down into ten pages posed more challenges than we had anticipated, but nonetheless, prospects of closure on this project were bright. A tragedy would intervene to dramatically change the scope and importance of our little media report.

Intense Media Coverage. We spoke earlier about the Coalition recently providing support for our program after highly publicized crime. Sarah Hansen was a 16-year-old honor student and cheerleader in a small community in western Kentucky. One Sunday evening in January she took the family's van to return some rented videotapes. She never returned. Her body was found in a lake the next day. Sarah had been raped. A young man in his early twenties was subsequently accused of and arrested for this crime. He had recently been released from prison after serving a five-year sentence on child sexual abuse charges. During his incarceration, he had participated briefly in the assessment phase of the SOTP, then dropped out of treatment.

Media coverage of this tragedy was intense. At the same time, the Judiciary Committee of the Kentucky State Legislature was meeting in anticipation of the biannual 1998 General Assembly session. Following is a sample of some of the overlapping coverage of the crime and proposed legislative responses in two of the state's major newspapers:

"A thousand people mourn the loss of small town's perfect child: Murder suspect-former sex offender." (*Louisville Courier-Journal*, January 25, 1997)

"Many sex offenders paroled without treatment: Support grows to make treatment mandatory." (*Louisville Courier-Journal*, February 20, 1997)

"New rules in sex crimes cases urged: Study asks at least two years of supervision after release." (*Lexington Herald Leader*, February 21, 1997)

"Make parole for sex offenders contingent on treatment." (editorial, *Louisville Courier-Journal*, January 25, 1997)

"State may toughen sex offender policy: (Governor) Patton concerned about parole, lack of treatment" (*Louisville Courier-Journal*, March 21, 1997)

Appropriate Documentation. Though we had no direct evidence of any specific initiatives under consideration, there was some concern within the administration of our program that someone in the legislature might propose the dissolution of the SOTP. As it happened, we would both eventually be called to testify before the joint House and Senate Judiciary Committee. We later sat on a Governor's Task Force charged with drafting Kentucky's community notification legislation. During January, February, and March, we were contacted almost daily by television, newspaper, and radio media for information and commentary. Our ten-page document suddenly became the object of interest, scrutiny, and suggestions from "above" in the Department of Corrections; it grew to well over thirty pages and now included, in addition to our study data, sections describing our treatment model, and other program activities such as preparation of presentence evaluations of risk and amenability to treatment, utilization data, and recommendations for legislative consideration. It was initially distributed in draft form and finally in finished form from the DOC media office.

Having this document close to being ready when so suddenly and sadly needed underscored the wisdom of our consultants' recommendations. We could readily speak to questions of service delivery and outcome, with reference to solid current data, and make informed interpretations and recommendations based on those data. I think we would have presented a far less professional picture of ourselves had we been under pressure to pull that information together on short notice. From our experience, we would recommend specifically that treatment programs and providers always be ready and able to speak to issues of (1) program philosophy and structure, (2) target client population characteristics, (3) program utilization (referrals, number of clients treated, reasons for dropouts), and (4) such efficacy or outcome data as might be available. Extending this proactivity and preparedness further to our association with the Coalition, it is useful not only to be thoroughly conversant with existing sex offender-relevant legislation but also to be knowledgeable about the legislative *zeitgeist* and with proposed legislation under consideration.

The Process Element. Our comments on proactivity and preparedness have thus far been in regard to treatment and legislative information in its many forms—that is, *content*. To extend this clinical frame, we have since reflected on the process element of several of our media experiences. We found some potential grist for the proactive mill there as well.

We begin by briefly recounting three (of many) specific media experiences: (1) a joint live television appearance on a cable news program; (2) a critique of a draft version of the media document by a local Louisville radio personality, for which we were not present; and (3) a joint appearance on another local radio station call-in talk show.

In the case of our television appearance, we were contacted by a staff person from broadcast headquarters in New York. The program was described as a live, half-hour interview show devoted to current issues in psychology. The show had obtained a copy of our program overview and wanted to discuss our findings and recommendations on the air. We assumed that we would be on the air for the full half hour and drove to Cincinnati where a network station affiliate had facilities for linking us to the program's hostess in New York for the actual broadcast. We had prepared assiduously, anticipated a variety of questions, and were well armed with much erudition to share with the viewing audience. Our actual experience entailed seven hurried (to us) minutes at the end of the broadcast, with little opportunity to elaborate on the rapid-fire questions that came our way. Although we must say that we were treated quite nicely throughout the process, it was, as a whole, disappointing. We went in expecting a leisurely, full meal of an interview and left feeling like we had gulped cheese on a Ritz cracker.

Our second experience initially came to us vicariously. A local morning radio personality had also obtained a draft copy of the program overview. He took vigorous

exception to some comments in our recommendations section about alternative sentencing possibilities for first-time incest offenders with no other criminal history. One
of our staff heard the broadcast and was able to tape much of it for us. Some representative comments were ". . . one strike, you're out . . .," ". . . mandatory life sentence . . .," ". . . throw away the key . . .," and ". . . grave doubts about the competence
of the Department of Corrections. . . ." An exchange that was particularly salient for
Jon Barnes was as follows:

> *Host*: "The people who put it [the program overview] together were Kathi
> Peterson and Jon Barnes. Now, Jon Barnes spells his name J-O-N. I would never
> trust a guy named Jon that didn't spell it J-O-H-N."
> *Newsman*: "Well, he had nothing to do with it. Blame his parents."
> *Host*: "Well, he should go have the damn thing changed."
> *Sidekick*: "Put an 'H' in it, baby!"

Dr. Peterson, who of the two of us has infinitely more media experience, found
this amusing. Jon Barnes, however, felt compelled to write the station manager a
thoughtful, reasoned note. He opined that Mr. Host was certainly entitled to his
extreme and uninformed opinions about appropriate legal dispositions for incest
offenders, that there is room in the universe for many views, and that the standards for
discourse and debate on commercial radio were perhaps lower than in more academic venues. He respectfully suggested that Mr. Host was moving away from the issue at
hand in his *ad hominem* disparagement of Jon's name, and politely questioned the sin-
cerity of his bombast. He went on to speculate that Mr. Host may have instead been
seeking to increase audience share through sensationalism. Mr. Station Manager subsequently passed this note along to Mr. Host. Several friends and colleagues who
heard Mr. Host's broadcast response used words like "rabid" and "insane" to characterize the performance qualities of his rebuttal.

Our third experience was with Joe Elliott, who has a long-running Louisville
evening radio call-in talk show. Like the other two media outlets, he had obtained a
copy of our program overview. We give Joe's name because he is a thoughtful, prepared, upfront person who asked us tough questions in a respectful way. He seemed
interested in the enormous complexity of the issues around treatment and legal
response to sex offenders. We had a variety of callers, including sexual abuse victims
and families of such individuals. Not everybody agreed, naturally, but we left feeling
as if we had been in a fair forum.

The Media as Client. One could ask how we might extract any unifying features from
three such disparate media encounters. In pondering this task while preparing for our
ATSA remarks, what finally clicked integratively was the extension of the
content/process clinical metaphor. If we were to have approached each media contact
as a client contact, what questions (assessment) would we have had, and how would
our behavior (intervention) have been shaped? Ideally without torturing the "media as
client" idea too painfully, here are some thoughts:

1. Ask why the interviewer is seeking you out. What is his agenda? The answers
   to the questions will be shaped by the media modality to some extent. For

example, a television reporter is more likely to be in pursuit of the pithy sound bite, the snippet of film that can spliced into the reporter's own commentary, whereas one might hope for a more fleshed-out rendering of comments from a print piece. A second relevant, and probably far less accessible, piece of information, involves the personal views of the reporter. "Objectivity" is a worthy aspirational goal, but those of us who have been the focus of a negatively slanted piece of reporting know how mythic can be the nature of the objective beast.

2. Like a good clinician, be able to set firm, respectful boundaries. Certainly the media has considerable ascribed authority in the eye of the public. So do we. Keep appropriate, nondefensive limits. Treat pushy, intrusive interview tactics much as you would a client with similar transference issues or with a hostile defensive style.

3. Remember that your goal is to communicate clearly with the media person and, by extension, his audience. Talk plain American. Use short, declarative sentences and nontechnical language. You probably don't speak to your clients the way you would to a professional peer.

With these simple guidelines in place, a quick evaluative review of our own contributions to our experiences might be instructive. In our seven minutes of televised fame, we would have been well advised to ask how long we would be on the air, and, in the best Rogerian tradition, to have met our interviewer "where she was." At the least we would not have had such dashed expectations. Diatribe and polemic are an enduring feature of the media landscape; with the wisdom of hindsight, it would have been far more appropriate to have accepted that reality and not entered into that media "client's" ideational system.

Conclusion

We can distill these reflections on our experiences into several conclusions. First, we can have a significant voice in shaping the laws and public perceptions that have an impact on our professional practice. Second, it is useful to be prepared in advance of dealing with the media. Have current, relevant data about the program available, and be prepared to manage the interview process professionally. We would enjoy hearing from our colleagues about their experiences in these domains as well.

Chapter 8

Sex Offender Recidivism and Risk Factors in the Involuntary Commitment Process

by Barbara K. Schwartz, Ph.D. and Henry R. Cellini, Ph.D.

Overview

One of the basic assumptions underlying involuntary commitment laws is that professionals are able to predict which sex offenders will reoffend. In this chapter, the authors review the literature regarding which offenders recidivate, with special emphasis on risk assessment instruments. An analysis of factors commonly thought to be associated with relapse shows that there is a great deal of contradictory information. The authors also review risk assessment instruments developed by a number of states in conjunction with public notification.

Introduction

States that decide to enact "involuntary commitment of sex offender" statutes must be prepared to develop a scientifically sound way of identifying individuals who will commit heinous sex crimes. Unlike being sentenced to life in prison, these individuals will not have the constitutional protections associated with a criminal trial. The individuals making the decision about fate of the alleged "sexually violent predator" will be greatly influenced by whatever set of dynamics is presented as forecasting the likelihood of reoffense.

The process must be defendable as both reliable and valid in the prediction of the type of behavior about which society is most concerned. For some individuals it is not that difficult to divine that sometime in the future they may reoffend. For example, a chronic exhibitionist who has continued his offensive behavior throughout a period of incarceration will probably engage in that behavior at some time in the future. However, is he the individual that society wants to spend hundreds of thousands of dollars each year to confine? Probably not. The individuals of whom society is most justifiably afraid are the very individuals who inspired these laws—repeat sex offenders who murder children. Certainly there are others as well—sadists, patterned violent rapists who may escalate to become serial murderers, fixated pedophiles with hundreds of victims. No one would question that society needs to be protected from these individuals. Unfortunately an increasing number of states have chosen to use involuntary commitment rather than the criminal justice system to deal with these persons.

Problems With Prediction

Prediction is an inadequate science at best. Serin (1996) found that there was a false-negative rate of 35.8% in a sample of 93 violent offenders. This false-negative rate refers to individuals who were predicted to be nonrecidivists but actually did recidivate. However, there was only a 3.7% rate of false positives, individuals who were predicted to recidivate but did not. Quinsey (1980, 1992) stated that accurate prediction of violent or sexual recidivism is possible even when there is a weak correlation if (1) there is an accurate estimate of the base rate, (2) the base rate is between 25% and 75% for the group, and (3) one is able to identify specific predictor variables (Furr, 1993). This statement assumes that flipping a coin would give a 50% hit rate but identifying variables that either mitigate or aggravate the hit rate would improve the prediction rate.

Base Rates

Base rates for sex offender recidivism are estimated at 19% (Hanson & Bussière, 1996), 25–50% (Davidson, 1984), and 36.4–51.5% for rapists (Beck & Shipley, 1987) to 13% (Hanson & Bussière, 1996) and 32.6–47.9% for child molesters (Beck & Shipley, 1987). Thus the estimates vary widely. According to Marshall, Jones, Ward, Johnston, and Barbaree (1991), who followed 13,000 sex offenders released in 1987, only 7% were actually reconvicted of another sex offense. These rates undoubtedly underestimate the real figure. Marshall and Barbaree (1990) report that "unofficial" sources show 2.4 times more "reoffenses" than do "official" reports.

However, involuntarily commitment is not concerned with preventing any sex offense. It is concerned with preventing the most frightening types of sex offenses. Fortunately, the worst types of sex offenses are the rarest. The base rate of sexual murder is extremely low compared to the impression that the media has created. The U.S. Department of Justice has reported that between 1976 and 1994 there were 405,089 murders in this country. The circumstances of the crime was known in 78.5% of the cases. Of these murders, 1.5% involved sexual assault. Contrary to the popular impression, this figure has actually been cut in half in recent years (*Crime statistic reports*, l996).

Legal Standard for Predicting Recidivism

Janus and Meehl (1997), in an article challenging involuntary commitment, have written a highly sophisticated analysis of the statistics involved in determining risk. In three states that have defended their involuntary commitments in court, all agree that their statute is designed to commit only the most dangerous. The Minnesota Supreme Court has interpreted this to mean that violence is "highly likely."[1] The Washington Supreme Court defined this as "extremely high."[2] The Wisconsin Supreme Court defined as "most likely," "distinctively dangerous," and "only the most dangerous of sexual offenders."[3] The Washington court established the standard of the 80% chance of reoffending to define "highly likely." Janus and Meehl assume that "likely" would be a 50% likelihood to reoffend. They then point out that there are basically two legal standards: the standard of proof, expressed in terms such as "clear and convincing evidence" or "preponderance of evidence," which refers to the fact finder's certainty about the evidence, and the standard of commitment, such as "likely" or "highly likely," which measures the likelihood of future behavior. They state, "We submit that the legal "standard of commitment" ought to be understood to include both types of uncertainty . . . the uncertainties arising from imperfect ability to perceive the world and those arising from the 'objective' indeterminacy of the world" (p. 43).

As Janus and Meehl (1997) point out, one method of predicting whether an individual will recidivate is to determine the likelihood that he belongs to a class of sex offenders whose base rate is known. For example, we might determine that a particular sex offender has a history of violence. If we know the base rate for violent sex offenders, then we have some idea about the offender's statistical probability to reoffend. However, the lower the base rate, the higher the proportion of false positives and the higher the likelihood that this individual will be predicted to reoffend but would not have. Reviewing the wide range of base rates and using Marshall and Barbaree's adjustment, these authors estimate a base rate between 20% and 70%.

We must then look at the accuracy of the prediction instrument, which ranges from 41% for the Sex Offender Screening Tool (Epperson, Kaul, & Huot, 1995) to 77% using Hanson's tool (Hanson & Bussière, 1996). Janus and Meehl (1997) then combine these two figures into a two-dimensional chart which shows what the accuracy of these two figures must be to produce a certain degree of likelihood of reoffense. For example, to achieve a 50% standard of commitment, one would have to use a tool or process that has a 70% accuracy rate and the base rate would have to be at least 30% However, this is not the standards to which the three courts have alluded.

Based on the mathematical formula, "Minnesota courts never attain a 50% probability of recidivism standard of commitment. Even on assumptions about the special
group that appear to be highly optimistic, 50% probability in the commitment class
will occur only on the most optimistic assumptions about base rates and prediction
accuracy" (Janus & Meehl, 1997, p. 58).

Some judges have totally rejected the concept of utilizing base rates to predict
recidivism. Justice Coyne, writing a dissenting opinion in *In re Linehan,* stated: "Not
only are the statistics concerning the violent behavior of others irrelevant, but it seems
to me wrong to confine any person on the basis not of that person's own conduct but
on the basis of statistical evidence regarding the behavior of other people" (cited in
Janus & Meehl, 1997, p. 63).

Studies of Factors Related to Recidivism

Numerous studies have evaluated factors related to recidivism in sex offenders.
Table 8.1 summarizes some of the more recent studies. However, readers should exercise caution in reading recidivism studies for a number of reasons. Studies differ widely in the quality of the research design. What were the criteria for success or failure?
Was there a control group? How long was the group followed and were the correct statistics used in analyzing time at risk? It must also be noted that each of these studies
utilized different types of sex offenders and studied a different, though possibly overlapping, set of variables.

Contradictory Findings

There are a great many contradictions within this research (see Table 8.2).
Although Beck and Shipley (1987) found that recidivism was not related to age when
paroled, Clark and Crum (1985), the Delaware Executive Committee (1984), and
Wallerstadt (1984) contradicted this. In fact, Grunfeld and Noreik (1986) suggest that
the older sex offender has a much more developed fixation and would therefore be
more likely to reoffend than a younger offender. The Delaware Executive Committee
(1984) found that the longer a person was incarcerated the higher the recidivism rate;
however, Beck and Shipley (1987) found just the opposite. Roundtree, Edwards, and
Parker (1984) and Boudouris (1983) found that race and recidivism were not related,
but Beck and Shipley (1987) and the Delaware Executive Committee (1984) studies
found that blacks had a higher recidivism rate. Greenfield (1985), Wilson (1985), and
the Delaware Executive Committee (1984) reported that males recidivate more than
females, but Roundtree et al. (1984) contradicted this finding. Eisenberg (1985) stated that participation in prison rehabilitative or vocational/technical programs had no
influence on recidivism whereas LeClair (1985) found that participants did significantly better. Eisenberg (1985) also reported that substance abusers had higher rates
of reoffense, but this finding was contested by a study conducted by the University of
Hawaii-Manoa (1984).

Quinsey, Chaplin, and Carrigan (1980) found that pretreatment penile response on
the plethysmograph was predictive of recidivism. Barbaree and Marshall (1988) found
the same result but when the sample was increased and the follow-up time lengthened,
the differences on this factor disappeared. Maletzky (1991) found that deviant arousal
greater than 80% predicted treatment failure. Eisenberg (1985) reported that those

Table 8.1
Studies of Factors Related to Recidivism

Study	*Factors Related to Recidivism*
Barbaree & Marshall (1988)	Deviant arousal, amount of force, penetration, number of victims, IQ, socio-economic status
Shaw, Herkov & Green (1995)	Reading ability, marital status
Quinsey, Rice & Harris (1995)	Married, violent convictions, PCL-R, admissions to corrections, property convictions (-*r*), sexual convictions, female victims, male child victims
Serin, Malcolm, Khanna, & Barbaree (1994)	Phallometric deviance Psychopathy, deviant arousal
Serin (1996)	Psychopathy
Rice & Harris (1997)	Psychopathy, sexual deviance
Hanson & Bussière (1996)	P-graph preference for child, elevated MMPI scale 5, victim stranger vs. acquaintance, deviant preference, negative relationship with mother, personality disorder, prior nonsexual offense, age under 30, never married, victim male child, diverse sex crimes, number of admissions to corrections, victim related child (-*r*), victim female child (-*r*)
Marshall & Barbaree (1990)	Age of offender (under 40 for nonfamilial child molesters), type of sexual contact, genital-genital or genital-anal contact, female victims
Hanson, Steffy, & Gauthier (1993)	Gender of and relationship with victim, never married, history of previous sex offenses
Abel, Mittelman, Becker, Rathner, & Rouleau (1988)	Molested both males and females as well as children and adolescents, failure to list increased communication with adults as a treatment goal, "hands on" and "hands off" offense behavior, divorced, familial and nonfamilial victims
Bench, Kramer, & Erickson (1997)	Number of felony convictions, number of arrests for sex offenses, fewer number of total arrests, increased number of arrests for non-sex offenses, greater number of felony arrests, failure to complete a sex offender treatment program
McGovern & Peters (1988)	Sexual deviation, victim of sexual abuse, cognitive impairment, substance abuse, relationship problems, employment problems, past violent felonies, past nonviolent fantasies, high density of sex offenses, multiple offense types, physical harm, weapons, minimization, attitudes condone act, negative attitude toward treatment
Hanson & Harris (1997)	Mixed victim types, elementary school maladjustment problems, not motivated for treatment, treatment dropout, total number of sexually deviant behaviors, PCL-R score
Epperson, Kaul, & Huot (1995, October)	Quick felony upon previous release, age of victims, number of victims, number of sex offense convictions, age at first conviction, chemical dependency during incarceration, number of felony convictions, length of sex offense history, discipline history, marginal performance in prior sex offender treatment
Prentky, Lee, Knight, & Cerce (1997) Prentky, Knight, & Lee (1997) Prentky, Lee, Knight, & Cerce (1995)	Rapists: impulsive lifestyle, offense planning, and pervasive anger Child molesters: fixation, paraphilias, and number of victims

offenders with previous stable employment records did better on release, but Roundtree et al. (1984) indicated that this variable was not relevant. Finally, the Oregon Crime Analysis Center (1984) reported that parolees who recidivate do so for crimes similar to those for which they were originally imprisoned, but Wallerstadt (1984) stated that parolees who recidivate commit offenses different from the ones they originally committed. All these contradictory findings involve dynamics that would intuitively be thought to be related to recidivism.

The lack of agreement in these studies is alarming given that they analyze the most commonly evaluated variables. For example, Marshall and Barbaree (1990) specifically found that socioeconomic status, number or prior offenses, age of victim, intelligence level and pre- and posttreatment indices of deviant sexual interests were not relevant to recidivism.

Factors Related to Subtypes of Sex Offenders

One possible reason for the amount of disagreement in these studies is that they may use a heterogeneous group of sex offenders in their analysis. Mixing an antisocial rapist with a socially skilled fixated pedophile with a developmentally disabled exhibitionist may indeed produce a hodgepodge of results. Accuracy may be improved by using a more homogeneous group of sex offenders.

Child Molesters. Rice, Quinsey, and Harris (1991) found that child molesters who recidivated had a history of past sex offenses, had more admissions to correctional institutions, were more likely to be diagnosed as personality disordered, were less likely to be married, and showed deviant arousal on an initial phallometric assessment.

Hanson, Steffy, and Gauthier (1993) identified the following predictors for recidivating child molesters:

1. Victims were most likely to be extrafamilial males and least likely to be intrafamilial;
2. Never having been married; and
3. Previous sex offense.

Another study of child molesters by Prentky, Knight, and Lee (1997) followed 111 child molesters released between 1960 and 1984 and found that degree of sexual preoccupation with children, number of paraphilias, and number of prior sex offenses predicted sexual recidivism, but juvenile and adult antisocial behavior, paraphilias, and low contact with children predicted crimes with nonsexual victims.

Rapists. In evaluating rapists Prentky, Lee, Knight, and Cerce (1995) analyzed the recidivism data from the Massachusetts Treatment Center and identified lifestyle impulsivity as highly predictive of reoffense in this group. They defined this factor as being a composite of the following:

1. Unstable employment;
2. Reckless behavior such as dangerous driving;

Table 8.2
Contradictory Studies of Factors Related to Recidivism

Factor	Positively Related	Not Positively Related
Offender type: rapist	Marshall & Barbaree (1990); Quinsey, Rice, & Harris (1995); Barbaree & Marshall (1988)	Shaw et al. (1995); Prentky (1997); Hanson & Bussière (1996); Abel et al. (1988)
Deviant arousal	Quinsey et al. (1995); Rice & Harris (1997); Hanson & Bussière (1996)	Marshall & Barbaree (1990)
Race	Roundtree et al. (1988)	Beck & Shipley (1987); Delaware Executive Committee (1984)
Prior sexual convictions	Quinsey et al. (1995); Bench et al. (1997); Hanson & Harris (1997); Epperson et al. (1995, October)	Marshall & Barbaree (1990)
Violent convictions	Bench et al. (1997); Epperson et al. (1995, October)	Marshall & Barbaree (1990)
PCL-R	Quinsey et al. (1995); Serin (1996); Rice & Harris (1997)	Marshall (1997)
Incarcerations	Quinsey et al. (1995), Hanson & Bussière (1996)	Serin (1996)
Other crimes	Hanson & Bussière (1996)	Quinsey et al. (1995); Bench et al. (1997); Marshall & Barbaree (1990)
Male victims	Hanson & Bussière (1996); Quinsey et al. (1995)	Marshall & Barbaree (1990)
Both sexes of victims	Hanson & Bussière (1996); Abel et al. (1988); Epperson (1995, October)	Hanson & Bussière (1996); Quinsey et al. (1995)
Age	Hanson & Bussière (1996); Marshall & Barbaree (1990)	Clark & Crum (1985); Shaw et al. (1995); Delaware Executive Committee (1984); Wallerstadt (1984)
Substance abuse	Eisenberg (1985); Epperson (1995)	University of Hawaii-Manoa (1984)
Sex offender treatment	LeClair (1985); Bench et al. (1997); Hanson & Harris (1997); Epperson et al. (1995, October); Steele (1995); Mander et al. (1996)	Eisenberg (1985); U.S. GAO (1996)
Length of incarcerations	Delaware Executive Committee (1984)	Beck & Shipley (1987)
Stable work history	Eisenberg (1985)	Roundtree et al. (1988)

3. Repeated instances of aggressive or destructive behavior;
4. Disruptiveness at school or work; and
5. A history of fighting.

The high-lifestyle-impulsivity rapists were twice as likely to reoffend as were the low lifestyle impulsivity rapists.

The base rate of this researched group (Prentky, Lee, Knight, & Cerce, 1997) is similar to the population being selected for civil commitment because of their potential dangerousness. According to these researchers, great variability exists in sex offender research regarding the likelihood of recidivism. This research used a data set of 251 sex offenders (136 rapist and 115 child molesters) who were discharged over a twenty-five-year time period from the Massachusetts Treatment Center for Sexually Dangerous Persons located in Bridgewater. The purpose of this research was to determine some of the reasons related to why there is such a great variation in research findings regarding recidivism rates among child molesters and rapists. The data indicate that child molesters and rapists do remain at risk to reoffend long after their release and that using simple percentages to calculate recidivism rates results in an underestimation. The degree of underestimation is considerable where, in their article, the authors indicate that "In sum, sexual recidivism was underestimated by 30–40% when rates were estimated using the simple proportion of new offenses." The authors (Prentky, Knight, & Lee, 1997; Prentky, Lee, & Knight, 1995) also state that certain simple concepts can discriminate groups of sex offenders who did and did not commit additional sexual offenses. These constructs are for:

- Rapists: impulsive lifestyle, offense planning, and pervasive anger; and
- Child molesters: fixation, paraphilias, and number of victims.

Dr. Rodney V. McCormick, in a review of the Prentky, Lee, Knight, and Cerce (1997) research, determined that the article is quite dense, and it appropriately addresses the methodological problems of ascertaining recidivism rates. By looking at accumulated "failure rates" over a very long period (twenty-five years), two different types of offenders, and three different levels of return to the corrections domain, they indicate how the recidivism rates have been underestimated. The statistical analysis they used remained primarily at the descriptive level, in order to describe their methodological approach. Inferential statistics were used to indicate that there was insufficient data to yield significant differences among time groups. Now, let us assume that a Weibull distribution (used in survival analyses) was used to describe failure rates over time, and the analysis implied that over the twenty-five-year span considered, sex offenders have a theoretically determinable "failure" rate. That is, they have a chance to reoffend per any given time period. So, previous studies of smaller duration underestimated this failure rate.

An example helps clarify why Weibull distribution is important to use when determining recidivism rates. Say over a two-year period, of 100 people 40 end up back in prison. The simple percentage rate is determined by dividing 40%/2, yielding 20% a year. But if it follows a Weibull distribution, say after the first year thirty are back in prison, leaving seventy, ten of whom are back in prison after the end of the second year. The rate the first year is 30%, the second is 14%. Thus a rough average is 22%, which demonstrates that the simple percentage underestimates the recidivism.

Additional Research Studies

Many studies have also found that dynamics predictive for one group of offenders do not predict for others. For example, Marshall's study (1997) reported that age was predictive for nonfamilial child molesters but not for incest offenders. Schwartz (1977) found that child molesters who positively responded to a treatment program were characterized by the variables of environmental stress, no previous criminal convictions, no history of alcoholism, and intact marriages whereas rapists were differentiated by the Rorschach Genetic Level Score, intact marriages, stable employment, and honorable discharge from the military. Simkins, Ward, Bowman, and Rinck (1989) found that denial was related to reoffense but only for treated offenders. Romero and Williams (1985) compared different types of offenders and found that pedophiles reoffended less than those convicted of sexual assault, but the highest rate was among exhibitionists. However, when Frisbie and Dondis (1965, quoted in Quinsey, 1977) made a more detailed study, they found that were significant differences in the reoffense rates of child molesters with those who molested males having the highest rate for this subgroup. In contrast, Abel, Mittelman, Becker, Rathner, and Roulear (1988) found that offenders who targeted males and females had the highest reoffense rate. Prentky (1990) found that impulsivity was highly predictive among repetitive rapists but was not a factor for child molesters. Alcohol is another variable that depends on offense type. For example, male-oriented pedophiles have a low rate of alcohol use whereas the use of alcohol was higher among extrafamilial female-target child molesters, rapists, and exhibitionists. (Rada, 1976)

Use of force has been found to be associated with recidivism by a number of researchers; however, the highest rate of recidivism is associated with hands-off offenses. Furthermore, highly fixated pedophiles who have the largest number of victims are not prone to extraneous physical force, preferring to rely on intimidation, trickery, and coercion. Offenders who have a stable support system and specifically are married are slightly less likely to reoffend (Abel, Mittelman, & Becker, 1985; Fitch, 1962; Hall, 1990). However, an incest offender whose wife colludes with his denial may be at more risk to reoffend. Although age is predictive for rapists, it is not predictive for child molesters (McGrath, 1991).

It must be remembered that the factors that emerge as predictive in any given study are largely dependent on the characteristics of the sample. For example, Marshall and Barbaree (1990) studied an outpatient group. This would not be comparable to Prentky's (1990) population, which consisted of highly repetitive or violent offenders. Rice and Harris's (1997) population consisted of individuals who were committed to a mental hospital and suffered major psychological problems in addition to sexual deviancy. To predict from a prison-incarcerated population, one should use only studies that were done on a prison-incarcerated sample. However, few studies have used that population (see Table 8.3).

Formal Systems of Risk Assessment

One of the most comprehensive systems of predicting risk is the Level of Service Inventory—Revised (LSI-R), which was developed by Andrews and Bonta (1994). This instrument was originally designed by Canadian researchers as an objective way

Table 8.3
Problems With Commonly Used Variables

Factor	Problem
Deviant arousal	Does not predict for rapists; research contradictory
Amount of force	Predicts for violent offenders but would not predict for patterned child molesters who are not violent
Number of victims	Would predict for offenders who are able to avoid detection; would not predict for more violent offenders who may have been caught relatively soon in their offending careers
Gender of victims	Rapists would have female victims; male victims are predictive in some studies for child molesters; both genders are predictive for child molesters in other studies
Married	Would not be predictive if wife was in denial
Social support	Depends on whether they are prosocial or antisocial and whether they in denial
Age	Would be predictive for impulsive offenders but not for compulsive offenders
Age of victims	Would be inversely related to age
Length of sex offending history	Depends on availability. Would not be predictive for rapists

of assigning probation officer caseloads with varying levels of supervision for all types of offenders. The instrument was found to be useful in identifying inmates' adaptation to halfway houses (predicting nine out of ten failures) and their likelihood to reoffend with those with a lower score recidivating at a rate of 15.8% versus a 48% rate for high scorers (Andrews & Bonta, 1994). The scale consists of fifty-four items covering criminal history, education/employment, financial, family/marital, accommodations, recreation/leisure, companions, alcohol/drugs, and emotional/personal and attitudes/orientation. One nice feature of this tool is its inclusion of numerous dynamic versus static variables that are responsive to change on the part of the offender. However, the assessment does not specifically address sex offenders.

Boer, Wilson, Gauthier, and Hart (1997) developed the Sexual Violence Risk—20 (SVR-20). This system is based on twenty factors covering psychosocial adjustment, sexual offending, and future plans. The authors have distilled these factors from recidivism research, but the validity of the assessment has not been researched.

Hare (1988, 1991) developed the Psychopathy Checklist—Revised, which is the most commonly used measure of psychopathy (Harpur, Hakstian, & Hare, 1988; Prentky & Knight, 1988; Harris, Rice, & Cormier, 1989; Patrick & Iacono, 1989; Gacono & Hutton, 1994; Salekin, Rogers, & Sewel, 1996; Cook, 1997). The assessment includes a records review and an interview. It measures two factors: Factor 1, which associated with "Selfish, callous and remorseless use of others," and Factor 2, "Chronically unstable and antisocial lifestyle, social deviance" (Hare, McPherson, & Forth, 1988; Hare, 1991). Serin and associates (1994) found psychopathy as measured by the PCL-R (Hare,1991) significantly related to recidivism for extrafamilial child molesters. In 1996, Serin reported that after following 93 sex offenders for two years there was a 10% rate of violent recidivism for his overall group, but for those identified as psychopathic, the rate was 25%. He also found that on the PCL-R, Factor 1 was related to violent recidivism and Factor 2 was related to overall recidivism. Psychopathy, however, is not the magic bullet of risk assessment. Marshall (1997) states that Canadian sex offender treatment programs in prisons have not noted higher recidivism among psychopaths. According to Furr (1993):

> The magnitude of the correlations between the PCL-R and violent recidivism in various studies range is between .25 and .35/ This is only a slight degree of correlation. The conclusion, therefore, is the PCL-R may be able to predict future violent re-offending only among groups of released offenders who have been convicted of a violent offense, who have a high base rate of re-offense, and where there is a long follow-up, but not among the general population of offenders. (p. 277)

Use of the PCL to predict various forms of recidivism has been tested in a number of articles. The cutoff values varied across studies, and the number of years of follow-up also varied. The distinction of psychopath versus nonpsychopath does significantly predict recidivism in general and violence and sexual offenses in particular (see Table 8.4).

Based on the articles examined, the PCL-R appears to be a both reliable and valid instrument for the populations surveyed. The analyses were for populations primarily found in Canada; thus if it can be shown that African Americans form a special class different than Caucasians on the psychopathology construct measured by the PCL-R, then further reliability and validity studies may be required.

Quinsey et al. (1995) have incorporated the concept of psychopathy into their Violence Risk Appraisal Guide. They found that psychopathy was related to deviance as measured by the penile plethysmograph and to previous convictions for other crimes but was not related to a history of sex offenses. These researchers first emphasized the importance of psychopathy and pretreatment phallometric results but later reported that these factors contributed only marginally to the accuracy of prediction. It may appear that these factors were relevant to some sex offenders but not to others: "Sexual deviance may be a more important factor for child molesters than for rapists,

Table 8.4
Projected Rates of Recidivism

Study	After # Years	Hare PCL-Rated Recidivism		
		Psychopaths	*Mixed*	*Nonpsychopath*
Hare (1985)	3	90%	62%	30%
Hart, Kropp, & Hare (1988)	not clear	33%	31%	7%
Harris, Rice, & Cormier (1991) 1. Violent	10	77%	Not defined	21%
Quinsey, Rice, & Harris (1995) 1. Violent	Survival analysis at 5 yrs.	62%	Not defined	19%
Serin (1996) 1. General recidivism 2. Violent reoffense	2.5	85% 25%	51% 7%	40% 0%
Rice & Harris (1997) 1. Violent (deviant/ nondeviant) 2. Sexual (deviant/ nondeviant)	Survival analysis at 5 yrs.	90% / 65% 90% / 75%	Not defined	60% / 40% 30% / 35%

whereas general criminal deviance, lack of self-control, and psychopathy may be more important for rapists" (Rice & Harris, 1997, p. 239).

Grubin and Wingate (1996) criticized the Quinsey et al. (1995) study by stating as follows:

[T]he authors claim that their method resulted in 72% correct decisions in relation to "violent failure" and 77% correct decisions in relation to sexual reconvictions, both of which represented a relative improvement over chance of just over 40%. The vast majority of the sample, however, had risk scores giving a probability of reoffending that was less than 40%, which, even if a significant improvement over chance, is not particularly helpful to those who must make decisions about release. Thus, although the 50% success rate of tossing a coin to decide who was going to reoffend would not be as good as their method, it would not be all that much worse. It is only for those with the highest scores that the probability of reoffending becomes clinically meaningful at around 85%, but this accounted for just six men, 3% of the sample. (pp. 353–354)

Public Notification Risk Assessment Systems Adopted by States

A number of states are attempting to develop risk assessment tools to determine the level of public notification. One might assume that a system designed to differentiate sex offenders so that the most dangerous trigger the widest public notification would be both reliable and valid. However, little long-term research has been conducted on these scales. (See Table 8.5, on pages 8-14 and 8-15.)

Numerous problems may be noted with these assessment tools in addition to the problems associated with contradictions surrounding the individual factors. The Washington adaptation of the Minnesota screen makes repeated use of the same factors such as number of sex offenses, age, marital status, and so on. This repeated use may reflect a desire to doubly weight those items but is a rather roundabout way of doing so. The overrides on both the Washington and the Massachusetts screen that refer to individuals who have children or "vulnerable victims" basically negate the rest of the instrument. The override related to "sexually predatory" behavior is extremely vague and the second half of that override probably captures all extrafamilial offenders. It would be more honest and certainly quicker to simply divide all sex offenders into intrafamilial and extrafamilial groups and classify all the latter at high risk and then to add those from the intrafamilial group who accosted children under a certain age. Of course, the result would have little relationship to reoffense rates. The Massachusetts screen also places in the highest-risk category anyone who previously participated in a sex offender program but is not doing so currently. There is no exception made for sex offenders who successfully completed sex offender treatment and were thus discharged, sometimes up to twenty years previously.

An additional problem is that records from sex offender treatment programs are often used to obtain relevant information. For example, we may know that an offender has twenty victims because he was truthful with his therapist. Contrast this scenario with one in which the offender has refused to participate in treatment and thus we are only aware of and can only score the crimes he has been convicted of rather than all the crimes he has committed. The treated offender will score higher on the assessment. However, is he really more dangerous? A system needs to be developed that does not penalize offenders who divulge information in treatment while rewarding offenders who refuse therapy.

Dynamic Variables

All the factors discussed so far have been static in the sense that they are part of an individual's basic characteristic, such as age, or are part of his history. Hanson and Harris (1997) researched dynamic factors that occur in the offender's life on a daily basis. Those that distinguished between recidivists and successful offenders at a .01 level of significance included individuals who:

1. Failed to show up for the initial interview;
2. Show attitudes tolerant of sexual offending including general excuses, justification, low victim empathy;

	Minnesota	Washington	New Jersey	Massachusetts
Number of sex/sex-related convictions	X	X	X	X*
Offense against a child or mentally retarded person				X*
Incarceration				X
Relation to victim				X
Felony convictions	X	X	X	
Sex/sex-related charges not resulting in convictions	X	X		
Age at first conviction	X	X	X	X*
Threat of or use of a weapon	X	X		X*
Total number of victims	X	X	X	
Age of victims (adult offender)	X	X	X	
Threats of or indication of plans to commit a sex offense				X
Past participation in a sex offender treatment program				X
Age of victims (juvenile offender)	X	X		
Use of force	X	X	X	
Other characteristics of the offense	X	X		
Length of sexual offending behavior	X	X		X
Felony committed on release from institution	X	X		
Alcohol/drug use	X	X		X
Compulsive behaviors				X
Impulsivity				X
Prior sex offender treatment	X	X		X
Number of significant/ marital relations	X	X		
Employment history	X	X	X	
School history	X	X	X	
Multiple paraphilias	X	X		

* Overrides.

(cont'd)

Table 8.5
Public Notification Risk Assessments

	Minnesota	Washington	New Jersey	Massachusetts
Release environment	X	X	X	X
Physical health				X
Age at release	X	X		
Discipline record while incarcerated	X	X		
Mental abnormality				X*
Chemical dependency treatment while incarcerated	X	X	X	
Length of time since last offense				X
Sex offender treatment while incarcerated	X	X	X	X
Vulnerable victim				X*
Sex offense of a predatory nature or offender used trust, authority, or professional relationship to facilitate the commission of a nonfamilial offense			X*	
Offender continued sexual acting-out during incarceration		X*		X
Gender of victim			X	
No supervision requirements upon release		X*		
Hanson Quick Risk Score (number of sex offenses, age at conviction, marital relationships, age at release, stranger victim, male victims)		X	X	

3. Expect sexual entitlement;
4. Demonstrated attitudes tolerant of rape/child molesting;
5. See themselves as not being at risk;
6. Show sexual risk factors;
7. Have access to victims;
8. Are exposed to positive social influences (*-r*);
9. Are exposed to negative social influences; and
10. Cooperate with supervision.

Factors that demonstrated that an offender under supervision was changing for the worse included:

1. Drinking or using drugs at initial interview;
2. Attended initial interview;
3. Feeling low;
4. Attitude changes for the worse;
5. Sees self at no risk;
6. Has access to victims;
7. Socially disengaged;
8. Manipulative; and
9. Misses sessions.

This information is extremely useful for supervising agents but less helpful for identifying individuals who are being screened for involuntary commitment while still in an institution.

Specifying Risk Assessment

Because the traditional manner of developing a risk assessment scale results in a jumble of factors that are related in different ways to different subgroups of offenders, perhaps a different approach could be taken. It is fairly easy to identify which types of sex offenders society would be most concerned about releasing. These might include:

1. Compulsive pedophiles who have exclusive arousal to children;
2. Pedophiles who have used kidnapping or violence with unknown children;
3. Repetitive rapists who use gratuitous violence;
4. Sadists; and
5. Individuals who have committed or attempted to commit murder.

First one would study the factors that separate recidivists from nonrecidivists for these subgroups and then develop assessment scales that would predict placement in the recidivism class of a particular subgroup. These instruments would attempt to predict not only whether a person would recidivate but how he would recidivate. Generic risk assessments are designed only to predict risk of reoffense; however, the easiest group to classify are exhibitionists, who are not candidates for involuntary commitment. Factors that predict those offenders who are society's worst nightmare are rarely studied. With the exception of Massachusetts, which incorporated some of these factors into assessment, they are rarely included in risk assessment scales because they rarely occur. Yet these factors would be highly predictive. Such factors include:

1. Committing a sexual assault while institutionalized;
2. Collecting offense-related pornography while institutionalized;
3. Preparing plans to commit a sex offense upon release;
4. Maintaining contact with untreated sex offenders who are in the community; and
5. Threatening their victims while institutionalized.

Studies have been conducted of sex offenders who escalate. The FBI has developed a profile of those who have committed increasingly violent or sadistic rapes. These factors include:

1. Evidence of an erotic fantasy being acted out;
2. Sexual pleasure having been experienced from inflicting pain or humiliation as opposed to acting out angrily or demanding that sexual urges be satisfied;
3. Torture, beating, or use of instruments (including the use of psychological torment or humiliation);
4. Planning involved;
5. Transportation of the victim to a different location;
6. Victim is a stranger;
7. Holding victim captive (twenty-four hours or more);
8. Bondage (beyond that needed to restrain), painful and/or sexual bondage
9. Forced fellatio, anal intercourse;
10. Recording of offenses (journal, photograph, etc.);
11. Keeping personal items belonging to the victim;
12. Cold, detached, unemotional interaction with the victim;
13. Acting in a "macho" manner; and
14. Not negotiating with or reassuring the victim.

A similar profile could be developed for sex offenders who assault unknown children and for each of the other relevant subtypes.

Conclusion

In attempting to classify the risk level of all sex offenders for purposes of either public notification or involuntary commitment, states have assumed a daunting responsibility. The prediction of human behavior is fraught with problems too numerous to mention here. However, one issue does encompass many of the others and that is *the price that society is willing to pay to keep certain events from occurring*. In our highly litigious society, no one wants to be sued in connection with a lurid sex crime. Yet when these events occur, the first impulse is to find someone or some flaw in the system to blame.

The public is so frightened by the thought that these events may not be controllable that public officials and politicians may go to any lengths to try to alleviate that fear. Thus are born public policies such as involuntary commitment and public notification.

States that decide to implement these policies must look at the statistical problems inherent in this process. Grubin and Wingate (1996) summarize the problem with all actuarial instruments developed to predict sex offender recidivism:

> Imagine that an actuarial technique is developed that can predict with 90% accuracy who will reoffend and who will not, a figure much greater than anything currently available. Given 4,000 sex offenders in prison with a recidivism rate of 10%, then 400 of these men will reoffend as opposed to 3,600 who will not. With an actuarial tool of 90% accuracy, 360 of the 400 will be identified successfully (and just 40 missed). We would also, however, incorrectly decide that 360 (i.e. 10%) of the 3,600 non-offenders will reoffend. Thus, we would identify a group of 720 men predicted to reoffend of whom just 360 (50%) will actually do so. What this means is that we would be making good decisions about who will not reoffend (in the above example, only about 1% of those let out would do so), and we would identify well a high-risk group for continued detention, but for individuals within the high-risk group the odds of any one individual reoffending are still 50/50, that is, similar to tossing a coin. (p. 354)

Unfortunately it would appear that policymakers wish to use the widest brush possible to paint all sex offenders as violent predators. Consequently, nonspecific factors are utilized that are guaranteed to produce the highest number of false positives. More appropriate risk assessment scales could be developed if they were targeted to specific behaviors. However, the reality is that the incidence of that behavior is extremely low. As a result, it would take large numbers of offenders followed over a lengthy period to begin to evaluate the validity of such an instrument. It is unlikely that any state or the federal government would be willing to delay implementation of these laws while the instrument was being developed.

However, in lieu of the fact that systems are being developed without the necessary statistical verification, an effort might be made to link the variables with the actual behavior one is trying to prevent. In doing so, policymakers must resist the urge to cast a net that covers every sex offender. In this case the object should be to catch only the sharks—not every creature in the sea. In developing risk assessment scales for involuntary commitment, the researchers involved must constantly keep in mind that they are dealing with depriving a person of their liberty for quite possibly the rest of his life, to say nothing of the actual cost of this incarceration, which is staggering. This entire process grew out of a political situation and remains fraught with political connotations. The least that can be asked is that a good faith effort be made to apply this policy to as few individuals as possible while addressing the issue of public safety with longer sentences for repeat offenders, better prevention, and treatment programs.

Footnotes

[1] See In re Linehan, 557 N.W.2d 171, 181 (Minn. 1996).
[2] See In re Young. 857 P.2d 989, 1008 (Wash. 1993).

[3] See Wis. Stat. § 980.01 (1996); State v. Post. 541 N.W.2d 115, 118 (Wis. 1995), *petition for cert. filed.* (U.S. March 7, 1996).

References

Abel, G. G., Mittelman, M., & Becker, J. (1985). Sex offenders: Results of assessment and recommendations for treatment. In J. Ben-Aron, S. Hucker, & C. Webster (Eds.), *Clinical criminology: Current concepts* (pp. 127–155). Toronto: M & M Graphics.

Abel, G. G., Mittelman, M., Becker, J., Rathner, J., & Roulear, J. (1988). Predicting child molesters' response to treatment. In R. A. Prentky & V. L. Quinsey (Eds.), *Human sexual aggression: Current perspectives* (pp. 223–234). New York: New York Academy of Science.

Andrews, D. A., & Bonta, J. L. (1994). *The psychology of criminal conduct.* Cincinnati, OH: Anderson.

Barbaree, H. E., & Marshall, W. (1988). Deviant sexual arousal, offense history and demographic variables as predictors of reoffense among child molesters. *Behavioral Sciences and the Law, 6,* 267–280.

Beck, A. J., & Shipley, B. E. (1987). *Recidivism of young parolees.* Washington, DC: U.S. Department of Justice, Bureau of Justice Statistics.

Bench, L. L., Kramer, S. P., & Erickson, S. (1997). A discriminant analysis of predictive factors in sex offender recidivism. In B. K. Schwartz & H. R. Cellini (Eds.), *The sex offender: New insights, treatment innovations and legal developments* (vol. II, pp. 15-1–15-14). Kingston, NJ: Civic Research Institute.

Boer, D. P., Wilson, R. J., Gauthier, C. M., & Hart, S. D. (1997). Assessing risk of sexual violence: Guidelines for clinical practice. In C. D. Webster & M. A. Jackson (Eds.), *Impulsivity: Theory, assessment and treatment* (pp. 326–342). New York: Guilford Press.

Boudouris, J. (l983). *The recidivism of releasees from the Iowa State Penitentiary at Fort Madison, IA.* Fort Madison: Iowa Department of Corrections, Bureau of Data, Research and Planning.

Clark, S. H., & Crum, L. (1985). *Returns to prison in North Carolina.* Chapel Hill: Institute of Government, University of North Carolina.

Cooke, D. J., & Michie, C. (1997). An item response theory analysis of the HARE Psychopathy checklist—revised. *Psychological Assessment, 9,* 3–14.

Crime statistics report. (1996). Washington, DC: Bureau of Justice Statistics.

Davidson, P. R. (1984). *Behavioral treatment for incarcerated sex offenders: Post-treatment outcome.* Unpublished manuscript. Kingston, Ontario: Regional Treatment Center.

Delaware Executive Committee. (1984). *Recidivism in Delaware after release from incarceration.* Dover: Delaware Executive Department Statistical Analysis Center.

Eisenberg, M. (1985). *Factors associated with recidivism.* Austin: Texas Board of Pardons and Parole.

Epperson, D. L., Kaul, J. D., & Huot, S. J. (1995, October). *Predicting risk for recidivism for incarcerated sex offenders: Updated development for the Sex Offender Screening Tool (SOST).* Poster session presented at the annual conference of the Association for the Treatment of Sexual Abusers. New Orleans, LA.

Fitch, J. (1962). Men convicted of sexual offenses against children: A descriptive follow-up study. *British Journal of Criminology, 3,* 18–37.

Frisbie, L. V., & Dondis, E. H. (1965). *Recidivism among sex offenders.* California Mental Health Research Monogram No. 5. Sacramento: California Department of Mental Hygiene.

Furr, K. D. (1993). Prediction of sexual or violent recidivism among sexual offenders: A comparison of prediction instruments. *Annals of Sex Research, 6,* 271–286.

Gacono, C. B., & Hutton, H. E. (1994). Suggestions for the clinical and forensic use of the HARE Psychopathology checklist—revised. *International Journal of Law and Psychiatry, 17,* 303–317.

Grubin, D., & Wingate, S. (1996). Sexual offense recidivism: Prediction versus understanding. *Criminal Behavior and Mental Health, 6,* 349–359.

Grunfeld, B., & Noreik, K. (1986). Recidivism among sex offenders: A follow-up study of 541 Norwegian sex offenders. *International Journal of Law and Psychiatry, 9,* 95–102.

Hall, G. C. N. (1990). Prediction of sexual aggression. *Clinical Psychology Review, 10,* 229–245.

Hall, G. C. N. (1995). Sexual offender recidivism revisited: A meta-analysis of recent treatment studies. *Journal of Counseling and Clinical Psychology, 63,* 802–809.

Hanson, R. K., & Bussière, M. T. (1996). *Predictors of sexual offender recidivism: A meta-analysis.* (User Report No.1996-4). Ottawa: Corrections Branch, Ministry of the Solicitor General of Canada.

Hanson, R. K., & Harris, A. J. R. (1997). *Dynamic predictors of sexual reoffense project 1997.* Presentation at the annual conference of the Association for the Treatment of Sexual Aggressor. Arlington, VA.

Hanson, R. K., Steffy, R. A., & Gauthier, R. (1993). Long-term recidivism of child molesters. *Journal of Consulting and Clinical Psychology, 61,* 646–652.

Hare, R. D. (1991). *The Hare PCL-R.* North Tonawanda, NY: Multi-Health Systems.

Hare, R. D., McPherson, L. M., & Forth, A. E. (1988). Male psychopaths and their criminal career. *Journal of Consulting and Clinical Psychology, 56,* 710–714.

Harpur, T. J., Hakstian, R., & Hare, R. D. (1988). Factor structure of the psychopathy checklist. *Journal of Consulting and Clinical Psychology, 56,* 741–747.

Harris, G. T., Rice, M. E., & Cormier, C. A. (1989, April). *Violent recidivism among psychopaths and nonpsychopaths treated in a therapeutic community.* Research report from the Penetanguishene Mental Health Centre VI(1), Penetanguishene, Ontario.

Harris, G. T., Rice, M. E., & Cormier, C. A. (1991). Psychopathy and violent recidivism. *Law and Human Behavior, 15,* 625–637.

Hart, S. D., Kropp, P. R., & Hare, R. D. (1988). Performance of male psychopaths following conditional release from prison. *Journal of Consulting and Clinical Psychology, 56,* 227–232.

Janus, E. S., & Meehl, P. E. (1997). Assessing the legal standard for predictions of dangerousness in sex offender commitment proceedings. *Psychology, Public Policy and Law, 3*(1), 33–66.

LeClair D. P. (1985). *The effect of community reintegration on rates of recidivism: A statistical overview of data for the years 1971–1982.* Boston: Massachusetts Department of Corrections.

Maletzky, B. M. (1991). *Treating the sexual offender.* Newbury Park, CA: Sage.

Mander, A. M., Atrops, M. E., Barnes, A. R., & Munafo, R. (1996). *Sex Offender Treatment Program: Initial recidivism study.* Anchorage: Alaska Justice Statistical Analysis Unit, Justice Center University of Alaska.

Marshall, W. (1997, August 22). *Assessment and treatment of the adult sexual offender: The state of the science.* Conference on Sexual offenders: Assessment, risk management and treatment. San Diego, CA.

Marshall, W., & Barbaree, H. E. (1990). Outcome of comprehensive cognitive-behavioral treatment program. In W. L. Marshall, D. R. Laws, & H. E. Barbaree (Eds.), *Handbook of sexual assault: Issues, theories, and treatment of offenders* (pp. 363–385). New York: Plenum Press.

Marshall, W. L., Jones, R., Ward, T., Johnston, P., & Barbaree, H. E. (1991). Treatment outcome with sex offenders. *Clinical Psychology Review, 11,* 465–485.

McGovern, K., & Peters, J. (1988). Guidelines for assessing sex offenders. In L.A. Walker (Ed.), *Handbook on the sexual abuse of children* (pp. 216–246). New York: Springer.

McGrath, R. (1991). Sex-offender risk assessment and disposition planning: A review of empirical and clinical findings. *International Journal of Offender Therapy and Comparative Criminology, 35,* 328–350.

Oregon Crime Analysis Center. (1984). *Recidivism of releases from Oregon corrections institutions.* Salem: Author.

Patrick, C. J., & Iacono, W .G. (1989). Psychopathy, threat, and polygraph test accuracy. *Journal of Applied Psychology, 74,* 347–355.

Prentky, R. (1990). *Sexual violence: A review.* Paper presented at the Ninth aAnnual Clinical and Research Conference on the Assessment and Treatment of Sexual Abusers, Their Families and Victims, Toronto, Canada.

Prentky, R., & Knight, R. (1988). *Antisocial personality disorder and Hare assessments of psychopathy among sexual offenders.* Unpublished manuscript.

Prentky, R. A., Knight, R. A., & Lee, A. F. S. (1997). Risk factors associated with recidivism among extrafamilial child molesters. *Journal of Consulting and Clinical Psychology, 65*(1), 141–149.

Prentky, R. A., Lee, A. F. S., Knight, R. A., & Cerce, D. (1995). Predictive validity of lifestyle impulsivity for rapists. *Criminal Justice and Behavior, 32*(2), 106–128.

Prentky, R. A., Lee, A. F. S., Knight, R. A., & Cerce, D. (1997). Recidivism rates among child molesters and rapists: A methodological analysis. *Law and Human Behavior, 21*(6), 635–659.

Quinsey, V. (1977). The assessment of treatment of child molesters: A review. *Canadian Psychological Review, 18,* 204–220.

Quinsey, V .L. (1980). The base rate problem and prediction of dangerousness: A reappraisal. *Journal of Psychiatry and Law, 8,* 329–340.

Quinsey, V. L. (1992, March). Presentation at Risk Prediction Workshop. Ontario Regional Psychologists, Correction Service Canada.

Quinsey, V., Chaplin, T., & Carrigan, W. (1980). Biofeedback and signaled punishment in the modification of sexual age preference. *Behavior Therapy, 11,* 567–576.

Quinsey, V. L., Rice, M. E., & Harris, G. T. (1995). Actuarial prediction of sexual recidivism. *Journal of Interpersonal Violence, 10*(1),85–105.

Rada, R. (1976). Alcoholism and the child molester. *Annals of New York Academy of Science, 273,* 492–498.

Rice, M. E., & Harris, G. T. (1997). Cross-validation and extension of the Violence Risk Appraisal Guide for child molesters. *Law and Human Behavior, 21*(2), 223–241.

Rice, M. E., Quinsey, V. L., & Harris, G. T. (1991). Sexual recidivism among child molesters released from a maximum security psychiatric institution. *Journal of Consulting and Clinical Psychology, 59,* 381–386.

Romero, J. , & Williams, L. (1985). Recidivism among convicted sex offenders: A 10-year follow-up study. *Federal Probation, 49,* 58–64.

Roundtree, G. A., Edwards, D. W., & Parker, J. B. (1984). A study of personal characteristics of probationers as related to recidivism. *Journal of Offender Counseling, 8,* 53–61.

Salekin, R. T., Rogers, R., & Sewel, K. W. (1996). A review and meta-analysis of the Psychopathy Checklist and Psychopathy Checklist—Revised: Predictive validity of dangerousness. *Clinical Psychology: Science and Practice, 3,* 203–215.

Schwartz B. K. (1977). *Factors associated with response to treatment in aggressive sex offenders.* Doctoral dissertation, University of New Mexico.

Serin, R. C. (1996). Violent recidivism in criminal psychopaths. *Law and Human Behavior, 20*(2), 207–217.

Serin, R. C., Malcolm, P. B., Khanna, A., & Barbaree, H. (1994). Psychopathy and deviant sexual arousal in incarcerated sexual offenders. *Journal of Interpersonal Violence, 9*(1), 3–11.

Shaw, T. A, Herkov, M. J., & Green, R. A. (1995). Examination of treatment completion and predicted outcome among incarcerated sex offenders. *Bulletin of the American Academy of Psychiatry and Law, 23*(1), 35–41.

Simkins, L., Ward, W., Bowman, S., & Rinck, C. M. (1989). The Multiphasic Sex Inventory: Diagnosis and prediction of treatment response in child sexual abusers. *Annals of Sex Research, 2,* 205–226.

Steele, N. (1995). Cost-effectiveness of treatment. In B. K. Schwartz, & H. R. Cellini (Eds.), *The sex offender: Corrections, treatment and legal practice* (vol. I, pp. 4.1–4.15). Kingston, NJ: Civic Research Institute.

U.S. General Accounting Office. (1996). *Sex offender treatment: Results inconclusive about what works to reduce recidivism.* Washington, DC: Author.

University of Hawaii-Manoa. (1984). *Recidivism of 1979 adult probation, Third Circuit Court.* Honolulu, HI: Youth Development and Research Center.

Wallerstadt, J. F. (1984). *Returning to prison.* Washington, DC: Bureau of Justice Statistics.

Chapter 9

Dynamic Predictors of Sex Offense Recidivism—New Data From Community Supervision Officers

by Andrew J. R. Harris, M.Sc. and R. Karl Hanson, Ph.D.

Overview

Most risk assessment inventories use static factors such as age, criminal history, and crime descriptors to predict reoffense. However, anyone who has ever worked with offenders on probation or parole realizes that the vagaries of everyday life are often the most telling factors when it comes to successful adjustment. Did the offender find a good job? Did he find a positive support system or a stable girlfriend? Did he start drinking? We have studied these dynamic factors and offer suggestions as to what supervisors should be looking for as forecasters for failure. (*Note:* This chapter presents an overview of a large and complicated national study and, as such, leaves many details and findings unreported.)

Introduction

The factors most proximally related to sex offender recidivism were compiled in a recent large-scale research effort and are reported in this chapter, in summary form. More than 300 parole and probation officers were asked to provide detailed accounts of the moods and behaviors they had observed while either successfully supervising sex offenders in the community or watching an offender slip toward his next sexual offense. Important factors included: general cooperation with supervision, manipulation, disengagement, and "no shows." These findings reveal the changing or "dynamic" predictors of sexual reoffense, which represent not only the "ripest" targets for treatment but also potential triggers for supervisory intervention.

Scope of the Problem

Parole and probation officers do the bulk of sex offender supervision in the community. Canada has approximately 17,000 sex offenders under community supervision (Correctional Service of Canada, 1997). Using rough math, there would be at least ten times that number under supervision in U.S. communities.

Sex offender recidivism attracts disproportionate and sensationalist media attention and the general concern of the public. Although sex offenders do not recidivate as quickly, as often, or as violently as do general criminal offenders (Hanson, Scott, & Steffy, 1995), long-term follow-up studies do find, in a fifteen- to thirty-year period, that 35% of sex offenders commit another sexual offense. This means that over the next fifteen to thrity years Canada will observe at least 5,950 new sex offenses from sex offenders currently under community supervision and that U.S. cities can expect to observe at least 59,500 new sex offenses from sex offenders currently under community supervision.

Importance of Dynamic Risk Predictors

Dynamic risk predictors are changeable personal factors having a causal or moderator effect on criminal behavior. These factors provide the best treatment targets and should guide community supervision of the offender. Dynamic risk predictors, when changed, should modify an offender's level of risk to reoffend.

Risk predictors for all offenders can be grouped into three broad classes: (1) static factors (fixed historical predictors which cannot be changed), such as criminal record and gender; (2) stable dynamic factors (persistent personality and behavioral traits which are potentially changeable), such as antisocial attitudes and deviant sexual preferences; and (3) acute dynamic factors (rapidly changing factors, such as negative mood or alcohol intoxication), which are obvious targets for supervisory based interventions. A recent meta-analysis (Gendreau, Little, & Goggin, 1996) reviewed 131 studies of general criminal recidivism and found that dynamic predictors of reoffense outpredicted static predictors.

Quinsey, Lalumière, Rice, and Harris (1995) state that "the most important need at present is the identification and evaluation of dynamic predictors" (p. 133) and that the most useful dynamic predictors will reflect criminogenic needs such as compliance with supervision. Quinsey et al. (1995) state that research on dynamic factors will eventually allow us to gauge how effectively a particular course of action would reduce a sex offender's likelihood of recidivism.

Research has shown that supervision and treatment are most effective when applied to higher-risk cases (Andrews et al., 1990). By matching the level of intervention to the offenders' level of risk we may more effectively target/deploy already scarce treatment and supervisory resources (Andrews & Bonta, 1994).

Studying Dynamic Factors

The true participants in this study were more than 300 Canadian parole and probation officers who gave of their time and experience to answer detailed questions about sexual offenders on their caseloads. Officers completed a structured interview commenting on 409 sex offenders under community supervision in Canada. These sex offender cases were drawn from federal parole offices across Canada and from the offices of nine provincial probation services.

Divided into two main subsamples (see Table 9.1), the first sex offender group consisted of 208 sex offenders who had committed another sexual offense, been charged with another sexual offense, had their parole or probation breached due to a sexual incident, or had self-disclosed another sexual offense while under community supervision.

The second sex offender subgroup consisted of 201 men who had not reoffended or self-disclosed another sexual offense while under community supervision. Both

Table 9.1
Types of Sexual Offenders

Participant Groups **N = 409**	Recidivistic Sex Offenders	Nonrecidivistic Sex Offenders
Boy-object child molesters	$n = 61$	$n = 61$
Girl-object child molesters	$n = 76$	$n = 74$
Sexual assault of adult women	$n = 71$	$n = 66$

of these main subgroups were further divided into boy-object child molesters, girl-object child molesters, and rapists of adult women. Due to their generally low recidivism rates (Hanson et al., 1995), pure incest offenders were not included in this study.

Collecting Data From Community Supervisors

Parole and probation offices were asked to identify suitable cases for inclusion in the study. Trained data collectors then interviewed individual officers. As part of the subject selection process, offenders were roughly matched on relevant risk factors.

This project had three data collection tasks: (1) the recording of static risk variables from the offender's file, (2) a structured interview conducted with the parole/probation officer assigned to the case, and (3) a review of acute dynamic risk factors observed over the last eight months of supervision.

Coding of the Static Variables. First, demographic and historical static variables were copied from the offender's official file into a paper-based coding manual. In those cases in which sufficient historical background was present, a Psychopathy Checklist—Revised (PCL-R; Hare, 1991) was coded based on file information (Wong, 1984). The coding of static information was extensive and covered a broad base of risk-related areas. These static variables were collected to ensure parity in basic static risk between the recidivistic and the nonrecidivistic groups.

Coding of the Officer Interview Information. Second, a structured interview was conducted with the parole or probation officer involved with the case. The officer was asked to give his opinion as to the number of social contacts that were evident in the offender's life at that time and whether these contacts were, in the view of the officer, positive or negative. Next, slightly adapted items from the Psychopathy Checklist: Screening Version (PCL:SV; Hart, Cox, & Hare, 1995) were read out loud to the officer and the officer was asked whether the "flavor" of the paragraph generally referred to the offender. Officers were also asked whether, in their opinion, the offender held attitudes favoring sex with children, whether the offender would endorse rape myths, or whether the offender would feel entitled to sexual gratification from others.

Coding of Dynamic Predictors of Sexual Reoffense. As part of the interview process, officers were presented with a time graph and asked to draw a freehand representation of their "gut" feeling about the offender's risk for sexual recidivism (see Figure 9.1). The officers rated their impressions, with 100 representing "complete confidence that the offender would not recidivate in a sexual manner" and "0" representing no confidence that the offender would stay out of sexual trouble. As shown in Figure 9.1, the officer's subjective impression of the offender's risk for sexual recidivism is represented by the curved line starting at [S] (early February 1996) and moving across the page to the date of the sexual recidivism [R] (around the third week of February 1997). The interviewer would then delineate two periods for the officer by drawing vertical lines on the graph.

Referred to as "T2," the second period represented the last six to eight weeks of

Figure 9.1
The Interview Time Graph

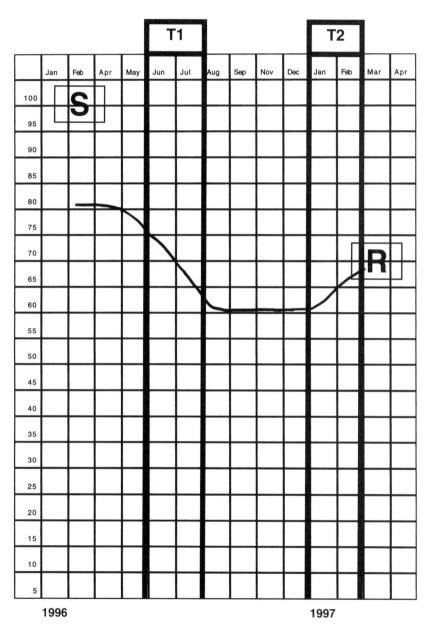

Please graph your "gut" feeling about this offender's risk for sexual recidivism while under your supervision.

S = Start of supervision; R = Recidivism, end of February.

supervision for nonrecidivistic offenders and the six to eight weeks of supervision just prior to reoffense for recidivists. Four clear months were allowed prior to this period and then another period was outlined containing another six- to eight-week period. This period was referred to as "T1" (see Figure 9.1).

This technique, summarized below, created a stable period across which to judge change in an extensive list of dynamic risk factors.

- Drinking/drugs;
- Negative attitudes;
- Seeing self as "at no risk to reoffend";
- Access to victims;
- "No shows" and personal commitments;
- Disengaged from supervision; and
- Manipulative of supervisor.

The time graph (Figure 9.1) was displayed in front of the officer at all times and the questions were asked in the following format. For example, the officer was asked if he had ever been concerned about an offender's substance abuse during the entire course of the offender's supervision. If the officer answered "yes," the officer was then asked: "When were you more concerned about substance abuse, during period T1 or T2?" A code was then entered which indicated whether substance abuse was more of a concern right before recidivism (T2) or six to eight months previously (T1). This code was used to assess whether the offender presented a stable risk throughout the supervision or whether there were observable patterns across the two periods that could be assessed as "getting worse" just prior to recidivism.

Results of Static Variables

Comparisons on static risk factors estimate the similarity of the recidivistic and nonrecidivistic groups. As can be seen in Table 9.2, the recidivists and the nonrecidivists were well matched on important variables: age, marital status, and race. Recidivists did not score as highly as nonrecidivists on standard assessments of IQ. The incidence of psychotic-type disorders was small and the same in both groups.

The recidivists had a slightly greater number of total victims, but this was not statistically significant. More recidivists than nonrecidivists had offended against victims of diverse ages and genders. Recidivists also had a higher number of established paraphilias. There were, however, no group differences in having a diagnosis of sexually deviant preference, either clinically reported or by phallometric diagnosis. The same percentage of recidivists and nonrecidivists had attended treatment programs and both groups had tried treatment the same number of times. However, the recidivists were noted as demonstrating lower motivation and they more often dropped out of treatment.

The two groups had experienced similar levels of physical abuse as children. However, the recidivists had experienced more sexual abuse and emotional neglect, had more often suffered a significant separation from their parents prior to age 16, and had more often been apprehended by child protection services.

Recidivists and nonrecidivists were comparable on criminal history before and at the time of their index offenses. Prior to the index offense there were no significant dif-

Table 9.2
Comparison of the Recidivists and Nonrecidivists on Static, Historical Variables

Measure	Recidivists	Nonrecidivists	Sig.
Sample size	208	201	
Demographic factors			
Age at index offense	34.2	34.9	ns
Ever married	59.2%	62.8%	ns
Minority race	14.0%	11.5%	ns
Clinical assessement			
IQ	94.4 (14.6)	100.1 (14.5)	< .001
Any psychotic disorder	5.3%	5.0%	ns
Total known victims			
mean (SD)	9.4 (20.1)	7.8 (27.2)	ns
median	5	3	
Sexual deviance			
Diverse victim types (age/sex)	53.8%	33.3%	< .001
Number of paraphilias (voyeurism, exhibitionism, fetishes, etc.)	1.5 (1.5)	1.0 (1.1)	< .001
Any diagnosis of deviant sexual preferences	51.0%	43.0%	ns
Sex offender treatment history			
Ever attended	76.3%	77.1%	ns
Number of different programs	2.1 (1.8)	1.9 (1.4)	ns
Poor treatment candidate (low motivation, dropout)	2.6 (6.4)	1.2 (6.8)	< .001
Family background			
Physical abuse	46.8%	40.5%	ns
Sexual abuse	61.3%	44.2%	< .001
Other abuse (emotional/neglect)	54.8%	36.8%	< .001
Any long-term separation from parents prior to age 16	42.8%	28.9%	.003
Apprehended by child protective services	26.9%	14.9%	.003

ferences between recidivists and nonrecidivists on the average number of sex offenses (means: 2.4 vs. 2.2) or on total number of criminal offenses (means: 11.6 vs. 10.3). Nor were there significant differences between recidivists and nonrecidivists at the time of index offense: not on average number of sex offenses (means: 3.1 vs. 3.2) or on the average number of total offenses (means: 4.2 vs. 4.3). The recidivists, by design, had significantly greater post-index levels of sexual and general criminality ($p > .001$).

Results of Interview Evaluation of Stable Variables

As Table 9.3 illustrates, the nonrecidivists had almost twice the number of positive community-based social contacts to negative social contacts. The recidivists, however, displayed the reverse pattern. Recidivists had more information on file that would potentially indicate a diagnosis of personality disorder. Based on an adapted oral presentation of the PCL:SV (Hart et al., 1995), the officers judged the recidivistic group to contain significantly more psychopaths (35.6%) than did the nonrecidivistic group (6.6%). File review of PCL-Rs (Wong, 1984) also estimated that there were more psychopaths (Hare, 1991) in the recidivistic group (20.5%) than in the nonrecidivistic group (6.6%).

Results of Interview on Dynamic Variables

The "EVER" Results. Because information was collected on a large number of individual variables, the variables were first organized into meaningful categories with the intent of creating clinically useful scales. Data reduction techniques, such as factor analysis, were used to minimize redundancy between similar questions. Cronbach's alpha (Cronbach & Meehl, 1955) was used to assess internal consistency. The officers told us what factors had "EVER" been a concern during the supervision of their given offender.

All attitudinal measures differentiated recidivists from nonrecidivists (see Table 9.4). In general, the recidivists showed little remorse or concern for their victims, endorsed rape myths, thought that having sexual relations with children was accept-

Table 9.3
Comparison of the Recidivists and Nonrecidivists on Officer Verbal
Response Variables

Measure	Recidivists	Nonrecidivists	Sig.
Community social contacts			
Positive	1.1 (1.3)	2.1 (2.0)	< .001
Negative	1.3 (.72)	.72 (1.1)	< .001
Antisocial personality disorder			
Antisocial personality (scored from file) (% displaying disorder)	88%	60.2%	< .001
Officer scored PCL:SV			
Mean (SD)	14.7 (5.3)	8.7 (6.0)	< .001
% > 17	35.6 ($n = 205$)	6.6 ($n = 166$)	
File scored PCL-R			
Mean (SD)	23.4 (6.8)	16.5 (8.7)	< .001
% > 29	20.5 ($n = 190$)	6.6 ($n = 166$)	

Table 9.4
Factors to Pay Attention to When Supervising a Sex Offender in the Community

---

Attitudes
- Low remorse/victim blaming
- Rape attitudes
- Child molester attitudes
- Sexual entitlement

Self-management
- Sees self as "no risk" to roeffend
- Victim access

Sexual deviancy
- Sexual risk factors

Cooperation with supervision
- Overall co-operation
- Disengaged (scale)
- Manipulative (scale)
- No show/late (scale)

Factors the Same in Both Recidivistic and Nonrecidivistic Groups

Psychological symptoms
- Negative mood
- Anger
- Life stress
- Psychiatric symptoms (any)

Note: All variables in the "pay attention" section significantly differentiate the two groups $p > .001$ and all variables in the "same in both" section did not show significant differences between groups.

---

able, and that, on the whole, they were entitled to sexual gratification from others. Officers told us that the recidivists more often viewed themselves as "at no risk" to sexually reoffend. In comparison to nonrecidivists, recidivists more often arranged their world to allow themselves ready access to victims and more often engaged in sexually risky behaviors, such as attending massage and strip parlors. Recidivists displayed a general lack of cooperation in supervision and presented as disengaged and manipulative and were significantly more likely to be late for supervision or not to show up at all.

None of the measures of general psychological symptoms differentiated recidivists from nonrecidivists (see bottom of Table 9.4). Negative mood, anger, and general life stress were equally common in both groups. The rates of serious psychiatric symptoms (hallucinations, major depression) were similar in both groups, but this was expected given our attempt to match offenders on psychiatric history. Contrary to expectation, no overall difference in the frequency with which the recidivists and nonrecidivists were known to associate with other sexual offenders was detected.

The "T1"–"T2" Results. The "T1"–"T2" time differential was used to determine what factors "got worse" just before recidivism (see Table 9.5). In the period just before they reoffended, recidivistic offenders showed more substance abuse, displayed negative attitudes that distanced them from their crime, saw themselves as "at no risk to reoffend" sexually, and tested known risk factors. They tended to arrange their world to increase their ready access to victims and may have acquired goods or taken up hobbies/activities to facilitate that access.

When supervising a sex offender, an empty chair should give the supervisor a sinking feeling. The guys who go bad, in general, do not show up or are often late for appointments. In the course of supervision they appear disengaged, attempting to distance themselves from the supervisory process, and may try to manipulate the supervisory relationship.

Results Suggest What Community Supervisors Should Watch For

Our results indicate that community supervision officers perceived substantial differences between those offenders who did and those who did not go on to commit a new sexual offense. In comparison to nonrecidivists, the recidivists had a greater history of sexual deviance, had more antisocial characteristics, were less cooperative with supervision, and had less social support in the community. Importantly, the officers frequently noticed that the recidivist's behavior deteriorated prior to reoffending. The identification of such acute dynamic risk factors suggests that careful community supervision can contribute to community safety by timing interventions to periods of increased risk.

Limitations to Study

Memory bias is the most obvious criticism that can be leveled at this study. We asked officers what they remembered about offenders before they recidivated and all the officers knew that the offender had recidivated while "on their watch." Hence, there is a concern that the officer may be reconstructing memories. In an attempt to counter this phenomenon, we scored the officers' daily contact notes on the same questions we used in the interview. We did this to see whether the factors that the officers told us about in the interview were present in their contact notes. We also did this to see what factors the officers felt were important enough to include in a supervision note. On the whole, the officers' notes were scarce and often did not reflect information related to sexual recidivism. However, some of the dynamic factors did appear, which supports the contention that officers did perceive some of the behavioral changes at the time and were not just reconstructing "bad guys" from memory.

Conclusion

Overall, these results represent the accumulated experience of more than 300 seasoned community supervision officers. We believe these findings to be sensible in light of both theoretical (Andrews & Bonta, 1994) and empirical (Hanson & Bussière, 1996) knowledge. Consequently, community supervision officers may want to use the factors identified in this study to guide their interviews with sexual offenders. For example, officers could check whether offenders were "same as always" or "worse" on the factors listed in Table 9.5. An accumulation of negative marks may indicate the need to reassess the supervision strategy.

Table 9.5
Factors That "Got Worse" Just Before Sexual Recidivism

Drinking/Drugs
- Is he using illicit drugs?
- Is he drinking more?

Negative Attitudes
- He holds attitudes that are tolerant of sex crimes
- He believes that sex crimes are acceptable in certain circumstances
- He does not "own" his crimes
- He engages in victim blaming
- He shows low victim empathy
- He shows no remorse
- He engages in minimizing and justifying his crimes
- He denies his offense
- He fails to understand how his sexual behavior affects others

Sees self as no risk
- He sees himself as at no risk to reoffend or fails to recognize that risk
- He will not make personal sacrifices to avoid high-risk situations
- He will test known risk factors
- He fails to acknowledge and understand his sexual problems
- He says: "I'm not a pervert, I need to put this behind me, why do you always bring this up?" (with reference to his offense)
- He says "I only pled guilty because my lawyer told me to"
- He says "Everything is fine/great/no problem," but you feel he is covering things up

Access to victims
- You feel he has ready access to victims
- You worry he is cruising or creating opportunities to reoffend
- He may be grooming victims

- He has a flashy bicycle/4X4/motorcycle/flashy car (i.e., he's a kid magnet)
- He has hobbies which attract children: cameras/fishing/kites/boats
- He has a computer/surfs the net

No show
- He is late for appointments with you
- He "no shows" with you
- He "no shows" with other commitments
- He makes requests to reschedule appointments with you
- He has broken the conditions of his supervision

Disengaged
- You feel he is "just going through the motions"
- He is not open to talking about treatment
- He is not invested in treatment
- He is silent and nondisclosing
- He keeps secrets from you
- You feel he is not working with you
- You feel that you don't, generally, know what is going on with this offender

Manipulative
- You find inconsistencies between what the offender tells you and what the treatment team tells you
- He tries to manipulate you
- You get the feeling the offender is "being phony" with you
- He tries to "play the system"
- He tries to take control of the interview
- He wants to be "buddy-buddy" with you
- He attempts to focus the interview on irrelevant issues

Note. All correlations with recidivism significant past the $p < .001$ level.

Note

The complete report may be requested by contacting either of the authors or by downloading the report from the following website: http://www.sgc.gc.ca.

References

Andrews, D. A., & Bonta, J. L. (1994). *The psychology of criminal conduct.* Cincinnati, OH: Anderson.

Andrews, D. A., Zinger, I., Hoge, R. D., Bonta, J. L., Gendreau, P., & Cullen, F. T. (1990). Does correctional treatment work? A psychologically informed meta-analysis. *Criminology, 28,* 369–404.

Correctional Service of Canada. (1997). *Basic facts about corrections in Canada: 1997 edition.* Ottawa, Canada: Ministry of Supply and Services.

Cronbach, L. J. & Meehl, P. F. (1955). Construct validity and psychological tests. *Psychological Bulletin, 52,* 281–302.

Gendreau, P., Little, T., & Goggin, C. (1996). A meta-analysis of the predictors of adult offender recidivism: What works! *Criminology, 34*(4), 575–607.

Hanson, R. K., & Bussière, M. T. (1996). *Predictors of sexual offender recidivism: A meta-analysis.* (User Report No. 1996-04). Ottawa: Corrections Branch, Ministry of the Solicitor General of Canada.

Hanson, R. K., Scott, H., & Steffy, R. A. (1995). A comparison of child molesters and nonsexual criminals: Risk predictors and long-term recidivism. *Journal of Research in Crime and Delinquency, 32*(3), 325–337.

Hare, R. D. (1991). *Manual for the Revised Psychopathy Checklist.* North Tonawanda, NY: Multi-Health Systems.

Hart, S. D., Cox, D. N., & Hare, R. D. (1995). *Manual for the Psychopathy Checklist: Screening Version (PCL-SV).* Toronto: Multi-Health Systems.

Quinsey, V. L., Lalumière, M. L., Rice, M. E., & Harris, G. T. (1995). Predicting sexual offenses. In J. C. Campbell (Ed.), *Assessing dangerousness: Violence by sexual offenders, batterers, and child abusers.* Thousand Oaks, CA: Sage.

Wong, S. (1984). *The criminal and institutional behaviors of psychopaths.* (User Report No. 1984-87). Ottawa: Ministry of the Solicitor General of Canada.

Chapter 10

Total Quality Management Implications for Sex Offender Program Planning, Implementation, and Evaluation

by Scott Blankenship, M.S.W.

Overview

Private industry must constantly search for ways to improve its product in order to compete in a capitalist economy. However, this has not been the case in many human service organizations until recent years, when the public has begun to demand more accountability in this area. The field of sex offender treatment is particularly susceptible to public scrutiny and demands for ever-improving treatment and treatment delivery systems. Total quality management (TQM) offers a system for constantly evaluating and improving these types of programs.

Introduction

The evolution of sex offender treatment and policy in the United States has reached a crossroads. Group therapy, psychoeducational training, plethysmography, covert sensitization, and so on are widely implemented forms of relapse prevention–oriented sex offender treatment. Measures that prioritize community safety and victims' needs have resulted in new state and federal policies involving various community notification processes, lifetime parole, and even civil commitments. These strategies have now become the established benchmarks of treatment and policy on which a new era of continuous quality improvement (CQI) may be built. A major challenge now becomes using these approaches to implement a comprehensive system. For instance, as stated in the title of Massachusetts's master plan, No More Victims (Massachusetts Association for the Treatment of Sex Abusers, 1997), maximum safety—to the point of zero victims—is the simple, common goal of improving sex offender treatment and policy. The goal of "no more victims" is rather optimistic, but it is not overly idealistic as a goal insofar as maximum safety must direct public policy. Victims, neighborhoods, courts, departments of correction, probation, and parole, among others, are the customers of sex offender treatment. They all have in common the need for maximizing the safety of sex offenders. Furthermore, they all need to be able continuously improve any system that may be implemented. TQM is the management tool that may addressed this need for continuous, maximum improvement.

The Concept of Total Quality Management

The word "total" may seem somewhat pretentious, but the management of quality needs to be as complete and total as possible for improvement to be substantial and continuous. In extremely difficult and risk-oriented endeavors such as sex offender programming, improvement is not easily substantiated; thus opportunities to improve must be seized.

TQM's singular purpose of continuously increasing quality must be understood and accepted across an organization for it to be successful. Otherwise, TQM initiatives die off. Therefore, the entire organization dealing with sex offenders must direct its focus toward continuous improvement by its direct-service staff, its supervisors, its middle managers, its executives, its boards of directors, and—when applicable—even its stockholders. TQM theorists emphasize that this focus toward CQI will be a dramatic shift from the traditional focus on productivity. Gunther and Hawkins (1997) compared the culture of quality that can exist in human service organizations to the culture of productivity that has traditionally existed. This shift from productivity to quality involves the following:

> changes from market focus to customer focus, from vertical organizational structures that are segmented and centralized to horizontal organizational structures that are integrated and aligned, from outcome monitoring to process monitoring, from vertical and rational sequences of decision making to statistically based decision making, from regimented thinking to creative thinking, from individual performance and orientation to collective performance and

orientation, from changing individuals to changing processes, and from organizational conformity to organizational innovation, among others. (p 15)

As an organization's focus begins to change from productivity to quality, the roles and responsibilities of managers and supervisors change. The entire organization must be trained to act differently. Managers and supervisors need to act less autocratically and more cooperatively. They need to pursue less regimented standards of productivity and more flexibly active roles as option provider, coach, even cheerleader. Because of this aspect of TQM, managers and supervisors who refuse to or cannot perform these roles often either leave or are directly involved in the failure of organizations' TQM initiatives. The roles of direct-service employees also change to include increased responsibility and creativity in service improvement. Shared responsibility and creative opportunities motivate and empower direct-service staff and, thus, prevent such problems as burnout, poor morale, disconnectedness from work, resentment, sabotage, and other acting-out behaviors common in traditional, predominantly productivity-oriented organizations.

As an organization shifts priorities from productivity to quality improvement, managerial and direct-service staff need to work together far more often and in far more ways than previously. And, despite the focal shift away from productivity, thoroughly implemented TQM initiatives involving these shared responsibilities and open creativity for improved quality just so happen to improve productivity as well. This organizational/policy phenomenon in TQM parallels the clinical/treatment phenomenon of paradoxical intervention in which clients are pushed away from objects that therapists hope they will approach. That is, TQM paradoxically directs an organization's focus toward quality and away from productivity—and, in so doing, substantially increases the organization's productivity as its qualitative successes improve customer satisfaction. Increased customer satisfaction leads to increased service use and valuation by customers—monetary valuation and otherwise. And, at this time in its history, when little is allocated and yet much is expected of programs, sex offender treatment has a great need for valuation. However, to reap these rewards of TQM, traditional organizations must be prepared to change from productivity-oriented to quality-oriented cultures with compatible policies and procedures.

Organizational Preparation for TQM

Many organizations are most likely quite unprepared for TQM. For example, sex offender programs operating within institutional settings can be particularly unprepared for TQM initiatives because they must also receive autocratic orders from correctional staff and other institutional authorities. TQM can succeed regardless of outside influences, though, if an organization is adequately prepared. Moreover, organizations must be particularly prepared to manage obstacles of resistance, conflict, and lethargy within and among their own members. As direct-service staff are called on by TQM practices to increase their responsibility, their initiative, and their creativity, managers and administrators will be called on to decrease their autocratic controls and their reliance on traditional policies and procedures. Either or both of these organizational strata may resist these changes. Both will to some extent resist stepping outside their strata to do the teamwork that is required once TQM is initiated. These problems in initiating TQM can be overcome, though, if an organization is able to focus on the needs to improve which it does have. But, the needs for improvement must cross a cer-

tain threshold and reach a critical mass across the organization so that the organization is motivated to attempt changes. Needs must be sufficiently compelling to genuinely commit to the "radical transformation" of TQM in response to its needs to
improve—and it must be able to go from the stages of uninformed optimism to
informed pessimism and then on to hopeful realism or else it will fail. Jablonski
(1992) explained the ways organizations fail to move from informed pessimism to
hopeful realism due not only to the expected resistances, conflicts, and negative attitudes and comments but also simply to the dramatic directional changes that everyone
involved in the organization must undergo in TQM. A wide variety of assessment tools
have already been developed to determine an organization's preparedness. For example, Appendix A in *Total Quality Management in Human Service Organizations*
(Gunther & Hawkins, 1997) presents a series of questions that serve as a guide to
TQM implementation. To illustrate the general issues involved in organizational
preparation for TQM initiatives, following are Gunther and Hawkins's stages of TQM
implementation for human services:

TQM Assessment and Readiness

- How will you assess the readiness of your organization to implement TQM
  on the organizational and customer level[s]?

- Who will be the key players in the decision to introduce TQM to your organization? What role will they play?

- What methods will you use to prepare your organization for TQM?

- What kind of resistance will you experience in preparing your organization
  for TQM?

- What is the nature of the understanding and commitment that you have
  from "top" management toward this TQM initiative?

- What kind of organizational resources are committed to the TQM initiative?

Think of the various people involved in an organization and their rankings. By
applying these questions to the organizational dynamics, light should be shed on what
early TQM initiatives in a program would be like.

It is highly recommended that any program considering TQM hire a consultant
with TQM expertise. Just as sex offender programs routinely hire consultants to provide clinical and other expertise, so must these programs hire management expertise
to assess the organization, prepare it for TQM, and then oversee the development of
TQM across these programs. Faced with challenges to substantiate their successes and
to justify the resources allocated to them, sex offender programs need to be prepared
to take advantage of the opportunities for improvement that TQM provides.

Challenges in Implementing TQM

However, misunderstandings about TQM impede and often nullify TQM initiatives. For example, many professionals involved in the field of sex offender treatment

and policy have indeed heard of TQM but do not have an in-depth understanding of the concepts. These individuals might say, "Oh yes, we do TQM-type teamwork naturally because we're always trying to improve the quality of our treatment." Similarly, many administrators have said, in effect, "TQM is fine for homelessness programs or whatever, but these are sex offenders we're dealing with . . . we can't afford to get fancy with these offenders." The primary objective of this chapter is to clarify how TQM and the benefits of TQM can exist within the context of total organizational implementation, top to bottom, and in all areas. Not only must the organization be assessed for preparedness, but TQM must be operationally understood and consistently used at all levels and areas of the organization. Certainly, many sex offender treatment teams do high-quality work and improve regularly. But, despite the best intentions of treatment teams and others, TQM never happens "naturally." TQM must be implemented deliberately and thoroughly.

The other basic objective here is to clarify that TQM is, in fact, especially suited for sex offender treatment and policy. Because of factors such as high burnout in sex offender therapists and the need to continuously reduce recidivism rates, organizational and management tools that measurably facilitate CQI are sorely needed. TQM is designed to meet that need, present in all human services—but present in abundance in organizations responsible for making uniquely dangerous populations of sex offenders as safe as can be. TQM initiatives will be increasingly applied to sex offender programs via (1) team actions to solve problems common to sex offender treatment, such as high unprocessed countertranferance toward sex offenders, inadequate boundaries and therapeutic alliances between treatment staff and sex offenders, inconsistent applications of therapeutic modalities, varied completeness in discharge planning, and so on; and (2) statistical and graphic indications of progress or regression in program functioning so that decision making can be based on facts rather than on the impressions that have traditionally guided clinical programs.

Human service organizations are now beginning to "catch on" to TQM initiatives that have been successful in almost all other areas of business administration, but sex offender treatment and other clinical programs have been particularly slow to explore the opportunities that TQM presents. TQM will not encroach on or impede clinicians' professionally trained treatment approaches unless it is implemented incorrectly. TQM is a management, not a treatment, approach.

Freeman-Longo and Knopp (1992) articulated the importance of a "management, not cure" approach to sex offender treatment and policy:

> Without doubt, sex offender programs should be encouraged to engage in both process evaluation and outcome evaluation using standardized procedures. Programs suspected of being ineffective should be rigorously reviewed and examined for the design, content, and format of their operation to reflect current standards, knowledge, methods, models, and technology in the field. However, the purported findings of poorly designed outcome studies, based on outdated and/or ineffective treatment methods, should not be accepted as reliable evidence that specialized sex offender treatment programs portray a dismal picture. (p. 149)

Unfortunately, some powerful people and organizations have accepted anecdotal evidence that has projected a dismal picture for sex offender treatment. This is just one reason why sex offender treatment programs (and the communities they are charged with making less dangerous) do deserve the opportunities TQM presents. And, although only relatively few sex offender treatment programs have actually begun TQM initiatives, we can see the characteristics that programs are likely to have both before and after. (See Table 10.1.)

These ten areas of sex offender program functioning involve initial service delivery benchmarks beyond which TQM initiatives will continuously build improvement and community safety. TQM seems panacean at first. But once the increases in individual and organizational responsibilities for problem solving and creativity become clear, the opportunities for such substantial and continuous improvement should also become clear.

Defining the "Customers" of Sex Offender Treatment and Policy

TQM enables all "customers" to become increasingly invested in the material and intrinsic satisfaction derived from the total relative success of sex offender treatment and policy. TQM provides structural and functional access to CQI within and among organizations by motivating all participants in the service process to actively pursue satisfaction. Who, besides sex offenders, are the "customers" of sex offender treatment and policy? TQM differentiates between internal and external customers. Table 10.2 differentiates the internal and external customers of sex offender treatment and policy. Traditional definitions of service customers are far less broad than TQM's definitions.

An internal customer's roles involve being a direct recipient of service delivery, and an external customer's roles involve being less directly or indirectly a recipient of services. Sex offenders as treatment patients or clients are clearly internal customers. Employees, however, are also internal customers because they can expect to receive a number of things in exchange for their work, including a competitive salary and other material benefits, a wide variety opportunities to grow professionally, and other intrinsic rewards.

With TQM, the broadest applicable definition of a service's customers is necessary to direct management of these services in ways that correspondingly broaden the service's value to customers. Table 10.2 shows a total of eighteen types of customers of sex offender treatment and policy. Some are internal customers in one setting, and then external customers in another setting.

Statistical Montitoring in TQM

By determining service improvement and customer satisfaction using statistical charts, TQM provides a critical element of measurability contrated to the often vague organizational issues of improvement and satisfaction. National Seminars, Inc. (1992) identified the seven basic tools for TQM as follows:

1) Cause-and effect diagrams . . . typically used to depict causes of certain problems and to group them according to categories;

Table 10.1
Characteristics of TQM Programs (Before and After)

Before	*After*
1. Substantial variations in the contents of psychoeducational classes and modules on victim empathy, anger management, social skills, personal victimization, clear thinking, stress management, understanding sexual assault, relapse prevention, etc.	1. Standardized elements of psychoeducational classes and modules resulting in sex offenders being more completely prepared for the intensive group therapy that enables relapse prevention.
2. Substantial variations in amounts of confrontational vs. supportive group therapy interventions which result in variations of appropriate boundaries, therapeutic alliance, accountability for harm to victims, etc.	2. Standardized balance of confrontational and supportive group therapy resulting in clear boundaries, boundaries, secure therapeutic alliance, and accountability for for harm to victims, etc.
3. Substantial variations in the development and maintenance of therapeutic communities (TCs) in institutional/correctional treatment settings.	3. Standardized use of "round-the-clock" TC peer observations and confrontations, presentations of deviant cycles to the TC, and behavioral contracts addressing past and present acting out behaviors.
4. Substantial variations in the completeness of discharge planning, implementation and follow-up resulting in poor continuity of assessment and treatment as sex offendersgo on to less restrictive environments and circumstances.	4. Standardized elements to fully complete discharge planning, implementation and follow-up, provide mazimum continuity of assessment and treatment in less restrictive settings and circumstances.
5. Varied use of risk assessment.	5. Standardized use of risk assessment
6. Substantial variations in the clinical processing of transference and countertransference between sex offenders and treatment staff that results in risks of undermining treatment, risk of abuse and harm, etc.	6. Standardized assessments and interventions of clinical supervision to fully process transferance and countertranserance resulting in minimizing risks.
7. Substantial variation in the management of treatment staff "burnout" and other morale problems resulting in high staff turnover.	7. Standardized use of supervisor monitoring and creative problem solving (e.g., flexible scheduling,workloads oriented to individuals' strengths, etc.) to assist treatment staff in allaying the effects and causes of"burnout" and other moraleproblems and issues.
8. Substantial variations in the training and licensure of sex offender treatment providers.	8. Standardized hiring of staff who meet or exceed requirements for licensure with requirements of education in sex offender-specific treatment.
9. Substantial variations in the cooperation between sex offender treatment programs, problems between sex offender treatment departments of correction, probation, parole, programs and all entities linked to the courts, etc., resulting in diminished treatment opportunities and increased hostility in these entities toward sex offender treatment.	9. Standardized monitoring of functioning between all agencies which results in decreased interagency hostility and more treatment and supervison.
10. Substantial variations in the policies and procedures which sex offender treatment programs use to educate public entities about necessities and effectiveness of fully treating sex offenders.	10. Standardized policies and procedures for querying public entities as to their levels of satisfaction and concerns regardingthe necessity and efficacy of treating sexoffenders. These policies and procedures will increase the public's understanding and support of necessary treatment.

Table 10.2
Defining the Customers of Sex Offender Treatment and Policy

	Internal Customers	External Customers
Community-based settings	• Sex offenders • Therapists, supervisors, etc. • Parole or probation officers • Case workers • Residential service providers • Law authorities	• Victims/families • Neighborhoods • Local governments • State government • Federal government • Society at large
Institutional settings	• Sex offenders • Doctors, administrators, etc. • Therapists, instructors, etc. • Case workers • Parole or probation officers • State government or privatized facility	• Victims/families • Neighborhoods • law authorities • justice systems • Local governments • State government if facility is private • Federal government • Society at large
Correctional settings	• Sex offenders • Justice systems • Law authorities • Correctional staff and administration • Therapists, instructors, etc. • Parole boards • State government or privatized facility	• Victims/families • Neighborhoods • Local governments • State government if facility is privatized • Federal government • Society at large

2) flow charts or process-flow diagrams . . . [that] are the visual representation of the steps in a process . . . particularly useful in the service industries, where work involves unseen steps;

3) simple bar charts used after data collection to rank causes so that priorities can be assigned. They give rise to the 80-20 rule—that 80 percent of the problems stem from 20 percent of the causes;

4) run (trend) charts [that] simply show the results of a process plotted over a period of time;

5) histograms . . . used to measure [frequencies];

6) scatter diagrams [used] to illustrate the relationship between two variables;

7) control charts [that] are the most advanced of the seven basic tools and are used reflect variation in a system. They are run charts with statistically determined upper and lower limits. As long as the process variables fall within the range, the system is said to be "in control" and its variation to stem from a

common cause. The goal is to narrow the range from the upper and lower limits by seeking to eliminate the common causes that occur day in and day out. Controlling variation equates to controlling cost and conforming to requirements. (pp. 49–50)

Problem-solving tasks are assigned to teams of staff who use statistical results and diagrams to direct service delivery toward customer satisfaction with less variability. Variation is wasted energy, misdirected resources. Consequently, TQM's statistically based decision making does save money. But, the information generated has its greatest value in organization's increased abilities to find its way most directly to their particular areas of needed improvement.

The use of concrete, objective information in statistical monitoring, charts and diagrams will enable sex offender treatment programs to hone "best practices" into standardized service delivery processes. Teams will continuously develop the following:

1. The most complete psychoeducational preparation of all the program's sex offenders for fully confrontational as well as fully supportive group therapy.
2. The most thorough implementation of each therapeutic community initiated by the program.
3. The most comprehensive discharge planning, implementation and follow-up.
4. The fullest assessment and management of risks.
5. Complete and appropriate peer and supervisory monitoring of treatment staff needs and problems.
6. The most far-reaching and diplomatic efforts to cooperate with public entities and other links to programmatic functioning.
7. Complete licensure and creatively challenging training of staff at all levels of the program.

For instance, Figure 10.1, a process flow chart, represents a program that might use a "rework" intervention already common to sex offender treatment in which remedial psychoeducational classes and earlier-staged group therapy are clinically indicated. TQM teamwork involves the use of flow charts to diagram all organizational processes so that incomplete processes can be "scrapped" (a term associated with being unburdened by previous methods), then reworked before the detrimental effects of such varied methods compound.

A broader view of programatic functioning is gained using cause-and-effect charts such as the one in Figure 10.2, which indicates four problematic effects as examples. Cause-and-effect charts are read left to right for tracing the effects of problems back to their causes or sources.

As more sex offender treatment programs develop TQM initiatives, it will be interesting to see the applications these programs use to gather statistical information and use graphical representations to understand their problems better and to generate CQI. Even in these early stages of TQM initiatives, sex offender treatment programs will benefit from the use of statistical monitoring to educate themselves and the public entities on which they depend for support. Toward the middle stages, however, they will begin to accumulate the newly measureable improvement that the customers of sex offender programs require.

Figure 10.1
Process Flow Examples

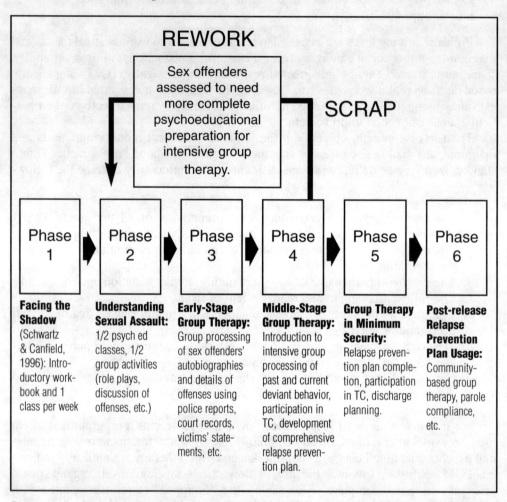

Employee Empowerment in TQM

Success in the service sector depends on the performance and behavior of employees. Other areas of organizational functioning are important, too, but the work of direct-service employees is particularly central in the field of human services. Further, in the field of sex offender treatment, direct-service employees are faced with treating offenders who have committed horrendous crimes and broken our society's deepest taboos.

Clearly, these employees need substantial empowerment so they can provide services adequate enough to maximize the safety of such dangerous offenders. Empowered sex offender therapists, supervisors, and administrators are necessary to meet the enormous societal need for increased safety. But, unfortunately, motivation and morale are common problem areas for these employees. TQM language would translate this as follows: Morale satisfaction and motivational satisfaction of staff customers need to increase in order for the safety of sex offenders to improve via increased service delivery quality. Notice the constructive, problem-solving implications in this language, which is usually used in TQM-oriented employee interactions.

Employee empowerment increases when this approach is used because it comes from a strengths perspective rather than the traditional deficiency perspective of the medical models most clinical settings still employ today. Quality training and education are ongoing and elemental processes of TQM in which improvement opportunities are identified in employees' work processes and then offered to employees as immediately as possible. An operant effect is created as employees experience increased power after taking advantage of the learning opportunities regularly presented to them. The weekly in-service programs and the occasional workshops and conferences, for example, commonly offered sex offender treatment staff are basically "one-size-fits-all" approaches to training. These occasional interventions cannot be expected to increase service delivery quality nearly as well as the ongoing improvement opportunities TQM provides. And, as these opportunities are offered "on the job" as a part of TQM's regular service delivery processing, they are more applied and less abstract than traditional training and education methods.

TQM employs strengths perspectives especially in its methods of team formation.

Figure 10.2
Cause-and-Effect Chart

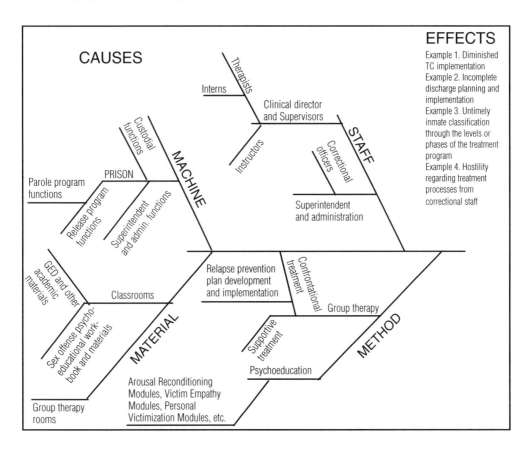

Quality improvement tasks and problem-solving tasks are taken up by teams of employees to use their various individual strengths. All people in organizations want to be creative and contribute well to service delivery, and TQM exploits this basic drive. Many staff develop poor morale in traditional standardized procedures because they have few opportunities to exercise this basic drive. These staff members are often quite excited about TQM initiatives and go on to shed their morale problems.

Continuous Quality Improvement of Sex Offender Treatment and Policy

Sex offender programs interact closely with, for example, state departments of Correction, Rehabilitation, Probation, Parole, Social and Human Services, and these organizations can be directly involved in quality improvement initiatives for sex offender treatment and management.

Ohio, for example, has implemented a Quality Services through Partnership (QStP) program through its Department of Rehabilitation and Correction. Ritchie-Matsumoto (1997) described the steps taken to introduce quality improvement methods:

> [It] began with the offering of QStP training to all 13,000 employees. Basic instruction was provided through a top down or cascading strategy. Every employee was involved through training at all levels. Next, quality steering committees were created to guide ongoing local training and provide overall guidance. The quality steering committees' mission was to support on-site, front-line teams that were then created to monitor and improve specific processes—teams such as Process Improvement Teams (PIT) and Problem Solving Process Teams (PSP). Today, the teams operate in every prison, every parole office, and community service site as well as in the central office. They devise new strategies to improve the quality of services offered. (p. 5)
>
> [As a result,] hundreds of different types of teams were formed to correct a specific problem or exploit an opportunity. Problem Solving Process teams were set up at the Southern Ohio Correctional Facility (Lucusville, Ohio) to further develop Residential Treatment Units and mental health programming. Their goals include initiating daily program structures, treatment plans, activity therapy, program development, and the application of technologies. (p. 5)

The teamwork in service delivery processing and service adjustment creates CQI. CQI in sex offender treatment involves successive benchmarking based on the proven contemporary methods of relapse prevention (Pithers & Cumming, 1995) and models that integrate (Schwartz, 1995) comprehensive approaches to sex offender treatment and policy. These methods and models should therefore be considered the baseline of quality improvement in the field. Benchmarked improvement needs to be built on this baseline of treatment and policy. As this improvement occurs now and in the future, sex offender programs should face less controversy about services.

Conclusion

Sex offender programs continue to face reduced resource allocations, expectations to do more with less, and problems substantiating treatment and policy successes.

They need tools to facilitate reliable improvement from statistically based decision making. TQM has been proven to provide these tools in a variety of human service organizations, but up to this point it has been initiated in sex offender treatment programs only rarely.

For sex offender programs to benefit from the continuous quality improvement that results from successful TQM initiatives, they must be prepared to make many changes in managerial roles and direct-service responsibilities. These changes can be upsetting, so preparations must be made, but organizations can adjust to TQM and come to appreciate the satisfactions that result from its focus on a full spectrum of customers. Increased customer satisfaction leads to increased service use and increased valuation of sex offender treatment, critical areas of need for almost all sex offender programs existing today and in the foreseeable future.

References

Freeman-Longo, R. E., & Knopp, F. H. (1992). State-of-the-art sex offender treatment outcome and issues. *Annals of Sex Research, 5,* 141–160.

Gunther, J., & Hawkins, F. (1997). *Total quality management in human service organizations.* New York: Springer.

Jablonski, J. R. (1992). *Implementing TQM.* San Diego: Pfeiffer.

Massachusetts Association for the Treatment of Sexual Abusers. (1997). *No more victims: A master plan for addressing the problem of sexual assault in the Commonwealth of Massachusetts.*

National Seminars, Inc. (1992). *Total quality management: A supervisor's handbook.* Bethesda, MD: National Press Publications.

Pithers, W. D., & Cummings, G. F. (1995). Relapse prevention: A method for enhancing behavioral self-management and external supervision of the sexual aggressor. In B. K. Schwartz & H. R. Cellini, (Eds.), *The sex offender: Corrections, treatment and practice* (vol. I, pp. 20-1–20-32). Kingston, NJ: Civic Research Institute.

Ritchie-Matsumoto, P. (1997). Quality improvement for a demanding correctional environment. *Offender Programs Report, 1*(1), 5–13.

Schwartz, B. K. (1995). Introduction to the integrative approach. In B. K. Schwartz & H. R. Cellini (Eds.), *The sex offender: Corrections, treatment and practice* (vol. I, pp. 1-1–1-13). Kingston, NJ: Civic Research Institute.

Schwartz, B. K., & Canfield, G. M. S. (1996). *Facing the shadow.* Kingston, NJ: Civic Research Institute.

Chapter 11

Forcible Confinements and Sexual Assault of Staff in a Correctional Environment

by Sharon M. Williams, Ph.D., C. Pysch.

Overview

Working in a correctional environment carries with it the potential risk of common assault, forcible confinement, sexual assault, and even death. This chapter focuses exclusively on forcible confinement and examines issues such as incidence, offender characteristics, strategies for reducing the potential for forcible confinement, survival strategies, and the impact of forcible confinement on correctional staff.

Introduction

Forcible confinement (often described as hostage takings) is not a recent phenomenon. Furthermore, the stress of captivity has been studied in considerable detail (Herman, 1992; Crelinstein, 1977). However, the literature does not reveal a similar interest in forcible confinement in a correctional context (Needham, 1977), and no studies focusing on the impact of forcible confinement on staff members could be identified.

"Forcible confinement" is defined as a situation in which any person—staff, visitor, or inmate—is held against his or her will by an inmate(s) seeking to escape, gain concessions, or achieve other goals, such as publicizing a particular cause, gaining recognition, or creating change. The underlying assumption is that the confined individual is currency that can be used as barter for various purposes. However, a number of recent internal investigations carried out by Correctional Service of Canada determined that there was an emerging trend for "hostage takers" to forcibly confine staff members for sexual gratification. These forcible confiners appeared to target noncustodial female staff, had few demands, and, unlike the more traditional hostage taker who confines in order to trade his hostage for specific benefits, committed the forcible confinement for the primary purpose of sexually assaulting the staff member. A study conducted by Williams (1995) focused on all forcible confinements that occurred between 1993 and 1995 with a view to identifying better procedures for dealing with potential hostage takers, providing staff with better training, and generally improving the strategies used to deal with crises.

Rates of Forcible Confinement in Canada

The incidence of forcible confinement of Canadian federal correctional staff is relatively low compared with other assaults. An examination of the major security incidents that occurred in Canadian federal prisons between 1986 and 1995 revealed that there were as few as one (1987–1988) and as many as seven (1989–1990) in a one-year period. The mean was 3.9 per year, and the median 4.0. Unfortunately, this number should be considered an underestimate as some incidents were not reported, some were reported but not placed on the computerized offender management system, and others were identified as minor incidents because only physical injuries were identified as major prior to 1995. Subsequent to the study reported here, forcible confinement resulting in psychological impact has been classified as major, which will improve our future understanding of the frequency and characteristics of this type of offense.

Characteristics of Forcible Confinements

Williams found that most perpetrators acted alone and eleven of twelve incidents involved single victims. Offenders ranged from 30 to 50 (mean 35), were between 13 and 20 at first offense (mean 19) and all were serving sentences for violent offenses. Three quarters of the forcible confinements involved an offender with a history of sexual violence. This number is disproportionately large because sex offenders comprise 25% of the incarcerated population in Canada. All the sex offenders who forcibly confined had previously committed a sexual assault against an adult woman, and two thirds had committed more than one. Both the median and mod were three. Furthermore, all but one were serving an indefinite sentence (no defined release date) or a long finite sentence (mean nine years). More than half had previously confined staff members. Most offenders carried a weapon, which was most frequently a knife. Victims were most commonly women and only one of the women was a correctional officer.

When men with violent histories (non–sex offenders) forcibly confined, their victims were male, demands were made, and sexual assault did not occur. In contrast, when perpetrators were sex offenders, their choice of victim was exclusively female, and in all but one case, sexual assault was either attempted or completed. Most had earlier indicators of distress (e.g., love letters, stalking behavior, recent reconviction, detention, or suicidal intent).

Training Necessary to Ensure Staff Safety

The primary recommendation of this 1995 paper was that staff receive training to help them to become more aware of potentially dangerous situations by teaching them how to deal with forcible confinements more effectively and how to cope with the social and emotional aftermath of these critical incidents. Other recommendations involved more general issues related to both negotiation and crisis management.

Staff can deal more effectively with the enhanced risk of forcible confinement by discussing the issue with family and friends, becoming more alert within their workplace, and having information on survival strategies which can improve their ability to avoid, escape from, and deal with confinement.

Working in a correctional setting requires alertness to one's environment. Over time, correctional workers tend to adapt to anxiety-provoking situations. This is known as habituation or adaptation and is generally considered a normal process. Constant vigilance or edginess not only would increase stress-related illnesses, such as high blood pressure, but would result in staff who are unable to carry out the everyday functions that are required to meet the terms of their continued employment. However, becoming too habituated or relaxed can result in a loss of alertness to potentially dangerous situations, especially in medium- and maximum-security settings.

Being a member of a helping profession does not seem to be a protective factor, because forcible confiners seem to be more motivated by opportunity and self-gratification than by either their relationship to the victim or the consequences of the act to themselves or others.

Preparation

Outside the Workplace. Being prepared involves discussion with one's family and friends of the potential for forcible confinement in the workplace. A frank discussion about the dangers inherent in the workplace, clear instructions about responsibilities to children and pets should a forcible confinement occur, and an updated will can reduce distraction and anxiety should a forcible confinement occur.

In the Workplace: Know Your Environment. If staff are likely to be in an office, group room, library, lab, or treatment room, they should be aware of the physical layout of the room, proximity to the door, how the door locks, how the door opens, and the presence of potential weapons. The desk should be located so that the staff member is facing the door and is physically closest to it. Some offices or interview/treatment rooms are equipped with a fixed alarm. It should be placed close to the desk, so it can be pushed inobtrusively.

Staff members are often issued a personal portable alarm (PPA), which can be worn on a belt or placed in a pocket. Some staff members may object to wearing it because it may imply that they are intimidated by offenders; others are concerned that it will not be useful if depressed outside the office location. The first concern can be dealt with by having all staff members wear PPAs as policy. The second concern is more difficult to address as PPAs are most useful to staff who remain in a specific location.

Offenders may ask staff members to place a piece of paper over a window to increase privacy. As the window is one's main visual contact point with correctional officers or colleagues working in the area, it should never be obscured. Paper cannot be secured over a window if there is no tape in the office. Tape dispensers can also make an effective weapon. Staff might wish to keep tape in a central location rather than as a standard desk accessory.

Offenders may also request that the door be closed to ensure privacy and confidentiality. Keeping the door slightly ajar improves the officer's or colleague's ability to hear signs of distress, and a closed door should be a signal that a forcible confinement may be in progress.

Each staff member should survey his or her office to determine whether there are objects on the desk which could be used as weapons. Letter openers, staple dispensers, glass picture frames, and even pens and pencils can be used or broken to create impromptu weapons.

Staff members should be aware of the timing of routine walks or security checks. If possible, when a high-risk or potentially violent offender is scheduled for an appointment, the officer should be notified and may determine that increased visual contact is necessary. In some instances, staff members will determine that the offender should be interviewed in a more secure environment.

Knowing each offender's characteristics can be invaluable. Information regarding a prior history of violence, sexual violence, prior forcible confinement of staff while incarcerated, and current dynamic factors, such as recent divorce, death in the family, stalking behaviors, or love letters to staff members, should be noted.

It is also extremely important to evaluate one's own strengths and weaknesses. If one is forcibly confined, would one respond by talking, running, or fighting? Although each situation is different and will require variations in responding, there is some advantage to determining one's most likely response.

If staff members have a physical illness which requires medication, this should be on a record that will be accessible in case of such an emergency. Breathing difficulties such as asthma or emphysema are particularly important because they may compromise the use of airborne agents, such as tear gas, should a physical assault be necessary.

Once a Staff Member Is Confined

Because each forcible confinement is different, and each staff member is equipped with different strengths and weaknesses, there is no right or wrong way to deal with a forcible confinement. However, being observant and having a range of behaviors in one's repertoire is probably the most adaptive response. For example, the staff member should determine whether the offender is intent on confining him or whether the offender can be "talked down." Assessing whether there is a clear route to the door and whether the door is open or locked will help to determine whether escape is possible. Similarly, the presence or absence of a potentially lethal weapon (e.g., a knife or gun) and the proximity of other staff members can also help to determine whether shouting or fighting might be successful strategies.

If circumstances are favorable, pushing the fixed alarm or PPA, yelling, or running could dissuade the offender or might increase the likelihood of an early resolution of the confinement. In the study described earlier, Williams (1995) found that different staff members had tried strategies such as yelling, fighting, talking, or quietly awaiting rescue, and most were satisfied with their own response.

Once the confinement is under way, the staff member should be made aware that the first fifteen to forty-five minutes are likely to be the most stressful and the most dangerous to his or her physical safety. Confiners who have taken a hostage to be bartered for various "payoffs" will be physiologically aroused by the realization that they have accomplished their goal. If the offender has confined the staff member for sexual motives, a sexual assault is likely to be attempted or carried out within the first twenty minutes (Williams, 1995).

It is generally agreed that during the early part of a confinement, victims should be quiet and not attract attention to themselves. Although it may sound like a formidable challenge, relaxing (through focused breathing and imagery) and observing details of the offender's behavior, clothing, and weapons and the location of other victims may help to refocus attention in a more constructive way and thereby decrease anxiety. An effort should be made to speak to the offender (especially when spoken to) and to try to take the offender's perspective, especially if the offender has particular views of the "system" which have potentiated the forcible confinement.

Strategies for Dealing With Sexually Motivated Confiner

If the offender has sexual motives, the staff member can try a variety of strategies to discourage him, although the likelihood of success will vary. I have ordered these along a continuum ranging from least to most intrusive.

It seems most reasonable to try to verbally defuse the situation and follow this strategy with verbal resistance and finally physical resistance. As stated earlier, each situation is different because offenders and staff members have different motives and skills and, as a result, focus, observation, and flexibility are key.

At a verbal level, the confinee can appeal to the offender's better judgment, ask the offender to consider the impact of his acts, talk about her children, and generally try to establish empathy. For offenders who have cognitive distortions about women in general or about the staff member in particular, it might be useful for the confinee to reiterate that she is not a willing participant and that the cues which the offender believes are indicative of sexual interest or provocation did not occur or were misinterpreted.

One approach that may be useful with sex offenders with low self-esteem is for the confinee to say that her previous interactions with the offender led her to believe that the offender would treat her with respect and fairness. Verbalizing this expectation may discourage assault.

As a last resort, some individuals have been able to distract the offender by asking for toilet facilities, coffee, or water or were able to force themselves to vomit or faint. In some cases, the victim is so frightened that passive compliance is her only option. When all else has failed, several victims fought with offenders in order to avoid sexual assault. The drawback to this approach is that the offender may become even more angry, which increases potential for both physical and sexual assault.

Strategies for Dealing With Nonsexually Motivated Confiner

When the forcible confinement is for nonsexual purposes, the staff member should be aware of the Stockholm Syndrome. The Stockholm Syndrome can be defined as the rapport or relationship that grows between confiner and confinee. The confiner may begin to feel responsible for the victim's well-being, while the victim may feel that the confiner has good reasons for taking this extreme reaction, especially if the hostage is being bartered for escape or better conditions. Anger resulting from the slowness of negotiation and fear of the assault team can contribute to the positive relationship or bond between confiner and victim. Prolonged negotiation tends to exhaust the offender and strengthen the bond, thereby decreasing the chance that the victim will be harmed by the offender.

The development of a bond can be enhanced by making eye contact, agreeing with the offender's perspective, and asking the offender for food, medication, water, or blankets, among other things. Requests should be made quietly and infrequently.

If the confinement continues for a prolonged period, staff members should try to relax, sleep, eat and drink, physically exercise, and keep their minds active by doing mental arithmetic, recalling poetry, or rehearsing positive events. Having a routine and maintaining self-respect are important survival strategies.

Organizational Responses

While the confinement is under way, considerable activity is occurring inside the institution. Most facilities have a "crisis management model" for dealing with emergencies such as a forcible confinement. These models generally involve a crisis manager or decision maker (who may have one or more advisers), a negotiator who attempts to make contact with the offender and acts as a go-between for the crisis manager and offender, and an assault team, whose role includes gathering "intelligence" or information and developing a feasible assault plan which will remove the victim without endangering his or her life. Although the victim(s) may feel extremely isolated, all other staff members in their facility will be focused on their safe release. Most facilities wish to preserve the victim's life at all costs and will attempt to resolve the crisis through negotiation. It is only when this process breaks down, or when there is good reason to believe that the victim's life is in danger, that an assault will be carried out by the emergency response team. In most cases, the assault team will need to be mobilized, briefed, and have reasonable plans before the team will use assault. By the time release can be obtained, either through negotiation or assault, the victim nay have been confined for many hours, and if the object of the confinement was sexual assault, it is likely to have occurred at least once.

If an assault team is used, plans are limited to three main approaches:

1. Use of a chemical agent such as tear gas, which is either thrown in by grenades,

sprayed, or fired into the room by a gas gun. In the ensuing confusion, the team will remove the victim and perpetrator.

2. Use of physical assault, where the door, window or wall is breached to allow physical entry and removal of victim and perpetrator.

3. Use of lethal force, where the assault team uses a handgun or rifle.

These approaches can be used together: tear gas is fired into the room, the door/wall is breached, and lethal force is used if necessary.

The Aftermath of Confinement

When the forcible confinement has been resolved, whether by negotiation or by the assault team, there are a number of psychological sequelae. A recent study of staff who have been taken hostage (Seidman & Williams, 1997) indicates that most experience a number of symptoms. The most frequent are anxiety (89%), hypervigilance (81%), sleep disturbance (74%), hostility (74%), feelings of powerlessness (70%), shock (67%), fears/phobias (67%), feelings of isolation (63%), and nightmares (63%). Some of these symptoms are transient; others remain problematic. One third of the sample in the study had severe difficulties with multiple symptoms. These survivors were, on the average, confined for a lengthy period (four to sixty hours) and 80% had been victims of severe physical and/or sexual assaults. Nonetheless, two thirds of the survivors were able to return to work, most frequently within one to three weeks, and most within twelve months.

Return to psychological health can be augmented by having supportive family, friends, coworkers, and administration. Often coworkers feel awkward dealing with the survivor, as they are uncertain about how much to say or ask. A simple comment, such as "We're glad to see you are back," or questions, such as "How are you feeling?" or "Do you feel like talking about it?," would help the survivor to feel more comfortable at work. Often victims feel that they were responsible for the forcible confinement. This may occur because people like to believe that the world is a fair place, where "bad" things do not happen to "good" people. If they were to believe that forcible confinements could happen to nondeserving victims, then similar events could beset them. Staff training should be aimed at helping staff to deal with survivors in a more humane fashion.

The Correctional Service of Canada recently developed a film, *Forcible Confinement: A Survivor's Story*. It is a dramatic tool to enhance staff training for front-line staff, administrators, negotiators and assault team members. This would be a useful adjunct to staff training.

Conclusion

In summary, although forcible confinement of staff members occurs infrequently, when it does occur it can be extremely traumatic for the immediate victim, his or her family, and colleagues. In the Canadian correctional environment, sexual assault has become an increasingly frequent accompaniment to forcible confinement. This chapter outlines the characteristics of offenders who confine staff for both sexual and nonsexual motives and discusses methods of increasing one's alertness to the work environment, as well as tactics for dealing more effectively with the forcible confinement and its aftermath.

References

Crelinstein, R. D. (Ed.). (1977). *Dimensions of victimization in the context of terrorist acts.* Montreal, Canada: International Centre for Comparative Criminology.

Herman, J. I. (1992). *Trauma and recoveyr.* New York: Basic Books.

Needham, J. P. (1977). Neutralization of prison hostage situations. *Criminal Justice Monograph, 8*(1).

Seidman, B. T. , & Williams, S. M. (1997, August). *Hostage-takings of Correctional Service of Canada (CSC) staff: Psychological impact and institutional management.* Internal publication.

Williams, S. M. (1995, August). *Review of sexual assaults and forcible confinements.* Internal publication.

Chapter 12

The Grand Alliance— Probation Officer and Therapist

by Rebecca Palmer, M.S. and Terry Childers, L.I.C.S.W.

Overview

Treating and supervising court-mandated sex offenders is a grueling task. Clinical emphasis and treatment plans are much more potent when the treatment provider has a working relationship with the referring probation officer and a fundamental understanding of the criminal justice and court system. Likewise, the probation officer benefits from a clear, concrete understanding of the therapy process. Providing treatment and supervision to sex offenders in the absence of an alliance between therapist and probation officer is like raising a child in the absence of parental communication.

Introduction

The community is at risk when the monitoring of convicted sex offenders is insubstantial. Therapists have an obligation to the community at large to provide treatment and to assist the courts in monitoring sex offender behavior. Probation officers are sworn to protect the community and enforce the conditions of probation and supervision as stipulated by the courts. The alliance between the therapists and the probation officer enhances both the safety to the community and the services provided to the offender.

Therapy vs. Probation

Table 12.1 outlines the basic responsibilities required of the probation officer and the therapist. This tool can assist both parties in recognizing the differences that exist for each professional. Recognizing that the therapist and probation officer have different roles and responsibilities allows for both professionals to collaborate and maximize the most appropriate treatment plan. Because the object of discussion is court-mandated sex offenders, the first domain on which to focus is that of the referring agent. Most often, that person is the probation officer.

Probation Officer as Referral Agent

Providing treatment to a sex offender without the close assistance and support of a probation officer is like playing tennis with a ping-pong paddle. It can be done, but it is not very effective. The probation officer by his authority and office is responsible for the supervision of the offender. He uses many tools to ensure that the offender complies with supervision and does not recidivate. One of these tools is treatment. More often than not, what a therapist knows about a client is what the client reveals (Smith, 1995; Quinsey & Lalumière, 1996; Salter; 1988). It is not the role of the therapist to corroborate or verify the veracity of what the offender says. However, in sex offender treatment, it is imperative that the therapist knows many aspects of the offender's history, present circumstances, living arrangements, and so on. The probation officer has ready access to this information and is in the position to share it with the therapist.

Table 12.1
Responsibilities of Therapist and Probation Officer

	Therapy	*Probation*
Goals	Client acknowledges abusive behavior and works toward resolving factors that contribute to and maintain abusive behaviors	Discovery of facts, ensures client will adhere to parameters of probation
Strategies	Group, individual, family/couples therapy, communication with probation officer	Home visits, office visits. communication with all involved systems, case manager
Tools	Objective tests, polygraph, Abel screening, plethysmograph	Court order
Consumer	Client, court, and community	Client, court, community, and referral source

At no point in the therapeutic process is this sharing of information more important than at the time of initial referral. At that point, the therapist knows nothing about the offender whereas the probation officer knows a great deal. The type of information to which he is privy, and which will enhance the referral process, includes:

- *Details of the offense.* What did the offender do to the victim? What kind of sexual activities did he engage in? What did he say to the victim? What was the victim profile? This is information about which the probation officer should be intimately aware.
- *Criminal history.* Has the offender been arrested before the sex offending or sex offending–related offenses? Is there a history of violence? Have there been arrests for other crimes not sex related?
- *Psychiatric history.* Does the offender suffer from a psychiatric disorder? Is he maintained on any type of psychotropic medication? Is he in treatment elsewhere? Has he ever been in treatment, and if so, where?
- *Drug history.* Does the offender have a history of substance abuse? If so, what are his drugs of choice? Is he currently receiving treatment for drug abuse?
- *Medical history.* Does the offender suffer from any medical problems? If so, is he currently in treatment or taking medications?
- *Family history.* This is particularly important in incest cases. Does the offender still live with the victim? What are the sleeping arrangements in the house? How has the victim responded to the abuse?
- *Offender's residence.* Probation officers make home visits. Are there any items in the home related to the offending behavior? This would include but is not limited to video materials, toys, books, and so on. Does the offender live near a school or day-care center? What kind of car does he drive? For example, a van can be used as a place to abuse; a convertible would be very accommodating for an exhibitionist.

The probation officer has all this information, and conveying it to the treatment provider at the time of the referral expedites the process and ensures a timely and appropriate treatment plan.

After the referral is made, it is also imperative that the probation officer meet in person with the therapist and the offender. Such a meeting gives all parties the opportunity to clarify treatment goals. The issues to be addressed at this initial meeting should include the following:

- Frequency and length of therapy sessions;
- Modality of treatment (will the offender be expected to be in group, individual, family therapy, etc.?);
- Cost and method of payment;
- Medication issues;
- Use of plethysmograph or polygraph; and
- Confidentiality issues.

Of most importance at this time is that the therapist and the probation officer present as a united front. Their goal is the same: *the successful treatment of the offender resulting in no more victims.* But their methods are different. It is the complementarity of their roles that must be conveyed to the offender. In particular, the offender should sense that he would be unable to split the alliance, turning the therapist against the probation officer and vice versa.

Pretreatment Planning

The best prognosis for providing effective, sound therapy is to have a solid foundation. Pretreatment planning is the foundation that allows the therapist to construct a solid therapeutic relationship with the offender (Morrison, Erooga, & Beckett, 1994; Trepper & Barrett, 1989). The first order of business in pretreatment planning is to develop clear and consistence communication with the probation officer. Such communication instills trust in the probation officer and also conveys to the offender that the alliance is in place. As addressed later in this chapter, many times throughout treatment the therapist needs to rely on the probation officer for information, direction, and support.

There are many benefits to maintaining an alliance with the probation officer, one of which is to reinforce the offender's belief that the length of treatment coincides with the length of supervision. At times, that is not be the case, and the supervision might be scheduled to terminate before the treatment is completed. In those situations, the therapist might convey concerns to the probation officer that the offender is still at risk to the community, providing possible cause to continue the period of supervision (Salter, 1988).

An additional benefit for having consistent communication with the probation officer is to avoid splitting, a strategy often used by court-mandated clients. Offenders often seek to minimize their culpability and the work expected of them in therapy, as well as incessantly complain about the undue burdens placed on them by the probation officer (Finkelhor, 1984). When a strong and obvious alliance does not exist between the therapist and the probation officer, the offender perceives a lack of communication. This provides fertile ground for the offender to rupture the probation officer–therapist relationship, thus causing minor to significant chaos.

The Role of the Probation Officer in the First Stage of Treatment

The first stage of treatment creates a context for change. The goal of the therapist at this stage is to create a safe environment for the client (Trepper & Barrett, 1989). Feeling safe allows the offender to establish trust in the therapist and in the therapeutic process. This trust enhances the therapeutic relationship and assists the client in taking necessary risks in being honest about his offending behavior and assuming responsibility for his conduct. Creating a safe therapeutic environment does not prohibit confronting the offender's behavior, but it does allow the offender to explore and learn healthy coping mechanisms. It is important for the offender to know what the treatment expectations are, and this is an area that should be addressed by all parties—the offender, the therapist and the probation officer. It is imperative at this pretreatment stage that all the parties are "on the same page."

Inasmuch as he is privy to so many aspects of the offender's life and responsible for enforcing supervision conditions, the probation officer is the quintessential case manager. He is at the absolute center of the offender's life. Figure 12.1 illustrates this point. When the offender's relational environment is envisioned as a wheel, the probation officer becomes the hub of the wheel. In that center position, the probation officer is the liaison between all the other spokes in the wheel—the other people involved in the offender's life.

The function that the probation officer plays in the ongoing treatment process is similar to the role he assumed during the referral stage. He provides information to the therapist, corroborates information, and supervises the offender. Again, the therapist will mostly know what the offender reveals. The probation officer, having wider access to the community, can provide critical information in the following areas:

- *Offender's employment.* The therapist may not know for certain where the offender works. Conversations with the offender's supervisor could reveal relevant material for the therapist. If the offender is searching for employment, the probation officer can inform the therapist where he is seeking employment and the sorts of job in which he is interested.
- *Local police.* Is the offender suspected of crimes for which he has not been charged? Is he under surveillance?
- Offender's family. Is there a marital problem? Does the family even know the offender is in treatment? The probation officer can be liaison between family and therapist.
- *Other treatment providers.* It is not uncommon for offenders in supervision to be receiving a variety of services from different treatment providers, including the sex offender therapist. The probation officer can provide necessary communication between these professionals.
- *Victims.* The probation officer will have information about the victim to which

Figure 12.1
Responsibilities of Probation Officer

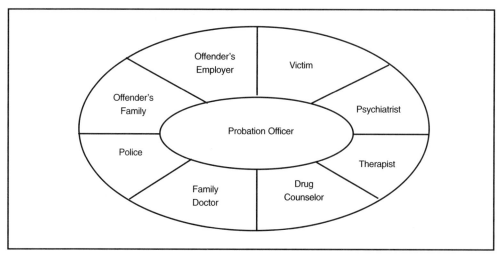

the therapist will not normally have access, such as addresses, phone numbers, and so on. At times, information from the victims might be needed to address treatment issues.

- *Home visits.* The probation officer may visit the offender at home at any time. On those occasions, he might note materials such as pornography and sexual paraphernalia that could contribute to the offending cycle. The treatment provider must know this information to deal with it in therapy.
- *Neighborhood.* The probation officer has access to the offender's neighborhood and can describe it to the therapist, paying particular interest to potential spots for reoffending behavior to occur, such as playgrounds, arcades, parks, school yards, and so on.

Finally, the probation officer is the enforcer. He is the officer of the court or the parole authorities. As such, he is in a position to enforce compliance with supervision guidelines and initiate consequences when the offender refuses to comply with supervision, including treatment. Neither the probation officer nor the therapist can "make" an offender participate actively and appropriately in treatment. However, the probation officer can certainly ensure consequences for the offender who refuses to participate.

A course of treatment is predicated by the needs of the offender. These needs are determined by an extensive sex offender evaluation. Accordingly, an evaluation should be conducted before any kind of ongoing therapy is begun. After the evaluation is completed, the recommendations should be discussed with the probation officer and the offender. If it is deemed that the offender have no contact with children, the probation officer is in the position to legally enforce this recommendation. Moreover, the probation officer is expected to question the offender regarding his cycle of offending, use of pornography, sexual activity, and fantasies and report these things to the therapist. Because the probation officer is often the best source of information about the offender's environment, the therapist should look to the probation officer for information to address cognitive distortions, thinking errors, fantasies, and seemingly unimportant decisions that the offender might be making in the community.

The goal of successful treatment of the offender—"no more victims"—is prevalent throughout the treatment community (Goldstein, 1987). To that end both the probation officer and therapist must communicate about the progress and prognosis for the offender. Stage one of treatment is completed when the offender has made a commitment to treatment and acknowledges a willingness to change.

The Role of the Probation Officer in the Second Stage of Treatment

The assistance of the probation officer is also necessary in stage two of treatment. In that stage, the offender will be expected to understand his cycle of offending and be able to share this understanding with his spouse or significant other. A relapse prevention plan begins when the treatment commences, and in stage two the offender is challenged to inform those persons with whom he lives that he has a sexual problem. This information will enable family members to participate in his treatment and to assist him from participating in behaviors that could trigger relapse and reoffending. This is a critical stage of treatment as this kind of disclosure could result in rejection of the offender by his loved ones, leading to depression and possible self-destructive behavior. Or, the offender could possibly turn on his family and harm them. As the probation officer has ready access to the offender's home and family, he could easily monitor this situation and provide feedback to the therapist.

The Role of the Probation Officer in the Final Stage of Treatment

In the third or last stage of treatment, the probation officer spends time with the offender and his significant others reviewing what has changed throughout the course of treatment. The probation officer makes predictions regarding potential triggers of offending behavior and reinforces the relapse prevention plan. As mentioned earlier in this chapter, many offenders assume treatment is complete when probation has ended. It is critical that the therapist convey any concerns to the probation officer weeks prior to the end of probation. Both therapist and probation officer need to remember that they are making decisions as a team. An important goal of the therapist is to help the offender understand that treatment is not meant as a punishment but is a significant instrument in assisting him to take responsibility and change his abusive behaviors.

Conclusion

The alliance of the probation officer and the therapist will result in the best possible treatment and supervision of the court-mandated offender. An outside support system is an integral component to relapse prevention, and the probation officer is in a unique position to validate information provided by the offender to the therapist. Moreover, the therapist has an understanding of the offender, which can be communicated to the probation officer, assisting the officer in more selectively and judiciously supervising the offender.

References

Finkelhor, D. (1984). *Child sexual abuse.* New York: Free Press.

Goldstein, S. (1987). *The sexual exploitation of children.* CRC Press.

Morrison, T., Erooga, M., & Beckett, R. (1994). *Sexual offending against children: Assessment and treatment of male abusers.* London and New York: Routledge.

Quinsey, V., & Lalumière, M. (1996). *Assessment of sexual offenders against children.* Thousand Oaks, CA: Sage.

Salter, A. (1988). *Treating child sex offenders and victims.* Newbury Park, CA: Sage.

Smith, R. (1995). Sex offender program planning and implementation. In B. K. Schwartz & H. R. Cellini (Eds.), *The sex offender. Corrections, treatment and legal practice* (vol. I, pp. 7-1–7-13). Kingston, NJ: Civic Research Institute.

Trepper, T., & Barrett, M.J (1989). *Systemic treatment of incest: A therapeutic handbook.* New York: Brunner/Mazel..

Chapter 13

The Sex Offender, the Polygraph, and Community Corrections

by Pryor Green, B.S. and Billy Franklin, B.S.

Overview

Polygraphy has long held a controversial role in criminal justice. Although the field has progressively gotten more sophisticated and reliable, evidence has continued to be excluded from trials, giving the impression that the technique is a combination of science and magic. However, states particularly in the Northwest have long used polygraphy in the monitoring of sex offenders. Often just the thought of the procedure is enough to deter offenders from certain high-risk behaviors. In this chapter, the authors, a probation officer and a polygrapher, discuss in detail the use of this technology in the effective monitoring of this population.

Introduction

A basic condition of treating sex offenders is to promote honesty in participants, because sex offenders can be quite convincing in their denial and projection of blame onto others. One major goal of treatment is to expose an offender's deviant sexual history as quickly as possible. In the review of available options, it appears that the use of polygraph testing is the most direct method of accomplishing this goal.

A basic principle of community supervision of sex offenders for the Newport News Probation and Parole Department is to require them to fully accept responsibility for both their conviction and their deviant sexual history. Clearly, it is extremely difficult to effectively supervise and treat sex offenders without their taking full responsibility for their actions. The polygraph is a powerful tool to end the cycle of sex offender manipulation.

History of Polygraph Testing

The history of civilization is filled with attempts to detect lies and verify the truth by various means, including torture and trial by ordeal. Some of these ancient tests reflect a shrewd understanding of psychology or physiology, but they were hardly reliable or scientific. The earliest scientific approach to lie detection was developed by the Italian criminologist Cesare Lombroso. In 1895, Lombroso conducted experiments in the detection of deception by recording changes in a subject's blood pressure with a device called "Lombroso's Glove." Around the same period, another Italian scientist, Mosso, conducted investigations of blood volume changes during deception tests through the use of a crude device called "Mosso's Cradle."

In the early 1900s, a third Italian, Vittorio Benussi, conducted experiments in lie detection with a device that measured and recorded the rate and depth of the subject's respiration. These experiments convinced Benussi that distinct changes in the respiratory pattern occur during attempts to deceive.

The first American to become directly involved in the field of lie detection was Dr. William M. Marston, a psychologist. The U.S. government commissioned him to devise a method to interrogate prisoners of war during World War I. Using a sphygmomanometer (the device physicians use to take blood pressure), Marston conducted experiments by taking intermittent blood pressure readings during interrogation periods. In 1921, inspired by the success of Dr. Marston, Dr. John A. Larson, a psychiatrist, developed the forerunner of the modern-day polygraph, which made the first continuous, permanent record of blood pressure, pulse, and respiration.

As a result of Dr. Larson's work, a young psychologist, Leonard Keeler, developed his own instrument. His apparatus added the feature of measuring changes in the skin's resistance to electricity (the "Galvanic skin response"). Keeler is generally recognized as the true pioneer of modern-day polygraphy. Keeler refined its application to police work, introduced it into the field of business, and taught the technique to many others (Barefoot, 1974).

The polygraph technique began to be used in the United States in 1921. Since then, its use in official investigations has spread nationally to virtually all police departments. Today almost every major police department in the United States uses polygraph in criminal investigations as well as in applicant screening.

History of Sex Offender Polygraph Testing

Born out of the frustration of high rates of recidivism, reoffending probationers, and insufficient resources of supervision, Illinois Judge Clarence E. Partee introduced polygraph testing of sex offenders in 1966. His program required that participants agree to take annual polygraph examinations as a condition of their probation.

In 1969, Judge John C. Tuttle developed a similar plan in Walla Walla, Washington. Probationers were periodically polygraphed to determine whether they were violating the terms of their probation. This program was characterized as "an inexpensive twenty-four hour tail," which served as a deterrent to further antisocial behavior.

In 1973, Oregon Judge John Beatty initiated the polygraph surveillance program and began to effectively use disclosure polygraph testing. The advantages of this test were that it broke through the offender's denial, and allowed testers to obtain the names of victims. As a result of participant admissions made prior to the test and after it, much of their denial was reduced or even eliminated.

In Jackson County, Oregon, corrections departments, polygraphists, therapists, courts, district attorneys, and victim services used a unique procedure of close interaction. Of 173 offenders who had been supervised by corrections sex offender specialists, the following statistics were reported:

- 95% were free of new crime convictions;
- 96% were free of new felony convictions;
- 89% were crime free in testing of any criminal convictions; and
- 65% experienced no parole/probation revocations (Abrams & Abrams, 1993).

Today, other states, including Hawaii, Texas, Colorado, Florida, Massachusetts, and California, have instituted polygraph testing programs for sex offenders.

Why Polygraph Sex Offenders?

In the field of community corrections a thorough risk assessment is necessary for the community supervision of sex offenders. The polygraph examination is an indispensable part of that assessment. For example, a probation/parole officer and treatment provider were confronted with two new sex offender cases referred for supervision. Initially, both sex offenders made the same claim: this conviction was the first time they had ever committed a sex offense act. Without having to depend exclusively on self-reporting, the use of a polygraph examination can lead to striking differences between the treatment of both offenders.

The experience of the Newport News Sex Offender Program was that the polygraph revealed that the first offender had actually committed only one act and was caught whereas the second offender who had made the same claim had perpetrated hundreds of deviant sexual acts on approximately twenty-five victims. Based on the new information revealed by the polygraph, different treatment and supervision plans were established for the sex offenders. In this time of limited resources it is extremely important to compile accurate information on sex offenders, which can help create better treatment plans for all participants.

Sex Offender Testing in Newport News, Virginia

In 1993, Newport News Probation and Parole initiated the Newport News Sex Offender Community Protection Program. Newport News Probation and Parole secured the services of Franklin Security Systems, Inc., a private agency, to provide polygraph examinations. This combination proved to be highly successful to the program.

The Newport News program uses a team approach that incorporates the participation of a polygraph examiner, therapist, and a sex offender specialist from the probation and parole department. The team relies on the involvement and support of the local courts, the local Commonwealth's Attorney, the Virginia Parole Board, and victim services providers.

Once a sex offender begins the program, he is apprised that his time can be revoked or sanctions imposed depending on his choice about accepting responsibility for both his present offense and past deviant behavior in a timely fashion. The polygraph has been an invaluable risk assessment tool in getting offenders to accept responsibility for their actions and to participate more honestly in treatment.

From January 1993 through December 31, 1997, the polygraph testing by Franklin Security Systems, Inc., yielded the following statistics:

Number of disclosure tests conducted	136
Number of additional incidents of criminal sexual misconduct admitted to by the sexual offenders (136) prior to their polygraph tests	653
Number of individual incidents of sexual misconduct admitted to by the sexual offenders (136) during their respective polygraph tests (see Figure 13.1)	137,918

In 1997, thirty-three offenders were tested for number of victims. Before the polygraph they admitted to 40 victims; during the polygraph they admitted 498 victims (see Figure 13.2).

In addition to admissions of criminal sexual misconduct during their polygraph tests, the 136 offenders also admitted to engaging in other instances of misconduct and/or deviant behavior, including: arson, alcohol and drug abuse, obscene phone calls, thefts of women's underclothing, bestiality, transvestitism, coprophilia, urophilia, and fetishes.

From January 1, 1993, through December 31, 1997, fifty-eight periodic maintenance polygraph examinations were also conducted for Newport News Probation and Parole. Three of the offenders tested on the polygraph admitted committing sexual crimes while under active supervision. These three individuals were removed from the program and subsequently returned to prison.

Achieving Effective Results

For a sex offender management team to establish appropriate supervision and treatment plans, it is absolutely essential for the sex offender to understand that all elements of the team (probation and parole, the treatment provider, and polygraph examiner) are working together and share all information. From the beginning, the probation/parole officer and treatment provider inform sex offenders that they have sixty to ninety days to complete disclosure of their offense of conviction and deviant sexual history. The sixty- to ninety-day period allows sex offenders to learn about their treatment program and to deal with issues of shame and embarrassment relating to their

Figure 13.1
Polygraph as a Tool: Sexual Offenses Admitted

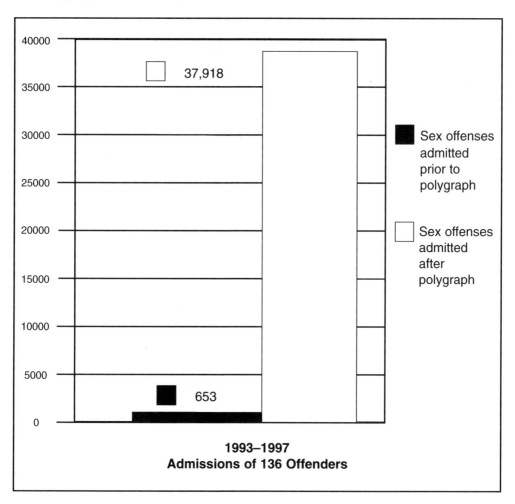

offending behavior. During the initial sixty- to ninety-day period before taking the disclosure polygraph, sex offenders are constantly reminded that they will take a polygraph examination to verify their self-reported sexual deviant history.

The primary goal for this phase of the process is for the sex offender to pass the polygraph; then an effective risk assessment can be conducted on the case, all of which is explained to the participant. The risk assessment shapes both the treatment and supervision plan for the sex offender.

The treatment team shares the possible consequences/sanctions of a deceptive test with the offender in order to stimulate his cooperation in passing the examination. For example, depending on the severity of the deception, the sex offender could be returned to the sentencing court to face a probation revocation hearing. Other sanctions might involve placing the offender on a curfew, home electronic monitoring, or increased reporting to the probation/parole officer. During this process, the

Figure 13.2
Polygraph as a Tool: Number of Victims

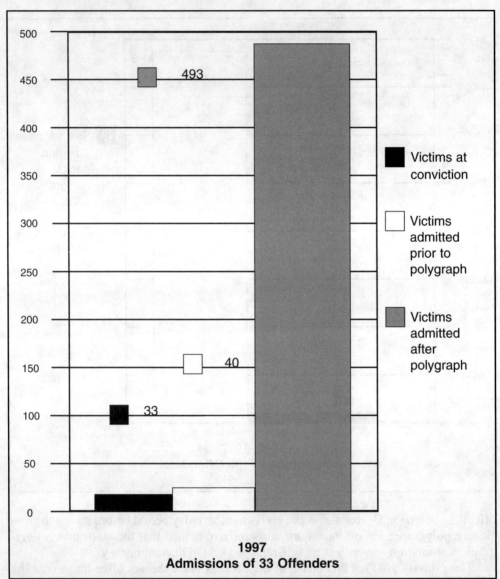

sex offender team must review and confront sex offenders with inconsistencies from their self-disclosures. The team should utilize previous sex offender statements, presentence reports, police reports, and victim statements when challenging offenders about their concealed sexual history. The sex offender team members need to communicate and support each other during this process. This team approach tactic keeps the pressure on the sex offender for full disclosure, which in the Newport News Sex Offender Program is labeled a "stress continuum." This flow is depicted as follows:

Probation/parole officer confronts sex offender on current offense and past sexual history.

Treatment provider confronts sex offender on current offense and past sexual history.

Together probation/parole officer and treatment provider confront sex offender and explain use of polygraph.

During the next sixty to ninety days, probation/parole officer and treatment provider encourage truthfulness for disclosure and continue to remind offenders of impending polygraph.

Probation/parole officer and treatment provider fully discuss with sex offender possible consequences/sanctions for deceptive test.

Probation/parole officer whenever possible must be present during polygraph exam.

If polygraph exam is deceptive, polygraph examiner and probation/parole officer immediately confront offender on deceptive answers.

If the sex offender further discloses, he is reexamined by polygraph examiner.

At the Newport News Sex Offender Program, this model has been found to be effective in promoting honest self-disclosure, discouraging deception, and achieving positive treatment results.

Importance of Polygraph Examinations

Clearly, the polygraph is a critical component of the treatment team's program. The Newport News Program utilizes a highly skilled professional polygraph examination team of two licensed examiners, one male and one female, with more than fifty-five years of combined experience and more than 50,000 polygraph tests successfully completed. Their expertise in working with sex offenders plays a significant role in the treatment and supervision of this group of offenders.

As noted previously, the polygraph examinations free the treatment team from reliance on self-reports and help direct the treatment toward its goals, which involve the participants' honest disclosure of the true nature of their offenses, as well as all related deviant sexual behavior. The polygraph examiners provide all information reported during a polygraph examination to the probation/parole officer and the treatment provider. This information assists the probation and parole officer in assessing risk to community and compliance with supervision and provides the therapist with information on compliance with treatment directives. In sum, the polygraph examination provides a measure of compliance with treatment and supervision. At the same time, the offender learns that all behavior will be continually evaluated for the duration of supervision.

The polygraph examination also enables the treatment team to be proactive in identifying precursors to possible sex cycles or patterns of abuse. When signs of deviant behavior patterns emerge, the team is quick to act on them to reduce the possibility of a reoffense.

Types of Examinations

In the Newport News Program, we administer three types of treatment-related polygraph examinations.

Full Disclosure Polygraph Examinations. The primary purpose of full sexual history disclosure examinations is twofold:

1. To verify that the offender has fully disclosed the kinds and frequency of sexual acts/abuse involving himself and the victim of record; and
2. To verify that the offender has fully disclosed the number of victims and acts of his sexual abuse, including all sexually motivated crimes, not just those similar to his crime of conviction.

As noted earlier, full disclosure of an offender's present offense as well as past sexual deviant history is essential to forming any effective treatment plan.

Maintenance Polygraph Examinations. The purpose of this "periodic" examination, every six months or less, is to determine whether the offender has complied with probation/parole and treatment conditions. Unauthorized contacts with minors or victims is especially scrutinized.

Specific Issue Examinations. Another type of polygraph test available to our program is a focused examination usually pertaining to a specific crime or accusation. These tests make up the majority of the polygraph tests conducted by police examiners. If an offender in our program was observed engaging in behavior that violated probation or parole and he denies the prohibited act, we might conduct an examination focused on that single issue.

Use of Polygraph Disclosures

Before an offender undertakes a polygraph, the team has already given him every reasonable opportunity to disclose all the relevant matters in treatment. For example, during the pretest interview the offender is given another opportunity to disclose any information that he has not previously divulged to the therapist, sexual offender group, or probation/parole officer. Quite often he makes new disclosures here.

If, subsequently, the polygraph test results expose deception, the examiner confronts the offender, which may prompt futher disclosures from the offender. The examiner notifies the probation/parole officer and the therapist via a written report, which also includes the relevant questions, all information divulged during the pre-test and post-test interviews, and the polygraph examiner's conclusions regarding the offender's truthfulness or deception. If results suggest a significant community or treatment concern, the examiner consults the probation/parole officer and therapist immediately.

Tests showing significant deception are presented to the group by the therapist, and the group confronts the offender. The probation/parole officer also addresses these issues separately with the offender and subsequently confers with the therapist and examiner. If further disclosures are forthcoming, they are documented and a follow-up polygraph is conducted to determine whether the offender is now telling the truth to the issues in question. Decisions to expel from treatment are left to the probation/parole officer in consultation with the therapist. This is a powerful example of the essential character of the teamwork exercised in the program.

The polygraph should be used as an investigative, risk assessment, and treatment tool, not as a final arbitrator of guilt or innocence. Admissions of new crimes or violations, or treatment failures, not polygraph failures, are reported to the releasing authorities and other appropriate local and state agencies involved in community safety.

Determining Questions Directed to the Offender

The determination of the issues to be covered during any examination is a collective decision made by the parole officer, therapist, and polygraph examiner. The parole officer and therapist are encouraged to suggest questions to be asked during the examination. However, the final determination of which questions are asked is the sole responsibility of the polygraph examiner.

The accuracy of any polygraph test depends in large part on the polygraph examiner's ability to properly phrase questions in order to elicit the appropriate response during the test. Polygraph examiners are trained to prepare questions worded in language that the subject understands. These questions deal directly with conduct and are specific to a particular behavior. The clearer the issue, the more identifiable the answer will be on the examination as either truthful or deceptive. Vague or nonspecific questions, for example, "Did you improperly touch Sarah?" or "Did you sexually offend Sarah?" can be confusing to the subject and difficult or impossible for the polygraph examiner to interpret. If the offender is able to cognitively distort a question, he may be able to "pass" or appear truthful on that question. He may rationalize, "I love Sarah, so I did not sexually offend her," and pass this question.

Polygraph questions are best when they are single meaning and short and precise in wording, for example, "Did you touch Sarah's vagina?" or "Did you put your finger in Sarah's vagina?" The direct questions, for example, "Did you touch Sarah's vagina?" do not allow the offender to use his distorted thinking.

Information Provided to the Polygraphist

Adequate background information is critical to the polygraph examiner when he is preparing to conduct any polygraph examination.Complete information concerning the crime or crimes committed as well as any other known sexual deviancy by the offender should be provided to the examiner.

All information available regarding the offender's general background should also be provided.

1. Offender's presentence report;
2. Police offense report;
3. Victim's statement;
4. Offender's statement;
5. Comments by parole officer; and
6. Comments by therapist.

Having adequate pretest information enables the polygraph examiner to properly select the right questions to ask during the instrumental phase of the examination. Unless the proper questions are asked during the test, results can be confusing and invalid.

Knowledge of the offender's overall background also enables the polygraph examiner to select the proper approach to use to solicit admissions during any post-test interrogation. Expert interrogation is, after all, nothing more than "the art and science of asking questions." When performed properly, questioning is a science, not random, and becomes the art of painting pictures with words (Arther & Caputo, 1959).

Finding a Qualified Polygraph Examiner

Not all probation/parole officers possess the qualifications or the desire to deal with sex offenders and not all polygraph examiners are qualified to successfully examine high-risk sex offenders. The selected polygraphist should be a highly qualified examiner trained to deal with sex offenders and must be a skilled interrogator.

It is advisable to check the prospective polygraphist's reputation in the professional community. The great majority of polygraph examiners in practice are competent and ethical and should be proud to share their professional credentials. Inquiries about the polygraphist's formal education and specialized training and experience—in particular, experience in testing sex offenders—are advisable.

Professional societies with membership limited to qualified polygraphists invite inquiries. The American Polygraph Association, which is the national association of qualified examiners, and the Academy of Certified Polygraphists, are organizations open to selected individuals. Both of these associations are happy to confirm whether a polygrapher is a member in good standing.

Conclusion

Polygraphy has moved from a method viewed with suspicion mixed with awe to a valuable tool in the supervision of sexual aggressors. Polygraphers work in concert with probation and parole officers to provide an integrated network of professionals who know and understand the individual offender and his high-risk situations. This is known as the containment approach (English, Pullen, & Jones, 1996), and a number of states are adopting this method as a way of maximizing public safety.

References

Abrams, S., & Abrams, J. (1993). *Polygraph testing of the pedophile.* Portland, OR: Ryan Gwinner Press.

Arther, R. O., & Caputo, R. R. (1959). *Interrogation for investigators.* New York: William C. Copp & Associates.

Barefoot, J. K. (Ed.). (1974). *The polygraph story.* Anniston, AL: American Polygraph Association.

English, K., Pullen, S., & Jones, L. (1996). *Managing adult sex offenders: A containment approach.* Denver: Colorado Division of Criminal Justice & American Probation and Parole Association.

Chapter 14

Two Measures for Tracking Participation in Treatment and Behavior Change in a Residential Sex Offender Program

by Nancy H. Walbek, Ph.D.

Overview

In 1992, Minnesota Security Hospital faced the challenge of rapidly developing a comprehensive treatment program to address the needs of a growing population of individuals with a history of sexual offending. This challenge was precipitated by a rapid increase in the number of men being committed for treatment under a 1939 sexual psychopathic personality statute. The rate of commitment under this and later similar legislation grew from one per year during the 1980s to one or two per month in the 1990s. Most of these new commitments came to the hospital after completing lengthy prison terms for their most recent offenses. This practice of confining an essentially criminal population under civil commitment statutes, which was originally done under the old sexual psychopaths laws, is being reinstituted across the country. This chapter describes the author's experience in assessing the participation in treatment and behavior change of this population within the context of a long-term locked treatment program. Ideally, her experience will be useful to others facing a similar challenge.

Introduction

In 1990, a vicious attack on a young boy in the state of Washington instigated the reenactment of involuntary commitment of sex offenders on the premise that these individuals suffer from a mental disorder that predisposes them to commit sexually violent acts. Consequently, they should be involuntarily committed for a day to life for treatment for this condition. Minnesota had one of the original sexual psychopath laws and when Washington repopularized this public policy, Minnesota's program suddenly was revitalized. Because these individuals must prove that they have successfully completed treatment before they can be released, the measurement of treatment progress is extremely important and is often the focus of legal battles between the offender who desires release and the State that is pursuing continued confinement.

Developing a Program for Involuntarily Committed

Minnesota's program was designed to be a nonpunitive therapeutic community that offers a variety of structured opportunities to develop social competencies. The interventions developed drew on social learning theories and include relapse prevention strategies. Review of the literature available at that time (especially Knopp, 1984; Laws, 1989; Marques, Day, Nelson, Miner, & West, 1991; Marshall, Jones, Ward, Johnston, & Barbaree, 1991; Pithers, 1982) and the staff's previous experience treating offenders provided the basis for our efforts. Patients are required to successfully complete four phases of the treatment program and demonstrate the capacity to successfully reintegrate into society before staff will support a provisional discharge to a less secure setting. (See Farnsworth, Seely, & Walbek, 1996, for a more complete description of the development and substance of this program.)

Given the strong public sentiment about sexual offenses and the intrusiveness of indefinite commitment, all components of this program are subject to intense scrutiny. This scrutiny comes from both the community, as represented in a panel that reviews requests for provisional discharge, and the patients themselves, who are often pursuing shortcuts to discharge. This environment makes it very important to maintain high levels of professionalism in the evaluation and treatment of patients. The thorough assessment and reassessment by qualified professionals from several disciplines and delivery of needed treatment services that characterized the hospital's programs for forensic patients were extended to committed sex offenders.

Awareness of the special needs of this program prompted enhanced efforts to monitor service delivery, patient participation, and progress toward treatment goals. The two empiric ratings described here were developed prior to the program's implementation and their routine administration has continued through more than four years of program operation. This consistency of data collection may prove valuable in future efforts to relate participation and evidence of observable behavioral change while in a locked program to later adjustment in the community.

The Measures of Treatment Progress

Daily Participation Rating Scales. Maintaining good records of daily program delivery and participation is a basic building block in evaluating both treatment programs and residents. This instrument was designed to document both the delivery of group-based services and characteristics of each individual's participation in each session of various treatment programs. Entry of the daily observations into a data base provided the means to summarize observations over time, both for the individual and for the comparison group of other residents participating in the same program.

Clinical staff from the departments of psychology, behavior analysis, and social services collaborated in the development of the instrument. Prior experience with ratings of group participation had highlighted the difficulty of using a single scale. Too many different types of behavior are evident in a single program event to permit meaningful rating on a one dimensional scale. For example, a midpoint score on a general scale of group participation may reflect (1) moderate levels of both support of others and self-examination; (2) exemplary support of others, no self-examination; or (3) insightful and open self-examination, no response to others' issues.

These concerns led to the decision to rate participation in each day's groups on several dichotomous decisions rather than a multilevel one-dimensional scale. For each group member, each of the following questions is answered yes or no following each group session:

1. Did he attend the session?
2. Did his hygiene meet minimum standards for grooming and dress for the activity?
3. Did he bring what was needed for the activity, e.g., pen or pencil, written assignments, or whatever else is needed for the particular program activity? This item is answered yes unless the rater observes a lack of some needed item.
4. Did he remain awake throughout the group and not disrupt the general flow by dominating, distracting, or diverting from the topic?
5. Did he make at least one verbal comment during the activity?
6. Did he verbalize support of others by making at least one positive comment to another person involved in the activity?
7. Did he confront others by offering an alternative perspective to another group member or describing the negative impact of another's behavior at least one time?
8. Did he address his personal treatment issues at least once during the session?
9. Was he open to feedback in at least one instance of being receptive to learning how he impacts or is seen by others or how his behavior might be improved?

Professional staff rate each member after each session. Collaboration between co-leaders to determine ratings is encouraged, but is not universally practiced. One data collection sheet is used for each group session. Group identification information including the group's code, date of group session, duration in minutes, and staff present to lead that group is recorded on a single sheet which also provides a grid for ratings of "1" (yes) or "0" (no) on all nine items for each of each of the residents assigned to the group.

Data collection sheets are turned in daily and entered into a database program by evening clerical staff. Weekly monitoring of data entry with reminders to submit missing data encourages staff to report all group sessions. Service delivery is monitored by comparing the frequency with which groups are reported as delivered to the program's design for frequency of service delivery. This practice is an important tool in quality management and insures prompt identification of areas where staff needs assistance in delivering the program as designed.

The information is tabulated in a variety of ways beyond monitoring service delivery. Summaries of ratings are printed at regular intervals (approximately every six weeks in this program), and these form the basis for routine entries in each man's medical record. At the end of each review period group leaders receive a packet of single page computer generated reports which include both individual and group summaries of participation during that reporting period. Individual reports list the date and duration of all sessions offered, whether or not the individual was present, and scores on items two through nine. The total score across these eight items is calculated and presented as a final column of data. Scores on this total can range between zero and eight.

Beneath the daily data, a summary for each of the ratings during the time period is calculated. Total number of sessions attended and total number of hours in session are the first two summary scores. For all other ratings, the sum of ratings in all sessions is divided by the number of groups attended. For all but the total score, these averages may vary between 0.00 and 1.00 and represent the proportion of times present that each of the remaining behaviors was evident. The average total score can range between zero and eight and reflects the average number of the eight rated positive behaviors displayed in groups attended during the time period. It can be seen that summarizing dichotomous ratings over numerous group sessions provides a continuous variable which is capable of reflecting more subtle differences than possible with single dichotomous ratings.

Group reports print a single row of date for each individual which includes his name and average scores during the reporting period. These group reports provide the group norms to which each individual's performance may be compared as group leaders prepare individual comments to supplement the printed data in describing the resident's group participation.

At the end of each reporting period, group leaders write their comments beneath each resident's computer generated report. The group leaders use their group's norms to describe each man's relative level of participation and supplement reporting based on the ratings with comments regarding the quality of participation and evidence of progress toward treatment goals. Similar reports are prepared for all group-based interventions and are placed in the resident's medical record and reviewed by his treatment team.

Sex Offender Rating Scales. The second of the two measures developed by this program attempted to move beyond the microscopic examination of daily participation in therapeutic programming to an assessment of the degree to which the outcomes targeted by treatment are manifest in daily behavior, both in treatment groups and in general hospital life. These scales represent an effort to quantify in vivo observations of residents of a long-term residential treatment program for sex offenders. Ratings reflect observation of both verbal and nonverbal behaviors in a variety of settings. The items were designed to address behaviors that are both observable and changeable within the institution. Relevance to the problems leading to hospitalization, scale reliability, and ease and economy of frequent administrations of the scale were principles guiding this effort.

Unknown to this author, a similar effort to develop an indicator of progress in sexual offender treatment was underway in Connecticut concurrent with our work (Anderson, Gibeau, & D'Amora, 1995). The instrument, called the Sex Offender Treatment Rating Scale, relies on therapists' ratings on 6-point scales with behavioral descriptors of six variables: insight, deviant thoughts, awareness of situational risks, motivation, victim empathy, and offense disclosure. Clearly both efforts were motivated by a perceived need for better measures of progress in sex offender treatment, and there is considerable overlap of the concepts addressed. One difference between the two instruments is that the one developed by Anderson et.al. focuses on verbal behavior within the setting of the treatment session. In contrast, the measure developed in Minnesota attempts to quantify behavior evident in a wider variety of settings.

In Minnesota, five scale areas were identified by program staff as universally important issues for this population:

1. Accountability (expression of an internal locus of control for the offense and appreciation of the impact of his behavior on others);
2. Impulse Control (thinking before acting);
3. Adult Daily Living Skills (daily self-care and time-structuring);
4. Relationships (quality of interaction with program peers and staff); and
5. Sexuality (openness in discussing sexuality and evidence of a process of self-management in this area).

Table 14.1 illustrates the twenty-five items used for this scale. Ideas for items came both from similar rating scales used by other treatment providers and from years of clinical experience with inpatient sex offenders. After several initial trials and revisions, four to six items were selected for each of the scale areas. All items are rated on a five-point incidence of observation scale ranging from "never" to "consistently." Higher scores always reflect more positive behavior.

Independent ratings of seventy-four residents were made by the psychologist and one other professional member of the treatment team working with each of four residential units to assess inter-rater reliability. For the full twenty-five-item instrument, correlation coefficients ranged between .54 and .80 (average = .74) for four replications, each including between sixteen and twenty-two patients. The single pair of raters generating a reliability coefficient less than .78 reported having limited opportunity for observation of the same behavior samples. Reliability coefficients for the subscales were lower, but for the three replications where the two raters had ample common observations they averaged between .66 and .69.

Three times each year, ratings on this scale are completed independently by five staff who work with each resident. At least three of the ratings are done by unit-based staff, one each from the classifications of security counselor, recreation therapist and nurse. The remaining two ratings are done by a psychologist or behavior analyst and a social worker. If the resident is involved in groups or psycho-educational groups with leaders from these disciplines, these ratings are done by people leading at least one of these groups. For men not participating in groups, the unit-based psychologist or behavior analyst and social worker complete the rating. Raters are instructed to

Table 14.1
Items Comprising the Sex Offender Rating Scales

Accountability
1. Verbalizes need to make specific personal changes.
2. Openly acknowledges historical and current hurtful behaviors.
3. Accurately describes magnitude and causes of his historical and current hurtful behaviors.
4. Clearly acknowledges impact of his behaviors on others.
5. Expresses remorse for hurt his behaviors have caused others.

Impulse Control
6. Pursues wants and needs in a reasonable manner.
7. Abstains from verbal and/or physical outbursts of feelings.
8. Displays restraint in spending and eating.
9. Discusses possible outcomes of decisions before acting.
10. Makes choices which minimize exposure to high-risk situations.

Adult Daily Living Skills
11. Maintains adequate personal hygiene.
12. Maintains responsible involvement in education and/or work.
13. Engages in a variety of leisure time activities.
14. Displays competence in activities such as cooking, laundry, maintaining living
    space.

Relationships
15. Maintains egalitarian peer relationships.
16. Expresses thoughts and feelings assertively.
17. Respects others' personal boundaries.
18. Verbalizes an awareness of others' point of view.
19. Collaborates with formulating and pursuing his own therapeutic interventions.
20. Communicates an understanding of the differences between abusive and
    nonabusive behavior.

Sexuality
21. Clearly discusses history of perpetrating sexual abuse.
22. Clearly describes current sexual thinking and behavior.
23. Reports a variety of nonabusive sexual thoughts.
24. Details personal process to modify sexual fantasy.
25. Current sexual behavior appears to be appropriate.

base their responses on their observations of the resident during the two weeks preceding observation.

   These ratings are entered into a data base and summarized on a computer printed
report. Each row of the report lists the date of that rating, the initials and discipline of

the rater, the average rating on the four to six items comprising each of the five sub-scales (possible range is between 0 and 4) and a total of all ratings (total can vary between 0 and 100). A summary row presents an average of the ratings provided by the five staff members.

These printed reports provide the basis for a note prepared by the psychologist working with that individual's treatment team and printed directly below the summary data. The psychologist has access to data which allows preparation of a note comparing current average total ratings to those earned previously by that individual and to the current norms for others in the same phase of the treatment program. The note may reflect further interpretation of the results by discussing the different sub-scales and the perspective from which the rating was made. For example, unit staff offer a valuable perspective on impulse control, adult daily living skills and relationships since the treatment team is interested in the generalization of these characteristics outside of the group therapy setting. On the other hand, group leaders are probably the best source of information on the scales assessing accountability and sexuality since these are the types of issues most often addressed in groups. These notes with both empirical and interpretive information are filed in each resident's medical record.

Relationship Between These Measures and Progress in Treatment

Some work has been done to assess the extent to which scores on these instruments correlate with broader clinically based decisions regarding placement and progress in treatment. It is important to note that in many cases the professional staff who rate program residents on these two instruments are also members of the treatment teams which make decisions about treatment placement and promotion. Even when the same staff are not involved, the reports using these two instruments are two of many sources of information considered as treatment teams review patient progress and make decisions about placement and promotion. Moreover, staff making the ratings are aware of each residents' assignment within the program's phases of treatment. Consideration of the findings presented below must bear in mind that the two variables are not fully independent. Indeed, to provide for full independence of ratings and treatment team decisions would require sufficient professional staff to permit two parallel subsets, one to apply the ratings without knowledge of the individual's program placement and the other to determine program placement without knowledge of the ratings. Settings offering this redundancy of staff are not known to this writer.

Total scores on both Daily Participation Rating Scales and Sex Offender Rating Scales show a positive association with current placement in the treatment program. In an assessment of this association, the average mean Daily Participation score across thirteen weeks of programming was 5.7 within a group of thirty-one early phase patients, 6.5 in the group of twenty-six Phase II patients, and 7.4 in the sixteen patients assigned to Phases III and IV of the program. When the frequency of falling above or below the overall median of Daily Participation scores was tabulated against these three levels of placement, the resulting chi square of 27.79 (2 df) has a probability value of less than .001.

Similar results were obtained for total scores on the Sex Offender Rating Scales. On three different replications of rating the entire program population, averages for residents in the introductory level of treatment varied between 25 and 31; in Phase I the group average ranged from 32 to 38; the average rating of men assigned to Phase II fell between 48 and 49, whereas the group average for Phase III patients varied between 61 and 77. The size of the group on which these means were based was twenty-five or greater in all but two of the twelve groups. For one of replication of Sex Offender Rating Scales administration, ratings of seventy-three residents were classified by treatment phase and lowest, middle and upper third of the distribution of scores. The resulting chi square was 72.59 (6 df), which has a probability value of less than .001.

Preliminary work suggests that the ratings may also be capable of predicting promotions from one treatment phase to the next. It appears that within the group of residents in the early phases of treatment, residents who earn promotion at their next team review have significantly higher scores on both measures than those who do not earn promotion. The Sex Offender Rating Scales seem to be more powerful predictors of promotion than are Daily Participation Ratings.

Conclusion

These findings indicate that two relatively simple rating systems show a great deal of agreement with a clinical team's more complicated assessment of program residents' current placement on a continuum from beginning treatment to nearing readiness for discharge. The results reported here need replication and additional research is also needed to sort out the relative value of different components of the ratings. Even in the absence of this research, the measures have served a need to clearly document service delivery and resident participation as well as to provide a system for quantifying observations of movement toward important treatment objectives. When the measures were first adopted, some staff voiced concern that communicating expected outcomes so clearly would make it easy for residents to insincerely comply with staff expectations. After several years of experience with these instruments, even the most skeptical of the staff acknowledge that the standards are too high and too pervasive across situations to make shallow compliance likely.

References

Anderson, R. D., Gibeau, D., & D'Amora, D. A. (1995). The sex offender treatment rating scale: Initial reliability data. *Sexual Abuse: A Journal of Research and Treatment, 7,* 221–227.

Farnsworth, M. G., Seely, R. K., & Walbek, N. H. (1996). *Evolution of sexual psychopath laws and design of a sex offender program in Minnesota.* St. Peter: Minnesota Security Hospital.

Knopp, F. H. (1984). *Retraining adult sex offenders: Methods and models.* Syracuse, NY: Safer Society Press.

Laws, D. R. (1989). *Relapse prevention with sex offenders.* New York: Guilford Press.

Marques, J. K., Day, D. M., Nelson, C., Miner, M. H., & West, M. A. (1991). *The sex offender treatment and evaluation project: Report to the legislature.* Sacramento: California Department of Mental Health.

Marshall, W. L., Jones, R., Ward, T., Johnston, P., & Barbaree, H. E. (1991). Treatment outcome with sex offenders. *Clinical Psychology Review, 11,* 465–485.

Pithers, W. D. (1982). *The Vermont Treatment Program for Sexual Aggressors: A program description.* Waterbury: Vermont Department of Corrections.

Chapter 15

Posttreatment Recidivism Rates in Sexual Aggressors—A Comparison Between Dropout and Nondropout Subjects

by Jean Proulx, Ph.D., Marc Ouimet, Ph.D., Bruno Pellerin, M.Sc., Yves Paradis, M.Sc., André McKibben, M.Sc., and Jocelyn Aubut, M.D.

Overview

The aim of the current study was to assess the impact of a treatment program (dropout, completed, extended) on the posttreatment recidivism rates of sexual aggressors. The treatment program included relapse prevention, social skill training, sex education, behavioral techniques to alter sexual preferences, anger management training, stress management training, and antiandrogenic treatment. Data on three types of recidivism (sexual; violent; criminal) were gathered for 102 child molesters and 70 rapists. During logistic regression analyses, we controlled for the impact of the following variables: subject's age, criminal history, gender of the last victim, follow-up period, and type of setting (inpatient, outpatient). The criminal recidivism rate for child molesters who completed the treatment program (5.7%) was lower than for those of the child molesters who did not complete the treatment (33.3%). As to the rapists, the criminal recidivism rate was lower for those who underwent an extended treatment program (38.5%) than for the other two groups (dropout: 70.8%; completed: 65%). These data showed that a cognitive behavioral treatment program reduced the recidivism rates in sexual aggressors. The optimal duration of treatment, however, varied according to the type of offender.

Introduction

During the last years, a debate has been going on regarding the efficacy of treatment programs for sexual aggressors. To the question "Can sexual offenders be effectively treated to reduce recidivism," the answer by W. L. Marshall is: "We believe that the evidence provides an unequivocally positive answer to this question although equally clearly, not all programs are successful and not all sex offenders profit from treatment. Comprehensive cognitive-behavioral programs and those programs that utilize antiandrogen in conjunction with psychological treatments seem to offer the greatest hope for effectiveness and future development. However, even here not all versions of these programs are equally effective and those that are, do far better with child molesters and exhibitionists than with rapists" (Marshall, Jones, Ward, Johnston, & Barbaree, 1991, p. 480). On the other hand, the answer by V. L. Quinsey is: "The effectiveness of treatment in reducing sex offender recidivism has not yet been scientifically demonstrated. To demonstrate the effectiveness of sex offender treatment, more well controlled outcome is required that can be evaluated with meta-analytic techniques" (Quinsey, Harris, Rice, & Lalumière, 1993, p. 512). How can it be that two such well-known researchers in the field of sexual aggression, Marshall and Quinsey, have such divergent opinions concerning the effectiveness of treatment programs for sexual offenders, especially as their opinions are based on a review of the same outcome studies? To clarify this controversy, we present the results of these outcome studies and analyze how both researchers and their colleagues interpreted the results.

Studying Dropout Rates

Marques et al. (1994) presented data regarding dropout subjects. Among 106 treated subjects, 7 child molesters and 1 rapist were considered dropouts because they stayed less than one year in the treatment program. Owing to the small number of dropouts, no separate data were provided for rapists and child molesters. The sexual recidivism rate was statistically significantly higher in the dropout group (37.5%) than in the group that completed the treatment program (8.2%). In addition, the violent recidivism rate was statistically significantly higher in the dropout group (37.5%) than in the group of subjects who completed the treatment program (8.2%). The results of two other studies indicated that the recidivism rate is higher in dropout groups than in the groups of subjects who completed their treatment program (Hildebran & Pithers, 1992; Miner & Dwyer, 1995). Unfortunately, in these two studies, no separate data were provided for rapists and child molesters. Nevertheless, these results indicated that dropouts are at higher risk of recidivism than sexual aggressors who completed cognitive-behavioral treatments.

Because none of the dropout studies carried out to date provided separate data for aggressors of women and child molesters, the aim of the current study was to verify whether posttreatment recidivism rates differ between dropout and nondropout rapists and child molesters.

Selection of Subjects

Between 1978 and 1993, 172 men with an official record of at least one hands-on sexual offense in Canada were treated at the Institut Philippe Pinel de Montréal, a maximum security psychiatric hospital (fifty-nine rapists and thirty-four child molesters) or at the outpatient clinic affiliated with this hospital (eleven rapists and sixty-eight child molesters).

Based on police and clinical reports obtained during their last sentence, those who had sexually assaulted adult women, pubescent girls under 18 years of age, or both, were classified as rapists ($n = 70$). Those who had molested girls or boys under 13 years of age, pubescent boys under 18 years of age, or a combination of these types of victims were classified as child molesters ($n = 102$). We use the term "sexual aggressors" to include both rapists and child molesters because they committed hands-on sexual offenses. Excluded from this study were subjects who were intellectually limited or suffering from serious mental disorders (affective or psychotic disorders) and those whose records consisted of noncontact sexual offenses such as exhibitionists and voyeurs.

The duration of the treatment program was two years. The sexual aggressors who were treated for less than twelve months were classified as dropouts (twenty-four rapists, thirty-nine child molesters); those who were treated between twelve and twenty-four months were classified as having their treatment completed (twenty rapists, thirty-five child molesters) and those who were treated more than twenty-four months were classified as having their treatment extended (twenty-six rapists, twenty-eight child molesters).

The treatment program was changed between 1978 and 1991. In 1991, the main components of the treatment program were as follows: (1) relapse prevention, (2) social skill training, (3) sex education, (4) behavioral techniques to alter sexual preferences, (5) anger management training, (6) stress management training, (7) antiandrogenic treatment, and (8) drug and alcohol abuse management training (Aubut, Proulx, Lamoureux, & McKibben, 1998).

Instruments Used in Assessment

Phallometric Assessment. Since the introduction in 1984 of phallometric assessments, initial phallometric data have been gathered on 124 subjects in our sample. The results of twenty-eight of these, however, were excluded from data analyses because these subjects had not shown penile increases of over 1 mm of diameter, representing approximately 10% to 15% of a full erection, depending on the size of the penis. These exclusions were necessary because a penile response of less than 10% of a full erection is considered uninterpretable (Castonguay, Proulx, Aubut, McKibben, & Campbell, 1993). The remaining ninety-six subjects consisted of thirty-seven rapists and fifty-nine child molesters.

The stimuli used for the rapists were French translations of English-language audiotaped recordings used by Abel, Blanchard, Becker, and Djenderedjian (1978). These stimuli have been demonstrated to differentiate rapists from nonrapists (Earls & Proulx, 1986; Proulx, Aubut, McKibben, & Côté, 1994). The audiotapes were categorized as follows: (1) mutually consenting sexual relationship, (2) rape, (3) nonsexual physical aggression, and (4) nonsexual, nonaggressive control stimulus. At each assessment, two audiotapes for each of the categories were used. The average duration of the audiotapes was 208.57 sec (SD = 29.82 sec.).

Audiotaped recordings, French translations of the Quinsey and Chaplin (1988) stimuli, were used for child molesters. These audiotaped stimuli were categorized as follows: (1) sexual interaction with a consenting adult, (2) passively consenting sexual relations (the child does not resist precoital caressing), (3) coercive sexual activities (child is not consenting to precoital caressing), (4) violent sexual behavior (nonconsenting child, physical violence used to achieve anal or vaginal coitus), (5) nonsexual violence (aggressor used violence without sexual activities), and (6) nonviolent, nonsexual control stimuli. Each assessment included eleven tapes, one of each category for both men and women. The average duration of the stimuli was 121.81 sec (SD = 12.89 sec).

Penile responses were measured with a mercury-in-rubber strain gauge (Bancroft, Jones, & Pullan, 1966). Electrical conductance changes in the gauge, resulting from changes in penile circumference, were recorded with a Grass poligraph (Model 7D). Penile responses were recorded during stimulus presentation only. For further details of the stimuli, the apparatus, and the procedure, see Castonguay et al. (1993), Proulx (1989), Proulx et al. (1994), and Proulx, Côté, and Achille (1993). For each subject, the raw scores were used to calculate deviance indices.

For the rapists, the rape index consisted of a ratio of maximal penile response obtained during rape stimuli as the numerator and maximal penile response to mutually consenting sexual activities stimuli as the denominator. The aggression index consisted of a ratio of the same denominator and maximal penile response obtained during nonsexual physical aggression stimuli as the numerator.

For the child molesters assessed with audiotape recordings, seven pedophilic indices were calculated: three for heterosexual stimuli, three for homosexual stimuli, and one for both types of stimuli. The three heterosexual pedophilic indices were ratios of maximal penile response during the heterosexual adult stimulus as the denominator and maximal penile response obtained during each of the heterosexual pedophilic stimuli (passively consenting sexual activities, coercive sexual activities, and violent sexual behavior) as the numerators. The three homosexual pedophilic indices were calculated the same way as the heterosexual pedophilic indices. The global pedophilic index consisted of a ratio of maximal penile response to any of the pedophilic stimuli as the numerator and maximal penile response to any of the adult stimuli as the denominator.

Psychometric Assessment. The psychometric assessment set for sexual aggressors was introduced at the Institut Philippe Pinel de Montréal in 1987. Consequently, initial psychometric data were compiled for fifty-three subjects only (twenty rapists, thirty-three child molesters). The psychometric assessment set included a French version of the following questionnaires: State–Trait Anxiety Inventory (Spielberger, Gorsuch, & Lushene, 1970), Beck Depression Inventory (Beck, Ward, Mendelson, Mock, & Erbaugh, 1961), Anger Inventory Questionnaire (Novaco, 1975), Miller Social Intimacy Scale (Miller & Lefcourt, 1982), Satisfaction with Life Scale, Rape Myth Acceptance (Burt, 1980), and Abel and Becker Cognitive Scale (Abel et al., 1989).

Criminal History. Criminal history variables were collected from all the subjects to obtain the following information: (1) total of previous charges for sexual offenses, (2) total of previous charges for nonsexual violent offenses, (3) total of previous charges for nonsexual, nonviolent offenses, (4) total of convictions before initial assessment, (5) duration of last sentence, (6) number of victims involved in the last conviction, (7) age of the last victim involved in the last conviction, (8) relationship between aggressor and last victim involved in the last conviction, and (9) gender of last victim involved in the last conviction. These variables were coded from institutional files and from the Fingerprint Service of the Royal Canadian Mounted Police.

Demographic Data. This section includes the subjects' ages and relationship status. Subjects who were single, divorced, or separated at the time of the last offense were coded as living alone. Subjects who were married or living with a partner were coded as not living alone. These variables were coded also from institutional files.

Measuring Outcome

The main source of information for outcome variables was the Fingerprint Service of the Royal Canadian Mounted Police. For all subjects, the follow-up time ended in 1994 but began at different times between 1978 and 1993 (mean, 55.9 months; range, 1–155 months). For incarcerated subjects, the follow-up time was estimated to start after two thirds of their sentence had been served, this being the usual time of their release under mandatory supervision. For sujbects assessed at the outpatient clinic, the follow-up time started on the day of the initial assessment.

Recidivism was defined in three ways: sexual recidivism, violent recidivism, and criminal recidivism. The first type of recidivism referred to a new conviction for at least one sexual offense committed during the follow-up period. Violent recidivism referred to a new conviction for at least one offense against a person (sexual or nonsexual violent offenses). Criminal recidivism referred to any conviction regardless of the type of offense (sexual or nonsexual violent or nonsexual nonviolent). Due to plea bargaining, we used a cumulative hierarchy in which each additional category included new information and subsumed that of previous categories. In fact, some subjects may have had nonsexual charges following a sexual offense (Rice et al., 1991).

Treated Child Molesters Show Lower Recidivism

Table 15.1 shows recidivism rates (sexual, violent, criminal) of child molesters for three treatment durations (dropout, treatment completed, treatment extended).

Table 15.1
Recidivism Rates (Frequency) of Child Molesters for Three Types of Treatment Duration

	Treatment Duration		
Type of recidivism	Dropout (n = 39) (0–11 months)	Treatment completed (n = 35) (12–24 months)	Treatment extended (N = 28) (more than 24 months)
Sexual	20.5% (8)	5.7% (2)	21.4% (6)
Violent	20.5% (8)	5.7% (2)	28.6% (8)
Criminal	33.3% (13)	5.7% (2)	32.1% (9)

Logistic regression analyses were carried out to verify whether differences in recidivism rates were statistically significant. During these analyses, at the first step we controlled for the impact of variables demonstrated to be related to recidivism rates in child molesters: (1) subject's age, (2) previous convictions for a sexual offense, (3) previous convictions for a nonsexual nonviolent offense, (4) gender of the last victim, (5) duration of follow-up period, and (6) type of therapeutic setting (Proulx et al., 1997). At the second step of these analyses, we assessed the impact of treatment duration on recidivism rates.

Table 15.2 shows statistics (model chi square, degree of freedom, significance) for the two steps in the logistic regression for three types of recidivism. For sexual recidivism, the model chi square for the variable treatment duration (step 2) is marginally significant ($p = .05$). Regarding violent and criminal recidivism, however, models chi square for the variable treatment are statistically significant; as to the violent recidivism the subjects having completed their treatment had a significantly lower recidivism rate than did those having their treatment extended [R (partial correlation coefficient) = .27, wald = 7.37, $p < .01$]. Regarding criminal recidivism, the subjects

Table 15.2
Statistics (Model Chi Square, Degree of Freedom, Significance) for Logistic Regressions for Three Types of Recidivism of Child Molesters

Type of Recidivism	Step in the Logistic Regression	X^2	df	p
Sexual	Step 1 (control)	21.8	6	.001
	Step 2 (treatment duration)	5.9	2	.05
Violent	Step 1 (control)	19.4	6	.004
	Step 2 (treatment duration)	10.8	2	.005
Criminal	Step 1 (control)	29.1	6	.001
	Step 2 (treatment duration)	19.3	2	.002

Figure 15.1
Survival Rates (Violent Recidivism) for Child Molesters in Three Types of Treatment Duration

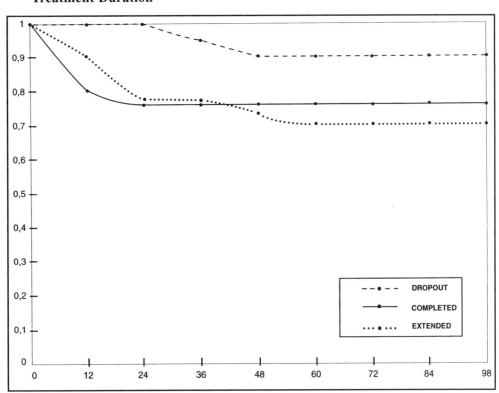

who completed their treatment had a significantly lower recidivism rate than the dropouts (R = .19, wald = 4.71, $p < .05$) and those having their treatment extended (R = .29, wald = 8.52, $p < .01$). Therefore, in child molesters, violent and criminal recidivism rates varied with treatment duration. The child molesters who completed their treatment had the lower rate of recidivism.

Figure 15.1 shows survival rates (violent recidivism) for child molesters in three types of treatment duration. The child molesters who completed their treatment did not recidivate before forty-eight months, whereas those in the two other treatment duration started to recidivate twelve months after treatment completion. Survival curves for sexual and criminal recidivism have the same shape as those for violent recidivism.

As to the phallometric and psychometric variables, child molesters who completed their treatment were not significantly different from those in the two other groups (dropout, extended treatment). Statistical powers in those comparisons, however, were low due to small numbers of subjects in each group. Consequently, some differences among the groups, although important, did not reach statistical significance. Specifically, the child molesters having their treatment extended had a mean pedophilic index (passively consenting) of 3.8, whereas those in the two other groups had a mean pedophilic index of 2.2. Furthermore, the child molesters having their treatment extended had a mean score of 118.0 at the Abel and Becker Cognitive Scale,

Table 15.3
Recidivism Rates (Frequency) of Rapists for Three Types of Treatment Duration

	Treatment Duration		
Type of recidivism	Dropout (n = 24) (0–11 months)	Treatment completed (n = 20) (12–24 months)	Treatment extended (N = 26) (more than 24 months)
Sexual	20.8% (5)	35.0% (7)	23.1% (6)
Violent	54.2% (13)	50.2% (10)	26.9% (7)
Criminal	70.8% (17)	65.0% (13)	38.5% (10)

whereas the dropouts had a mean score of 103.2 and those who completed their treatment had a mean score of 108.9.

Rapists in Extended Program Do Best

Table 15.3 shows recidivism rates (sexual, violent, criminal) of rapists for three treatment duration (dropout, treatment completed, treatment extended). Logistic regression analyses were carried out to verify whether differences in recidivism rates were statistically significant. During those analyses, at the first step we controlled for the impact of variables that have been demonstrated to be related to recidivism in rapists: (1) subject's age; (2) previous convictions for sexual offenses; (3) previous convictions for nonsexual, violent offenses; (4) previous convictions for nonsexual, nonviolent offenses; and (5) duration of the follow-up period (Proulx et al., 1997). At the second step of the analyses, we assessed the impact of treatment duration on recidivism rates.

Table 15.4 shows statistics (model chi square, degree of freedom, significance) for the two steps in the logistic regression for three types of recidivism. For the three

Table 15.4
Statistics (Model Chi Square, Degree of Freedom, Significance) for Logistic Regressions for Three Types of Recidivism of Rapists

Type of Recidivism	Step in the Logistic Regression	X^2	df	p
Sexual	Step 1 (control)	16.1	5	.007
	Step 2 (treatment duration)	1.5	2	.47
Violent	Step 1 (control)	34.8	5	.001
	Step 2 (treatment duration)	2.1	2	.35
Criminal	Step 1 (control)	33.1	5	.001
	Step 2 (treatment duration)	2.3	2	.33

Figure 15.2
Survival Rates (Violent Recidivism) for Rapists in Three Types of Treatment Duration

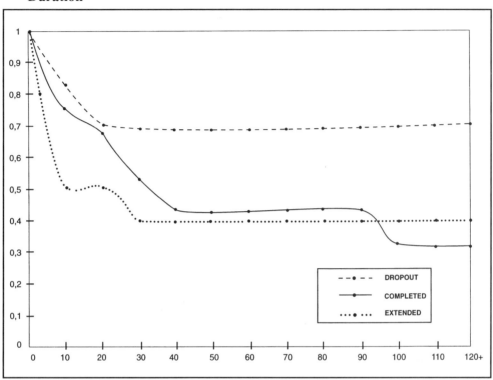

types of recidivism, the model chi square for the variable treatment duration (step 2) is not significant. Therefore, in rapists, recidivism rates did not varied with treatment duration.

Figure 15.2 shows survival rate (criminal recidivism) for rapists in three types of treatment duration. Rapists in the first three groups recidivated during the first twelve months of the follow-up period. For those having an extended treatment program, however, there was no more recidivism after twenty-four months of follow-up. For the other two groups (dropout, treatment completed) survival rate diminished up to forty-eight months of follow-up. Survival curves for sexual and violent recidivism had the same shape as those for criminal recidivism.

As to the phallometric and psychometric variables, rapists who had their treatment extended were not significantly different from those in the two other groups (dropout, treatment completed). Statistical power in those comparisons, however, was low owing to the small numbers of subjects in each group. Consequently, some differences among the groups, although important, did not reach statistical significance. Specifically, the rapist dropouts had a mean score of 109.5 ($SD = 4.1$) on the Rape Myth Acceptance Questionnaire, whereas those who completed the treatment program had a mean score of 94.2 ($SD = 17.5$) and those who had their treatment extended had a mean score of 90.3 ($SD = 16.6$). Furthermore, the rapist dropouts had a mean score of 302.0 ($SD = 80.2$) on the Novaco Anger Inventory, whereas those who completed the treatment program had a mean score of 291.4 (SD = 51.1) and those who had their treatment extended had a mean score of 274.6 (SD = 47.1).

Different Patterns of Recidivism Noted

In our sample of treated child molesters, the sexual recidivism rate was higher in dropouts (20.5%) than in those who completed a cognitive-behavioral treatment program (5.7%). The difference between the two groups is marginally significant. The results of Marques et al. (1994), however, indicated that the recidivism rate of sexual aggressors (seven child molesters, one rapist) who dropped out (28.6%) was statistically significantly higher than the rate of those who completed the cognitive-behavioral treatment program (7.9%). Therefore, our results as to the sexual recidivism rate agree with those obtained by Marques et al. (1994). The differences between the two studies, as to the statistical significance, may be owing to the low statistical power (Cohen, 1992) in recidivism studies (Barbaree, 1997; Hanson, 1997; Weisburd, Petrosino, & Mason, 1993). Because violent recidivism in child molesters who dropped out and those who completed the treatment program consisted mainly in sexual recidivism, no separate discussion is necessary.

In our sample of treated child molesters, the criminal recidivism rate was statistically significantly higher in dropouts (33.3%) than in those who completed the treatment program (5.7%). Such results give the impression that a treatment program designed to reduce sexual recidivism rates do better with the criminal recidivism rate. A probable explanation for these results is that the base rate for criminal recidivism is higher than for sexual recidivism. Consequently, the statistical power is higher for the analyses on criminal recidivism than for those for sexual recidivism (Barbaree, 1997; Marshall & Pithers, 1994).

Beyond the controversy as to the base rate and the statistical power, we must explain why a treatment program designed to reduce sexual recidivism is also effective for other types of crimes. A possible explanation is that child molesters learned social skills during the course of their treatment program. Consequently, they may cope appropriately with social and occupational stressful situations rather than using antisocial means to achieve their goals.

The survival curves indicate that child molesters in our study were at risk of recidivism for many years. Recidivism rates, however, were higher during the first four years of follow-up than in the following years. Other studies have also found such results (Hanson, Steffy, & Gauthier, 1993; Marques et al., 1994).

In our sample of child molesters, violent and criminal recidivism rates were higher for those having an extended treatment program than for those who completed the regular treatment program. A possible explanation for these unexpected results is that the child molesters who had an extended treatment were the most deviant and required longer supervision than did the other aggressors. In support of this hypothesis, our results indicated that the child molesters who had an extended treatment were more deviant (sexual preferences for children, cognitive distortions justifying sexual contacts with children) than those in the other two groups. Because current treatment programs, although extended, seem to be ineffective in reducing recidivism in child molesters, additional management strategies must be considered (e.g., chemical castration and preventive incarceration).

In our sample of treated rapists, the violent recidivism rates were higher in dropouts (54.2%) and in those who completed the regular treatment program (50.2%) than in those who received an extended treatment program (26.9%). Furthermore, the criminal recidivism rates were higher in dropouts (70.8%) and in those who completed the regular treatment program (65.0%) than in those who received an extended treatment program (38.5%). These differences among the groups, however, are not significant when we statistically control for the impact of factors related to recidivism rates (step 1 in the logistic regressions).

Regarding the statistical power in the analysis carried out with the rapists' data, we noted that it is decreased by the small number of subjects but increased by a high base rate of recidivism (Barbaree, 1997). Therefore, the statistical power in these analyses is low. Consequently, our data seem to indicate that an extended cognitive-behavioral treatment program (more than two years) may be necessary to reduce recidivism rates in rapists. Data from other studies, which indicated that treatment programs of less than two years are ineffective in reducing recidivism rates in rapists (Marshall et al., 1991; Marques et al., 1994), support this conclusion.

Conclusion

Our study is the first to separately investigate recidivim rates in rapists and in child molesters who dropped out of a cognitive-behavioral treatment program. Furthermore, our study included groups of sexual aggressors who received an extended treatment program. Unfortunately, owing to ethical and administrative restrictions, a random assignment procedure has not been used to form a control group of untreated aggressors. Therefore, a full assessment of the efficacy of the cognitive-behavioral treatment program of the Institut Philippe Pinel de Montreal requires further studies.

Note

The research reported in this paper was funded by the Ministry of the Solicitor General of Canada (9514-IN/525). The views expressed are those of the authors and are not necessarily those of the Ministry. The authors wish to thank Elvira Stahl for her substantive and stylistic editing and Louise Grenier for providing us with criminal records.

References

Abel, G. G., Blanchard, E. B., Becker, J. V., & Djenderedjian, A. (1978). Differentiating sexual aggressives with penile measures. *Criminal Justice and Behavior, 5,* 315–332.

Abel, G. G., Gore, D. K., Holland, C. L., Camp, N., Becker, J. V., & Rathner, J. (1989). The measurement of the cognitive distortions of child molesters. *Annals of Sex Research, 2,* 135–153.

Aubut, J., Proulx, J., Lamoureux, B., & McKibben, A. (1998). Sexual offenders' treatment program of the Philippe-Pinel Institute of Montreal. In W. L. Marshall, Y. M., Fernandez, S. M. Hudson, & T. Ward (Eds.), *Sourcebook of treatment programs for sexual offenders* (pp. 221–233). New York: Plenum Press.

Bancroft, J., Jones, H. G., & Pullan, B. R. (1966). A simple transducer for measuring penile erection with comments on its use in the treatment of sexual disorders. *Behaviour Research and Therapy, 4,* 239–241.

Barbaree, H. E. (1997). Evaluating treatment efficacy with sexual offenders: The sensitivity of recidivism studies to treatment effect. *Sexual Abuse: A Journal of Research and Treatment, 9,* 111–128.

Beck, A. T., Ward, C. H., Mendelson, M., Mock, J., & Erbaugh, J. (1961). An inventory for measuring depression. *Archives of General Psychiatry, 14,* 561–571.

Becker, J. V., & Hunter, J. A. (1992). Evaluation of treatment outcome for adult perpetrators of child sexual abuse. *Criminal Justice and Behavior, 19,* 74–92.

Burt, M. R. (1980). Cultural myths and support for rape. *Journal of Personality and Social Psychology, 38,* 217–230.

Castonguary, L. G., Proulx, J., Aubut, J., McKibben, A., & Campbell, M. (1993). Sexual preference assessment of sexual aggressors: Predictors of penile response magnitude. *Archives of Sexual Behavior, 22,* 325–334.

Cohen, J. (1992). A power primer. *Psychological Bulletin, 112,* 155–159.

Earls, C. M., & Proulx, J. (1986). The differentiation of francophone rapists and nonrapists using penile circumferential measures. *Criminal Justice and Behavior, 13,* 419–429.

Furby, L., Weinrott, M. R., & Blackshaw, L. (1989). Sex offender recidivism. *Psychological Bulletin, 105,* 3–30.

Hall, G. N. C. (1995). Sexual offender recidivism revisited: A meta-analysis of recent treatment studies. *Journal of Consulting and Clinical Psychology, 63*(5), 802–809.

Hanson, R. K. (1997). How to know what works with sexual offenders. *Sexual Abuse: A Journal of Research and Treatment, 9,* 129–145.

Hanson, R. K., & Bussière, M. T. (1998). Predicting relapse: A meta-analysis of sexual offender recidivism studies. *Journal of Consulting and Clinical Psychology, 66,* 348–362.

Hanson, R. K., Steffy, R. A., & Gauthier, R. (1993). Long-term recidivism of child molesters. *Journal of Consulting and Clinical Psychology, 61,* 646–652.

Hildebran, D. D., & Pithers, W. D. (1992). Relapse prevention: Application and outcome. In W. O'Donohue, & J. H. Geer (Eds.), *The sexual abuse of children: clinical issues* (vol. 2, pp. 365–393), Hillsdale, NJ: Erlbaum.

Kelly, R. J. (1982). Behavioral reorientation of pedophiliacs: Can it be done? *Clinical Psychology Review, 2,* 387–408.

Marques, J. K., Day, D. M., Nelson, C., & West, M. A. (1994). Effects of cognitive-behavioral treatment on sex offender recidivism: Preliminary results of a longitudinal study. *Criminal Justice and Behavior, 21,* 28–54.

Marshall, W. L., & Barbaree, H. E. (1988). The long-term evaluation of a behavioral treatment program for child molesters. *Behaviour Research and Therapy, 26,* 499–511.

Marshall, W. L., Jones, R., Ward, T., Johnston, P., & Barbaree, H. E. (1991). Treatment outcome with sex offenders. *Clinical Psychology Review, 11,* 465–485.

Marshall, W. L., & Pithers, W. D. (1994). A reconsideration of treatment outcome with sex offenders. *Criminal Justice and Behavior, 21,* 10–27.

Meyers, L. C., & Romero, J. J. (1980). *A ten-year follow-up of sex offender recidivism.* Philadelphia: J. J. Peters Institute.

Miller, R. S., & Lefcourt, H. M. (1982). The assessment of intimacy. *Journal of Personality Assessment, 66,* 514–518.

Miner, M. H. (1997). How can we conduct treatment outcome research. *Sexual Abuse: A Journal of Research and Treatment, 9,* 95–110.

Miner, M. H., & Dwyer, S. M. (1995). Analysis of dropouts from outpatient sex offender treatment. *Journal of Psychology and Human Sexuality, 7,* 77–93.

Nicholaichuk, T. (1997). *Does participation in treatment reduce recidivism.* Paper presented at the National Conference: Community notification and other techniques for managing high-risk and dangerous offenders. Winnipeg, Canada.

Novaco, R. W. (1975). *Anger control.* Lexington, MA: Lexington Press.

Peters, J. J., & Roether, H. A. (1971). *Success and failure of sex offenders.* Philadelphia: American Association for the Advancement of Science.

Proulx, J. (1989). Sexual preference assessment of sexual aggressors. *International Journal of Law and Psychiatry, 12,* 275–280.

Proulx, J., Aubut, J., McKibben, A., & Côté, M. (1994). Penile responses of rapists and non rapists to rape stimuli involving physical violence or humiliation. *Archives of Sexual Behavior, 23,* 295–310.

Proulx, J., Côté, G., & Achille, P. A. (1993). Prevention of voluntary control of penile response in homosexual pedophiles during phallometric testing. *Journal of Sex Research, 30,* 140–147.

Proulx, J., Pellerin, B., Paradis, Y., McKibben, A., Aubut, J., & Ouimet, M. (1997). Static and dynamic predictors of recidivism in sexual aggressors. *Sexual Abuse: A Journal of Research and Treatment, 9,* 7–27.

Quinsey, V. L., & Chaplin, T. C. (1988). Penile responses of child molesters and normals to descriptions of encounters with children involving sex and violence. *Journal of Interpersonal Violence, 3,* 259–274.

Quinsey, V. L., Harris, G. T., Rice, M. E., & Lalumière, M. L. (1993). Assessing treatment efficacity in outcome studies of sex offenders. *Journal of Interpersonal Violence, 8,* 512–523.

Rice, M. E., Harris, G. T., & Quinsey, V. L. (1993). Evaluating treatment programs for child molesters. In J. Hudson & I. V. Roberts (Eds.), *Evaluation research in canadian justice programs.* Calgary: University of Calgary Press.

Rice, M. E., Quinsey, V. L., & Harris, G. T. (1991). Sexual recidivism among child molesters released from a maximum security psychiatric institution. *Journal of Consulting and Clinical Psychology, 59,* 381–386.

Spielberger, C. G., Gorsuch, R. L., & Lushene, R. D. (1970). *Manual for the State–Trait Anxiety Inventory (self-evaluation questionnaire).* Palo Alto, CA: Consulting Psychologist Press.

Weisburd, D., Petrosino, A., & Mason, G. (1993). Design sensitivity in criminal justice experiments. In M. Tonry (Ed.), *Crime and justice: A review of research* (vol. 17, pp. 337–378). Chicago: Chicago University Press.

Part 3

Adolescent Sex Offenders

Adolescent sex offender treatment was once relatively uncommon compared with programs for adult offenders, but it has flourished in the last ten years. Numerous community-based and residential sex offender programs that specialize in the treatment of adolescents have sprung up. These programs seem to have more public support and may be easier to sell to a skeptical public, which may still have some hope for children and teens who act out sexually. Also, the term "sexually reactive children" elicits sympathy as it is a reminder that these "offenders" started out as "victims."

There are a number of controversies surrounding the treatment of adolescent offenders that are argued among those who supervise and treat juvenile sex offenders. Are juvenile sex offenders psychologically just small adult sex offenders, which would imply that they need the same treatment, supervision, and public policies? Or, are they unique, and if so, in what ways? If we assume that you cannot "cure" a sex offender—that is, it will be a problem all of their lives—is the same true for juveniles? Is it effective and prudent public policy to try adolescents who commit sex offenses as adults and place them in prisons with adult offenders? Does it enhance public safety to issue public notification bulletins on adolescent sex offenders?

Adolescent sex offenders are complicated, with multiple overlapping problems. Rarely can their treatment focus solely on their sexual acting out. Usually they have been victims of a variety of types of abuses. They often suffer from concomitant problems, such as various types of emotional problems, addictive disorders, and a variety of behavioral issues. Thus, their treatment must be multimodal. In addition, treatment must include family members, who are usually still responsible for these children and must be taught how to reinforce therapeutic gains and provide appropriate supervision.

Not only must treatment for juvenile sex offenders focus on their multiple problems, but it must also be geared to the learning needs of this population. Many of these clients may have learning disabilities or may have had negative school experiences. They may have difficulties sitting still in groups or talking through their problems. Therapy needs to accommodate these differences and be able to adapt to individuals who may need more experiential and physically active types of treatment.

Public policies must also be geared for the heterogeneous nature of this group. It is true that some juvenile offenders are sophisticated psychopaths who are indistinguishable from adult criminals, but there are other juvenile offenders of the same age who are still children. These individuals are not sophisticated criminals. They are still malleable. Incarcerating them in adult prisons may well have disastrous results for the offenders and eventually for the public.

Fortunately, most states do not include juveniles in their Megan's Law policies. However, a number of states do not distinguish between adults and juveniles in their public notification procedures. Is it reasonable to expect that these individuals will be able to attend school, participate in extracurricular activities, or otherwise adjust to the community when everyone with whom they are likely to interact knows all about their history of sexual acting out. The reasonableness of public notification will not be debated here, but all the criticisms for this public policy are magnified when it is applied to adolescents and their families.

Part 3 provides information on developing programs for adolescent sex offenders. David P. Fago has conducted a study that analyzes the proportion of juvenile sex offenders that also suffer from attention-deficit/hyperactivity disorder (ADHD). He correlates the symptoms of this problem with the characteristics of juvenile sex offenders. Both groups show a lack of empathy and sensitivity to others. Both are vulnerable to substance abuse and have a variety of difficulties controlling their behavior. Both groups tend to be "sensation seekers" and to show hypersexuality. However, juveniles with ADHD are suffering from a neurological disorder that cannot be adequately treated without medication. Thus, an investigator attempting to treat a juvenile sex offender who is also afflicted with this comorbid disorder will be significantly handicapped. Dr Fago urges adequate assessment for this condition and recommends treatments for the two disorders.

Collette Corcoran, Alexis O. Miranda, Kathleen W. Tenukas-Strebla, and Ben D. Taylor discuss the inclusion of the family in the treatment of the adolescent sex offender. Although the rationale behind this premise is obvious, some treatment programs do not give this issue adequate attention. This is particularly important given the high percentage of adolescent sex offenders who are charged with offending against other family members. The family will not only have to offer protection to other siblings of the youthful offender but must be thoroughly familiar with the offenders' relapse prevention plan and high-risk situations. The authors discuss the challenge of treating these families, which are often dysfunctional and may even include other offenders. They outline a schedule of phases for this important work.

Fred Schmidt and Laura Heinz present a follow-up study on the efficacy of their treatment program for adolescent sex offenders. They offer a review of other treatment programs for this group. They then discuss the outcome of thirty-three juveniles followed from twelve to fifty-four months. An interesting aspect of this study is that it contrasts sexual recidivists with non–sexual recidivists and draws some interesting implications.

James M. Yokley presents ideas on how to modify the experiences found in therapeutic communities (TCs). This author and his colleagues devised an interesting model, utilizing a day treatment model combined with therapeutic foster homes. Although their patients were not living in a residential unit, the therapists were able to adapt many of the techniques used in TCs. They conducted a study in which they alternatively introduced and then withdrew the use of these modalities. Yokley also discusses using these techniques with preteen abusers. The focus here is on creating a model of a functional family.

Adolescent sex offenders present a quandary for society. At one extreme they are seen as highly dangerous, predatory criminals who, if charged with certain crimes, are to be automatically bound over as adults and sent to adult prisons. Unfortunately few departments of corrections are prepared to deal with this population. If these adolescent offenders are placed in specialized sex offender treatment programs, they are exposed to seasoned pedophiles who may prey on them. If not offered treatment, they may simply continue to indulge in deviant fantasies and become progressively worse. On the other hand, they may be seen as children involved in innocent exploration and what is truly offending behavior may be ignored. Fortunately, a number of specialized programs are becoming available. Now, education for the judiciary, probation, and evaluators is necessary to help sort out which juvenile sex offenders need to be treated as adults, which need actual sex offender treatment, and which need only minimal counseling and education regarding their sexual behavior.

Chapter 16

Comorbidity of Attention-Deficit/Hyperactivity Disorder in Sexually Aggressive Children and Adolescents

by David P. Fago, Ph.D.

Overview

In a retrospective field study of thirty-five children and adolescents evaluated for sexually aggressive behavior (nonconsensual sexual touching of another child or adult), a significant majority of the children and adolescents were determined to have a diagnosis of attention-deficit/hyperactivity disorder (ADHD). This incidence was found to be significantly greater than (1) the base rate diagnosis of ADHD for all children and adolescents evaluated at this facility during the same period, and (2) the incidence for ADHD reported for the general population. The author discusses these findings in terms of (1) the possible role of ADHD as an etiological factor in childhood sexual aggression and (2) the importance of screening for ADHD in the evaluation and treatment of child and adolescent sexual offenders.

Introduction

The existing research on juvenile and adult sexual offenders has identified several factors that are positively correlated with sexual aggression and assault. These include (1) a history of sexual or other abuse to the offender (Barnard, Robbins, Newman, & Hutchinson, 1985; Finkelhor, 1988; Freeman-Longo, 1985; Groth, 1979;

Langevin, Wright, & Handy, 1989; Petrovich & Templer, 1984; Pierce & Pierce, 1987; Seghorn, Prentky, & Boucher, 1987; Smith, 1988); (2) a history of family dysfunction (Monastersky & Smith, 1985; Lewis, Shankon, & Pincus, 1985; Smith, 1988); (3) deficits in the offender's personality, particularly in social and interpersonal competence (Blaske, Borduin, Henggeler, & Mann, 1989; Fehrenbach, Smith, & Monastersky, 1986; Figia, Lang, Plutchik, & Holden, 1987; Groth, 1977); (4) previous exposure to pornography and/or sexual violence (Becker & Stein, 1991; Candeon & Nutter, 1988; Carter, Prentky, Knight, Venderveer, & Boucher, 1987; Ford & Linney, 1995; Pynoos & Nader, 1988); and (5) the offender's use of "cognitive distortions" (i.e., distortions in thinking and feeling that potentiate the sexually aggressive behavior) (Hayashino, Wurtele, & Klebe, 1995).

Although some studies have noted the frequent presence of long-standing learning problems in sexual offender populations (Awad & Saunders, 1991; Lewis et al., 1979; Pierce & Pierce, 1987; Tarter, Hegedus, Alterman, & Katzgaar, 1983), only a few (Kavoussi, Kaplan, & Becker, 1988; Ryan, 1991; James & Neil, 1996) have briefly mentioned the possible role of ADHD (ADHD or ADD) in childhood sexual aggression. Moreover, a recently published literature review (Hall & Barongan, 1997) of the causes of sexual aggression actually minimizes the importance of childhood learning problems or neurodevelopmental deficits as contributory factors to sexual aggression. Nevertheless, children and adolescents with ADHD are of special interest in this regard because (1) such youngsters frequently display coñmorbid antisocial-spectrum disorders (Hinshaw, 1987; Lynam, 1996), exceeding 50% in many samples (Biederman, Newcorn, & Sprich, 1991), and (2) ADHD is, by itself, a strong predictor of delinquency and conduct disorders in adolescence and adulthood (Klein & Manuzza, 1991). The possible role of ADHD in sexual aggression is implicated further by a body of anecdotal, clinical information that associates ADHD in adulthood with episodes of hypersexuality and inappropriate sexual acting out (Hallowell & Ratey, 1994).

ADHD: A Neurodevelopmental Disorder

Of the three features identified as hallmarks of ADHD (impulsivity, distractibility/attention deficits, and hyperactivity; see American Psychiatric Association, 1994, and Connors, 1994), impulsivity is thought to be the significant catalyst to antisocial behavior in the ADHD population (Hinshaw, Simmel, & Heller, 1995; White et al., 1994). Recent brain-imaging studies (Zametkin, Nordahl, Gross, & King, 1990; Zametkin, Liebenauer, Fitzgerald, & King, 1993) have used positron emission tomography (PET) to establish a clear neurobiological process in ADHD. In these studies PET has been used to evaluate brain metabolism in children and adults with ADHD, with a finding of pronounced metabolic imbalance in crucial brain areas of subjects diagnosed with ADHD. One prominent theory (Barkley, 1994) states that the metabolic instability observed in ADHD leads to a problem of "inhibitory capacity," that is, a failure in the child's or adult's ability to inhibit behaviors, thoughts, actions, and emotions. As Hallowell and Ratey (1994) have described:

> The social intrusiveness that is so characteristic of those who have ADD is the inability to stop at the other's boundaries. The failure to form intimate relationships is the inability to pause long enough even to listen to the other per-

son, let alone to understand and respect the other's needs. The impulsivity, the lack of planning, and the outbursts [of emotion] are the inability to restrain the flow of action and feeling. (p. 282)

Children and adolescents with ADHD are known for their tendency to act impulsively, without considering possible outcomes or consequences, and without weighing the needs or feelings of others. This proclivity results in seemingly endless interpersonal wrangles for the ADHD child, as evidenced by frequent conflicts with family and at school. Later, in adulthood, these conflicts often emerge with marital partners, employers, and legal authorities.

Theoretical Considerations

A possible etiological pathway between ADHD and the emergence of sexually aggressive and assaultive behaviors is intuitively reasonable in several respects. First, many children, adolescents, and adults with ADHD and comorbid conduct disorders share multiple characteristics with individuals who commit sexual aggression. These characteristics include (1) a frequent lack of interpersonal sensitivity and empathy, more generally demonstrated by emotional immaturity; (2) a vulnerability to chemical dependency and addictive behavior; (3) an attraction to dangerous, highly stimulating, and high-risk behavior; (4) a tendency, in some, toward hypersexuality; and (5) a difficulty or deficit in imposing limits, structure, and direction on their own behavior. The presence of ADHD may also explain the occurrence of sexual acting out in children who have never been abused—sexually or otherwise—and have not been exposed to sexual violence or severe family dysfunction. ADHD, when coupled with exposure to sexual stimulation, which is ubiquitous in our media-oriented culture, may be sufficient to evoke an imitative response that results in sexual aggression and misconduct in young children.

Youngsters with ADHD are well-known for impulsively reenacting dangerous and highly stimulating behavior that they have observed elsewhere. Although impulsivity may be instrumental to a child's initial forays into sexual misconduct, particularly when other traumatic influences are absent, it is not likely to be the factor that propels this sexual behavior into a lifelong, adulthood pattern. In fact, impulsivity may be a key variable in differentiating episodic, thoughtless acting out from calculated, remorseless psychopathy (Hinshaw, 1994). This formulation also is consistent with Groth's (1982) original distinction between chronic, "fixated" pedophiles (who are known to carefully plan their offenses and to "groom" their victims) and the more episodic, "regressed" offender (who seems more often to be driven by thoughtless or unconscious impulses).

What may be necessary for impulsive episodes to develop into chronic patterns of planned behavior is the comorbid presence of interpersonal and social deficits, referred to by some as a deficit in "emotional intelligence" (Goleman, 1995). If a child or adolescent is severely lacking in interpersonal and emotional understanding and skills, it is unlikely that the child will develop more appropriate and mature forms of sexual expression. Instead, it may be more likely that existing forms of sexual expression—however primitive or maladaptive—will become fixed. It is therefore also useful to note the well-established finding that some children with ADHD also have major deficits in social skills and in processing social information (Moffett, 1990; Milrich &

Dodge, 1984). It is certainly reasonable that such deficits, if not ameliorated, could contribute to lifelong problems with sexual intimacy and healthy sexual expression.

The presence of cognitive deficits associated with the processing of social and emotional information may be instrumental to the creation of "cognitive distortions" that maintain a chronic pattern of sexual misconduct. Hence, children with ADHD, by virtue of their impulsivity, may be more vulnerable to reenacting inappropriate sexual behavior during childhood and adolescence and may be more likely to continue this antisocial behavior into adulthood when they also lack the cognitive skills essential to their social and emotional development. In fact, this paradigm is particularly congruent with existing research that has shown that children with both ADHD and verbal learning disabilities/social skill deficits present a more serious risk for sustaining their antisocial behavior through adolescence and into adulthood (Moffett, 1990).

Implications for Evaluation and Treatment

Results from the present study suggest that in a substantial percentage of cases, sexually aggressive/assaultive behavior in children and adolescents may be symptomatic of a more fundamental attention-deficit/hyperactivity disorder. The results would also appear to indicate that the presence of ADHD is even more likely to be found in sexually aggressive children who are under the age of 13. Therefore, if the present findings are replicated, it will become essential that clinical evaluations of child and adolescent sexual offenders also include screenings for ADHD. Presently, many professionals who perform offender evaluations are not trained in the evaluation and treatment of ADHD and may lack an understanding of the disorder's potential contribution to the child's sexual aggression, as well as its implications for the child's long-term adjustment and predisposition to antisocial behavior. Without adequate evaluation, a significant component of these childrens' behavioral difficulties could go undetected, resulting in insufficient treatment and enhanced risk of continued antisocial behavior.

When ADHD is detected in sexually aggressive children, it is imperative that it be treated clinically, using the same comprehensive strategies that are indicated for attention-deficit disorders in general. These strategies generally include (1) various school interventions, (2) parent education and training, (3) individual and/or group counseling for the child, (4) cognitive training strategies, and (5) medication, most commonly a central nervous system stimulant, antidepressant, or other mood stabilizer. Education and counseling for the child and family are typically included in offender treatment, as is some type of cognitive retraining. These interventions can be easily supplemented to include information and counseling related to ADHD. Also, it may be important for clinicians to recognize ADHD's potentially profound effect on academic performance, and its subsequent influence on long-term social and emotional adjustment. These effects may require clinicians to act as advocates at school and with teachers, to ensure that the child receives all the academic services and supports that are appropriate and necessary for the child's success.

Finally, the important role of medication must not be overlooked. Although considerable misinformation and misunderstanding about drug treatment for ADHD persistently appears in the media, a sizable body of research (see, e.g., Hinshaw, Henker, Whalen, Erhardt, & Dunnington, 1989) has demonstrated the significant positive effects of stimulant medication on multiple target symptoms of ADHD, including aggressive behavior. Hence, it is also important for clinicians to be familiar with the various pharmaceutical treatments for ADHD and to be able to consult with pediatricians and psychiatric physicians concerning the sexually aggressive child's medication needs.

Conclusion

Many of the characteristics of juvenile sex offenders also describe children with ADHD. This condition has a neurological base which must be addressed in therapy if any of the sex offender specific techniques are expected to be intregrated by the client. Thus it may become essential for clinicians to broaden their assessment and treatment repertoire so they can provide truly comprehensive and effective services for sexually aggressive and assaultive children and their families.

References

American Psychiatric Association. (1994). *Diagnostic and statistical manual of mental disorders* (4th ed.). Washington, DC: Author.

Anderson, J., Williams, S., McGee, R., & Silva, P. (1987). DSM-III disorders in preadolescent children. *Archives of General Psychiatry, 44,* 69–76.

Awad, G. A., & Saunders, E. B. (1991) Male adolescent sexual assaulters: Clinical observations. *Journal of Interpersonal Violence, 2,* 3–25.

Barkley, R. A. (1994). Impaired delayed responding: A unified theory of attention-deficit hyperactivity disorder. In D. K. Routh (Ed.), *Disruptive behavior disorders in childhood: Essays honoring Herbert C. Quay* (pp. 11–57). New York: Plenum Press.

Barnard, G. W., Robbins, L., Newman, G., & Hutchinson, D. (3985). Differences found between rapists and child molesters. *Psychiatric News, 20,* 34–35.

Becker, J., & Stein, R. M. (1991). Is sexual erotica associated with sexual deviance in adolescent males? *International Journal of Law and Psychiatry, 14*(1–2), 85–95.

Berger, D., & Berger, L. (1991). *We heard the angels of madness.* New York: William Morrow.

Biederman, J., Farone, S. J., Spencer, T., Wilens, T., Norman, D., Lapey, K. A., Mick, E., Lehman, B. K., & Doyle, A. (1993). Patterns of psychiatric comorbidity, cognition, and psychosocial functioning in adults with attention-deficit disorder. *American Journal of Psychiatry, 150*(12), 1792–1798.

Biederman, J., Newcorn, J., & Sprichs, M. (1991). Comorbidity of attention deficit hyperactivity with conduct, depressive, anxiety and other disorders. *American Journal of Psychiatry, 148,* 564–577.

Blaske, D., Borduin, C. M., Henggeler, S. W., & Mann, B. J. (1989). Individual, family and peer chacteristics of adolescent sex offenders and assaultive offenders. *Developmental Psychology, 25,* 846–855.

Brown, T. E. (in press). *Brown Attention Deficit Disorders Scales.* San Antonio, TX: Psychological Corporation.

Candeon, M. K., & Nutter, D. E. (1988). A preliminary examination of the pornography experience of sex offenders, paraphiliacs, sexual dysfunction patients, and controls based on Meese Commission recommendations. *Journal of Sex and Marital Therapy, 14,* 285–298.

Carter, D. L., Prentky, R. A., Knight, R. A., Vanderveer, P. L., & Boucher, R. J. (1987). Use of pornography in the criminal and developmental histories of sexual offenders. *Journal of Interpersonal Violence, 2,* 196–211.

Connors, C. K. (1989). *Connors Rating Scale manual.* Toronto: Multi-Health Systems.

Connors, C. K. (1994). *Attention deficit hyperactivity disorder: Assessment and treatment for children and adolescents.* Toronto: Multi-Health Systems.

Fehrenbach, P. A., Smith, W., Monastersky, C., & Deisher, R. W. (1986). Adolescent sexual offenders: Offender and offense characteristics. *American Journal of Orthopsychiatry, 56,* 225–233.

Figia, N. A., Lang, R. A., Plutchik, R., & Holden, R. (1987). Personality differences between sex and violent offenders. *International Journal of Offender Therapy and Comparative Criminology, 31,* 211–226.

Finkelhor, D. (1988). The trauma of sexual abuse: Two models. In G. Wyatt & G. Powell (Eds.), *Lasting effects of child sexual abuse* (pp. 61–82). Newbury Park, CA: Sage.

Ford, M E., & Linney, J. A. (1995). Comparative analysis of juvenile sexual offenders, violent nonsexual offenders, and status offenders. *Journal of Interpersonal Violence, 10*(1), 56–70.

Freeman-Longo, R. E. (1985). The adolescent sexual offender: Background and research perspectives. In E. M. Otey & G. D. Ryan (Eds.), *Adolescent sex offenders: Issues in research and treatment* (pp. 130–146). Rockville, MD: Department of Health and Human Services.

Friedrich, W. N. (1994, August 12). *Psychological assessment of sexually abused children: The case for abuse-specific measures.* Paper presented at the annual convention of the American Psychological Association, Los Angeles.

Goleman, D. (1995). *Emotional intelligence: Why it can matter more than IQ.* New York: Bantam Books.

Groth, A. N. (1977). The adolescent sexual offender and his prey. *International Journal of Offender Therapy and Comparative Criminology, 21,* 249–254.

Groth, A. N. (1979). Sexual trauma in the life histories of rapists and child molesters. *Victimology: An International Journal, 4,* 10–16.

Groth, A. N. (1982) The incest offender. In S. M. Sgroi (Ed.), *Handbook of clinical intervention in child sexual abuse* (pp. 215–239). Lexington, MA: Heath.

Hall, G. C. N., & Barongan, C. (1997). Prevention of sexual aggression: Sociocultural risk and protective factors. *American Psychologist, 52*(1), 5–14.

Hallowell, E. M., & Ratey, J. J. (1994). *Driven to distraction: Recognizing and coping with attention-deficit disorder from childhood through adulthood.* New York: Simon & Schuster.

Hayashino, D. S., Wurtele, S. K., & Klebe, K. J. (1995). Child molesters: An examination of cognitive factors. *Journal of Interpersonal Violence, 10*(1), 106–116.

Hinshaw, S. P. (1987) On the distinction between attention deficits/hyperactivity and conduct problems/aggression in child psychopathology. *Psychological Bulletin, 101,* 443–463.

Hinshaw, S. P. (1994). Conduct disorder in childhood: Conceptualization, diagnosis, comorbidity, and risk status for anti-social functioning in adulthood. In D. Fowles, P. Sutker, & S. Goodman (Eds.), *Psychopathy and antisocial personality: A developmental perspective* (pp. 3–44). New York: Springer.

Hinshaw, S. P., Heller, T., & McHale, J. P. (1992). Covert antisocial behavior in boys with attention-deficit hyperactivity disorder: External validation and effects of methylphenidate. *Journal of Consulting and Clinical Psychology, 57,* 636–643.

Hinshaw, S. P., Henker, B., Whalen, C. K., Erhardt, D., & Dunnington, R. E. (1989). Aggressive, prosocial, and nonsocial behavior in hyperactive boys: Dose effects of methylphenidate in naturalistic settings. *Journal of Consulting and Clinical Psychology, 57*(5), 636–643.

Hinshaw, S. P., & Melnick, S. (in press). Peer relationships in children with attention-deficit hyperactivity disorder with and without comorbid aggression. *Development and Psychopathology.*

Hinshaw, S. P., Simmel, C., & Heller, T. L. (1995). Multimethod assessment of covert antisocial behavior in children: Laboratory observations, adult ratings, and child self-report. *Psychological Assessment, 7,* 209–219.

James, A. C., & Neil, P. (1996). Juvenile sexual offending: One-year period prevalence study within Oxfordshire. *Child Abuse and Neglect, 20*(6), 477–485.

Kavoussi, R. J., Kaplan, M., & Becker, J. V. (1988). Psychiatric diagnoses in adolescent sex offenders. *Journal of the American Academy of Child and Adolescent Psychiatry, 27*(2), 241–243.

Klein, R., & Manuzza, S. (1991). Long-term outcome of hyperactive children: A review. *Journal of the American Academy of Child and Adolescent Psychiatry, 30,* 1120–1134.

Langevin, R., Wright, P., & Handy, L. (1989). Characteristics of sex offenders who were sexually victimized as children. *Annals of Sex Research, 2,* 227–253.

Lewis, D. O., Shankok, S. S., & Pincus, J. H. (1979). Juvenile male sexual assaulters. *American Journal of Psychiatry, 136,* 1194–1196.

Loney, J. (1987). Hyperactivity and aggression in the diagnosis of attention deficit disorder. In B. B. Lahey & A. E. Kazdin (Eds.), *Advances in clinical child psychology* (vol. 10, pp. 99–135). New York: Plenum Press.

Lynam, D. R. (1996). Early identification of chronic offenders: Who is the fledgling psychopath? *Psychological Bulletin, 120*(2), 209–234.

Millich, R., & Dodge, K. A. (1984). Social information processing in child psychiatry populations. *Journal of Abnormal Child Psychology, 12,* 471–489.

Moffitt, T. E. (1990). Juvenile delinquency and attention deficit disorder: Boys' developmental trajectories from age 3 to age 15. *Child Development, 61,* 893–910.

Monastersky, C., & Smith, W. (1985). Juvenile sexual offenders: A family systems paradigm. In E. M. Otey & G. D. Ryan (Eds.), *Adolescent sex offenders: Issues in research and treatment* (pp. 130–146). Rockville, MD: Department of Health and Human Services.

Murphy, W. D. (1990). Assessment and modification of cognitive distortions in sex offenders. In W. L. Marshall, D. R. Laws & H. E. Barbaree (Eds.), *Handbook of sexual assault: Issues, theories, and treatment of the offender* (pp. 331–342). New York: Plenum Press.

Patterson, G. R., Reid, J. B., & Dishion, T. J. (1992). *Antisocial boys.* Eugene, OR: Castalia.

Petrovich, M., & Templer, D. I. (1984). Heterosexual molestation of children who later become rapists. *Psychological Reports, 54,* 810.

Pierce, L. H., & Pierce, R. L. (1987). Incestuous victimization by juvenile sexual offenders. *Journal of Family Violence, 2,* 351–364.

Pynoos, R. S., & Nader, K. (1988). Children who witness the sexual assaults of their mothers. *Journal of the American Academy of Child and Adolescent Psychiatry, 27,* 567–572.

Ryan, G. D. (1991) Incidence and prevalence of sexual offenses committed by juveniles. In G. D. Ryan & S. Lane. (Eds.), *Juvenile sexual offending: Causes, consequences, and correction* (pp. 9–19). Lexington, MA: Lexington Books.

Sandberg, S., Weiselberg, M., & Shaffer, D. (1980). Hyperkinetic and conduct problem children in primary school population: Some epidemiological considerations. *Journal of Child Psychology and Psychiatry, 21,* 293–311.

Seghorn, T. K., Prentky, R. A., & Boucher, R. A. (1987). Childhood sexual abuse in the lives of sexual offenders. *Journal of the American Academy of Child and Adolescent Psychiatry, 26,* 262–267.

Smith, W. R. (1988). Delinquency and abuse among juvenile sexual offenders. *Journal of Interpersonal Violence, 3,* 400–413.

Stermac, L. E., & Segal, Z. V. (1989). Adult sexual contact with children: An examination of cognitive factors. *Behavior Therapy, 20,* 573–584.

Tarter, R. E., Hegedus, A. M., Alterman, A. I., & Katzgaar, L. (1983). Cognitive capacities of juvenile violent, non-violent, and sexual offenders. *Journal of Nervous and Mental Diseases, 171,* 564–567.

White, J. L., Moffitt, T. E., Caspi, A., Bartusch, D., Needles, D., & Stouthamer-Loeber, M. (1994). Measuring impulsivity and examining its relationship to delinquency. *Journal of Abnormal Psychology, 103,* 192–205.

Widon, C. S. (1995, March). V*ictims of childhood sexual abuse—Later criminal consequences. Research in brief.* Washington, DC: U.S. Department of Justice.

Zametkin, A. J., Liebenauer, L. L., Fitzgerald, G. A., & King, A. C. (1993). Metabolism in teenagers with attention-deficit hyperactivity disorder. *Archives of General Psychiatry, 50*(5), 333–340.

Zametkin, A. J., Nordahl, T. E., Gross, M., & King, A. C. (1990). Metabolism in adults with hyperactivity with childhood onset. *New England Journal of Medicine, 323*(20), 1361–1366.

Chapter 17

Inclusion of the Family in the Treatment of Juvenile Sexual Abuse Perpetrators

by Colette L. Corcoran, M.Ed., Alexis O. Miranda, Ph.D.,
Kathleen W. Tenukas-Steblea, L.I.C.S.W., and
Ben D. Taylor, M.A.

Overview

Much research has been done on the individual characteristics of juvenile sexual abuse perpetrators (JSAPs). Although many programs include family therapy, minimal research has been done on the characteristics of these families. This chapter describes the characteristics of JSAPs and their families used to design and implement a model that includes the family in treatment.

Introduction

Camp and Thyer (1993) reported an increase in the sexual abuse committed by juveniles. Groth, Longo, and McFadin (1982); Abel, Mittelman, and Becker (1985); and Davis and Leitenberg (1987) suggested that many sexual abuse perpetrators begin a career of sexual deviance in childhood or adolescence. Groth and Loredo (1981) found that the first sexual offense for many perpetrators occurred between the ages of 8 and 16. Similarly, Lee and Olender (1992) found that 60% to 80% of adult sexual abuse perpetrators reported their first perpetration during adolescence.

The Task Force on Juvenile Sexual Offenders and Their Victims (TFJSOV, 1996) suggested that the incidence of sexual abuse by juveniles decreased with treatment in a specialized counseling program. Some recent research findings confirmed the effectiveness of early interventions to stop or decrease juveniles' abusive behaviors (Gerber, 1994; Morenz & Becker, 1995; Sapp & Vaughn, 1990). Particularly promising have been treatment programs that recognized the role of the family in originating and maintaining deviant sexual behavior (Ryan, & Lane, 1991). Hence, comprehensive treatments that include the family have been most effective for JSAPs. Because information is available about the unique characteristics of JSAPs and their families, this information was used to develop the treatment model described in this chapter.

Characteristics of Juvenile Sexual Abuse Perpetrators

Although Smith, Monastersky, and Deisher (1987) characterized JSAPs as a heterogeneous group, others found common characteristics among them. Gender, sexual arousal and gratification, histories of sexual abuse victimization and maltreatment, maladaptive cognitive patterns and use of defense mechanisms, lack of empathy for victims, and psychiatric impairment are common JSAP characteristics cited in the literature that deserve individual attention when treating juveniles.

Gender. The literature reflects that the majority of JSAPs are males. Brown, Flanagan, and McLeod (1984) indicated that females accounted for only 7% of the sex offenders and 2% of the rapists. Similarly, Camp and Thyer (1993) found that females accounted for less than 5% of the JSAP population. McCarty (1986) noted a lower representation of females in the sexual abuser population in a retrospective study of adult female sexual abusers. In this study none of the participants reported committing sexual abuse in childhood or adolescence.

Although fewer female juvenile sexual abuse perpetrators have been identified, adult female perpetrators usually commit serious sexual offenses against children. Fehrenbach and Monastersky (1988) provided evidence that adult female sex offenders reported committing serious and persistent sexual abuse against children who were under their care.

Sexual Arousal and Gratification. It appears that sexual gratification is not the aim of JSAPs when they abuse. Hunter and Becker (1994) suggested that sexual gratification was not the only correlate to the development or maintenance of deviant sexual arousal for JSAPs. Similarly, Gerber (1994) reported that juveniles, unlike adult sexual abuse perpetrators, rarely offended solely for sexual reasons. Rather, sexual perpetrations by juveniles appear to be related to two traumatic experiences these individuals had suffered: maltreatment and previous sexual abuse victimization.

History of Sexual and Physical Abuse Victimization. Hunter and Becker (1994) found the rate of sexual abuse victimization among JSAPs to be between 50% and 80%. The high incidence of sexual abuse victimization among JSAPs supported the theoretical association between victimization and subsequent sexual abuse perpetration. Theoretically, the connection between victimization and subsequent perpetration represents a deviant and sexualized attempt on the part of the juvenile to integrate the abuse experience into a coherent world view (DiGiorgio-Miller, 1994). A noteworthy assumption of DiGiorgio-Miller's connection between victimization and perpetration was that sexually victimized JSAPs replicated the abuse they suffered; that is, what was done to them is what they did to others.

Hunter and Becker (1994) found that sexually victimized JSAPs were more likely to sexually abuse victims of either gender. Impartiality for the victim's gender was associated with psychopathological conditions and greater potential for further abuse perpetrations.

Becker and Stein (1991) also addressed the connection between sexual abuse victimization and subsequent sexual abuse perpetration. In their study, Becker and Stein found that juvenile males who had been sexually abused as children had higher numbers of victims than did those who had no history of sexual abuse. The study further revealed that physical abuse victimization was a common experience among the JSAPs and that JSAPs with a history of physical abuse had more victims than those who did not.

Maladaptive Thinking Patterns and Use of Defense Mechanisms. Goocher (1994) reported two components of the JSAP's cognitions: power and control. Similarly, DiGiorgio-Miller (1994) suggested that powerlessness was a fundamental dimension of sexual abuse perpetration. For DiGiorgio-Miller, powerlessness resulted from the experience of abuse victimization.

Gerber (1994) reported that JSAPs avoided responsibility for their abusive behavior, using denial, projection by blaming others, and minimization of responsibility as defense mechanisms. Also, Ryan and Lane (1991) suggested that JSAPs dissociate from their feelings to avoid the experience of uncomfortable emotional states.

Lack of Victim Empathy. The majority of JSAPs lack the ability to feel empathy for others, especially their victims. Gerber (1994) attributed the JSAPs' ability to maintain sexual arousal during abuse incidents, despite the victim's pain and discomfort, to the lack of victim empathy. Also, the lack of empathy reflects the inability of JSAPs to realize that sexual abuse is a severe violation of another's personal boundaries. Katz (1990) emphasized the importance of victim empathy, suggesting its central role in any treatment of sexual abusers.

Psychiatric Impairment. Goocher (1994) found that many JSAPs were diagnosed with conduct disorder, antisocial personality disorder, or posttraumatic stress disorder. In addition, Becker, Kaplan, Tenke, and Tartaglini (1991) found in their study of 246 adolescent sex offenders that 42% showed symptoms of major depressive disorder This percentage was twice as high as that found in the control group.

Exposure to Sexually Explicit Material. Becker and Stein (1991) found that 74% of the JSAPs sampled reported the frequent use of sexually explicit material from magazines, videotapes, television, and books. The JSAPs who used sexually explicit material reported that such material increased their sexual arousal.

Low Self-Esteem and Inappropriate Social Skills. Gerber (1994) suggested that most JSAPs' relationships with peers and adults were unhealthy. JSAPs' low self-esteem was attributed to the instability of their relationships. For DiGiorgia-Miller (1994), the social isolation that ultimately affected self-esteem did so in two ways. First, JSAPs were frequently rejected by peers and family because of the sexual abuse committed. Second, JSAPs experienced peer rejection because of inappropriate social skills.

Sensation Seeking. Samenow (1984) found that sexual abuse perpetrators were twice as likely to be aroused by environmental stimuli than individuals from the general population. This hypersensitivity to environmental stimuli explained the low impulse control that characterizes JSAPs (Smith, Monastersky, & Deisher, 1987).

Characteristics of Families of Juvenile Sexual Abuse Perpetrators

Ryan and Lane (1991) suggested that the JSAP's family life was characterized by exposure to aggressive models and sexual behaviors, neglect, and lack of positive role models. There has been some empirical support for these characteristics.

Exposure to Aggressive Models and Sexual Interactions. Van Ness (1984) reported that 79% of adolescent sex offenders witnessed intrafamilial violence. In contrast, only 20% of juvenile delinquents who did not commit a sexual offense witnessed intrafamilial violence. Gray and Pithers (1993) found that JSAPs often witnessed physical violence within the family and experienced sexual and physical abuse victimization in greater proportion than did their cohorts. Similarly, Fagan and Wexler (1988) found that JSAPs were more likely than others to come from families in which exposure to domestic violence, child abuse, and child sexual molestation were the norm.

Smith and Israel (1987) found that JSAPs often came from highly sexualized family environments characterized by sexual interplay between siblings, parents, and extended family members. Notable in Smith and Israel's study was that a highly sexualized family environment predicted how JSAPs later acted in intra- and extrafamilial interactions.

Parental Neglect. Fehrenback, Smith, Monastersky, and Deisher (1986) suggested that parental neglect played the principal role in the development of sexual abuse behavior among juveniles. Van Ness (1984) provided support for Fehrenback et al. in an earlier study that showed that 41% of the sex offenders reported a history of physical abuse or neglect. In contrast, only 15% of the controls reported histories of physical abuse or neglect.

Hunter and Becker (1994) assumed that neglect originated from parental loss in many juvenile incest perpetrators' families. Interestingly, Hunter and Becker's findings showed that the juveniles felt rejected or neglected by family members before as well as after they committed sexual abuse perpetrations.

Lack of Positive Role Models. Ryan and Lane (1991) suggested that circumstances, experiences, and parental models in the JSAP's early life were conducive to the development of sexual deviance or acted as inhibitors to the ability to empathize with others. Smith and Israel (1987) found, in their study of twenty-five sibling incest perpetrators' families, that the parents were often distant, inaccessible, and secretive.

Treatment Model for JSAPs and Their Families

Rationale. The proposed treatement model is holistic and based on the guidelines of the Association for Treatment of Sexual Abusers (ATSA, 1997) and the previously mentioned studies. The model's rationale rests on the assumption that the individual and family characteristics unique to the JSAP population need individual clinical attention. Furthermore, Cashwell and Carusso (1997) considered most effective those treatments conducted in group, that included the family, and used individual counseling as a supplement.

Structure and Operation. The principal goals of the treatment are the prevention of more abuse and the increase of adaptive family functioning. Treatment begins with a psychosocial evaluation of the family and a psychological evaluation of the JSAP. The psychosocial evaluation focuses on familial and abuse variables. The JSAP psychological evaluation includes standard psychological assessment instruments to identify potential influences on treatment (e.g., cognitive abilities and personality disorders). Also, psychological assessment of constructs related exclusively to sexual issues is often necessary (e.g., hostility and impulse control).

Structurally, the treatment is divided into two phases: (1) JSAP treatment and (2) family treatment. The family treatment phase is further divided into the orientation and unification subphases. The orientation subphase for the families is implemented concurrently with the JSAP treatment phase using the same format (e.g., small groups that meet weekly for approximately one and a half hours). Frequently, JSAP participants are six to ten juveniles between the ages of 13 and 17. The number of participants in the family treatment group depends on the number of JSAPs in treatment.

At the end of the JSAP treatment the family joins the JSAP for the unification

Table 17.1
Treatment Issues and Goals for the JASP Treatment Phase

Issues	Goals
Trust	Development of trust in others.
Accountability	Admission of responsibility for abusive incident(s).
Self-esteem and self-awareness	Increase in positive feelings toward self.
Victimization	Recognition of harm to the victim.
Feeling identification and mastery	Recognition and attention to anger management and feelings about own victimization (if applicable).
Impulse control	Identify contributing factors to the abuse incident.
Problem identification and problem solving.	Development of problem solving skills and stress-coping resources.
Risk factors	Identification of one's own cycle of abuse; development of impulse control strategies.
Communication skills	Development of appropriate communication skills.
Social skills	Development of respect for personal boundaries.
Sex education	Development of knowledge about sexual issues.
Relapse prevention	Identification and use of relapse prevention strategies.
Empowerment	Recognize positive personal attributes and contributions.
Assertiveness skills	Recognition of need for external and lasting social support systems.

subphase. The unification subphase involves JSAPs and their families in weekly family therapy. The unification subphase lasts approximately four to six months. Each phase of treatment has its own focus and goals.

Phase A: The JSAP Treatment. The aim of the JSAP treatment is the accomplishment of goals that focus on issues unique to JSAPs. Table 17.1 depicts the JSAP treatment's issues and goals. The achievement of the treatment goals is obtained by the completion of clinical tasks presented on Table 17.2.

Phase B: The JSAP's Family Treatment. Family treatment begins with an orientation subphase in which the group addresses issues specific to sexual abuse and family dynamics. The format is psychoeducational and process oriented. For example, factual information about the cycle of abuse and sexual abuse risk factors is discussed. Also, the discussions allow personal reflection and the expression of emotions. The aim of the orientation phase is to educate the family about abuse and family dynamics and to encourage active participation in treatment.

Table 17.2
Clinical Areas and Tasks in the JASP Treatment Phase

Area	Tasks
Responsibility	Adherence to clinical regimen (weekly individual and group counseling).
	Payment for counseling sessions.
	Disclosure of events related to the perpetration(s).
	Recognition of defense mechanisms used to deal with perpetration(s) and perpetrator status.
	Acceptance of abuse's impact on others.
Empathy	Recognition of consequences of abuse on victim(s).
	Discussion of own abuse issues.
	Reparation and apology to victims(s) and other(s) affected by the abuse.
	Interaction with guest speakers (e.g., adult survivor of sexual abuse who discusses the impact of the abuse).
Skills	Development of social and communications skills.
	Development of strategies to recognize and modify negative thinking patterns.
Relapse prevention	Development of knowledge and understanding about the sexual abuse cycle.
	Development of appropriate stress coping resources mechanisms.
	Development of models for adaptive decision-making processes.
	Identification of factors and strategies to avoid high-risk behaviors.
	Strategies to access environmental and social supports.

The orientation subphase often leads to the expression of support, cohesion, and confirmation of the shared emotions and experiences among the participants, important dynamics of group counseling work (Yalom, 1985). Furthermore, these discussions facilitate the confrontation of denial that family members failed to recognize the abuse, that a family member is a sexual abuser, and that family dynamics may contribute to and maintain abusive incidents (Schlank & Shaw, 1997).

In family treatment, members are introduced to the clinical issues and goals presented in Table 17.3. This sample of clinical issues and their respective goals represent the dynamics cited in the aforementioned studies and issues commonly experienced by JSAPs' families.

Following termination of the JSAP treatment phase, each JSAP meets with his family to address issues unique to that system. Also, family counseling addresses and encourages the use of skills developed during previous treatment. For example, the family members and the JSAP are encouraged to identify high-risk situations and define the role that each family member may play to avoid them. The emotional and

Table 17.3
Sample Salient Issues for JSAP's Families and Treatment Goals

Issues	Goals
Physical and sexual abuse within the family	Identification of physical or sexual abuse histories within the family.
	Recognition and establishment of emotional and physical boundaries between family members.
	Termination of drug use.
Access to sexually explicit material	Decrease availability and access to sexually explicit material or sexual interactions by JSAP.
Family involvement	Increase JSAP's access to familial and external positive models.
	Increase JSAP's involvement in school and extracurricular activities.
Immediate reaction to the abuse incident	Formulate and implement strategies to deal with emotional reactions to the abuse (e.g., anger and abuse shock).
	Develop strategies to prevent further abuse (e.g., changing children's sleeping arrangements).
Legal involvement	Identify strategies to confront legal involvement (e.g., necessity for legal representation).
Shame and guilt	Determine association and relationship to perpetrator (e.g., appearances in court, supervision of JSAP's with contact other children, inclusion of JSAP's name in sexual abuser registry).
Victim safety	Formulate strategies to monitor JSAP's interactions with potential victims.
	Identify need and obligation to inform others about JSAP's potential to abuse (e.g., school personnel and extended family members).

cognitive reactions resulting from the practice of new skills and behaviors are explored in follow-up weekly counseling sessions. Treatment culminates with a clinical evaluation of the treatment's efficacy.

Treatment Efficacy Evaluation. Because many professionals are involved in this comprehensive treatment, and because the treatment model is long-termed and multifaceted, the treatment evaluation is dynamic and tailored to the uniqueness of each family and JSAP. The efficacy of each treatment component is evaluated individually, several times during the course of treatment. However, a final evaluation requires all the mental health professionals involved in the treatment of each JSAP and family. Multiple evaluations from multiple sources (i.e., counselors from the JSAP treatment groups and from the family group treatment) allow the evaluation of the accomplishment of each goal. Multiple evaluations also allow a comprehensive view of JSAPs and their families and the efficacy of each treatment component. Although the program currently relies heavily on clinical experience to determine the efficacy of each treatment component, objective studies are being conducted to empirically evaluate treatment efficacy.

Conclusion

This chapter presented the characteristics of JSAPs and their families used to develop and implement a treatment model with two distinct phases. The aim of treatment is the accomplishment of specific goals for two phases of treatment: treatment for JSAPs and for their families. McConaghy, Blaszczynski, Armstrong, and Kidson (1989) found that JSAPs were more resistant to treatment than were adult sex offenders, as evidenced by the higher abuse recidivism rate following treatment. Although the model presented here is not appropriate for all JSAPs or their families, evidence supports the effectiveness of programs that intercept deviant sexual patterns early andcomprehensively and interrupt the reinforcing cycle (Gerber, 1994).

References

Abel, F., Mittelman, M., & Becker, J. (1985). Sex offenders: Results of assessment and ecommendations for treatment. In J. Ben-Aron, S. Hucker, & C. Webster (Eds.), *Clinical criminology: Current concepts* (pp. 127–155). Toronto: M & M Graphics.

Association for the Treatment of Sexual Abusers. (1997). *Ethical standards and principles for the management of sexual abusers.* Beaverton, OR: Author.

Becker, J. V., & Hunter, J. A. (1993). Aggressive sex offenders. *Child and Adolescent Psychiatric Clinics of North America, 2*(2), 477–487.

Becker, J. V., Kaplan, M., Tenke, C., & Tartaglini, A. (1991). The incidence of depressive symptomatology in juvenile sex offenders. *Child Abuse and Neglect, 15,* 531–536.

Becker, J. V., & Stein, R. V. (1991). Is sexual erotica associated with sexual deviance in adolescent males? *International Journal of Law and Psychiatry, 14*(1–2), 85–95.

Brown, E. J., Flanagan, T. J., & McLeod, M. (1984). *Sourcebook of criminal justice statistics—1983.* Washington, DC: Bureau of Justice Statistics.

Camp, B. H., & Thyer, B. A. (1993). Treatment of adolescent sex offenders: A review of empirical research. *Journal of Applied Social Sciences, 17*(2), 191–206.

Cashwell, C. S., & Carusso, M. E. (1997). Adolescent sex offenders: Identification and intervention strategies. *Journal of Mental Health Counseling, 19*(4), 336–348.

Davis, G., & Leitenberg, H. (1987). Adolescent sex offenders. *Psychological Bulletin, 101,* 417–427.

DiGiorgio-Miller, J. (1994). Clinical techniques in the treatment of juvenile sex offenders. *Journal of Offender Rehabilitation, 21*(1–2), 117–126.

Fagan, J., & Wexler, S. (1988). Explanations of sexual assault among violent delinquents. *Journal of Adolescent Research, 3,* 363–385.

Fehrenbach, P. A., & Monastersky, C. (1988). Characteristics of female adolescent sexual offenders. *American Journal of Orthopsychiatry, 58,* 148–151.

Fehrenbach, P. A., Smith, W., Monastersky, C., & Deisher, R. W. (1986). Adolescent sexual offenders: Offender and offense characteristics. *American Journal of Orthopsychiatry, 56,* 225–233.

Gerber, J. (1994). The use of art therapy in juvenile sex offender specific treatment. *Arts in Psychotherapy, 21*(5), 367–374.

Goocher, B. E., (1994). Some comments of the residential treatment of juvenile sex offenders. *Child and Youth Care Forum, 23*(4), 243–250.

Gray, A. S., & Pithers, W. D. (1993). Relapse prevention with sexually aggressive adolescents. In H. E. Barbaree, W. L. Marshall, & S. M. Hudson (Eds.), *The juvenile sex offender* (pp. 289–320). New York: Guilford Press.

Groth, A., Longo, A., & McFadin, J. (1982). Undetected recidivism among rapists and child molesters. *Crime and Delinquency, 28,* 450–458.

Groth, N., & Loredo, C. M. (1981). Juvenile sex offenders: Guidelines for assessment. *Journal of Offender Therapy and Comparative Criminology, 25,* 31–39.

Hunter, J. A., & Becker, J. V. (1994). The role of deviant sexual arousal in juvenile sexual offending: Etiology, evaluation, and treatment. *Criminal Justice and Behavior, 21*(1), 132–149.

Katz, R. (1990). Psychological adjustment in adolescent child molesters. *Child Abuse and Neglect, 14,* 567–575.

Lee, D. G., & Olender, M. B. (1992). Working with juvenile sex offenders in foster care. *Community Alternatives: International Journal of Family Care, 4*(2), 63–75.

McCarty, L. M. (1986). Characteristics of the offender. *Child Welfare, 65,* 447–458.

McConaghy, N., Blaszczynski, A., Armstrong, M. S., & Kidson, W. (1989). Resistance to treatment of adolescent sex offenders. *Archives of Sexual Behavior, 18*(2), 97–107.

Morenz, B, & Becker, J. V. (1995). The treatment of youthful sexual offenders. *Applied and Preventive Psychology, 4,* 247–256.

Ryan, G. D., & Lane, S. (1991). *Juvenile sexual offending: Causes, consequences, and corrections.* Lexington, MA: Lexington Books.

Samenow, S. E. (1984). *Inside the criminal mind.* New York: Times Books.

Sapp, A. D., & Vaughn, M. S. (1990). Juvenile sex offender treatment at state-operated correctional institutions. *International Journal of Offender Therapy and Comparative Criminology, 34*(2), 131–146.

Schlank, A. M., & Shaw, T. (1997). Treating sexual offenders who deny: A review. In B. K. Schwartz, & H. R. Cellini (Eds.), *The sex offender: Corrections, treatment, and legal practice* (vol. I, pp. 6-1–6-7). Kingston, NJ: Civic Research Institute.

Smith, H., & Israel, E. (1987). Sibling incest: A study of the dynamics of 25 cases. *Child Abuse and Neglect, 11*(2), 325–341.

Smith, W. R., Monastersky, C., & Deisher, R. M. (1987). MMPI-based personality types among juvenile sexual offenders. *Journal of Clinical Psychology, 43,* 422–430.

Task Force on Juvenile Sexual Offenders and Their Victims. (1996). *Juvenile sexual offenders and their victims.* Tallahassee, FL: Author.

Van Ness, S. R. (1984) Rape as instrumental violence: A study of youth offenders. *Journal of Offender Counseling Services and Rehabilitation, 9,* 161–170.

Yalom, I. D. (1985). *The theory and practice of group psychotherapy* (3rd. ed.). New York: Basic Books.

Chapter 18

Treatment Success of a Community-Based Program for Young Adolescent Sex Offenders

by Fred Schmidt, Ph.D., and Laura Heinz, B.A.

Overview

The Thunder Bay Adolescent Sex Offender Program studied the posttreatment adjustment of thirty-three youths who had completed at least twelve months of their treatment program. They were followed for an average of twenty-eight months. The differences between offending and nonoffending juveniles were studied.

Introduction

The early and effective treatment of adolescent sex offenders is critical given what is known about sexually offending behavior. Current statistics indicate that roughly 30% of child sexual abuse cases are committed by adolescents (Ryan & Lane, 1997) and that between 58% (Abel, Mittelman, & Becker, 1985) and 80% (Bremer, 1992) of adult offenders begin their deviant sexual arousal and offending behavior as an adolescent. By intervening at a young age, youth who have developed or are developing sexually abusive patterns of behavior can be helped to stop and prevent the devastating victimization of untold numbers of children and adults. Early intervention is also likely to make treatment more successful because deviant and abusive behavioral patterns have not yet become entrenched, as is commonly found with adult sex offenders. However, to be effective, interventions must be critically evaluated to ensure that they are successful.

Treatment Effectiveness Studies

When compared to the evaluation of adolescent sex offender treatment, considerably more evaluation and longer term follow-up work has been done with adult sex offenders. Several recent comprehensive review articles suggest that when taken as a whole, the treatment of adult sex offenders is effective in reducing sexually abusive behavior (Hall, 1995; Hanson & Bussière, 1996). Hall's (1995) recent meta-analysis of treatment studies revealed a small but strong treatment effect size. Across studies and types of offenders, the 27% sexual recidivism rate for untreated offenders was significantly higher than the 19% recidivism rate for treated offenders. In another meta-analysis using an average five-year follow-up period, Hanson and Bussière (1996) found an overall recidivism rate of 13.4%. Sexual recidivism was found to be much less common than general nonviolent recidivism (M = 36%) but similar to nonsexual violent recidivism (M − 12%). Hanson and Bussière (1996) also found that the strongest predictors of sexual recidivism were characteristics related to sexual deviance and, to a lesser extent, general criminological variables. Moreover, the nonsexual recidivism for sexual offenders was predicted by the same variables that predicted recidivism among nonsexual offenders. Although many factors were identified as being related to sexual and nonsexual recidivism, no factor was strong enough on its own to justify using it as a single predictor. Consequently, it appears that risk assessment must consider a range of relevant factors and also examine the cumulative or interactive effect of multiple risk factors.

Adolescent Treatment Efficacy Studies

Only a handful of recidivism studies have investigated adolescent sex offenders, and most of them have very short follow-up periods. Table 18.1 provides a brief summary of the most representative studies that have been completed. In general, these studies suggest that sexual recidivism for adolescents is lower than that reported in the adult literature. Reoffending rates vary from as low as 1.9% (Brannon & Troyer, 1991) to as high as 43.7% over a three-year period for a small sample of treated high-risk offenders (Borduin, Henggeler, Blaske, & Stein, 1990). Treatment outcome studies that have been based on a broad and representative sample of adolescent sex offenders have generally found sexual reoffending rates to be below 15% (Knopp, 1982; Smith & Monastersky, 1986; Becker, 1990; Kahn & Chambers, 1991; Shram, Milloy, & Rowe, 1991; Bremer, 1992; Lab, Shields, & Schondel, 1993). Similar to adult findings, nonsexual recidivism rates tend to be higher with a low of 11% (Lab et al., 1993) to a high of 89% in a sample of sexually aggressive youth (Rubinstein, Yeager, Goodstein, & Lewis, 1993).

Table 18.1
Summary of Adolescent Sex Offender Recidivism Studies

Study	Sample Size	Treatment Setting (C, R)	Mean Length of Follow-up (in Months)	Recidivism (%)	
				Sexual	Nonsexual
Knopp (1982)	80	R	n.s.	5.0	11.0
Smith & Monastersky (1986)	112	C	28.9	14.3	34.8
Becker (1990)	52	C	12.0	9.6	n.s.
Borduin et al. (1990)	16	C	37.0	43.7	37.5
Kahn & Chambers (1991)	221	both	20.4	7.5	37.3
Brannon & Troyer (1991)	53	R	n.s	1.9	32.1
Shram et al. (1991)	197	both	74.0	10.2	47.7
Bremer (1992)	193	R	n.s.	6.0	n.s.
Rubinstein et al. (1993)	19	n.s.	96.0	37.0	89.0
Lab et al. (1993)	155	C	n.s.	3.2	18.7

Note. C = community treatment; R = residential treatment; n.s = not specified

As illustrated in Table 18.1, many of these studies found that roughly one-third of their sex offenders nonsexually reoffended.

In addition to the small number of studies, a number of methodological problems exist which make interpretation and generalization to all adolescent sex offenders difficult. Many of these studies are characterized by small sample sizes, short follow-up periods, and apparent heterogeneity in the types of adolescent sex offenders studied. For example, Rubinstein et al. (1993) followed a small sample of sexually violent youths with significant histories of sexual victimization, while Lab et al. (1993) reported on adolescent sex offenders whose history of abuse and violence in their lives was much less prominent. Such a wide range of characteristics makes interpretation and comparison of recidivism rates difficult at best. Not surprisingly, studies that exclusively sampled chronic delinquent sex offenders (Borduin et al., 1990) or sexually aggressive youths (Rubinstein et al., 1993) obtained significantly higher recidivism rates for both sexual and nonsexual offenses. Moreover, other than the study by Smith and Monastersky (1986), recidivism studies with adolescent sex offenders have not progressed to the point where predictors of sexual and nonsexual offending behavior have been studied. It is not known whether adolescents have the same or different risk factors from those identified in adult sex offenders or whether the factors related to nonsexual recidivism are the same between adolescents who commit sex offenses and those who commit only nonsexual offenses.

Other Studies Related to Juvenile Sex Offenses

In addition to treatment outcome, it is also necessary to describe and understand the life circumstances of offenders and the nature of their offending behavior. Early information about adolescent sex offenders and their offending behavior (Davis & Leitenberg, 1987; Fehrenbach, Smith, Monastersky, & Deisher, 1986) is similar to the more recent and comprehensive data collected by Ryan, Miyoshi, Metzner, Krugman, and Fryer (1996). Ryan et al. (1996) reported on the profiles of more than 1,600 sexually abusive youth through the Uniform Data Collection System (UDCS) developed by the National Adolescent Perpetrator Network. This latter data set suggests that almost all of the sexually abusive youths referred into treatment are male (97%), with only 54% living in a two-parent home. Traumatic experiences are common in the life history of adolescent sexual abusers, with as many as 42% being victims of physical abuse, 26% having been neglected, and 39% having been sexually abused. In addition, 63% of the youth had also witnessed some form of family violence. Many of the youths (63%) had previously committed a nonsexual offense and almost half had previously been involved in therapy (46%). These youths committed a wide range of sexual offenses with an average of 7.7 victims per offender and 30% using force to complete their offense(s). Victims were two times more likely to be females than males with 63% of the victims being younger than 9 years of age.

Initial Treatment Effectiveness Study

The limited information available regarding treatment success with adolescent sex offenders suggests that further evaluation of community-based treatment programs, as they are commonly delivered, is essential to shaping and improving current interventions. This chapter provides the initial treatment effectiveness findings for the Thunder Bay Adolescent Sex Offender Program (TBASOP).

Thunder Bay Adolescent Sex Offender Program. TBASOP is a multiagency initiative sponsored jointly by children's mental health, child protection services, probation, and a specific young offender treatment program. This community-based program has been in operation since December 1990 and provides intervention to Phase I adolescent sex offenders (ages 12 to 15) who have been mandated into treatment. The treatment model is primarily cognitive-behavioral in orientation but takes an eclectic approach to the simultaneous delivery of group, individual, and family therapy. A high priority is placed on supervising and supporting the offenders while they are involved in the treatment program. Supervision and support are provided on a monthly basis through case conferences held with the youth, parents, and treatment providers in order to continually modify and adjust each youth's treatment plan. During these monthly case conferences, probation, mental health, and child protection services provide representation. TBASOP is the only treatment service for Phase I adolescent sex offenders in the city of Thunder Bay, a community of roughly 120,000 people.

Participants. The present results are based on those adolescent sex offenders who participated in TBASOP between December 1990 and December 1995. Offender and victim characteristics are provided for the forty-two youths who participated in this program during the five-year treatment period. Recidivism results were obtained for the thirty-three youths who had completed the treatment program for a period longer than twelve months.

On average, the adolescent sex offenders entering treatment were 15.3 years of age, with 97% being male. Roughly 38% of the offenders were of aboriginal background with the remainder being caucasian. At the time of their conviction, an equal number of offenders were living with two biological parents and a single parent (34%), with a smaller number living in a stepfamily (22%), with relatives (5%), or in foster care (5%).

Approximately 70% of the offenders came from families in which abuse or family violence had occurred. Specifically, 45% of the offenders had themselves been sexually victimized prior to their involvement in TBASOP. Roughly half of the offenders (52%) had received counseling prior to their conviction for a sexual offense, with 22% also having had involvement with child protection services at some time in their childhood. Clearly, most of these youths had experienced traumatic events during their life and, despite receiving prior help and intervention, continued to develop unhealthy and sexually abusive behavioral patterns.

None of the offenders had been convicted of a prior sexual offense. Thirty-seven percent, however, had committed a prior nonsexual offense, with an average of 3.2 offenses per offender for those with a delinquent history.

Offending Characteristics. A significant number of the adolescent offenders reported having only one victim (45%), with an overall average of 1.7 victims per offender. There was a great deal of variance, however, in the number of repeat offenses committed against any one victim with a range of 1 to 50 offenses (M = 5.3 offenses) per victim. Even at this young age a number of adolescent offenders had repeated their offenses on many occasions, suggesting significant risk for an offending lifestyle if intervention was not put in place. Victims tended to be young in age (M = 10.8 years), with 31% being 6 or younger, 41% falling within the ages of 6 and 12, and the remaining 28% being over the age of 12. Seventy-eight percent of the victims were female, with all male victims being under the age of 12.

The majority of offenses occurred in the victim's home (62%), with another 16% occurring outdoors, 9% on school property, and 5% in the offender's home. In almost all circumstances, the offender was someone known to or responsible for the care of the victim. In 32% of the cases the offender was a family member or relative, 41% of the time the offender was an acquaintance, 24% of the time the offender was in charge as a babysitter, and in only 3% of the cases was the offender a stranger to the victim. Althogh few of the offenses occurred when the offender was under the influence of alcohol or drugs (9%), 42% used either physical force or threats of physical harm in order to complete their offenses. Each offense frequently involved a number of different sexual acts, with genital fondling being the most common offense type (61%) and intrusive sexual acts such as intercourse (25%) and oral-genital contact (19%) also occurring very often. Table 18.2 provides a description of offense type frequency according to the victim's age.

Sexual and Nonsexual Recidivism. Only the thirty-three youths who had finished the treatment program for longer than a twelve-month period were included in the exam-

Table 18.2
Frequency of Offense Type by Age of Victim

Offense Type[a] (%)	Age Categories (in Years)				
	0–6 (%)	6–12 (%)	13–18 (%)	18+ n	Total (%)
Genital fondling (60.9)	61.9	78.6	58.3	0.0	42
Intercourse (24.6)	14.3	35.7	33.3	0.0	17
Oral-genital contact (18.8)	19.0	32.1	0.0	0.0	13
Nontouch (14.5)	9.5	3.6	8.3	100.0	10
Digital penetration (8.7)	14.3	3.6	16.6	0.0	6

[a] Offense types are not mutually exclusive for each victim.

ination of recidivism. The average length of follow-up time for these youths was twenty-eight months (range of twelve to fifty-four months). This follow-up was in addition to the 16.7 months of treatment time taken by the average youth who completed the program. Significant is the finding that 19% of the youths who began treatment were suspended and unable to comply with the demands of a community-based intervention program. These noncompliant youths were brought back before the courts.

Only 3% of the adolescent sex offenders were convicted of a sexual offense following their involvement with the treatment program. Examination of nonsexual recidivism indicated that 37% of the offenders went on to commit a nonsexual offense. On average, the nonsexual offenses did not occur until seventeen and a half months after completion of the treatment program (range of four to thirty-nine months). Roughly 75% of the reoffenses were of a nonviolent nature, with a smaller number involving assaults (25%). Additional information obtained on these nonsexual reoffending youth indicated that they were high-risk delinquent youth even prior to the start of treatment. For example, 58% of these nonsexual reoffenders had committed a nonsexual offense prior to their conviction of a sexual offense. This statistic differed significantly from the 25% of youth in the nonoffending group who had committed a prior nonsexual offense (X^2 (1,32) = 10.93, $p < .05$). Moreover, of those youths who were suspended from the treatment program, 63% went on to commit a nonsexual reoffense. Thus, a large proportion of the recidivism came from youths who had histories of delinquent behavior and/or were unable to benefit from and comply with a community-based intervention program.

Important Differences Between Sexual Recidivists and Nonsexual Recidivists

The initial steps of any program evaluation must be to evaluate all attempts at intervention and then to proceed to examine and validate the effectiveness of specific components within the treatment program. The similarity found in offender and offense characteristics in this sample and those reported by Ryan et al. (1996) in a large national sample suggests that the current results are based on a representative sample of adolescent sex offenders. Only 3% of youths in this study were found to commit another sexual offense in the twenty-eight-month follow-up period. These early results are promising. They suggest that intensive sex offender–specific treatment is successful in averting the continuation of sexual offending behavior in high-risk adolescents who had multiple victims and/or had committed numerous offenses on the same victim. This also implies that this treatment program is able to prevent relapses in offending behavior and reduce the potential pool of adult sex offenders by helping these youths move along a healthier and less abusive developmental pathway. Although longer recidivism studies have been completed (Rubinstein et al., 1993; Borduin et al., 1990), their results were based on small nonrepresentative samples of adolescent sex offenders. There are only two published recidivism studies with a longer follow-up period using a representative sample of adolescent sex offenders (Bremer, 1992; Shram et al., 1991). Bremer (1992) found that there was no relationship between length of follow-up and likelihood of reoffending. She interpreted this result to mean that relapse is related to specific stressful events in an offender's life that are unpredictable. In contrast, Shram et al. (1993) found treated adolescent sex offenders to be at greatest risk for reoffending during the first year after treatment was completed. Given that these are the only longer-term studies that have addressed this question, further research is needed. As the current sample of adolescent sex offenders grows in number and the length of follow-up time increases, reexamination of recidivism data for TBASOP will allow for a more in-depth investigation of risk factors and will also provide a more valid account of sexual recidivism for this treatment program.

The descriptive information contained in these results with respect to nonsexual reoffending behavior points to the need for a broader intervention focus for some adolescent sex offenders. Adolescent sex offenders with strong criminogenic characteristics appear to require more specific and intensive services directed toward those factors related to nonsexual delinquent behavior. The TBASOP program appears to be very successful when dealing with sexually abusive behavior, but its success was less apparent for nonsexual offending behavior. This was largely due to those youths who were unable to comply with the expectations of a community-based program and did not follow through with treatment.

Despite these treatment failures, it is important to note that the 37% nonsexual recidivism rate found in this study is no different from that found in other outcome studies of adolescent sex offenders. When these results on nonsexual recidivism are taken together with previous studies, evidence suggests that it will be critical to assess and effectively treat criminogenic factors such as those identified by Hoge and Andrews (1996) in the Risk/Need Assessment form. Addressing these needs would not only be helpful in clinical work but would also provide the opportunity to assess whether the same criminogenic variables are able to predict nonsexual recidivism in sexual and nonsexual offenders. Results of the adult sex offender literature suggest that criminogenic variables do predict recidivism. As discovered in this evaluation, a small but important number of offenders do require greater structure and more intensive intervention before delinquent patterns of behavior can be stopped.

Conclusion

In light of the skepticism with which sex offender treatment is held, it is important that treatment providers take pains to study the efficacy of their programs. In an ideal world program administrators would be able to compare their treated patients with a match sample of untreated individuals, but this is rarely possible for community programs. It would require a group of sex offenders of equal severity to be released without treatment into the community. Given the unlikelihood of this occurrence, program administrators should nevertheless attempt to document the outcome of their treatment. Studying the differences between recidivists and nonrecidivists is another way of gaining insight into the treatment process. This study found several differences between the youths who committed sexual reoffenses and those who committed nonsexual reoffenses, a finding that has interesting implications for treatment.

Note

The authors gratefully acknowledge the encouragement and support of each member of the Thunder Bay Adolescent Sex Offender Program for making this research possible.

References

Abel, G. G., Mittelman, M. S., & Becker, J. V. (1985). Sex offenders: Results of assessment and recommendations for treatment. In H. Ben-Aaron, S. Hacker, & C. Webster (Eds.), *Clinical criminology: Current concepts* (pp. 127–155).Toronto: M&M Graphics.

Becker, J. V. (1990). Treating adolescent sexual offenders. *Professional Psychology: Research and Practice, 21,* 362–365.

Borduin, C. M., Henggeler, S. W., Blaske, D. M., & Stein, R. J., (1990). Multisystemic treatment of adolescent sexual offenders. *International Journal of Offender Therapy and Comparative Criminology, 34,* 105–113.

Brannon, J. M., & Troyer, R. (1991). Peer group counseling: A normalized residential alternative to the specialized treatment of adolescent sex offenders. *International Journal of Offender Therapy and Comparative Criminology, 35*(3), 225–234.

Bremer, J. F. (1992). Serious juvenile sex offenders: Treatment and long-term follow-up. *Psychiatric Annals, 22*(6), 326–332.

Davis, G. E., & Leitenberg, H. (1987). Adolescent sex offenders. *Psychological Bulletin, 101,* 417–427.

Fehrenbach, P. A., Smith, W., Monastersky, C., & Deisher, R. W. (1986). Adolescent sex offenders: Offender and offense characteristics. *American Journal of Orthopsychiatry, 56,* 225–233.

Hall, G. N. C. (1995). Sexual offender recidivism revisited: A meta-analysis of recent treatment studies. *Journal of Consulting and Clinical Psychology, 63*(5), 802–809.

Hanson, R. K., & Bussière, M. T. (1996). *Predictors of sexual offender recidivism: A meta-analysis.* (User Report No.1996-4). Ottawa: Corrections Branch, Ministry of the Solicitor General of Canada.

Hoge, R., & Andrews, D. A. (1996). *The Youth Level of Service/Case Management Inventory (YLS/CMI): Intake manual and item scoring key.* Carleton University, Ottawa, Canada.

Kahn, T. J., & Chambers, H. J. (1991). Assessing reoffense risk with juvenile sexual offenders. *Child Welfare, 70,* 333–345.

Knopp, F. (1982). *Remedial intervention in adolescent sex offenses: Nine program descriptions.* Syracuse, NY: Safer Society Press.

Lab, S. P., Shields, G., & Schondel, C. (1993). Research note: An evaluation of juvenile sexual offender treatment. *Crime and Delinquency, 39,* 543–553.

Rubinstein, M., Yeager, C. A. Goodstein, C., & Lewis, D. O. (1993). Sexually assaultive male juveniles: A follow-up. *American Journal of Psychiatry, 150,* 262–265.

Ryan, G., Miyoshi, T. J., Metzner, J. L., Krugman, R. D., & Fryer, G. E. (1996). Trends in a national sample of sexually abusive youths. *Journal of the American Academy of Child and Adolescent Psychiatry, 35*(1), 17–25.

Ryan, G. D. (1991). Incidence and prevalence of sexual offenses committed by juveniles. In G. D. Ryan & S. Lane (Eds.), *Juvenile sexual offending: Causes, consequences, and correction* (pp. 9–19). Lexington, MA: Lexington Books.

Schram, D. D., Milloy, C. D., & Rowe, W. E. (1991). *Juvenile sex offenders: A follow-up study of reoffense behavior.* From the Washington State Institute for Public Policy, Evergreen State College, Olympia, WA.

Smith, W. R., & Monastersky, C. (1986). Assessing juvenile sexual offenders' risk for reoffending. *Criminal Justice and Behavior, 13,* 115–140.

Chapter 19

Using Therapeutic Community Learning Experiences With Youth Sex Offenders

by James M. Yokley, Ph.D.

Overview

Traditional therapeutic communities (TCs) are most frequently associated with highly confrontational substance abuse treatment. A number of specific techniques have been developed for use in this type of situation. In this chapter, the author describes how these techniques are used within the TC environment. Here he reports the results of a clinical trial of TC experiential methods with youth sex offenders exhibiting multiple problems. These youth were living in specialized foster care and were highly responsive to the TC methods. The author also discusses how these experiences can be adapted for preteens.

Introduction

Programs for youth offenders are offered in a residential setting, which may be a state facility for delinquents, a private residential treatment program, or a traditional outpatient clinic setting. Typically the residential programs while trying to maintain a therapeutic environment, would not claim to be operating TCs, which use special techniques and approaches that have been developed for use in that setting (TC learning experiences). TCs encourage the development of responsibility and the utilization of new therapeutic tools in a unique experiential way.

One problem with using TCs and their associated learning experiences with youth offenders is that traditional clinicians view them too confrontational for use with young offenders. However, existing research suggests that youth offenders benefit from being held accountable for their behavior through the TC learning experiences (Pompi, 1994) and do not suffer adverse emotional impact (see section "Consumer Satisfaction and Emotional Well-Being," later in this chapter).

Application to Multiple Abusers Referred for Youth Sex Offender Treatment

Youth Sex Offenders Have Much in Common With Youth Substance Abusers. The rationale for adding TC social learning experiences that were originally developed for substance abusers to the cognitive-behavioral interventions used with multiple abusers referred for sex offender treatment relates to the similarity of these treatment populations. This similarity includes a lack of empathy, social immaturity, problems delaying gratification, lying, and manipulation (DeLeon, 1989). In addition to the "lack of empathy," which is considered to be the hallmark of sexual abusers (Sgroi, 1982, p. 253), the multiple abuser population exhibits extreme social "immaturity" and associated irresponsible acting out, which are considered to be hallmarks of substance abusers receiving treatment in residential TCs (DeLeon, 1989, p. 181). TC youths have been described as characterologically difficult clients whose impulsive, self-destructive acts create constant crises (Bratter, Bratter, Radda, & Steiner, 1993).

TC residents have been characterized as follows:

They include . . . low tolerance for all forms of discomfort and delay of gratification; inability to manage feelings (particularly hostility, guilt and anxiety); poor impulse control (particularly sexual or aggressive); poor judgment and reality testing concerning consequences of actions; unrealistic self-appraisal in terms of a discrepancy between personal resources and aspirations; prominence of lying; manipulation and deception as coping behaviors; problems with authority; social and personal irresponsibility, i.e., inconsistency or failure in completing expected obligations. (DeLeon, 1989, p. 181)

Both Populations Include Many Antisocial Personalities and Have a High Percentage of Character Disorders. Study results reveal that as many as half of drug/alcohol addicts may have a co-occurring antisocial personality (e.g., Blume, 1989; Calsyn, Fleming, Wells, & Saxon, 1996; Calsyn & Saxon, 1996; Craig & Olson, 1990). Personality testing has also indicated similarities between TC residents and multiple abusers referred for sexual offenses in terms of antisocial characteristics. The mean Minnesota Multiphasic Personality Inventory (MMPI) profile for TC residents is the elevated 4-8 code (DeLeon, 1989; Jainchill, 1994). The mean and highest frequency MMPI profile for sex offenders, particularly those who also tend to be physically aggressive (i.e., multiple abusers exhibiting both sexual and physical abuse), has also been the elevated 4-8 code in a number of studies (e.g., Armentrout & Hauer, 1978; Ericson et al., 1987; Langevin, Paitich, Freeman, Mann, & Handy, 1978; Radar, 1977). Along with other features, individuals with elevated 4-8 MMPI profiles exhibit authority resentment, impulse control problems, hostility, antisocial acting out, promiscuity, sexual deviation, drinking/drug abuse, exaggerated attention and affection needs, impaired empathy, manipulation, rationalization, blaming, and responsibility problems (Graham, 1977).

Many youth sex abusers suffer from "pan immaturity" in emotional/social adjustment (Fehrenbach, Smith, Monastersky, & Deisher, 1986; Shoor, Speed, & Bartelt, 1966) and character disorders. Becker, Kaplan, Cunningham-Rathner, & Kavoussi (1986) reported that 55% of their youth sex abuser sample were diagnosed as having character disorder and 50% had prior arrests for nonsexual crimes indicating a history of antisocial behavior. Awad, Saunders, and Levene (1984) also reported a history of character disorder symptoms in their youth sex abuser sample (e.g., lying, impulsive behavior, and unhappiness) and also reported that 50% of their sample had been arrested for nonsexual crimes. Fehrenbach et al. (1986) reported that 44% of their youth sex abusers sample committed at least one earlier non-sexual offense. Shoor et al. (1966) reported that 63% of their youth sex abuser sample exhibited previous delinquent activity. Awad et al. (1984) concluded that the same factors that have been found to contribute to juvenile delinquency in general seem to be found with youth sex abusers. The hypothesis that in youth, pure violence and sexual violence may reflect similar etiologies has been put forth by Lewis, Shankok, and Pincus (1979). Fehrenbach et al. (1986) concluded that youth sex abuse should be viewed not only as a potentially repetitive problem behavior but as a reflection of other adjustment and developmental problems. This social and emotional immaturity and character disorder is conceptualized as "pathological social immaturity" (Yokley, 1996) in the present study.

Many Youth Sex Offenders Are Multiple Abusers. It has also been established that many youth sex abusers are multiple abusers (i.e., of people, their property, and substances). Becker et al. (1986) reported that 41% of their youth sex abuser sample exhibited previous property abuse (i.e., burglary, robbery, trespassing, petty theft, and car theft) and 9% had previous substance abuse charges. Awad et al. (1984) also reported an extensive history of property abuse (i.e., breaking into homes, 30%; robbery, 8%; theft, 41%; vandalism, 16%; and arson, 12%) and a similar degree of substance abuse (i.e., 8%) in their youth sex abuser sample. Van Ness (1984) reported that 86% of the incarcerated youth sex abusers in her sample also evidenced a history of physical abuse (i.e., four or more aggressive attacks on others) and 52% had histories of substance abuse. Fehrenbach et al. (1986) reported that 44% of their youth sex abusers sample exhibited previous property abuse or physical abuse (i.e., theft, 38%; robbery or assault, 36%; and both, 26%).

Multiple abusers have significantly more sexual abuse victims (Yokley, 1996) and are thought to be at higher risk for reoffense. The more types of abuse problems a youth exhibits, the higher the probability of slipping up and committing one type of abuse. The abstinence violation effect dictates that when multiple abusers commit one type of abuse, they are likely to tell themselves "Because I've already violated my probation/parole, I might as well keep going," and then go on to commit another (usually more severe) type of abuse.

Traditional TC learning experiences are applicable with little modification to multiple abusers referred for sexual offense. Multiple abusers seem to have problems with vicarious learning. Their action-oriented style requires participant modeling and experiential learning. Hence, social and emotional learning experiences appear to fit their treatment needs best. The TC view and goal for substance abuse treatment along with the characteristics of that treatment population are consistent with the treatment needs and characteristics of multiple abusers referred for sexual abuse treatment.

Types of TC Learning Experiences

Therapeutic learning experiences include:

- *House meeting* (i.e., a gathering of all residents and staff to discuss important, serious matters).
- *Job function* (i.e., learning the work ethic and responsibility).
- *Pull-up* (i.e., a pull-up means pull someone up to your level of awareness by telling them something important that you have observed about their behavior or attitude that they need to "tighten up"). It is usually a brief, courteous, constructive criticism given by another resident.
- *Encounter group* (i.e., groups in which individuals encounter the feelings of themselves and others through "confrontation with concern"). Encounters help residents develop emotional and social maturity. Encounters exercise and expand the limits of emotional expression, self-control, and emotional endurance (i.e., "develop a callous on your belly"), as many abusers are selfish and insensitive to the impact of their behavior on others but hypersensitive to any minor personal affront directed toward them.) Encounter groups cycle through two levels with each person addressed.
  — *Level 1* (confrontation). Involves direct verbal confrontation of all the problem behaviors or situations caused by the group member who is being confronted. Confrontations or "ndictments" are handled in rank order with the person expressing the most intense feeling going first).
  — *Level 2* (concern). After all group members have completed "getting their feelings off" during the indictment, no further raised voices are allowed. To show concern and promote honesty, this level of the group, known as "the patch-up," focuses on support through identification and problem solving.
- *Spoken to*. A "spoken to" is a verbal reprimand, which includes three important components that are delivered consecutively (i.e., the behavior incident, the atti-

tude which set the occasion for the incident, and what the resident needs to do to change the attitude in order to prevent further incidents).

- *Haircut* (i.e., higher-intensity formal feedback). A "haircut" is a more intense verbal reprimand during which the resident has "about an inch of bad attitude taken off the top."
- *Bench* (i.e., extended time out for self-reflection and introspection). When on the bench, a resident is not allowed to speak or leave for any reason. If necessary, the resident must eat meals on the bench and get permission from an expediter (i.e., staff assistant) to go to the bathroom.
- *Sign* (i.e., written reminder). Artificial reminders must be constructed to symbolize the problem and remind the abusers because they "forget" and cannot remind themselves. The reminder must remain in place long enough to develop an appropriate emotional association with the problem behavior in order to help the abuser learn from the experience.
- *Contract.* A commitment contract mandates a commitment task designed to regain the trust of the rest of the residents so that the offender can be reintegrated into the TC. The object of the commitment task is to demonstrate a genuine commitment to treatment. Two basic types of commitment tasks are "work" and "spare parts." A work contract usually involves more physical work and a spare parts contract usually involves more emotional work.

(For a more complete and detailed list of TC learning experiences along with the theoretical underpinnings that support these tools, see Chapter 25 of this volume.)

Clinical Trial of TC Learning Experiences With Multiple Abusers

To date there have been no published outcome studies on sex abuser programs designed specifically to treat multiple abusers and the pathological social immaturity that underlies their multiple forms of abuse. The purpose of the present study was to develop a treatment program that targets the pathological social immaturity in youth sex abusers who exhibit multiple types of abuse and conduct an outpatient clinical trial of that program. An outpatient clinical trial helps isolate the impact of the TC learning experiences from the combined effect of the learning experiences and milieu therapy of the residential TC, which has already been demonstrated to be quite effective in previous studies.

The mean age of the multiple abusers in the present study ($n = 13$) was 16.3 ($SD = 1.5$), 92% were male and 77% were caucasian. All were referred for youth sex offender treatment and placed in an intensive outpatient treatment program with therapeutic foster care. The mean number of different types of abuse exhibited per abuser was 3.4 ($SD = .77$). Fifty-eight percent exhibited the same four types of abuse (i.e., problems with sexual abuse, physical abuse, property abuse, and substance abuse). Sixty-nine percent were on parole from a state correctional institution.

Traditional TC learning experiences were selected as the method of behavior management and social maturity development for the multiple abusers in the present study. These learning experiences were integrated into a treatment program that targets the pathological social immaturity that underlies multiple abuse behavior through confrontation with concern and by reinforcement of competing prosocial/family values (i.e., honesty, trust, loyalty, concern, and responsibility). All the basic traditional TC learning experiences were employed in the present study without changes except the highly structured commitment contract. The commitment contract used in the present study was a work contract modified slightly to fit current juvenile justice practices and relabeled "abbreviated boot camp."

The military trains individuals to work together for the protection of the country. Military personnel are used in abbreviated boot camp to train abusers to work together in group treatment for the protection of the community. The military basic training team building, "leave no man behind" attitude and emphasis on self-discipline fits well with the TC contract goals of reunification, "you are your brother's keeper," and serious effort toward positive life change. In both cases, the goal is to save lives and protect people.

Because the commitment contract was the most intense and highly structured intervention, a separate study on that learning experience was conducted. The results of a one-year study on the use of abbreviated boot camp as a commitment contract revealed significant benefits to abusers with no adverse impact (Yokley, Laraway, & Clough, 1997).

In addition to the implementation of TC learning experiences, the typical abuse behavior conceptualization of understanding the relapse cycle was replaced with the abuse development triad (Yokley, 1996). The abuse development triad is an expanded conceptual model that addresses more of the components necessary to meet the TC goal of an overall lifestyle change. This conceptual model helps multiple abusers understand how they acquired, maintained, and generalized their abuse behavior. The acquisition component of the abuse development triad involves the chain of events that led to abuse. The maintenance component involves the stress-abuse cycle that maintained the behavior and helped develop a pathological level of social and emotional immaturity. The generalization component includes the anatomy of interacting social and emotional immaturity components that set the occasion for multiple forms of abuse.

The study was carried out in sequential steps.

- *Implementation period 1 (two months).* TC learning experiences were implemented in addition to more traditional psychoeducational abuser treatment program interventions such as group discussion of problem issues, relapse prevention, and skill building, which were in effect throughout the study.
- *Partial learning experience withdrawal (one month, unannounced).* TC learning experiences were organized into five levels (A through E) according to intensity. During this study period every attempt was made to avoid using the more intense (i.e., levels D and E) learning experiences which were used on only two occasions. Abusers, foster parents and staff were not informed of this treatment plan change.
- *Full learning experience withdrawal (two weeks, announced).* No TC learning experiences were used. Abusers, foster parents, and staff were informed that there would be no further use of learning experiences. The length of this condition was cut short by an alarming rise in behavior incidents requiring that the learning experiences be restored to avoid a danger to the safety and security of the community.
- *Implementation period 2 (two months).* The use of all TC learning experiences was restored.

Results Confirm Effectiveness of TC Learning Experiences

Behavior Management. During the periods that learning experiences were implemented, each abuser had an average of two to three behavior incident reports every month. Behavior problem reports went up by a factor of 2 during the unannounced partial learning experience withdrawal (step 2) and continued to increase dramatically during full learning experience withdrawal (step 3; see Figure 19.1). A repeated measures analysis of variance (ANOVA) revealed a significant incident report effect, $F(3, 9) = 36.6$, $p < .001$. Newman–Keuls multiple comparisons indicated that there were significantly more behavior problem incident reports during full learning experience withdrawal (step 3) than during any other study condition. When only serious behavior incident reports were evaluated, the results revealed that during periods of partial and full learning experience withdrawal (steps 2 and 3) there were more parole,

Figure 19.1
Treatment Outcome: Incident Report Frequency During Four Study Conditions

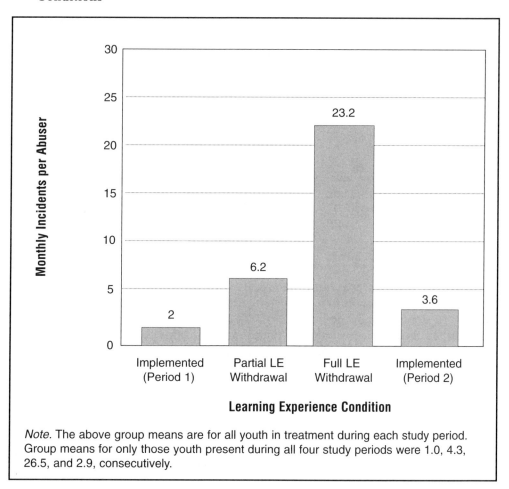

Note. The above group means are for all youth in treatment during each study period. Group means for only those youth present during all four study periods were 1.0, 4.3, 26.5, and 2.9, consecutively.

probation, or legal violations (see Figure 19.2) and more sexual, physical or property abuse incidents (see Figure 19.3).

Treatment Participation. The percentage of abusers turning in treatment homework assignments decreased 25% during full learning experience withdrawal (i.e., step 3;

Figure 19.2
Treatment Outcome: Probation, Parole, or Legal Violation During Four Study Conditions

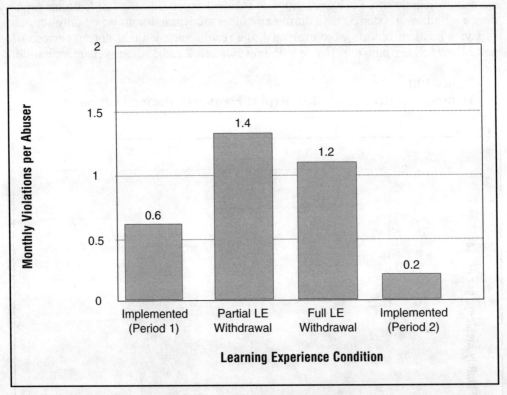

see Figure 19.4). There was some decrease in abusers helping themselves through group therapy discussion during periods of partial and full learning experience withdrawal (i.e., steps 2 and 3; see Figure 19.5). The percentage of abusers helping others during group therapy decreased 15% during partial learning experience withdrawal (step 2) and 30% during full learning experience withdrawal (step 3; see Figure 19.6). Peer-assigned group participation grades dropped one grade level during full learning experience withdrawal (step 3; see Figure 19.7). All study treatment participation measures increased after the TC learning experiences were restored.

Consumer Satisfaction and Emotional Well-Being. A paired-comparison *t*-test revealed that consumers (i.e., program residents, foster parents, and social workers) reported the treatment program as significantly more effective in managing abuser behavior with the learning experiences implemented than when the learning experi-

Figure 19.3
Treatment Outcome: Physical, Sexual, or Property Abuse During Four
Study Conditions

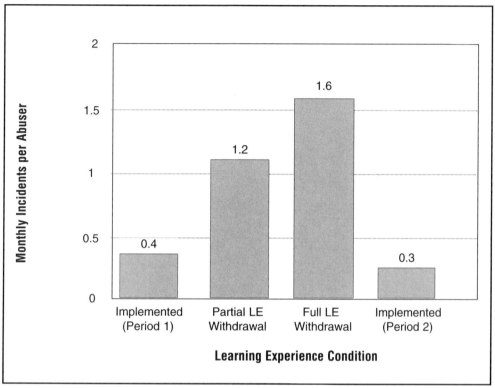

ences were withdrawn, t(9) = 7.7, *p* < .001. Both the program residents and staff reported more effective behavior management with the learning experiences implemented. Consumer ratings on behavior management during learning experience implementation and withdrawal appear in Table 19.1. A paired comparison *t*-test revealed that consumers reported the treatment program behavior intervention intensity as "Just about right" with the learning experiences implemented but significantly "too weak" when the learning experiences were withdrawn, t(9) = 9.8, *p* < .001. Both the program residents and staff reported the behavior intervention intensity as "Just about right" with the learning experiences and "too weak" without them. Consumer ratings on intervention intensity during learning experience implementation and withdrawal appear in Table 19.2. There were no significant increases in abuser levels of depression, t(4) = .52, *p* = .63, anxiety, t(4) = 1.36, *p* = .24, state anger, t(4) = .08, *p* = .94, or trait anger, t(4) = 1.05, *p* = .35 after the learning experiences were restored (i.e., implementation period 2). Measures of abuser emotional well-being appear in Table 19.3.

Discussion of the Effect of Learning Experiences

Although the present study involved a single group clinical trial and generalization of the results must be done with caution, the outcome was quite encouraging.

Figure 19.4
Treatment Participation: Homework Completion During Four Study Conditions[a]

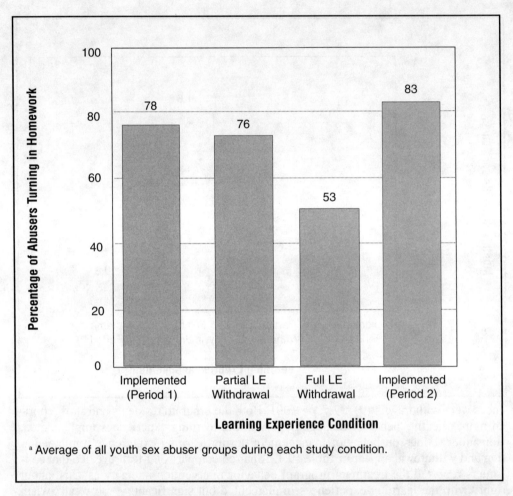

[a] Average of all youth sex abuser groups during each study condition.

Specifically, the results revealed that the combination of traditional TC learning experiences with an expanded abuse conceptual model (i.e., The Abuse Development Triad) and an intensive outpatient therapeutic foster family treatment milieu was a viable treatment approach for multiple abusers who have been referred for outpatient sexual abuse treatment. The learning experiences produced clinically significant improvements in abuser behavior management, treatment participation and treatment satisfaction without an adverse impact on abuser emotional wellbeing. There was dramatic deterioration in abuser behavior control during the announced full withdrawal of all learning experiences (step 3) when compared to the unannounced partial withdrawal (step 2) period. This stark contrast tends to indicate that the learning experiences have a deterrent effect. Simply knowing that the learning experiences are in place appears to help abusers motivate their internal self-control resources. When the learning experiences were implemented, consumer satisfaction ratings on the treat-

Figure 19.5
Treatment Participation: Helping Self Through Group Discussion During
Four Study Conditions[a]

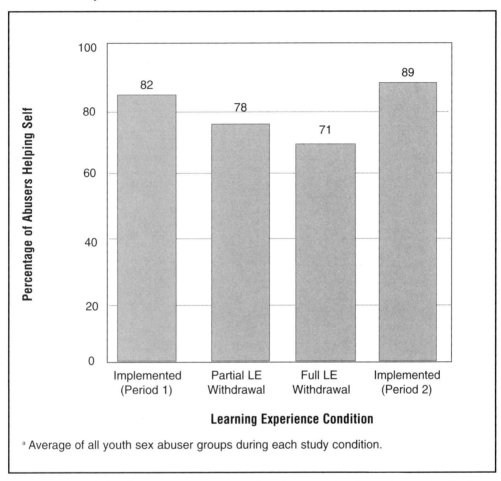

[a] Average of all youth sex abuser groups during each study condition.

ment program behavior management as well as intervention intensity tend to indicate that these experiences improve feelings of safety and security in the abusers in addition to their caretakers. The emotional stress and hard work involved when the learning experiences were implemented did not increase the abusers psychological test measures of depression, anxiety or anger. Thus, implementing high intensity level TC Learning Experiences in the outpatient setting does not appear to set up a situation where abusers are likely to act feelings out on others in the community. In fact, the present behavior incident data reveal the reverse to be true.

The present intensive outpatient clinical trial allowed a demonstration of the impact of TC learning experiences without the additive effect of the powerful residential TC positive peer culture milieu. TC learning experiences require positive peer culture support. Substituting an intensive outpatient treatment with a closely coordinated group of therapeutic foster families allowed the treatment providers to generate enough of the TC positive peer culture milieu to achieve the necessary additive

Figure 19.6
Treatment Participation: Helping Others in Group Therapy During Four Study Conditions[a]

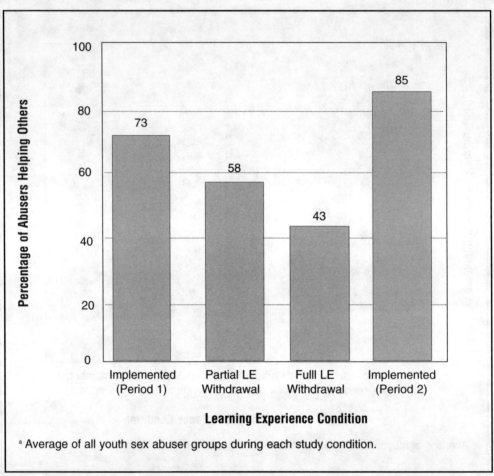

^a Average of all youth sex abuser groups during each study condition.

impact. The present results tend to indicate that the impact of the TC learning experiences may be strong enough to allow substituting alternative support systems for the learning experiences which have been traditionally supported by a strong residential group home milieu. These results have positive implications for the use of TC learning experiences in other outpatient or day treatment settings.

Application to Preteen Abusers Referred for Sex Offender Treatment

Although the present clinical trial did not include preteen abusers, a number of factors support the application of TC learning experiences to this population. The preteen abusers referred to in this section are mutually sexually reactive children who molest (Van Eys, 1997) and exhibit multiple abuser characteristics (i.e., multiple forms of abusive acting out). Removal of aggressive, maladjusted children from their

Figure 19.7
Peer-Assigned Group Grades During Four Study Conditions[a]

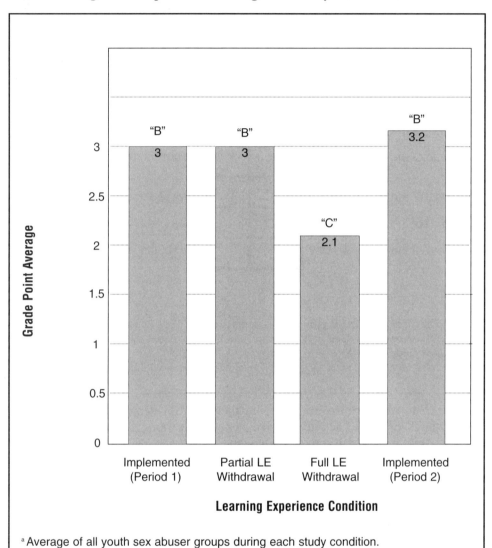

^a Average of all youth sex abuser groups during each study condition.

pathological setting and placement in a therapeutic community where family-type unity is encouraged and treatment problems do not bring rejection through discharge was recommended some time ago (Lowenstein, 1982). Like the traditional TC population, a large proportion exhibit comorbid conduct disorder and substance use disorder (Reebye, Moretti & Lessard, 1995). As predicted, action-oriented participant modeling has demonstrated better learning results than passive modeling of sexual abuse material with young children (Wurtele, Marrs & Miller, 1987). There has been a long-standing treatment of preteens with activity based therapy and the therapeutic milieu (e.g., Faux & Dixon, 1967; Kutschinski, 1977). Despite the similarity of this popula-

Table 19.1
Consumer Satisfaction Reports on Abuser Behavior Management During Learning Experience Implementation and Withdrawal

Learning Experiences Implemented			Full Learning Experience Withdrawal[a]
Able to control behavior of:			Able to control behavior of:
none of the youth abusers		57%	none of the youth abusers
some of the youth abusers		43%	some of the youth abusers
most of the youth abusers	27%		most of the youth abusers
almost all of the youth abusers	46%		almost all of the youth abusers
all of the youth abusers	27%		all of the youth abusers
	100%	100%	

Note. Consumers were TASC program residents and staff (i.e., foster parents and social workers). There were no significant differences between resident ratings and staff ratings during each study conditions.
[a] Traditional interventions such as group discussion of problem behavior remained in use.

tion to traditional TC abusers along with their cognitive/emotional maturity level which requires repetitive activity-based experiential learning, there are apparently no published reports of TCs for preteen offenders.

The more recently modified TC has addressed concerns that the TC procedure of giving responsibility for all house functions to the residents could recreate a dysfunctional family of parentialized children. The modified TC has allowed for all forms of supervised assisted living in small surrogate family units where residents are only assigned responsibilities that are appropriate for their developmental level or diagnostic condition. For example, instead of learning to purchase groceries and prepare their own meals, since food has special nurturance meanings to children, preteens can learn through interaction with the kitchen staff preparing their meals (Roberts & Bushaw, 1978).

Building a Functional Family Model

The TC was founded on basic family values such as honesty, concern and responsibility, which are the ideal building blocks for the healthy development of the preteen offender. Encounter groups have the potential to build self-efficacy in preteens who feel helpless about their natural family situation. The modified TC organization of the surrogate support families combined with the encounter group focus on the present

Table 19.2
Consumer Satisfaction Reports on Behavior Intensity During Learning Experience Implementation and Withdrawal

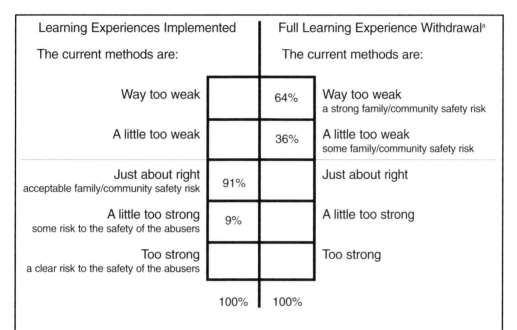

Learning Experiences Implemented			Full Learning Experience Withdrawal[a]	
The current methods are:			The current methods are:	
Way too weak		64%	Way too weak a strong family/community safety risk	
A little too weak		36%	A little too weak some family/community safety risk	
Just about right acceptable family/community safety risk	91%		Just about right	
A little too strong some risk to the safety of the abusers	9%		A little too strong	
Too strong a clear risk to the safety of the abusers			Too strong	
	100%	100%		

Note. Consumers were TASC program residents and staff (i.e., foster parents and social workers). There were no significant differences between resident ratings and staff ratings during each study conditions.
[a] Traditional interventions such as group discussion of problem behavior remained in use.

and on one's behavior marks a clear boundary between the TC family and the natural family. For older children, earning reentry status and a community job may be replaced with earning the right to be trusted to help others through appropriate community service (Brendtro, 1985; 1985b). The preteen helplessness about the dysfunctional family relationships that they can't change (Kelly, 1986) is addressed by their TC family where they can change both the behavior of themselves and of significant others through Encounter groups, Pull-ups and other learning experiences. Negative home experiences in prior dysfunctional family settings can be addressed through the TC view of residents as extended family. Family can be redefined as those that you can count on to show you honesty and concern. The modified TC milieu is capable of reducing isolation, mediating damaged trust and providing a sense of belonging to a prosocial group that provides the corrective attachment experience needed to stop children from victimizing others (Friedrich, 1993).

Modifying Learning Experiences for Preteens

Since some of the psychological shame research points to adult problems as the result of childhood shaming experiences, TC learning experiences need to be modi-

Table 19.3
Measures of Abuser Emotional Well-Being: Mean Test Raw Scores During Learning Experience Implementation and Withdrawal

Test Administered	Full LE Withdrawal	Implementation (Period 2)
Beck Depression Inventory	7.8	5.6
Beck Anxiety Inventory	7.7*	3.1
State–Trait Anger Expression Inventory		
State Anger	13.4	13.2
Trait Anger	15.0	18.2

Note. Measures of depression, anxiety, and anger were taken twice during each study condition. The mean raw scores listed are the average of all abusers on both measures during each condition. Abuser anxiety was elevated slightly (i.e., at the lower end of the "mild" elevation range) during full LE withdrawal.
*Clinically elevated test scores.

fied accordingly for this population. However, caution must be exercised not to completely remove disapproval of deviant behavior as this could escalate existing problems. The cooperative, team building group games, role plays, stories and exercises currently used with prepubescent sexual aggressors (e.g., Van Eys, 1997) are entirely consistent with the experiential milieu of the modified TC. In addition to attention-deficit/hyperactivity disorder, preteen abusers exhibit comorbid PTSD (Van Eys, 1997). Posttraumatic stress disorder (PTSD) research indicates that experiential activities with children may uncover problems by replicating a body pose that triggers emotional connections. Experiential activities where the child is allowed to express negative affect (e.g., encounter groups) or act out perceived control of the situation can provide relief (Nadar & Pynoos, 1991). The modified TC for mentally retarded/developmentally disabled offenders has already had its daily activities, learning experiences and coping skill requirements scaled back from adult expectations to preteen developmental levels. Thus, it appears that a good deal of the groundwork for a functional preteen offender TC has already been laid.

Because the learning experiences described in this chapter are easily translated into outpatient versions, the therapeutic foster care setting for preteen offenders would be an ideal setting to implement an intensive outpatient or day treatment version. This is particularly promising in light of the positive results obtained using TC learning experiences with youth multiple abusers in therapeutic foster care (Yokley & Laraway, 1996). The fairly recent "foster family clusters" approach where every family in the cluster has a role in every child's life (Eckstein, 1995) appears to be able to provide the additional support needed by preteens. "It takes a village to raise a child" and an intensive outpatient TC program using foster family clusters could provide the entire surrogate family, extended family support system and adult male role models necessary (Lund, 1995) to accomplish this task. The foster family cluster approach allows for the development of an entire surrogate extended family support system. Given the host of supportive factors outlined, clinical and research application of modified TC principles to the preteen offender population are strongly recommended.

Conclusion

One of the major problems in sex offender treatment is ascertaining whether the tools that the therapist is teaching in classes and groups are being utilized in daily life. To successfully change the sex offender, his daily interactions must change. He must begin to take responsibility for every decision he makes. The learning experiences that were first developed in generic and substance abuse–oriented TCs are ideal for helping individuals monitor their behavior and integrate what they are learning in treatment. They address offenders' learning deficits and limited insight through action-oriented learning experiences that are consistent with their personality style. This chapter has discussed the application of these residential group home experiential activities to out-patient treatment environments. It has also provided initial research evidence that these approaches can change behavior without an adverse emotional impact.

Note

A portion of the material contained in this chapter was presented at the fifteenth annual research and treatment conference of the Association for the Treatment of Sexual Abusers.

References

Armentrout, J., & Hauer, A. (1978). MMPIs of rapists of children and non-rapist sex offenders. *Journal of Clinical Psychology 34*(2), 330–332.

Becker, J. V., Kaplan, M., Cunningham-Rathner, J., & Kavoussi, R. (1986). Characteristics of adolescent incest perpetrators: Preliminary findings. *Journal of Family Violence, 1,* 85–97.

Blume, S. (1989). Dual diagnosis: Psychoactive substance dependence and the personality disorders. *Journal of Psychoactive Drugs, 21*(2), 139–144.

Bratter, B., Bratter, T., Radda, H., & Steiner, K. (1993). The residential therapeutic caring community. *Psychotherapy, 30*(2), 299–304.

Brendtro, L. (1985). Synergistic relationships: The powerful "SR" of reeducation. *Milieu Therapy, 4*(1), 3–12.

Calsyn, D., Fleming, C., Wells, E., & Saxon, A. (1996). Personality disorder subtypes among opiate addicts in methadone maintenance. *Psychology of Addictive Behaviors, 10*(1), 3–8.

Calsyn, D., & Saxon, A. (1990). Personality disorder subtypes among cocaine and opiod addicts using the Millon Clinical Multiaxial Inventory. *International Journal of the Addictions, 25,* 1037–1049.

Craig, R. J., & Olson, R. E. (1990). MCMI comparisons of cocaine and heroin addicts. *Journal of Clinical Psychology, 15*(1–2), 231–237.

DeLeon, G. (1989). Psychopathology and substance abuse: What is being learned from research in therapeutic communities. *Journal of Psychoactive Drugs, 21*(2), 177–187.

Eckstein, M. (1995). Foster family clusters: Continuum advocate home network. In L. Combrinck-Graham, (Ed.), *Children in families at risk: Maintaining the connection* (pp. 275–298). New York: Guilford Press.

Ericson, W., Luxenberg, M., Walbek, N., & Seely, R. (1987). Frequency of MMPI two-point code types among sex offenders. *Journal of Consulting and Clinical Psychology, 55*(4), 566–570.

Faux, E., & Dixon, D. (1967) Children in the therapeutic community. *Diseases of the Nervous System, 28*(3), 170–177.

Fehrenbach, P., Smith, W., Monastersky, C., & Deisher, R. (1986). Adolescent sexual offenders: Offender and offense characteristics. *American Journal of Orthopsychiatry, 56,* 225–233.

Friedrich, W. N. (1993). Foreword. In E. Gil & T. Johnson (Eds.), *Sexualized children: Assessment and treatment of sexualized children who molest.* Rockville MD: Launch Press.

Graham, J. (1977). *The MMPI: A practical guide.* New York: Oxford University Press.

Jainchill, N. (1994). Co-morbidity and therapeutic community treatment. In F. Tims, G. DeLeon, & N Jainchill (Eds.), *Therapeutic community: Advances in research and application* (pp. 209–231) (NIDA Monograph No. 144, NIH Publication No. 94-3633). Rockville, MD: National Institute on Drug Abuse.

Kelley, S. (1986). Learned helplessness in the sexually abused child. *Issues in Comprehensive Pediatric Nursing, 9*(3), 193–207.

Kutschinski, W. (1977) Milieu therapy under the primary caretaker system at the University of Michigan's Children's Psychiatric Hospital. *Child Psychiatry and Human Development, 8*(1), 31–42.

Langevin, R., Paitich, D., Freeman, R., Mann, K., & Handy, L. (1978). Personality characteristics and sexual anomolies in males. *Candian Journal of Behavioral Science, 10,* 222–238.

Lewis, D. O., Shankok, S., & Balla, D. (1979). Perinatal difficulties, head and face trauma, and child abuse in the medical histories of seriously delinquent children. *American Journal of Psychiatry, 136*(4-A), 419–423.

Lewis, D. O., Shankok, S., & Pincus, J. (1979). Juvenile male sexual assaulters. *American Journal of Psychiatry, 136,* 1194–1196.

Lowenstein, L. (1982). The treatment of aggressive behaviour in maladjusted children. *National Council for Educational Standards Bulletin. No. 5,* pp. 15–20.

Lund, D. (1995). Matrilineal descent and juvenile offender counseling. *International Journal of Offender Therapy and Comparative Criminology, 39*(1), 43–46.

Pompi, K. (1994). Adolescents in therapeutic communities: Retention and posttreatment outcome. In F. Tims, G. DeLeon, & N. Jainchill (Eds.), *Therapeutic community: Advances in research and application* (pp. 128–161) (NIDA Research Monograph 144, NIH Publication No. 94-3633). Rockville, MD: National Institute on Drug Abuse.

Radar, C. (1977). MMPI profile types of exposers, rapists and assaulters in a court services population. *Journal of Consulting and Clinical Psychology, 45*(1), 61–69.

Reebye, P., Moretti, M., & Lessard, J. (1995). Conduct disorder and substance use disorder: Comorbidity in a clinical sample of preadolescents and adolescents [Special issue on child and adolescent psychiatry]. *Canadian Journal of Psychiatry, 40*(6), 313–319.

Roberts, M., & Bushaw, E. (1978). Food for thought: Participation of kitchen staff in milieu treatment. *Child Care Quarterly, 7*(3), 242–249.

Sgroi, S. (1982). Handbook of clinical intervention in child sexual abuse. Lexington, MA: Lexington Books.

Shoor, M., Speed, M., & Bartelt, C. (1966). Syndrome of the adolescent child molester. *American Journal of Psychiatry, 122,* 783–789.

Van Eys, P. (1997). Group treatment for prepubescent boys with sexually aggressive behavior: Clinical considerations and proposed treatment techniques. *Cognitive and Behavioral Practice, 4,* 349–382.

Wurtele, S., Marrs, S., & Miller-Perrin, C. (1987). Practice makes perfect? The role of participant modeling in sexual abuse prevention programs. *Journal of Consulting and Clinical Psychology, 55*(4), 599–602.

Yokley, J. (1996, March). *The development of abuse in youth sex offenders: A conceptual model with treatment implications.* Twelfth Annual Conference of the National Adolescent Perpetrator Network, Minneapolis.

Yokley, J., & Laraway, C. (1996, November). The use of therapeutic community learning experiences in the treatment of youth sex offenders: An outpatient clinical trial. Fifteenth Annual Research and Treatment Conference of the Association for the Treatment of Sexual Abusers, Chicago.

Yokley, J., Laraway, C. , & Clough, A. (1997, November). Behavior therapy and criminal justice: The controversy over boot camp treatments. Thirty-first Annual Convention of the Association for the Advancement of Behavior Therapy, Miami, FL.

Part 4

Developmentally Disabled Offenders

If sex offenders are challenging to treat, developmentally disabled sex offenders may be even more challenging. However, these individuals are not drastically different from their peers with higher-functioning levels. In many ways they may be easier to treat in that they may not engaged in elaborate intellectualized games and manipulations.

Throughout the country an increasing number of professionals are specializing in dealing with this special population. However, many areas still lack the special services needed to provide treatment to these offenders. Also, a number of individuals with intellectual limitations have difficulty controlling their sexual impulses but never receive specialized treatment because they are never processed through the criminal justice system. Agencies that deal with the developmentally disabled are just now beginning to realize that they are responsible for individuals who are difficult to place and supervise because of their sexual impulsivity. However, these agencies may be reluctant to seek out "sex offender treatment" for their clients as they feel the clients will then be labeled. If these people are residing in the community, neighbors may become upset; group homes may be pressured to move or, in turn, may bar these individuals; sheltered workshops may view these individuals as liabilities. Yet without specialized treatment, these individuals will probably not learn to control their behavior.

The professionals who contributed chapters to Part 4 have developed and/or adopted special techniques for dealing with developmentally disabled sex offenders. Lisa Coston and Joyce F. Lakey enthusiastically embrace treating these individuals and recognize their special strengths, including uncomplicated defense systems and sense of humor. They discuss the basic treatment goals, which include helping these individuals examine their defense systems, helping them adapt to change, enhancing coping skills, understanding cognitive distortions, and enhancing social skills. These goals are not markedly different from the treatment goals of normally functioning sex offenders. However, presentation of these skills must be modified to compensate for various learning difficulties.

Julie Brown and Andy Pond suggest that interventions must be focused, concrete, and specific. It is easy to believe that an intellectually limited individual understands what the therapist is presenting. These authors point out that these clients often manifest the "nod of incomprehension." The therapist must develop ways of testing whether there is any real comprehension. These individuals often also have a limited ability to regulate affect and control their impulses. Many of the techniques that have been developed to deal with emotional dysregulation in borderline personalities can be used effectively with this population. Often these clients show little, if any, ability to recognize emotions or degree of emotional arousal. In addition, these clients also need training in thought and behavioral awareness skills.

Nancy M. Stacken and Jim Shevich work with intellectually disabled, socially inadequate sex offenders within a regular prison. In this situation not only is there the challenge inherent in treating this population but there is also the problem of keeping these individuals physically safe and psychologically intact in a dangerous environment. These authors have been able to establish a secure therapeutic setting that enhances the treatment process. They have also developed special techniques including the visual crime scene, personal drawing of sexually deviant behavior, and "old me/new me" techniques.

Finally, James M. Yokley presents ways of adapting the traditional therapeutic community (TC) for this population. He stresses the use of repetitive experiential learning experiences. He suggests ways of adapting the TC for individuals who will live in supervised situations. He also gives specific suggestions for modifying traditional TC modalities.

The intellectually challenged sex offender probably has no higher a recidivism rate than does the sex offender with normal intelligence. He may well be a refreshing change from the highly manipulative antisocial or psychopathic offender. The therapist and the probation or parole officer need to meet the challenge of adapting their approach to fit the learning style of this population, which can be quite a creative and rewarding undertaking.

Chapter 20

Creative Therapy With Intellectually Disabled Male Adolescent Sex Offenders

by Lisa Coston, M.S. and Joyce F. Lakey, M.A.

Overview

Too often treatment professionals focus on the deficits of their clients and ignore or pass lightly over their strengths. This is especially true if the clients are expected to be resistant and slow to internalize complex concepts. Cambone (1995) suggested that troubled children are often viewed strictly from the framework of their deficits rather than their strengths. The purpose of this chapter is to identify some attributes of intellectually disabled male adolescent sex offenders that invite creative techniques. It also seeks to illustrate that treating these individuals can be a humbling, enriching, and challenging experience.

Introduction

Intellectually disabled male adolescent sex offenders exhibit a splendid array of positive qualities that a knowledgeable therapist can use to develop appropriate moral values, empathy, and remorse. The remarkable and delightful surprise in treating this population is that they exhibit many qualities that enrich treatment for themselves and their therapists. Harnessing those resources by utilizing a variety of therapeutic techniques can be a poignant growth journey laced with humor and growth for both client and practitioner. These observations are based on our thirteen years of combined experience treating clients between the ages of 12 and 17 in a private, nonprofit, residential setting for delinquent boys.

Examining the Defense System

The defense system of an intellectually disabled adolescent sex offender is usually much less complicated than that of an individual who is endowed with normal cognitive functioning. According to Haaven, Little, and Petre-Miller (1990), such a person "may be quick to anger, and, lacking verbal and social skills, have fewer ways to cope with his environment or divert anger through catharic release" (p. 5). For example, in an obvious use of reaction formation, a client pretended that he hated another boy when, in fact, he was sexually acting out with him. To express their frustrations, other students have hidden under beds or in closets, torn toilets off the wall, ripped clothes, or become encopretic in fits of anger. These incidents are usually best handled in a low-key fashion or through the structure provided in a controlled environment. Often humor can be used to deescalate such situations.

These clients show tendencies to use anger to avoid reality. This tendency contributes to their unpredictability. However, it might be an adaptive way to deal with a dysfunctional environment. Perhaps the reality that these offenders create for themselves facilitates their survival in a hostile environment and that strength can be exploited in therapy.

One student was using his own version of reality when he created a fictitious report card on the computer to boost his own pride. He was planning to send the altered report card to his mother so that she would be proud of his good grades. Staff praised him for his creativity on the computer and encouraged him to route his newly found skill in a more appropriate way.

Managing Change

Intellectually disabled male adolescent sex offenders need maximum structure as they generally adapt poorly to change. They can become aggressive, sad, manic, sometimes even suicidal quite suddenly without any apparent connection to a specific event. They may sexually act out when none of their precursors or predictors are apparent. Eventually, after a great deal of observation, therapists can identify a cycle and then a cyclical pattern. Through the creation of a stable environment and calm repetition and consistency, the clients may become gradually more open to change. Often the use of humor and role playing, not as a put-down but to mirror negative behavior, can prompt slow change. Relevant cartoons, comics, poetry, therapeutic stories, and articles of current events can be introduced to identify thinking errors and suggest socially acceptable behavior in response to change.

Enhancing Coping Skills

Coping skills related to external and internal changes are scarce in this population. These individuals are usually unsophisticated in the ways of the world and naive with little or no insight. Haaven et al. (1990) stress the need to "link emotion to the learning process" and suggest that offenders will "retain what they are taught if the learning experience is fun, dramatic or bizarre" (p. 22). These authors have developed a number of highly creative methods of presenting treatment materials to their patients.

This population may have little ability to generalize values or moral beliefs to assist in controlling behavior. For example, an adolescent sex offender was in a bus station when he was solicited by a drug dealer. He refused to buy anything, and he excitedly reported his experience to a policeman who arrested the dealer. The boy was an instant hero. He was puzzled by the praise of peers and staff.

"Doesn't everyone turn in drug dealers?" he asked. He had a clear picture of good and evil in this situation yet he was unable to make that distinction when he molested a neighbor girl. The morality issues of both situations only became clear to him after a discussion of his offense and the bus stop experience, noting common elements in each. Of course, this sort of disparity between the application of morals and values in one situation (the bus station) versus another situation (the neighbor child) is not unique to the intellectually challenged and is practically a hallmark of sex offender behavior.

Intellectually impaired adolescent sex offenders demonstrate poor social skills (Davis & Leitenberg, 1987; Stermac & Sheridan, cited in Barbaree, Marshall, & Hudson, 1993) with little sense of propriety. One client casually used an obscene word as an invitation to his therapist to have a sexual relationship with no awareness of how inappropriate his behavior was. Another client angrily called his therapist an obscene name. Her unexpectedly firm but friendly response caught him off guard, and he did not repeat the name calling.

Being Aware of Cognitive Deficits

One can never assume what basic information these clients might possess. A client said that he felt discouraged and hopeless. The therapist started to tell the children's story of *The Little Engine That Could*. "The little engine that what?" he exclaimed. Only one offender in a group of twelve had ever heard that favorite tale about persistence, and there was confusion over the use of the word "could."

Therapists must constantly evaluate how well intellectually disabled clients are processing new information. The therapist must be prepared to repeat that information over and over again. In discussing sexuality, intellectually disabled clients may mistakenly believe that they are not to have a sexual life at all because they have difficulty sorting out appropriate sexual thoughts from inappropriate ones and decreasing their deviant arousal patterns. They conclude that any sexual thought or feeling is bad. Thus monitoring and correcting these impressions on a daily basis is important.

Along the way therapists must take care that clients are not taking messages literally. Intellectually disabled clients invariably believe in many myths, usually acquired from families or peers or based on misperceptions. One way to assess a client's social and sexual knowledge is to use the team-oriented Quiz Bowl, a game show exercise that includes myths and truths and clarifies both of them.

Typically these clients are not as sophisticated about the use of language as a source of humor. However, creative therapy introduces puns and plays on words, which some pick up quickly despite limited vocabularies. A student who was proud of some of the new words he just learned was planting small rectangles of sod. "See," he called proudly to his therapist, "I'm doing sodomy."

Fortunately, these clients are able to laugh at themselves most of the time, a most endearing quality for anyone. Their spelling provides a light moment:

human beings	human beans
contraceptives	counterseptives
LaMaze classes	Liberace class
naked	neckade
paranoid	pearanoid
tubal ligation	tubal litigation
penance card	penis card
Whitney's cotton gin	Winnie's cotton grin

A "Different" Sense of Humor

Intellectually impaired adolescent sex offenders are often funny without knowing they are funny and their humor is elementary, sometimes crude, but it may open small windows of insight and feelings. They laugh at what would be considered rude, immature antics such as body sounds and gestures, including belching (produced on command), flatulence, snapping their fingers in another's face, imitating gun and car noises, picking at one's private parts, and making silly faces. Here again, role playing a person who may be behaving in an offensive manner may stimulate a discussion of alternative conduct.

Disgusted with a student who was constantly grabbing his crotch, one therapist grabbed hers and threw the therapeutic group into an uproar of shock and protests, but the lesson hit home. Repeated exposure to a wide range of social skills and occasionally unexpected but purposeful therapist behavior can help this population modify their behavior.

Harnessing Creativity

Breer (1987) suggested that adolescent sex offenders have a large "reservoir of creativity" (p. 194), and intellectually disabled offenders are no exception. Tapping into hidden talents of drawing, painting, crafts, writing memories and stories, and designing challenging projects offers valuable moments for introspection which might inspire questions and eventually insight. Invariably, clients are able to express feelings through these modalities in a way that they may not allow to surface verbally.

One client's self-portrait revealed a large, macho figure. It was drawn about the time the student had fantasies of raping a female staff member. Another client wrote about his family in ideal "Brady Bunch" terms when in reality the family was highly dysfunctional, with all of the children having been physically or sexually abused. The message communicated through these modalities reveal issues that may never have been discussed verbally.

Helping the Client Become Open to New Experiences

Because intellectually disabled adolescent sex offenders have a narrow, limited frame of reference from which to draw, they are usually open to new experiences even though beliefs in myths and thinking errors make them uncertain and anxious (Lakey, 1995). They are not necessarily threatened by new experiences, but they do have difficulties with changed routines. Many have never visited a state park, zoo, art gallery, historical museum, or beach; they may never have had a picnic or colored Easter eggs or dined in a restaurant with table cloths. Recreating wholesome and ordinary childhood experiences which they have never had and witnessing their joy is as satisfying to the therapist as the event itself, and it usually leaves a positive imprint on the client. In addition, team and adventure-based activities encourage the development of leadership and resourcefulness.

Developing New Social Skills

Many clients have had few people in their lives who advocated for them or consciously taught appropriate behavior. Thus, therapists are not only educators but sometimes finds themselves in the role of the parent, ombudsman, and confidant. For example, these clients may have poor hygiene habits. One 14-year-old had to be shown how to bathe. Some need guidance regarding general grooming and selection and care of clothing. Usually their table manners are primitive and inconsiderate. It is imperative that they become interested in these daily liviing habits in order to refrain from offending others and to attract appropriate peers. Reinforcement must be constant as interest in change occurs slowly in small increments.

Intellectually disabled clients often do not have the assertiveness to protect themselves from manipulative peers or adults. They need to practice saying "no" loudly and role play situations in order to develop assertiveness. Such skills are difficult for them to master because they often have been victims of extreme abuse and feel helpless in controlling their bodies and environments. The complicated problem of being a victim as well as a perpetrator places extra responsibility on therapists to teach the ability to appropriately stand up for one's self and thus reduce aggression.

Understanding Prosocial Behavior

These clients may be stunned by small acts of kindness directed toward them. Most likely they have lived on the fringe of societyand have been called names, shunned, and demeaned in a variety of ways. Schwartz, Gilperin, and Masters (1995) reported that some clients have been given the "implicit message that one must barter one's body for safety such that any act of kindness by an authority figure becomes interpreted as something sure to be followed (sooner or later) by a demand for payment" (p. 21).

Some are visibly touched when told that someone has inquired about them, or when a staff member gives them a treat or offers them a napkin because they forgot to get one. Taking a client to an upscale restaurant during a court hearing became an event that one adolescent repeatedly recounted.

One student, age 16, found a necklace with a pendant that had fallen in the gravel. The therapist owner gave him a thank you note, which he immediately shared with his peers. He was not "showing off" with it or bragging, but rather, he took genuine pride that someone had acknowledged his good deed, and he cherished the written evidence. This particular quality in intellectually disabled adolescent sex offenders easily lends itself to verbal reinforcement and is a constant reminder of "doing the right thing."

Implications for Treatment

Intellectually disabled male adolescent sex offenders can be unpredictable, refreshingly innocent and trusting, unsophisticated, humorous, creative, and appreciative. Though they are often difficult as clients and their treatment requires infinite patience, they also have lessons to teach.

An uncomplicated defense system sometimes makes it easier for a therapist to help an adolescent sex offender examine his motivations and needs in light of his relationships with others. Innocence and lack of knowledge offer the opportunity to introduce new, appropriate adventures which are legal and nonthreatening and promote a more global view of responsibility. Correcting mythical and magical thinking leads to more logical perceptions and decision making.

Expressions of a "different" sense of humor provide momentary relief from intense, repetitive, slowed-down therapy and can be used to teach clients how to interact and attract others. The creativity of these clients frequently surfaces in their ability to draw. They may not be able to verbalize their feelings, but they can often draw their own and even portray those of others. Some can journal and should be encouraged to do so. The fact that they are often open to and appreciative of new experiences and demonstrated kindnesses offers special chances for counseling which can nurture commitment to change.

Conclusion

There is nothing more exciting than watching a client relate to a concept or feeling that the therapist is trying to explain. It is especially rewarding when a client begins to use appropriate names for body parts, masters acceptable eating habits, makes an insightful comment in group therapy, or shows signs of empathy and remorse. Although sex offenders, adolescent offenders, and intellectually disabled offenders are all difficult to treat, the combination of all three makes the therapeutic task particularly challenging. However, it is certainly not without its unique rewards.

References

Barbaree, H. E., Marshall, W. L, & Hudson, S. M. (1993). *The juvenile sex offender.* NewYork: Guilford Press.

Breer, W. (1987). *The adolescent molester.* Springfield, IL: Charles C. Thomas.

Cambone, J. (1995). Rethinking how we think about troubled children. *Journal of Emotional and Behavioral Problems, 3*(4),12–14.

Davis, G. E., & Leitenberg, H. (1987). Adolescent sex offenders. *Psychological Bulletin, 101,* 417–427.

Haaven, J., Little, R., & Petre-Miller, D. (1990). *Treating the intellectually disabled sex offender: A model residential program.* Orwell, VT: Safer Society Press.

Lakey, J. F. (1995). Myth information and bizarre beliefs of male juvenile sex offenders. *Journal of Addictions and Offender Counseling, 13*(1), 2–10.

Schwartz, M. F., Galperin, L. D., & Masters, W. H. (1995, October). *Post-traumatic stress, sexual trauma and dissociative disorders: Issues related to intimacy and sexuality.* Paper presented at the Annual Conference of the Association for the Treatment of Sexual Abusers, New Orleans.

Chapter 21

"They Just Don't Get It"— Essentials of Cognitive-Behavioral Treatment for Intellectually Disabled Sexual Abusers

by Julie Brown, L.I.C.S.W. and Andy Pond, L.I.C.S.W.

Overview

The intellectually disabled sex offender is often an individual with multiple problems whose treatment must accommodate a variety of cognitive and affective problems. Therapists must be cognizant of ways to accommodate intellectual limitations and present complex materials in comprehensible formats. In this chapter, Brown and Pond present a variety of innovative approaches to reach this population.

Introduction

"We have tried to work with this guy, and he's been in treatment for a while, but he just doesn't get it!" This is a common lament from service providers who are frustrated with the lack of progress they see with intellectually disabled clients. We have, we admit, been guilty of saying similar things about our own clients when we feel that all our hard work seems to have little effect. Of course, the real failure to "get it" is likely to be ours: We may have failed to provide treatment at the appropriate level and pace; thus the client is unable to learn and generalize the skills necessary to function as a more responsible member of society. The clinician who attempts to provide cognitive-behavioral sexual offender treatment for a developmentally disabled adolescent or adult perpetrator will be challenged. Our clients may be stereotyped as "simple" by society, but these clinical cases are anything but straightforward. Our intent in this brief chapter is to highlight a few of the essential aspects of treating intellectually disabled sexual abusers, providing these individuals with the opportunity to lead safer, offense-free lives.

Who Is the Intellectually Disabled Sex Offender?

The clients we are treating fall in the mild to moderate range of mental retardation or have borderline intellectual functioning. Those with intellectual impairment may be experiencing broad ranges of difficulties, including organic brain dysfunction, brain injury, and the sequelae of Fetal Alcohol Syndrome. In addition to these handicaps, the "typical" client has often experienced environmental stressors that include neglect, sexual abuse, physical abuse, witnessing domestic violence, familial drug/alcohol abuse, poverty, or stigmatization due to the disability. Psychiatric disturbances are not uncommon. The client may also be coping with an affective disorder, psychosis, or a character disorder that further clouds the clinical picture. Significant impairment leads to varied presentations, making assessment difficult—layers of issues affect the client's functioning. The clinician must review these factors throughout treatment in order to establish realistic expectations and effective interventions.

Effective Cognitive-Behavioral Treatment With Intellectually Disabled Sexual Abusers

A client must understand many challenging concepts and integrate them into his repertoire of behavior in order to refrain from sexually abusive behaviors. The offender must do the following:

- Accurately report his offense history;
- Understand his offending pattern;
- Learn about thinking errors;
- Report fantasies;
- Stop deviant thoughts;
- Control arousal and urges;
- Learn to be accountable for his actions; and

• Demonstrate relapse prevention strategies.

The client must also replace deviant behaviors with prosocial coping strategies. Adaptive coping in social situations requires a person to be able to do the following:

• Accurately interpret the environment and situations;
• Label and express feelings appropriately;
• Reflect on thoughts, options and consequences;
• Use self-talk;
• Make choices for behavior;
• Self-evaluate actions;
• Accept responsibility for actions;
• Tolerate difficult emotions; and
• Value and respect himself and others.

Each of these aspects of treatment is a complex multistep, multiskill process. Learning and integrating these new patterns of behavior is challenging for any sexual abuser, and it is especially challenging for an individual with limited cognitive abilities.

Within each task, the client self-reflects and makes choices that promote his offense-free lifestyle. Feelings, thoughts, and behavior awareness skills are the fundamental building blocks for self-reflection. The sexual abuser must put together the proper progression of skills to successfully complete a complex, multistep coping strategy. If he "misses" one basic skill, treatment is compromised.

Special Considerations in Treatment Design

Although each person is different, many intellectually disabled sexual abusers share certain traits. A client with developmental disabilities generally perceives the world as "black and white." He has limited ability to understand abstract concepts. Thus, interventions must be focused, specific, and concrete. Teaching skills in a progression of steps generally enhances the learning experience.

The intellectually impaired client has difficulty learning new information. A slower pace, simple vocabulary, and repetition of concepts can increase the effectiveness of therapeutic activities. Visual cues and aids can help the intellectually disabled client to understand difficult concepts. The clinician should attempt various types of interventions, adapting to the client's individual learning style.

A common coping mechanism is the "nod of incomprehension" when facing a difficult concept. When asked if he understands a given concept or skill, the intellectually impaired client is likely to nod his head and reply "yes," even if he has no real grasp of the material.

The clinician must probe and test the client's skills, never allowing a cursory review to suffice. If the client feels lost, a common reaction is to shut down and disengage from the session. The clinician must continually assess the design, pace, and expectations of each activity. The client may be displaying resistance and manipulation, or he may not comprehend the information. In either case, the clinician must evaluate and make adjustments as necessary.

The Importance of Appropriate Intervention

Generally, when the client begins treatment, he has very little awareness of his internal experience. Because an intellectually impaired individual is generally adept at compensating for or hiding his disability, it is easy for the clinician to erroneously assume that a client understands basic feelings, thoughts, and behavior awareness skills. Without increased competence in each of these areas, the client will not change dangerous patterns, and under stress he will revert to old patterns of coping. Kimball, Nelson, and Politano (1990) explore the problem of providers paying insufficient attention to the developmental status of a client. They note that "within the cognitive-behavioral framework, the importance of developmental differences often has been overlooked . . . cognitive-behavioral treatment procedures need to be tailored to the developmental level of the individual, either child or adolescent" (p. 25). They stress that it is critical to understand how the client comprehends social information, such as verbal labeling, sequencing, organizing, attention, retention, and the ability to read social and internal cues. Therapists must assess cognitive functioning to "determine which abilities, under what circumstances, contribute to or interfere with adequate conduct" (p. 26). This is not an easy task, but it is essential to effective treatment.

Inability to Regulate Impulses and Affect Interferes With Adequate Conduct

A developmentally disabled sexual abuser often has limited ability to adequately regulate his affective states and control his impulses. The abuser does not have the necessary skill to cope with his feelings; thus he may act out his emotions. He often attributes the responsibility to others for his emotional difficulties through abusive behaviors (Jenkins, 1994). Insufficient modulation skills are a key force that drives and perpetuates the client's offending patterns. Unless this problem is addressed, the client will continue to have exaggerated emotional responses that tend to "override" any cognitive controls and lead to dangerous behaviors. Cognitive-behavioral sexual offender treatment should help the client build basic feelings, thoughts, and behavior awareness skills that are the preliminary steps for learning to regulate behavioral responses to emotion.

Linehan (1993) carefully examines the elements of emotional dysregulation in patients with borderline personality disorder. Though Linehan's work is not specifically aimed at our group of clients, we believe her useful analysis also applies to many intellectually disabled sexual abusers. Linehan notes that her typical client is highly sensitive to emotions and reacts quickly to affective stimulation. The emotionally dysregulated client is also highly reactive to emotions, and the reactions are extreme. Once emotionally escalated, the dysregulated client returns slowly to baseline. These reactions are prolonged, and the client is highly sensitive to the next stimulus. A key concept is that high affective arousal interferes with cognitive processing—an obvious difficulty for a client who is already struggling with cognitive impairment. Using some of Linehan's concepts, and drawing from the standard repertoire of cognitive-behavioral strategies, we may adapt our treatment to meet the needs of this population.

Feelings, Thoughts, and Behavior Awareness Skills

Basic cognitive-behavioral therapy theory postulates that feelings mediate cognitions and cognitions mediate feeling in affecting behaviors. Treatment must address all three areas to affect behavioral change.

Feelings Awareness Skills. This area has five components.

Feelings Language Development. The client's goal is to expand his ability to label and communicate his internal experiences. Initially, the client's feelings vocabulary usually consists of "mad" and "happy." Emotions that are very difficult to tolerate (such as feelings of shame, sadness, hurt, rejection, abandonment, and betrayal) are labeled as "mad" by the client. Learning to differentiate between various positive emotions is important, as well. Beginning with a list of six to ten "primary" feelings can help the client begin to slowly label and organize his affective experiences. In time the client can further expand his feelings vocabulary. Using third-person scenarios can be an effective way to help engage the client to examine and label his feelings.

Feelings Rating Scale. We use a 0–1–2–3–4–5 rating scale to help clients understand the progression of intensity of feelings. As the client become proficient at evaluating feelings with the scale, the 0-5 system can be used in various ways to concretize and organize related, abstract concepts. It is important to clearly define each number: 0 = no feeling; 1 = a tiny feeling; 2 = a small feeling; 3 = a medium feeling; 4 = a big feeling; 5 = overwhelming feeling that leads to out-of-control behavior, such as offending or assaultiveness. The feeling intensity should be linked to some concrete behavior: A "4" would be a strong feeling but contained with perhaps some minor nondirected swearing, or "storming" behavior.

An emotionally dysregulated and cognitively impaired client commonly reports emotions as either a "0" (a numbed absence of feelings) or a "5" (an exaggerated response for a relatively minor stimulus). Group activities, such as team competitions or discussions about labeling emotions, can be effective in helping clients to "fill in the gaps" between these extremes. Benefits of group work include practicing talking about feelings with other people, listening to other people's impressions about feelings, offering an opportunity for the clients to learn that feelings are complicated and subjective, and learning that discussing feelings can be a positive experience.

Associating Body Sensations Wth Feelings. The client needs to become aware of his physiological responses to emotions. Early detection and labeling can cue the client to use self-control strategies if he is beginning to experience uncomfortable feelings. It is important that the client intervene prior to becoming emotionally and cognitively dysregulated. This type of training is the foundation for relapse prevention work; without basic feelings awareness, cognitive strategies are likely to be less useful.

Many drawing and experiential activities can make learning about how people react to feelings interesting and educational. Groups can create brainstorm lists of all feelings. As each word is shared, the client assigns the feeling to a place on a roughly drawn body shape on the board. Group members can discuss and share their experiences of the feeling. Playing "feelings charades" is fun and effective. A group leader whispers a feeling and a rating number (0–5) to a group member. The client acts out the feeling and the group guesses the emotion and the intensity rating of the feeling from the performance. The performer demonstrates the ability to report his internal experience and communicates emotions within a controlled environment. The group members practice reading and interpreting social cues, which is an important aspect in the development of empathy skills (Ryan & Lane, 1997).

Learning About Having Mixed or Multiple Emotions. The client needs to understand that he may experience a myriad of conflicting emotions in a given situation. Scenarios about individuals having a wide range of emotions make for rich group discussions.

Understanding the Function and Nature of Emotions. Clients need to discover that emotions are a natural part of the human experience and that feelings serve an important purpose in daily life. We teach our clients that a feeling often builds and then reduces in intensity over time, and that different experiences may produce varying responses. Pictures of "feelings waves" create a visual representation of the course of a feeling. A diagram can help make an abstract concept, like the pattern of an emotion, more understandable for a developmentally disabled client. This is an important lesson in teaching the client to tolerate affective states. For an emotionally dysregulated person, even a minor feeling (2) can seem catastrophic and quickly escalate to an out-of-control emotion (5). The pictures educate and help desensitize clients to tolerate experiencing feelings. The message to the client is this: Emotions come and go, and difficult feelings are survivable.

Thoughts Awareness Skills. Understanding the role of thoughts is another important aspect of sexual offender treatment. A client must recognize deviant thoughts, acknowledge thinking errors, change his thoughts, and replace the deviant cognition with positive self-talk in order to avoid sexually abusive behaviors. In addition to preliminary skill-building activities that prepare the client for addressing his deviant sexual behaviors, he must learn about the role his thoughts play in adaptive coping. The next items address some helpful thought awareness skills, which are the building blocks for learning to make "new-me" (see sections "Labeling thoughts" and "Recognizing 'choice points'") coping choices. When discussing the concept of "choice," Lawler (1992) notes that "in choice situations, cognitions mediate all emotions" (p. 335). Several exercises are designed to help prepare the client to self-reflect and make positive choices.

Understanding That Thoughts Are Separate From Feelings. Generally, the client has difficulty telling the difference between a feeling and a thought. The client becomes overwhelmed and driven by affect; his awareness of thoughts is often very poor. He generally has reacted quickly in situations, so slowing down to be aware of his thoughts is a critical step for the client.

Linking Emotions to Thoughts. The client needs to begin to understand that he has thoughts following experiences and emotions. He needs to become aware of the many negative ingrained patterns of thinking he has. By reviewing his cognitive responses to emotions, the client can begin to understand the connections between feelings and thoughts.

Linking Thoughts and Behaviors. In the beginning of treatment, the client is usually resistant to the idea that his thoughts lead him to have behaviors; to him, actions just happen "out of the blue." Educating clients about how thoughts can lead an individual to actions is an important step. They can then begin to see that by noticing and changing what they think about, they can gain control of their offending behaviors.

Labeling Thoughts. Using the framework of "old me and new me" (Haaven, Little, & Petre-Miller, 1990) is an effective way for a client to label and qualify his thoughts in terms of his treatment. "Old-me" thoughts are thoughts that lead a client to have abusive behaviors. "New-me" thoughts are cognitions that promotes adaptive choices and actions. We recommend that all treatment providers familiarize themselves with Haaven's work with this population (Haaven et al., 1990).

Recognizing "Choice Points." The client needs to realize that each thought or action is a "choice point." At any choice point, he can choose the "new-me" or the "old-me" options. The idea of a choice point teaches clients that they need to stop and think, prior to acting. As in all relapse prevention strategies, the client learns about ways to halt and readjust potentially dangerous thoughts and actions.

Becoming Aware of the First Thought in a Situation. The client needs to continually reflect on his internal experience. Being aware of his first thought in every situation is important. The client may not be able to control the first thought, but how he proceeds from there is within his control.

Assessing Situations: 0–5 Rating Scale for Intensity of a Situation. The client has spent most of his life misreading situations. Accurately assessing situations is the foundation for making prosocial decisions. Using the 0–5 scale can help clients learn to evaluate the importance and/or the intensity of a situation.

Behavior Awareness Skills. Initially, the client is likely to have minimal awareness about what leads to his behavior. There are a few basic strategies that enhance this awareness.

Recognizing the Goal or Function of a Behavior. The client needs to begin to observe behaviors more objectively and learn about the factors that motivate him. It is important to teach clients to look beyond the surface of an action to examine what the goal of the behavior is. The client may have a reasonable goal, but he may be unable to comprehend his feelings, organize his thoughts, and choose behaviors in the proper progression of steps to reach the goal. The client needs to gain increased clarity about his goals of his behaviors in order to make informed choices. There is a delicate balance to maintain while treating the developmentally disabled sexual abuser. The client needs to learn to accept himself and his past "old me" while realizing that the deviant behaviors must change. The client needs to realize that he, as an individual, is acceptable; abusive behaviors, on the other hand, are not.

Labeling Behaviors as "Old Me." or "New Me." Reflecting on and labeling behaviors is an important exercise. As the client develops the skill of labeling his thoughts and behaviors objectively, he will become better able to accurately self-evaluate. Learning to self-monitor and report his internal experience to others is a critical skill. Intellectually impaired clients often have had a poverty of opportunity to acquire adaptive self and social skills. The emphasis on learning about "new me" must be equal to the emphasis on increasing awareness about "old me." Keeping the treatment focused on the positive aspects of his learning new skills will help the intellectually impaired client build improved self-regard. The client needs to increase his sense of positive personal power to replace the negative sense of power gained by abusing.

Examine How the Environment Responds to Various Behaviors and Choices. The developmentally disabled sexual abuser often has unrealistic perceptions about the social and legal consequences of his behaviors. This lack of understanding may be reinforced by inconsistent messages from his environment. Cognitive distortions cloud realistic perceptions about consequences of behaviors. He must understand that he, rather than the environment, controls his actions. The client has to begin to envision the short- and long-term consequences of his actions. There are positive and negative results of behaviors, and he must be able to list these in a concrete fashion as part of his relapse prevention plan.

Examine the Effects of Behavior on Self and Others. There are often far-reaching ramifications of actions, some overt and others more subtle. Ideally, the client should become aware of the various levels on which he and others are affected by actions. However, treatment usually focuses on how the client experiences consequences, due to his typically limited capacity for empathy. Helping the client to consider the effects of his actions on his relationship with himself and others can help him begin to incorporate these questions into a process of self-reflection and change.

Conclusion

Developing appropriate treatment strategies is hard work for the clinician, who must break down and carefully elaborate approaches that are difficult enough to apply to clients who are not cognitively impaired. The reward is seeing clients begin to "get" the treatment, grasping concepts and learning skills that have eluded them in the past. This population does have the ability to change, to grow, and to be safer members of society. We hope that the outline of issues presented in this chapter encourages other providers to research, develop, and share their own strategies—leading to a more comprehensive treatment model for the cognitively impaired client.

References

Haaven, J., Little, R., & Petre-Miller, D. (1990). *Treating intellectually disabled sex offenders: A model residential program.* Orwell, VT: Safer Society Press.

Jenkins, A. (1994). *Invitations to responsibility.* Adelaide, Australia: Dulwich Centre Publications.

Kimball, W., Nelson, W. M., & Politano, P. (1990). The role of developmental variables in cognitive behavioral interventions with children. In A. J. Finch, W. M. Nelson III, & E. Ott (Eds.), *Cognitive behavioral procedures with children and adolescents: A practical guide* (pp. 20–35). Boston: Allyn & Bacon.

Lawler, E. J. (1992). Affective attachments to nested groups: A choice-process theory. *American Sociological Review, 57,* 327–339.

Linehan, M. M. (1993). *Skills training manual for treating borderline personality disorder.* New York: Guilford Press.

Ryan, G. D., & Lane, S. (Eds.). (1991). *Juvenile sex offending: Causes, consequences, and correction.* Lexington, MA: Lexington Books.

Chapter 22

Working With the Intellectually Disabled/Socially Inadequate Sex Offender in a Prison Setting

Nancy M. Stacken, M.A., L.P. and Jim Shevich, B.A.

Overview

The intellectually disabled/socially inadequate sex offender is often neglected, abused, and manipulated in the prison environment. Few programs have been designed to respond to their unique needs. In this chapter the authors describe a program specifically developed to present sex offender treatment to this population in a manner designed to match the learning style of this population.

Introduction

As a result of the closing of state hospitals and concerns for public safety, it is becoming more and more likely that sex offenders who are labeled intellectually disabled/socially inadequate will be sent to prison. In a prison setting, this group may consist of intellectually disabled, socially inadequate, learning disabled, developmentally disabled, developmentally delayed, "low-functioning," mentally retarded, those within the "borderline" range of intellectual functioning, mentally ill, or those who act out in a fashion that is disturbing but does not qualify them as mentally retarded or mentally ill. Perhaps the most encompassing term is "psychosocially challenged."

More often than not, these individuals are excluded from the conventional sex offender treatment programs (Murphy, Coleman, & Haynes, 1983) or are pushed through them with the hope that the program has done them some good. A 1989 survey by Knopp and Stevenson indicated that "43% of the identified specialized sex-offender treatment programs in the United States provide some sort of services for the intellectually disabled clients, but that they are rarely adequate or comprehensive" (p. 19). A 1994 report of the Program Evaluation Division of the Office of the Legislative Auditor in Minnesota found that "three-quarters of outpatient treatment programs would not accept developmentally disabled offenders (those with an IQ less than 70). In addition, half of the outpatient programs would not accept offenders who were intellectually 'low-functioning' with IQs above 70 but below 80 or 85. Treatment providers told us that offenders need a minimum level of intellectual ability to succeed in treatment because they must retain certain concepts and sometimes function in the abstract." The report went on to say, "Similarly, county and state correctional facilities . . . were not prepared to treat offenders who did not meet the low-functioning criterion. An official from one Department of Corrections treatment program told us that the program occasionally accepted low-functioning offenders because they were too vulnerable in the prison's open population" (p. 68).

Specialized programs have been developed around the country, such as Oregon State Hospital's Social Skills Program (SSP); Behaviour Management Services, York Central Hospital Program-Ontario; Vermont Center for the Prevention and Treatment of Sexual Abuse; and Alaskan Specialized Education and Training Services (ASETS). The Minnesota Department of Corrections has also developed a prison-based program track for low-functioning offenders. Development began in 1994 in response to the legislative auditor's report cited previously.

The lack of programming for this population may be a result of the following beliefs:

1. Successful sex offender treatment requires high IQ and ability to verbally express oneself and use abstract thinking.
2. This population drains already limited resources (i.e., time, money, and staff).
3. The societal prejudice that people with developmental disabilities function at one extreme or the other of the sexual continuum: either as asexual children or as sexual monsters (Knopp, 1990).
4. Inaccurate identification of this population.
5. Lack of the awareness of their differences.

For these reasons, this population has been "warehoused" and ignored, and consequently members of this population have "fallen through the cracks" in the system. It is vital that all sex offenders be held responsible for their behavior. "The issue of accountability is very important for normalization" (Ward et al., 1992, p. 8).

The issue of normalization takes even a further twist in the prison setting. Prisons demand order. Both staff and prisoners alike rely on a structured and consistent routine. There are rules and schedules to abide by. Anything or anyone who is seen as "odd" or "unusual" upsets the normal order. Both inmates and staff can react strongly and sometimes forcefully to the unpredictable nature of the intellectually disabled inmate. For example, if Johnnie is standing in the group room cussing and yelling, the staff would try to redirect his behavior. But, if Johnnie stood in the dining room and started cussing and yelling, he would be immediately detained and escorted to the segregation unit. Although the response to an inmate's behavior depends on the setting and the institution, the client-centered approach of the mental health professional and the correctional officer's responsibility to keep order and control can blend together to create a setting that facilitates the goals of community safety and rehabilitation.

Prison administrators generally respond to this concern by creating separate housing units for these individuals. Although this approach addresses security concerns, problems arise when these units become "warehouses." Too often, these units lack programming and the inmates are given meaningless tasks to keep them busy. Time that could have been used constructively becomes "dead time."

Schwartz (1995) talks about another problem—the differences that exist between the prison culture and the environment necessary for effective treatment:

1. Prisons encourage dependency while treatment focuses on responsibility.
2. Prisons often isolate men from women, while treatment tries to facilitate more appropriate interaction with women.
3. Prisons encourage distrust, while treatment encourages trust. (p. 8-5)

Schwartz (1995), citing Knopp (1984), points to "the attitudes of secrecy, defensiveness and denial that the prison value system encourages. Idle time is spent reinforcing deviant attitudes and fantasies. Expressing emotions or admitting problems is perceived as weakness. Individuals may acquire certain problems while they are in prison that they did not have before they entered the institution. These problems include drug abuse, alcoholism, criminal thought patterns, bitterness, and anger toward the system" (p. 8-5).

One might ask whether or not sex offender treatment can be successfully provided in a prison setting. This chapter describes a variety of activities and techniques we have found useful when working with the intellectually disabled/socially inadequate sex offenders in our prison program.

Intelligence: Asset or Liability

Schwartz (1995) comments:

[T]herapists disagree about whether high intelligence is an asset or a liability in the treatment of sex offenders.. . . Limited intelligence may prevent an individual from remembering, assimilating, or utilizing what he has learned in treatment. It may be difficult to rely on heavily verbal modalities or aim for the acquisition of insight.. . . However, individuals of high intelligence who lack true motivation, abdicate responsibility, or lack remorse may use their innate abilities to manipulate others. They may be able to learn all the appropriate jargon and theories and say exactly what therapists wish to hear. (p. 8-3)

Many specialized treatment providers concur that the "borderline" intellectually disabled sex offenders are surprisingly amenable to treatment. Even though their progress can be slow, it is more likely to be real and genuine (Haaven, Little, & Petre-Miller, 1990; Fried, 1986; Gafgen, 1988; Safer Society Program, 1988).

Clinicians typically approach treatment with a cognitive perspective that relies on tapping intelligence (IQ) and insight. Working with low-functioning sex offenders, the clinician must tap into other forms of intelligence. Gardner (1983) refers to multiple intelligences, such as linguistic, logical/mathematical, intrapersonal, spacial, musical, bodily/kinesthetic, and interpersonal.

Lakey (1996) identifies characteristics of low-functioning male adolescent sex offenders that she believes can help the therapeutic process. These include "artistic; creativity; uncomplicated defense system[s]; innocence, lack of knowledge [and] naivete; sense of humor; open to new experiences; appreciation of kindness directed to him; spontaneous; unpredictability." Although these characteristics may be seen as liabilities in the general prison population, they can be reframed as assets in the therapy group.

Constructing a Safe Treatment Environment

Creating a safe environment in which treatment can occur is a difficult task in a prison, but Griffiths, Quinsey, and Hingsburger (1989) and Willis (1980) support the idea that environments can be restructured to encourage appropriate expression and can be designed specifically to foster behavioral and cognitive change. Blending the needs for security and treatment is a constant challenge. This blending can be accomplished in a variety of innovative ways.

At the Moose Lake Correctional Facility, the sex offender program has fifty beds of a 100-bed unit. The treatment program area contains the group rooms, staff offices, and living areas. All sex offender programming takes place here. Education, recreation, dining, canteen, and religious services are shared with the general population. The sex offender program has two tracks: one for long-term intensive treatment of nondisabled sex offenders (forty beds) and Track A-Alternatives (ten beds) for the men identified as intellectually disabled/socially inadequate (those with an IQ greater than 65 but lower than 85). Together, the two tracks make up a therapeutic community. At least once a week, they all meet to address community issues. They are expected to hold each other accountable for their attitudes and behaviors. In this way, the lower-functioning inmate has the opportunity to develop assertiveness skills, increase self-esteem, be looked up to and respected, and have a place and purpose in the community rather than be seen as a burden or a "misfit." For the nondisabled sex offenders, it provides an opportunity to reach out to someone else, show compassion and concern, practice empathy, and break down stereotypes.

Prisons, which are generally cold, noisy, concrete buildings, do not foster a sense of ownership or responsibility and do not provide the "psychological space" needed to make change. As a way to combat this phenomenon, the program area needs to be a space that generates a sense of calm and quiet. The low-functioning inmates in our program have a group room that is accessible only to them. None of the other offenders in the program can use this room. It is set up to be warm and inviting. The chairs are soft and comfortable and large windows provide light as well as a view of the yard outside. Carpeting adds warmth and deadens sound. Esthetically pleasing plants also provide an opportunity for the offenders to nurture and care for something. The offenders are empowered to make this space their own. Everything in the room is personal and related to treatment. Handmade posters, collages, and hobby craft items are expressions of the offenders and the issues on which they are working in treatment. Reference is made to the posters during group sessions as a way to address treatment concepts. This fosters a sense of ownership and commitment.

The living area contains a large day room and inmates' bunkrooms. The men share three-man rooms. Although single rooms are preferable, the physical layout does not allow it. However, there are some positive aspects to three-man rooms. Having roommates allows various issues to surface, such as interpersonal relationships, conflict resolution, "support/buddy" system for assignments, and helping each other act responsibly, and it deters the inmates from sexually acting out with one another.

What Works: Treatment Techniques

"To enhance the resident's ability to retain what he has learned, programming emphasizes the affective element of the learning process, using play as an approach to teaching life and treatment skills. Residents retain what they are taught if the learning experience is fun, dramatic, or bizarre" (Haaven et al., 1990, p. 22).

Visual Crime Scene. The phrase "a picture is worth a thousand words" exemplifies our approach to helping the low-functioning sex offender describe his offense(s). This technique arose from the ongoing struggle to get accurate and consistent information from the offender regarding his sexually assaultive behaviors. Most sex offender programs require the offender to either read or describe the details of his offenses. The presentence investigation (PSI) reports are often used to support what the offender is admitting he did or to challenge his denial. Low-functioning offenders have problems with this task due to their limitations with language and comprehension. They often cannot put their thoughts into words, so their verbal description of their offense(s) is not always congruent with the information provided by the PSI and other sources. As a result, therapists often mislabel their behavior as resistant, defensive, and uncooperative. The "visual crime scene" assignment is a tool the offender can use to recreate the crime scene on paper. When used in conjunction with other records and reports, the therapist gets a clearer understanding of how the offender perceives his behavior, is able to point out discrepancies, and sometimes gets information about the offender's current sexual thinking and behavior. In addition, the information obtained through this assignment can be used in the ongoing process of assessing and evaluating the offender's dangerousness and amenability to treatment.

For this assignment, the offender is asked to draw a picture of his offense. He is told to include all the victims, where the crime took place, any weapons he might have used, and anything else that was sexually stimulating. He is told to draw it to the best of his ability using simple figures. He is also encouraged to write a few words or phrases next to the drawings/figures to foster recall and tracking when he is presenting the assignment in group. The offender is given poster paper and colored markers. He is given whatever length of time he needs to finish the assignment. The therapist monitors the offender's progress. Group members are encouraged to support and provide feedback through the "buddy system." Once the offender has completed his drawing, he brings it to a group session and presents it to the group. This session is typically videotaped for future use in group therapy. The drawing is placed on an easel and the offender stands in front of the group and talks about each detail of his drawing. Peers and therapist ask questions throughout the presentation. We have been surprised by the unexpected amount of information that has been revealed by offenders who otherwise were unable to describe their behavior. The following example illustrates the process:

> Mark is a 29-year-old pedophile. He attempted to present his PSI three times in the group by reading it from the report. On at least one other occasion, the therapist read the report to him. He sat in his chair expressionless, looking at the floor and stuttering. He read through the report quickly and once finished, only responded to questions by saying "I guess so" and "If you say so" and then by being silent. He showed no emotion and appeared to be lost. After his peers challenged him, he became sarcastic, angry, and frustrated. The end result was a lack of ownership of his behavior and failure. The group members were frustrated and wanted to kick Mark out of treatment. The therapist, looking for another way to work with him, told Mark: "Draw what you did. Keep it simple. Take your time. I will have a group buddy assist you with this. Have some fun using whatever color markers you want. I'm going to have you teach us what you did." Mark responded by showing enthusiasm and investment in completing the task. He was given the freedom to work on it at his own pace and he worked on it with a great deal of interest and pride. When he presented it to the group, he showed confidence and the words flowed. He provided a great amount of detail about his offense, as well as information about paraphilic behavior that was previously unknown.

As the example shows, the end result was an increase in Mark's responsibility for his behavior, greater motivation, and investment. We noticed a rippling effect in other areas of his treatment. Mark became more verbal, used more "I" statements, became willing to confront others, spent more time working on assignments, and sought out projects. His behavior became more self-directed and purposeful. We believe that by saying "teach us about you" instead of "I'll teach you about you" the therapist empowers the offender to actively engage in the treatment process. The offender is allowed to discover his abilities rather than live within the confines of what others think he can or cannot do.

Personal Drawings of Sexually Deviant Behaviors. One of the issues every therapist faces is how to keep track of the offender's current sexual behaviors and fantasies. Fantasy logs are not useful with this population because they are often inaccurate, and the offenders become obsessed with their sexual thoughts and urges. We have found that continuous questioning of the low-functioning offender is not helpful either because it generally leads to immediate denial or simple "yes or no" answers. The more the therapist prods, the more confusing and frustrating it becomes to the offender, and both the offender and therapist become embattled.

The "personal drawing of sexually deviant behaviors" assignment is an offshoot of the "visual crime scene" assignment and is approached in the same manner. The therapist says, "Draw for me all the sneaky, deviant sexual behaviors you are involved in on the unit." The therapist is not actually asking the offender to draw behaviors but rather figures or images that represent behaviors. The offender writes a brief description under each figure. When the offender is working on his drawing, it gives him time to think about his behaviors. Thus, when he presents it to the group, he is more prepared to talk openly about his behaviors. This openness enables him to take further risks in disclosing his behaviors. One of the keys to this technique is allowing the offender to stand in front of the group and point to the drawings as he describes his behaviors. Because these offenders typically act out of emotions, impulses, and bodily sensations, movement, such as pointing, standing and pacing, acts as a catalyst for their thought processes. Physical movement helps the thoughts flow. We have also used this method to investigate an inmate's sexual behavior. The following is an example of such a situation:

> Joe, an offender with "borderline" IQ, was suspected of being involved in sexual activity with another inmate. Because there was concern about his vulnerability, it was very important to sort out who was responsible for initiating the sexual behavior. After attempting to get clear information from Joe by asking him direct questions, it became obvious that he was giving conflicting and inconsistent answers. The therapist then chose to ask Joe to draw a picture of what happened between him and the other inmate. Joe sat at the table and drew a picture that also had words to describe it. He then talked about his picture with the therapist. Using this technique, Joe was able to describe behaviors without making contradictory statements. The therapist did not have to probe for additional details. Consequently, the appropriate interventions were made and the problem was resolved.

Identity. Haaven et al. (1990) talk about using an "old me, new me" identification process as a way of helping the offender "relate to himself and the world." The offender learns how to establish a new identity and discard the old identity. Using this idea, we ask the offenders to make collages representing their "old me," the offending self, and the "new me," the nonoffending self. All group members present their personal collages to the group.

We also use this identification process when teaching various treatment concepts. For example, when addressing the concept of "consent," we use the "Rules of Consent" developed by the Metropolitan Community Mental Health Center (MCMHC; 1996) in Minneapolis. Instead of posting these rules only in written form, the group creates a collage of pictures representing both "old me" and "new me" behaviors. The "old me" collage has pictures of children, individuals who might be vulnerable due to a physical disability, older women, and families and pictures depicting rape, exhibitionism, and unprotected sex. The "new me" collage has pictures of couples, adults, and a condom and pictures that depict self-sufficiency and privacy.

Another way to address identity is by using icons (visual representations). The Be Cool series (Stanfield, 1992) uses icons to symbolize effective and ineffective responses to coping with difficult people and situations. The Be Cool series uses three male characters, described as "cold," "cool," and "hot," who are paired with three pictures—ice, clouds, and fire—that represent typical responses to difficult situations: cold (ice), cool (clouds) and hot (fire). The offenders in our group expanded the concept by giving each of the figures a name: "Whimpy," "Mr. Smooth," and "Dudley." "Whimpy" (passive) and "Dudley" (aggressive) represent the "old me" offending identity; "Mr. Smooth" (assertiveness) represents the "new me" nonoffending identity. By labeling these figures, the offenders in our group created an emotional connection with the concepts. The therapist can refer to the offender's behavior as being like "Whimpy," "Dudley," or "Mr. Smooth." Likewise, the offenders describe their behaviors by using the names of the offender with whom they identify. For example, "Mr. Smooth" has become their role model. Someone they want to become. "Mr. Smooth" is not criminal but, rather, someone who is respectful and effectively handles his daily problems.

The "Mr. Smooth" icon is also helpful when the therapist talks about hygiene and personal appearance. "Mr. Smooth" models a clean-cut appearance. He shaves everyday or keeps his beard trimmed. He keeps his hair clean and combed. His clothes are clean and he comes to the group sessions dressed appropriately.

The "Nerf" Ball. Some cultures have a tradition of "talking circles." In these circles, participants pass around a stick. Whoever has the "talking stick" is given the full attention of everyone else in the circle. We have adopted this idea for our group sessions, but instead of using a "talking stick" we use a "Nerf" ball. The "Nerf" ball is used for the following reasons:

1. To cue and remind the offender who struggles with his verbal skills to join in and contribute to the group.
2. To build confidence by identifying the offenders as important, giving them permission to talk.
3. To quiet those who attempt to monopolize the group.
4. To tap into kinesthetic senses.

Holding the ball seems to help the offenders focus their thoughts. As a result, their speech is more goal directed and fluent.

Intonation. Keeping the low-functioning sex offender's attention focused on the task at hand is not always easy. Changing intonation, rather than speaking in a monotone or predictable style, draws the offender's attention to the therapist and keeps the offender interested. Changing the volume and intensity in one's voice generates an emotional response in the offender which the therapist can then tap into.

Movement. Therapists and offenders typically sit in the group setting. We have found that the therapist can maintain the offender's attention span more effectively by periodically standing, pacing, moving to a chair closer to the offender to whom he or she is talking , writing on the board, pointing to a poster, or gesturing. In addition, requiring the offender to move by standing, pacing, walking to the center of the circle, sitting or lying on the floor, or walking over to a poster on the wall and reading it empowers him to become more actively involved in the group process. Our experience is that the offenders are more verbally involved when they are prompted to move around the room.

Touch. The use of touch in the therapy setting is controversial at best. Few would argue that touch is an essential human need. However, the irresponsible behavior of some therapists has made touch taboo in the therapy setting. We believe that some forms of touch in the therapy setting are appropriate, but there must be respect for the readiness and the values of the offender and the stage of the group's development. Touch should never be forced or imposed; rather, the therapist must have earned the offender's trust and permission before engaging in any use of touch. The therapist must take into account the gender and sexual orientation of the offenders in the group, as well as their own gender and sexual orientation. In addition, the therapist must be aware of what personal needs he or she may be attempting to fulfill.

The following two scenarios illustrate how we have used touch in our program:

Bill, an offender with flat affect, showed no awareness of the impact of his behavior on the victim. Whenever he watched any videos focusing on victim impact, his eyes had a glossy, drifting look to them. He would always respond to questions asked of him with "yes or no" answers and showed no remorse. He could not emotionally attend to other group members who were showing feelings. In attempting to try something different, the therapist asked Bill to place his hands on the shoulder's of another group member who was crying. Bill was told to look at the crying man's face and to try to feel the man's emotions. After a few minutes, Bill was able to talk with this man rather than to him. He showed increased eye contact and support for the other man's emotions.

Jim is a hypersensitive and rather paranoid man who would typically tremble and shake whenever he was challenged or confronted. During one group session in which his behavior was the focus of the group's discussion, Jim started to shake uncontrollably and then bolted out of the room. The therapist immediately attended to Jim outside the group room by approaching Jim in a calm and supportive manner and placing his hand on Jim's shoulder. He encouraged Jim to return to the group room and reassured Jim that he was not in trouble. Jim was still shaking when he walked into the group room. In an effort to redirect Jim's focus and help him regain composure, the therapist accompanied Jim to the window. With his hand on Jim's shoulder, the therapist told Jim to softly place his hands on the cold window pane. When Jim did this, the therapist asked him to feel the cold sensation. While continuing to reassure Jim, the therapist prescribed the desired outcome by describing to Jim how he was now becoming calm and relaxed. When the therapist pointed out that Jim was no longer shaking, Jim affirmed this by smiling and acknowledging that it was true. Jim then was able to rejoin the group.

In the latter scenario, tapping into a different tactile sensation stimulated a shift or redirection of Jim's thoughts, feelings, and behaviors. When, in the past, his behavior might have escalated to the point where he was dangerous to himself or others, in this case, Jim was able to regain control of his impulses. Jim continues to use this technique whenever he feels he is becoming agitated and stressed.

A variety of sources in a group room can be creatively used to tap or rechannel different bodily sensations. Rather than using human touch, a therapist might ask the offender to feel the heat coming out of the heat register, feel the texture of a plant, touch a smooth cool surface like a tabletop, feel the rough texture of the carpeting, or even put his finger in a glass of water to feel the wetness. Whatever the case, with the appropriate timing and support of the offender's process, touch can be a valuable treatment tool.

Upward Arm Raise. The "upward arm raise" is a technique used to close the group session. At the end of the group session, the therapist and all the group members stand together in the middle of the circle. One by one, they place both their hands on top of each other's hands and recite the ACTION acronym: **A**void victims, **C**ontrol deviant urges, **T**hink clearly, **I**nvolve others, **O**ne day at a time, **N**o pornography (Little, 1992). They then yell out "one, two, three—Action" and raise their arms upward. This is a group ritual that combines touch, movement, and intonation for the purpose of bonding, group closure and integration of relapse prevention concepts.

Other Helpful Techniques. Some of the basic therapeutic techniques such as paraphrasing, role playing, redirecting, homework and goal setting are also helpful when working with this population. Using multimedia presentations such as flip charts, overheads, slides, videos, charts, and posters provides a visual reinforcement of the discussion topics. Nature and relaxation music, appropriate humor, daily affirmations, and video and audiotaping are also useful. It is important, no matter what is used, to keep it simple. Ferguson and Haaven (1990) address this need to "keep it simple." In the group room, we have a poster with the acronym KISS hanging above the door. The acronym stands for **K**eep **I**t **S**urprisingly **S**imple.

Support: Helping Them Achieve Their Potential

Support and confrontation go hand in hand. For the therapist to be supportive, he or she must use care and concern when confronting. Authentic confrontation is not an attack but, rather, a means to draw the offender's attention to his resistance and denial and to the discrepancies between what he says and what he does. It is a way to point out the games and manipulations. Offenders will not respond to confrontation in a positive way if trust and respect have not been established. This is a particular concern when working with the low-functioning offender who is generally hypersensitive to criticism. Egan (1973) stated, "Confrontation without support is disastrous, support without confrontation is anemic" (p. 132). We simply describe it as the "fist" and the "high five." The "fist" is the confrontation and the "high five" is the support.

The therapist may find him/self asking, What am I? a helper? a friend? an advocate? an information giver? an agent of the court? a protector of society? There is no easy answer. The environment, the clientele, the therapist's characteristics and training, and the type of treatment dictate the role the therapist will play. In a prison setting, the therapist's function and role are further complicated. The therapist is required to work within the constraints of security and due process while maintaining an environment that is conducive to treatment and rehabilitation. Civil commitment and community notification laws have further exacerbated this problem.

Regardless of the role, the essential aspects of therapy, especially when working with the low-functioning offender, are to help these clients recognize their own strengths, help them develop an identity based on these strengths, and accentuate their potential. In order to accomplish this, both the therapist and offender need to assume responsibility for the offender's therapy:

Like a canoe on the river, the canoe (offender) is supported by the river (therapist), pushed along by the water, sometimes gently and sometimes forcefully, through calm pools and rapids, always flowing toward some destination. The canoe floats effortlessly when its movements are in synchrony with the flow of the water, the banks providing boundaries and the weather (outside forces) changing the direction of the canoe. "Don't push the river." "Go with the flow." The offender sometimes paddles upstream (resistance). Sometimes he stops and puts his anchor down. He might have lunch on a rock, bask in the sun, explore the surroundings, and have a moment's thought. Then, if he decides to move on, he gets back in the canoe and continues the journey.

Conclusion

This chapter has described some of the techniques used in our work with the low-functioning offender. The intention is not to provide gimmicks but to encourage treatment providers to be creative, to invent techniques that are an extension of themselves and their sensitivity to the offender's needs. Therapists should pay attention to what they resonate to in the offender and the offender will give them clues about what will be effective for him. It is also necessary for therapists to be aware of the impact of their behavior on the offender. Therapists have a great deal of influence on the offenders with whom they work. The qualities that the therapist brings to the therapeutic relationship affect the offender's ability and willingness to engage in the process. Truax and Carkhuff (1967) wrote that "research seems consistently to find empathy, warmth and genuiness characteristic of human encounters that change people—for the better" (p. 141). In addition, therapists who offer low levels of these "therapeutic conditions" produce either deterioration or no change in clients. Further research suggests that when warmth and interpersonal skills are combined with a cognitive-behavioral approach, the impact is even more significant (Andrews & Kiessling, 1980).

A prison may not appear to be a setting conducive to doing sex offender treatment, much less conducive to meeting the therapeutic needs of the intellectually disabled/socially inadequate sex offender. However, as the number of incarcerated intellectually disabled/socially inadequate sex offenders increases, therapists are faced with the task of providing programming for this population. Collaboration between the security staff and therapists results in an improved environment throughout the prison.

Perhaps more important, however, is the belief that with some creativity, patience, and openness to the needs of this population, the therapist can effectively work with the intellectually disabled/socially inadequate sex offender in any setting. As clinicians, we often feel pressured by the community's expectation that we "cure" the sex offender. When the intellectually disabled/socially inadequate sex offender does not respond to the cognitive-behavioral approaches, we tend to give up on them. Instead, we opt to work with the "brighter" offender who is more capable of telling us what we want to hear. With the techniques described in this chapter and openness and flexibility on the therapist's behalf, we believe that working with this population can be effective and rewarding.

References

Andrews, D. A., & Kiessling, J. J. (1980). Program structure and effective correctional practices: A summary of the CaVIC research. In R.R. Ross & P. Gendreau, (Eds.), *Effective correctional treatment* (pp. 441–463). Toronto: Butterworths.

Egan, G. (1973). *Face to face.* Monterey, CA: Brooks/Cole.

Ferguson, E., & Haaven, J. (1990). On the design of motivating learning environments for intellectually disabled offenders. *Journal of Correctional Education, 41*(1), 33.

Fried, E. R. (1986, May). *A multimodal treatment of developmentally disabled sex offenders.* Paper presented to the Fourth National Conference on the Sexual Victimization of Children, New Orleans.

Gafgen, J. (1988, October). [Taped interview by F. H. Knopp].

Gardner, H. (1983). *Frames of mind: Theory of multiple intelligences.* New York: Basic Books.

Griffiths, D. M., Quinsey, V. L., & Hingsburger, D. (1989). *Changing inappropriate sexual behavior: A community-based approach for persons with developmental disabilities.* Baltimore: Paul H. Brookes.

Haaven, J., Little, R., & Petre-Miller, D. (1990). *Treating intellectually disabled sex offenders: A model residential program.* Orwell, VT: Safer Society Press.

Knopp, F. H. (1984). *Retraining adult sex offenders.* Syracuse, NY: Safer Society Press.

Knopp, F. H. (1990). Introduction. In J. Haaven, R. Little, & D. Petre-Miller (Eds.), *Treating intellectually disabled sex offenders: A model residential program.* (pp. 2–9). Orwell, VT: The Safer Society Press.

Knopp, F. H., & Stevenson, W. F. (1989). *A nationwide survey of juvenile and adult sex-offender treatment programs and models, 1988.* Orwell, VT: Safer Society Press.

Lakey, J. F. (1996, November). *Creative therapy for low-functioning adolescent sex offenders.* Paper presented to the Association for the Treatment of Sexual Abusers (ATSA), Chicago.

Little, R. (1992, November). *Assessment and treatment of intellectually disabled sex offenders.* ACTION Group, Burlington, VT.

Metropolitan Community Mental Health Center. (1996, March 6–7). *Strategies for community-based treatment of sex offenders with special needs.* Workshop, Eveleth, MN.

Murphy, W. D., Coleman, E. M., & Haynes, M. R. (1983). Treatment and evaluation issues with the mentally retarded sex offender. In J. G. Greer & I. R. Stuart (Eds.), *The sexual aggressor: Current perspectives on treatment* (pp. 22–41). New York: Van Nostrand Reinhold.

Program Evaluation Division. (1994). *Sex offender treatment programs.* St. Paul, MN: Office of the Legislative Auditor.

Safer Society Program. (1988, March 25–27). *A summary of selected notes from the working sessions of the first national training conference on the assessment and treatment of intellectually disabled juvenile and adult sexual offenders.* Presented under the auspices of Ohio Youth Services Network, Safer Society Program, and other related Ohio agencies, Columbus, OH.

Schwartz, B. (1995). Decision making with incarcerated sex offenders. In B. K. Schwartz & H. R. Cellini (Eds.), *The sex offender: Corrections, treatment, and legal practice* (vol. I, pp. 8-1–8-18). Kingston: NJ: Civic Research Institute.

Stanfield, J. (1992). *Be cool: Coping with difficult people.* Santa Barbara, CA: Author.

Truax, C., & Carkhuff, R. (1967). *Toward effective counseling and psychotherapy.* Chicago: Aldine.

Ward, K. M., Heffern, S. J., Wilcox, D. A., McElwee, D., Dowrick, P., Brown, T. D., Jones, M. J., & Johnson, C. L. (1992). *Managing inappropriate sexual behaviors: Supporting individuals with developmental disabilities in the community.* Anchorage: Alaska Specialized Education and Training Services.

Willis, V. (1980, July). Design considerations for mental health facilities. *Hospital and Community Psychiatry, 31*(7), 483–490.

Chapter 23

Therapeutic Community Learning Experiences: Applicaton to Mentally Retarded/Developmentally Disabled Sexual Abusers

by James M. Yokley, Ph.D.

Overview

Traditional therapeutic communities are usually associated with the treatment of fairly sophisticated criminal groups. Treatment techniques for multiple abusers are often heavily confrontational. This is hardly the setting one would associate with developmentally disabled individuals. However, with some modifications the techniques from those therapeutic settings can be adapted for use with this population.

Introduction

Traditional therapeutic community (TC) programs have been modified for application to a number of settings and special populations (DeLeon, 1995a). Modified TCs typically treat dual-diagnosis clients. Traditional TC learning experiences require some modification to meet the special needs of the mentally retarded or developmentally disabled (MR/DD) abuser referred for sexual offense. There has been a general trend in modified TCs toward decreasing length of stay (DeLeon, 1995b) and intensity of confrontation while increasing the use of cognitive-behavioral techniques. In contrast to the trend toward a shorter length of stay, the longer TC residents stay in treatment, the lower the probability of relapse. This is true of both traditional TC residents and MR/DD offenders (e.g., Condelli & Hubbard, 1994; Haaven, Little, & Petre-Miller, 1990).

Need to Modify TC Learning Experiences for the MR/DD Population

The conceptual match between the needs of the MR/DD offender and the repetitious experiential learning provided in the TC are nearly ideal. Despite this obvious conceptual match, there is a paucity of research in this area, with apparently only one published study describing a modified TC for the MR/DD sex offender (Haaven et al., 1990).

It is a "different world" for the MR/DD offender who will not transition into fully independent living after treatment. Thus, the TC philosophy of "making the inside of your house like the outside world" requires that learning experiences be modified to promote adjustment to assisted living in the community. The highly structured TC format needs to remain, but tolerance training (DeLeon, 1988) through unannounced change needs to be built in within a stable living routine. Thus, responsibility is emphasized while change is planned and processed. In general, traditional TC learning experiences need to be reduced in intensity to the lowest level that will still produce target behavioral change. Although this adjustment requires some trial and error with each new group of offenders, the modifications in basic TC learning experiences that are discussed here are recommended as guidelines for use with the MR/DD offender population. These guidelines are for the most part consistent with the relatively successful MR/DD modified TC reported by Haaven et al. (1990).

Adapting Specific Learning Experiences

Following is a list of TC learning experiences which need to be adapted from their traditional form for use with the MR/DD population. (Chapter 25, in this volume, provides a description of these learning experiences in their original form.)

House Meeting. It is important for abusers to develop and maintain a sense of environmental support from everyone in treatment. However, in contrast with multiple abusers, the MR/DD offender's need for acceptance and belonging already includes everyone and is not typically limited to negative peers. Thus, prosocial dependence does not need to be cultured or developed further during house meetings. In fact, care must be taken to ensure that MR/DD offenders do not become overly dependent on the community, which could inhibit personal problem solving. In addition, large group issues discussions and the overall concept of "we" or community may be too over-whelming and abstract to be beneficial. This situation requires concrete problem solving as opposed to abstract issue processing in small groups. In special education class sizes, less is more. Dividing the house into surrogate families is considered more beneficial and is recommended for the MR/DD offender (Gerhard & Dorgan, 1970). Community house meetings are more appropriately reserved for affirming procedures such as accomplishment or promotion announcements.

Job Function. The traditional TC philosophy of having a self-sufficient house where all necessary functions are performed by the residents is an extremely important part of treatment for the MR/DD offender. Job functions need to be modified to emphasize basic adaptive living skills (e.g., hygiene upkeep, service crew tasks, and kitchen crew tasks). The expediter (i.e., staff assistant) job function needs to be broken down into its different responsibilities, with one assigned to each resident (work checker, hygiene checker, behavior checker, etc.). Residents need to shift "learning how to learn" from being open to feedback to learning how to ask questions until they understand the task. Staff need to shift from explanation once to demonstration many times, with successive approximations rewarded by verbal praise. As in the traditional TC, residents develop self-awareness by reviewing actual behavior interactions with others during their job function, but feedback needs to be immediate and with the support of staff, not delayed until an encounter group where residents can decide if they want to give feedback. The traditional TC full workday on a single job function needs to be broken up with other experience-based learning activities so that no resident's attention span is exceeded. Supervision of the MR/DD population is paramount. Giving "strength" (i.e., supervision by residents in higher phases of treatment) to new residents is a must. Orientation, primary treatment, and community reentry phases need to be adjusted in length to accommodate anticipated learning problems.

Pull-up. Strict adherence to traditional TC rules about giving "pull-up" feedback to others without cursing must be maintained. Staff needs to help reframe and rephrase so that feedback is beneficial to both parties. "I" statements with concrete requests need to replace traditional brief pull-up statements. For example, the pull-up confrontation "Deal with your feelings" might be stated as follows: "I would like you to lower your voice," or "I think you should talk to staff." The "concern for others" obligation (i.e., "You are your brother's keeper") needs to be operationalized into concrete requirements (e.g., two helpful pull-ups per day) which are recorded. Problem thoughts and attitudes need to be (1) limited to the basics (i.e., the fewer the better that cover the program's basic criteria), (2) translated (e.g., "victim stance" referred to as "poor me"), (3) illustrated (e.g., with a picture depicting each one), and (4) posted (e.g., on the wall in the most prominent area such as the group room).

Encounter Group. Encounter group learning needs to be modified to accommodate the limited intellectual ability of the MR/DD population. In general, as intellectual level and associated coping ability drops, group frequency needs to be increased while confrontation intensity is decreased. Traditional TC tolerance training (DeLeon, 1988), which requires learning to cope with built-up emotions and delay gratification until an encounter group, which could be two days later, needs to be modified significantly for the MR/DD population. Instead of having encounter group every other day, the schedule must provide ongoing opportunity to unload problems and vent feelings. Leaning to hold on to feelings needs to be replaced with learning to deal with feelings right away so that emotional buildup and consequent acting out is minimized.

Traditional TC tolerance training (DeLeon, 1988), which requires learning to cope with intense confrontation by others, also needs to be modified. A 2:1 ratio of concern to confrontation feedback needs to be maintained. These parameters are generally recommended for the child population, which roughly matches the MR/DD offender in mental age.

Encounter group level 1 confrontation points need to be reinforced by repetition, not intensity, during communication. Staff members need to help reframe and rephrase repetitions to maximize understanding and add coping statements for the resident. Seating is critically important and in order to maintain the strict no-contact rules, staff should separate residents known to be in conflict.

Encounter group level 2 concern needs to focus on help offered by other residents through concrete suggestions that have resulted from guided discovery by staff and been repeated by the resident receiving the concern. Identification and feedback acceptance need to be fostered by staff prompting, such as "Raise your hand if you have ever made that mistake," or "Tell us how that applies to you." Staff need to ask the resident receiving the concern if they appreciate the help and would like to thank the group. Empathy development needs to be concrete and to stay focused on role-reversal ability in here-and-now group situations, not abstract exercises like reviewing victim recounts of trauma and imagining that experience. Cognitive abilities involving similarities and discrimination are limited in the MR/DD offender. Thus, imagining victim trauma is probably too close to actual deviant fantasy material for this group to separate.

Spoken To. Staff cannot assume that MR/DD offenders will understand that the incident about which they are being "spoken to" has been chosen because it reflects a problem behavioral pattern. Teaching the abstract concept these offenders need to change by understanding their attitude and how to modify it is not likely to be beneficial. Thus, the "spoken to" needs to be changed from giving three different pieces of information about one behavioral pattern (i.e., incident, attitude, and what to change) to having three different examples of the same behavior repeated with the same suggestion for each. At the end, staff need to request that residents repeat back what they learned in a nonthreatening, face-saving manner that models responsibility ownership and will not embarrass residents who do not understand. For example, "Sometimes I ramble on too much, get off the track and don't make sense, so tell me what you think I said so I know I said it right."

Haircut. The verbal "haircut," which requires that the resident demonstrate self-control by remaining totally inactive and not reacting under confrontation stress, needs to be replaced with a "haircut" where the resident is reinforced for positive action. The incident portion of the haircut, which is designed to hold the resident's emotional attention through loud confrontation, needs to be replaced with an exciting, fun, dramatic, or bizarre behavior that relates to the incident and will hold emotional attention. The three-stage one-sided interaction of the verbal haircut needs to be reduced to a two-stage problem-solving interactive role-reversal haircut where the focus is on seeing what the problem looks like and doing something about it. Staff need to help the resident arrive at an adaptive solution using prompting and guided discovery.

For example, if MR/DD resident Larry had several aggressive outbursts toward his sheltered workshop supervisor, he would be told to wait outside the staff door in the same manner as he would be told during a typical "verbal haircut." However, when called in, Larry would observe one staff member wearing Larry's own hat and workshop apron with his name on it while reenacting a safe version of his outburst by banging loudly on the supervisor's table with a ruler. A second staff member would be sitting at the supervisor's table trying to get agitated Larry to stop and would ask the resident to "help me calm Larry down!" Reinforcement of appropriate behavior would be applied. Agitated Larry would beat loudly when his fellow staff member gave suggestions and stop when the resident gave suggestions. The fellow staff would continue triggering banging outbursts by offering suggestions to agitated Larry until the resident offered an appropriate coping suggestion. At that point agitated Larry would stop, put down his ruler, tell the resident that he was feeling like his good self again, and thank him for his help. The second staff member would then shift to the final change portion of the haircut by pointing out, "Just like you were the only person who could stop this problem today, you're the only person who can stop your outbursts at the workshop. Let's talk about how you can stop your outbursts at the workshop." This procedure has been effective with special abuser youth when the youth who had the aggressive school outbursts was dressed in suit and tie and sat at the principal's desk while each group member entered the office one at a time and recreated the aggressive outburst. This technique required the aggressive youth to manage someone else exhibiting his behavior by using problem-solving skills from the perspective of the individual receiving that behavior. In summary, the resident observes an attention-holding reenactment of his problem, is reinforced for finding an appropriate solution, and tells the staff member how he can use that solution for his own problem.

Bench. Techniques that use lengthy periods in which to reflect on one's behavior or other abstract issues, such as one's entire negative lifestyle, are not the forte of the MR/DD offender. The value of the "bench" for this group is to interrupt destructive behavior before it progresses. Thus, it is far more valuable to use many short trial-and-error bench stays to consider minor problems than to let frustration build up to the point where a traditional lengthy bench intervention is required. Time out on the bench should be in a low-activity area and reduced for the MR/DD population. For example, offenders with a preteen mental age need to be started with the standard five to ten minutes while those with the mental age of young teens may receive up to twenty minutes. If an aggressive act is brewing and more than twenty minutes away from environmental triggers is needed, provision of a room or space where offenders may stand and stretch their legs a bit is desirable. In addition, residents should always be instructed as to the specific reasons why they are on the bench, and they should be asked to repeat these reasons when staff comes to take them off the bench. Of course, any institutional or departmental policies covering "time outs" or "sequestration" must be adhered to.

Sign. Although a large sign may be cumbersome and irritating to MR/DD offenders, they are not likely to be self-conscious enough about a cool image and appearance to quickly change problem behaviors in order to have the sign removed. For the MR/DD offender, the value of the "sign" learning experience lies in its ability to function as a behavioral queue or prompt. However, to function in that capacity, the MR/DD offender needs to be able to read the sign. Reading the sign presents a problem if the offender is wearing it on his chest. Historically, traditional TC residents who were unable to "keep things up front" (i.e., stay aware of their behavioral patterns) with a regular sign to help remind them would receive a "Ding-a-ling" sign. This "Ding-a-ling" sign is on a note card mounted on a coat hanger and worn on a tennis headband. Thus, the abuser has the reminder message suspended in front of his face at all times. This type of sign is considered too dangerous for MR/DD, children, or other residents who are likely to have coordination problems with obstructed vision.

The MR/DD offender literally needs to be able to "read the handwriting on the wall." Thus, the sign learning experience needs to be modified so that the MR/DD resident can help to develop a sign that illustrates his problem in a way that is meaningful to him. Signs need to be simple, direct, and illustrated with a picture or symbol (i.e., a trademark) that the resident puts after his name on all written assignments he turns in during the "sign learning experience." When a suitable sign has been created, the resident needs to post that sign in the target area in which the behavior is most likely to occur. If the behavior trigger is a person, the sign needs to be posted in an area where the target person is most often found. If the problem is likely to occur in more than one area, more than one sign needs to be posted. Each time the problem behavior is exhibited, the resident constructs another sign and posts it in that area. If necessary, wrist reminders with the same sign message can be warn around the wrist with a rubberband to keep them in place. The sign(s) should come down after the first day of behavior maintenance or the first demonstration of behavior change.

Contracts. The commitment contract needs to be modified for the MR/DD offender to focus on brief interventions with specific behaviors. The two basic types of contracts (work and spare parts) need to be adapted. Work contracts need to focus more on repeating prosocial behaviors during work tasks as opposed to developing self-control through different work assignments. Spare parts contracts need to focus more on basic reinforcement and creative consequences as opposed to repeating the problem behavior with spare parts reminders until problem behavior satiation occurs. The commitment to a positive identity needs to be simplified to good behavior. The image adjustment portion (i.e., making the person look more positive to authorities or less "cool" to negative peers) of the contract needs to shift from external appearance-oriented interventions to prosocial behaviors. One work contract example would be a required respect image adjustment where the resident is required to "go to the opposite extreme" of courtesy (e.g., using "excuse me, may I say something" prior to speaking, and "it was very nice to speak to you" at the end of each conversation, along with "please" and "thank you" during every conversation). Having to always hold the door and offer others one's seat or place in line would also be included.

Activity therapy time might include positive role practice in playing frustration tolerance games. For example, the resident could play "Thank You" Uno. Uno is a game in which the opponent prevents the player from winning by playing cards that require the player to draw more cards. Because the object is to discard all cards, the game is frustrating and typically elicits emotional outbursts in young children. "Thank You" Uno has players saying "thank you" for each unwanted card they must draw; that is, they are thanking the opponent who is frustrating them.

Traditional contracts often include a relating table each night at which residents talk to the person on contract about their problem. The "sign" or "spare parts" (objects used as reminders) are probably better than a relating table for the MR/DD offender. Like the sign, it is important that spare parts be easily seen, which for the most part rules out wearing items.

The contract commitment task for the MR/DD offender needs to be brief, fit the behavior, and be instructive. In a work contract example, the resident who is not giving his required number of daily pull-ups and not keeping up his hygiene might receive the commitment task of hygiene expediter for the following day. Each day that his hygiene is acceptable and he meets his hygiene pull-up quota with others, the resident is excused from hygiene expediter duties. Having residents give pull-ups about their own problem areas to others helps them "keep their problem up front," as well as promotes learning (i.e., "If you want someone to learn something, have them teach it to others").

A version of differential reinforcement of other behavior needs to be added to the spare parts contract for the MR/DD offender. The typical spare parts contract procedure of prescribing repetition of the maladaptive role that the offender is displaying needs to be changed to neutralizing that role while reinforcing the opposite in others. The first step is to neutralize and contain the maladaptive role by removing the reinforcing audience. Then, because MR/DD offenders have an easier time observing others than themselves, the competing behavior of others is reinforced instead of reinforcing a competing response made by the offender. For example, the resident trying to provoke a physical confrontation by refusing a time out for abusive group behavior would be handled by stating, "OK if you won't leave, then the rest of you leave." After the rest of the group has left the room, the defiant resident is told, "You refused to leave here, so stay here" and the door is closed. The rest of the group members are quietly taken to the canteen for an ice cream sundae. After they are done and return to the group room, which has in effect been turned into a time-out setting, the defiant resident discovers the consequences of his refusal role. This substitution of the paradoxical "assign them their maladaptive role" procedure has the added advantage of reinforcing the compliant while providing a consequence for the defiant. This procedure has been effective with special abuser youth by taking the rest of the group shopping as differential reinforcement. To maximize the intervention, the rest of the group was told that they had one hour to buy any T-shirt they wanted as long as they all agreed on it and would wear it to the next three group sessions. This required group compromise and problem solving. When the shoppers returned to group that day and for the next three sessions all wearing the same designer T-shirt, the difference between the compliant and the defiant was underscored in powerful nonverbal language. The defiant high-functioning MR teenager never refused a time out again.

Conclusion

This chapter has been devoted to recommendations for modifying basic tradition-al TC learning experiences to meet the needs of MR/DD sex offenders. These learn-ing experiences are free standing and may be applied in the inpatient, day treatment, or outpatient setting. Teaching treatment concepts to the MR/DD offender requires using visual, auditory, and motor sensory input channels (Dutta, 1979), which means integrating art, music, recreation, and other activity therapies. Art therapy activities are easily integrated into the TC action-oriented, experiential format (e.g., Donnenberg, 1978; Gerritsen, 1995). This can be seen when residents illustrate life problems on sign learning experiences. This is not the case with drama therapy tech-niques, which may be applied to violence reduction (Count-Van Manen, 1991) but must be seriously modified to fit the strict TC no-contact rules and interaction regu-lations. These rules inhibit the spontaneity of drama therapy but must remain in place for safety and security. Haaven et al. (1990) provide a good example of how to inte-grate art therapy and activity therapy into a modified TC model for the intellectually disabled offender, along with a detailed description of a well-structured residential treatment program.

References

Condelli, W., & Hubbard, R. (1994). Client outcomes from therapeutic communities. In F. Tims, G. DeLeon & N Jainchill (Eds.), *Therapeutic community: Advances in research and application* (pp. 80–98) (NIDA Research Monograph 144, NIH Publication No. 94-3633). Rockville, MD: National Institute on Drug Abuse.

Count-Van Manen, G. (1991). Drama-imagery processes as socialization: An interdisciplinary per-spective. Imagery and sociology [Special issue]. *Journal of Mental Imagery, 15*(1–2), 243–293.

DeLeon, G. (1988). *The therapeutic community and behavioral science* (NIDA Research Monograph 84). Rockville, MD: National Institute on Drug Abuse.

De Leon, G. (1995a, January–March). Residential therapeutic communities in the mainstream: Diversity and issues. *Journal of Psychoactive Drugs, 27*(1), 3–15.

DeLeon, G. (1995b). Therapeutic communities for addictions: A theoretical framework. *International Journal of the Addictions, 30*(12), 1603–1645.

Donnenberg, D. (1978). Art therapy in a drug community. *Confinia Psychiatrica, 21*(1–3), 7–44.

Dutta, T. (1979). Education for problem children [Special issue]. *Indian Psychological Review, 18*(1–4), 31–34.

Gerhard, R., & Dorgan, R. (1970). A catchment milieu training-service model for the mental retar-dation sector: A documented proposal. *International Journal of Social Psychiatry, 16*(3), 221–227.

Gerritsen, M. (1995). Art therapy: The real art is the process. *Therapeutic Communities: International Journal for Therapeutic and Supportive Organizations, 16*(1), 25–35.

Haaven, J., Little, R., & Petre-Miller, D. (1990). *Treating intellectually disabled sex offenders: A model residential program.* Orwell VT: Safer Society Press.

Part 5

Treating the Adult Sex Offender

This section covers recent innovations in practical applications for treating the adult sex offender. These applications range from new approaches to follow-up to the development of treatments for dealing with exhibitionists. Steven P. Sawyer, of Project Pathfinder in Minneapolis, saw the need not only to follow up on recidivism but also to evaluate whether the men are actually using what they learned in treatment. To do this, program staff contacted 100 men who had completed treatment up to five years previously. Subjects were interviewed at six months and one year after treatment and annually thereafter. Graduates of the treatment program were questioned regarding their relapse prevention plans, including precursors and interventions, family and relationship adjustment, substance abuse, work adjustment and contact with the law. Interesting data emerge as to how these individuals have adjusted and what appeared to be helpful in easing adjustment. Finally, the study includes the program's recidivism data.

Therapeutic communities (TCs) are a treatment approach that has been shown to be useful with a variety of offender groups. Besides simply housing offenders who are participating in treatment together, TCs have evolved a number of special techniques by which to confront offenders over their daily behavior. The strength of the TC is that it aids in helping the participants learn to be more responsible, develop prosocial attitudes, and form nonabusive interpersonal relations. James M. Yokely has outlined a variety of these techniques. He discusses how to establish different types of contracts and use different confrontational techniques.

Phallometric assessments have been the standard tool for assessing deviant arousal in sex offenders for at least fifteen years. However, this technique is inherently controversial as it is fairly intrusive and there have been long-standing arguments regarding stimulus materials. Gene Abel developed an alternative method, which skirts many of the problems with the p-graph. However, is it accurate? Can it be easily faked? Scott A. Johnson and Alan Listiak of the Minnesota Department of Corrections have compared the two techniques. This chapter should be useful to therapists and programs trying to decide between the two approaches.

Sex offenders are frequently woefully ill informed on the basics of human sexuality. Sex education is almost always a basic component of sex offender treatment. Nancy H. Walbek and Richard K. Seely surveyed more than 300 treatment programs as to their approaches to teaching human sexuality. In addition, they surveyed the programs on restriction of pornography. The authors share their findings and make recommendations on developing curriculum in this area.

Treating exhibitionists can be an extremely frustrating undertaking. These individuals appear to be highly compulsive. Because they are often in community-based treatment programs as a result of being charged with misdemeanors rather than felonies, they can cause therapists many sleepless nights worrying about their high risk of reoffending. Moreover, these clients often are individuals with a tremendous amount to lose should their behavior continue. Carol J. Ball and Theoharis K. Seghorn of New England Forensic Associates have developed a treatment program that combines behavioral treatment with medication to help these individuals.

Sexually offending clergy have outraged the public and devastated many congregations. Donald R. Hands, in his chapter, "Beyond the Cloister," focuses on some of the practices of the Roman Catholic Church that he believes may contribute to the problems of sex-abusing clergy. This chapter has been included in this volume with the hope that some of these issues can be evaluated in the light of the extent of the problem; however, readers should be reminded that many sex offenders enter the ministry because it offers access to children. It may well be that a combination of improved screening of applicants and a fresh look at some of the shame-enhancing techniques will reduce the extent of this tragedy.

Chapter 24

Measuring Treatment Efficacy Through Long-Term Follow-up

by Steven P. Sawyer, M.S.S.W.

Overview

The posttreatment functioning and reoffense rate of 100 men who completed long-term outpatient sex offender treatment was assessed utilizing official criminal records and follow-up interviews. The subjects, 100 men, ages 18 to 72 and mostly Caucasian, had committed or been convicted in criminal court of sex or sex-related crimes. Most were child molesters (80%), 8% committed exhibitionism, voyeurism, or obscene telephone calls, and 12% committed rape or attempted rape. Two hundred forty-nine follow-up interviews were conducted with 87 of the 100 subjects at intervals from six months to five years posttreatment. Questions were asked pertaining to reoffense precursors and coping strategies, family and relationship adjustment, chemical use, work adjustment, and any contact with the law. Official criminal records were reviewed annually for all subjects. Results from 249 structured interviews and criminal records checks that included sex-related and non–sex-related convictions are presented. An overall criminal reoffense rate of 6% was found: 2% for sex-related convictions and 4% for non–sex-related convictions. Subjects showed positive posttreatment adjustment and the ability to name precursors and coping mechanisms that would occur early in a reoffense cycle.

Research on Efficacy of Treatment

Research studies have assessed factors associated with treatment success and failure (Maletzky, 1993; Simkins, Ward, Bowman, & Rinck 1990), recidivism of randomized, matched groups of incarcerated offenders (Marques, Day, Nelson, & West, 1994), and recidivism of outpatient programs (Dwyer & Rosser 1992; Hanson, Steffy, & Gauthier 1993). Furby, Weinrott, and Blackshaw (1989) and Nagayama-Hall (1995) also conducted meta-analyses.

The efficacy of the treatment of adult sex offenders has become a much discussed topic in the professional literature and popular press (*Wall Street Journal*, 1996; *Star-Tribune*, 1991; *Glamour,* 1996). The viability of treatment programs is a topic of concern in many states. Programs are under pressure from funding agencies and the public to demonstrate positive outcome. The demand to demonstrate that treatment reduces the reoffense rate of those treated has resulted in an increasing number of published studies and debates in the literature regarding treatment efficacy. Marshall and Pithers (1994) asserted that "to be maximally effective . . . treatment must be comprehensive, cognitively-behaviorally based, and include a relapse prevention component." Prentky and Burgess (1990) argued that even utilizing a conservative "failure rate" calculation model, which defines a failure as a charge versus an arrest, conviction, or any reincarceration or parole violation, to calculate reoffense rate for treated and untreated child molesters, it is cost-effective to treat sex offenders.

Outcome and recidivism studies have yielded varied results depending on the type of treatment approach, offense type, and length of time at risk. The generalizability of results is limited given the differences in length and type of treatment, offense histories of research subjects, and study design. These limitations suggest that each facility treating sex offenders should conduct the best possible outcome study for its treatment approach and population. Treatment results measured by review of official criminal record, posttreatment testing, or posttreatment interviews provide the treatment program with information that can be used to evaluate program effectiveness. Effectiveness of these measures can be augmented when used in combination with each other.

Purpose of Study

The purpose of this ongoing study was to assess the posttreatment adjustment and occurrence of reoffense of men who completed an outpatient sex offender treatment program. The study utilized structured interviews and official criminal record checks. The study was based on the following hypothesis: Effective treatment would reduce the risk for reoffense and the rate of recidivism if:

1. Clients learn to manage day-to-day life difficulties that could be precursors to a reoffense.
2. Clients ameliorate underlying psychosocial, biological, relational, lifestyle, and behavioral difficulties or symptoms.
3. Clients know precursors to a reoffense and have strategies to manage those circumstances.
4. Clients are able to intervene on their difficulties early in the chain of events that could lead to another offense.

Treatment Goals

The outpatient treatment program, operated by a community-based nonprofit agency, was based on a multiple strategy approach utilizing cognitive-behavioral, family systems, and psychodynamic theory and techniques. The treatment format was structured around weekly group therapy and twice monthly individual, conjoint, or family therapy. Treatment was open ended; clients remained in group and individual therapy until all treatment goals were completed.

Prior to admission to treatment, all clients were assessed using clinical interviews, standardized psychological testing, and review of all relevant legal documents. Psychological testing was also administered prior to treatment completion.

The following psychological testing and assessment procedures were used pre-treatment: Minnesota Multiphasic Personality Inventory (MMPI-II), Millon Multiaxial Clinical Inventory III (MCMI III), Multiphasic Sex Inventory (MSI), Measure of Psychosocial Development (MPD), and Shipley Institute of Living Scale.

In addition, the following were used on a case-by-case basis when clinically appropriate: polygraph, phallometric exam, Wechsler Adult Intelligence Scale—Revised (WAIS-R), Beck Depression Inventory, Test of Variable Attention (TOVA), Rorschach, and the Hare Psychopathy Checklist—Revised (PCL-R).

The following psychological testing and assessment procedures were used post-treatment: MMPI-II, MCMI III, MSI, and MPD.

All treatment expectations were given in writing at the beginning of the treatment process. The treatment consisted of nineteen goals, each representing a specific issue or task to be accomplished by the client. Some goals required the inclusion of a spouse, family member or significant other. The issues covered by the goals included the following:

- Take a history of all illegal behavior.
- Identify the sequence of the behaviors, thoughts, and emotions that were associated with the current and prior offenses.
- Resolve minimization and or denial.
- Identify offense cycles or patterns.
- Identify and resolve shame or self-denigrating thoughts.
- Understand the meaning of the offense.

- Recognize other aggressive behaviors that were part of the offense pattern.
- Develop healthy sexuality.
- Express victim empathy.
- Develop expressive and receptive communication skills.
- Resolve family-of-origin conflicts.
- Enhance moral development.
- Build prosocial relationships.
- Repay the victim and community.
- Develop and implement a relapse prevention plan.

Referral to an aftercare group was made according to an individualized treatment plan. Group composition was heterogeneous by age and offense with the exception of a special focus group of young men whose offense involved consensual sex with a known underage female. All groups were facilitated by a male and female co-therapy team.

Interview Procedure

Upon completion of treatment, a verbal description of the study was given and clients were asked if they would be willing to participate in the study. If they agreed, they signed a consent form outlining the process and limits of confidentiality. At six, twelve, twenty-four, thirty-six, forty-eight, and sixty months posttreatment, clients received a letter asking them to contact the interviewer. Interviewers placed follow-up phone calls if the client did not contact them. Interviews were conducted in person or by telephone. This interview was based on a protocol developed by Dwyer and Amberson (1985) and Dwyer and Rosser (1992).

Interview topics included incidents of reoffense or near offense, reoffense warning signs, strategies and techniques to manage warning signs, offense-related fantasies, quality of relationships at work and with family, any contact with the law, and chemical use pattern. In addition, interviewers asked three questions regarding the client's experience in the treatment program.

The interview consisted of closed-end questions requiring a "yes" or "no" answer, such as "Have there been any situations where you felt you were close to another sex offense?", and questions asking for a description, such as "Can you describe early warning signs or red flags that would be clues you may be headed toward another offense?" The responses to questions regarding knowledge of precursors and strategies to manage warning signs were categorized into thoughts, emotions, behaviors, and situations. Thoughts were defined as cognitive processes of mental manipulation or concept formation that cannot be directly observed (i.e., desire, sexualizing, attitudes, or self-dialogue). Emotions were defined as an acute or momentary condition, subjectively experienced, affect-laden states (i.e., nervousness, depression, low self- esteem, urges, or loneliness). Behaviors were defined as acts, activities, responses, movements, or any measurable action (i.e., being defensive, body language, going to or leaving a situation). Situations were defined as a place, locale, or position or set of circumstances (i.e., stress, isolation, or "at home alone").

Study Compliance

Interviews were conducted with 87 of the 100 subjects who agreed to participate. Of the thirteen subjects who were not interviewed, one requested to be dismissed from the study prior to the first interview and one was deceased prior to the first interview. Official criminal records were reviewed on all 100 subjects. The social functioning and reoffense data were drawn from official criminal records and 249 interviews. The time posttreatment was six months to five years.

Initial Results

Subjects. The subjects were primarily Caucasian, high school educated and employed (Table 24.1). Their mean age was 33. More than half (61%) were in a relationship at the time of discharge from treatment. The sexual offenses committed by this population included intrafamilial and extrafamilial child molestation, exhibitionism, rape, attempted rape, other nonrape sexual assault, obscene telephone calls, and voyeurism.

Table 24.1
Demographic Profile

	Child Molest Intrafamilial n = 24	*Child Molest Extrafamilial n = 56*	*Rape[a] n = 12*	*Other[b] n = 8*
Age				
Range	22–62	19–72	20–32	25–40
Mean	40	36	25	30
Race				
Caucasian	22	48	11	8
Non-Caucasian	2	8	1	0
Relationship Status @ Discharge				
Married/couple	15	30	10	6
Not coupled	9	22	2	2
Education (years)				
0–11	5	12	10	2
12 or GED	15	32	8	0
13–15	3	3	27	5
16 +		9	1	1
Unknown		1		

[a] Rape includes rape, attempted rape, and nonrape sexual assault.
[b] Other includes exhibitionism, voyeurism, and obscene phone calls.

Victims. Victims (Table 24.2) were primarily prepubescent, adolescent, and adult females; however, 11.6% of reported victims were male. Several subjects reported multiple victims.

Table 24.2
Victim Age and Gender by Offense Type

	Child Molest Intrafamilial n = 24		Child Molest Extrafamilial n = 56		Rape[a] n = 12		Other[b] n = 8	
	n	%	n	%	n	%	n	%
Female victim								
< 12	0	40	27	47	0	0	0	0
12–17	9	36	22	38	3	25	1	13
Adult	0	0	0	0	9	75	7	87
Male victim								
< 12	6	24	2	3	0	0	0	0
12–17	0	0	4	7	0	0	0	0
Adult	0	0	0	0	0	0	0	0
Totals[c]	25		58		12		8	

[a] Rape includes rape, attempted rape, and nonrape sexual assault.
[b] Other includes exhibitionism, voyeurism, and obscene phone calls.
[c] Total $N = 103$ victims as some subjects had multiple victims.

Treatment Variables. The mean length of time in treatment for all offense types was thirty-two months with some variation between offense categories. Approximately 33% were less than twenty-three months posttreatment, 46% were twenty-four to sixty months posttreatment, and 21% percent were more than sixty months posttreatment at the time of the most recent criminal record check. Table 24.3 describes attendance rate and length of time posttreatment by offense category and interview interval.

Definition of Reoffense

Reoffense was defined as any self-report of any criminal behavior, sex related or not sex related, and any misdemeanor or felony arrest or conviction found in official records. Consequently, positive results were defined as an absence of sex or non–sex-related criminal behavior, an absence of situations close to a reoffense, a demonstrated ability to name reoffense precursors early in a likely reoffense chain, an ability to identify a variety of named strategies to manage precursors, and positive relationship functioning within family and work relationships.

Six subjects were found to have committed eight incidents of criminal reoffense; two sex-related reoffenses and six non–sex-related offenses. All eight were found by official record; three were also self-reported. From official sources, one sex-related record consisted of two instances of exhibitionism by the same subject. The other con-

Table 24.3
Number of Months in Treatment, Posttreatment, and Number of Interviews

	Child Molest Intrafamilial n = 24	Child Molest Extrafamilial n = 56	Rape[a] n = 12	Other[b] n = 8
Months in Treatment				
Mean	39	30	23	33
Range	12–59	14–73	20–50	13–34
Attendance Rate[c]				
Mean %	92	90	85	78
Months Posttreatment				
6–23	4	20	2	7
24–35	6	9	0	1
36–47	5	14	0	0
48–59	2	7	1	1
60 +	7	6	5	3
Total Number of Interviews[d]	75	131	22	21

[a] Rape includes rape, attempted rape, and nonrape sexual assault.
[b] Other includes exhibitionism, voyeurism, and obscene phone calls.
[c] Attendance rate is number of treatment sessions attended divided by total possible sessions.
[d] No interviews with thirteen subjects.

sisted of one instance of invasion of privacy (voyeurism). Both cases of exhibitionism were self-reported. Three cases of drug- or alcohol-related criminal reoffense were reported by official record: two for driving under the influence; one for possession of a narcotic. One case of disorderly conduct (also alcohol related) and two driving violations were also found. Counting all subjects who committed any reoffense yielded a sex-related reoffense rate of 2% (2/100), a non–sex-related reoffense rate of 4% (4/100), and an overall criminal reoffense rate of 6% (6/100).

Self-Reports by Offenders

Investigators found positive self-reported results in a number of areas. An important finding was the ability of the subjects to name multiple reoffense precursors at each interview interval (Table 24.4). Many subjects named precursors that would occur at the beginning of a reoffense chain, as described by Pithers (1988) and Pithers and Cumming (1996). Examples of negative emotional states named as precursors included "felt rejected," "felt lonely," and "felt angry." Few subjects named precursors imminent to a reoffense, such as watching children at a playground, cruising or stalking victims, or arranging time alone with children. Subjects named behavioral precursors most frequently (36.8%) and thoughts (27.6%), emotions (21.8%), and situations (13.7%) less frequently.

Likewise, most subjects were able to name multiple strategies to intervene in a reoffense pattern. Strategies were also categorized into behaviors, thoughts, emotions,

Table 24.4
Strategies and Precursors Named by Interview Period

	Child Molest Intrafamilial n = 24		Child Molest Extrafamilial n = 56		Rape[a] n = 12		Other[b] n = 8	
Months Posttreatment	*n*	*avg.*	*n*	*avg.*	*n*	*avg.*	*n*	*avg.*
Precursors								
6	71	3	169	3	20	3	15	3
12	65	3	137	4	17	3	15	3
24	41	3	74	4	15	5	17	4
36	41	4	50	3	6	3	16	5
48	20	3	17	3	10	5	12	6
60	12	3	0	0	5	5	16	5
Strategies								
6	76	3	167	3	23	3	19	4
12	63	3	136	4	24	4	24	5
24	46	4	73	3	8	3	14	4
36	34	3	60	3	12	6	10	3
48	20	3	25	4	6	3	3	2
60	15	4	0	0	5	5	8	3

[a] Rape includes rape, attempted rape, and nonrape sexual assault.
[b] Other includes exhibitionism, voyeurism, and obscene phone calls.

and situations. Subjects named behavioral strategies most often (69.5%), followed by thoughts (27.4%), situations (2.4%), and emotions (.7%). Subjects named early behavioral interventions, such as "talk with my wife" or "tell someone if I am angry," or thoughts such as "recognize depression." Some also named more immediate behavioral strategies, such as "leave the situation." This response pattern suggests an action-oriented approach to managing risk.

Relationships with family or significant others (Table 24.5) and at work (Table 24.6) were queried and found to be generally positive or improved. Overall, subjects reported having difficulty with any member of their family of origin in sixty-nine (27.7%) of the interviews. Few reported difficulty with more than one family member or difficulty across multiple interviews. Across all interviews, difficulty with father or mother was reported with equal frequency (6.8% vs. 6.4%) whereas reports of difficulty with siblings were higher (14.5%). Reports of quality of relationship with spouse or partner were positive. Across all interviews with all subjects, 29% reported having difficulty with a partner. Having difficulty with a partner ranged from 19% to 34% across the six interview intervals. Approximately 23% reported having difficulty with children.

Overall, subjects reported improved relationships at work in 69% of the interviews with little change across the five-year time span. About half reported increased productivity at work. They attributed their improved relationships to having better communication skills, higher self-esteem, or improved self-confidence.

Table 24.5
Interview Results: Family Relationship Difficulties

	W/Father % Yes	W/Mother % Yes	W/Siblings % Yes	W/Partner/ Dating % Yes	W/Children % Yes
Months Posttreatment					
6 (*n* = 84)	9	4	17	19	19
12 (*n* = 67)	6	10	9	15	23
24 (*n* = 41)	5	5	13	34	18
36 (*n* = 33)	3	3	6	28	16
48 (*n* = 16)	7	6	13	23	14
60 (*n* = 8)	25	38	38	29	17

Note. Percentages reflect interview results where subjects had a relationship or children, or when parents were living.

Table 24.6
Interview Results: Work Relationships and Productivity

	Relationships at Work % Better	% Same	% Worse	Productivity at Work % Better	% Same	% Worse
Months Posttreatment						
6 (*n* = 84)	51	25	4	44	31	4
12 (*n* = 67)	57	34	1	36	39	2
24 (*n* = 41)	73	20	2	51	37	5
36 (*n* = 33)	68	8	0	49	24	3
48 (*n* = 16)	56	31	6	31	56	6
60 (*n* = 8)	87	13	0	75	25	0

Note. Data reflect interviews with employed subjects only.

Subjects reported a decrease in occurrence of offense-related fantasies compared to the rate of offense-related fantasies prior to treatment. When asked to estimate the percent of offense-related fantasies prior to treatment, subjects reported a mean of 35.5% (SD, 33.6; range 0–100). When asked to estimate percent of offense-related fantasies posttreatment subjects reported a mean of 2.9% (SD, 8.7; range 0–75).

Simkins, Ward, Bowman, and Rinck (1990) found that the total number of sessions attended and therapy attendance rate were critical factors affecting therapy progress. Attendance rate was calculated for each offense category utilizing a method described by Simkins et al. (1990) and was found to be 78–92%.

Treatment Results Related to a Decrease in Stressful Situations

These initial results suggest that this treatment approach had a positive impact on factors that were related to increased risk for reoffense. For example, most subjects reported positive social, relational, and employment circumstances. Reports of relationship conflict were limited to cases in which a divorce occurred during or after treatment or in which chronic conflict had been the norm. Many subjects reported positive relationships and work functioning over multiple interviews, which suggests stability in these areas. Contact with the law was limited to traffic violations and the criminal violations identified in official records.

Eleven percent reported having felt close to a reoffense at least one time, although only 1% reported this circumstance in consecutive interviews. This appears to be a positive outcome because many subjects named precursors early in their reoffense cycle; however, it is likely that others have, at one time or another, felt close to another offense but did not report these instances.

Social and Work-Related Skills

Social and work-related functioning reflect the overall social skills and competence of the subjects. Many subjects reported increased work productivity and most reported improved relations at work. In describing this phenomenon they noted improved self-esteem and communication skills and greater self-confidence as contributing factors. The treatment model ties improved social skills to a lower level of risk. Therefore, a goal of treatment is to improve social skills and relationship competence. A positive outcome occurs when subjects gain greater satisfaction from their employment or benefits from improved conflict management skills.

Family Relationships

Subjects reported improved relationship functioning. Few subjects reported chronic family problems that persisted over time, and few reported problems with all members of their family. This suggests that in general, subjects experienced their family as a potential source of support and few subjects were experiencing alienation from their family. Although an indirect measure, job satisfaction and relational success are related to a high degree of self-efficacy, which is an important component of self-esteem (Bandura, 1997).

Expected Level of Reoffense

Is the current sex-related reoffense rate (2%) viable and reasonable for this population? The current sex offense was the first for most subjects. Most did not have any prior criminal record. None carried a diagnosis of pedophilia—exclusive type, according to the fourth edition of *Diagnostic and Statistical Manual of Mental Disorders* (American Psychiatric Association, 1994). This population was treated in the community where they were expected to be employed, to pay for at least a portion of the cost of treatment, to include family members in the treatment program, and to report to their probation officer on a regular basis. In a meta-analysis published in 1995, Hall reported a sex offense recidivism rate of 19% for treated sex offenders in twelve studies of 1,313 offenders in community and institutional programs. Studies by Schwartz and Cellini (1995) of six community-based programs treating less violent sex offenders showed a range of recidivism from 3% to 14.9% for treated sex offenders who committed a new sex offense.

Dynamics of Therapy

This treatment approach was long term and comprehensive. It was designed to assess and treat the thoughts, behaviors, affect, and relationship context of each client. The client was expected to demonstrate change over time. The client was expected to move from an external locus of control at the beginning of treatment to an internal locus by the end of treatment. When this shift happens, a client develops his own motivation for gaining benefit from the treatment process, and begins to parallel mainstream psychotherapy patients who benefit from long-term psychotherapy, as observed by Seligman (1996).

This was an outpatient population who lived in the community. Many had families and children. Although many were incarcerated in local jails as a judicial sanction for their offense, most received probation and few were incarcerated in state penal institutions. A probation population has been assessed to be more likely to remain stable in the community. As a population with a low occurrence of risk factors, a relatively low rate of reoffense could be expected.

Significance of Noncooperation

What was the meaning of study dropouts ($N = 1$) and subjects who failed to respond to the request for a follow-up interview or were not located ($N = 11$)? Did these men drop out of the study for a particular reason? Were they avoiding the additional scrutiny inherent in the follow-up questions? The reasons for lack of follow-through can only be conjectured. Some subjects who were interviewed commented that the interviews reminded them of being in treatment, suggesting the possibility that nonresponders did not want to be reminded of treatment. Nonresponders were included in official criminal record checks and accounted for two reoffenses; one sex related and one drug/alcohol related. The eleven interview nonresponders represented all offense behaviors and a range of ages.

Limitations of the Current Study

Interview data on social functioning and reoffense was based on self-report. There may be varying motivations for reliable responses to the interview questions. One could hypothesize that the interview results would be of higher reliability when a subject was cooperative and less reliable than when a subject did not follow through or was resistant.

The range of time at risk was six months to more than five years with 33% of the subjects being less than twenty-four months posttreatment. Research has demonstrated the likelihood of underreporting of sex crimes in general. Consequently, the occurrence of additional crimes may be underreported, leading to inaccuracy in the criminal records.

The principal investigator was the treating clinician in some cases and the supervisor or agency administrator for all cases. This relationship could have influenced the responses of some subjects. However, there were instances of subjects making negative comments about their therapist or aspects of the treatment program as well as instances of self-report of fantasies of the offense behavior, lending credibility to the interview data.

All subjects were informed of the limits of confidentiality inherent in the design and execution of the study. Consequently, any instance of known or suspected abuse of a child was subject to reporting to local authorities. This reporting requirement was not minimized nor was any advice offered to aid the subjects in avoiding this issue. Compliance with this law by the interviewer created a situation that may have reduced the admission of reoffense for fear of the legal consequences.

A priority was placed on interviewing as many subjects as possible. Because some subjects were unable or unwilling to complete the interview in person, some interviews were completed over the telephone. Although there is no immediate evidence of bias as a result of this methodology, all efforts were made to conduct interviews in person as often as possible during the five-year period.

Conclusion

Program evaluation, recidivism studies, or outcome studies contribute to an understanding of treatment impact, risk for reoffense, and factors that deteriorate over time and contribute to increased recidivism. Prior studies have demonstrated the relationship between precursors to a sexual offense and the importance of early intervention on a reoffense pattern. Marshall (1990) and others have discussed the antecedents to sexual offense and the contribution of other life stressors. Comprehensive treatment approaches target the improvement of communication skills, self-esteem, and appropriate sexual and relational outlets, in addition to eliminating deviant and abusive outlets.

The initial results from this study support a comprehensive approach to the treatment of sex offenders. Subjects reported improved social and relational skills, improved self-esteem, job stability, an ability to name reoffense warning signs and strategies to manage risk situations, and a low reoffense rate. Further study is warranted to validate these results.

References

American Psychiatric Association. (1994). *Diagnostic and statistical manual of mental disorders* (4th ed.). Washington, DC: Author.

Bandura, A. (1997). Self-efficacy. *Harvard Mental Health Letter, 13*(9), 4–6.

Dwyer, M., & Amberson, J. I. (1985). Sex offender treatment program: A follow up study. *American Journal of Social Psychiatry, 4,* 56–60.

Dwyer, S. M., & Rosser, B. R. S. (1992). Treatment outcome research: Cross referencing a six month to ten year followup study on sex offenders. *Annals of Sex Research, 5,* 87–97.

Furby, L., Weinrott, M. R., & Blackshaw, L. (1989). Sex offender recidivism: A review. *Psychological Bulletin, 105,* 3–30.

Hall, G. C. N. (1995). Sexual offender recidivism revisited: A meta analysis of recent treatment studies. *Journal of Consulting and Clinical Psychology, 63*(5), 802–809.

Hanson, R. K., Steffy, R. A., & Gauthier, R., (1993). Long-term recidivism of child molesters, *Journal of Consulting and Clinical Psychology, 61,* 646–652.

Henry, L. (1992, October). Should rapists ever be set free? *Glamour,* pp. 275, 294–297.

Maletzky, B. M. (1993). Factors associated with success and failure in the behavioral and cognitive treatment of sexual offenders. *Annals of Sex Research, 6,* 241–258.

Marques, J. K., Day, D. M., Nelson, C., & West, M. A., (1994). Effects of cognitive behavioral treatment on sex offender recidivism: Preliminary results of a longitudinal study. *Criminal Justice and Behavior, 21,* 28–54.

Marshall, W. L., & Barbaree, H. E. (1990). An integrated theory of the etiology of sexual offending. In W. L. Marshall, D. R. Laws, & H. E. Barbaree (Eds.), *Handbook of sexual assault: Issues, theories and treatment of the offender* (pp. 257–275). New York: Plenum Press.

Marshall, W. L., & Pithers, W. D. (1994). A reconsideration of treatment outcome with sex offenders. *Criminal Justice and Behavior, 21,* 10–27.

Mehta, S. N. (1996, May 24). Treating sex offenders becomes an industry, but does it work? *Wall Street Journal,* pp. 1, A6.

Pithers, W., & Cumming, G. F. (1995). Relapse prevention: A method for enhancing behavioral self-management and external supervision of the sexual aggressor. In B. K. Schwartz & H. R. Cellini (Eds.), *The sex offender: Corrections, treatment and legal practice* (pp. 20-1–20-32). Kingston, NJ: Civic Research Institute.

Pithers, W., Cumming, G., Beal, L., Young, W., & Turner, R. (1988). Relapse prevention. In B. K. Schwartz (Ed.), *A practitioner's guide to treating the incarcerated male sex offender—breaking through the cycle of abuse* (pp. 123–140) Washington, DC: U.S. Department of Justice, National Institute of Corrections.

Prentky, R., & Burgess, A. W. (1990). Rehabilitation of child molesters: A cost benefit analysis. *American Journal of Orthopsychiatry, 60*(1), 250–261.

Schwartz, B. K., & Cellini, H. R. (Eds.). (1995). *The sex offender: Corrections, treatment and legal practice* (vol. I). Kingston, NJ: Civic Research Institute.

Seligman, M. E. P. (1996). Long term psychotherapy is highly effective: The Consumer Reports study. *Harvard Mental Health Letter, 13*(1).

Short, A., & Halvorson, D. (1991, November 10–12). Free to rape. *Star-Tribune,* p. 1.

Simkins, L., Ward, W., Bowman, S., & Rinck, C. M. (1990). Characteristics predictive of child sex abusers' response to treatment: An exploratory study. *Journal of Psychology and Human Sexuality, 3*(1), 19–55.

Chapter 25

The Application of Therapeutic Community Learning Experiences to Adult Abusers

by James M. Yokley, Ph.D.

Overview

Therapeutic communities (TCs) are widely used with offender populations to target criminal abuse. In this residential setting whether in a prison or in the community TC members have the obligation to hold each other responsible for their everyday behavior. These residential communities are closed to the public. Thus sex offenders are rarely exposed to situations that set the occasion for relapse. However, they continue to carry their abuse lifestyle with them in the absence of abuse opportunities. The precursors to their offenses along with their criminal thinking and pride are readily observed in the positive TC setting, where confrontation with concern helps them to become aware of the motivations behind their actions (i.e., "where they are coming from") and to learn to intervene. This chapter focuses on the exercises and therapeutic interventions (TC learning experiences) that are used in these abuse treatment settings.

Introduction

TC learning experiences are relevant for abusers who exhibit pathological social and emotional immaturity related to their abuse behavior pattern, personality style, developmental disability, age, or some combination of these factors. The pronounced social and emotional immaturity of this population, along with their extreme role reversal deficit, inhibits both empathy development and positive vicarious learning. This condition requires repetitious experiential learning. Special offender populations that exhibit the aforementioned characteristics and for whom the TC learning experience is a logical application include (1) pathologically immature, action-oriented multiple abusers; (2) mentally retarded/developmentally disabled (MR/DD) abusers and; (3) preteen abusers referred for sexual offense.

History and Original Target Population

Initially Developed at Synanon. TC learning experiences were first implemented in 1958 by Charles Dederich, the founder of Synanon. This TC provided residential treatment for socially immature, irresponsible, character-disordered substance abusers (usually heroin addicts/abusers) who engaged in multiple forms of abuse and crime (Yablonsky, 1969). Synanon was faced with the problem of developing interventions capable of containing and modifying the behavior of it's multiple-abuser residents. Like many of today's sex offender therapists, Dederich faced considerable resistance from the community, which did not want the abusers. Thus the community behavior of those abusers was critical. Problems from one could mean eviction of the entire group. Dederich had to formulate methods to modify and maintain multiple-abuser behavior at alevel that would make the surrounding skeptical community view these abusers as model citizens.

TC Focus on Changing the Whole Person. TCs target the abuser's socially immature and irresponsible lifestyle by viewing substance abuse as a whole-person disorder, encompassing problems in conduct, attitudes, values, moods, and emotional management (DeLeon, 1989, 1995a). The focus on what can be controlled and changed (i.e., one's behavior and the present) as opposed to what cannot be controlled and changed (i.e., other people's behavior and the past) makes becoming aware of "where you are coming from" (i.e., self-awareness of behavior, emotions, and motivations) an essential goal. However, developing self-awareness is only one part of changing from maladaptive to adaptive by "learning to learn." Learning to learn involves the abuser learning to accept teaching and coaching as well as the observations of others in order to become more aware of his attitudes and behavior so that positive change can take effect. In the TC, drugs/abuse is not viewed as the problem but, instead, as a poor solution for the problem. The focus is on learning to develop a positive lifestyle by changing negative behavior patterns, thoughts, and feelings that predispose drugs/abuse (DeLeon, 1995a). TC learning experiences were implemented to develop a positive lifestyle by teaching prosocial/family values and behaviors to antisocial abusers. In TCs, the positive-lifestyle-change view of right living (i.e., "Getting yourself together")-emphasizes values such as truth and honesty, responsible concern to others (i.e., "you are your brothers keeper"), the work ethic, economic self-reliance, personal accountability, and good citizenry (DeLeon, 1995a).

TC learning experiences consist of a combination of natural and logical consequences which can be viewed as behavior therapy or social learning within the context of a positive peer culture and experiential framework. The goal of the twelve- to twenty-four-month TC treatment is "the development of a prosocial lifestyle marked by abstinence and the elimination of antisocial behaviors and attitudes" (DeLeon, 1989, p. 179). TC treatment outcome has been related to time in treatment with completion of at least one year, which is considered necessary for antisocial/multiple abusers (Messina et al., 1997). The eighteen- to twenty-four-month planned treatment duration has been found to be the optimal amount of time to achieve some level of internalized change (DeLeon, 1995a).

Effectiveness of TCs. TC learning experiences serve the purpose of protecting the safety and security of the community while benefiting the abuser. Extensive research has been conducted on TC treatment. Significant decreases in criminal involvement after treatment has been demonstrated for both adults and adolescents in the community setting (DeLeon, 1984, 1987; Pompi, 1994) and for inmates in the corrections setting (e.g., Wexler & Love, 1994). TC learning experiences have been quite successful in the treatment of drug addicts with criminal lifestyles. In many cases, traditional TC learning experiences proved so effective that the antisocial abusers in treatment were viewed as model citizens by the neighbors who originally protested against their presence in the community. Empirical study results from random assignment of substance abusers with and without antisocial personality disorder to traditional or abbreviated/modified TC facilities revealed that the TC is effective with antisocial abusers (Messina et al., 1997). Antisocial abusers were as likely to complete TC treatment as those without that diagnosis (Messina et al., 1997). However, consistent with the research indicating that time in TC treatment is a strong predictor of outcome, abusers in the abbreviated facility were more likely to recidivate than those in the traditional

TC (Messina et al., 1997). (See DeLeon, 1995b, for further information on the TC structure and framework.)

Over the past forty years, TC programs have expanded beyond their original community group home setting and have been implemented in prisons, shelters, and psychiatric as well as general hospitals (Galanter et al., 1993; Wexler & Love, 1994). To meet the funding needs of these settings, the original eighteen- to twenty-four-month planned duration of residential TC treatment has been reduced. An estimated 80,000 admissions per year occur in programs that subscribe to the basic TC perspective (Therapeutic Communities of America, 1994).

General Description of Therapeutic Community Environment

TC learning experiences are implemented to eliminate abuse behavior by developing social maturity and responsibility as competing responses to immature, irresponsible abuse behavior. Learning experiences develop social and emotional maturity and appropriate social behavior control through a broad range of experiential techniques. TC learning experiences get the abuser in touch with the feelings of others, provide role reversal experiences, and develop emotional expression responding which satisfies the three-component model of empathy (Feshbach & Feshbach, 1982). Learning experiences range from low-intensity procedures similar to basic communication feedback and participant modeling of responsibilities to high-intensity procedures involving prolonged exposure to real pressures designed to "develop a callous on your belly" (i.e., stress inoculation and frustration tolerance building). These learning experiences also include natural and logical consequences which address the socially immature, irresponsible acting out involved in multiple forms of abuse/crime.

In general, the TC emphasis is on "making the inside of your house like the outside world," which promotes treatment generalization. For maximum generalization to occur, the training environment needs to be as close as possible to the target (real- world) environment. Thus, to help with their control and power authority issues, abusers need to encounter authorities who are just as directive and controlling as those found in the real world. Stress inoculation by placing the abuser in a more difficult training environment that requires more self-control and self-discipline than would be expected in the real world is preferred. To foster an easier adjustment to the demands of community living, efforts are made to set responsibilities above community standards. Residents are taught that "you have to go to the opposite extreme in order to meet the median," which means they must put just as much energy into doing the right thing in the TC as they invested in doing the wrong thing on the street. This has some similarity to the behavioral overcorrection procedure but includes attitude as well as behavior.

In order to promote the ability to adapt to the unexpected, whenever possible responsibilities are changed as soon as residents become comfortable (i.e., residents are taught that "nothing is constant but change," which could be considered a form of the behavioral stress inoculation procedure). This also redirects the energy buildup from the comfort-triggered boredom that is often invested in relapse planning into adapting to the new environmental demands. Although most high-intensity learning experiences appear to provide as much structure as they do pressure to change (i.e., stress), residents are able to tolerate these experiences well due to the underlying concern that is apparent. The issue is not amount of stress but amount of stress for what purpose. The emphasis is on implementing learning experiences that maximize doing things in order to match the social and emotional limitations and action-oriented style of the abuser.

Character-disordered substance abusers engage in multiple forms of abuse/crime and do not seem to learn from their mistakes. Because these abusers learn best by experience, traditional TCs (e.g., Daytop Village, Delancey Street, and Synanon) have employed direct confrontation along with experiential treatment approaches or social "learning experiences" that frequently require prosocial action on the part of the abuser. For example, if a resident stomps up the stairs after being told to go up there and clean the bathrooms again, behavioral advice might be to look at the compliance behavior (i.e., the resident went up to do it) and ignore the stomping. In the TC, residents are required to "go to the opposite extreme" by paying attention to both their behavior and their attitude. A resident would receive an incident report for "reacting on the floor" if he stomped up the stairs to complete an assigned responsibility.

The treatment outcome literature has revealed that the social learning experiences used in TCs are successful in modifying the behavior and psychological symptoms of immature abusers (described in the TC treatment literature as substance abusers with antisocial, narcissistic, borderline, and oppositional personality features) who were referred for substance abuse treatment (e.g., Bratter et al., 1993; DeLeon, 1985, 1989; Holland, 1983).

Although TC learning experiences were developed by abusers to address the special problems of abusers, the combination of natural and logical consequences involved in TC learning experiences can be viewed as behavior therapy or social learning in the context of a positive peer culture and experiential framework. Socially immature abusers seem to have problems with positive vicarious learning. Their maladaptive thinking style of "paying attention to only what suits them" (Yochelson & Samenow, 1977, p. 362) coupled with their criminal image, pride and values allows only for negative vicarious learning. This situation underscores the importance of providing an environment where peers model and reinforce prosocial/family values. TC learning experiences confront negative images and maladaptive behaviors, not valuable people.

Basic Traditional Therapeutic Community Learning Experiences

The following basic learning experiences are common to most traditional TCs. However, different TCs may vary some on their emphasis, frequency, and intensity of these learning experiences.

House Meeting. The house meeting is where all residents gather to discuss important, serious "community" problems that affect everyone in the TC. Discussing how things are going with the house helps instill a strong sense of belonging and community where fellow house residents are viewed as actual extended family (i.e. "brothers and sisters"). This is important for traditional TC residents, who often dropped out and rejected their community, assuming a nonconformist, counterculture "I don't need anyone" attitude. However, only the community and the authorities that represent the community values are rejected. The residents' "I don't need anyone" attitude coexists with a sick need for acceptance by negative peers. The TC stresses accept-ance of everyone. Practices such as "salt and pepper" seating (i.e., Caucasians and minorities not sitting together as separate groups) discourage subgroups or "cliques." New residents are introduced in house meetings. "You are your brother's keeper" is reinforced in house meetings, where group consequences such as the "house ban" (i.e., total loss of privileges and service crew GI cleaning assignment for the entire house) are announced.

TC residents and staff are well aware that "people don't appreciate anything they don't ask for." This is especially true of abusers who are court ordered to rehabilita-tion programs that they do not want and do not appreciate. Therefore, residents who have committed serious violations of TC rules, are failing their treatment obligations, and want a second chance must ask for help from the entire house during a house meeting. The plea for help from others is critical for immature TC residents who proj-ect the image of an unrealistically self-assured, authority-defiant, rebelliously inde-pendent iconoclast. Multiple abusers require extra emphasis on learning to trust and depend on reliable people in addition to allowing themselves to experience a sense of belonging (i.e., pushing past their fear of losing their image and criminal identity).

Job Function. Learning the work ethic (e.g., accepting responsibilities, earning what you get, finishing what you start, and taking pride in a job well done) is accomplished through the assignment of necessary job functions. To "make the inside of the house like the outside world" and to address the abuser's sense of entitlement, residents start at the bottom. They work their way up the job function ladder, receiving more impor-tant responsibilities as they mature. New residents on orientation status are placed on the service crew where they are given "strength" (i.e., they are supervised or shadowed by a responsible resident for the entire day). An outpatient example of the concept of "strength" would be "shadowing." Probably the best publicized example of "shadow-ing" is the alternative school use of the technique which appeared on the CBS televi-sion show *48 Hours* ("Discipline: When is it too much?") on January 20, 1995. In that broadcast, school administrators had parents of unruly children sign behavior contracts and follow their children around the school all day when they were having behavior problems.[1] The criminal abuser's action-oriented style makes him more likely to ben-efit from social and emotional learning experiences. Learning experiences emphasize experiential learning and the participant modeling practice of prosocial behaviors under real and/or stressful conditions. This contrasts with typical skills training, which occurs in a stress-free individual therapy session with symbolic modeling and abstract explanations. A suitable analogy for this difference might be on-the-job training ver-sus classroom learning. This action-oriented trial-and-error learning where residents must engage in the behavior that produces positive outcomes as well as mistakes has been referred to as efficacy training (DeLeon, 1995a).

Completing high school is the primary job function of teenage residents. TCs may have many different job functions. In keeping with the outside world, each type of job consists of the workers, their immediate supervisor, and a department head. Following are some basic house job functions listed in rank order:

- Service crew: cleans house, stocks bathrooms, empties trash, etc.
- Maintenance crew: builds, paints, and does repair work.

- Kitchen crew: prepares meals, makes grocery lists, and purchases food.
- Administration: files, makes appointments, keeps records, etc.
- Public relations: handles speaking engagements, solicits contributions.
- Expediters: "the eyes and ears of staff," who patrol the house twenty-four hours a day, completing an incident log. Expediters make hourly bed checks throughout the night.

Work therapy exposes residents to real coworker and supervisor interaction stress while teaching appropriate emotional-behavior control during job performance situations (Zavolta & Rogoff, 1990). After working themselves up the ladder of such house jobs as the ones listed here and showing enough progress to warrant promotion to a community reentry phase of treatment, residents may move to a community job function. Residents are taught not to feel entitled to any privilege they receive (i.e., "If you abuse it, you lose it"). Residents also must learn to maintain the effort they put into obtaining a job promotion to avoid being "shot down" (demoted). No one has nicknames. Everyone's given name is used. For example, Jim is referred to as James. The object is to get down to the real person for who he is, not the image he is projecting. To help residents learn to take their responsibilities seriously, careful follow-up with a "do it right once or do it right twice" approach by expediters is implemented.

Pull-up. A "pull-up" (i.e., informal peer feedback) occurs when another resident pulls someone up to his level of awareness by telling him something important that was observed about his behavior or attitude that he needs to "tighten up." It is usually a brief, courteous, constructive criticism given by another resident. Self-control pull-ups like "drop a slip" or "deal with it" involve being told to delay the gratification of venting feelings until an appropriate time and place. For example, if a resident is "reacting" (i.e., losing control of his or her temper) "on the floor" (i.e., anytime outside an encounter group), he or she is told to "drop a slip." This involves having residents put their name along with the name of the person they have feelings for and the reason or type of feeling on a slip of paper. The slip is dropped into a locked encounter box, which staff use to organize groups, so that residents will be put in the same group as the people listed on their slips.

Because TC residents spent much of their pretreatment time and energy in negative/antisocial activity which required little self-discipline, the house structure consists of an extremely positive/prosocial peer culture that requires serious self-discipline. Everything is tightly controlled right down to the number of cups of coffee allowed per day. Pull-ups are given constantly for the slightest of infractions. Residents are told, "You have to go to the opposite extreme in order to meet the median," which is a general self-discipline overcorrection procedure designed to prepare the resident for positive community adjustment. For multiple abusers, the "stinking thinking" (Rosellini, 1985) beliefs and addict attitude pull-ups typically made in TCs need to be expanded to include criminal thinking errors (Yochelson & Samenow, 1977).

Encounter Group. In the traditional TC, the encounter group (where individuals encounter their own feelings and the feelings of others through "confrontation with concern") is the heart of the program. "You are your brother's keeper" is seen in the confrontation with concern of encounter groups as well as giving "strength" to new residents. Encounters help residents develop emotional and social maturity. Encounters exercise and expand the limits of emotional expression, self-control, and emotional endurance (i.e., "develop a callous on your belly") as many abusers are selfish and insensitive to the impact of their behavior on others but hypersensitive to any minor personal affront directed toward them. Because the victim-stance thinking of abusers prevents them from accepting personal responsibility for their actions, the first step is for them to develop enough emotional endurance so that they are able to hear about their actions without becoming too defensive to learn (e.g., blocking others out or reacting aggressively). The second step, accomplished through direct confrontation is to increase their empathy by developing awareness, acceptance, and understanding of the thoughts, feelings and needs of others. A basic two-level group process is used to accomplish these goals. Strict adherence to the group rules (i.e., no violence, no threats of violence, and stay in your seat at all times) is required.

Level 1 (confrontation). This level involves direct verbal confrontation of all the problem behaviors or situations caused by the group member who is being confronted. Confrontations or "indictments" are handled in rank order with the person expressing the most intense feeling going first. Although all indictments begin at once as soon as staff state that the group is open, residents who have less intense feelings yield to the one who is obviously most upset. The person being "indicted" is required to remain silent throughout this emotionally charged level in order to prevent him from diverting energy into a verbal defense of his behavior, which should be focused on becoming aware of the impact of his behavior. Every member who has feelings about the impact of the behavior of the person being indicted expresses those feelings directly, using "I" statements and labeling their feelings so that everyone can understand the negative impact on others. "Engrossment" is used to hold the person's full attention and make a point by exaggerating feelings or reframing the situation to help the person being indicted get enthralled in a larger-than-life picture of his problem. Engrossment holds the residents' emotional attention and counters the automatic tendency to discount or minimize feedback. It is residents' responsibility to ask to change seats if they are sitting next to someone they intend to confront.

Level 2 (concern). After all group members have completed "getting their feelings off" during the indictment, no further raised voices are allowed. To show concern and promote honesty, this level of the group, which is referred to as "the patch-up," focuses on support through identification and problem solving. A resident in tears is always encouraged by all to keep talking in order to put words to the feelings so that they make sense and will lead to an after-group feeling of emotionally drained relief, not humiliation or anger. Those who have had or observed similar problems give positive suggestions about changes that can be made in order to modify the attitude (and other contributing factors) that caused the problems. Residents identify with having experienced similar problems and disclose what they did about it. Thus, the same people who were screaming at a resident who behaved badly toward them may later tell that person that they had the same problem themselves and may end up giving that person helpful advice on how to handle the problem.

The best defense in an encounter is honesty, which prevents a return to confrontation. Residents are taught the "window concept" (i.e., take in everything everyone says; hold on to the information that applies to you; shovel the rest out the window) to help them manage difficult feedback. They are taught the value of other people's feedback (i.e., "Other people see you better than you see yourself"). Readers may recognize this process as the "blind self" quadrant of the Johari window of self-awareness (Luft, 1970, p. 11). The "blind self" is those things about ourselves that others know but we are not aware of.

Residents are also taught not to ignore or use the window concept on feedback just because they do not like it (i.e., "If ten people say you're a horse, you're a horse"). After it is clear that the residents being confronted understand what they were indicted for and how they need to change their behavior, the residents are afforded the opportunity to indict any of the other group members about problem incidents (i.e., they have "earned the right to complain" about the incidents/behavior of others). Multiple abusers who have been sexually offended and victimized typically do better with confrontation than with showing concern. Generally, they are making sure that other offenders do not view their kindness as weakness and try to take advantage of them. Encouraging them to discuss their fears of being "groomed" or set up for victimization usually helps, along with constant reinforcement of their obligation to practice showing concern as a competing behavior against abusiveness and the strict no-contact rules.

Because abusers have difficulty dealing with their feelings constructively, the encounter box can fill up with conflict slips rapidly. Thus, encounter groups need to be fairly frequent. Having groups Monday, Wednesday, and Friday provides a balance between the need to learn to delay gratification of feeling expression and not bottling things up so much that abusive outbursts occur. Encounter groups typically have eight to twelve people and run until everyone who has dropped a slip has dealt with his or her feelings constructively.

Spoken To. A "spoken to" (i.e., formal feedback) is a verbal reprimand which includes three important components that are delivered consecutively (i.e., the behavior incident, the attitude which set the occasion for the incident, and what the resident needs to do to change the attitude in order to prevent further incidents). While receiving a "spoken to," the resident must stand at attention several feet in front of the staff and senior-phase residents who remain seated during the confrontation of their behavior. During the "spoken to," staff and senior-phase residents address residents in a normal tone of voice, but the residents are not allowed to move and can only speak if they are requested to respond. Residents are required to look at each person who is speaking to them without reacting. In general, a "spoken to" is more likely than a pull-up to be delivered in private. Residents may "forget" rational, reasonable feedback from positive models during a "spoken to." It is considered helpful to hold their emotional attention at the end by telling residents where their behavior is leading them and giving them specific examples of consequences they are likely to face if they choose not to change.

Haircut. A "haircut" (i.e., higher-intensity formal feedback) is a more intense verbal reprimand where the resident has "about an inch of bad attitude taken off the top." The basic differences between a verbal "haircut" and a "spoken to" are that (1) the resident is not allowed to speak at any time for any reason after the haircut is started, and (2) the resident's emotional attention is held at the beginning, not at the end. After the resident acknowledges that he knows why he is there, the behavior incident component is delivered in a loud, forceful manner, designed to hold the resident's emotional attention, in a voice congruent with the wrongfulness of the act. This portion must be brief or the resident will acclimate and the procedure will fail. No voices are raised during the remaining two components covering the attitude that led to the incident and how to change.

The TC resident who exhibits a pattern of enjoying "Pushing your buttons" by provoking authorities to the point where their behavior is confronted in a raised voice may receive a role reversal Haircut where they give themselves a Haircut in the mirror. Having to confront themselves deprives their button pushing self-fulfilling prophecy that "all the authorities ever do is get on your back". The Haircut emphasis is on imparting serious life saving information in a confrontation with concern format to residents who are resisting treatment and are headed towards relapse. Multiple abusers often have a dysfunctional family or environment history that helped develop selective listening. For example, in some cases the stimulus overload of constant chaotic interaction required only paying attention to those things that held their emotional attention such as loud noise. These abusers frequently require the use of the "Two by Four" concept (i.e., brief loud noise which grabs your survival instinct attention like slapping a table with a Two by Four board) to hold their emotional attention so that they will listen to what is being communicated to them. It is critically important that staff voice intonation and body language impart sincere concern for the abusers welfare after holding their emotional attention during the incident portion of the Haircut or that attention is likely to be lost.

Bench. The "bench" is a hard-backed wooden chair or bench. This learning experience (i.e., extended time out for self-reflection and introspection) can vary in intensity (duration) from hours to days. When on the bench, a resident is not allowed to speak or leave for any reason. If necessary, the resident eats meals on the bench, and he must receive permission to go to the bathroom from an expediter. The bench is situated in an area that allows the resident to be easily observed at all times. Generally, the bench is used for reflection on serious issues that deserve all of the resident's attention (e.g., whether he intends to stay in treatment or quit on himself).

Sign. Residents can feel genuinely bad after exhibiting abusive behavior particularly when they receive a consequence for that behavior. However, their emotional immaturity leaves them with childlike stress reactions (i.e., they appear to get upset easily and get over it easily). This component is the emotional part of their vicarious learning deficit. When coupled with their action-oriented cognitive style, vicarious learning is impaired. This vicarious learning deficit prevents residents from reminding themselves or "keeping it up front." Because their genuine feelings are transient, fleeting, and momentary, like a child's, residents require a tangible reminder to help them stay in touch with the appropriate feeling after the problem behavior consequences. Thus, because they "forget" and cannot remind themselves, artificial reminders must be constructed to symbolize the problem and remind the abusers. To help residents learn from the experience, the reminder must last long enough for them to develop an appropriate emotional association with the problem behavior.

In order to accomplish this, residents wear a cardboard sign around their neck as a constant reminder of the serious behavior problem that they need "to keep up front" (i.e., to stay aware of and not cover up). The sign learning experience (i.e., written reminder) can vary in intensity (size) from a small single-sided chest-sized sign to one of the large, double-sided, sandwich-style head-to-toe signs that were originally used for street advertising in big cities. Signs are worn at all times except when outside the treatment environment for necessary purposes (e.g., a doctor's appointment). Outpatient examples of this learning experience include the "creative sentencing" of shoplifters to carry a sign identifying their problem in front of the store from which they stole (e.g., Cornick, 1996) along with the pocket self-monitoring logs that behavior therapy clients carry. Learning experience signs require tailoring to the individual and therapists are only limited by their creativity.

Contract. The contract (a commitment contract demonstrated by honesty, serious effort, and self-discipline) is a criminal-abuse-cycle interruption method typically applied to maladaptive roles that lead to treatment failure and relapse. The contract avoids stigmatization from treatment discharge and/or incarceration. The contract is able to dissipate acting-out energy invested in maladaptive roles. This dissipation minimizes the use of more restrictive containment procedures, such as seclusion and restraint. Abusers are often stigmatized as "born losers," society's "throwaway" quitters who lack tenacity and "will never amount to anything." They frequently have a history of not making commitments and rarely finishing what they start. They have often looked for the easy way out of a situation, manipulating the system by acting out to escape responsibility. If school was too hard, instead of trying harder they had an abusive outburst, got suspended, and enjoyed sitting home watching cartoons on television. Although it is routine for substance abuse programs to eject failing residents, it is counter to theory which indicates that "addictive behavior is more likely to ensue when a person is cast out of the group of origin for the outcast will find a compatible, but possibly substance abusing, subculture with which to attach" (Houts, 1995, p. 26).

Contract Used Rather Than Termination

When TC residents commit an abuse relapse behavior (one that is not an imminent danger to the safety and security of others), staff do not give them an easy way out by expelling them from treatment. Instead of requiring less from the abuser by treatment dismissal, staff require more of the abuser by increasing the intensity in treatment and teaching tenacity (i.e., "when the going gets tough, the tough get going"). When TC residents "give up on themselves," act like losers, and return to destructive behavior, the attitude of the staff and other residents is not "once a loser always a loser," followed by expulsion. The abuser is not discarded and stigmatized but instead reintegrated into the TC through a commitment contract that demonstrates serious effort, self-discipline, humility (as a first step toward remorse), and other prosocial/family values of the community.

In addition to their sick need for excitement, TC residents typically have a sick need for acceptance (usually by negative peers). This sick need causes them to hold on to their maladaptive, criminal, negative role too long and initially form "negative contracts" (i.e., "I'll cover your back when you do something wrong if you cover my back when I do something wrong"). However, the same strong need also helps them work toward gaining acceptance by adopting a positive role after they have accepted a contract and made a commitment to let go of their negative/criminal image.

TC residents on a contract are not suspended from treatment activities until they complete that commitment. They continue to attend encounter groups where they process their learning experience, deal with their feelings, and are observed for progress. Three basic components are usually involved in a treatment commitment contract: (1) an image adjustment, (2) a problem reminder, and (3) a commitment task.

Image Adjustment Modifies Self-Concept

An *image adjustment* involves helping the resident let go of his criminal pride and develops social maturity by redirecting the person to the importance of internal as opposed to external values. Removal of all belongings including jewelry (and make-up if female) is typical. Contact lenses are replaced with glasses. In the 1960s era of long hair and bell-bottom pants, an image adjustment would involve getting a shaved head (or stocking cap if female) and wearing baggy bib overalls. In today's era of short crewcuts and baggy, saggy pants, an image adjustment might involve getting glasses and a businessman haircut and wearing a business suit with white shirt and tie. The object of the image adjustment is to get down to the real person for who he is, not who he is trying to look like. This is accomplished by removing the current cool, tough, negative criminal image and replacing it with a clean-cut look that will attract positive influences and deflect negative ones. During the course of the contract, social maturity is supposed to grow in place of the tough criminal image.

Problem Reminders Focus Attention on Issue

The *problem reminder*, or "keeping the problem up front" (a life priority, which should be constantly on the mind of the resident), is typically done with a *sign* (described previously), *spare parts*, or a *relating table*. Spare parts are items or props used to symbolize the resident's problem. For example, residents with repeated "baby fits" might carry a baby rattle in their pocket at all times. Every time they get up, sit down, or walk too fast, the noisy rattle calls unwanted attention to them. At the relating table, residents are required to discuss an assigned problem issue with others as well as what they are learning about it. For example, the resident sits at a table in the dining room every evening for a specified amount of time with a sign on the table that says, "Please talk to me about my baby tantrums." "You are your brother's keeper" makes everyone in the house responsible for ensuring that there is someone at the relating table at all times discussing the problem(s) with the person.

The *commitment task* is designed to regain the trust of the rest of the residents so that the offender can be reintegrated into the TC. The object of the commitment task is to demonstrate a genuine commitment to treatment through effort and to get down to real people for who they are, not who they are trying to act like. The task must be difficult enough to demonstrate a serious commitment to change. The commitment task is necessary because offenders frequently lie about their commitments and fail to finish what they start. "Talk is cheap" to other residents, who must first see actual self-discipline before the offender is accepted back into their community. Two basic types of commitment tasks are "work" and "spare parts." Because the commitment contract is the most serious learning experience in the traditional TC, there is less variance in intensity between contracts, but in terms of difficulty, a work contract usually involves more physical work and a spare parts contract usually involves more emotional work.

During a work contract, the resident receives an intensive daily work detail from the time he gets up to the time he goes to bed. Because many abusers have serious problems with accepting obligations, completing responsibilities (i.e., job or treatment), doing what they are told, and feeling entitled to a living, the most common commitment task is strenuous work. The work detail usually involves thoroughly cleaning the entire facility. This cleaning includes removal of all furniture; scrubbing walls, ceiling, floors, and windows; and vacuuming, mopping, stripping, and waxing the floors. A work contract also typically includes the "dish pan" (i.e., washing, drying , and putting away all the dishes after each meal) and the "bum squad" (i.e., straightening up the house after dinner and just before bed). Maintaining a high-quality level for this type of mundane work requires a great deal of tenacity and self-discipline. Expediters issue work assignments, constantly follow up, and conduct inspections. They also give pull-ups along with standing haircuts for lack of effort, failure to complete responsibilities, not doing exactly what was told, and incomplete or substandard work.

"Spare Parts" Symbolize Problem

A "spare parts" contract involves the use of household items, props, and other "spare parts" which symbolize or relate to the resident's problem. These spare parts are used as tools in the commitment contract to help get residents in touch with their problem behaviors and feelings. The spare-parts contract is used in cases in which a vicarious learning deficit coupled with immaturity and an action-oriented style requires that the resident become his problem and act it out in order to work through it. In contrast with drama therapy, where actors may touch each other, TC residents on a spare-parts contract are not touched by anyone at any time for any reason. When working under a spare-parts contract, residents' problems are dissipated by their acting out their problems. This is a form of "be careful what you ask for because you just might get what you want," where the staff stop trying to get residents to abandon their destructive role and assign that role to them as part of a learning experience.

For example, the resident with repeated aggressive tantrums may receive the spare-parts task of displaying that baby role. The self-centered "King Baby" attitude— "what's right is what I want to do and the reason it's right is because I want to do it" —is the source of baby fits which, if left unchecked, can quickly escalate into serious forms of abusive behavior.

Lack of appropriate social behavior control, low frustration tolerance, inability to delay gratification, and lack of effort toward suppressing urges are common abuser/addict problems. This pathological social and emotional immaturity or set of "King Baby" characteristics (Cunningham, 1986) includes "my way" thinking (Hutchens, 1989) along with a control and power obsession (Yokley, 1996) that results in emotional outbursts; angry, immature acting-out; and other childish traits that accelerate abuse relapse. Pathological social and emotional immaturity is a serious force to be reckoned with and in its extreme form is associated with a primitive egocentric Piaget thought stage in which the individual comprehends the world only from his own point of view.

Given this situation, TC residents are routinely confronted about their "baby feelings" and other "King Baby" characteristics. When pull-ups, encounters, and other interventions fail to curb primitive, aggressive baby outbursts, the resident may end up on a spare-parts contract with a commitment task of having to assume and act out his or her "King Baby" problem role. The "King Baby" role is typically supported with the aid of one or more props as exemplified in the section on contract problem reminders. By reframing intimidating aggression as a "Baby Huey" act, it loses its shock value and associated disruptive thrill. Respondents may feel that they can gain status by frightening everyone through a "tough guy" aggressive outburst that demands the instant attention of all authorities. However, having to throw the same baby fit again and again is not frightening. This baby role is not viewed as cool by even the newest of residents who are still subject to negative peer influences and have not yet accepted the positive peer culture In another form of treatment disruption, the resident who makes no treatment gains because he keeps "punching holes" (i.e., stating why treatment suggestions or concepts won't work for him) might receive the spare-parts task of emptying a lake using a bucket with holes punched in the bottom. Like emptying a lake with a bucket, recovery from serious ingrained abuse patterns is almost impossible, but hole punching makes it completely impossible. When residents ends up getting entirely frustrated and fed up with their spare-parts task, they are ready to talk about what this behavior has done to their recovery.

Refusal to take treatment seriously, disrupting group, or deliberately rescuing other residents with inappropriate joking is a destructive, authority-defiant, immature role that holds the resident back in treatment. When other interventions fail, the resident may receive a spare-parts contract with a clown role commitment task. Spending time as the character Bozo "punches a hole" in the resident's sick need for rebellious excitement. By making clowning a mundane job responsibility, it loses its disruptive thrill. Criminal pride is reinforced when an individual receives negative peer respect by disrupting the group with inappropriate joking, but having to tell the same joke over and over again for a week is not funny and not viewed as cool even by negative peers. Because there is a strictly enforced TC rule that if you laugh at someone's learning experience, you get that learning experience, there is little chance of being reinforced for acting out the clown role. In another form of holding yourself back, residents who make treatment gains but are locked into a self-defeating "break what they make" gains sabotage because they are afraid (e.g., of responsibility, change, or others' expectations) might receive a spare-parts task that involves always returning to where they started (e.g., climbing to the top of a ladder or set of stairs and then turning around and going right back down or digging a deep hole and then filling it back up).

Spare-parts props and commitment tasks require tailoring to the individual resident's problem, and therapists are only limited by their ability to identify and creatively address relapse or treatment-resistance problem roles. TC learning experiences are treated seriously. Traditional TC residents refer to their learning experiences, concepts, and terms as life-saving methods which provide them with a last chance to avoid ending up dead of an overdose, dead in a drug-related shootout, or dead in prison (see Nielsen & Scarpitti, 1995, for further information describing TC language, terms, and methods).

Theoretical Underpinning of Selected TC Learning Experiences

A complete discussion of the theoretical underpinnings of all the TC learning experiences would be extensive and beyond the scope of this chapter. However, because the commitment contract, particularly the spare-parts version, is the most intense TC learning experience, some discussion of the mechanisms involved in the procedure is warranted. DeLeon (1988, 1990–1991) has pointed out the similarity between TC learning experiences and behavioral science principles. Certain TC procedures do mirror such cognitive-behavioral techniques as satiation, aversive behavior rehearsal, and paradoxical intention. However, TC learning experiences incorporate other methods as well.

In satiation of deviant behaviors, the socially unacceptable thoughts or behavior are repeated over and over in private (e.g., Laws, 1995; Marshall, 1979). Satiation repetition is done in a condition that ensures that the reinforcing thrill is diminished, that is, in a "postorgasm-induced, relative refractory state" (Marshall & Eccles, 1993, p. 126), and prevents self-reinforcement of deviant behavior. Because the reinforcing thrill is diminished and the offender considers the problem behavior egodystonic as well as socially unacceptable, the satiation experience is able to extinguish the arousal value of the deviant themes. Satiation has been described as the only masturbatory conditioning procedure that has generated empirical support (Marshall & Eccles, 1993, p. 126) and as "devastating" by one heterosexual pedophile who has experienced no arousal to heterosexual pedophile material since using it (Maletzky, 1991, p. 89).

Aversive behavior rehearsal or "shame aversion therapy" (Server, 1970) involves repeating in front of others a deviant behavior that the offender considers egodystonic and socially unacceptable. Like satiation, versions of aversive behavior rehearsal have demonstrated impressive effectiveness in case studies (e.g., Maletzky, 1991, pp. 34, 88, 201) as well as in research studies (e.g., Wickramasekera, 1976) with no adverse side effects reported when the offender asks for help and follows a special protocol (Smith & Wolfe, 1988).

In summary, aversive behavior rehearsal and satiation share "the production of extreme anxiety and shame with a total or partial re-creation of the offense" (Maletzky, 1991, p. 89) along with a dramatic impact on deviant behavior.

The spare-parts contract uses similar procedures, as described earlier, but has modifications that allow it to address more common immature, abusive criminal behaviors. More common criminal behaviors, such as "tough guy" aggressive outbursts, treatment disruption ,or other authority defiance, are considered ego syntonic, and offenders routinely "build themselves up" by private rumination and rehearsal of these self-reinforcing criminal pride traits. In addition, these more common criminal behaviors are socially acceptable to negative peers from whom the offender has a reinforcement expectancy when he displays the behavior publicly.

Because standard satiation and aversive behavior rehearsal are approaches that involve exact repetition of problems, they are not an option with common criminal behaviors which are egosyntonic and socially acceptable to negative peers. Without modification, these procedures are likely to receive reinforcement, which defeats their behavior extinction ability. An amplification, spin, or reframing of common

criminal behaviors must be conducted prior to rehearsal in order to remove their reinforcement value. Engrossment including props is used in the spare-parts contract to
exaggerate and reframe the offender's behavior into a role that is close enough to the
original behavior to be understood as representative of the problem but no longer
socially acceptable to the offenders or their peers. This allows the satiation and aversive behavior rehearsal extinction mechanisms to take hold and terminate the problem behavior.

Performing (i.e., as opposed to stopping) the problem behavior as a requirement
of a spare-parts contract is a version of "prescribing the symptom" that may be viewed
as paradoxical intention (Ascher, 1980). However, the extended intense energy and
effort required in actually having to assume the problem behavior role, complete with
appropriate wardrobe and other props, shares some components of a paradoxical
ordeal (Haley, 1984). Ordeal therapy is based on the premise that "if one makes it
more difficult for a person to have a symptom than to give it up, the person will give
up the symptom" (Haley, 1984, p. 5). The ordeal is a technique originally attributed to
Milton Ericson. The ordeal must be appropriate to the problem, like a consequence
should fit a behavior, but the main requirement of an ordeal is that it provide motivation for change by causing "distress equal to or greater than that caused by the symptom" (Haley, 1984, p. 6). It is fairly clear that it takes a lot more effort to fully engage
in the "baby" or "clown" roles than it does to avoid those ordeal-like commitment contract tasks by controlling baby outbursts or disruptive clowning. The work-contract
learning experience could be viewed as a "Straightforward Task Ordeal" (Haley, 1984,
p. 7) that addresses failure to complete responsibilities by flooding with responsibility. Ordeal therapy requirements that are satisfied by the commitment-contract learning experience are a clear problem definition, a commitment to change, a commitment
task (i.e., ordeal), a rationale for the commitment task, termination of the contract
only when the problem behavior changes, and social support of the behavior change.
Depending on how they are implemented, it may be possible to view other TC learning experiences (e.g., the bench, sign, and haircut) as ordeals as well.

In ordeal therapy, going through the ordeal provides motivation to give up the
problem, which expends less effort than continuing the ordeal. Setting up a situation
in which a TC resident ends up doing the right thing for himself and others by "taking the easy way out" is absolutely tailormade for this population. However, a contract
learning experience appears to involve more than satiation and ordeal processes. Not
only does the commitment contract help the resident abandon "negative" (deviant,
immature, maladaptive, and antisocial/criminal) problem roles, but it offers a way for
residents to be reintegrated into the positive peer culture of the TC by proving themselves through a commitment task which requires demonstration of "positive" (i.e.,
appropriate, mature, adaptive, or prosocial) behavior roles. This process is consistent
with the theory of reintegrative shaming (Braithwaite, 1989). According to this theory, "shaming is the most potent weapon of social control unless it shades into stigmatization" (Braithwaite, 1989).

Healthy reintigrative shaming is powerful "disapproval dispensed within an ongoing relationship with the offender based on respect" (Braithwaite, 1993, p. 1) and
"bounded by ceremonies to reintegrate the offender back into the community of
responsible citizens" (Braithwaite, 1989, p. 4). "Shaming and reintegration do not
occur simultaneously but sequentially" (Braithwaite, 1989, p. 101). Healthy reintigra-

tive shaming is temporary and separates the person from his negative behavior choices by shaming the negative behavior when it is selected.

> Contrary to the claims of some labeling theorists, potent shaming directed at offenders is the essential necessary condition for low crime rates. Yet shaming can be counterproductive if it is disintegrative rather than reintegrative. Shaming is counterproductive when it pushes offenders into the clutches of criminal subcultures; shaming controls crime when it is at the same time powerful and bounded by ceremonies to reintegrate the offender back into the community of responsible citizens. The labeling perspective has failed to distinguish the crime-producing consequences of stigma that is open-ended, outcasting, and person- rather than offense-centered from the crime-reducing consequences of shaming that is reintegrative. This is why there is such limited empirical support for the key predictions of labeling theory. (Braithwaite, 1989, p. 4)

Stigmatization is unhealthy shaming that combines disapproval, disrespect, and excommunication or shunning without reinforcing positive alternative behavior by offering a chance or method to earn reintegration.

Stigmatization is the permanent shaming of the entire person as a stereotype and does not separate people from their negative choices. Stigmatization shaming outcasts the person as a member of a group that has little hope of achieving lasting change and is thus considered unworthy of any rehabilitation/reintegration effort (e.g., "stone cold junkie," "career criminal," or antisocial personality disorder). "Concerns have been raised that the diagnosis [antisocial personality disorder] may at times be misapplied to individuals in settings in which seemingly antisocial behavior may be part of a protective survival strategy" (American Psychiatric Association, 1994, p. 647). This "born loser," "waste of time," "throwaway" stigmatization "pushes offenders into the clutches of criminal subcultures" (Braithwaite,1989, p. 4) and creates a self-fulfilling prophesy on the part of professionals when the outcasts decide to identify with criminal peers who do not reject them.

Formal criminal punishment is an ineffective weapon of social control partly because it is a degradation ceremony with maximum prospects for stigmatization (Braithwaite, 1989, p. 14).

> The theory of reintegrative shaming posits that the consequence of stigmatization is attraction to criminal subcultures. Subcultures supply the outcast offender with the opportunity to reject her rejectors, thereby maintaining a form of self-respect" (Braithwaite, 1989, p. 14). "If I am a young black gang member who is stigmatized in all of my other relationships as a gang member, I am likely to cut myself off from those relationships. In fact I may do more than cut myself off from caring about what my teachers and family think of me; out of resentment at the way they stigmatize me, I may seek to do exactly the opposite to that which they would approve." (Braithwaite, 1993, p. 15)

Braithwaite (1989) gives an example of a self-fulfilling prophecy: "They think because you're a used car dealer you're a liar. So they treat you like one and lie to you. Can you blame the dealer for lying back?" (p. 128).

The specific nature of shame, along with the relationship of shame to offending behavior and psychopathology, has been a topic of much debate. In general, the psychological research has indicated that shame as a trait is associated with deviance such as alcoholism, aggression, or domestic violence (e.g., Tangney et al., 1995) whereas criminal justice research has shown that expected shame decreases motivation to offend (e.g., Grasmick, Bursick, & Kinsey, 1991). "One likely explanation for these inconsistent results is the existence of multiple forms of shame that appear to have differential effects on individual perceptions and behavior" (Tibbetts, 1997, p. 235). This explanation is particularly obvious in the case of healthy reintegrative shaming versus unhealthy stigmatization shaming. One might expect different outcomes from an addict/abuser who was shamed as an unmotivated "failure" and permanently expelled as opposed to an addict/abuser whose lack of effort on treatment responsibilities was shamed and who was offered a commitment contract to earn his way back into treatment.

In addition to its logical appeal, the expectation of a positive outcome from healthy reintegrative shaming has both research and theoretical support. Research indicating that shame-induced violence is related to factors including whether or not the rejection is of self or an aspect of self (Thomas, 1995) supports the practice of shaming problem choices or behavior as opposed to the whole person as a stereotype. The self-psychology emphasis on belonging as an antidote to both shame and addiction (Potter-Efron, 1993) supports the need to couple reintegration with shaming. Finally, research on the shame experiences of abusive men revealed recollections of public scolding, random punishment, and generic criticism (Dutton, van Ginkel, & Starzomski, 1995), whereas reintegrative shaming as applied to the TC is private (i.e., not outside the program), predictable, and specific.

Treatment Provider Issues, Experience, Therapeutic Characteristics

There are strong conceptual similarities between drug and alcohol treatment issues and sex abuser treatment issues. Although sexual abuser treatment is still in its infancy, as a result of these similarities, the tendency has been to apply drug/alcohol treatment techniques to sex abuser treatment almost from the start. Traditional Twelve-Step substance abuse/addiction groups were extended to sexual behavior problems (Hope & Recovery, 1987). Cognitive-behavioral substance abuse concepts and interventions were also readily applied to sexually abusive behavior. This is particularly apparent in the area of relapse prevention where concepts from Marlatt and Gordon's (1985) model of substance abuse relapse (based primarily on tobacco and alcohol research) were widely adopted in sexual abuser treatment programs. Having treatment staff with experience in drug/alcohol treatment and cognitive-behavioral intervention is useful.

Special population abusers (multiple abusers, MR/DD, and children) frequently have unrefined and ill-defined abuse patterns (see Chapter 23, in this volume). Unlike typical adult pedophiles who have a well-defined target victim age group, sex, appearance, race, and other fantasy characteristics, this group exhibits both intra- and inter-abuse-type scatter. Intraabuse-type scatter is more prevalent in the child and MR/DD groups which are less discriminating, targeting male, female, child, and adult victims (e.g., Griffiths et al., 1985). Interabuse-type scatter is the defining characteristic of the multiple abuser. Special abuser problems with cognitive, emotional, and social maturity support a general self-discipline, self-control, and role-reversal deficit that sets the occasion for following urges and allows displacement of feelings. These urges and feelings are acted in multiple forms of abusive behavior toward others as well as multiple forms of problem behavior within a single type of abuse. Having staff with experience in general impulse control issues and criminal/delinquent treatment is useful.

The Role of ADHD. Many special population abusers have a history of attention-deficit/hyperactivity disorder (ADHD) (e.g., Lahey, Loeber, Hart, Frick, & Applegate, 1995; Pearson, Norton, & Farwell, 1997; Van Eys, 1997; Zagar, Arbit, Hughes, & Busch, 1989), brain dysfunction/closed head injury (e.g., Burke,1980; Lewis, Shanok, & Balla, 1979; Petersen et al., 1982; Templer et al., 1992; Segalowitz & Brown, 1991), and special education (i.e., severely behaviorally handicapped or learning disabled) class placement (e.g., Brier, 1989; Lopez, Forness, MacMillan, Bocian, & Gresham, 1996; Pullis, 1991; Segal, 1973) which often occur together. These conditions interact with family problems and peer influence to predispose the special population abuser for serious problems with appropriate social behavior control and social maturity development. Dysfunctional abuser families were unable to provide prosocial values training (e.g., honesty, trust, loyalty, concern, and responsibility) and the functional ones were not able to provide it at a level that could override negative peer influence. In addition, some prosocial values were not adaptive survival skills for the abuser (e.g., honesty in the dysfunctional family brought aversive consequences). Having treatment staff with child mental health center experience including ADHD, MR/DD, special students, and dysfunctional families is useful.

Use of Action-Oriented Techniques. Special population abusers in treatment often exhibit a positive vicarious learning deficit. Most have problems internalizing or making a lasting emotional connection with what they have learned through reading or listening in the traditional treatment setting. This problem is thought to relate to the fact that the traditional mental health treatment methods used (1) are often highly verbal/cognitive, (2) are usually not associated with an emotional experience, (3) do not require action (i.e., performance, practice or implementation) in the treatment setting, and (4) lack immediate practical value and consequent motivation to adapt (i.e., concepts are not taught in a treatment environment in which they are valuable as social survival skills—there is nothing in it for the abuser to change). As a result, not only do abusers need to "actively engage in the behaviors and attitudes to be changed, they must feel the feelings associated with this engagement, understand the meaning or value of the change, and come to see themselves, others, and the world differently" (DeLeon, 1995a). The special population abuser requires participant modeling and other action-oriented experiences that set up a situation in which he can learn while doing. Treatment provider creativity in implementing experiential interventions along with ability to be openly enthusiastic, animated and engaging is very important.

Traditional Treatment. Traditional mental health professionals are commonly trained using methods developed in university research settings on YAVIS (i.e., Young, Attractive, Verbal, Intelligent, and Socialized) college student clients by academic professionals. TC learning experiences were developed in the abuser treatment setting on multiple abusers (i.e., pathologically immature, action-oriented, verbally limited, maladaptive thinkers with antisocial values) by ex-abusers. TC interventions make honesty a survival skill by reducing consequences for self-disclosure (i.e., "getting honest" or "holding yourself accountable") while increasing consequences for problem behavior discovered by others in a positive peer culture. TC residents observe positive role models (i.e., staff and residents) actually model the appropriate emotion (e.g., anger and righteous indignation) and attitude (i.e., show appropriate prosocial values) toward socially immature, abusive, destructive, antisocial behavior in order to teach social maturity and combat criminal pride. Criminal thinking errors include assuming that if individuals do not confront or challenge what they say or do, one accepts it or approves. Thus, remaining "neutral" or "objective" with abusers reinforces their behavior and is damaging to them and to the community. This is sometimes a problem with professionals who were taught to maintain a position of clinical detachment. For this group, purposeful emotion modeling is easily viewed as unintended, unprofessional "countertransference," and honest attitudes/opinions are easily viewed as "value judgments." Clinical detachment is not realistic and may not be possible during participant modeling of prosocial attitudes and values. Applying the traditional therapeutic approach to the treatment of delinquent children and young adults with severe personality disorders has long been criticized (Abruzzi, 1975). Mental health professionals who apply only traditional psychotherapy techniques to members of special abuser populations are not considering the special problems and needs of this population. Treatment provider ability to "be real," drop the professional persona, and connect through an open, honest expression of feelings and opinions is a very important attribute.

Abusers tend to selectively attend and block things out automatically, paying attention only to what suits them. They minimize, deny, and rationalize. Experiential learning (i.e., actually having to do a new behavior or being put through an experience to become aware of the emotions attached to that situation) through social and emotional learning experiences addresses these abuser treatment problems. Social and emotional learning experiences are designed to address the special needs of the abuser population by holding abusers emotional attention to help them (1) stay aware of situations they tend to avoid, (2) break out of treatment resistance ruts (i.e., wake up, become aware of what they are doing, where they are coming from, or where they are headed), (3) interrupt antisocial/relapse behavior patterns (i.e., by getting and holding the abuser's emotional attention), and (4) redirect attention to the important priority issues needed to develop social maturity (e.g., honesty and concern) and maintain appropriate social behavior control. Treatment provider comfort using confrontation with concern and the anger of abusers toward their "authority" is very important.

Redirection of antisocial values reinforced by negative peers requires appropriate emotional display of prosocial/family values reinforced by staff and positive peers. Abusers are typically insecure people who need rigid structure. That structure needs to be provided through the actual daily work routine as well as appropriate emotional response modeling and confrontation with concern on the job on the spot. This "therapeutic authority role" may be uncomfortable for some professionals who correctly imagine being played against colleagues by abusers taking the victim stance in an attempt to get out of learning experiences. This therapeutic authority role may be uncomfortable for other professionals who correctly imagine the abuser having a strong emotional outburst in their presence. Professionals are humans too, but being professional means pushing past the fear of professional criticism or angry outbursts and being an effective member of the treatment team. Professionals who choose to maintain "clinical detachment" and not assume the "therapeutic authority role" duty need to make sure that there are ample staff on board already assigned to that duty. It is critically important for professionals to include diverse models (e.g., parole officers, foster parents, and ex-abusers) of appropriate values, behavior, attitudes/opinions, and emotion. Some professional groups are trained to make prosocial value judgments based on a strong code of honor, sense of right and wrong, and adaptive family values or team-building skills. They adhere strongly to a "leave no man behind," "all souls are worth saving" reintegrative position that inhibits giving up on others through premature discharge. They are proud to display and teach prosocial/family values to abusers who lack direction in their life. Military drill instructors and clergy are professional groups that deserve consideration as treatment team members. Treatment provider ability to assemble and work side by side with a diverse treatment team of professional and paraprofessional staff is critically important.

Vocational Rehabilitation. In the mental health setting, vocational rehabilitation has been strictly separated from psychotherapy. Vocational rehabilitation and occupational therapy have traditionally focused on learning new job skills or adapting to a disability to regain old job skills. Outside the TC, the only institution that regularly teaches self-discipline and team building during job skills training is the U.S. military. Although mental health professionals have been willing to view other activities as having psychotherapeutic value (e.g., art, drama, music, and recreational therapy), there is currently no established "work therapy" in mental health treatment. Except for a few techniques such as participant modeling and graduated exposure, mental health therapy has focused on problem solving by the removed abstract approach of talking about a stressful situation which is imagined while in an office safely away from that situation. This is a problem for abusers who need to watch it, do it, and teach it in order to learn it. These three repetitions are critical to social maturity development, which is an important form of emotional intelligence needed for success in life (Goleman, 1995). Abusers fail to make the connection between treatment focus on self-control under stress and the real world where they envision themselves without stress as the result of beliefs that they will be able to do what they want to do when they want to do it for the reason they want to do it. This fractured connection based on unrealistic expectations demands a work therapy that induces real life stress (e.g., Zavolta & Rogoff, 1990). Only under these training circumstances will self-control techniques be meaningful enough to adopt. Treatment provider willingness to continue to learn and to be open to a new perspective is perhaps most important with the special abuser population.

Mental health professionals working in TCs need further education to become effective with this population. The professional education and training of the increasing number of mental health professionals working in TCs has created problems by introducing "differences in concepts, language and methods which are often counter to or subvert the fundamental self-help features of the TC. These non-TC staff must have theoretical as well as experiential training in the 'traditional' TC in order to be effectively integrated into the TC Approach" (DeLeon, 1995b, p. 1634).

Conclusion

Adult abusers referred for sexual offense exhibit pathological social and emotional immaturity along with role-reversal deficits that impair empathy and positive vicarious learning. These problems require the type of repetitious experiential learning found in TC learning experiences. This chapter outline the basic traditional TC learning experiences for the adult abuser population. This chapter also discussed the history and theoretical underpinnings of TC learning experiences along with treatment provider issues.

Footnotes

[1] For a transcript of the *48 Hours* broadcast, call 800-777-text. For a videotape copy, call 800-338-4847.

References

Abruzzi, W. (1975). Severe personality disorders in an institutional setting. *American Journal of Psychoanalysis, 35*(3), 269–277.

American Psychiatric Association. (1994). *Diagnostic and statistical manual of mental disorders* (4th ed.). Washington, DC: Author.

Armentrout, J., & Hauer, A. (1978). MMPIs of rapists of children and non-rapist sex offenders. *Journal of Clinical Psychology, 34*(2), 330–332.

Ascher, L. (1980). Paradoxical intention. In A. Goldstein & E. B. Foa (Eds.), *Handbook of behavioral interventions: A clinical guide* (pp. 261–321). New York:Wiley.

Awad, G., Saunders, E., & Levene, J. (1984). A clinical study of male adolescent sexual offenders. *International Journal of Offender Therapy and Comparative Criminology, 28,* 105–115.

Becker, J., Kaplan, M., Cunningham-Rathner, J., & Kavoussi, R. (1986). Characteristics of adolescent incest perpetrators: Preliminary findings. *Journal of Family Violence, 1,* 85–97.

Blume, S. (1989). Dual diagnosis: Psychoactive substance dependence and the personality disorders. *Journal of Psychoactive Drugs, 21*(2), 139–144.

Braithwaite, J. (1989). *Crime, shame and reintegration.* Melbourne, Australia: Oxford University Press.

Braithwaite, J. (1993). Shame and modernity. *British Journal of Criminology, 33*(1), 1–18.

Bratter, B., Bratter, T., Radda, H., & Steiner, K. (1993). The residential therapeutic caring community. *Psychotherapy, 30*(2), 299–304.

Brendtro, L. (1985a). Making caring fashionable: Philosophy and procedures of service learning. *Child Care Quarterly, 14*(1), 4–13.

Brendtro, L. (1985b). Synergistic relationships: The powerful "SR" of reeducation. *Milieu Therapy, 4*(1), 3–12.

Brier, N. (1989). The relationship between learning disability and delinquency: A review and reappraisal. *Journal of Learning Disabilities, 22*(9), 546–553.

Burke, A. (1980). A cross cultural study of delinquency among West Indian boys. *International Journal of Social Psychiatry, 26*(2), 81–87.

Condelli, W., & Hubbard, R. (1994). Client outcomes from therapeutic communities. In F. Tims, G. DeLeon & N Jainchill (Eds.), *Therapeutic community: Advances in research and application* (pp. 80–98) (National Institute on Drug Abuse Research Monograph 144, NIH Publication No. 94-3633). Rockville, MD: National Institute on Drug Abuse.

Cornick, M. (Producer). (1996, October 18). Sentences of public humiliation as punishment. *20/20.* New York: ABC News.

Count-Van Manen, G. (1991). Drama-imagery processes as socialization: An interdisciplinary perspective [Special issue]. *Journal of Mental Imagery, 15*(1–2), 243–293.

Cunningham, T. (1986). *King baby.* Center City, MN: Hazelden.

Curry, S., Marlatt, G A., & Gordon, J. (1987). Abstinence violation effect: Validation of an attributional construct with smoking cessation. *Journal of Consulting & Clinical Psychology, 55*(2), 145–149.

DeLeon, G. (1984). The therapeutic community: Study of effectiveness (NIDA Research Monograph, DHHS Publication No. ADM 84-1286). Washington, DC: U.S. Government Printing Office.

DeLeon, G. (1985). The therapeutic community: Status and evolution. *International Journal of the Addictions, 20*(6–7), 823–844.

DeLeon, G. (1987). Alcohol use among drug abusers: Treatment outcomes in a therapeutic community. *Alcoholism, Clinical and Experimental Research, 11*(5), 430–436.

DeLeon, G. (1988). *The therapeutic community and behavioral science* (NIDA Research Monograph 84). Rockville, MD: National Institute on Drug Abuse.

DeLeon, G. (1989). Psychopathology and substance abuse: What is being learning from research in therapeutic communities. *Journal of Psychoactive Drugs, 21*(2), 177–187.

DeLeon, G. (1990–1991). The therapeutic community and behavioral science [Special issue: Substance user treatment for research, practice, and policy]. *International Journal of the Addictions, 25*(12A), 1537–1557.

De Leon, G. (1995a, January–March). Residential therapeutic communities in the mainstream: Diversity and issues. *Journal of Psychoactive Drugs, 27*(1), 3–15.

DeLeon, G. (1995b). Therapeutic communities for addictions: A theoretical framework. *International Journal of the Addictions, 30*(12), 1603–1545.

Donnenberg, D. (1978). Art therapy in a drug community. *Confinia Psychiatrica, 21*(1–3), 37–44.

Dutta, T. (1979). Education for problem children [Special issue]. *Indian Psychological Review, 18*(1–4), 31–34.

Dutton, D., van Ginkel, C., & Starzomski, A. (1995). The role of shame and guilt in the intergenerational transmission of abusiveness. *Violence and Victims, 10*(2), 121–131.

Eckstein, M. (1995). Foster family clusters: Continuum advocate home network. In L. Combrinck-Graham (Ed.), *Children in families at risk: Maintaining the connections* (pp. 275–298.) New York: Guilford Press.

Ericson, W., Luxenberg, M., Walbek, N., & Seely, R. (1987). Frequency of MMPI two-point code types among sex offenders. *Journal of Consulting and Clinical Psychology, 55*(4), 566–570.

Faux, E., & Dixon, D. (1967) Children in the therapeutic community. *Diseases of the Nervous System, 28*(3), 170–177.

Fehrenbach, P. A., Smith, W., Monastersky, C., & Deisher, R. W. (1986). Adolescent sexual offenders: Offender and offense characteristics. *American Journal of Orthopsychiatry, 56,* 225–233.

Feshbach, N., & Feshbach, S. (1982). Empathy training and the relation of aggression: Potentialities and limitations. *Academic Psychology Bulletin, 4,* 399–413.

Freeman-Longo, R., Bird, S., Stevenson, W., & Fiske, J. (1994). 1994 Nationwide survey of treatment programs and models serving abuse-reactive children and adolescent and adult sex offenders. Brandon, VT: Safer Society Press.

Friedrich, W. (1993). Foreword. In E. Gil & T. Johnson (Eds.). *Sexualized children: Assessment and treatment of sexualized children who molest* (pp. x–xii). Rockville, MD: Launch Press.

Galanter, M., Egelko, S., DeLeon, G., & Rohrs, C. (1993). A general hospital day program combining peer-led and professional treatment of cocaine abusers. *Hospital Community Psychiatry, 44,* 644–649.

Gerhard, R., & Dorgan, R. (1970). A catchment milieu training-service model for the mental retardation sector: A documented proposal. *International Journal of Social Psychiatry, 16*(3), 221–227.

Gerritsen, M. (1995). Art therapy: The real art is the process. *Therapeutic Communities: International Journal for Therapeutic and Supportive Organizations, 16*(1), 25–35.

Goleman, D. (1995) *Emotional intelligence: Why it can matter more than IQ.* New York:Bantam Books.

Graham, J. (1977). *The MMPI: A practical guide.* New York: Oxford University Press.

Grasmick, H., Bursick, R., & Kinsey, K. (1991). Shame and embarrasment as deterents to noncompliance with the law. *Environment and Behavior, 23,* 233–251.

Griffiths, D., Hinsburger, D., & Christian, R. (1985). Treating developmentally handicapped sexual offenders: The York behavior management services treatment program. *Psychiatric Aspects of Mental Retardation Reviews, 4,* 49–54.

Haaven, J., Little, R., & Petre-Miller, D. (1990). *Treating intellectually disabled sex offenders: A model residential program.* Orwell VT: Safer Society Press.

Haley, J. (1984). *Ordeal therapy.* San Francisco: Jossey-Bass.

Hope and recovery: A twelve step guide for healing from compulsive sexual behavior. (1987). Minneapolis, MN: CompCare.

Houts, S. (1995). Explaining alcoholism treatment efficacy with the theory of reintegrative shaming. *Alcoholism Treatment Quarterly, 13*(4), 25–38, 1995.

Hutchens, L. (1989). *Restitution, treatment and training. R.T.A.T. manual* (available from RTAT Inc., P.O. Box 800, Ontario, OR 97914).

Jainchill, N. (1994). Co-morbidity and therapeutic community treatment. In F. Tims, G. DeLeon, & N. Jainchill (Eds.), *Therapeutic community: Advances in research and application* [NIDA Monograph No. 144] (NIH Publication No. 94-3633, pp. 209–231). Rockville, MD: National Institute on Drug Abuse.

Jenkins-Hall, K. D., & Marlatt, G. A. (1989). Apparently irrelevant decisions in the relapse process. In D. R. Laws (Ed.), *Relapse prevention with sex offenders* (pp. 47–55). New York: Guilford Press.

Kelley, S. (1986). Learned helplessness in the sexually abused child. *Issues in Comprehensive Pediatric Nursing, 9*(3), 193–207.

Kutschinski, W. (1977), Milieu therapy under the primary caretaker system at the University of Michigan's Children's Psychiatric Hospital. *Child Psychiatry and Human Development, 8*(1), 31–42.

Lahey, B., Loeber, R., Hart, E., Frick, P., & Applegate, B. (1995). Four-year longitudinal study of conduct disorder in boys: Patterns and predictors of persistence. *Journal of Abnormal Psychology, 104*(1), 83–93.

Langevin, R., Paitich, D., Freeman, R., Mann, K., & Handy, L. (1978). Personality characteristics and sexual anomalies in males. *Candian Journal of Behavioral Science, 10,* 222–238.

Laws, D. R. (1995). Verbal satiation: Notes on procedure, with speculations on its mechanism of effect. *Sexual Abuse: Journal of Research and Treatment, 7*(2), 155–166.

Lewis, D. O., Shankok, S., & Balla, D. (1979). Perinatal difficulties, head and face trauma, and child abuse in the medical histories of seriously delinquent children. *American Journal of Psychiatry, 136*(4-A), 419–423.

Lewis, D. O., Shankok, S., & Pincus, J. (1979). Juvenile male sexual assaulters. *American Journal of Psychiatry, 136,* 1194–1196.

Lopez, M., Forness, S., MacMillan, D., Bocian, K., & Gresham, F. (1996). Children with attention deficit hyperactivity disorder and emotional or behavioral disorders in primary grades: Inappropriate placement in the learning disorder category. *Education & Treatment of Children, 19*(3), 286–299.

Lowenstein, L. (1982). The treatment of aggressive behaviour in maladjusted children. *National Council for Educational Standards Bulletin No. 5,* pp. 15–20.

Luft, J. (1970). *Group processes: An introduction to group dynamics.* Palo Alto, CA: Mayfield.

Lund, D. (1995). Matrilineal descent and juvenile offender counseling. *International Journal of Offender Therapy and Comparative Criminology, 39*(1), 43–46.

Maletzky, B. M. (1991). *Treating the sexual offender.* Newbury Park, CA: Sage.

Marlatt, G. A. (1989). Feeding the PIG: The problem of immediate gratification. In D. R. Laws (Ed.), *Relapse prevention with sex offenders* (pp. 56–62). New York: Guilford Press.

Marlatt, G. A. (1990). Cue exposure and relapse prevention in the treatment of addictive behaviors. *Addictive Behaviors, 15*(4), 395–399.

Marlatt, G. A. (1996). Section I. Theoretical perspectives on relapse: Taxonomy of high-risk situations for alcohol relapse: Evolution and development of a cognitive-behavioral model. *Addiction, 91*(Suppl.), S37–S49.

Marlatt, G. A., & Gordon, J. R. (Eds.). (1985). *Relapse prevention: Maintenance strategies in addictive behavior change.* New York: Guilford Press.

Marshall, W. L. (1979). Satiation therapy: A procedure for reducing deviant sexual arousal. *Journal of Applied Behavior Analysis, 12*(3), 377–389.

Marshall, W L., & Eccles, A. (1993). Pavlovian conditioning processes in adolescent sex offenders. In H. E. Barbaree, W. L. Marshall, & S. Hudson (Eds.), *The juvenile sex offender* (pp. 118–142). New York: Guilford Press.

Messina, N., Wish, E., & Nemes, S. (1997, November). *The efficacy of therapeutic community treatment for substance abusers with co-occuring antisocial personality disorder.* American Society of Criminology Annual Conference, San Diego, CA.

Nadar, K., & Pynoos, R. (1991). Play drawing techniques as tools for interviewing traumatized children. In C. Schaefer, K. Gitlin, & A. Sandgrund (Eds.), *Play diagnosis and assessment* (pp. 375–389). New York: Wiley.

Nielsen, A., & Scarpitti, F. (1995). Argot use in a therapeutic community. *Deviant Behavior: An Interdisciplinary Journal, 16,* 245–267.

Pearson, D., Norton, A., & Farwell, E. (1997). Attention-deficit hyperactivity disorder in mental retardation: Nature of attention deficits. In J. Burack & J. Enns (Eds.), *Attention, development, and psychopathology* (pp. 205–221). New York: Guilford Press.

Petersen, K., et al (1982). EEG antecedents of thievery. *Acta Psychiatrica Scandinavica, 65*(5), 331–338.

Pompi, K. (1994). Adolescents in therapeutic communities: Retention and posttreatment outcome. In F. Tims, G. DeLeon, & N. Jainchill (Eds.), *Therapeutic community: Advances in research and application* (pp. 128–161) (NIDA Monograph No. 144, NIH Publication No. 94-3633). Rockville, MD: National Institute on Drug Abuse.

Potter-Efron, R. (1993). Three models of shame and their relation to the addictive process. *Alcoholism Treatment Quarterly, 10*(1–2), 23–48.

Pullis, M. (1991). Practical considerations of excluding conduct disordered students: An empirical analysis. *Behavioral Disorders, 17*(1), 9–22.

Radar, C. (1977). MMPI profile types of exposers, rapists and assaulters in a court services population. *Journal of Consulting and Clinical Psychology, 45*(1), 61–69.

Reebye, P., Moretti, M., & Lessard, J. (1995). Conduct disorder and substance use disorder: Comorbidity in a clinical sample of preadolescents and adolescents. Special Issue: Child and Adolescent Psychiatry. *Canadian Journal of Psychiatry, 40*(6), 313–319.

Roberts, M., & Bushaw, E. (1978). Food for thought: Participation of kitchen staff in milieu treatment. *Child Care Quarterly, 7*(3), 242–249.

Rosellini, G. (1985). Stinking thinking. Center City, MN: Hazelden.

Segal, S. (1973). Retarded readers and anti-social young people: An English study. *International Journal of Offender Therapy & Comparative Criminology, 17*(3), 297–302.

Segalowitz, S., & Brown, D. (1991). Mild head injury as a source of developmental disabilities. *Journal of Learning Disabilities, 24*(9), 551–559.

Serber, M. (1970). Shame aversion therapy. *Journal of Behavior Therapy and Experimental Psychiatry, 1,* 213–215.

Sgroi, S. (1982). *Handbook of clinical intervention in child sexual abuse.* Lexington, MA: Lexington Books.

Shoor, M., Speed, M., & Bartelt, C. (1966). Syndrome of the adolescent child molester. *American Journal of Psychiatry, 122,* 783–789.

Smith, T., & Wolfe, R. (1988). A treatment model for sexual aggression [Special issue: The sexually unusual: Guide to understanding and helping]. *Journal of Social Work and Human Sexuality, 7*(1), 149–164.

Tangney, J., Burggraf, S., & Wagner, P. (1995). Shame-proneness, guilt-proneness and psychological symptoms. In J. P. Tangney & K. W. Fischer (Eds.), *Self-conscious emotions: The psychology of shame, guilt, embarrassment and pride* (pp. 343–367). New York: Guilford Press.

Templer, D., Kasiraj, J.,Trent, N., Trent, A., Hughey, B., Keller, W., Orling, R., & Thomas-Dobson, S. (1992). Exploration of head injury without medical attention. *Perceptual and Motor Skills, 75*(1), 195–202.

Therapeutic Communities of America. (1994). *Paradigms:Past, present and future.* Proceedings of the Therapeutic Communities of America 1992 planning conference, Chantilly, VA.

Thomas, H. (1995). Experiencing a shame response as a precursor to violence. *Bulletin of the American Academy of Psychiatry and the Law, 23*(4), 587–593.

Tibbetts, S. (1997). Shame and rational choice in offending decisions. *Criminal Justice and Behavior, 24*(2), 234–255.

Van Eys, P. (1997). Group treatment for prepubescent boys with sexually aggressive behavior: Clinical considerations and proposed treatment techniques. *Cognitive and Behavioral Practice, 4,* 349–382.

Van Ness, S. R. (1984). Rape as instrumental violence: A study of youth offenders. *Journal of Offender Counseling, Services and Rehabilitation, 9,* 161–170.

Wexler, H., & Love, C. (1994). Therapeutic communities in prison. In F. Tims, G. DeLeon, & N Jainchill (Eds.), *Therapeutic community: Advances in research and application* [NIDA Monograph No. 144] (NIH Publication No. 94-3633, pp. 181–208). Rockville, MD: National Institute on Drug Abuse.

Wickramasekera, I. (1976). Aversive behavior rehearsal for sexual exhibitionism. *Behavior Therapy, 7*(2), 167–176.

Wurtele, S., Marrs, S., & Miller-Perrin, C. (1987). Practice makes perfect? The role of participant modeling in sexual abuse prevention programs. *Journal of Consulting and Clinical Psychology, 55*(4), 599–602.

Yablonsky, L. (1969). *Synanon: The tunnel back.* Baltimore: Pelican Books.

Yochelson, S., & Samenow, S. (1977). *The criminal personality, Vol. 1: A profile for change.* New York: Jason Aronson.

Yokley, J. (1996, March). *The development of abuse in youth sex offenders: A conceptual model with treatment implications.* Twelfh Annual Conference of the National Adolescent Perpetrator Network, Minneapolis, Minnesota.

Yokley, J., & Laraway, C. (1996, November). *The use of therapeutic community learning experiences in the treatment of youth sex offenders: An outpatient clinical trial.* Fifteenth Annual Research and Treatment Conference of the Association for the Treatment of Sexual Abusers, Chicago.

Yokley, J., Laraway, C., & Clough, A. (1997, November). *Behavior therapy and criminal justice: The controversy over boot camp treatments.* Thirty-first Annual Convention of the Association for the Advancement of Behavior Therapy, Miami Beach, FL.

Zagar, R., Arbit, J., Hughes, J., Busell, R., & Busch, K. (1989). Developmental and disruptive behavior disorders among delinquents. *Journal of the American Academy of Child and Adolescent Psychiatry, 28*(3), 437–440.

Zavolta, H., & Rogoff, S. (1990). An overview of the vocational rehabilitation process in a long-term drug rehabilitation program [Special issue]. *Journal of Applied Rehabilitation Counseling, 21*(3), 40–44.

Chapter 26

The Measurement of Sexual Preference— A Preliminary Comparison of Phallometry and the Abel Assessment

by Scott A. Johnson, M.A., L.P. and Alan Listiak, Ph.D., L.I.C.S.W.

Overview

Penile plethysmography has been the recognized way of measuring deviant arousal. However, many programs have been unable to use this technology because of its controversial and intrusive nature. At last an alternative technique has been developed. However, many treatment specialists are reluctant to replace one with the other. This chapter discusses the relative measures of each technique.

Introduction

One of the most theoretically developed concepts specific to the etiology of sexual offending is that of sexual motivation. Often operationalized as "sexual preference," it is hypothesized that persons who are more sexually aroused or responsive to "deviant" stimuli than they are to normative stimuli will be motivated to gratify their sexual drive by employing deviant themes in fantasy and masturbation and by enacting them in actual sexual behavior (Barbaree, 1990; Barbaree & Marshall, 1991; Hall, Shondrick, & Hirschman, 1993; Hunter & Becker, 1994; Laws & Marshall, 1990; Maletzky, 1991; Murphy, Haynes, & Worley, 1991). Of course, whether or not this motive actually prompts sexually criminal behavior depends on a variety of mediating variables that may encourage or disencourage the act.

Current theories of sexual offending incorporate a multifactorial perspective and present a set of selected concepts that organize the existing empirical and clinical research. Some theories are phrased at a general level and attempt to describe the offense process through mostly motivational factors (Hall & Hirschman, 1991; Knight & Prentky, 1990) or a combination of motivational and contextual factors (Finkelhor, 1984; Lanyon, 1991; Malamuth, Heavey, & Linz, 1993; Marshall & Barbaree, 1990). Others theories are phrased at the microlevel and present a similar combination of factors to describe the decision-making process involved in the sexual offense cycle or reoffense process (Pithers, 1990; Ward, Louden, Hudson, & Marshall, 1995).

Recently a significant meta-analysis of the sex offender treatment outcome research reported that several of the top correlates of recidivism are indices of sexual motivation. Hanson and Bussière's (1996) analysis of sixty-one data sets composed of 28,972 sex offenders followed for a median of four years identified sixty-nine predictor variables of sexual reoffense. The variable with the highest correlation to recidivism was "erections to children," the fourth highest correlation was "deviant sexual preference," and the twelfth highest correlation was "erection to boys." These data underscore the importance of assessing sexual preference as part of the evaluation and treatment of sex offenders.

Use of Phallometry

The measurement of sexual preference has proven to be rather complex. Subjective methods that rely on self-report have been found to be limited in obtaining reliable and valid information from sex offenders. However, several studies have found that self-reported sexual interest or arousal is more reliable and valid than other researchers have indicated (see, e.g., Bradford, Boulet, & Pawlak, 1992; Hall, Binek, & DiTomasso, 1985; Haywood, Grossman, & Cavanaugh, 1990). Until recently, the only "objective" method that has proven useful as an index of sexual arousal in males has been the measurement of erectile response to sexual stimuli by a plethysmograph (Rosen & Beck, 1988; Pithers & Laws, 1995; Harris & Rice, 1996; Howe, 1995; Murphy & Barbaree, 1994). This procedure, often termed "penile plethysmography" or "phallometry," has become the standard in the field for the objective measurement of sexual preferences, and is considered by some to be an "essential" technology in the assessment and treatment of sex offenders (Pithers & Laws, 1995). An extensive body of research has investigated the measurement of erectile response in males as an index of sexual arousal (or stimulus control) and sexual preference.

Several reviews have indicated that phallometry has adequate reliability and validity compared to other psychometric tests and that it is more accurate than any other measure at classifying sexual offenders. These reviewers have also indicated that the utility of the procedure is limited by relatively large error rates, ineffectiveness with particular subpopulations, and several measurement issues. They caution that the results of the procedure must be carefully interpreted within the context of a comprehensive assessment or treatment plan (see, e.g., Castonguay, Proulx, Aubut, McKibben, & Campbell, 1993; Howe, 1995; Murphy & Barbaree, 1994; Murphy & Peters, 1992; O'Donohue & Leterneau, 1992). Several other reviewers have been more critical of the results of phallometric assessment and have both questioned the validity and reliability of the procedure and raised ethical concerns about forensic interpretation (see, e.g., Blader & Marshall, 1989; McConaghy, 1993; Simon & Shouten, 1991, 1992; Travis, Cullen, & Melella, 1988). However, recently Quinsey and his colleagues (Harris, Rice, Quinsey, Chaplin, & Earls, 1992; Lalumière & Quinsey, 1994; Quinsey & Lalumière, 1996) have published several studies indicating that if proper sexual stimuli, scoring methods, and procedures are used, phallometric erectile measures have acceptable reliability, convergent validity, and divergent validity. Moreover, the responses of child molesters and rapists can be consistently differentiated from non-sex offenders. However, the use of the procedure in the field has been constrained by a variety of factors. These include the expense of purchasing the plethysmograph, space and time requirements to administer the procedure, intrusiveness of measuring erectile response, and ethical and legal concerns regarding stimulus materials.

Abel Assessment for Sexual Assessment

Recently, an alternative procedure to measure sexual preference has been introduced that does not rely on the measurement of erectile response. The Abel Assessment for Sexual Interest™ (AA) instead measures the length of time a subject spends viewing a set of sexual stimuli as the physiological index of sexual response or interest. (There is a small base of research that indicates consistent correlations between sexual response and length of time spent viewing a visual sexual stimulus [see, e.g., Abel, Hoffman, Warberg, & Holland, 1998; Harris, Rice, Quinsey, & Chaplin, 1996; Langevin, 1985]). Using this measure is less intrusive and requires less space and time than do plethysmographic procedures. In addition, a set of visual sexual stimuli on slides have been developed that include only non-nude models, and the scoring methodology has been standardized. Research reported by Abel indicates that the measure of visual reaction time has a high degree of reliability. Validity is also reported to be good, based on significant correlations between visual reaction time and both diagnosis and self-report. In addition, the use of multiple measurements for each stimulus category and data analysis based on the relative weights placed by clients on different categories of stimuli is reported to make it difficult to manipulate or fake response times (Abel, 1995; Abel, Lawry, Karlstrom, Osborn, & Gillespie, 1994).

Abel et al. (1998) also conducted research comparing the new procedure with the measurement of erectile response using a circumferential transducer and plethysmograph. The sample included 157 men who were alleged to have been sexually abusive and were referred to Abel's outpatient clinic for evaluation. All the men completed the Abel Assessment and fifty-six of them also men completed phallometric assessment. Both procedures presented pictorial stimuli on slides. The phallometric procedure used the Multisite Study Slides set (Laws, Gulayets, & Frenzel, 1995) whereas the AA used the specially developed slide set described earlier. Both procedures were found to be internally consistent, indicating that each procedure was highly reliable. Both procedures also demonstrated strong validity. Each procedure had significant correlations between the physiological measures and (1) self-reported sexual interest, (2) therapist categorization of sexual interest, and (3) prediction of sexual interest. For each of these three variables, the AA performed marginally better than the phallometric procedure. Based on this early research, the AA appears to be a promising new tool in the assessment of sexual preferences.

Methods Contrasted

This chapter reports preliminary data from an ongoing study intended to replicate and extend the comparative research on the two objective measures of sexual preference: erectile response as measured by a plethysmograph and visual reaction time as measured by a specially designed computer program in the AA. The analysis presented here is of necessity limited to a number of basic observations and comparisons. More in-depth and sophisticated analysis is precluded at this time because of differences in the two computerized measurement systems and the formulas used to calculate scores. These differences do not allow a direct comparison of response scores between the two systems. For example, both systems calculate z-scores, but they are based on different measures and different formulas and, as such, cannot be compared to each other beyond simple directionality and relative magnitudes. Consequently, it is not possible at this time to compare the two procedures on a case-by-case basis or to aggregate response scores for statistical manipulation. As the study proceeds, a data analysis program will be created to facilitate more direct comparisons of the procedures and to evaluate a number of issues, including comparative reliability and discriminant validity.

Nonetheless, the preliminary findings reported here are both interesting and suggestive. For this chapter, the analysis examines the erectile and reaction time responses evoked by the stimuli and measured by each procedure. The following data are presented: (1) the overall distribution of responses for each procedure by sex/age category, (2) the amount of agreement/disagreement between each procedure for responses by sex/age category, (3) an examination of how the low and nonresponders on the plethysmograph responded on the AA, and (4) the accuracy of each procedure to classify subjects on the basis of the sex/age category of their victim(s).

A Note About Stimulus Materials

Recently, a number of ethical and legal concerns were raised about the widely used Multisite Study Slides and other visual materials that depict nude adults and children. The result of these concerns was that the distributor of the Multisite Study Slides withdrew them from distribution. Moreover, the Association for the Treatment of Sexual Abusers (ATSA) recommended that the use of such visuals be discontinued (Laws et al., 1995; Card & Olsen, 1996; Laws, 1996). The Abel stimulus materials were developed in direct response to these concerns and seek to alleviate them by using nonnude models in visual pictorial depictions in slide format. There are currently no visual materials in slide format available for use with the plethysmographic procedure that meet these concerns. Although it would be possible to create a such a set, the cost, time, and effort involved are too prohibitive for a state agency. Recently, two commercially produced visual stimulus sets for use with the plethysmographic procedure have been marketed that respond to these concerns. These materials are on videotape and use nonnude models in both pictorial and active depictions. One set includes only active models in standardized vignettes; the other set includes compound sexual stimuli composed of both pictorial and non-pornographic audio components. These materials are not directly comparable to the AA slide set, but they are the only reasonable alternative for visual stimuli for the phallometric procedure. As such, these two new stimulus sets were incorporated into the research design for this study. Unfortunately, the use of two differing types of stimulus materials makes the comparison of the two procedures less direct and more complicated; the comparison must be much grosser and at a more general level than we would like. Nonetheless, the comparison is useful and reveals interesting trends.

Measuring Sexual Preferences

Subjects. The sample reported here consists of twenty-six adult male sex offenders incarcerated at a medium-security prison in Minnesota. All are participants in a sex offender treatment program. The authors and clinical staff recruited the sample from a large group meeting at which they described the project. They described the project as a research investigation of two methods of measuring sexual preferences that would provide participants with an opportunity to learn more about their sexual interests and sexual behavior. They also described the project as being conducted for research purposes only, and they said that the results would be shared with the participants but not with the administration of the prison treatment program. Participation was voluntary to program members.

The first subjects who completed both procedures reported that the debriefings conducted after the procedures were informative and useful. They wanted the results to be incorporated into their treatment and shared with the program staff. They were informed that if this information was placed in their clinical files, it would be available for any future evaluation for determining community risk levels or possible civil commitment referral. Even with the possibility that the assessment results could be used against them, the subjects wanted the results to be incorporated into their treatment. From this point forward, all potential subjects were informed that the results would be shared with their primary therapist and that a copy of the results would be placed in their clinical file. This has not hampered the volunteer rate. It was discussed that even a "deviant" arousal profile is not necessarily a negative result. Cooperation in treatment and indications of progress partially mitigate risk factors and often have a positive impact on legal proceedings. This alleviated a significant demand characteristic of the prison setting. However, potential response bias for subjects to present themselves in a way they believed would help their case in terms of treatment reports and early release remained. However, all subjects were "admitters"; that is, they all admitted to at least the conviction crime and its basic details, in particular, the details about the victim. Moreover, as discussed later, we used certain strategies to control for and reduce response bias.

Each subject was assessed with both the penile plethysmograph and the AA, administered at different times. The minimum period between the administration of the two procedures was one week. A structured interview was conducted with each subject to gather information about how each procedure was experienced, opinions on what they found to be useful and not useful, and any preference for one procedure over the other. The results of these interviews are not reported here.

Each subject was classified into a sexual crime category on the basis of the sexual crime for which he was sentenced. This information was obtained from the criminal complaint or police report in the clinical files. Both authors reviewed each case and had complete agreement on categorical assignment of subjects. For this chapter, four basic offense categories are used. Although historical and self-reported information indicated that a number of subjects had committed sexual crimes in several of the categories, the classification of subjects for this report was based on the nature of the crime and victim(s) as reported in the criminal conviction located in the subject's file. The categories are defined in the following manner:

1. *Incest.* The subject's victim was age 13 or less and was related to him or the subject had a relationship with his victim that involved some adult or parental role. Fifteen subjects were incest offenders.
2. *Child molester.* The subject's victim was age 13 or less and not related to him, or the subject's relationship with his victim did not involve some adult or parental role. Sixteen subjects fit this category.
3. *Sexual assault.* The subject's victim was age 14 to adult and the subject used persuasion or coercion but not physical force. Eight subjects are in this category.
4. *Rape:* The subject's victim was age 18 or older and the subject used significant instrumental coercion or physical force and attempted or achieved oral, anal, or vaginal penetration. Nine subjects were rapists.

Table 26.1 presents the categories and the number of subjects in each category. Table 26.1 also presents information about the sex of the victims of the subjects based on their criminal convictions.

Plethysmograph Apparatus and Procedure. Erectile response was measured as a function of change in the circumference of the subject's penis as recorded by a sterilized Mercury tube–type strain gauge (manufactured by the D. M. Davis Company) in

Table 26.1
Classification of Subjects by Sexual Offense Category

Category of Sexual Offense	N = 48
Incest	
Female victim under 13 only	10
Female victim over 14 only	1
Female victim under and over 13	1
Male victim under 13 only	2
Male victim over 14 only	1
Total incest offenders	**15**
Child Molester	
Female victim under 13 only	9
Female victim under and over 13	1
Male victim under 13 only	5
Both female and male victims	1
Total child molesters	**16**
Sexual Assault	
Female victim 14–18 only	3
Female victim adult only	2
Male victim 14–18 only	3
Total sexual assaulters	**8**
Rape	
Female victim adult only	6
Female victim under 13 only	1
Female victim over 13 only	1
Both female and male victims under 13	1
Total rapists	**9**

response to a variety of sexual stimuli. The gauge was connected to a Farrall Instruments CAT-600UL computerized plethysmograph using version 6.0 of the Male Assessment Software developed by Behavioral Technology, Inc. As noted previously, no specific transformations of the tumescence responses are conducted for this report beyond conversion to the number of millimeters increased over a baseline measure of the circumference of the flaccid penis and as the relative percentage of the maximum erection, or tumescence, evoked in the assessment. To be scored as a clinically significant response, penile circumference must increase by 5 millimeters. Also recorded was the subject's respiration and galvanic skin response (GSR).

The procedure was explained to the subject using a standardized instruction set. The subject was instructed to allow himself to respond openly to the stimuli and to allow his thoughts/fantasies and interests to develop without censoring them. Any questions raised by the subject were answered. The subject signed a statement of informed consent and was asked if he understood the procedure and the limits of confidentiality. The subject was given a structured interview prior to the procedure that inquired about his anxiety level, use of medications, recent sexual activity, and other background information. The procedure was conducted in accordance with the *Guidelines for the Use of the Penile Plethysmograph* (ATSA, 1997).

The subject was seated in a private room where he placed the respiration, GSR, and strain gauges appropriately and was then instructed to relax so that the gauges could stabilize. When the gauges stabilized, the presentation of the stimulus materials began. The examiner was in verbal but not visual contact with the subject during the assessment. The subject's psychological or subjective sexual response to the plethysmographic stimuli was measured through his answers to particular questions asked after the presentation of each stimulus. He was asked to rate his psychological sexual response to the stimuli on a seven-point scale. This scale ranges from 1 to 7, with 1 indicating extreme dislike or disgust and 7 indicating extreme sexual interest or response; 4 indicates a neutral subjective sexual response. The subject was also asked to provide a subjective estimate of the degree of erection evoked by each stimulus on a scale of 0 to 100%.

The length of time required for phallometric assessment has been noted as a problem with the procedure. Time added a confounding factor to the phallometric assessments in this study. Presenting two separate stimulus sets required one three- to four-hour block of time (with breaks) or two separate meetings. Due to a combination of prison scheduling, technical difficulties, and strong erectile responses and long detumescence times, a number of phallometric assessments were pressed for time for completion. Rather than cut the assessment short and eliminate the vignettes that were the last to be presented, selected vignettes were chosen to be eliminated so that later vignettes could be presented. The choice of vignettes was based on a review of previous responding to select a vignette to which a low or nonresponse was expected and which was not in the sex/age category of the subject's victim. In two cases, intense responses and long detumescence times to many vignettes pushed the time limit and required elimination of several vignettes that would have been expected to produce strong responses. Again, the vignettes eliminated were chosen on the basis of dissimilarity with sex/age category of the subject's victim. This procedure minimizes the impact of the incomplete presentation of all stimuli.

Plethysmograph Stimulus Material. Two newly developed, commercially available sets of stimulus materials were employed. These materials were developed to alleviate the ethical and legal issues involved in the use of nudity, especially of children, in visual materials as noted earlier. The first set is produced by Northwest Media, Inc. (NW) and is composed of eleven video vignettes depicting female and males models ranging in the following age categories: kindergarten, 6–7, 8–9, teenage, and young adult.

Each vignette in the NW stimulus set runs for approximately two and one-half minutes. The first vignette is a neutral scene that is used to establish baseline penile response. The other vignettes are presented in standardized random order. They open with a single model in a swimsuit sitting in a folding chair. The model gets up and walks to a raised swimming pool and sits on the steps, eats of piece of fruit, then walks along the pool deck, sits with on the edge of the pool with his or her feet in the water and splashes water on him- or herself. The model then stands up again and uses a towel to dry off. The vignettes include closeups of genital areas and breasts but contain no nudity or sex acts. The only audio is background music. Each sex/age category include Caucasian, African-American, and Hispanic models. The vignettes are presented in a fixed random order.

The second set of stimulus materials is version 5A, Randomization 1 of the Adult Projective Audio-Video Tape Set produced by Behavioral Technology, Inc. (BTI). The set consists of twenty-two to twenty-five vignettes presented in fixed random order. The first vignette describes a neutral scenario that is used to establish baseline penile response. The other vignettes are presented in standardized random order. The last vignette contains a series of sixteen pictures of nude/seminude adult females with no audio, as a "normal" heterosexual stimulus. A similar vignette is optionally available for adult males. The remaining twenty vignettes begin with a picture of a male or female (nonnude) ranging in age from infant to adult presented for five seconds. The picture is removed and the screen goes blank while an eighty-five-second audio scenario is presented that describes compliant/consenting or coercive sexual interactions with a person of the same sex and age as in the preceding picture. Following this audio scenario, four still pictures of persons (nonnude) also the sex and age of the person in the first picture and described in the audio scenario, are presented for ten seconds each. For vignettes with compliant/consenting scenarios the age categories are infant, 2–5, 6–10, 12–17, and adult for both females and males. For vignettes with coercive sexual scenarios the age categories are the same except infants are not included.

Response bias or deliberate manipulation of erectile response is a noted problem in phallometric assessment. There are various techniques used in the field to limit such efforts. The BTI stimulus set has "attention cues" just for this purpose embedded randomly throughout the audio scenarios and the 40-second presentation of pictures after the audio scenarios. The cues are auditory beeps in the audio scenario and the appearance of a star somewhere near the periphery of the pictures. When a cue is presented, the subject is required to respond by moving a lever to indicate his awareness of the cue. This movement is recorded by the computer software. Also to minimize response bias, the subject was asked to describe each vignette to the examiner after it was presented and to provide the ratings of sexual arousal. Due to the comparative and descriptive nature of the study at this time, such techniques as instructing the subject to deliberately enhance or suppress his response were not implemented. In addition, as noted earlier, respiration and GSR were recorded as measures of response bias.

Both the NW and the BTI stimulus sets use nonpornographic stimuli that are designed to evoke discriminant sexual responses rather than a maximal sexual responses. The NW stimulus set is primarily oriented to evoke a sexual response to the age and sex of the models in the vignettes. The BTI stimulus set is more complicated in design and uses compound sexual stimuli that combine age and sex of the "partner" with descriptions of sexual interaction that have different degrees of consent. The stimuli use both audio and visual components. As described in recent research (Card & Dribble, 1995), the BTI set is based on the assumption that sexual offenders have developed an internal response pattern based on their sexual fantasies, experiences, and patterns of reinforcement. The sexually "deviant" or nonnormative audio scenarios are written as offender "self-talk" and are intended to be "projective" rather than explicit and pornographic. The suggestive "deviant" narrative is hypothesized to allow, even trigger, sex offenders to project or complete the details of the scenario based on their internal sexual response patterns. Non-sex offenders, who presumably do not have such response patterns, are expected to respond minimally, if at all, to the narrative. The visual stimuli are provided to further discrimination by enhancing responses depending on the nature of the sexual interest that is evoked.

Abel Assessment Apparatus and Procedure. The Abel Assessment consists of two parts. The first part requires the subject to answer a questionnaire covering twenty-one areas. The questionnaire includes such areas as demographics, social history, family stability, school problems, sexual development, sexual victimization, sexual perpetration, physical assault, cognitive distortions, sexual interests, and social desirability. In the second part, the subject views a set of slides and moves from slide to slide by pressing a key on a Macintosh Powerbook which is linked to the slide tray and controls the movement of the slides. The subject also enters his psychological sexual response on the same seven-point scale as used in the plethysmographic procedure. The computer uses a specially designed program to record the viewing time and psychological rating for each slide. The reactions times are converted to z-scores for scoring and interpretation. To be recorded as a clinically significant response, visual time must be at least 33% of the maximum z-score achieved in the assessment in the appropriate racial category.

The procedure was explained to the subject using a standardized instruction set. Any questions raised by the subject were answered. The subject signed a statement of informed consent and was asked if he understood the procedure and the limits of confidentiality. The subject then completed the questionnaire and underwent the objective portion the same day or no later than the following day. The objective portion consists of a practice and clinical component. In the practice component the examiner walks the subject through the procedure using a tray of fifteen slides two times. The subject operates the computer and rates his psychological sexual arousal to the models in the slides on a seven-point scale like the one used on the phallometric assessment. The subject is encouraged to respond openly to the stimuli and the examiner discusses the subject's responses with him. No responses are recorded in the practice component. When it appears that the subject understands the procedure the clinical component is started. The subject views two trays of eighty slides in privacy two times. The first time he views the slides with the understanding that he is simply becoming familiar with the content of the slides. During this period, his viewing time is being recorded. The second time he rates his psychological sexual arousal for each slide on the seven-point scale. After each slide tray is completed, the examiner is notified and changes the tray.

Abel Assessment Stimulus Materials. Like the stimulus materials used in the phallometric procedure, the slide set used in the AA was developed to avoid the legal and ethical issues involved in the use of nudity, especially of children, in visual materials. Unlike the materials reported in previous research (Abel et al., 1998), the slide set used in this procedure consisted of 160 slides placed in two carousels of 80 slides each. Both Caucasian and African-American models are used in the set. The set assesses twenty-two categories of sexual interest, including four age categories: 2–4, 8–10, 14–17, and adults over 22 years of age, two categories of sex, and two categories of race. Each age category contains seven male and female models of each race. The models are clothed in lingeries or in swimwear and are presented against a neutral background. Also included are categories of exhibitionism, voyeurism, fetishism, frotteurism, and sadism toward males and sadism toward females. Each of these categories also contains seven slides. There are also twenty-six slides (thirteen in each carousel) of models that are used as extras or "fillers." Responses to these slides are not incorporated into the final scores.

For the purposes of this report, only the sex/age categories for males and females for each stimulus set are examined. As noted, the AA uses four such categories, the NW set uses five, and the BTI uses five. The NW and BTI categories are adapted to conform to the AA categories. Only the BTI compliant/consenting stimuli are utilized in the analysis.

Results Suggest That Both Methods Are Comparable in Measuring Deviant Arousal

In comparing the measurement of erectile response with visual reaction time, the use of different stimulus sets in each procedure complicates interpretation. The AA slides considered in this report are designed to evoke responses to the sex and age of the models. Of the two phallometric sets, only the NW set is designed to evoke responses solely to the sex and age of the models in the vignettes. The BTI stimulus set, as noted previously, is composed of compound sexual stimuli that present not only pictorial sex and age cues but audio descriptions of sexual scenarios with compliant/consenting partners and sexual cues. Interpreting responses to these stimuli involves discriminating the responses to the various excitatory and inhibitory cues.

Several cases of the phallometric assessment indicated possible response bias or attempts to manipulate erectile response. It is not known how many other subjects may have been successful in faking responses. However, the admitter status of all subjects, pattern of their responses, and correlations with self-reported arousal indicate that this was not a major problem. Early research with the AA indicates that it may be harder to fake than the phallometric procedure. This is an area that will be investigated in the future.

Analyzing Age and Sex Preferences. The first step in the analysis examines the distribution of measured responses for each procedure by sex/age category. Table 26.2 presents the total number of responses for each stimulus set and procedure. Responses are dichotomized as "significant response" and "no response." A significant response is recorded when visual reaction time or erectile response is at or above the clinical significance threshold. No response is recorded when the measured visual reaction time or erectile response is negligible or below the clinical significance threshold. Overall, the AA slides evoked more significant responses in all sex/age categories compared to the NW videos measured by erectile response. In particular, the AA was more evocative for females ages 2–4 and for all male categories. However, there were marked differences between the AA and the BTI videos. The BTI videos evoked more

Table 26.2
Distribution of Responses in Total Sample by Sex/Age Category

N = 48

Sex/Age Category	Abel Assessment		NW Media		BTI Compliant/Consenting	
	Significant Response	Nonresponse	Significant Response	Nonresponse	Significant Response	Nonresponse
F/2–4	19 (40)	29 (60)	7 (15)	41 (85)	30 (62)	17 (35) [1]
F/8–10	28 (58)	20 (42)	18 (33)	30 (56)	27 (56)	19 (40) [2]
F/14–17	43 (90)	5 (10)	36 (75)	12 (25)	31 (65)	13 (27) [4]
F/Adult	41 (85)	7 (15)	34 (71)	14 (29)	37 (77)	11 (23) [0]
M/ 2–4	11 (23)	37 (77)	4 (8)	44 (92)	13 (27)	29 (60) [6]
M/8–10	14 (29)	34 (71)	6 (13)	42 (87)	18 (37)	28 (58) [2]
M/14–17	15 (31)	33 (69)	6 (13)	42 (87)	21 (44)	23 (48) [4]
M/Adult	12 (25)	36 (75)	3 (6)	44 (92) [1]	22 (46)	26 (54) [0]

Note. Numbers in parentheses ( ) are percentages. Numbers in brackets [ ] are the number of stimuli for that category that were not presented in an assessment for that particular set.

Table 26.3
Rate of Measurement Agreement for Responses in Each Sex/Age Category:
Abel Assessment Slides vs. Plethysmograph/Northwest Media Video
Vignettes

Sex/Age Category	Total Measurement Agreement for Both Procedures (N = 48)	Significant Response on Both Procedures	No Response on Both Procedures
F/2–4	30 (63)	4	26
F/8–10	33 (68)	15	18
F/14–17	41 (85)	36	5
F/Adult	37 (77)	32	5
M/2–4	35 (75)	1	34
M/8–10	34 (71)	3	31
M/14–17	36 (75)	4	32
M/Adult	38 (79)	3	35 [1]

Note. Numbers in parentheses ( ) are percentages. Numbers in brackets [ ] are the number of stimuli for that category that were not presented in an assessment for that particular set.

responses for females ages 2–4 and for all male categories. Both the AA and the BTI videos were more evocative than the NW videos for females ages 2–4 and for all male categories.

Measuring Agreement Between Procedures and Stimulus Sets. The next step in the analysis examines the amount of agreement between the procedures/stimulus sets for measured responses. Table 26.3 presents the number of clinically significant and non-significant responses in each sex/age category that were measured on both the AA slides and the NW videos. There is moderate to high agreement between the two for all responses, ranging from 63% to 85% in sex/age categories. The highest level of agreement for all responses was for females ages 8 to adult and all categories of males. Table 26.4 presents the number of clinically significant responses that are common to both procedures and unique to each. The AA measured more responses to its slides in all sex/age categories than the plethysmograph did to the NW video vignettes, ranging from seven to eleven more responses.

Comparing Slides and Videos. Tables 26.5 and 26.6 present the same comparison for the AA slides and the BTI video vignettes. In this case, the video vignettes are, as noted earlier, compound sexual stimuli that combine pictorial presentations with audio narratives. Hence, the responses to these materials are more complex because of the mixture of a variety of sexual cues and inhibitory cues. The agreement rate on measured clinically significant responses is somewhat lower than for the NW video vignettes, ranging from 55 to 77%. However, unlike the case of the NW videos, here each procedure recorded responses to stimuli that the other did not. In particular, the BTI

Table 26.4
Unique Clinically Significant Responses for Abel Assessment Slides vs.
Plethysmograph/Northwest Media Video Vignettes
$N = 48$

Sex/Age Category	Total Significant Responses to Abel	Significant Response to Abel Only	Total Significant Responses to NW	Significant Responses to NW Only
F/2–4	19	15	7	3
F/8–10	28	13	18	2
F/14–17	43	7	36	0
F/Adult	41	9	34	2
M/2–4	11	10	4	3
M/8–10	14	11	6	3
M/14–17	15	10	6	2
M/Adult	12	9	3	0 [1]

Note. Numbers in brackets [ ] are the number of stimuli for that category that were not presented in the assessment.

Table 26.5
Rate of Measurement Agreement for Responses in Each Sex/Age Category:
Abel Assessment Slides vs. Plethysmograph/BTI Compliant/Consenting
Video Vignettes

Sex/Age Category	Total Measurement Agreement for Both Procedures (N = 48)	Significant Response on Both Procedures	No Response on Both Procedures
F/2–4	26 (55)	14	12 [1]
F/8–10	32 (70)	20	12 [2]
F/14–17	32 (70)	29	3 [4]
F/Adult	37 (77)	34	3
M/2–4	28 (67)	4	24 [6]
M/8–10	29 (63)	7	22 [2]
M/14–17	23 (52)	6	17 [4]
M/Adult	26 (54)	6	20

Note. Numbers in parentheses ( ) are percentages. Numbers in brackets [ ] are the number of stimuli for that category that were not presented in the assessment.

evoked fourteen significant responses in the female 2–4 category from subjects who did not respond similarly to the AA slides in the same age category, but the AA slides evoked three responses in this category from subjects who did not respond to the corresponding stimuli in the BTI set. For the remaining female categories, the AA gener-

Table 26.6
Unique Clinically Significant Responses for Abel Assessment Slides vs.
Plethysmograph/BTI Compliant/Consenting Video Vignettes

$N = 48$

Sex/Age Category	Total Significant Responses to Abel	Significant Response to Abel Only	Total Significant Responses to BTI	Significant Responses to BTI Only
F/2–4	19	5	30	14 [1]
F/8–10	28	6	27	8 [2]
F/14–17	43	10	31	2 [4]
F/Adult	41	7	37	4
M/2–4	11	6	13	8 [6]
M/8–10	14	6	18	11 [2]
M/14–17	15	6	21	15 [4]
M/Adult	13	6	21	16

Note. Numbers in brackets [ ] are the number of stimuli for that category that were not presented in an assessment.

ated more significant responses that were unmatched on the BTI stimuli. For the male categories, both procedures generated between six and sixteen unique responses.

Measuring Low Responders. The third area of analysis deals with the problem of low or nonresponders often found in plethysmographic assessment. It is reported that between 10 and 20% of the men who undergo this procedure do not respond at a clinically significant level to any of the stimuli. Low responders are subjects for whom there were only a few measured erectile responses with the maximum response reaching borderline clinical significance. To date in this study, there have been eight low responders. Five of them were child molesters, one was a sexual assaulter, and two were rapists. In the preassessment interview, four of these low responders reported difficulty in achieving an erection, four reported medications that affected erectile ability, and two reported both erection difficulty and medications. Three were over age 55. Nonresponders are subjects for whom there were no clinically significant measured erection responses. To date in this study, there have been six nonresponders. Two were child molesters, one an incest perpetrator, and three were rapists. In the preassessment interview, none of these nonresponders reported problems with erectile response. One of the rapist nonresponders reported no erectile difficulty or medications but was nonresponsive to all stimuli until the presentation of the BTI vignette describing the rape of an adult female. The subject became so emotionally distraught when listening to this scenario that the procedure was stopped. The subject said that the scenario was so similar to the rape he had committed that he was flooded with shame and guilt about his crime. He was counseled by program staff immediately upon cessation of the

Table 26.7
Low and Nonresponders on Plethysmograph and Their Responses on the Abel Assessment

$$N = 48$$

Sex/Age Category	Low Responders on NW and BTI (N = 8)	Significant Responses on Abel Assessment of Low Responders	Significant Responses on Abel Assessment of Nonresponders on NW and BTI (N = 6)
F/2–4	2	3	3
F/8–10	2	4	3
F/14–17	7	8	4
F/Adult	6	7	5
M/2–4	0	2	1
M/8–10	2	4	1
M/14–17	3	4	3
M/Adult	2	2	3

assessment. Table 26.7 presents the number of significant responses of the low responders to both the NW and BTI stimuli as measured by the plethysmograph and their corresponding significant responses to the slides of the AA. The AA evoked slightly more significant responses in each sex/age category. The last column in Table 26.7 presents the significant responses on the AA of the three nonresponders on the plethysmograph. The AA evoked responses from all six subjects who did not respond significantly to any stimuli presented with the plethysmograph.

Accuracy in Classifying by Offense Category. The fourth and last area of analysis examines the accuracy of each procedure in classifying subjects in terms of their sexual offense category. Table 26.8 presents each sexual offense category and the number of clinically significant responses that matched the sex/age of the subjects' victims as described in the current conviction.

The BTI videos obtained responses that matched the sex/age of all ten of the incest offenders who had victims under the age of 13 only. For the remaining age categories of victims there are only one or two subjects and all three measures performed equally. It should be noted that none of the measures identified the one incest offender who had a male victim under age 13. Also, the AA and BTI identified both incest offenders who had adolescent male victims older than 13. For the child molester category, the AA matched the sex/age of the victims of 94% of the subjects. The NW and BTI videos correctly matched 62% of victims' sex/age. It should be noted that none of the measures are capable of differentiating incest from child molestation, other than specifying the sex/age of the identified victim.

For the category of sexual assault, all three measures performed well. The AA slides evoked responses that matched the sex/age of all eight subjects, whereas the

Table 26.8
Number of Responses in Subject's Sexual Offense Classification and in Sex/Age Categories of Victims

Category of Sexual Offense	Abel Assessment	NW	BTI
Incest			
Female victim over 13 only (*n* = 1)	1	1	1
Female victim under 14 only (*n* = 10)	5	5	10
Female victim under and over 13 (*n* = 1)	1	1	1
Male victim 13 or under only (*n* = 1)	0	0	0
Male victim under 13 only (*n* = 2)	2	0	2
Total incest offenders = 15			
Child Molester			
Female victim under 14 only (*n* = 9)	9	5	7
Female victim under and over 13 (*n* = 1)	1*	1*	0
Male victim under 13 only (*n* = 5)	4	4	3
Both female and male victim (*n* = 1)	1	0	0
Total child molesters = 16			
Sexual Assault			
Female victim 14–18 only (*n* = 3)	3	2	2
Female victim adult only (*n* = 2)	2	2	2
Male victim 14–18 only (*n* = 3)	3	2	3
Rape			
Female victim adult only (*n* = 6)	6	2	3
Female victim under 13 only (*n* = 1)	0	0	0
Female victim over 13 only (*n* = 1)	1	1	1
Both female and male victims under 13 (*n* = 1)	1 (female only)	0	0

[a] One subject had female victims under and over age 13 but responded only to the category of females over 13.

NW and BTI matched six and seven subjects, respectively. In the rape category, the AA slides obtained responses more consistently that the other two measures.

Different Methods Measure Different Preferences

The AA was relatively more effective at evoking clinically significant responses to teenage and adult females among this sample. For prepubescent females, the AA and BTI video vignettes evoked relatively good response rates given that over half the sample had victims in these categories. The NW videos were the least effective, especially for the very young female category (ages 2–4). For prepubescent males, the AA slides and BTI videos were comparable, whereas for adolescent and adult males the subjects were somewhat more responsive to the BTI videos than to the AA slides. The subjects were least responsive to the NW male stimuli. The overall level of agreement of clinically significant responses between the AA and the NW sets was over 70% for every sex/age category except for the very young female (ages 2–4), which was 42%. The AA set generated more clinically significant responses to both females and males not matched by the NW set. The overall level of agreement of clinically significant responses between the AA and the BTI sets was moderate 55 to 71 %). In this case, the BTI set generated three to fourteen clinically significant responses not matched by the AA set. However, the AA set generated three to eleven clinically significant responses not matched by the BTI set. At this point, it is not clear how to interpret these unique responses.

Conclusion

To summarize, the results obtained by the Abel Assessment are comparable with those of the phallometric assessment. Some interesting trends and differences have emerged that will be explored in the future. Further investigation will involve discussing the results in more detail with each subject to clarify response trends. In addition, we plan to examine the following areas as our subject pool increases: (1) identification of possible trends on the AA that may indicate a possible interest or arousal to sexual and nonsexual violence; (2) response bias and susceptibility to faking and manipulation; (3) reliability and validity; and (4) the subjects' reported experience with each procedure.

References

Abel, G. G. (1995). *Abel Assessment for Sexual Interest™: Therapists' product information.* Atlanta, GA: Abel Screening, Inc.

Abel, G. G., Huffman, J., Warberg, B., & Holland, C. L. (1998). Visual reaction time and plethysmography as measures of sexual interest in child molesters. *Sexual Abuse: A Journal of Research and Treatment, 10*(2), 81–95.

Abel, G. G., Lawry, S. S. Karlstrom, E., Osborn, C. A., & Gillelspie, C. F. (1994). Screening tests for pedophilia. *Criminal Justice and Behavior 21*(1), 115–131.

Association for the Treatment of Sexual Abusers. (1997). *Ethical standards and principles for the management of sexual abusers* (rev. ed.). Beaverton, OR: Author.

Barbaree, H. E. (1990). Stimulus control of sexual arousal: Its role in sexual assault. In W. L. Marshall, D. R. Laws, & H. E. Barbaree (Eds.), *Handbook of sexual assault: Issues, theories and treatment of the offender* (pp. 115–142). New York: Plenum Press.

Barbaree, H. E., & Marshall, W. L. (1991). The role of male sexual arousal in rape: six models. *Journal of Consulting and Clinical Psychology, 59,* 621–630.

Blader, J. C., & Marshall, W. L. (1989). Is assessment of sexual arousal in rapists worthwhile? A critique of current methods and the development of a response compatibility approach. *Clinical Psychology Review, 9,* 569–587.

Bradford, J. M. W., Boulet, J., & Pawlak, A. (1992, March). The paraphilias: A multiplicity of deviant behaviors. *Canadian Journal of Psychiatry, 37,* 104–108.

Card, R. D., & Dribble, A. (1995). Predictive value of the Card/Farrall stimuli in discriminating between gynephilic and pedophilic sex offenders. *Sexual Abuse: A Journal of Research and Treatment, 7*(2), 129–142.

Card, R. D., & Olsen, S. E. (1996). Visual plethysmograph stimuli involving children: Rethinking some quasi-legal issues. *Sexual Abuse, 8*(4), 267–271.

Cohen, F. (1995). Therapeutic uses of sexually explicit material and the plethysmograph. In B. K. Schwartz & H. R. Cellini (Eds.), *The sex offender: Corrections, treatment, and legal practice* (vol. I, pp. 29-1–29-10). Kingston, NJ: Civic Research Institute.

Finkelhor, D. (1984). *Child sexual abuse.* New York: Free Press.

Hall, G. C. N., & Hirschman, R. (1991). Towards a theory of sexual aggression: A quadripartite model. *Journal of Consulting and Clinical Psychology, 59,* 662–669.

Hall, G. C. N., Shondrick, D., & Hirschman, R. (1993). The role of sexual arousal in sexually aggressive behavior: A meta-analysis. *Journal of Consulting and Clinical Psychology, 61,* 1091–1095.

Hall, K. S., Binik, Y., & DiTomasso, E. (1985). Concordance between physiological and subjective measures of sexual arousal. *Behaviour Research and Therapy, 23,* 297–303.

Hanson, R. K., & Bussière, M. T. (1996). *Predictors of sexual offender recidivism: A meta-analysis.* (User Report No.1996-4). Ottawa: Corrections Branch, Ministry of the Solicitor General of Canada.

Harris, G. T., & Rice, M. E. (1996). The science in phallometric measurement of male sexual interest. *Current Directions in Psychological Science, 5,* 156–160.

Harris, G. T., Rice, M. E., Quinsey, V. L., & Chaplin, T. C. (1996). Viewing time as a measure of sexual interest among child molesters and normal heterosexual men. *Behaviour Research and Therapy, 34,* 389–394.

Harris, G. T., Rice, M. E., Quinsey, V. L., Chaplin, T. C., & Earls, C. (1992). Maximizing the discriminant validity of phallometric assessment data. *Psychological Assessment, 4*(4), 502–511.

Haywood, T. W., Grossman, L. S., & Cavanaugh, J. L. Jr. (1990). Subjective versus objective measurements of deviant sexual arousal in clinical evaluations of alleged child molesters. *Psychological Assessment, 2,* 269–275.

Hunter, J. A., & Becker, J. V (1994). The role of deviant sexual arousal in juvenile sexual offending: Etiology, evaluation, and treatment. *Criminal Justice and Behavior, 21*(1), 132–140.

Knight, R. A., & Prentky, R. A. (1990). Classifying sexual offenders: The development and corroboration of taxonomic models. In W. L. Marshall, D. R. Laws, & H. E. Barbaree (Eds.), *Handbook of sexual assault: Issues, theories and treatment of the offender* (pp. 23–52). New York: Plenum Press.

Lalumière, M. L., & Quinsey, V. L. (1994). The discriminability of rapists from non-sex offenders using phallometric measures: A meta-analysis. *Criminal Justice and Behavior, 21*(1), 150–175.

Langevin, R. (Ed.). (1985). *Erotic preference, gender identity, and aggression in men: New research studies.* Hillsdale, NJ: Erlbaum.

Lanyon, R.I. (1991). Theories of sexual offending. In C. R. Hollin & K. Howells (Eds.), *Clinical approaches to sex offenders and their victims* (pp. 35–54). Chichester: Wiley.

Laws, D. R. (1993, April). The president's column. *ATSA Newsletter, 5*(2), 2–4.

Laws, D. R. (1996). Marching into the past: A critique of Card and Olsen. *Sexual Abuse, 8*(4), 273–278.

Laws, D. R., Gulayets, M. J., & Frenzel, R. R. (1995). Assessment of sex offenders using standardized slide stimuli and procedures: A multisite study. *Sexual Abuse, 7*(1), 45–66.

Laws, D. R., & Marshall, W. L. (1990). A conditioning theory of the etiology and maintenance of deviant sexual preference and behavior. In W. L. Marshall, D. R. Laws, & H. E. Barbaree (Eds.), *Handbook of sexual assault: Issues, theories and treatment of the offender* (pp. 209–229). New York: Plenum Press.

Malamuth, N. M., Heavey, C. L., & Linz, D. (1993). Predicting men's antisocial behavior against women: The interaction model of sexual aggression. In G. C. N. Hall, R. Hirschman, J. R. Grahaj, & M. S. Zaragoza (Eds.), *Sexual aggression: Issues in etiology, assessment and treatment* (pp. 63–97). Washington, DC: Taylor & Francis.

Marshall, W. L., & Barbaree, H. E. (1990). An integrated theory of the etiology of sexual offending. In W. L. Marshall, D. R. Laws, & H. E. Barbaree (Eds.), *Handbook of sexual assault: Issues, theories and treatment of the offender* (pp. 257–275). New York: Plenum Press.

McConaghy, N. (1993). *Sexual behavior: Problems and management.* New York: Plenum Press.

Murphy, W. D., & Barbaree. H. E. (1994). *Assessments of sex offenders by measures of erectile response: Psychometric properties and decision making* (rev. and updated). Brandon, VT: Safer Society Press.

Murphy, W. D., Haynes, M. R., & Worley, P. J. (1991). Assessment of adult sexual interest. In C. R. Hollin & K. Howells (Eds.), *Clinical approaches to sex offenders and their victims* (pp. 77–92). New York: Wiley.

Murphy, W. D., & Peters, J. M. (1992, March). Profiling child sexual abusers: Psychological considerations. *Criminal Justice and Behavior 19*(1), 24–37.

O'Donohue, W., & Leterneau, E. (1992). The psychometric properties of the penile tumescence assessment of child molesters. *Journal of Psychopathology and Behavioral Assessment, 14,* 123–174.

Pithers, W. D. (1990). Relapse prevention with sexual aggressors. In W. L. Marshall, D. R. Laws, & H. E. Barbaree (Eds.), *Handbook of sexual assault: Issues, theories and treatment of the offender* (pp. 343–361). New York: Plenum Press.

Pithers, W. D., & D. R. Laws. (1995). Phallometric assessment. In B. K. Schwartz & H. R. Cellini (Eds.), *The sex offender: Corrections, treatment, and legal practice* (vol. I, pp. 12-1–121-18). Kingston, NJ: Civic Research Institute.

Quinsey, V. L., & Lalumière, M. L. (1996). *Assessment of sexual offenders against children.* Thousand Oaks, CA: Sage.

Rosen, R., & Beck, J. G. (1988). *Patterns of sexual arousal: Psychophysiological processes and clinical applications.* New York: Guilford Press.

Simon, W. T., & Schouten, P. G. W. (1991). Plethysmography in the assessment and treatment of sexual deviance: An overview. *Archives of Sexual Behavior, 20,* 75–91.

Simon, W. T., & Schouten, P. G. W. (1992). Problems in sexual preference testing in child sexual abuse cases: A legal and community perspective. *Journal of Interpersonal Violence, 7*(4), 503–516.

Travin, S., Cullen, K., & Melella, J. (1988). The use and abuse of erection measurements: A forensic perspective. *Bulletin of the American Academy of Psychiatry and the Law, 16*(3), 289–299.

Ward, T., Louden, K., Hudson, S. M., & Marshall, W. L. (1995). A descriptive model of the offense chain for child molesters. *Journal of Interpersonal Violence, 10,* 453–473.

Chapter 27

Sex Education and Sexually Explicit Media in Residential Treatment Programs for Sex Offenders

**by Nancy H. Walbek, Ph.D., L.P. and
Richard K. Seely, L.I.C.S.W.**

Overview

Sex education is almost universally included as one of the treatment modalities offered in programs for sex offenders. In the Safer Society's 1994 survey of 1,394 programs treating either adult or adolescent male sex offenders, more than 85% of respondents identified sex education as a component of their program (Freeman-Longo, Bird, Stevenson, & Fiske, 1995). Despite the widespread use of this type of intervention, little has been written describing the specific goals, content, and processes of this treatment component. A related issue is how programs control access to sexually explicit media both within the context of sexuality education and during residents' leisure time. The authors have witnessed treatment programs struggle with this issue, often in an emotionally charged context. The literature offers virtually no guidance on current practice in treatment programs. This chapter presents a rationale for bolstering sexuality education that includes sexually explicit media in residential treatment programs for offenders. The authors provide a detailed outline of the type of program recommended, together with a listing of resource material. The second part of the chapter describes a survey of providers of residential sex offender treatment regarding the sex education component of their programs and their rules regarding access to media with sexual content. Enhanced understanding of how these issues are handled in sex offender programs across the country may be helpful to individual programs.

Introduction

Clinicians working with persons with sexual dysfunctions, including sexual involvement with children or other aggressive sexual behavior, often report that these individuals tend to be anxious about sexual matters and have a tremendous amount of ignorance, confusion, distortion, and anxiety regarding human relationships and human sexual functioning (Lakey, 1992). Given the premise that most sexual attitudes, values, and behaviors are learned, clinicians often describe both juvenile and adult sex offenders as harboring an incredible amount of misinformation, strange beliefs, and attitudes regarding sexual matters. These observations provide compelling arguments for the inclusion of comprehensive education on age-appropriate healthy human sexuality in the treatment of all persons suffering from victimization, dysfunction, and sexual aggression issues. Our experience with sex offender treatment has constantly reinforced the premise that the more knowledge people have about an issue, the more likely they are to make sound decisions about their behavior associated with that knowledge.

Enhancing Sex Education With Sexual Aggressors

Many children grow toward adulthood with experiences similar to those of persons who become sex offenders, which have left them naive, anxious, and confused about sexual matters, yet they do not become sexually aggressive or victims of sexual aggression. Our experience indicates that those whose lives and sexuality have been severely traumatized by sexual abuse issues appear to respond positively to accurate information regarding the impact that misinformation and trauma have had on their lives.We have concluded that the sex offenders with whom we have worked have responded favorably to the opportunity to learn accurate information about sexual issues. In 1972, the sex offender program developed the first known comprehensive sex education curriculum to be offered to sex offenders; it included explicit films and slides in the curriculum. The course evolved in a manner that specifically addressed developmental sexuality and culturally sensitive information as we attempted to offer healthy sexuality information to clients with very diverse experiences, interests, and dysfunctions.

Each opportunity we have had to present this material to staff, sex offenders, and their families has resulted in favorable feedback from the participants. Staff members often acknowledged that they had received little or no training that prepared them to discuss sexual matters openly; that their bias, prejudices, knowledge, and beliefs had never been so challenged as when they were confronted with the beliefs of the offenders and their families with whom they worked. Sex offenders would often tell us that other programs in which they had unsuccessfully participated did not talk about sexual matters. Family members of offenders reported a much deeper understanding of the attitudes and dysfunction of offenders after participating in the course. All participants, while acknowledging that sexual assault is not only about sexual feelings and attitudes that have gone awry, expressed a clearer understanding of how healthy sexuality and the development of a healthy sexuality plan may play a significant role in the therapeutic process.

Sexual Misconceptions

Sex offenders harbor a number of misconceptions, some of which directly contribute to their deviant behavior. One offender , when telling about his ongoing sexual abuse of his 8-year-old daughter, was asked by the treatment team about his masturbation history. He immediately responded, "I don' t do that. It's a sin." Another offender, when asked what he believed to be the average size of a man's penis, responded "ten to twelve inches." He then shared that he felt very cheated and inadequate in that area and that he had no experience with sexual behavior with adults and had significant fears of engaging in sexual behavior with an adult woman. He was quick to share that the children with whom he had been sexual complained that his penis was too big. He was skeptical when we shared the accurate information with him. These two examples demonstrate common themes in offender's thoughts that are remediated through accurate information about sexual matters.

Building a Curriculum

The curriculum developed for both staff and clients was derived from Kinsey's work, from the work of Masters and Johnson, and, most recently, from several new textbooks Table 27.1 (on p. 27-4) lists a number of the resources useful to curriculum development. The curriculum blends classroom instruction with elements of the Sexual Attitude Reassessment (SAR) developed by Ted McIllveny of the National Sex and Drug Forum. The comprehensive course we developed for both staff and clients identifies three goals: (1) increase accurate knowledge about human sexuality, (2) foster critical examination of prejudices and myths, and (3) develop greater sexual self-knowledge, acceptance, and responsibility. The objectives identified for the course include the following:

1. Provide an opportunity to explore sexual beliefs and values with others.
2. Provide an opportunity to learn to become more comfortable in discussing sexual issues.
3. Provide accurate information regarding sexual anatomy, physiology, function and dysfunction, and specifically a reference point of healthy sexuality.

Explicit visual media that are developmentally appropriate are used to encourage reality-based discussion.

We recommend that any curriculum pay specific attention to the biological, psychosocial, cultural, behavioral, and clinical aspects of human sexuality. We further recommend that all aspects of the course be co-taught by a male and female teaching team and that a minimum of four hours be spent in each unit as follows:

Table 27.1
Sexuality Education Resources

Books

Ansuini, C. G., Fiddler-Woite, J., & Woite, R. S. (1996). The source, accuracy, and impact of initial sexuality information on lifetime wellness. *Adolescence, 31,* 283–289.

Berne, L. A., & Huberman, B. K. (1995). Sexuality education: Sorting fact from fiction. *Phi Delta Kappan, 229*(4), 77.

Chilgren, R. A., & Briggs, M. M. (1973, May). On being explicit: Sex education for professionals. *SIECUS Report, 1*(5).

Crooks, R., & Baur, K. (1996). *Our sexuality* (6th ed.). Pacific Grove, CA: Brooks/Cole.

Mayden, B. (1995, October–November). Access to sexuality information for out-of-home youth. *SIECUS Report, 24,* 13–15.

Ogletree, R. J., Rienzo, B. A., Drolet, J. C., & Fetro, J. V. (1995). An assessment of 23 selected school-based sexuality education curricula. *Journal of School Health, 65,* 186–190.

Planned Parenthood Federation of America. (1996a). *Human sexuality: What children should know and when they should know it.* http://www.ppfa.org/ppfa/kids-pub.html.

Planned Parenthood Federation of America. (1996b). *What you should know about sexuality education.* http://www.ppfa.org/ppfa/sexed-mm.html.

Reinisch, J. M. (1990). *The Kinsey Institute new report on sex.* New York: St. Martin's Press.

Sexuality Information and Education Council of the United States. (1996). *Sexuality education and the schools: Issues and answers.* http://noah.cuny.edu/sexuality/siecus/fact5.html.

Videos

Better Sex Video Series, P.O. Box 8855, Chapel Hill, NC 27515.

Focus International, Inc., 13-A Jules Lane, New Brunswick, NJ 08901.

Multi-Focus, Inc., 1525 Franklin Street, San Francisco, CA 94109-4592; (415) 673-5100, (800) 821-0514.

- Unit 1: Healthy Sexual Functioning—Anatomy, Physiology, Body Image, Sexual Response Cycle;
- Unit 2: Risks and Protections—Birth Control, Sexually Transmitted Infections;
- Unit 3: Healthy Sexuality: Developmental Sexuality (Childhood, Adolescent, Adult Sexuality), Fantasy, Masturbation;
- Unit 4: Sexual Choices (Sex as Communication, Sex as Weapon, Dehumanization), Continuums (Sexual Preference, Birth to Death, Hyposexuality/ Hypersexuality,Variations),Communicating About Sexuality; and
- Unit 5: Sexual Function and Dysfunctions—Male and Female Dysfunctions Paraphilias, Sexual Assault, Lovemaking, Pleasuring, and Intimacy.

Using Sexually Explicit Material in Sex Education

There has been considerable controversy over the use of sexually explicit material in sex offender treatment. Some practitioners are concerned that this material will arouse deviant fantasies in the program participants. Others are concerned that the media may misinterpret and sensationalize the use of this material. There certainly have been miunderstandings regarding the use of explicit stimulus material in phallometric assessment. To evaluate the use of this type of material in other programs, we conducted a survey.

Survey Method and Response Rate. The survey population was defined by the address labels of residential treatment programs for sex offenders purchased from the Safer Society Program for the explicit purpose of conducting this study. The letter requested that a person familiar with the sex education curriculum at the facility complete the survey and return it along with a course description of any sex education program offered and policies governing resident access to media. Surveys were sent to 163 programs serving male adolescents and 144 programs for adult males in late May with a remailing to nonresponders in late July 1996. The rate of return of usable questionnaires was 42% ($n = 60$) for the adult programs and 40% ($n = 65$) for the adolescent programs.

Supplementary materials describing sex education programs, were received from nine adolescent and fifteen adult programs. Thirteen adult programs sent policies or statements regarding restriction of media. No policies were sent by adolescent programs; one respondent indicated his program was in the process of preparing a policy; another wrote a few sentences reporting the practices in his program.

Survey Results. Sex education as one component of treatment was reported by 78% of respondents. A larger proportion (85%) of programs for adolescents reported presenting sex education than did programs for adults (70%). All these findings are between 7 and 11 percentage points lower than those obtained in the Safer Society's 1994 survey. The difference may be related to the fact that the current study surveyed exclusively residential programs, which offer longer-term treatment and are more often managed by corrections than are outpatient programs. It seems likely that programs offered by human service agencies would be more likely to include sex education.

Table 27.2 (on p. 27-6) presents responses to the survey questions dealing with sex education. The total number of hours of sex education presented to each resident varied widely, from 1 to 300 hours reported by adolescent programs and 2 to 200 hours reported by adult programs. Of those programs reporting the total number of hours of sex education, adolescent programs were more likely to report twenty or more hours than under twenty hours of instruction. Among the adult programs, offering less than twenty hours was slightly more likely than offering over twenty hours. Chi-square analysis of this distribution of frequencies was not significant.

Responses to the questions about the types of media used in sex education for residents are presented in the second section of Table 27.2. The majority of programs report using diagrams of sexual systems and still pictures of genitals, but less than one-fourth include still or moving pictures of sexual behavior. In general, programs treating adolescents reported greater use of media.

These findings parallel an analysis of the twenty-four descriptions of sexual education curricula received from respondents. Although all programs included content on the names and functions of sexual organs, reproduction, and fundamentals of safe sex, only thirteen specifically addressed sexual behaviors and how they related to the societal values detailed in twenty-one of the twenty-four curricula received.

A minority of programs reported including sex education in their staff training. As seen in the lowest portion of Table 27.2, programs treating adolescents are substantially more likely to provide sex education to some or all of their staff than are programs treating adult offenders. This difference in frequencies is statistically significant ($X^2 = 9.74$, 1 df, $p < .01$).

Table 27.2
Sex Education Offered to Resident and Staff

	65 Adolescent Treatment Programs		60 Adult Programs	
	N	%[a]	N	%[a]
Amount of Sex Education Offered Residents				
None	10	15.4	19	30
1–18 hours	15	23.1	14	23.3
Some, hours not specified	21	32.3	15	25
20–66 hours	18	27.7	12	20.0
200–300 hours	1	1.5	1	1.7
Media Used in Sex Education for Residents				
Diagrams of sexual systems	50/54	92.6	29/40	72.5
Still pictures of genitals	35/53	66.0	26/40	65.0
Still pictures of sexual theories	10/54	18.5	9/39	22.5
Sexually explicit movies or videos	12/55	21.8	4/40	10.0
Provision of Sex Education to Staff				
Required of all staff	14/63	22.2	3/58	5.2
Required for some staff	12/63	19.1	6/58	10.5
Not offered to staff	37/63	58.7	49/58	84.5
When provided, hours offered: Mean range (should be divided in two)	1.1		7.0	
	1.2		3–18	
Staff training includes same or more media as used with residents	14/25			

[a]The base for percentages is the number of surveys on which that single item was answered.

Program Restrictions on Media. Figures 27.1 and 27.2 present program restrictions on various types of media. The data reflect the widespread practice of exercising at least some restriction on both print and moving media. No restrictions on print media were reported by 16% of the adult and 5% of the adolescent programs. With reference to moving media, 22% of the adult and 3% of the adolescent programs reported no restrictions. Across both adult and adolescent settings, even such widely available media as news and geographic magazines and "G"- or "PG"-rated movies were reported as being restricted by at least 10% of respondents. Restrictions were far more frequent in adolescent than in adult programs. The only exceptions to this difference were teen magazines and "PG"- and "G"-rated movies, which were more often restricted in adult programs.

Figure 27.1
Programs' Restriction of Printed Media

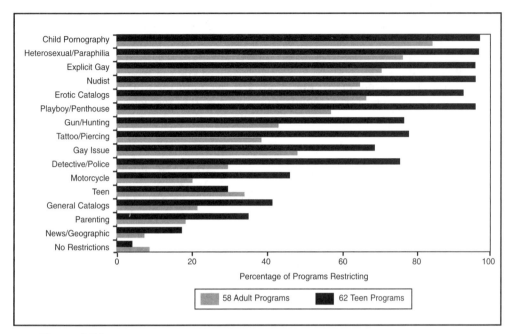

Figure 27.2
Programs' Restriction of Electronic Media

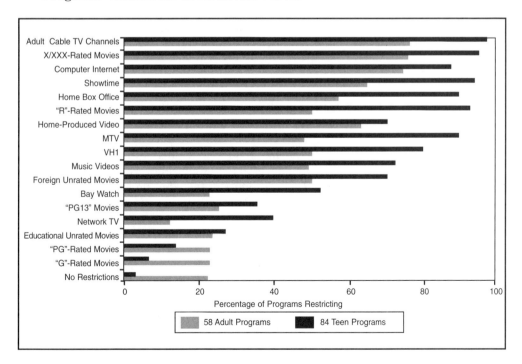

Responses from adolescent programs showed widespread agreement regarding the restriction of several types of media including child pornography, explicit gay and nudist magazines, *Playboy/Penthouse* magazines, movies with an "R" or higher rating, the MTV channel, and adult cable channels. Even the televised prime-time teen favorite *Baywatch* was restricted by approximately 50% of adolescent treatment programs.

Within adult programs, there was less consensus about a wide range of restricted media; only child pornography was restricted by more than 80% of the programs responding. Roughly half of the adult programs reported restricting residents' access to *Playboy/Penthouse*, gay issue magazines, "R"-rated movies, and the MTV channel.

Sexually Explicit Material Defined as Contraband. The policies or other information regarding sexually explicit contraband which were sent by thirteen adult programs varied widely. Five respondents described restricted material with phrases such as "any erotica," "any sexually explicit material," depictions of "people in the nude, seminude, or in a way that can be used to objectify human beings in a sexual way." Five respondents specified only specific displays such as same-gender or pedophilic behavior, bestiality, bondage, masturbation ,or photos in which the "sex act can be construed." One restricted mail "offensive to accepted local standards of decency or appealing to prurient interest," another restricted X-rated videos and other material as individually determined. The final program wrote a brief description regarding how the privilege of having magazines is available after assessment of meeting treatment objectives, television is not permitted, and the content of videos, not just the rating, is evaluated.

The two adolescent programs commenting on rules regarding media indicated restriction of "R"-rated videos. One reported restricting "television programs that depict sexually explicit or insinuate sexuality." The other wrote that "printed pornography and sexually explicit materials are not allowed, and staff discretion is encouraged when censoring television programs, magazines, music and books."

Conclusion

It is clear from these results that simply knowing a sex offender treatment program includes sex education communicates very little information about the details of this intervention. Respondents identifying sex education as a part of their program provided a wide range of answers to items that requested details of the time and content of this treatment component. The time devoted to sex education varied from 1 to 300 hours in adolescent programs and 2 to 200 hours in the adult programs. Most of the respondents who reported that sex education was offered in their programs used diagrams of sexual systems, but fewer than one in five used still pictures of sexual behaviors. All the curricula received address the anatomy, physiology, and health aspects of sex, and approximately half reported directly discussing sexual behaviors.

Responses to these surveys reflect relatively little emphasis on providing sex education to the staff working in these sex offender treatment programs. Fewer than half of the respondents from adolescent programs reported offering any sex education to staff; this proportion fell to 16% in the adult programs. Those programs that include some sex education in their staff training offer an average of six hours of training and do not require it for all staff. Apparently there is widespread confidence that employees' preemployment education offers adequate (or nearly enough) training in sexuality to work with this population.

The results of this survey indicate that restricting the media available to residents of treatment programs is a more widely practiced approach to treatment than is offering sex education. Restrictions were reported by a higher proportion of programs (88%) than was providing sex education (78%). The discrepancy was evident in both adolescent and adult programs, though slightly higher in the results from the adult programs. Although this survey indicates that control of media exposure is almost universally practiced in sex offender treatment programs, it has not been identified as a treatment modality in previous surveys of treatment programs (Freeman-Longo, Bird, Stevenson, & Fiske, 1995). We have been unable to locate literature that details procedures for implementing media restriction or which presents research supporting this practice in the treatment of sex offenders.

Unfortunately, the present survey does not provide information about the amount of staff time devoted to enforcing rules regarding media access. The authors' experience working in residential sex offender programs suggests that restricting media requires substantial ongoing vigilance and enforcement by program staff.

References

Freeman-Longo, R. E., Bird, S., Stevenson, W. F., & Fiske, J. A. (1995). *1994 nationwide survey of treatment programs and models serving abuse-reactive children and adolescent and adult sex offenders.* Brandon, VT: Safer Society Press.

Lakey, J. F. (1995). Myth information and bizarre beliefs of male juvenile sex offenders. *Journal of Addictions and Offender Counseling, 13*(1), 2–10.

Chapter 28

Diagnosis and Treatment of Exhibitionism and Other Sexual Compulsive Disorders

by Carol J. Ball, Ph.D. and Theoharis K. Seghorn, Ph.D.

Overview

The classification of paraphilia according to the revised third edition of the *Diagnostic and Statistical Manual of Mental Disorders* (DSM-III-R; American Psychiatric Association, 1987) includes a wide variety of disorders whose primary commonality is a superficial association to sexuality. This leads to two mistaken conclusions about etiology, dynamics, and treatment. Recently, professionals working with offenders have concentrated their efforts on the development of effective treatment for other sex offenders (e.g., sexual abusers of children). This chapter discusses diagnostic issues that differentiate exhibitionism and similar sexually compulsive disorders from other paraphilias and presents a comprehensive behavioral treatment approach that stresses the role of such paraphilias as maladaptive attempts at regulation of anxiety and/or depression.

Introduction

For the sake of descriptive convenience, paraphilias are classified in DSM-III-R (American Psychiatric Association, 1987, p. 279) as sexual disorders, along with disturbances of sexual desire, arousal, and sexual dysfunction. Paraphilias are characterized by "an arousal in response to sexual objects or situations that are not part of normative arousal-activity patterns and that in varying degrees may interfere with the capacity for reciprocal, affectionate sexual activity" (American Psychiatric Association, 1987). Although this classification seems logical and conceptually consistent, it may lead to the erroneous conclusion that paraphilic disorders (which include pedophilia, exhibitionism, voyeurism, transvestitism, frotteurism, and sexual sadism, among others) are indeed disturbances of sexual functioning. This erroneous conclusion has led to much confusion about appropriate treatment.

Furthermore, to understand these seemingly senseless, and often bizarre behaviors, we must give up our focus on the meaning of this behavior—understanding the underlying symbolism may be an interesting intellectual exercise, but even if such connections were valid, that insight is not likely to provide a method to help bring about a decrease in the client's inappropriate behavior.

More important, we must ask ourselves, "What function does this behavior serve in the client's life?" Although the obvious answer would appear to be "But of course, it's sexual gratification," the overwhelming majority of such paraphiliacs do not masturbate to orgasm during the deviant behavior, but, rather, they report a sense of "relief" or an intense "rush" upon completion of the behavior. Indeed, often such offenders report that it is engaging in the deviant ritual itself that produces the pleasure, not the orgasm. The function of the behavior appears to serve either to reduce anxiety or to be used as a self-soothing mechanism—temporary relief from the emptiness, loneliness, or other anomic feelings associated with a low-level chronic depression.

Early Attempts at Understanding Paraphilias

Psychoanalytic theorists were among the first to study "sexual perversions" (paraphilic behavior). Freud, for example, theorized that a complex interaction of ego defense mechanisms of "fixation" and "repression" produced paraphilias (Guttmacher, 1951). Even Freud was puzzled about the etiology of the perversions. Freud (1905/1953) concluded that "the unsatisfactory conclusion however that emerges from these investigations of the disturbances of sexual life is that we know far too little concerning the biological processes constituting the essence of sexuality to be able to construct from out fragmentary information, a theory adequate to the understanding of normal and pathological conditions" (p. 243). Writing directly about exhibitionism, Freud posited that this paraphilia was strongly dependent on the "castration complex," and that by exhibiting himself to the female, the male invited her to exhibit her genitals and then experienced the infantile satisfaction that the female has no penis (Jones, 1953). In his footnote relating to a discussion of exhibitionism, Freud (1905/1953) acknowledged, however, that "analysis reveals that this perversion, just as most others has a surprising variety of motives and determinants" (p. 157).

Krafft-Ebing (1912) categorized exhibitionists into two general groups: (1) those in whom exposure is a symptom of a recognized mental illness leading to a general behavioral deterioration, and (2) those in whom exposure arises out of an impulsive-compulsive drive (Mohr, Turner, Jerry, 1964). Other researchers followed Krafft-Ebing's thinking and delineated similar classifications systems (e.g. Ellis, 1933; Hirschfeld, 1948).

Karpman (1926) studied extensively the psychopathology of exhibitionism and observed that the disorder was consistently seen in persons who had compulsive personality characteristics. Rickles (1950) concurred with this hypothesis, emphasizing that the exhibitionist be regarded as "neurotic rather than depraved" (p. 87) and concluded that the "exhibitionist is a compulsive neurotic by all accepted definitions" (p. 88). Mohr et al. (1964), in their study of fifty-four exhibitionists, examined more than twenty characteristics, including age of onset of deviant behavior, country of birth, religion, relationship with parents, birth order, and marital status but were not able to reach any conclusions about the etiology of such disorders.

The Addiction Model

In recent years an addiction model that was originally applied to alcoholism and drug addiction has shown some currency in the popular literature. Originally, addiction was narrowly defined as a physiological dependence on a foreign substance, typically a drug or alcohol, that had both physiological and emotional components. More recently, a range of other maladaptive behaviors has been classified as "addictions" on the basis of having common characteristics. These maladaptive behaviors involve some repetitive form of indulgence for short-term pleasure or satisfaction at the expense of longer-term adverse effects (Miller, 1980).

Carnes (1983), who first proposed that paraphilic behavior was another form of addiction, drew a parallel between his definition of alcoholism or drug dependency as a "pathological relationship with a mood-altering chemical" (p. 4) and the paraphilic patient's relationship with a mood-altering "experience." Like Miller (1980), Carnes (1983) suggested that people get caught up in an "addictive system" that starts with a belief system of faulty assumptions, myths, and values and results in "delusional" thought processes that insulate the addiction cycle from reality. This addiction cycle consists of four phases: (1) preoccupation, (2) ritualization, (3) sexual compulsivity, and (4) despair. Carnes also proposed that other self-destructive behaviors, such as shoplifting, gambling, spending, and overwork, are also part of this addiction system.

Carnes (1991) reported survey data on 289 sex addicts who had had at least three years of recovery. This sample was predominately male (82%), white (93%), and professional (63%). The survey simply asked respondents to indicate the frequency of certain sexual activities or the prevalence of certain attitudes about sex. For example, one item asked, " Do you spend time fantasizing about past or future sexual experiences?" (p. 416). Ninety percent of the males responding endorsed this item.

Perhaps because of its face validity and the existence of an intervention model (in the form of Alcoholics Anonymous and its offshoots), the sexual addiction model received wide acceptance, and currently there are numerous self-help programs modeled after the Twelve Steps of Alcoholics Anonymous across the United States and Canada. However, there is a dearth of empirical research to support the efficacy of the addiction model for explaining paraphilic behavior.

Obsessive-Compulsive and Related Anxiety Disorders

DSM-III-R defines the obsessive-compulsive disorder (OCD) as "recurrent obsessions or compulsions sufficiently severe to cause marked distress, be time consuming or significantly interfere with the person's normal routine, occupational functioning, or usual social activities or relationship with others" (p. 245). OCD is included under the general classification of anxiety disorders because the obsessions and resulting compulsions are understood to function to neutralize or prevent discomfort by discharging tension. In a typical OCD case, the course of the condition begins with obsessions (e.g. persistent ideas, thoughts, impulses, or images) that are experienced, at least initially, as intrusive or senseless.

These obsessions are highly anxiety provoking, and it is only through the compulsive behaviors that the obsessive thinking is counteracted and temporarily relieved. For example, a patient with developing OCD may initially experience worries about contracting a fatal illness and develop a heightened awareness to situations in which he or she might be exposed to a contagious disease. As these thoughts become more frequent, the individual experiences an increasing fear of places or objects where he or she might come in contact with germs. As the thoughts become increasingly more intrusive the degree of anxiety escalates. In attempt to reduce the anxiety, the individual seeks methods of eliminating contaminants. It is in this fashion that, for example, hand washing becomes adopted as a method of reducing the potential for contamination but, more important, as a means of temporarily reducing the anxiety. The course of the syndrome is such that the remedy provides only a transient solution (i.e., short-lived reduction in anxiety). The irrational fears are not eliminated and the problem escalates. Fear and thoughts of contamination lead to more intense obsessions and ever increasing anxiety. Thus, the obsessive-compulsive cycle is established.

Sexual Compulsive Disorder as a Variant of OCD

Several writer have noted the similarities between paraphilias—and nonparaphilic sexual addictions—and obsessive-compulsive disorders. Coleman (1990, 1992) defined compulsive sexual behavior as behavior driven by anxiety-reduction mechanisms rather than sexual desire and supported the theory that sexual compulsive disorder (SCD) is a variant of OCD. This idea is further strengthened by the findings reported by Marshall et al. (1991) that exhibitionists do not have deviant sexual arousal. Jenike (1989) and Pearson (1990) concurred with Coleman in stating that the most compelling theory is that compulsive sexual behavior is a symptom of an underlying OCD in which the anxiety-driven behavior happens to be sexual in nature. In an attempt to clarify the relationship between paraphilias, sexual addictions, and OCD a group of researchers (Stein et al., 1992) conducted a retrospective review of thirteen patients with paraphilias, sexual addictions, or sexual obsessions who were treated with serotonin reuptake blockers, clomiprimine, fluoxetine, or fluvoxamine. The paraphilic patients had no improvement in their sexually compulsive symptoms but did show some improvement in their OCD symptoms, whereas the nonparaphilic sexual addiction patients showed mixed results with improvement in symptoms in two of the five patients in this group. In the small sample of patients with sexual obsessions and compulsions, only two of three showed improvement in both OCD symptoms and sexual obsessions and compulsions. The authors of this study suggested that although serotonin reuptake blockers may be effective, additional medications as well as psychotherapy may be necessary for a therapeutic effect.

However, Kafka (1991; Kafka & Prentky, 1992), following a treatment protocol found to have some efficacy in the treatment of other obsessional disorders, treated twenty male nonparaphilic sexually addicted patients with fluoxetine and found significant response to the medication, with a decrease in sexually compulsive behaviors. Kafka (1991), however, suggested that compulsive sexual behavior is best understood as a drive dysregulation syndrome found in association with a primary mood disorder and that affective spectrum disorders may be broader in scope and may include obsessive-compulsive disorders as well as eating disorders. Other case reports (Cesnik & Coleman, 1989; Kashkin, 1990) have also found evidence for sex offenders' positive response to serotonergic antidepressant pharmacotherapy.

Work continues toward further understanding the underlying neurocortical substrate for both obsessive and sexually compulsive behaviors. Coleman (1990) speculated that abnormalities in the basal ganglia and/or prefrontal cortex may underlie such behaviors. Money (1981) reported that a reduction in serum testosterone levels through the use of antiandrogens also can reduce paraphilic fantasies and result in an improvement of impulse control . The relationship between neurophysiology and neurochemistry of sexuality is still unknown, but sex drives and impulse control are most certainly not direct correlates of sex hormone levels alone (Gorzalka, Mendelson, & Watson, 1990). It is possible that increased understanding of the relationship between neuroendocrinology and neurotransmitters, such as serotonin, may give us new insights into the complexity of these paraphilic and nonparaphilic disorders.

Jenike et al. (1990), in summarizing recent research in the area, noted that a number of brain studies pointed to a neurological basis for OCD, and they postulated that SCD and various eating disorders, addictive gambling, and body dysmorphic syndrome may be related to OCD as well. Pearson (1990) supported this view. She described paraphilias as having as an essential feature, recurrent and persistent fantasies about deviant sex with a sense of mounting tension prior to committing the act. Although there may be some gratification or sexual release at the time, guilt and remorse often immediately follow.

Behavioral Research

With the continued development of behavior theory and therapy, deviant sexual behavior became an area of interest to behaviorists. Serber and Wolpe (1961), in presenting several case studies of successful treatment of various paraphilias using counterconditioning techniques, postulated that such behaviors were caused by an internal anxiety state. According to Serber and Wolpe, however, some deviant behavior is not anteceded by anxiety but is a learned response that is triggered by specific external stimuli. In discussing one of their cases, they suggested that an urge to fondle a woman's breast, for example, if not accompanied by overt sexual arousal, could be simply a learned response that could quickly respond to counterconditioning treatment methods.

Kurt Freund (1983), a pioneer in researching sex offenses and their treatment, hypothesized that voyeurism, exhibitionism, and obscene telephone calling were all distorted aspects of what he believed to be four normal phases of human male courtship behavior: (1) location and initial appraisal of a potential partner; (2) pretactile interaction, such as smiling at or talking to a prospective partner; (3) tactile interaction; and (4) effecting genital union. Freund's studies of 950 males found that multiple sexual anomalies were often found in the same individual, leading him to posit the existence of a discrete syndrome that he labeled courtship disorder (Freund & Blanchard, 1986). In a later study, Freund (1987) compared men who engaged in exhibitionism, voyeurism, obscene phone calling, or frotteurism with rapists and normal controls to determine their phallometric responses to various erotic stimuli. His results indicated that courtship disorder is related to an abnormally strong agonistic component in sexual interaction.

Other researchers have suggested that exhibitionism and other related paraphilias are part of a narcissistic personality disorder. Langevin et al. (1979) found that the need for admiration was a primary motivation of exhibitionists. Langevin and his colleagues (Lang, Langevin, Checkley, & Pugh, 1987) compared thirty-four male exhibitionists and twenty nonviolent non-sex offender controls on measures of gender identity and sexual and criminal history. They found that although 41% of their exhibitionist group also engaged in transvestitism, their gender identity was nonetheless masculine. However, frequency of exhibiting was not correlated with desire for consequent intercourse with the victim. Nearly all exhibitionists hoped the unsuspecting female victim would enjoy the experience, and more than half indicated that they would have dated the victim if she had responded favorably or otherwise showed interest. According to the authors (Lang et al., 1981), these findings supported the conclusion that narcissism, rather than courtship disorder, was associated with exhibitionist behavior.

In another recent study, Marshall, Payne, Barbaree, and Eccles (1991) assessed the sexual preferences of forty-four male exhibitionists and twenty matched nonoffender control subjects. Erectile responses of both groups were measured as they listened to six audiotaped descriptions of sexual activities—three audiotapes described mutually consenting sexual activities between an adult male and an adult female and three others described an adult male exposing his penis to an unwilling adult female. They found that exhibitionists have higher arousal to descriptions of exhibiting than do normal men but that both groups have significantly higher arousal to scenes of consenting sex. Only 13.6% of the exhibitionists had scores that classified them as deviants in need of treatment for the deviant arousal patterns. Marshall et al. (1991) concluded that reduction of deviant sexual arousal would not likely be a significant factor in the treatment of exhibitionists. However Maletzky (1991) in his study of 770 exhibitionists did find significant deviant arousal (68%) in the group of exhibitionists.

How a Paraphilia Develops

The basic principle of operant learning theory is that if a behavior (response) is followed by a positive event (reinforcement), that behavior is likely to occur again—

and if further reinforcement again occurs, the behavior will become overlearned and habituated. For instance, autoerotic stimulation of the genitals is a pleasurable activity and is a part of the normal repertoire of behaviors of many young children. The behavior is pleasurable and the pleasure serves as a positive reinforcer of the behavior. A young boy who is unhappy in a dysfunctional family where parents are abusive or neglectful finds that masturbation is calming and soothing. Thus an otherwise normal sexual behavior is used as a coping strategy—to manage the anxiety, pain, or sadness—rather than only for its pleasurable physical sensation. The young boy learns to gain relief from anxiety (or depression) by this physical stimulation. Rather than turning to other people for nurturance, or learning more appropriate ways to deal with his stressful environment, such as verbalizing his feelings and using cognitive means to resolve the stress, the boy withdraws further into his one way of self-soothing. Of course, in abusive homes, talking about feelings may actually elicit more anger or abuse from the abusing parent, making the choice to use means such as rational discussion even more probable, and it also increases the likelihood of the boy's being seduced into a sexual relationship by a pedophile. As the young boy matures, he may continue to use masturbation as a stress (anxiety or depression) reliever and may enhance his sexual thoughts with pornography. If, perhaps through happenstance, he finds violent, aggressive sexually explicit materials, he may, through repeatedly reinforced fantasies about these themes, increase his attraction to thoughts of aggression, and these aggressive fantasies ultimately may lead to assaultive behaviors.

Or, instead of developing an interest in aggressive themes, the boy may continue to use masturbation to cope with negative feelings and stress. Years later, perhaps after a disagreement with his employer, he experiences the "urge" to masturbate while driving home from work, and while engaged in this, by chance a woman in the adjacent automobile notices him. The man may distortedly interpret her glance as a sign of approval. ("I really believe the women enjoyed watching"). Now there is a secondary reinforcer, social approval. This perceived approval, enhanced by his own masturbatory fantasies is an even stronger secondary reinforcer, with the result that masturbating while driving is reinforced, and the chain of behavior continues to develop.

Diagnosing Sexual Compulsive Disorders

The Clinical Interview. SCD can be defined as a history of one or more inappropriate, self-destructive, or self-defeating sexual behaviors that the client has unsuccessfully tried to control. Persons suffering from SCD may be involved with the criminal justice system if their behavior has violated laws. But he or she may also be self-referred (precipitated by the realization of the often high-risk nature of many sexually compulsive behaviors) or as the result of the impact of the disorder on family relationships or career. Whatever the point of entry, it is important to provide a psychologically safe environment in which clients can explore their sexually compulsive behavior disorder—frequently the client has never been able to confide in any other person about the extent of his disorder. The client may initially appear defensive, but often this is the result of intense underlying feelings of shame and guilt that almost always accompany such behaviors.

To determine the extent and intensity of the SCD it is important to do a sensitive, in-depth clinical history that focuses both on the range of sexually deviant acts and the frequency and intensity of the client's involvement with them. For instance, it is not unusual for the pattern to have its roots early in preadolescence, as the young boy finds adult pornography or, in his yearning for tactile closeness, discovers his mother's or sister's lingerie, with touching sometimes leading to actual wearing of the undergarments. As the young boy enters adolescence, he may discover that he he becomes aroused by voyeurism, or exhibitionism. In one instance, a boy, in a family in which the father was sadistic toward his youngest son, discovered that he became excited by being nude in his backyard. This behavior soon escalated. As he searched for excitement to help him escape from feelings of anger and despair, he started to venture out into his neighborhood late at night, to see if he could run around the block while naked, and avoid being caught.

The family histories of SCD clients are typically dysfunctional. The father is frequently emotionally, if not physically, absent. This dynamic often results in a greater risk of being sexually victimized by an adult male, or by an older peer. Sometimes the client can recall incidents in which he was sexualized by siblings. For instance, one exhibitionist was sexually abused by an older brother, and another client, a transvestite, recalled enjoying the attention of older sisters who would dress him in girls' clothing as part of their play. Still another client with a complex fetish involving women's hair had a vivid early memory of his sister's long hair brushing his face as she leaned over his bed.

During adolescence there is often an escalation of sexual acting out by making obscene phone calls and engaging in episodes of indecent assault and battery (e.g., running up behind females and touching their breasts or genitals) and voyeurism. Treatment providers should also question clients about sexual experimentation with pets, and although it is difficult for clients to speak about, their ability to confide in the therapist often significantly lifts their guilt, as does the ability to speak of sexual involvement with children.

Although there may be a subsidence of such feelings as the client enters adulthood, as the stresses of adulthood—career, marriage, family—build, the feelings and urges reappear, often with renewed intensity and urgency. This resurgence of symptoms may be accompanied by a number of feelings that are not normally associated with sexual acting out. The clinician should inquire about feelings of boredom and restlessness or a need for excitement, all potential signs of an underlying depression. Clients may also acknowledge that they never feel truly happy, that they are usually disappointed with life, and that they always feel that something is missing from their life.

On the other hand, the client may exhibit signs of OCD: He may be a perfectionist, a workaholic, and have an excessively high need to achieve. Such patients tend to be self-critical, rigid, and moralistic. Such clients present a restriction of the range of feeling, with anger being the most predominant emotional response.

Use of Psychological Testing. Various psychological and sexual tests can play a useful role in treatment planning. The New England SCD Scale (adapted from the Yale-Brown Obsessive Compulsive Disorder Scale and reprinted in Prentky and Edmunds, 1997) is useful in evaluating the intensity of sexual obsessions and compulsions and the short-term strength of behavioral control over acting-out urges. The Millon Multiaxial Clinical Inventory (MCMI-III; Millon, 1994) is useful in screening for underlying major mental illness, and the presence of dysthymic or obsessional problems. The results of these two instruments, combined with the interview data, are the basis for the strength of the recommendation that the client be referred for psychopharmacological consultation and possible adjunctive psychopharmacological management.

If the deviant behavior involves exhibitionism or frotteurism, it is important that the client undergo a penile plethysmograph assessment as part of the intake process. This assessment uses standardized, auditory stimulus materials from the Association for the Treatment of Sexual Abusers (ATSA). Using age-appropriate, mutual, and consenting sex with a peer as a baseline, it is important to include scenarios of exhibitionism to children as well as to adults. Given some of the offense spillover observed in sexually compulsive clients, it is wise to include at least some stimulus scenarios describing sexual assaults on adult women and sexual abuse of children to rule out deviant arousal by such behaviors. Currently, we also are using the Abel Screening Assessment as part of the assessment process, to cross-validate this promising new procedure with the penile plethysmograph assessment process.

Treatment

Behavior Therapy. A similar treatment protocol is used with many sexually compulsive behaviors including the compulsive use of pornography, sexual promiscuity with prostitutes, transvestitism, and sex offenses, such as exhibitionism, voyeurism, and rape. This section focuses specifically on exhibitionism but can be adapted for other problem behaviors as well. For the more compulsive clients, behavior therapy (in combination with medications) is a necessary precursor to other treatment modalities to stabilize the patient in order to minimize the risk of relapse until more stable controls are established and internalized.

The course of aversive behavior therapy involves approximately twenty weeks of individual sessions. This treatment can be carried out in a group setting, but we prefer to meet individually with the client, as it provides us with the opportunity to know the client in greater depth and to develop a strong therapeutic alliance with him. The first few sessions are spent in history taking and in gathering specific details about the client's pattern of acting out. At this point, if the client is struggling to maintain control of his deviant impulses, he is referred for psychopharmacological consultation.

The weekly, fifty-minute sessions focus on educating the client about the concepts of cognitive behavior therapy—especially about the connection between thoughts and feelings and their effect on behavior. It is important that the client understand the rationale for these procedures so that he can gain confidence about their effectiveness in helping him control his compulsive behavior. The client is instructed to keep daily frequency counts of total sexual experiences, including inappropriate sexual thoughts (thoughts about engaging in the deviant behavior), deviant urges (defined as something stronger than a simple thought, e.g., driving aimlessly around looking for a victim), frequency of masturbation, and frequency of appropriate sexual activity. This log is the client's weekly homework assignment and continues throughout the aversive behavior therapy. In addition to maintaining the frequency count, we assign additional reading and homework. We find that the Bays-Longo (1989) book is useful with outpatients to provide a further introduction to relapse prevention.

Ammonia aversion (Abel, 1990) is introduced during the fourth or fifth session. The most current treatment protocol is adapted from Abel, but with several modifications. As noted previously, exhibitionists, voyeurs, obscene phone callers, and other compulsively disordered men generally do not have deviant sexual arousal; that is, they are not aroused by children or by aggressive stimuli. They generally do demonstrate some inappropriate arousal to scenes describing exhibitionistic, voyeuristic behaviors. Therefore, presentation of the aversive stimulus is paired with either the thought or urge to engage in the inappropriate behavior rather than with the sight of the victim or with the deviant act itself (Cautela, 1985).

The client is first instructed to compose several typical scenarios describing his deviant behavior, beginning with the antecedents to the acting out (e.g. "I'm driving home from work . . . feeling angry and frustrated because the boss criticized my work . . ."). The scenario must be detailed and specific, and it must include the client's thoughts and feelings and corresponding behaviors that lead up to the deviant act. The scripts should be written in the first-person, present tense, as though the feelings and behavior are actually occurring at that moment. The script stops just prior to the client's engaging in the deviant act. We avoid allowing the client to describe the deviant act itself because in our experience this can be overstimulating and actually can become reinforcing to the client.

The client is then instructed to relax and allow himself to fantasize the scene while speaking the scenario into a tape recorder. At any point in the scene, if the client begins to experience arousal, he is instructed to interrupt the scene and break and inhale the ammonia capsule. If he does not experience arousal during the exercise, he completes reciting the scenario into the tape recorder up to the point in the fantasy where he is about to engage in the deviant behavior. At that point, he stops, breaks the capsule, and inhales the noxious odor. Continuing to record, he then reaffirms his desire to give up the behavior ("I am doing this homework to give up my urges to expose myself" (make obscene phone calls, look in windows, etc.).

Homework requires daily recording of three such deviant scenarios (using a variation of the deviant behavior in each scene). However, the basic script is not altered. Simple boredom is likely to be a secondary treatment effect, which increases the effectiveness of this procedure. Over the course of approximately twenty weeks, these scenes are gradually shortened, moving backward along the behavioral chain to earlier links in the deviant behavior chain and ending with the very first thought or impulse to engage in the behavior. This first link may actually occur several days before the client engages in the behavior—some time during the earliest planning stage. For example, the script might now read: "I am going on a business trip and will have some free time on Friday afternoon. I can cruise around looking for women to expose myself to."

Each week, along with his log, the client is required to bring in his taped record of seven days' homework to the session. The therapist listens to segments of the recording, checking for compliance with the homework and for cognitive distortions and exploring and refining new offense scenario links that are uncovered as the client repeatedly relives the deviant behavior. He is now instructed to keep a log rating the intensity of the aversive stimuli ("how painful was it") and the clarity of the image ("how real was the fantasy"). In addition to listening to the taped homework, the weekly session includes review of the client's sexual output log, specifically focusing on details of any inappropriate thought, urges, or behaviors and educating the client about antecedents to these occurrences. Specific note is made of any increase or decrease in the frequency of the inappropriate thoughts or feelings. Written homework from assigned readings is also discussed. If the client's deviant thoughts and urges appear to be increasing, a concrete and detailed safety plan is put in place, and the client and therapist work to understand the environmental stressors that may be causing the increase.

In later stages of the individual behavior therapy, the client is instructed to begin carrying the ammonia capsules with him at all times. He is instructed to use the ammonia at any point at which he is in a high-risk situation and finds that he is having a deviant thought. This assignment is more effective if it comes later in the course of behavior therapy as the client is not likely to use the ammonia at all in the early stages of treatment if he finds himself in a risky situation because the impulse to engage in the behavior is generally too strong to respond to any intervention.

Ongoing Offender Group Treatment. Once the client has the behavior under some control, he is ready to move to the next phase of treatment—relapse prevention group therapy. The timing of when the client begins group varies with the individual, based on his clinical needs, his having reached some (but not necessarily total) stability in being able to control his acting out, and the availability of a group placement. Often there is a several-weeks overlap of both group and behavior therapy. Ultimately, however, the behavior therapy sessions are gradually faded out, and the group therapy becomes the primary treatment modality.

Group treatment serves multiple purposes, and combines principles of relapse prevention with more classical, insight-oriented group work. Group also becomes a major support system as the client struggles with slips and relapses in his move toward stable control over acting out. As urges are dealt with in the group, each member revisits relapse prevention principles, again confronts his own cognitive distortions, and finds acceptance and support, along with confrontation, from his group. Groups vary in the degree of structure they require, and in some groups work may be facilitated by using reading and homework assignments from several workbooks that are available (Longo & Bays, 1988; Bays & Longo; 1989; Bays, Longo, & Hildebran, 1990; Schwartz & Canfield, 1996). Other groups respond better to a less structured approach. For several reasons, whenever possible we recommend that sexually compulsive clients not be placed in the same group as sexual abusers of children. First, there are few real similarities between the offenses of each and between the personality organizations of the offenders themselves. In most cases there are few similarities between the compulsive urges that exhibitionists struggle with and the chronic emotional and physical attraction of pedophiles to children.

Case Study 1: Peter

Peter is a 32-year-old married man who had an extensive history of making obscene telephone calls and exhibitionism. He is the third oldest child in a family of four with two older brothers and one younger sister. One older brother has been diagnosed as manic depressive and another brother is alcoholic. Peter's home life was filled with anxiety and tension, as Peter's father was domineering and threatening, although he only infrequently resorted to physically punishing his children.

Peter's acting out began at age 15 when he began making obscene phone calls.

Later, after reading a story about a woman who exposed herself to a neighbor to arouse him, Peter began duplicating this behavior to his neighbors. He was subsequently charged with exhibitionism, but the arrest did not deter him from continuing the deviant behavior. Ten years later, he was referred to us for treatment after his fourth arrest. He had been in two difference sex offender group treatment programs but had not received specialized behavior therapy or any pharmacological interventions.

The MCMI-III showed no evidence of major mental illness, but there was an elevation on the Dysthymia scale along with negativistic personality characteristics. Testing on the penile plethysmograph showed clear arousal to stories involving mutually consenting sexual contact with adult women, as well as to scenarios that described exposing to female adults. However, Peter did not show arousal to the more aggressive scenes depicting rape of an adult woman.

Peter completed six months of individual behavior therapy, usng ammonia aversion therapy. He kept a log of inappropriate thoughts and urges and times when he masturbated to thoughts of deviant behavior, as well as recording any relapses. Inappropriate thoughts and urges are defined as "any thoughts about exposing or making obscene phone calls" (as this was also reported as a prior deviant behavior). Appropriate thoughts and urges are defined as "thoughts about engaging in age appropriate, sexual contact with a consenting adult."

At intake, Peter was referred for medication and was prescribed Prozac, with the ultimate level of 60 mg. After the initial period of about four weeks to bring the dosage up to therapeutic levels, Peter reported a dramatic decrease in his inappropriate thoughts and urges, although the medication alone did not give him complete control. He relied on the behavior therapy, carrying the ammonia capsules with him and using them *in vivo*, any time he experienced the beginning signs of a relapse cycle, which for him was staring at women or thoughts about driving aimlessly to "check out" women.

Four months after Peter began treatment, he was assigned to an SCD group with other men who had similar problems with exhibitionism. Ideally, patients would begin both group and individual therapy simultaneously, but the practicalities of the financial burden of being in both modalities is managed by first helping the patient get the deviant behavior under control with the behavior therapy and then, when those individual meetings can be scheduled less frequently, assigning the patient to a group, which becomes the primary treatment modality. The focus here was on relapse prevention training, as well as on learning more adaptive ways to manage daily stress and improving communication skills. Peter is continuing in group therapy but has successfully completed the behavior therapy treatment. At one-year follow-up, Peter has had no relapses and reports that this is the longest period without acting out since the compulsive behavior began more than fifteen years ago.

Case Study 2: Jim

Jim is a 35-year-old married male who was referred for treatment subsequent to his arrest for making harassing phone calls. He was caught after he attempted to meet one of his victims (he had been making frequent calls to a local college dormitory, and the female students had been alerted to be on guard for these intrusive calls). Jim reported that he was not certain what he intended to do when he met this woman. She had invited him to meet as part of the entrapment plan. He indicated that his fantasy was that they would have consenting sex.

Jim's behavior was unique in that during these phone calls, he did not initially make lewd remarks but posed as a marketing research person collecting information about female sanitary products. His goal was to engage the unsuspecting female to disclose personal information about herself, particularly her habits around her menstrual cycle. He did not masturbate during these phone calls but used the information as material for his sexual fantasies at a later date.

Jim indicated that for the past five years he had been spending an increasing amount of time making phone calls from his office, thus neglecting his work duties. (He had a high-level position in the banking industry.) Jim also reported that he frequently went into women's bathrooms looking for discarded sanitary napkins which he would use in his masturbatory fantasies. The phone "surveys" were an extension of the initial fixation on sanitary products.

Jim is the second oldest of five children from a middle-class family. His family life was chaotic with frequent arguments resulting in Jim's father physical abusing Jim's mother and Jim and his siblings. Jim's mother tried to compensate for the abusive environment by protecting the children as best she could, but she was not able to stand up to her husband. Eventually, as Jim grew older, he became quite protective of his mother, and at one point, had a physical altercation with his father.

Jim received no sex education at home and learned about sex from his peers. He recalls that he began masturbating at age 12 or 13 while looking in the bathroom door at his mother and older sister. He developed a curiosity for their menstrual cycles, and after finding sanitary pads in the bathroom, he began masturbating with them. This fetishistic behavior continued off and on during his adult life, particularly during times when he felt sad or lonely. In high school, Jim began abusing marijuana. His marijuana use continued to the current time. He reported that he needed to get high to help him cope with the daily stresses in his life.

At age 13, Jim met his future wife, Sue. They developed an intense dating relationship and were married immediately on graduation from high school at age 18. The couple appeared to have a very dependent relationship on one another. Jim became quite demanding in his sexual needs, and although he never used physical force, he was quite manipulative in getting his wife to agree to sexual activity on a daily basis. Upon intake, the couple had been married for nineteen years and had three sons.

The MMCI-II showed a primary diagnosis on Axis I of dysthymia with elevations on anxiety and substance abuse. Axis II showed a personality configuration of compulsive and passive-aggressive personality features. Beck Depression Scale scores were also in the moderate to severe range of depression, and the Beck Anxiety Scale showed scores in the range of severe anxiety. Penile plethysmograph assessment was not done because there were no stimulus materials specific to the range of deviant behaviors.

Jim completed twenty-six weeks of individual behavior therapy, using ammonia aversion techniques as well as structured weekly homework and relapse prevention training. Because of Jim's serious mood disorder and his continued urges to engage in deviant compulsive behavior, Jim was immediately referred for a psychopharmacological consult to help him manage his mood disorder (both anxiety and depression) and his compulsive behavior. Over the course of a few weeks, Jim reached an optimal level of antidepressant medication (selective serotonin reuptake inhibitors), which also helped reduce his sexual urges. After four months of individual behavior therapy and when Jim was stabilized, as he had gone through several weeks of severe depression, including a suicide attempt, he then began sex offender group therapy with six others who also had sexual compulsive disorders.

At the end of six months after a period of gradually reducing the frequency of his ammonia aversion homework sessions, the behavior therapy was terminated. Jim continued in ninety-minute, weekly group therapy where he focused on relapse prevention, anger management, and communication skills to address his passive-aggressive communication style. Jim continued in weekly group therapy for approximately two years. During that time, although he had reports of deviant thoughts during times of stress, he had no reoccurrence of the deviant behavior that brought him into treatment. A three-year follow-up assessment shows no reoccurrence of his deviant behavior by his own self-report, and there has been no report of his being arrested for any such behavior. Jim has remained on antidepressant medication and stresses continue in his marriage. The couple are now currently in couples therapy.

Conclusion

Sex offender treatment has focused on developing a comprehensive approach to treating offenders and protecting society. This approach, demonstrated to have high success rates, emphasizes relapse prevention skills in the context of long-term group treatment. Our work indicates that this model, with some modification, has applicability to the treatment of other sex offenses and paraphilias that we subsume under the classification of SCD. In contrast to the disturbances in adult relationships that lead to the sexualization of children, for sexually compulsive men the behaviors are used as a means of regulating and discharging anxiety and/or depression. Such disorders respond best to a combination of behavioral techniques and psychopharmacological management of the underlying emotional states, to effect short term control over acting out while more long-term relapse prevention strategies can be consolidated and stabilized.

References

Abel, G. G., & Rouleau, J. L. (1990). Male sex offenders. In M. E. Thase, B. A. Edelstein, & M. Hersen (Eds.), *Handbook of outpatient treatment of adults* (pp. 271–290). New York: Plenum Press.

American Psychiatric Association. (1987). *Diagnostic and statistical manual of mental disorders* (rev. 3rd ed.). Washington, DC: Author.

Association for the Treatment of Sexual Abusers. (1993). *Auditory stimuli for penile plethysmograph.* Beaverton, OR: Author.

Bays, L., & Freeman-Longo, R. (1989). *Why did I do it again?* Brandon, VT: Safer Society Press.

Bays, L., & Freeman-Longo, R. (1990). *How can I stop?* Brandon, VT: Safer Society Press.

Carnes, P. (1991). *Don't call it love; recovery from sexual addiction.* New York: Bantam Books.

Carnes, P. (1983) Out of the shadows: Understanding sexual addiction. New York: Norton.

Cesnik, J., & Coleman, E. (1989). Use of lithium carbonate in the treatment of autoerotic asphyxia. *American Journal of Psychotherapy, 43,* 277–286.

Coleman, E. (1990). The obsessive-compulsive model for describing compulsive sexual behavior. *American Journal of Preventative Psychiatry and Neurology, 2,* 9–13.

Coleman, E. (1991). Compulsive sexual behavior: *New Concepts and Treatments. Journal of Psychology and Human Sexuality, 4*(2), 37–52.

Ellis, H. (1933). *Psychology of sex.* London: Heinemann.

Freeman-Longo, R., & Bays, L. (1988). *A guided workbook for clients in evaluation and beginning treatment.* Brandon, VT: Safer Society Press.

Freud, S. (1953). Three essays on the theory of sexuality. In J. Strachey (Ed. and Trans.), *The standard edition of the complete works of Sigmund Freud* (Vol. 7, pp. 225–243). London: Hogarth Press.

Freund, K. (1987). Courtship disorder: Is this hypothesis valid. *Annals of the New York Academy of Sciences, 528,* 172–182.

Freund, K., & Blanchard, R. (1989). Phallometric diagnosis of pedophilia. *Journal of Consulting and Clinical Psychology, 57*(1), 100–105.

Freund, K., Scher, H., & Hucker, S. (1983). The courtship disorders. *Archives of Sexual Behavior, 12,* 369–379.

Gorzalka, B., Mendelson, S., & Watson, N. (1990). Serotonin receptor subtypes and sexual behavior. *Annals of the New York Academy of Sciences, 600,* 435–446.

Guttmacher, M. (1951). *Sex offenses. The problem, causes and prevention.* New York: Norton.

Haag, A., Schorsch, E., Galedary, G., & Hauch, M. (1985) Sexual perversions as diagnostic clues. *Nervenarzt, 56*(7), 373–378.

Hirshfield, M. (1948). *Sexual anomalies and perversions.* London: Francis Alder.

Jenicke, M. (1989). Obsessive-compulsive and related disorders. *New England Journal of Medicine, 321,* 539–541.

Jenicke, M, Baer, L., & Minichiello, W. (1990). *Obsessive-compulsive disorders, theory and management.* Chicago: Year Book Medical Publishers.

Jones, E. (1953). *Sigmund Freud: Life and work.* London: Hogarth Press.

Kafka, M. (1991). Successful antidepressant treatment of nonparaphilic sexual addictions and paraphilias in men. *Journal of Clinical Psychiatry, 52,* 60–65.

Kafka, M., & Prentky, R. (1992). A comparative study of nonparaphilic sexual addictions and paraphilias in men. *Journal of Clinical Psychiatry, 53*(10), 345–349.

Karpman, B. (1926). The psychopathology of exhibitionism. *Psychoanalytic Review, 13,* 64–97.

Kashkin, K. (1990). *Sex offenders treated with flouxetine: Preliminary results.* Poster presentation at the annual meeting of the American Psychiatric Association. Washington, DC: American Psychiatric Association.

Krafft-Ebing, R. (1912). *Psychopathis sexualis* (12th ed.). New York: Rebman.

Lang, R., Langevin, R., Checkley, K., & Pugh, G. (1987). Genital exhibitionism: Courtship disorder or narcissism? *Canadian Journal of Behavioural Science, 19*(2), 216–232.

Langevin, R., Paitech, D., Ramsay, G., Anderson, C., Kamrad, J., Pope, S., Geller, G., Pearl, L., & Newman, S. (1979). Experimental studies of the etiology of genital exhibitionism. *Sexual Behavior, 8(*44), 307–331.

Maletzky, B. M. (1991). *Treating the sexual offender.* Newbury Park, CA: Sage.

Maletzky, B. M. (1994). Exhibitionism. In C. Last & M. Hersen (Eds.), *Adult behavior therapy handbook* (pp. 235–257). New York: Plenum Press.

Marshall, W. L., Payne, K., Barbaree, H. E., & Eccles, A. (1991). Exhibitionists: Sexual preferences for exposing. *Behavioral Research and Therapy, 29*(1), 37–40.

Miller, W. R. (Ed.). (1980). *The addictive behaviors.* Oxford, UK: Pergamon Press.

Millon, T. (1994). *Millon Clinical Multiaxial Inventory—III manual.* Minneapolis, MN: National Computer Systems.

Mohr, J., Turner, R., & Jerry, M. (1964). *Pedophilia and exhibitionism.* University of Toronto Press: Toronto, Canada.

Money, J. (1981). Paraphilia and abuse-martyrdom: Exhibitionism as a paradigm for reciprocal couple counseling combined with antiandrogen. *Journal of Sex and Marital Therapy, 7*(2), 115–123.

Pearson, H. (1990). Paraphilias, impulse control and serotonin. *Journal of Clinical Psychopharmacology, 10*(3), 233.

Plassman, R. (1987). Supportive treatment of exhibitionism: A psychoanalytic approach. *Psyche-Zeitschrift-fur-Psychoanalyse und ihre-Anwendungen, 41*(2), 140–147.

Prentky, R., & Edmunds, S. (Eds.). (1997). *Assessing sexual abuse: A resource guide for practitioners.* Brandon, VT: Safer Society Press.

Rapoport, J. (1989). The biology of obsessive-compulsive disorders. *Scientific American, 260,* 83–89.

Rickles, N. (1950). *Exhibitionism.* Philadelphia: J. B. Lippincott.

Schwartz, B. K., & Canfield, G. M. S. (1996). *Facing the shadow.* Kingston, NJ: Civic Research Institute.

Serber, M., & Wolpe, J. (1966). *Behavior therapy techniques.* New York: Pergamon Press.

Stein, D., Hollander, E., Anthony, D., Schneir, F., Fallon, B., Liebowitz, M., & Klein, D. (1992). Serotonergic medications for sexual obsessions, sexual addictions, and paraphilias. *Journal of Clinical Psychiatry, 53,* 267–271.

Chapter 29

Beyond the Cloister— Shamed Sexuality in the Formation of Sex- Offending Clergy

Donald R. Hands, Ph.D.

Overview

In recent years the public has been shocked by the revelation that dozens of highly respected clergymen have been accused of child molestation. When children are sexually assaulted by their pastor or priest, not only is their trust of adults undermined but their faith in their God may alsobe eroded. This chapter suggests that certain practices of religious institutions may contribute to the number of priests accused of this crime.

Introduction

It is an anomaly that male clergy, the spokesmen for a normative and influential sexual morality, are being arrested and convicted for sexual assaults. The media have had a field day over the past decade and a half, highlighting this quite tragic irony. Estimates are that since 1980, more than 600 cases of sexual assault by male clergy are in various stages of adjudication (Berry, 1992). The victims are mostly adolescent boys; the perpetrators mostly single males, many but by no means all from Roman Catholic seminaries. In 1995, twelve Episcopal priests were in the criminal justice system for assaults against adolescent boys (Rider, 1994). Estimates are that 2% of Catholic priests are sexually attracted to children and another 4% are sexually attracted to adolescents (Sipe, 1990). The former percentage mirrors the general population, whereas the latter is higher. The statistics refer to attraction, not to perpetration, and they imply a disorder but not a crime. Marshall (1997) estimates that every adjudicated case of child molesting costs society more than $200,000. Some Catholic dioceses have been brought to bankruptcy due to damage and legal costs. This chapter examines the seminary formation that may have contributed to this sex offending. It is the contention of this chapter that seminarians of the 1950s through the mid-1970s had their sexuality abused by teachings and practices that increased their vulnerability to *shame*, which arrested their psychosexual development.

The Dynamics of Shame

Recently a good deal of attention has been paid to *shame* as a concept with its own dynamic processes and effects on personality (Kaufman, 1985). Over roughly the same period as the reported cases of clergy sexual assault, an understanding of the role of shame in shaping human behavior has been developing. This understanding has come from both the mental health and the addiction fields. Shame is distinguishable from guilt: guilt is a healthy response to having broken a rule or made a mistake—one admits the error, learns from it, and gets back on track without undue self-condemnation. Shame, on the other hand, is an unhealthy response to breaking a rule or making a mistake. Instead of getting back on track the shamed person experiences a downward spiral of self-loathing and despair. He feels defective in his core—he *is* a mistake more than he *made* a mistake. In addictions language, it is the difference between a lapse or a slip and a relapse. Shame is magnified by a sense of failure to live up to unrealistic expectations that have become internalized and learned. The shamed person's internal reaction to having failed to live up to an expected rule of behavior is to fear the exposure of his violation and to hide or become secretive and nondisclosive. This fear of exposure further pulls him downward in a continuing and cumulative spiral of self-condemnation, which he then relieves by engaging in what the rules forbid, followed by more shame, and so on.

Unrealistic Moral Expectations Contribute to Shame

In general, nonoffending clergy are prone to the ill effects of shame due to the increased level of moral expectations that come with the role and their heightened visibility. However, many sex-offending clergy may have internalized unrealistic, moral self-expectations that have been learned in their seminary training. These formative years exposed them both to teachings and to ascetical (i.e., spiritually disciplining) practices that created a shame cycle, generating conflict over their sexuality, and arresting their psychosexual development.

From the 1950s to the mid-1970s seminaries were filled with eager, idealistic adolescents recruited by the Church or religious orders at a pubescent or adolescent age. Some entered residential seminaries far from home; others attended commuter seminaries and lived at home. Some made permanent vows of poverty, chastity, and obedience while still teenagers. These adolescents in seminaries were given teachings about human sexuality and were expected to perform certain practices.

Celibacy vs. Chastity

The seminarians knew before admission that the overiding expectation was that they would be required to live lives of promised *celibacy* or of vowed *chastity*. The meaning of these terms is important, not only for the context of seminary and later clergy life but also for resolving some of the cognitive distortions used by clergy sex offenders. Celibacy is an historic promise made to one's Bishop not only not to marry but not to engage in *any* sexual behavior whatsoever, including with oneself. Chastity is a similar promise, but it is a more solemn vow made to a religious order to commit oneself to it for life. Likewise, it means not only not to marry but not to engage in any sexual behavior at all. Knowing this vocabulary is important for attacking the cognitive distortion used by clergy offenders that the promise of celibacy (or Vow of Chastity) only forbids marriage and that their sexual assault of a pubescent boy did not violate their vow. The canons (or rules) of the Catholic Church make this wider definition clear, that it is abstinence, or "continence," from all sexual activity that is required: "Clerics are obliged to observe perfect and perpetual Continence for the sake of the Kingdom of Heaven and therefore are obliged to observe celibacy, which is a special gift of God, by which Sacred Ministers can adhere more easily to Christ with an undivided heart and can more freely dedicate themselves to the Service of God and Humankind" (Sipe, 1995, p. 15).

Celibacy or continence is a lofty spiritual ideal and one that demands a high degree of psychosexual maturity for its selection and achievement. Unfortunately, seminaries did not foster this level of maturity, nor are the vast majority of priests able to live it out (Sipe, 1990).

Separation Between Body and Soul

The official position of the Catholic Church though rejected by many in the Church today is that if consented to, "every sexual thought, word, desire, and action outside Marriage is mortally sinful. Every sexual act within marriage not open to conception is mortally sinful. Sexual misbehavior constitutes grave matter in every instance" (Sipe, 1995, p. 38).

This teaching has its origins in dualistic philosophies that regard the body as a source of corruption or sin and the soul as the goodly core of the person entrapped by the body. This teaching raised masturbation up as the sin *par excellence* and the thermometer of spiritual and moral development, growth, and, above all, the focal preoccupation of the church. The price of masturbation was eternal damnation. The remedy offered was willpower, prayer, and confession to a priest. Daily confession was an option. Besides the sense of shame engendered by engaging in masturbation itself, the adolescent seminarian had to ward off an additional sense of moral recrimination when he failed to succeed in abstaining from masturbation. He was a moral weakling as well as a degenerate.

Church Stresses Personal Sin, Not Criminal Behavior

Another focus in the seminary's moral teaching about sexuality had to do with an emphasis on personal sin, or personal moral failure. Sexual misconduct was a selfish act on the part of the perpetrator with harmful, eternal consequences. It jeopardized his soul. This personal-moral view contrasts with the criminal justice system's interest in the abuse of sexual power and control over another. This interest is in a violation of another's rights by the abuse of sexual power on the part of an offender against a victim. The lack of mutual consent is crucial to the State's interest in sex. The presence of personal consent is critical to the Church's interest in sin. Victimization by sexual abuse has not been the salient seminary point of view about sexual sins. Masturbation and fornication (sex outside of marriage) were emphasized, not rape or child molesting. This was in some respects a reasonable omission, as it would have been astounding to admit that such sexual assaults would be perpetrated by clergy. In fact, the Church's own rules and policies across denominations—particularly on how to terminate a clergyperson—had been formulated to protect the clergy from being taken unfair advantage of by members of the congregation. These rules were not intended to remedy situations in which a clergyperson violates the rights of another.

Mortification of the Flesh Prescribed

In addition to the sexually shaming teachings, certain supplemental practices were their logical extensions. These practices are outlined below. The first two are examples of the "mortification" of one's body for the sake of imposing a discipline for regulation. This term means the "making dead" or "killing" of the body's sexual desires.

- *Self-flagellation.* This was the practice of whipping oneself with a braided half-inch-thick rope, three feet long, over the shoulder onto the back. Flagellation was done during seasons of Penance (e.g., Lent). There was a rule against the shedding of blood or breaking the skin. The whipping was to last one to two minutes, as long as it took to recite a formal prayer or two. It was done privately within one's own room.
- *Wearing metal chain-belts.* These were linked, wire belts with sharp barbs which were worn during times of Penance, in the early morning, from rising until after breakfast, a total of about three hours. They were worn either around one's waist or around one's upper thigh. They were also private, as they were worn under one's clothing. Again, rules forbade the breaking of skin or drawing of blood. The apparent theory behind this mortification was that the self-infliction of physical pain would tame sexual desire.

Close Friendships Discouraged

There was a prohibition against what was termed "particular friendships." This meant a ban on having any best friends. These friendships were seen as dangerous emotional attachments that would lead to sexual activity. Late adolescent seminarians spent four or more years of their life without healthy, intimate interpersonal relationships. Added to this relationship ban was a more specific homophobic proscription against two seminarians ever being alone together, the "Never-Two Alone" rule. This thinking set up a pervasive, hypervigilant, and hypersuspicious mentality which imagined sexual activity whenever two people were alone in a room. Consequently, room visiting was banned. The unintended consequence of this hypervigilance over possible sexual activity was that the fear of sexual acts prevented the development of healthy and intimate human friendship between men. The consequences are still evident today in the major complaint and distress of priests: loneliness. Sullivan mentioned this consequence as one of the failures to integrate sexuality and intimacy.

Furthermore, these homophobic practices were in the social context of an all-male environment which was assured through the practice of cloister. This was the banning of females from the private, living, and sleeping quarters. Females were limited to large visiting rooms. At worship, they were segregated from the males by some visual obstruction and separate seating arrangements. Thus another interpersonal barrier was erected with the unintended consequence of preventing the development of friendship and intimacy between men and women, again at the cost of loneliness.

Unfortunately for the sex-offending priests who believed in these sexuophobic teachings and practices, sexuality became an intolerable burden and a source of shame. Their belief in these teachings and practices arrested their emotional and psychosexual development at the level it was when they first entered the seminary. The awareness and understanding of these teachings and practices are necessary for those who offer therapy to these sex-offending clergy.

Ways of Coping With Sexual Frustration

A seminarian's sexuality was either split off from awareness and integration or acted out inappropriately. The splitting off was done by the dynamic, defense mechanisms of repression or suppression. Repression occurs when the seminarian pretends that he is not a sexual human being at all and, as Sullivan says, regards the area of his body from the navel to his knees as a "not me" area which somehow does not even exist. Sullivan says that this results in a "primary genital phobia" wherein any sexual thoughts, feelings, and impulses are immediately and almost reflexively ignored. What dynamic theorists believe, however, is that what is repressed can easily become obsessed, as two case examples illustrate. Suppression occurs by the conscious application of willpower to the struggle against consenting to any sexual thought, feeling, or urge. This was the preferred mechanism taught in seminaries. Prayer, the ascetical practices mentioned earlier, and confession were the weapons employed in the battle against lust. Some seminaries withheld hot bathing water for the first several years, hoping that cold showers would ward off sexual desires.

When a seminarian found himself in a state of heightened sexual interest or arousal, and tempted to masturbate, he was to engage these evil thoughts head on, fight to conquer, and be victorious. No matter that these practices kept him focused on the sexual release until he usually gave in, felt humiliated and shameful, and took another turn down the spiral of self-hatred. Others coped with this phobic atmosphere by gratifying and compartmentalizing their sexual impulses. These men masturbated regularly and engaged in homosexual activity discreetly, however forbidden and inappropriate in the celibate setting. They had to split off and closet their private practices from the public world in which they appeared to be virtuous and celibate.

Sublimation: The Defense Mechanism of Choice

The hoped-for outcome of celibacy was sublimation. The seminarian was to use his celibacy to free him for the service of others, a form of channeling of sexual energy into ministry. But in an atmosphere of repression and suppression, with the many sexual phobias and prohibitions, without positive models and instruction in the ways of integrating sexuality with healthy interpersonal relationships—where even healthy interpersonal relationships with other men or women were prevented—it was practically impossible to accomplish. This has left a generation of priests lonely and alienated, with many defections, and has resulted in the recent pattern of split-off, unintegrated, arrested sexual offending against minors.

Ephebophilia: Paraphilia or Sexual Disorder

As mentioned, celibate priests in the Catholic Church and single priests in the Episcopal Church are overrepresented in the ranks of those who offend against adolescent boys from the general population statistics (Sipe, 1995). *Ephebophilia* is an unofficial diagnostic label which many clergy offenders are given by Church hospitals or treatment centers. It is used as a subset of *sexual disorder*, which does not imply assault of a victim. Etymologically it means the love for a young male; clinically it means sexual attraction to postpubescent males. It is contrasted with *pedophilia*, which is officially defined as a *paraphilia* whose victim's upper age limit was set at pubescence and which implies a sexual assault against a non-onsenting victim. This label, ephebophilia, protects the clergy sex offender by implying that there was no sexual assault, only a personal sexual disorder. It misses the point that an assault occurred against an adolescent victim who was not able to give consent, a misuse of power and control.

Priests may not use physical force, but they do groom their victims with charm, gifts, and manipulation. This unofficial label further plays into the cognitive distortions used by priest offenders that the sex with a boy is mutual. It unfortunately gives an overoptimistic picture to Church leaders about low recidivism risk and even the possibility of reemploying priest offenders. The term does not appear and is not recognized by the official manual of psychiatric mental disorders: the American Psychiatric Association's fourth edition of *Diagnostic and Statistical Manual of Mental Disorders* (American Psychiatric Association, 1994). It is not so much the age of the victim that counts in assessing the risk potential of reoffending as much as the compulsivity; and having boy victims raises the risk more than having girl victims. This misuse of diagnosis has also contributed to a premature "flight into health" attitude on the part of clergy sex offenders who use it to continue minimization and denial processes.

Several case examples of clergy I have treated come to mind as victims of a seminary formation that did not promote psychological or psychosexual health or integration.

Case Study 1

The first case exemplifies arrest in psychosexual development and the sudden onset of sexual obsession following years of repression. The man was a 51-year-old vowed religious priest who had been teaching in a coeducational high school for twenty-five years. His seminary had the ban on "particular friendship," the cloister boundary, and the use of the whip. He wrote sexually explicit letters to a 14-year-old female student. He was removed from his teaching duties and sent for treatment. He had repressed and suppressed his sexuality for most of his adult life but found some release in periodic, ego-dystonic masturbation. He found himself obsessively preoccupied with this girl whom he sexually fantasized. He had never dated and entered a seminary when he was only 16 years old. He was retired from teaching and caused considerable damage to his school and religious community's reputation. No legal actions were taken. He was not charged with child enticement. He did well in treatment and realized that he was impoverished in terms of interpersonal relationships. He had colleagues but no friends. He understood his letters as a bizarre repression of a sexuality which was arrested at the age he entered the seminary. He reframed his entrance into his religious community as a search for the family he felt he never had at home. He was reassigned to a nursing home. A few years after his residential treatment and with the help of an outpatient therapist, he decided to leave his religious community and was dating an age-appropriate woman.

Case Study 2

The next case demonstrates an arrested psychosexual development, a confusion as to sexual orientation, and a diagnosis of ephebophilia. This is a priest whom I treated in a prison-based sex offender program. He is a 55-year-old celibate Catholic priest who was convicted of child enticement and second-degree sexual assault. He groomed a 14-year-old fatherless boy and lured him to a distant hotel. He then gave the boy alcohol during dinner and had him change into a bathing suit so he could take photographs. They then went swimming in the hotel pool, and he embraced the boy and started to fondle the boy's genitals. The boy was frightened and told the manager who called the police. The priest was dismissed from the priesthood and given a six-year prison sentence. He did well in treatment and clarified many of his cognitive distortions about the "mutuality" of this sexual activity. He had entered a residential seminary after high school and had experienced the teachings and practices outlined previously. He tried to both repress and suppress his sexuality. He became chronically lonely and isolated even though he performed his duties well and was well regarded. He turned to alcohol in his forties for relief of loneliness and abused it on and off. He had one fumbling and embarrasing heterosexual experience at age 16. He remains confused as to his basic sexual orientation and preference. He can be sexually aroused by both men and women. He realized that he psychologically distorted his relationship with the victim, making himself believe he was acting in a paternal manner. He was released from prison and is now exploring the world of sexual relationships with adults. Prior to incarceration he was treated in a Church-related center and told with congratulations from his therapist that he was not a pedophile and that he might be able to be reemployed in ministry.

Conclusion

The seminary teachings and practices outlined here may well have had the unintended effect of shaming and hiding these two offending priests' sexuality. These individuals may have tried to control their normal sexual urges by the use of the disciplines and mechanisms that kept them focused on an adolescent struggle against masturbation. This paralyzed them at an adolescent level of psychosexual development. When they entered midlife, they began to act out delayed sexual urges. Unfortunately, they acted out sexually by assaulting boys of the same age that they had been when they surrendered their sexuality at the seminary gates.

There are many reasons why members of the clergy become sex offenders. Some enter the ministry as fully developed pedophiles who see this career as providing easy access to children. However, institutions shoud look at practices that foster maladaptive sexual adjustments.

References

American Psychiatric Association. (1994). *Diagnostic and statistical manual of mental disorders* (4th ed.). Washington, DC: Author.

Berry, J. (1992). *Lead us not into temptation: Catholic priests and the sexual abuse of children*. New York: Doubleday.

Kaufman, G. (1985). *Shame: The power of caring*. Cambridge, MA: Schenkman Books.

Marshall, W. L. (1997, June 20). *Treating sex offenders*. Presentation to the Wisconsin Sex Offender Treatment Network, Madison, WI.

Rider, D. M. (1994). *Overview of sexual boundaries in ministry: Ethical, clinical and liability considerations*. New York: Episcopal Church Pension Fund.

Sipe, A. W. R. (1990). *A secret world: Sexuality and the search for celibacy*. New York: Brunner/Mazel.

Sipe, A. W. R. (1995). *Sex, priests, and power. Anatomy of a crisis*. New York: Brunner/Mazel.

Sullivan, H. S. (1953). *The interpersonal theory of psychiatry*. New York: Norton.

Part 6

Different Views on Denial

Denial is a key concept in working with sex offenders. Usually the professional working with these individuals associates denial with the initial response of almost all sex offenders when confronted with their assaultive behavior. However, denial presents in many forms and derives from many sources. Victims may be in denial for many years until the trauma manifests itself in a variety of different problems. When this memory emerges, families and professionals may be in denial and thus the current controversy regarding repressed memories. Families of sex offenders are often in denial. Medical, mental health, social service, and educational professional may be in denial and thus the tragedies of children who are abused despite obvious warnings. The criminal justice system may be in denial about what will happen to sex offenders who are simply locked away for a number of years and then released untreated and unsupervised. Finally, legislatures are frequently in denial when they pass high profile but misguided laws that often increase rather than decrease the danger which sex offenders present to the public.

This section is devoted to different views on denial. Anita Schlank, who works with highly challenging involuntarily committed sex offenders in Minnesota, has written on the assessment of cognitive distortions in sexual aggressors. Denial is composed of the many justifications, minimizations, and distortions that allow the sex offender to avoid taking responsibility for his or her behavior. Dr. Schlank has studied a variety of assessment devices that measure whether sex offenders are trying to present themselves in a socially desirable light, what distortions are being used, and the ability to empathize. Her research points out the strength of various devices and suggests strategies for dealing with denial.

One might assume that the type of cognitive distortion a sex offender chooses would depend on his or her level of intelligence, with brighter individuals opting for more sophisticated distortions while developmentally disabled individuals might utilize more primitive, less sophisticated thinking errors. Kalal, Nezu, Nezu, and McGuffin researched the types of cognitive distortions used by sex offenders with intellectual deficits and discovered that there were basically few differences between their subjects and sex offenders with normal intelligence.

William F. Northey's chapter presents a radically different approach to denial. Chapter 32 challenges some basic assumptions that are made in working with juvenile sex offenders. In fact, Dr. Northey does not refer to juvenile sex offenders but uses the term "juveniles accused of sex offenses," which reveals his willingness to acknowledge that some youths may have been falsely charged with sex offenses. Certainly many youthful offenders believe that they have been falsely accused, and this certainly has an impact on their treatment. Although most therapists take the approach that this denial must be challenged and broken down before treatment can really begin, Dr. Northey questions whether a therapist in attempting to break down denial is imposing his own presumptive realities on a situation about which he or she has no firsthand information. He also questions the practice of assuming that the victim's account is always truthful while the offender's account of the crime is always distorted. Although many therapists may bristle at the suggestions given in this chapter, they are presented in the interest of continuously challenging the field to engage in ongoing reevaluation of its basic assumptions.

Joan Zorza, an attorney working in the field of victim's rights, presents some discouraging facts regarding the continued presence of denial in our courts. Professionals in the field of sex offender treatment and supervision would like to believe that they have been successful in educating lawyers, judges, and the public who may someday serve as jurors to the trauma of child sexual abuse. However, current statistics suggest that particularly in custody cases, evidence of sexual assault may be ignored or minimized. For example, Zorza presents data that indicate that fathers who abuse their children get custody more frequently than those who do not.

She explores reasons that many courts remain in denial and offers suggestions for raising the awareness of sexual abuse among the legal profession and among generic mental health professionals.

Controversy surrounds how professionals involved with sex offenders deal with denial. Some will not deal with individuals in denial at all. Others suggest that this failure to deal with such individuals is tantamount to a doctor's deciding not to deal with individuals with colds who have runny noses. They believe that after all, denial is inherent when dealing with this population. Some professionals take a hard line in confronting individuals in denial; others advocate a much gentler approach. The controversy also extends to dealing with denial in public policy. Approaches vary in how to handle politicians, judges, parole boards, and the many other entities that interact with sex offenders. The chapters in this section present some new views on dealing with both individual and organizational denial.

Chapter 30

Issues in the Assessment of Sexual Offenders' Cognitive Distortions

by Anita Schlank, Ph.D.

Overview

One important goal of sex offender treatment is the identification and modification of cognitive distortions. Assessment of these distortions, however, can be difficult, especially given the lack of standardized scales that address maladaptive beliefs. This chapter reviews the available measures of cognitive distortions and offers suggestions concerning their use.

Introduction

Sex offender treatment can be quite challenging to the treatment participant and requires a high level of motivation to adhere to a rigorous treatment protocol. Treatment providers agree that an important early component of any program, and one

that can help provide necessary motivation for continuing in treatment, is the identification and modification of "cognitive distortions" (Abel, Becker, & Cunningham-
Rathner, 1984; Stermac & Segal, 1989; Murphy, 1990; Langevin, 1991; Ward ,
Hudson, Johnston, & Marshall, 1997). Cognitive distortions include an offender's
learned assumptions, self-statements, and attitudes which facilitate his minimization,
justification, and denial of his sexual offenses. These cognitive distortions allow the
offender to continue his behavior without experiencing feelings of guilt, anxiety, and
shame (Abel et al., 1984; Murphy, 1990).

Importance of Cognitive Restructuring in Treatment

Many studies have examined the various categories of cognitive distortions commonly seen in sexual offenders (Stermac & Segal, 1989; Hayashino, Wurtele, &
Klebe, 1995; Ward, Hudson, Johnston, & Marshall, 1997; Ward, Fon, Hudson, &
McCormack, 1998; Hartley, 1998). For example, Hartley identified the following categories: (1) cognitions related to sociocultural factors, (2) cognitions used to reduce
the fear of disclosure, (3) cognitions used to diminish responsibility, and (4) cognitions related to permission seeking. Other researchers have suggested slightly different categories. However, in general, studies have suggested that the cognitive distortions of sex offenders usually include those that perceive children in sexual terms and
minimize the harm caused to them by sexual abuse, those that stress sexual entitle-
ments of males and indicate that women are responsible for rape, and those that stress
that the particular circumstances surrounding the offender's crime were different from
the circumstances usually defined as an offense by society. Recently, though, Ward et
al. (1998) have noted that it is important to realize that not all offenders endorse all
types of cognitive distortions, and that there may be distorted thought processes
throughout the entire offense cycle. They encourage the study of those cognitive factors that are present during the initiation and maintenance of sexual offending and
suggest that, in the past, many treatment providers placed too much emphasis on those
distortions used following the offense as justification for the prior behavior.

Treatment outcome studies have suggested that modifications of cognitive distortions may be a primary positive outcome of relapse prevention–based therapy (Miner,
Marques, Day, & Nelson, 1990), and that failure to modify these cognitive distortions
is prognostic of poor treatment outcome (Simkins, Ward, Bowman, & Rinck, 1989).
Clinicians often view progress toward modification of these cognitive distortions as a
genuine indicator of treatment motivation, empathy, remorse, level of accountability,
and potential risk for recidivism (Marshall & Barbaree, 1990; Murphy, 1990; Pollack
& Hasmall, 1991). This belief persists despite the deficiency of psychometrically
sound assessment techniques for measuring cognitive distortions.

Assessment Measures

Despite the strong emphasis in treatment programs on the assessment of an
offender's adherence to cognitive distortions, relatively few empirically validated
measures exist which adequately assess these types of maladaptive beliefs. At this
time, the most commonly utilized measures include the following: the Abel and
Becker Cognitions Scale (Abel et al., 1989), the Burt Rape Myth Scale (Burt, 1980),

two subscales from the Multiphasic Sex Inventory (Nichols & Molinder, 1984), and the RAPE and MOLEST Scales (Bumby, 1996).

Abel and Becker Cognitions Scale. The Abel and Becker Cognitions Scale (Abel et al., 1989) is a twenty-nine-item self-report questionnaire which is intended to assess the cognitive distortions of adults who commit sexual offenses against children. Research using this scale has found that child molesters endorse significantly more cognitive distortions about a child's capacity to consent to sexual activity with an adult, and the long-term effects of child sexual abuse than do normative groups (Abel et al., 1989; Hayashino et al., 1995; Stermac & Segal, 1989). Although used quite frequently to assess maladaptive beliefs of child molesters, this scale was noted to be somewhat transparent and allowed for the possibility of a socially desirable response bias (Abel et al., 1989; Langevin, 1991; Murphy, 1990). The uniform direction of appropriate answers on the Likert scales also contributed to its transparency (Abel et al., 1989). In addition, it was noted that the odd number of Likert scale response options allowed for an individual to assume a "neutral" position on each item, possibly limiting the scale's usefulness (Bumby, 1996).

Burt Rape Myth Scale. The Burt Rape Myth Scale (Burt, 1980), a scale used to assess cognitive distortions about adult rape victims, is also commonly used with sex offender populations. It has been noted that there is little known about the discriminative utility of this test or the possibility of a socially desirable response bias. The face validity of the items suggests that it might be easy to guess what the "appropriate" answers are; however, Spohn (1993) found that this scale was not correlated with the Marlowe-Crowne Social Desirability Scale. One problem noted with the Burt Rape Myth Scale is that it includes several items that are not directly related to rape myths, such as those that assess a person's likelihood to believe reports of rape from various groups of people. Also, like the Abel and Becker scale, it is scored on a Likert scale that allows for an individual to select a "neutral" response to test items (Bumby, 1996).

Multiphasic Sex Inventory. The Multiphasic Sex Inventory (MSI) is a 300-item self-report questionnaire intended to assess many psychosexual characteristics of male sexual offenders (Nichols & Molinder, 1984). The test consists of twenty subscales and a portion of the test which provides a sexual history. One subscale, Cognitive Distortions and Immaturity (CDI), was designed to assess self-accountability. Specifically, it evaluates the degree to which an offender tends to take a "victim stance," including items such as "I feel like a victim as a result of the accusations made against me." Some difficulties have been noted with the CDI subscale, including its transparency and the fact that some of the items do not appear to be related specifically to sexual offenders (Murphy, 1990). In addition, some items do not appear to necessarily be indicative of a cognitive distortion. For example, items such as "During my adolescence I was secretly excited about sexual matters but I was embarrassed to talk about it to my friends," and "If I were artistic, I would like to draw children" do not appear to be related to a propensity to take a victim stance.

The "Justifications Scale." This scale is intended to assess the degree to which an offender justifies his behavior by projecting blame onto others, or onto stressors in his environment. For example, the scale includes items similar to the following: "The victim in my case did not tell the truth about what really happened," and "My sexual offense occurred as a result of my wife's lack of understanding of me and my needs." The Justification Scale is clearly related to an offender's tendency to minimize or project blame for his behavior; however, it is susceptible to a social desirability response bias (Bumby 1996). In addition, the Justification Scale is offense specific and does not assess general distortions about sexual abuse. It also will not provide any useful information about those offenders who completely deny committing any sexual offense (Nichols & Molinder, 1984).

Bumby MOLEST and RAPE Scales. Recently, Bumby (1996) introduced two new scales designed to assess the cognitive distortions of child molesters and rapists. Bumby's MOLEST and RAPE scales contain derivations of the Abel and Becker Cognitions Scale and the Burt Rape Myth Scale but appear less transparent and are scored on a four-point Likert-type scale, preventing a "neutral" or indifferent response. Preliminary investigation suggest that these scales are valid and reliable measures of the cognitive distortions of sex offenders and can discriminate between sex offenders and non–sex offenders. Results suggest that these two scales may be useful in assessing cognitive distortions prior to, during, and following treatment. It should be noted, however, that the RAPE and MOLEST scales do not include items that relate to the offender's specific offenses, and the items, like those in the Abel and Becker and Burt Rape Myth Scale, appear likely to be susceptible to a social desirability bias, including the uniform direction of the appropriate answers on the Likert scales.

Recent Research

Initial Testing. In a pilot study, twenty-two new admissions to a residential sex offender treatment program for civilly committed offenders were administered a test battery that included the Abel and Becker Cognitions Scale, the Burt Rape Myth Scale, and Bumby's MOLEST and RAPE Scales (Schlank & Bumby, 1997). Sixty-one percent of the subjects endorsed a higher percentage of cognitive distortions using the Bumby MOLEST Scale as compared to the Abel and Becker Cognitions Scale. When comparing the Bumby RAPE Scale with the Burt Rape Myth Scale, 64% of the subjects endorsed a higher percentage of cognitive distortions when using the MOLEST Scale. Ninety-one percent of the subjects endorsed a higher percentage of cognitive distortions on either the MOLEST or RAPE scales, as compared to their scores on the combination of the Abel and Becker Cognitions Scale and the Burt Rape Myth Scale. These results support the findings of Bumby (1996) and suggest that his scales might be more useful for treatment purposes than are the earlier scales, because cognitive distortions cannot be challenged until they are first identified.

The degree to which offenders endorsed more cognitive distortions using the Bumby scales is somewhat surprising given the apparent similarity of the items to those in earlier scales. Although the changes in items from earlier scales seem subtle, they do appear to be meaningful. This difference was perhaps best illustrated by one offender's responses. On the Abel and Becker Cognitions Scale, he mainly circled "5," suggesting that he did not endorse common cognitive distortions about child sexual abuse. However, on the Bumby MOLEST Scale, he not only endorsed many distortions but refused to answer some items and exhibited a highly emotional response to the test, writing messages about the items on every page. For example, he refused to answer item 3 ("Many children who are sexually assaulted do not experience any major problems because of the assaults.") and added a statement by that item which read, "Is every contact a sexual assault?" In response to the item which reads "Some people are not 'true' child molesters—they are just out of control and made a mistake," the offender again refused to answer and wrote next to the item: "A more apt question would be 'are all adults who sexually touch children molesters'? Answer yes—100%. Corollary, do all molesters damage children? Answer no." The offender summarized his thoughts about taking the test by adding the following statement to the top of the test: "I don't know who 'Bumby' is. I am uncomfortable with the way Bumby phrases questions.. . . I do not believe the implicit assumption . . . that every adult/child contact (of necessity) creates a 'victim' is an objectively valid fact."

This offender responded in a similar way on the RAPE Scale. There seemed to be something about these two tests that provoked in him a desire to strongly defend the cognitive distortions that support his abusive behavior. Despite the fact that this offender refused to answer some of the questions on the scales, he provided more information about his thought processes than do most offenders who complete every test item.

Because of the possibility of susceptibility to a social desirability bias, one addition to each of the Bumby scales was made during the previously mentioned pilot study (Schlank & Bumby, 1997). Because some of the new admissions had prior experience with sex offender treatment and were likely aware of society's view of sexual abuse, a "trick" question was added to each scale to assess whether those offenders who endorsed few cognitive distortions truly understood the concept of consent. On both the MOLEST Scale and the RAPE Scale, one item described a situation that was clearly not a sexual assault, but the offender was given the opportunity to label it as one. Also, the direction of the appropriate answer differed from the direction of the other test items. During the pilot study, 74% of the offenders answered the question on the MOLEST Scale incorrectly, and 52% answered the RAPE Scale item incorrectly. These results suggest that the Bumby scales might be improved by the addition of such a "trick" item, in order to counteract its susceptibility to a social desirability bias. In addition, the results suggest that treatment programs need to focus on teaching more completely about the concept of consent, including education about what is not a sexual assault. This is important because it appears likely that an offender who categorizes all sexual activity as a sexual assault may be just as prone to minimize the harmful effects as is an offender who does not label any activity as a sexually abusive.

Other Tests. McGrath, Cann, and Konopasky (1998) recently introduced some data on three new scales: the Sexual Social Desirability Scale (SSDS), the Empathy Scale (Empat), and the Child Molester Scale (CMS). The intent of the SSDS is to measure the degree to which offenders tend to present themselves in a socially desirable manner with regard to sexual issues. The Empat was described as a measure specifically of empathy for victims of child sexual abuse and may offer information specific to cognitive distortions concerning a tendency to minimize the impact of sexual assault. The CMS was developed to address the difficulty with the transparency of the Abel and Becker Cognitions Scale. It presents cognitive distortions similar to those on the Abel and Becker but makes them less transparent by offering justifications for the behaviors. In addition, the direction of the appropriate answers was varied, which would also help the scale be less transparent. Using a sample size of thirty, McGrath et al. (1998) found that the three scales had adequate internal consistency and were significantly correlated with each other. In addition, sexual offenders endorsed more cognitive distortions using these scales as compared to nonsexual offenders and controls. Unfortunately, McGrath et al. (1998) did not include detailed descriptions of the items in these scales, and further research on the usefulness of these scales is needed.

Other Assessment Issues

When conducting assessments of sexual offenders, it is important to include comprehensive assessments of both general cognitive distortions about sexual abuse and distortions specific to the offender's own offenses. In addition, it is useful to give all offenders scales that assess both cognitive distortions about child molestation and those that address the rape of adults. Although many offenders see themselves as solely fitting in one category, they often actually have cognitive distortions and fantasies that are quite similar to those offenders who target other types of victims. It is also not uncommon for an offender who has been convicted of one type of offense to later admit that he has committed many types of offenses or has at least come close to committing other types of offenses. This suggests that offenders should not be quickly "pigeon-holed" as either a child molester or a rapist of adults.

It is also useful when conducting assessments to administer the self-report questionnaires prior to any interview with the offender. Offenders who might become very closed and defensive during an interview about the thought processes surrounding their offending may be quick to endorse a cognitive distortion when it appears in print and it is apparent to them that many others have held similar beliefs. Therefore, it is likely that more cognitive distortions will be identified if the questionnaires are administered prior to the interview. An additional benefit of this order of administration is that it is then possible to go back to particular items on a test and ask for elaboration if the offender should become reluctant to discuss details during the clinical interview.

Conclusion

Before successful treatment of a sexual offender can be accomplished, it is important to understand the cognitive distortions that support the person's choice to commit offenses and are also used to justify the continued abusive behavior. Several scales currently exist to assist in this type of assessment, the most promising of which appears to be the Bumby MOLEST and RAPE scales. These two scales appear to adequately assess many types of cognitive distortions and appear to present a lowered risk for a social desirability bias in responses. In the future, researchers may wish to investigate the possibility of adding items to these two scales that would further decrease the chance of a social desirability bias and the possibility of including items related to the test taker's specific offenses. Also, future research on scales developed since the publication of the Bumby scales, such as the SSDS, Empat, and CMS scales (McGrath, et al., 1998), may find that these new tests address the limitations of past scales.

References

Abel, G. G., Becker, J. V., & Cunningham-Rathner, J. (1984). Complications, consent and cognitions in sex between children and adults. *International Journal of Law and Psychiatry, 7,* 89–103.

Abel, G. G., Gore, D. K., Holland, C. L., Camp, N., Becker, J. V., & Rathner, J. (1989). The measurement of the cognitive distortions of child molesters. *Annals of Sex Research, 2,* 135–153.

Bumby, K. M. (1996). Assessing cognitive distortions of child molesters and rapists: Development and validation of the MOLEST and RAPE scales. *Sexual Abuse: A Journal of Research and Treatment, 2*(1), 37–54.

Hartley, C. C. (1998). How incest offenders overcome internal inhibitions through the use of cognitions and cognitive distortions. *Journal of Interpersonal Violence, 13*(1), 25–39.

Hayashino, D. S., Wurtele, S. K., & Klebe, K. J. (1995). Long-term recidivism of child molesters. *Journal of Consulting and Clinical Psychology, 61,* 646–652.

Langevin, R. (1991). A note on the problem of response set in measuring cognitive distortions. *Annals of Sex Research, 4,* 287–292.

Marshall, W. L., & Barbaree, H. E. (1990). An integrated theory of the etiology of sexual offending. In W. L. Marshall, D. R. Laws, & H. E. Barbaree (Eds.), *Handbook of sexual assault: Issues, theories and treatment of the offender* (pp. 257–275). New York: Plenum Press.

McGrath, M., Cann, S., & Konopasky, R. (1998). New measures of defensiveness, empathy, and cognitive distortions for sexual offenders against children. *Sexual Abuse: A Journal of Research and Treatment, 10*(1), 25–36.

Miner, M. H., Marques, J. K., Day, D. M., & Nelson, C. (1990). Impact of relapse prevention in treating sex offenders: Preliminary findings. *Annals of Sex Research, 3,* 165–185.

Murphy, W. D. (1990). Assessment and modification of cognitive distortions in sex offenders. In W. L. Marshall, D. R. Laws & H. E. Barbaree (Eds.), *Handbook of sexual assault: Issues, theories and treatment of the offender* (pp. 331–342). New York: Plenum Press.

Murphy, W. D., & Stalgaitis, S. J. (1987). Assessment and treatment considerations for sexual offenders against children: Behavioral and social learning approaches. In J. R. McNamara & M. A. Appel (Eds.), *Critical issues, developments and trends in professional psychology* (vol. 3, pp. 177–210). New York: Praeger.

Nichols, H. R., & Molinder, I. (1984). *Multiphasic Sex Inventory manual: A test to assess the psychosexual characteristics of the sexual offender.* Tacoma, WA: Nichols & Molinder.

Pollack, N. L., & Hasmall, J. M. (1991). The excuses of child molesters. *Behavioral Sciences and the Law, 9,* 53–59.

Schlank, A., & Bumby, K. (1997, October). *Issues in the assessment of sexual offenders' cognitive distortions.* Paper presented at the Sixteenth Annual Research and Treatment Conference of the Association for the Treatment of Sexual Abusers, Arlington, VA.

Simkins, L., Ward, W., Bowman, S., & Rinck, C. M. (1989). The Multiphasic Sex Inventory: Diagnosis and prediction of treatment response in child sexual abusers. *Annals of Sex Research, 2,* 205–226.

Spohn, R. B. (1993). Social desirability correlates for acceptance of rape myth. *Psychological Reports, 73,* 12–18.

Stermac, L. E., & Segal, Z. V. (1989). Adult sexual contact with children: An examination of cognitive factors. *Behavior Therapy, 20,* 573–584.

Ward, T., Fon, C., Hudson, S. M., & McCormach, J. (1998). A descriptive model of dysfunctional cognitions in child molesters. *Journal of Interpersonal Violence, 13*(1), 129–155.

Ward, T. , Hudson, S. M., Johnston, L., & Marshall, W. L. (1997). Cognitive distortions in sex offenders: An integrative review. *Clinical Psychology Review, 17*(5), 479–507.

Chapter 31

Cognitive Distortions in Sexual Offenders With Intellectual Deficits

by David M. Kalal, M.A., Christine M. Nezu, Ph.D., Arthur M. Nezu, Ph.D., and Patrick McGuffin, Ph.D.

Overview

All sex offenders demonstrate cognitive distortions that allow them to justify and rationalize and thus continue their behavior. Intellectually impaired sex offenders also utilize cognitive distortions, but are these distortions qualitatively or quantitatively similar to those of nonimpaired offenders? This chapter reviews a study that measured matched groups of intellectually impaired and normal controls on the Abel Cognitions Scale. The chapter then discusses implications for treatment.

Introduction

Despite some change in public attitude toward sexuality, the subject of sexuality in persons with intellectual deficits remain controversial (Brantlinger, 1983; Schilling &

Schinke, 1989). Many people feel that these individuals should not be allowed to date, express their sexual needs, live with a sexual partner, or marry (Schilling & Schinke, 1989; Swanson & Garwick, 1990). Common misconceptions of persons with mental retardation include beliefs that they are children to be pitied or cherished, "holy innocents" and "chosen children of god," or dangerous, sexually impulsive "subhumans" (Morgenstern, 1973). In light of these beliefs, it becomes clear why the group of persons with intellectual deficits who commit sexual crimes are regarded with such suspicion (Marshall, 1983; Morgenstern, 1973). Even today, information on the actual prevalence of sexual offenders with intellectual deficits remains conflicting and inconclusive (Hawk, Rosenfeld, & Warren, 1993; Griffiths, Quinsey, & Hinsburger, 1989; Knopp, 1984; Murphy, Coleman, & Abel, 1983), while the intersection of individuals with intellectual deficits who commit sex crimes creates special problems for human service professionals and the court system (Schoen & Hoover, 1990).

Intellectually Deficient Offenders Present Special Challenge

Perske (1972) states that the increased freedom for persons with intellectual deficits granted by deinstitutionalization brings increased responsibility and the possibility of failure experiences—what he calls "the dignity of risk." However, as a result of this increased "risk" and responsibility, little action has been taken to understand individuals with intellectual deficits who engage in sexually deviant behavior. Specifically, research designed to identify the motivations that drive this behavior and their similarity or dissimilarity to those of sexual offenders without intellectual deficits, along with the creation of specialized treatment programs, has not been forthcoming (Knopp, Rosenburg, & Stevenson, 1986; Schoen & Hoover, 1990; Schilling & Schinke, 1989; Swanson & Garwick, 1990).

Definition of Intellectual Deficits

The *Diagnostic and Statistical Manual of Mental Disorders* (DSM-IV; American Psychiatric Association, 1994) defines mental retardation as a condition present in individuals who, before the age of 18, demonstrate significantly subaverage intellectual functioning with concurrent deficits in adaptive behavior. Adaptive behavior refers to the person's effectiveness in personal independence, self-care, and social responsibility appropriate to his or her culture and age group. According to both DSM-IV and the American Association on Mental Deficiency (Grossman, 1983), the four levels of mental retardation, which are based on psychological testing to produce an IQ score, are as follows:

Level of Mental Retardation	IQ Score
Mild	56–70
Moderate	41–55
Severe	26–40
Profound	25 and below

In addition, the category of borderline intellectual functioning is assigned when a diagnosis of mental retardation is not appropriate and the measured IQ score falls between 71 and 84, which is considered an intellectual deficit. In the study described in this chapter, individuals with intellectual deficits refer to both persons with mental retardation and those with borderline intellectual functioning (i.e., IQ scores from 41 to 84).

Definitions of Pedophilia

Hobson, Boland, and Jamieson (1985) define pedophilia as any sexual contact between an offender and a victim who, due to age and/or immaturity, is incapable of giving consent, either legally or realistically. The specific acts classified as pedophilic range from mutual touching and fondling to actual intercourse. Access to the victim is often achieved through pressure, coercion, or deception. DSM-IV (American Psychiatric Association, 1994) criteria for a diagnosis of pedophilia stipulate that the individual be at least 16 years of age and experience recurrent, intense sexual urges and sexually arousing fantasies involving sexual activity with a prepubescent child for a duration of at least six months. In addition, the person must have either acted on these urges or be markedly distressed by them. For the purposes of this study, the terms "pedophile" and "child molester" are used interchangeably, whereas the term "sexual offender" denotes a larger population that includes rapists, flashers, and so on.

Prevalence of Offenders With Intellectual Deficits

Studies that have attempted to specify the prevalence of sexual offenders with intellectual deficits have yielded a variety of conflicting findings, in part due to the many obstacles inherent in assessing sexual molestation (Hawk et al., 1993). Such obstacles include the child's fear, shame, or guilt; the family's reluctance to incur further victimization of the child by the justice system; perpetrators who are related or close to the family; and the fact that first offenses, especially involving offenders with intellectual deficits, are often ignored or given minor consequences (Swanson & Garwick, 1990; Travin, Bluestone, Coleman, Culler, & Melella, 1985). Some investigators conclude that offenders with intellectual deficits are not overrepresented among the general sex-offending population (Murphy, Coleman, & Abel, 1983), whereas others suggest that sexually deviant behavior may be more common among those with such deficits (Griffiths et al., 1989).

Another difficulty in determining an accurate estimate of the prevalence of these crimes stems from the practice of using prison populations to gather data. This procedure misses persons with intellectual deficits who are declared incompetent to stand trial and are referred away from the criminal justice system (Warren, Fitch, & Deitz, 1991) and, therefore, underestimates the prevalence of sex offenses in this population (Hawk et al., 1993; Murphy, Coleman, & Abel, 1983; Wolfe & Baker, 1980). To avoid this problem, Thompson (1988) analyzed pretrial forensic evaluations and found a disproportionately high number of sex offenses among individuals with intellectual deficits. Results indicated that 35% of such offenders were charged with sexual offenses compared to 10% of defendants with IQ scores in the normal range. In a similar investigation Hawk et al. (1993) found that the indictment ratio for sexual offenses was nearly twice as high among defendants with intellectual deficits (26%) compared to defendants with higher IQ scores (15%), although no differences were found in the nature of the crimes (felonies vs. misdemeanors, violent vs. nonviolent, against adults vs. children). The results of a survey of treatment providers reveal that 25% of their clients have some degree of intellectual deficits (Knopp, 1982). However, these findings stand in sharp contrast to a study by Swanson and Garwick (1991), which discovered that only 3% of recipients of county services had both severe sexual problems and intellectual deficits. These authors attribute the inflated prevalence rates found in other studies to stereotypes of those with intellectual deficits as sexually obsessed and believe that few data exist to indicate that the proportion of sexual crimes in this population of offenders is higher than that in sexual offenders with normal IQ scores. Such inconclusive findings highlight the need for gathering additional information regarding the characteristics of offenders with intellectual deficits.

Treatment for Offenders With Intellectual Deficits

Whatever the actual prevalence of sexual offenses among the population with intellectual deficits, sexual misconduct has serious consequences for both offenders and victims. Effective treatment in order to reduce the risk of reoccurrence is, therefore, critical, although, unfortunately, few treatment programs that are based on sound empirical evidence, rather than clinical experience, exist for offenders with intellectual deficits. A review of agencies that treat sex offenders indicated that of the 643 programs offered nationwide, only 148 provided services for clients with intellectual deficits (Knopp, Rosenburg, & Stevenson, 1986). And, although some research into the unique characteristics of offenders with intellectual deficits has been done, many treatment programs simply "water down" existing interventions that were designed for non-retarded offenders. Typical treatments for these individuals have included individual and group psychotherapy, behavior therapy, surgery, and medication (Berlin & Krout, 1986). Many of these interventions have also been used to treat offenders with intellectual deficits, despite a lack of evidence regarding their usefulness in this population. However, as discussed in the following paragraphs, specialized treatments do exist.

Haaven, Little, and Petre-Miller (1990) developed a comprehensive residential treatment program for sex offenders with intellectual deficits at the Oregon State Hospital. Their program employs a number of interventions, which include reparenting, cognitive restructuring, group therapy, covert sensitization, and plethysmography (the measurement of penile response to sexual stimuli). Program success is measured by tracking recidivism rates, although some studies have cast doubt on the usefulness of this type of measure (e.g., Furby, Weinrott, & Blackshaw, 1989; Quinsey, Harris, Rice, & Lalumière, 1993). The Haaven et al. (1990) data on recidivism from 1979 to 1988 indicate that after receiving one year of treatment, only 21% of clients had committed an additional sex crime, whereas 25% had reoffended after receiving less than a full year of treatment. No data are provided, however, for the recidivism rates of non-treated offenders.

Griffiths et al. (1989) developed a community-based treatment approach that includes social competency and relationship training, sex education, cognitive restructuring, and problem solving. In addition, these authors employ a relapse prevention model developed by Pithers, Marques, Gibat, and Marlatt (1983). No empirical studies, to date, have tested the efficacy of their treatment program.

Losada-Paisey and Paisey (1988) used a comprehensive, behavioral-based treatment program for seven adults with mental retardation displaying pedophilic behavior living in a residential treatment facility. Their treatment included academic and vocational training, sex education, a token economy, and individual behavior therapy, which utilized sexual reconditioning procedures. Of the seven participants, three attained the goal of unsupervised community living; two others achieved "significant progress."

Cognitive Distortions in Sexual Offenders

Cognitive distortions are personal beliefs used to explain and justify sexually deviant behavior. Abel et al. (1989) developed a scale designed to assess the presence and strength of distortions commonly found in pedophiles. Examples of such cognitive distortions include a belief that children can make their own decisions as to whether they want to have sex with an adult or not, that having sex with a child is a good way to teach the child about sex, that having sex with a child demonstrates love and affection to the child and can prevent the child from having sexual hangups in the future, and that a child who walks around with no or only a few clothes on is trying to arouse the individual (see Appendix at the end of this chapter for additional examples). Abel et al. (1989) speculate that these distortions are the product of conflict between external reinforcements (e.g., pleasure from pedophilic acts) and internal self-condemnation (e.g., guilt over culturally abhorred behaviors). Moreover, offenders often fail to receive feedback about their behavior from the children they molest, and the secrecy involved and fear of discovery prevent them from experiencing the negative attitudes of others around them. Cognitive distortions allow molesters to justify their ongoing sexual abuse without guilt, anxiety, or loss of self-esteem.

A common element in many of the treatment programs described here are multiple interventions that often include some type of cognitive restructuring (i.e., correcting distorted beliefs; Haaven et al., 1990; Griffiths et al., 1989). Other authors have also identified the correction of distorted cognitions in sex offenders as an important element in treatment (Abel, Becker, & Cunningham-Rathner, 1984; Knopp, 1982; Travin et al., 1986).

However, despite the fact that studies have consistently shown that cognitive distortions in sexual offenders play a role in the initiation and repetition of molesting behavior (Abel et al., 1984; Abel et al., 1989; Gudjonsson, 1990), it has not been shown whether individuals with intellectual deficits evidence such distortions in a similar manner. Caparulo et al. (1988) feel that the distortions of offenders with intellectual deficits should parallel those of nondisabled offenders, differing only in terms of sophistication. However, research had not yet been performed to test this hypothesis. Murphy, Coleman, and Haynes (1983) reported that sexual offenders with intellectual deficits presented with sexually deviant beliefs apparently more similar than dissimilar to their non-intellectually deficient counterparts in that they endorsed negative ideation toward women in a similar manner to a nonretarded comparison group. However, their variable, negative ideation, is different than the cognitive distortions described previously. These authors also underscore the need for additional empirical verification of the similarities and differences between offenders, with and without intellectual deficits, as much of the current knowledge is based on small numbers of case studies.

Rationale for the Study

Pursuant to the fact that a paucity of research on sex offenders with intellectual deficits has been done, specifically with regard to cognitive distortions, this study proposed to explore the possible differences in the frequency and intensity of distorted cognitions in pedophilic sexual offenders with intellectual deficits and in those without. It was predicted that pedophiles with intellectual deficits would significantly differ in both the amount and strength of distorted cognitions they endorse relative to pedophiles with higher IQ scores on a predesigned measure of cognitive distortions. This measure was administered to pedophiles from an outpatient clinic at Allegheny University of the Health Sciences that specializes in the treatment of offenders with intellectual deficits and to inmates from a facility in New Jersey that houses only individuals convicted of sexual crimes. The existence of significant differences between the two groups in the quantity and strength of distorted beliefs endorsed would, as hypothesized, suggest that intellectual level plays a role in the acquisition and maintenance of these beliefs, which are known to justify recurrent pedophilic behavior in offenders.

Exploring Types of Cognitive Distortions

Methods. Twenty-five male pedophiles participated and were assigned to the Intellectual Deficits Condition (IDC) or Comparison Condition (CC) on the basis of their IQ score. Only pedophiles were recruited, in part due to the nature of the questions on the measure and in part because of the qualitative differences between pedophilia and other types of sexual crimes, such as rape (Harry, Pierson, & Kuznetsov, 1993; Hobson, Boland, & Jamieson, 1985). Offenders were solicited from both the clinic and prison to participate in a larger research project designed to test a model of sexual offending. All participants were volunteers who underwent an informed consent and received no compensation. This project met criteria described by the National Commission for the Protection of Human Subjects regarding special populations (in this case inmates) in the 1994 Code of Federal Regulations. Confidentiality was ensured by assigning all participants identification numbers, which were used to mark all written documents, and keeping the names of the participants separate and in locked filing cabinets within the university.

Intellectual Deficits Group. The IDC consisted of ten individuals who met criteria for mild or moderate mental retardation or borderline intellectual functioning. The individuals in this group had been convicted of at least one episode of child molestation and/or had met DSM-IV criteria for pedophilia. Information regarding the nature of the offenses was elicited from a semistructured interview and from clinic/prison records. Potential participants were excluded from this group if their IQ test results suggested a diagnosis of severe or profound mental retardation or if their records indicated a history of any psychotic or substance use disorders. The presence of other psychological and personality disorders, however, would not have excluded an individual from the study, as it was predicted that other psychopathology would not interfere with the acquisition of deviant cognitions. None of the volunteers needed to be excluded on the basis of these criteria.

Comparison Condition. Fifteen individuals were assigned to the CC after intellectual assessment revealed an IQ score above 85, placing them within a normal IQ range. These offenders had also been convicted of at least one episode of child molestation or had met criteria for a DSM-IV diagnosis of pedophilia, although individuals with mixed convictions (e.g., adult rape and pedophilia) were excluded. Also excluded were individuals exhibiting current psychotic or substance use disorders. Participants with other diagnosable psychological conditions were not considered for exclusion, as previously outlined. No volunteers needed to be excluded on the basis of these criteria.

Measures. The Wechsler Adult Intelligence Scale—Revised (WAIS-R; Wechsler, 1981) is a test designed to measure adult intelligence. The WAIS-R contains eleven subtests grouped into a Verbal and a Performance section. Repeated administration of the test to the same subject has consistently produced relationships from .95 to .97 (test-retest reliability; Sattler, 1992). The WAIS-R also demonstrates a significant positive relationship, or correlation, with other intelligence tests, measures of academic achievement, and years of formal education, which suggests that the test is an adequate measure of general intelligence, also called *g*. Finally, the WAIS-R yields an IQ score from 45 to 150, which was sufficient to accurately identify the target population in this study. Because administration of the full WAIS-R was deemed overly time-consuming given the constraints of interviewing inmates, two subtests (Block Design and Vocabulary) were chosen to provide an extrapolated Full Scale IQ (FSIQ) score (Brooker & Cyr, 1986). The Block Design and Vocabulary subtests have moderate and high correlations, respectively, with the FSIQ, have consistently high test-retest reliability, and are good measures of *g* (Sattler, 1992). The two subtests when used together, however, have been shown to consistently overestimate the FSIQ in clinical samples by approximately 3 points (Margolis, Taylor, & Greenlief, 1986).

The Cognition Scale (Abel et al., 1984; see Appendix at end of this chapter) is composed of twenty-nine items designed to assess the distorted cognitions of child molesters. It has been used successfully to differentiate child molesters from samples of nonmolesting individuals (Abel et al., 1984; Abel, et al., 1989; Gudjonsson, 1990). The items are scored on a 5-point Likert scale, wherein a lower total score indicates more deviant cognitions. All items on the scale are "transparent" (e.g., no attempt was made to disguise the nature of the questions).

A factor analysis performed on the answers from one sample of child molesters yielded six reliable and valid factors, which accounted for 49.6% of the variance. Reliability tests yielded correlations from .64 to .77 with an overall test-retest reliability of .76. Because only the first factor accounted for a significant part of the variance (35.4%) the Cognition Scale can be used as a single-factor scale. Finally, the Cognition Scale demonstrated adequate validity throughout a number of tests. For example, in a "known groups" procedure, higher scores from child molesters on the Cognition Scale successfully discriminated this group from the general population.

Procedure for Evaluating Offenders. Assessment involved the administration of the two WAIS-R subtests, a semistructured interview, and the Cognition Scale. Inmates participated in two interviews separated by approximately one month, while the outpatient clients completed the measures prior to their regularly scheduled treatment sessions. All the tests were given by advanced students in the doctoral program in clinical psychology at Allegheny University of the Health Sciences The students underwent training in order to administer the measures and were under the supervision of the clinic co-director, Christine M. Nezu, Ph.D.

The assessment began with a brief explanation of the purpose of the study and an informed consent procedure. Next, completion of the WAIS-R subtests determined to which group the inmate would be assigned (WAIS-R FSIQ results were performed on the outpatient clients). Demographic information, including the nature of the sexual offense, was gathered from a semistructured interview and was verified using prison or clinic records. To eliminate any possible deficits in reading comprehension, participants were given the choice of having the measures read aloud. To avoid bias that may have resulted from discussions among potential participants with those who had already completed the study, debriefing forms will be distributed en masse after data collection for the entire study is completed.

Group Demographics. All data analyses were performed with the Statistical Package for the Social Sciences for Windows (SPSS). Participants in the IDC ($n = 10$) were 80% single and 40% Caucasian, 40% African-American, and 20% Hispanic. They had committed mostly nonincest pedophilia (60%) with female victims (60%). Forty percent of the sample denied committing the crime for which they had been sentenced. The CC participants ($n = 15$) were all Caucasian. Slightly under half were single (46.7%) while the remainder were mostly divorced or separated (46.7%; 6.7% married). Most (66.7%) had committed nonincest crimes with female victims (60%), while 33% had molested males (6.7 had molested both males and females). None were in denial of their crimes. Table 31.1 outlines additional demographic information.

Table 31.1
Means and Standard Deviations for Offender Demographics

Variable	Mean	SD	Range
IDC Group (n = 10)			
Age	38	8.9	25–52
Full Scale IQ	68	8.85	54–83
Education (years)	8	2.94	5–12
Number of victims	1.4	.70	1–3
Age of victims	9	3.68	4–15
CC Group (n = 15)			
Age	44	9.68	29–62
Full Scale IQ	102	10.42	88–122
Education (years)	13	3.33	7–19
Number of victims	1.87	1.13	1–5
Age of victims	11	3.	4–16

Results and Discussion Show Similarities in Cognitive Distortions

Independent t-tests for average (mean) values on the total Cognition Scale score and the totals of "Strongly Agree" and "Agree" answers revealed no significant differences between the IDC and CC groups ($t = 1.32$, $t = 1.28$, $t = 1.08$, respectively, all $p > .05$). Table 31.2 lists means and standard deviations for these variables. There were no missing scores.

Table 31.2
Means and Standard Deviations for Abel Cognition Scale Scores

Group	Total Scale Score	Strongly Agree	Agree
IDC	104 (26)*	2.1 (2.4)**	14.8 (18.9)***
CC	90 (33)*	2.9 (4.8)**	18.6 (14.6)***

* $t = 1.317$, $p = .263$; ** $t = 1.28$, $p = .268$; *** $t = 1.09$, $p = .306$.

Contrary to the original hypotheses, the offenders in the IDC did not endorse a significantly different number of distorted cognitions on the scale relative to offenders in the CC. One possible interpretation of this result is that the acquisition and maintenance of distorted cognitions in pedophiles may be the result of processes other than intellectual level. This finding appears to support the conclusions advanced by Caparulo et al. (1988) and Murphy, Coleman, and Haynes (1983) regarding the lack of differences between offenders with intellectual deficits and those without. It is important to remember, however, that the lack of significant differences in this study does not mean that such differences do not exist. If the null hypothesis (i.e., no differences) is replicated in further research, it suggests the possibility that processes and variables other than intellectual functioning are causal in creating the distorted beliefs that initiate and justify child molestation. However, other interpretations of these findings are possible, including the possibility that the limitations, discussed later, interfered with the results.

It is important to note the presence of the extremely large standard deviations within each group (see Table 31.2). The wide range of the differences within each group are much greater than the differences between the two groups, which further supports the idea that factors other than intellectual level may explain the presence of cognitive distortions. In addition, an absence of differences based on intellectual level would also be consistent with Abel et al.'s (1989) application of social learning theory (Bandura, 1973, 1977) to cognitive distortions.

Potential Limitations

Potential limitations in this study, however, may hinder the ability to draw accurate conclusions from the data. Aside from the relatively small sample sizes, most of the offenders had undergone treatment for their behavior. Many treatments, as mentioned earlier, address the correction of cognitive distortions as part of one of multiple interventions (Haaven et al., 1990; Gilby, Wolf, & Goldberg, 1989; Murphy, Coleman, & Abel, 1983). The effects of such treatment may caused offenders to change their previously distorted cognitions, although participants were asked to answer as they would have during the commission of their crimes. In addition, the stigma of holding beliefs may have caused the participants to reply to the questions in a socially appropriate fashion. In a 1991 study, Langevin used the Cognition Scale on a sample of pedophiles and found that more than 75% of subjects marked "Strongly Disagree" for all the items. He interprets this as a significant response bias and questions whether an unbiased scale that describes pedophilic sexual activity between in socially neutral terms is possible.

Schilling and Schinke (1989) indicate that apprehended sex offenders are likely to include a disproportionate number of individuals who are unskilled in avoiding arrest and are, therefore, potentially different from the overall population of pedophiles. Including only those offenders who have been indicted and either were placed on probation or are serving prison terms leaves the possibility open that qualitative differences exist between offenders who are caught and those who are able to escape detection.

Hawk et al. (1993) caution that offenders with intellectual deficits may be underrepresented in prison due to their being referred for treatment and probation rather than for incarceration. However, this possibility was minimized by using outpatient clients, all of whom displayed intellectual deficits. Only two of the ten participants in the IDC were inmates, which allows for the possibility that differences between an outpatient sample and an incarcerated sample exist.

Conclusion

The results of this study allow for an interpretation that the acquisition and maintenance of distorted cognitions in pedophiles may be the result of processes other than their intellectual level, although these conclusions must be adequately weighed against the limitations imposed on the study. Further research on the differences, or lack thereof, between pedophilic offenders with intellectual deficits and those without may provide more definitive answers. Additional research may also diminish some of the suspicion and stereotypes under which persons with intellectual deficits labor (Morgenstern, 1973; Marshall, 1983). In the long run, such research will produce more effective treatments, which can reduce the risk of offending and reoffending.

Finally, professionals who deal with individuals with intellectual deficits often have a tendency to believe that persons with mental retardation enjoy immunity from other types of psychopathology, or, conversely, they attribute any emotional problems as sequelae of the intellectual deficits (Nezu, Nezu, & Gill-Weiss, 1992). These misconceptions, called diagnostic overshadowing, may be particularly probable when addressing sexually deviant behavior. Therefore, it remains important when dealing with offenders with intellectual deficits to be cautious with overgeneralizations and assumptions and to be careful to assess each case individually.

References

Abel, G. G., Becker, J. V., & Cunningham-Rathner, J. (1984). Complications, consent, and cognitions in sex between children and adults. *International Journal of Law and Psychiatry, 7,* 89–103.

Abel, G. G., & Blanchard, E. B. (1974). The role of fantasy in the treatment of sexual deviation. *Archives of General Psychiatry, 30,* 467–475.

Abel, G. G., Gore, D. K., Holland, C. L., Camp, N. L., Becker, J. V., & Rathner, J. (1989). The measurement of the cognitive distortions of child molesters. *Annals of Sex Research, 2,* 135–153.

American Psychiatric Association. (1994). *Diagnostic and statistical manual of mental disorders* (4th ed.). Washington, DC: Author.

Bandura, A. (1973). *Aggression: A social learning analysis.* Englewood Cliffs, NJ: Prentice-Hall.

Bandura, A. (1977). *Social learning theory.* Englewood Cliffs, NJ: Prentice-Hall.

Berlin, F. S., & Krout, E. (1986). Pedophilia: Diagnostic concepts, treatment, and ethical considerations. *American Journal of Forensic Psychiatry, 7(*1), 13–30.

Berlin, F. S., & Meinecke, C. F. (1981). Treatment of sex offenders with anti-androgenic medication: Conceptualization, review of treatment modalities, and preliminary findings. *American Journal of Psychiatry, 138,* 601–607.

Brantlinger, E. (1983). Measuring variation and change in attitudes of residential care staff towards the sexuality of mentally retarded persons. *Mental Retardation, 21*(1), 17–22.

Brooker, B. H., & Cyr, J. J. (1986). Tables for clinicians to use to convert WAIS-R short forms. *Journal of Clinical Psychology, 42,* 983.

Caparulo, F., Comte, M., Gafgen, J., Haaven, J., Kaufman, K., Kempton, W., Sissala, L., Whitaker, J. M., & Wilson, R. (1988, March). *A summary of selected notes.* Presented at working sessions of the first national training conference on the assessment and treatment of intellectually disabled juvenile and adult sex offenders, Columbus, OH.

Code of Federal Regulations. (1994). Section 46.301.

Cooper, A. J. (1987). Medroxyprogesterone acetate (MPA) treatment of sexually acting out in men suffering from dementia. *Journal of Clinical Psychiatry, 48,* 368–370.

Fedoroff, J. P., Wisner-Carlson, R., Dean, S., & Berlin, F. S. (1992). Medroxy-Progesterone Acetate in the treatment of paraphiliac sexual disorders. *Journal of Offender Rehabilitation, 18*(3/4), 109–123.

Furby, L., Weinrott, M. R., & Blackshaw, L. (1989). Sex offender recidivism: A review. Psychological Bulletin, 105, 3–30.

Griffiths, D. M., Quinsey, V. L., & Hinsburger, D. (1989). *Changing inappropriate sexual behavior: A community-based approach for persons with developmental disabilities.* Baltimore: Paul H. Brookes.

Grossman, H. (1983). *Manual on terminology and classification in mental retardation.* Washington, DC: American Association on Mental Deficiency.

Gudjonsson, G. H. (1990). Cognitive distortions and blame attribution among paedophiles. *Sexual and Marital Therapy, 5*(2), 183–185.

Haaven, J., Little, R., & Petre-Miller, D. (1990). *Treating intellectually disabled sex offenders: A model residential program.* Orwell, VT: Safer Society Press.

Harry, B., Pierson, T. R., & Kuznetsov, A. (1993). Correlates of sex offender and offense traits by victim age. *Journal of Forensic Sciences, 38*(5), 1068–1074.

Hawk, G. L., Rosenfeld, B. D., & Warren, J. I. (1993). Prevalence of sexual offenses among mentally retarded criminal defendants. *Hospital and Community Psychiatry, 44*(8), 784–786.

Hobson, W. F., Boland, C., & Jamieson, D. (1985). Dangerous sexual offenders. *Medical Aspects of Human Sexuality, 19(*2), 104–123.

Knopp, F. H. (1982). *Remedial intervention in adolescent sex offenses: Nine program descriptions.* New York: Safer Society Press.

Knopp, F. H. (1984). *Retraining adult sex offenders: Methods and models.* Syracuse, NY: Safer Society Press.

Knopp, F. H., Rosenburg, J., & Stevenson, W. (1986). *Reports on nationwide survey of juvenile and adult sex-offender treatment programs and providers.* Syracuse, NY: Safer Society Press.

Langevin, R. (1991). A note on the problem of response set in measuring cognitive distortions. *Annals of Sex Research, 4,* 287–292.

Losada-Paisey, G., & Paisey, T. J. H. (1988). Program evaluation of a comprehensive treatment package for mentally retarded offenders. *Behavioral Residential Treatment, 3*(4), 247–265.

Margolis, R. B., Taylor, J. M., & Greenlief, C. C. (1986). A cross-validation of two short forms of the WAIS-R in a geriatric sample suspected of dementia. *Journal of Clinical Psychology, 42,* 145–146.

Marshall, W. I. (1983). The classification of sexual aggressives and their associated demographic, social, developmental, and psychological features. In S. N. Verdun-Jones & A. A. Keltner (Eds.), *Sexual aggression and the law* (pp. 3–13). Vancouver, BC: Criminology Research Center, Simon Frasier University.

Money, J. (1972). The therapeutic use of androgen-depleting hormone. *International Psychiatry Clinics, 8,* 165–174.

Morgenstern, M. (1973). Community attitudes toward sexuality of the mentally retarded. In F. F. de la Cruz & G. D. LaVeck (Eds.), *Human sexuality and the mentally retarded* (pp. 157–163). New York: Brunner/Mazel.

Murphy, W. D., Coleman, E. M., & Abel, G. G. (1983). Human sexuality in the mentally retarded. In J. L. Matson & F. Andrasik (Eds.), *Treatment issues and innovations in mental retardation* (pp. 581–644). New York: Plenum Press.

Murphy, W. D., Coleman, E. M., & Haynes, M. R. (1983). Treatment and evaluation issues with the mentally retarded sex offender. In J. G. Greer & I. R. Stuart (Eds.), *The sexual aggressor: Current perspectives on treatment* (pp. 22–41). New York: Van Nostrand Reinhold.

Nezu, C. M., Nezu, A. M., & Gill-Weiss, M. J. (1992). *Psychopathology in persons with mental retardation: Clinical guidelines for assessment and treatment.* New York: Guilford Press.

Persky, R. (1972). In W. Wolfensburger (Ed.), *The principle of normalization in human services.* Toronto, Canada: National Institute on Mental Retardation.

Pithers, W. D., Marques, J. K., Gibat, C. C., & Marlatt, G. A. (1983). Relapse prevention with sexual aggressives: A self-control model of treatment and maintenance of change. In J. G. Greer & I. R. Stuart (Eds.), *The sexual aggressor: Current perspectives on treatment* (pp. 214–234). New York: Van Nostrand Reinhold.

Quinsey, V. L., Harris, G. T., Rice, M. E., & Lalumière, M. L. (1993). Assessing treatment efficacy in outcome studies of sex offenders. *Journal of Interpersonal Violence, 8,* 512–523.

Sattler, J. M. (1992). *Assessment of children* (3rd ed.). San Diego, CA: Author.

Schilling, R. F., & Schinke, S. P. (1989). Mentally retarded sex offenders: Fact, fiction, and treatment. *Journal of Social Work and Human Sexuality, 7*(2), 33–48.

Schoen, J., & Hoover, J. H. (1990). Mentally retarded sex offenders. *Journal of Offender Rehabilitation, 16*(1/2), 81–91.

Swanson, C. K., & Garwick, G. B. (1990). Treatment for low-functioning sex offenders: Group therapy and interagency coordination. *Mental Retardation, 3,* 155–161.

Thompson, J. S. (1988, August). *Comparison of mentally retarded and non-retarded defendants referred for competency.* Paper presented at the annual meeting of the American Psychological Association, Atlanta, GA.

Travin, S., Bluestone, H., Coleman, E., Culler, K., & Melella, J. (1985). Pedophilia: An update on theory and practice. *Psychiatric Quarterly, 57*(2), 89–101.

Warren, J. I., Fitch, W. L., & Deitz, P. E. (1991). Criminal offense, psychiatric diagnosis and psycholegal opinion: an analysis of 894 pre-trial referrals. *Bulletin of the American Academy of Psychiatry and the Law, 21,* 63–69.

Wechsler, D. (1981). *Wechsler Adult Intelligence Scale—Revised.* San Antonio, TX: Psychological Corporation.

Wolfe, J., & Baker, V. (1980). Characteristics of imprisoned rapists and circumstances of the rape. In C. Warner (Ed.), *Rape and sexual assault* (pp. 265–278). Rockville, MD: Aspen Systems.

Appendix

Cognition Scale

Read each statement below carefully and then circle the number beside each statement that best describes how you feel about that statement. Please answer the way you would have answered before others (family, friends, the police) became aware of your deviant sexual behavior.

1. Strongly Agree
2. Agree
3. Neutral (neither agree or disagree)
4. Disagree
5. Strongly Disagree

1. If a young child stares at my genitals it means the child likes what she (he) sees and is enjoying watching my genitals.   1 2 3 4 5

2. A man (or woman) is justified in having sex with his (her) children or step-children, if his wife (husband) doesn't like sex.   1 2 3 4 5

3. A child 13 or younger can make her (his) own decision as to whether she (he) wants to have sex with an adult or not.   1 2 3 4 5

4. A child who doesn't physically resist an adult's sexual advances, really wants to have sex with the adult.   1 2 3 4 5

5. If a 13-year-old (or younger) child flirts with an adult, it means he (she) wants to have sex with an adult.   1 2 3 4 5

6. Sex between a 13-year-old (or younger child) and an adult causes the child no emotional problems.   1 2 3 4 5

7. Having sex with a child is a good way for an adult to teach the child about sex.   1 2 3 4 5

8. If I tell my young child (stepchild or
    close relative) what to do sexually and
    she (he) does it, that means the child will
    always do it because she (he) really wants to.   1 2 3 4 5

9. When a young child has sex with an
    adult, it helps the child learn to
    relate to adults in the future.   1 2 3 4 5

10. Most children 13 (or younger) would
    enjoy having sex with an adult, and
    it wouldn't harm the child in the
    future.   1 2 3 4 5

11. Children don't tell others about having
    sex with a parent (or other adult)
    because they really like it and want to
    continue.   1 2 3 4 5

12. Sometime in the future, our society
    will realize that sex between a child
    and an adult is all right.   1 2 3 4 5

13. An adult can tell if having sex with a
    young child will emotionally damage
    the child in the future.   1 2 3 4 5

14. An adult just feeling a child's body
    all over without touching her (his)
    genitals is not really being sexual
    with the child.   1 2 3 4 5

15. I show my love and affection to a
    child by having sex with him (her).   1 2 3 4 5

16. It's better to have sex with your
    child (or someone else's child)
    than to have an affair.   1 2 3 4 5

17. An adult fondling a young child or
    having the child fondle the adult
    will not cause the child any harm.   1 2 3 4 5

18. A child will never have sex with
    an adult unless the child really wants
    to.   1 2 3 4 5

19. My daughter (son) or other young child   1 2 3 4 5
    knows that I will still love her (him)
    even if she (he) refuses to be sexual
    with me.

20. When a young child asks an adult about   1 2 3 4 5
    sex, it means that she (he) wants to
    see the adult's sex organs or have sex
    with the adult.

21. If an adult has sex with a young child,   1 2 3 4 5
    it prevents the child from having
    sexual hangups in the future.

22. When a young child walks in front of   1 2 3 4 5
    me with no or only a few clothes on,
    she (he) is trying to arouse me.

23. My relationship with my daughter (son)   1 2 3 4 5
    or other child is strengthened by the
    fact that we have sex together.

24. If a child has sex with an adult, the   1 2 3 4 5
    child will look back at the experience
    as an adult and see it as a positive
    experience.

25. The only way I could do harm to a child   1 2 3 4 5
    when having sex with him (her) would
    be to use physical force to get her
    (him) to have sex with me.

26. When a child watches an adult masturbate,   1 2 3 4 5
    it helps the child learn about sex.

27. An adult can know just how much sex   1 2 3 4 5
    between him (her) and a child will
    hurt the child later on.

28. If a person is attracted to sex with   1 2 3 4 5
    children, he (she) should solve that
    problem himself (herself) and not talk
    to professionals.

29. There's no effective treatment for   1 2 3 4 5
    child molestation.

Chapter 32

The Politics of Denial— A Postmodern Critique

by William F. Northey, Ph.D.

Overview

In this chapter the author challenges some very basic assumptions about treating adolescents who have been charged with sex offenses. Rather than confronting a juvenile whose story does not match with the official version, this author suggests that the juvenile's view of what occurred should be considered therapeutically relevant. He also challenges the role that sex offender treatment providers should have with the criminal justice system. This chapter has been included to prompt sex offender providers to continually challenge their own most basic assumptions.

Introduction

Since the inception of specialized treatment for juveniles accused of sexual offenses (JASOs), denial has been an organizing principle. Most clinicians believe that "breaking through" denial is a necessary prerequisite for successful treatment. Unfortunately, there is little empirical evidence to support this claim. Further, when admitting to one's sexually offensive behavior in treatment becomes paramount, the risk increases that other therapeutic issues are neglected. This chapter calls attention to the limitations of using denial as an organizing principle and offers an alternative approach to working with youth who have difficulty taking responsibility for their sexual offending behavior. It is proposed that using "presumptive realities" as an organizing principle, rather than denial, helps to focus therapists on their role in the therapeutic process. When "presumptive realities" are used, the JASO's story or interpretation of the abuse event is considered therapeutically relevant and reflective of the context in which treatment occurs. Furthermore, and most important, the necessity of coercion is significantly minimized.

To date, few authors have considered the political aspects of denial. The ability to label someone as "in denial" has implications not only for those who can label but for those who get labeled. Denial, as it is currently used in the treatment of JASOs, is predicated on the belief that there is a reality that exists independent of the treatment provider, the victim, and the JASO, and this truth can be known. For purposes of this discussion, such a belief is not embraced; rather, it is assumed that reality is constructed (and reconstructed) constantly by each of us. Furthermore, what is generally referred to as "denial" is considered "a challenge" to the clinician's presumptive reality.

Presumptive Realities Are Therapeutic Constructions

"Presumptive realities" are the constructions created by a third party regarding an event in which that party did not participate, and that person's knowledge of the event is granted superiority relative to the knowledge of one of the participants (Northey, 1995). In the context of JASO treatment, presumptive realties manifest themselves when treatment providers use the information obtained from police reports, court reports, and the like to generate narratives about the sexually offensive behavior of JASOs. Presumptive realities as an organizing principle are based on a postmodern approach to therapy and treatment. Postmodernism, in its varied forms, has called attention to the limits and the sociopolitical aspects of knowledge.

The most serious critique promulgated by postmodern thinkers has focused on the belief in subject-object dualism (i.e., an independent, external reality). Although an independent, objective reality might exist, the human condition precludes the observer from "knowing" it (Dell, 1985).

Furthermore, some constructivists argue that "there is no independently existing reality. We literally create the world by living in it" (Kenny & Gardner, 1988, p. 15). The logical extension of the aforementioned tenets is that one can never know the "truth." Consequently, this means that JASO treatment providers can never know what "really" happened during an abuse event. Moreover, no inherent privilege can be granted to the a therapist's understanding over anyone else's. Lest I be misunderstood, this does not mean that the therapist's understanding is inherently inferior. It just means that each perspective is equally valid from the vantage point from which it is drawn. Accordingly, a postmodern perspective not only challenges us to consider the limitation of our own knowledge but also requires us to consider how those with power impose their knowledge on others.

Challenges to Presumptive Realities

Treatment providers hold a great deal of power over JASOs. Although power differentials can vary substantially relative to the treatment context and the relationship with the court, it is not unheard of for treatment providers to use various forms of coercion to get JASOs to comply with treatment (e.g., probation revocation and extended incarcerations). In fact, it is a commonly held assumption that JASOs are "not sufficiently uncomfortable with their behavior to follow through in treatment without external motivation to do so" (National Task Force on Adolescent Sexual Offending, 1988, p. 25). In spite of the potentially dire consequences, JASOs frequently challenge the presumptive reality held by the treatment providers. These challenges may vary from simply disagreeing about the time in which the abuse event occurred to complete dismissal of the alleged event. Generally, these challenges put forth by JASOs are summarily dismissed by clinicians as "denial." The dismissal of the JASO's challenge to the presumptive reality would not be so problematic if, the clinician presumptive reality was reliable and the JASO's challenge did not have clinical significance.

The Clinician's Knowledge Is Limited

The limits of what a clinician can know about a JASO or an abuse event are manifold. The issues to be considered here are what a clinician can realistically know about an abuse event and how we ascertain such information. Clinicians are rarely part of the investigative procedures.Consequently, their knowledge of the abuse is at best third hand. In most cases, the information gleaned by clinicians is based on police reports, court transcripts, assessments, interviews with the youths, and so on.

The common assumption is that the reports used by treatment providers accurately describe the events that resulted in the JASO's adjudication with little or no bias. Unfortunately, this assumption does not entertain the possibility of reporter bias, because rarely are these reports penned in the victim's own hand and rarely do treatment providers have direct contact with victims. These reports are commonly recorded by law enforcement or child protective workers, and discrepancies are rarely addressed. If the only issue was the possible bias related to the translation or transcription of the reports, concerns expressed by JASOs might be moot. However, an additional assumption that directly bears on the reliability of the presumptive reality has to do with the sociopolitical context in which law enforcement and child protective workers operate. These professionals are charged with protecting victims and the community. Accordingly, they are more likely to be interested in obtaining information that will result in an adjudication than in what happened from the JASO's perspective (especially when the JASO's version differs from the victim's).

Moreover, one must consider that a common assumption in the child sexual abuse field is that "victims of sexual abuse do not lie"; thus, if a child reports sexual abuse, it did in fact occur. Recently, this assumption has been challenged from two areas. First, more and more frequently child sexual abuse is being reported as a ploy among estranged spouses to gain custody of children, with concomitant coaching by the reporting spouse. Second, the literature on "false memory syndrome" (e.g., Loftus, 1993) suggests that therapists and investigators may contribute to the "construction" of a memory, resulting in an account that may be different from what "actually" happened.

In addition to "reporter bias," "interpreter bias" is also possible. Reading of any document can and usually does result in different interpretations depending on who reads it (Feixas, 1990). The question remains whether treatment providers read such reports critically and consider the sociopolitical context in which they were composed. Failure to do so is unwise given that there may be several sources of "error" in such reports. Several reasons can and most likely do account for the possible inaccuracies in these reports. The first is that the victim may have falsely accused the JASO. Contrary, to popular belief, victims are not above lying, embellishing, and/or misrepresenting their reports (Loftus, 1993). This is not to impute that victims lie. However, strict adherence to any written document has inherent flaws. Treatment providers who strictly adhere to a written document run the risk of creating presumptive realities that may not be accurate or complete or may not allow for a therapeutic frame.

Reports Usually Omit JASO's Perspective

It should also be noted that most, if not all, reports have an inherent gap in their accounts (i.e., the feelings, thoughts, and reactions of the JASO). Furthermore, to assume that the JASO's recollection of an abuse event can match, or will match, any type of report provided by the courts to treatment providers is unwise. Given that the focus of the investigation is on the abuse event, it is unlikely that aspects of the event that are not considered directly related to the sexual abuse will be included in those reports. That means that extenuating circumstances are likely to be excluded. The point is that any type of report is like a photograph, which only stops the action for a split second and, consequently, can only reveal part of the story. Exclusive reliance on any report, like exclusive reliance on a photograph to describe a parade, is incomplete and limiting.

Although it may appear that using presumptive realities requires that clinicians abdicate their responsbility in treatment, nothing could be further from the point. The idea is that clinicians must recognize not only the limitations of their clients' constructions (usually referred to as cognitive distortions or thinking errors) but their own as well. Just as clients get into "ruts," choosing to acknowledge the data that fit best with their understanding of events, clients often find themselves with similar routines. That is, they fail to hear the uniqueness attributable to most JASOs and the offense in which they are involved. It is my contention that treatment success is more likely to result from an appreciation and valuing of our clients than from fitting their experiences into predetermined narratives (e.g., offense cycles and relapse prevention plans). The focus on presumptive realities does not mean that JASOs will not admit or take responsibility; it just means that it is less likely to happen as the result of coercion or intimidation.

Further, there is no empirical support that JASOs cannot benefit from treatment without admitting. Sexually abusive behavior is a multidetermined phenomenon. Although understanding or insight may be more palatable—given our psychoanalytic roots—there is no evidence that insight is a necessary prerequisite for preventing reoffense. In fact, it is plausible that not admitting to one's most deviant sexual behavior to a group of strangers is a sign of mental health. If a youth refuses to admit to having committed a sexual offense, one might simply need to change tactics and work on how the JASO can prevent getting accused, arrested, and adjudicated in the future whether or not he or she admits to having committed the offense.

Challenging Relapse Prevention

I am well aware that such an approach does not fit well with some of the most common treatment approaches currently employed, namely, relapse prevention (RP) and sexual offense cycles. Rather than debate the merits of these types of approaches, I will make two points First, both RP and cycle work are insight-oriented and require JASOs to understand their offense patterns. As stated earlier, I am not convinced that insight is a necessary precondition of change. People change in a variety of ways and for a variety of reasons (Watzlawick, Weakland, & Fisch,1974). It is quite possible that some JASOs will simply not reoffend because they were caught the first time. Furthermore, it is possible that some youth may have a complete understanding of their offending behavior and go on to reoffend. RP and the like can be directly related to an addictions-oriented approach (Grey & Pithers,1993), which presumes an underlying psychopathology and the inevitability of continued sexual acting out. Unfortunately, there is virtually no empirical evidence in the JASO literature that supports such asser-tions. In fact, some studies report that there are no differences in outcome even when JASOs are placed in non–sex-offender-specific treatment (Brannon & Troyer, 1991, 1995) That is not to say that there are not juveniles who have deviant sexual interest (Hunter & Becker,1994) and may well become pedophiles, but the vast majority of youth are more similar to non-sexual offending delinquents (Bischof, Stith, & Whiney, 1995; Ford & Linney, 1995; Tartar, Hegedus, Alterman, & Katz-Garris ,1983) than to adult pedophiles (Hunter & Becker, 1994). Therefore, it may be best to reserve RP and some of the more intrusive behavioral techniques (e.g., aversive conditioning and mas-turbatory satiation) for the small number of youths with deviant sexual interest and to concentrate on increasing prosocial behavior among the other JASOs.

Anybody who has ever worked in a juvenile justice facility will tell you, "If you listen to the juveniles, none of them ever did what they are accused of." But one must also consider the possibility that perhaps the youth did not commit the offense for which he was adjudicated. I am unaware of any documentation on the number of juveniles who are falsely accused and convicted, but if this is possible in adult court, it is even more likely, given the less rigorous evidentiary procedures and disregard for basic civil rights, in juvenile courts (Schwartz, 1989).

The Relation of the Therapist to the Criminal Justice System

Treatment providers consistently report that they do not want to replicate the court proceedings by attempting to determine the guilt or innocence of a JASO in group; ergo, the youth must admit to the offense to receive treatment. The problem for most JASO treatment providers is that they want to extricate themselves from the court pro-ceedings, yet they want the threat of the court so that their clients will not leave ther-apy. To put it differently, treatment providers want to be thought of as therapeutic but do not want to consider themselves part of the criminal justice system. However, they want to use the consequences available to the court system (e.g., incarceration) to motivate their clients to attend therapy and do what the therapist says.

The most fundamental dilemma of this union is the presumptive realities that must be embraced if helpers are to work with court-referred clients. As Miller (1992) points out, therapists who do not subscribe to the belief that treatment and prosecution are compatible are systematically excluded from the process. When treatment providers accept court referrals, they are in essence accepting the presumptive realities that are thrust on them by the criminal justice system. Consequently, therapy, traditionally a process of exploring the gray and ambiguous areas of the human condition, becomes part of the "black and white" world of jurisprudence. Not succumbing to the certainty associated with this right-or-wrong, black-or-white, guilt-or-innocence mentality is no small feat for the therapist to accomplish.

JASO treatment, law enforcement, and the threat of prosecution have become inextricably interconnected (Miller, 1992). In many cases, the zeal to protect victims has resulted in the ability of treatment providers to use the coercion of the court to ensure treatment compliance. When coercion is employed, clinicians run the risk of failing to connect with or engage the JASO in therapy. The use of court sanctions to ensure compliance, in conjunction with presumptive realities about court-referred clients, may give license to therapists to "forget" how to engage clients or to blatantly abandon the most basic and vital aspects of therapeutic relationships. The use of court sanctions in therapy leaves clients vulnerable to potential violations of both civil rights and primary ethical principles. Consequently, basic values such as acceptance, agency, self-determination, and confidentiality can be seriously undermined by the association between helpers and the more adversarial criminal justice system (Miller, 1992).

This is not to say, however, that clinicians should not accept court-ordered clients. Most youth are not willing to discuss their sexual acting out if they do not have to. Consequently, it is unlikely that many JASOs will be forthcoming. The acceptance of court-ordered JASOs does mean that clinicians need to answer one basic question, "Who is my client?" Is the client the JASO? Is it the court? Or maybe the community?

Depending on the answer to this question different approaches will be brought to bear. For example, if one considers the JASO to be the client, it may not be in the best interests of the JASO to pursue the identification of additional victims, given mandatory reporting laws. One may argue that such revelations will help the client deal with "all" of his issues; however, in all likelihood it is going to result in additional, and possibly more severe, consequences. In the latter case, these additional consequences are clearly not in the best interest of the client.

It is the ethical responsibility of the clinician to clearly identify his or her client and to inform the JASO of this decision. All too often JASOs believe, or assume, they are the client when in fact the clinician views the community as his or her client.

Reasons for Challenging the Presumptive Reality

Heretofore the focus as been on the sociopolitical context, which may cast doubt on the veracity of the presumptive realities held by treatment providers. For the remainder of the discussion, let us assume that the presumptive realities created and used by clinicians are in fact accurate (granted we can never "truly" determine the accuracy). My research (Northey, 1995) has revealed that there are reasons why JASOs may challenge a clinician's presumptive reality regardless of its accuracy. The reasons why youth challenge the presumptive realities are based on interviews with forty incarcerated JASOs. These interviews were designed to elicit the experiences of the youth from the time they entered the system until they were interviewed. The major focus evolved into the exploration of how offense disclosures were incorporated into the treatment process.

Table 32.1
Reasons for Challenging the Presumptive Reality

Reason Category	N	Percent	Specific Reasons Mentioned
Affective reasons Fear Anxiety Pain or hurt Sensitivity	31	77.5	Shame or embarrassment
Issues of trust Confidentiality	11	27.5	Lack of history with group members
Protection of family Loss of relationships Disintegration	10	25	From embarrassment
Self-protection in a potentially hostile environment	8	20	Teasing Name calling Ridicule
Preservation of self-concept	8	20	Worth Humanness Identity
Protection of self Additional consequences	6	15	Physical harm
Maintenance of relationships	20	15	Loss of friends Treated differently
Forgetting Recall of the specific details Substance induced	4	10	Length of time between offense and treatment
Personality Entrenched value system Autonomy	4	10	Temperament characteristics
Offense characteristics	23	57.5	Gender of victim Relationship to victim Type of sexual behavior

Why JASOs May Have Difficulty Acknowledging Presumptive Realities

While exploring the process of offense disclosures, a number of reasons emerged that made disclosure difficult. The list of reasons contained in this chapter is not exhaustive, but it is illustrative of the numerous psychosocial issues that must be addressed when working with JASOs. Unfortunately, due to space limitations, an in-depth examination of the issues presented is not possible. The brief summary of reasons for challenging the presumptive reality is presented for consideration relative to the treatment process.

Table 32.1 contains the list of all of the "reasons" for challenging the presumptive reality presented by the forty JASOs who were interviewed. Overwhelmingly, the most common reasons why some JASOs did not disclose their sexual offense were affective. As might be expected, the shame and embarrassment usually expressed had to do mostly with being adjudicated on a sexual offense. The second most common reason mentioned by JASOs for why they had trouble accepting the presumptive reality was trust. Specifically, many of the participants reported that they were not sure they could trust the members of the group or the staff. Several of the youth mentioned that preservation of their self-concept was a motivating factor in challenging the presumptive reality. The attributions made to people accused or convicted of sexual offenses are severe in the United States. For a youth to accept the presumptive reality may require a complete revision of how he views himself as a person, particularly if he holds many of the same beliefs about "sex offenders" as does the larger culture.

In addition to emotional or psychological protection, challenges to the presumptive reality may protect the JASO from physical harm or further consequences. Similar to most people's response when they "get caught" at something they were not supposed to be doing, some of the youth reported that they challenged the presumptive reality so as not to get in trouble, or in any more trouble. Refusal to accept the presumptive reality may also have to do with issues related to protecting one's family. Just as being adjudicated on a sexual offense is embarrassing to the juvenile, it is likely to be equally embarrassing to the family, and particularly the parents. Challenging the presumptive reality allows the family to "save face" and offer alternative explanations for the son's incarceration (e.g., he was wrongly accused or someone wasout to get him). In addition to protecting family members, it also allows the youth to maintain relationships that would (from their perspective) need to be severed if they, in fact, had committed the alleged offense. Negative consequences with friends were more likely to be feared if the victim was a male, if the victim was a family member, or if the JASO was accused of rape. Many of the youth who had been adjudicated on charges for participating in homosexual offenses were concerned that their friends would not want to be around them because they would think the JASO was gay.

Forgetting was another reason why youth were unable to accept the presumptive reality. Only recently have personality characteristics or "temperament" been considered a possible reason why JASOs do not accept the presumptive reality (Ryan, 1995). There are youth who will not accept the presumptive reality because they are "stubborn," "independent," "autonomous," or the like. In addition to the aforementioned intrapersonal and interpersonal consequences, aspects of the offense seem to break out into an interactive and hierarchical schemata which may predict which youth will have more difficulty accepting the presumptive reality, regardless of its accuracy. These factors, in order of importance and with their dimensions in parentheses, are gender of the victim (male, female) (with the overtones of homosexuality and heterosexuality), relationship to the victim (first-order relative, second-order relative, non-relative), age difference between JASO and victim (significantly younger, extremely older, slightly younger, no age difference), type of sexual behavior (anal sex, vaginal intercourse, oral sex, fondling), and amount of aggression (excessive, minimal, none), amount of consent.

Conclusion

The use of the construct of "denial" in the treatment of JASOs raises several questions: Does the use of denial as an operating principle in the treatment of JASOs account for the concerns of all involved, including JASOs? What are the factors that lead to the use of "denial" (as it is currently understood) in the treatment of JASOs? Furthermore, are there legitimate reasons why some youth employ "denial"? The adoption of a postmodern paradigm allows for different answers to these questions and shifts the focus from the belief in a universe (right-wrong, black-white, either-or) to an appreciation of the multiverse (e.g., both-and) (Anderson & Goolishan, 1988). Acknowledging the existence of presumptive realities rather than a single "truth" not only allows therapists to address offense disclosures but allows for alternative perspectives that may shed light on other aspects of the JASO's life. Furthermore, the use of presumptive realities can allow for different types of interventions with JASOs which achieve most, if not all, of the same goals as when denial is the focus of treatment (e.g., victim empathy and taking responsibility for sexual offensive behavior). The major difference is that the reasons youth do not (or cannot?) take responsibility for the behavior early in the treatment process is as important, therapeutically, as when they can. Sexual offensive behavior does not occur in a political vacuum. Consequently, clinicians must be aware of sociopolicital aspects of sexual offending behavior and account for it in treatment.

References

Anderson, H., & Goolishian, H. A. (1988). Human systems as linguistic systems: Preliminary and evolving ideas about the implications for clinical theory. *Family Process, 27,* 371-393.

Dell, P. F. (1985). Understanding Bateson and Maturana: Toward a biological foundation. *Journal of Marital and Family Therapy, 11,* 1- 20.

Feixas, G. (1990). Personal construct theory and systemic therapies: Parallel or convergent trends? *Journal of Marital and Family Therapy, 16,* 1-20.

Kenny, V., & Gardner, G. (1988). Constructions of self-organizing systems. *The Irish Journal of Psychology, 9,* 1-24.

Loftus, E. F. (1993). The reality of repressed memory. *American Psychologist, 48,* 518-537.

Miller, J. G. (1992). On mitigating professional arrogance in the treatment of sex offenders. *International Journal of Medicine and Law, 11,* 485-491.

National Task Force on Adolescent Sexual Offending. (1988). Preliminary Report 1988. *Juvenile and Family Court Journal, 39,* 1–21.

Northey, W. F. Jr. (1995). *The use of presumptive realities in the treatment of incarcerated juveniles adjudicated on sexual offenses: A grounded theory study.* Unpublished doctoral dissertation, Kansas State University.

Ryan, G. (1995). *Resistance versus temperament: Characteristics which will not change.* Paper presented at the meeting of the National Adolescent Perpetrator Network, St. Louis, MO.

Schwartz, I. M. (1989). *Justice for juveniles: Rethinking the best interests of the child.* Lexington, MA: Lexington Books.

Chapter 33

Why Courts Are Reluctant to Believe and Respond to Allegations of Incest

by Joan Zorza, J.D.

Overview

This chapter examines why the family and divorce courts, which are supposed to operate in children's best interests, often fail to protect those who are victims of incest perpetrated by their fathers, particularly when the parents are separated. It further argues that because incest perpetrators are not cured quickly and often abuse other available children, all children in the family should be protected from the incest perpetrator, particularly from any unsupervised contact with him. In contrast, courts should attempt to strengthen the relationship between the children and their nonoffending mother to best help the children's recovery.

Introduction

Incest destroys the lives of thousands of individuals each year. Cohen (1998) has reported that victims of child sexual abuse account for half of the patients receiving mental health counseling at any given time. Yet courts continue to take a skeptical approach to actively prosecuting this crime. They may also be naïve as to ruling on custody and visitation rights in situations in which sexual abuse has been documented.

Courts' Awareness of Incest and Response

Even though public awareness of incest in the United States has fluctuated widely throughout history, child protection records have "found a constant level of 10 percent of cases involving incest" (Hooper, 1997, p. 338) from 1880 to 1960, with reductions only when many men are off at war and increases following their return home (Gordon, 1988). Public awareness of child sexual abuse and its devastating effects on its victims dates from the 1870s, beginning with the realization of how many prostitutes were incest and child sexual abuse survivors (Hooper, 1997). At that time, the emphasis was on controlling the female child's sexuality (Hooper, 1997), effectively blaming and punishing her for her father's abuse. Around the turn of the century the emphasis shifted to "diverting girls from 'promiscuity' towards responsible and healthy motherhood" (Hooper, 1997, p. 241). As scrutiny shifted, mothers began to be blamed for failing to protect their daughters, and the focus was more on the dysfunctional family (Hooper, 1997). All these erroneous views conveniently absolved the perpetrator father from responsibility and undoubtedly continued to reinforce the public's focus on children and mothers as blameworthy.

Custody Courts Skeptical of Allegations

Despite the high rates of incest cases and awareness of its harmful effects, many courts tend to disbelieve allegations that a father has perpetrated incest (Kelly, 1992; Myers, 1997). The Massachusetts Gender Bias Study, for example, found that most of the probate judges (who hear the state's divorce and custody cases) erroneously assume that mothers fabricate child sexual abuse allegations "to gain a bargaining advantage in the divorce process" (Abrams, 1989, p. 69), a view also held by the court's family service officers, who do most of the custody investigations and mediation for the court (Abrams, 1989). This unwillingness to credit reports of incest has been well documented in the custody and divorce courts in the United States (Winner, 1996; Armstrong, 1994; Myers, 1997; Chesler, 1986), Canada (Taylor, 1996), and still throughout the British criminal justice system (Hooper, 1997; La Fontaine, 1990). For exampe, a decade ago a Massachusetts General Hospital study found that 75% of children who claimed they had been sexually abused by a separated or divorced parent were not believed and none of the fathers were ever prosecuted (Armstrong, 1994).

The court determined that even semen found in a girl's vagina upon her return from visitation with her father was insufficient evidence of incest (Armstrong,1994). "All too commonly, complaints of incest are met with incredulity, whereas retractions are accepted on the flimsiest of pretexts" (Herman, 1981, p.166).

Not only do courts often refuse to consider or make findings that incest has occurred, divorce and custody courts often respond to mothers who make incest allegations by giving custody of the children to the fathers (Herman, 1981; Myers, 1997; Hartman, 1997), the very men who have abused them. Substantiating this bias, a study of custody determinations among women using California domestic violence programs found that the batterers who had not physically or sexually "abused their children actually won full custody less often (1,844) than fathers who were . . . sexually abusive (2,262)" of their children (Liss, 1993, p. 183). Even when courts find such allegations to be true, many courts refuse to prohibit the father from having visitation or to order appropriate supervised visitation which could protect the children. The Massachusetts General Hospital study found that 60% of the children sexually abused were forced to visit their alleged abuser, often overnight, with no or almost no supervision after the allegation (Armstrong, 1994). In 6,970 of the 9,557 California cases in which fathers sexually abused their children, the courts granted the incest perpetrator unsupervised visitation despite the evidence (Liss, 1993), with the result that 9,232 (96.6%) of the fathers who had sexually abused one or more children were awarded unrestricted access to their victims, because they had won either physical custody or unrestricted visitation. In addition, in many states "criminal stay-away order[s are] overridden by visitation orders" (Liss, 1993, p. 4) and mothers' allegations of family violence are ignored by the custody courts even after fathers have been criminally convicted (Liss, 1993).

Although the burden of proof to restrict or deny visitation to a parent is usually "clear and convincing" evidence (see, e.g., *Barron v. Barron*, 445 A.2d 1182 (N.J. 1982)), a difficult standard to meet but still easier than the "beyond a reasonable doubt" standard required for a criminal conviction, numerous lawyers have found that it is considerably easier to obtain a criminal conviction than to restrict or terminate an incest perpetrator's visitation because of the reluctance of custody and divorce courts to decide these issues. Incest victims are not protected from their perpetrator fathers when the custody and divorce courts are unwilling to seriously consider the accusations.

Why Many Courts Are Reluctant to Believe Allegations of Incest

Clear Evidence of Incest Seldom Exists. Courts expect evidence of child sexual abuse, including incest, to be corroborated by expert witnesses. Most courts expect such evidence to come from medical or mental health professionals (including child custody evaluators), or at least child protective service workers. Unfortunately, clear evidence proving sexual abuse of a child is often difficult to obtain (Schultz, 1997). Typically the abuse occurs in secret with the child, the only witness, being "too young, too shy, or too traumatized to testify. Medical and other corroborating evidence of abuse exists in only a small percent of cases" (Myers, 1997, p. 126) and is often inconclusive (Schultz, 1997). In one study of girl victims whose offenders admitted to vaginal penetration, "only normal appearing genitalia and nonspecific variation abnormalities were found in 39 percent of the girls" (Schultz, 1997, p. 172).

Just as medical evidence is usually lacking, there is no psychological test or device that determines whether a child was sexually abused or proves whether a particular man has sexually abused a child. (Myers, 1997). The presence or absence of posttraumatic stress disorder neither proves nor disproves sexual abuse (Schultz, 1997). Furthermore, even when there is medical evidence that a child was sexually abused, most children heal very rapidly, making it highly unlikely that the evidence will be detectable even a few weeks after the abuse occurred (Myers, 1997). This means that many if not most true cases of abuse, even when investigated by highly skilled professionals, are never substantiated. Clearly, those not knowledgeable in what to look for are far less likely to find clear indications of abuse.

Child sexual abuse is still a taboo topic for many people, including some professionals, with the result that even the minority of abused children who do disclose their abuse are often met with disbelief or even blame (Urbanic, 1993).

Just as there is no psychological assessment procedure that conclusively shows that a child has been sexually abused, there is none to prove that an alleged perpetrator did commit the offense (Dougher, 1995).

Few Professionals Trained to Find Incest. The reality is that few professionals who advise courts in custody determinations are actually knowledgeable about child sexual abuse, and especially about incest. A survey of all medical schools in the United States found that only half of them taught anything in their four-year curricula about any aspect of family violence students (Felder 1996). Furthermore, those that did include some training on the subject averaged less than twenty minutes during medical school and offered the information only to an elective class containing an average of twenty or fewer, with the result that few medical students learn much about any aspect of the subject, let alone are trained in the intricacies of child sexual abuse.

Most graduate programs in clinical and counseling psychology teach little about abuse, especially about sexual abuse of children (Pope, 1992). Indeed, even less is taught about any aspect of family violence in schools of psychology and family therapy than in medical schools (Felder, 1996). Substantiating this finding, the American Psychological Association's Presidential Task Force on Violence and the Family recently found that "many child protective service and mental health workers were not adequately trained or equipped to treat maltreated children." (American Psychological Association, 1996, p. 69). Not only are they not trained to treat family violence, but many of them "have not been trained to look for or assess for signs of abuse" (American Psychological Association, 1996, p.13). Many service providers and mental health workers harbor stereotypes that impede their ability to look for or find signs of child abuse (American Psychological Association, 1996).

Although therapists who treat child sexual abusers are usually very knowledgeable about the subject, and many treatment providers for incest victims are similarly knowledgeable, there is a strong preference in custody determinations for courts to rely on custody evaluators (Ackerman, 1996), although those psychologists and psychiatrists appointed to evaluate the family are far less likely to be knowledgeable (Liss, 1993). It is estimated that at most 10% of experienced child custody evaluators know enough about child sexual abuse not to be dangerous (Myers, 1997). Most of them have a strong joint custody bias (Ackerman, 1996), which makes them less able to consider child abuse accusations seriously. Indeed, a survey of the nation's most experienced psychologists who were custody evaluators showed that they recommended joint custody in 64% of cases (Ackerman, 1996). Because they hold a family dynamic perspective, few of them would be inclined to hold an abuser accountable for the incest, even though more than forty states require courts to consider family violence in making custody determinations (Zorza, 1997). Indeed, their responses indicated that they were eight times as likely to recommend sole custody to the parent who was accused of incest as against the accusing parent, without even any information about the accuracy of the allegation (Zorza, 1997). How cooperative parents are and how willing they are to foster a good relationship between the child and the other parent dominated as their main reasons for making custody recommendations. They gave these factors far more weight than family or domestic violence, which was checked by 27.7% of them, but only as a possible rationalization for not recommending joint custody. In contrast to the low importance they assigned to family violence when not recommending joint custody, 69.1% checked as a reason that parents do not cooperate/communicate and 57.4% checked that there was conflict or hostility between the parents (Zorza, 1997). Most custody evaluators blame the mother for family violence (Liss, 1993), which explains why most of them fail to hold even a proven abuser responsible.

Guardians ad litem in America, who represent the children's interests in the courts, are often inadequately trained in any aspects of family violence, including child sexual abuse, and many even lack adequate knowledge or training in child development (American Psychological Association, 1996) that might make them suspicious of inappropriate regression on the part of a child because of being abused. When they lack knowledge they cannot give courts reliable information about the abuse, how it affects the children, or what is needed to protect the children.

Further complicating matters is the fact that child protective workers tend to disbelieve children's incest allegations (Dziech, 1991). Many child protective service agencies refuse to respond when allegations of incest are made during custody disputes (Liss, 1993), further biasing the information that might come to the court's attention in making a custody determination.

Incest Perpetrators Deny and Manipulate. Not only do "almost all incest perpetrators lie about the incest, portraying themselves as the victim and threatening retaliation when exposed . . . [many of them] have now created an entire social movement [the False Memory Foundation] to protest their innocence, to disavow incest, and punish and discredit those who uncover it—patients and therapists alike" (Grand, 1995, p. 237; see also Armstrong, 1994). These threats from individual perpetrators and the False Memory Foundation have frightened many therapists (Brown, 1995), making fewer therapists willing to document incest or other abusive behaviors. These tactics of incest perpetrators negate the very existence of and further traumatize their victims (Grand, 1995), particularly when they successfully discredit their victim or their accuser.

In addition, abusive men often successfully manipulate mental health professionals, particularly the ones who have not been trained to understand how abusive and manipulative they are, confusing many professionals and causing them to blame the victim or believe that the abuser's problem is slight, nonexistent, or has been overcome

(American Psychological Association, 1996). The result is that courts that expect to be given accurate information may not receive it or, worse, may even be misled about what happened or its significance.

Many Myths Blind Professionals to Incest. Compounding the problem of courts not receiving accurate information about incest is the fact that significant numbers of professionals involved in custody matters (including some judges) have preconceived notions that make them unlikely to see or consider signs of child abuse, and incest in particular, even when the signs are blatant. This is particularly true when they are dealing with families that do not conform to their preconceived notions of where incest might happen (American Psychological Association, 1996) and when allegations involve middle- or upper-class families, although many researchers have found incest to be "more prevalent among more affluent families" (American Psychological Association,1996, p. 51). One study of 220 incest families found that 88% of the parents had at least a high school diploma, whereas another study involving 22 incest families had only one family receiving welfare (Patton, 1991). Similarly, many professionals falsely assume that incest is unlikely to occur in families that hold strong religious beliefs (Stout-Miller, 1997) or that the perpetrator is unlikely to abuse other children in the family (Prendergast, 1991).

Another problem blinding professionals to searching for or believing allegations of abuse is the myth that women frequently make false allegations of their own of a child's abuse and are particularly likely to do so for tactical gain in divorce and custody cases. Those believing this myth are especially reluctant to believe allegations when more than one type of abuse is alleged. However, women seldom make false allegations of domestic violence (Harrell, 1993; American Psychological Association, 1996) or child physical or sexual abuse (Thoennes, 1990; American Psychological Association, 1996). The Urban Institute documented that women filing for protection orders are abused an average of thirteen times in the year before they seek judicial relief, and that most women only come to court in desperation after everything else has failed to stop the abuse, and usually only after experiencing severe violence (Harrell, 1993) . In fact, women are far more likely to not report or underreport domestic violence than to falsely report it (American Psychological Association, 1996).

Also contrary to the myth that mothers frequently allege incest in contested custody cases, child sexual abuse allegations are made in only 2 to 3% of divorce cases (Thoennes 1990) and less than 10% of contested custody cases (American Psychological Association, 1996), and when those cases are objectively investigated, allegations are confirmed as often when custody is being disputed as when there is no divorce or custody case involved (McGraw, 1992). In fact, mothers do not even make the majority of child sexual abuse allegations (Myers, 1997). Unfortunately, many men who batter their wives also sexually abuse their children and vice versa (Edleson, 1993; American Psychological Association, 1996). After physical separation, many men feel an increased need to control their wives and partners (American Psychological Association,1996), increasing the likelihood that the wife will be beaten and the children physically or sexually abused. Indeed, fathers who have sexually abused their children often start to do so only after the parents separate or divorce (Myers, 1997; Armstrong, 1994). Men who abuse women are far more likely to seek custody of the children or to threaten to or actually abuse or abduct the children (American Psychological Association, 1996).

A related myth widely believed by many mental health professionals who advise courts in custody matters is that mothers often alienate their children against their fathers, and that incest allegations are the ultimate indication of "parental alienation syndrome." However, the American Psychological Association says that there is absolutely no scientific or other data supporting the popular psychological theory that mothers alienate their children (American Psychological Association, 1996), nor has this theory ever been subjected to peer review or been validated empirically (Berliner, 1993; Schultz, 1997). Nor has the theory ever been "listed among the diagnostic categories described by the American Psychiatric Association in *Diagnostic and Statistical Manual of Mental Disorders*" (Schultz,1997). The American Psychological Association instead cautions that courts and custody evaluators should not minimize violence or blame mothers or children for their anger against abusive fathers (American Psychological Association, 1996).

Another myth is the belief that anyone who was really abused would not retract his or her accusations, or its corollary that anyone who recants was not really abused. However, many children recant sexual abuse allegations, including many of those who were abused (American Psychological Association, 1996), and recanting does not mean that the abuse did not happen (Dziech, 1991). Similarly, some professionals still falsely believe that the consequences of child sexual abuse are not all that harmful to child victims, so that they dismiss any symptoms as exaggerated or presumptively not related to child sexual abuse.

Some Professionals Choose to Ignore Incest or Are Intimidated Into Not Reporting It. Even when professionals recognize abuse, some service providers, medical workers, and mental health workers are reluctant to invade the privacy or cause the breakup of an apparently successful family. Others are reluctant to risk ruining the father's reputation, especially if he is a successful wage earner, or believe that the effects of child sexual abuse are not sufficiently severe to warrant subjecting a family to intrusion. Moreover, they may fear for their own professional reputations should their accusation not be substantiated. Some feel that they may be subjecting the incest perpetrator to criminal charges and believe that this is not what the victim would want. In fact, prosecutions are rare even when the abuse is reported (Armstrong, 1994), although 87% of incest victims want the family member who sexually abused them to be prosecuted (Koss, 1992).

The American Psychological Association notes that many professionals required by law to report child abuse refuse or fail to report violence because they believe the process is burdensome or will interfere with any ongoing therapy or other intervention with the family. They doubt that the "outcome really will protect the victim, or they legitimately fear for their own physical or psychological safety" (American Psychological Association, 1996, p. 13) because retaliation by the offender is not that uncommon (Feldman-Summers, 1996; Grand, 1995; Armstrong, 1994; Zorza, 1996; Murphy, 1997).

Finally, some therapists have been remarkably tolerant of abuse toward women, and a few of them, mostly men, have themselves sexually abused female patients (Pope, 1996). Many of these therapists, as well as some of those taught or trained by them, might be less likely to look for or report incest or other sexual abuse.

Some Professionals May Protect Themselves From Vicarious Traumatization.
Vicarious traumatization is a phenomenon experienced by those exposed to victims of
trauma resulting from the transmission of the original trauma from the original victim
to those exposed. It is not caused by threats from the perpetrator, although such threats
probably would aggravate the vicarious traumatization. The effects of vicarious traumatization can be distressing and even debilitating (Zorza, 1998). To that extent, it is highly likely that a significant number of people protect themselves from vicarious traumatization and avoid being further emotionally affected by denying that the abuse happened or by blaming the victim for it (Dutton, 1992). Child sexual abuse, and particularly incest, has been found to be one of the most damaging traumas (Freyd, 1996).
People who have been previously exposed to severe trauma are at much higher risk of
vicarious traumatization (Zorza, 1998); as 9.5% of male and 16.4% of female therapists experienced child sexual abuse and 34.9% of male and 69.9% of female therapists
have experienced some form of abuse during their lifetimes (Pope, 1996), it is likely
that many of these professionals are at increased risk.

Some Medical Documentation Practices Confuse Lawyers. Many lawyers and
some judges do not know how to read medical records and many doctors use language
that is unclear or confusing (Schultz, 1997), further compounding the situation. The
term "history of sexual abuse" in a medical record only means that the doctor was told
that sexual abuse happened, not that the doctor made any findings (Schultz,1997).
Similarly, a doctor's usage of such terms as "diagnostic findings consistent with sexual abuse" or "consistent with abuse" could encompass normal findings which do not
prove abuse, because the findings do not rule out the sexual abuse allegation (Schultz,
1997). Because lawyers often interpret such statements as conclusive proof of abuse,
they and their clients are likely to be misled into thinking that they need no further
proof of the abuse, and they may not understand why an informed court does not find
in their favor regarding the sexual abuse issue raised.

Further Barriers to Courts Learning About Incest

Although courts usually never hear about the abuse because the child has never
disclosed the information, it can also happen in good faith because there are no signs
of abuse, or the child is too young or frightened to be more explicit, or because the
investigation was inconclusive. Knowing how punitive some courts can be against
mothers who raise incest allegations, or fearful of what the abuser might do to retaliate, the issue might never be raised because the mother or her lawyer is reluctant to or
dares not raise it.

In contrast to not hearing about the problem, when courts are repeatedly exposed
to misinformation, the myths and untruths are likely to become even more ingrained,
further impeding the ability of the system to find truth. In an atmosphere in which
myths that discredit women and children are regularly expressed without being cor-
rected, even those in the know may be intimidated into not challenging the myths.
Moreover, as many gender bias studies have noted, many courts have gender-biased
beliefs or practices that tend to discredit women, especially in cases involving allegations of rape or sexual abuse or custody disputes, trivializing her concerns and holding her to a far higher standard (Abrams, 1989; Gender 1991; Winner, 1996; Zorza,

1996a). This gender bias against women merely follows Western society's long tradition of disbelieving women's allegations of rape and sexual assault, an even more pronounced tendency when women or children allege incest (Myers, 1987).

Still other myths (e.g., that most mothers are co-conspirators in incest perpetrated by their partners [refuted in Urbanic, 1993]) cause blame to be wrongly focused on the mother and not on the incest perpetrator. Another myth holds that most mothers will never believe that the abuse happened and thus will not act to protect their abused children. Another popular belief is that incest happens because the mother does not sexually fulfill her partner's needs, causing him to be seek sexual gratification elsewhere (Johnson, 1992). In actuality, most male sex offenders "had the onset of their deviant sexual interest pattern during adolescence, which indicates a disposition to offending predating and independent of any family disruption" (Becker, 1994, p. 180).

Finally, judges and other court personnel on whom the court relies may hold the same types of myths that many other professionals hold, or may be psychologically unable to believe that abuse occurred, or be unwilling to recuse themselves when they are unable to act impartially. The result of any of these disabilities is that even when courts receive accurate information that should result in a clear findings of child sexual abuse, they may still be unable to impartially assess the weight of the evidence, seriously endangering the victims of child sexual abuse, particularly when a father is the perpetrator.

Effects of Incest Are Usually Devastating to the Child

Contrary to the myth that incest does not harm children, the reality is that the results are almost always extremely harmful, leading many of its victims to many "health and social problems including running away, prostitution, drug abuse, and mental health disturbances," as well as increasing their risk throughout life for engaging in or being victimized by violent criminal behavior or HIV infection (American Psychological Association, 1996, p. 52). Whereas only 5% of all rape victims suffer a major injury, 25% of parent-child rapes result in major injury (Greenfeld, 1997).

Child sexual abuse victims account for more than half of all individuals in the United States receiving mental health counseling or therapy, at an estimated cost between $8.3 billion and $9.7 billion in 1991 (Cohen, 1998, p. 106). More than three quarters (77.2%) of these 2,101,000 child sexual abuse victims in treatment were in treatment as adults (Cohen, 1998, p. 105). After murder, child sexual abuse is the most serious and expensive crime to the victim and society, including lost productivity, averaging $125,000 per survivor (Miller, 1996). Briere (1992) notes that greater long-term psychological trauma is frequently associated with sexual abuse involving "greater duration and frequency of the abuse . . . physically forced sexual contact . . . abuse at an earlier age . . . molestation by a perpetrator substantially older than the victim . . . [and] the victim's feelings of powerlessness, betrayal, and/or stigma at the time of the abuse," all factors more likely to be present in incest cases.

Not treating the original effects of child sexual abuse only "tend[s] to compound [them] over time, causing additional problems for the adult survivor" (American Psychological Association, 1996, pp. 54–55). (A minority of victims do not seem to have long-term effects as adults from child sexual abuse or even from incest [Meyers, 1997]). Furthermore, children do far better when they are treated as soon as possible

(Myers, 1997; American Psychological Association, 1996) and when they have supportive mothers (Myers, 1997; American Psychological Association, 1996) or do not have to "keep the abuse 'bottled up inside'" (Myers, 1997). Thus, preventing a nonoffending mother from supporting her child incest victim or from being in treatment is likely to compound the child's recovery. Moreover, such prohibitions cannot be justified by the "parental alienation syndrome," which has no scientific basis (American Psychological Association, 1996, p. 40; Schultz, 1997), or any of its equally baseless progeny, such as the "malicious mother syndrome (Smith, 1997).

How Courts Can Protect Incest Victims

Once a determination has been made that a child has been sexually abused by his or her father, it is important to protect all the children in the family lest the abuse continue. Any unsupervised visitation can be considered only if the perpetrator is in treatment and his therapist agrees that he is ready for this responsibility, and if it will not negatively affect the nonoffending mother from being able to support the child. However, courts need to realize that "child molesting is like other addictive behavior in that the risk to reoffend seems to extend over a long period of time if not a whole life span" (Finkelhor, 1988, pp. 133–134). Courts also need to know that it is unrealistic to assume that abuse will end upon discovery (La Fontaine, 1990; Herman, 1981); that children can protect themselves, even if they are in therapy (Chalk, 1989); or that even criminal prosecution will deter the abuser from reoffending (Chalk, 1989). The belief that most incest perpetrators only offend against their own children has been discredited, with new data showing an enormous overlap among the men who perpetrate incest and those who abuse unrelated children, and even those who sexually abuse or rape adults; in addition, they may target both males and females, again contradicting earlier assumptions (Becker, 1994). Castration is likely to work for only a small percentaage of compulsive offenders, and few incest perpetrators are of this variety (Chalk, 1998; Leberg, 1997). Moreover, those castrated, whether surgically or through use of chemicals, can completely circumvent the intended effects by taking the male hormone testosterone, which is readily purchasable on the street (Prentky, 1997).

Treatment Must Also Deal With Related Issues

Men who sexually abuse children often abuse their adult partners as well, including physically, sexually, and psychologically (American Psychological Association, 1996, p. 89). Because so many of these problems are interrelated and involve power and control, failure to address any of them means that the offender has not been adequately treated. However, although anger management must be an important component of any family violence treatment, it is not sufficient as a single treatment because of the complex nature of family violence (American Psychological Association, 1996).

Conditions for Reunification

"The safety of the child must not be compromised in an attempt to protect the legal rights of the accused perpetrator" (American Psychological Association, 1996,

p. 89). Every child exposed to violence in the home, even if the particular child has not been physically or sexually abused, has been psychologically maltreated by the abuser (American Psychological Association, 1996). For family therapy to be appropriate, both parents must be supportive of the child, the nonoffending parent and the child must agree to the treatment, and the perpetrator must have been in treatment and have accepted responsibility for the mistreatment (American Psychological Association, 1996). Contact should only be considered in families that agree that they want to reestablish contact and are willing to undergo family therapy (the mother's consent is most essential), and only if (1) the perpetrator has been successfully treated for any spousal violence and other anger issues; (2) the mother has been given sole authority to control and discipline children, with the perpetrator not allowed to criticize or undermine her; (3) the offender will never be alone with children; and (4) the family joins or is included in family group therapy. Much later, if the everyone in the family still wishes to resume a closer relationship, overnight visits can be considered, but only with trusted, responsible adult supervision and only if offender agrees (1) never to be in house alone without this supervision, (2) never to be in children's presence without this supervision (e.g., at night, the offender is not to leave his bedroom unless the supervisor is also up), and (3) children have locks on their doors (even if they choose not to use them) and the father has no right to compromise the lock's safety) (Wolf, 1988). This is for normal children; any child with a physical or mental disability is at much higher risk for being abused, and the aftermath of such abuse is far more complicated and devastating (American Psychological Association, 1996).

Because no on one can claim to "cure" incest, at most being able to keep the behavior under control" (Herman, 1989, p. 41), restoration of the incestuous family must center on the mother-daughter relationship. It is only when the mother feels strong enough to protect herself and her children and when the abused daughter feels she can turn to her mother for protection that it is at all possible to establish safety for the child. The choice of letting the father return to the family after he is ready should rest with the mother after the mother-daughter bond has been restored, and neither the mother nor the daughter should feel intimidated (Herman, 1989) If the father has admitted and taken full responsibility for the incest and the child's feelings of safety and well-being are restored and her distress symptoms gone, reunification is possible to consider . However, because "[t]he father's internal controls should never be considered sufficient to ensure safety for the child" (Herman,1989, p. 42), resumption of any relationship should only be considered if the mother and daughter are explicitly prepared to resume the relationship. No therapy should have as its goal preservation of the parents' marriage, as a decision to divorce is as valid as one to try to rebuild the parents' marriage (Herman,1989 p. 41). "Probably the best gauge of successful treatment is the child victim's subjective feeling of safety and well-being, the disappearance of her distress symptoms, and the resumption of her interrupted normal development" (Herman, 1989, p.41). Safety of the child will not be "established simply by improving the sexual or marital relationship of the parents; it is established only when the mother feels strong enough to protect herself and her children, and when the daughter feels that she can turn to her mother for protection" (Herman, 1989, p. 41). It is important to remember that children who have a strong relationship with their mothers heal far more quickly from abuse (American Psychological Association, 1996).

Because of the intergenerational cycle of abuse, children with abusive fathers may be at risk for abuse from the paternal grandparents (American Psychological Association, 1996), and it is unreasonable to expect members of the perpetrator's family to be able to supervise visitation. Putting children in foster care is far from an ideal situation because they are likely to be at high risk for abuse from the adults and other children in foster care (American Psychological Association, 1996).

Courts Need Not Find That Incest Occurred to Protect the Children

In some cases in which incest is suspected but not proven, one or more children in the family may still be afraid of the father. Even when there is not sufficient proof of incest to conclude that it happened, when child sexual abuse was known to have happened but there is insufficient proof that the father was the perpetrator, or when another child was abused but not this particular one, the court can still act to protect the child on a best-interest-of-the-child theory. Courts can respond to a child's fear with legitimate restrictions or infer that without protection a child could be at risk of incest. In such cases the court should not award sole or joint custody to the alleged perpetrator but should give the father supervised visitation that will offer any needed safety for the child. This makes far more sense than to punish a mother who makes an allegation in good faith (Thoennes, 1990) or to not protect or even punish a child by restricting the mother's authority over the child when the child needs the mother's support to best adjust (American Psychological Association, 1996).

Conclusion

Despite all the attention that sexual assault has received in the past few years, courts in many areas of the country are still reluctant to face the issue of incest. Children are still being placed with fathers who have had serious allegations of sexual abuse leveled against them. Courts are even ordering that children be forced to visit their convicted sex offender fathers in prison. Although it is certainly true that mothers can bring unsubstantiated charges against fathers in custody battles, it is too often the case that these allegations are dismissed out of hand. It is hoped that this chapter will serve as a wake-up call to courts to consider the well-being of children above all else and to realize that incest is not an anomaly but a frighteningly frequent occurrence.

References

Abrams, R. I., & Greaney, J. M. (1989). *Report of the gender bias study of the Supreme Judicial Court* [of Massachusetts].

Ackerman, M. J., & Ackerman, M. C. (1996). Child custody evaluation practices: A 1996 survey of psychologists. *Family Law Quarterly, 30*(3), 565–586.

American Psychological Association. (1996). *Violence and the family: Report of the American Psychological Association Presidential Task Force on Violence and the Family.* Washington, DC: Author.

Armstrong, L. (1994). *Rocking the cradle of sexual politics: What happened when women said incest.* New York: Addison-Wesley.

Becker, J. V. (1994). Offenders: Characteristics and treatment. *Sexual Abuse of Children, 4*, 176–197.

Becker, J. V., & Coleman, E. M. (1988). Incest. In V.B. Van Hasselt et als (Eds.), Handbook of family violence (pp.187–205). New York: Plenum Press.

Berliner, L., & Conte, J. (1993). Sexual abuse evaluations: Conceptual and empirical obstacles. *Child Abuse and Neglect, 17*, 111–129.

Brown, L. S. (1995). The therapy client as plaintiff: Clinical and legal issues for the treating therapist. In J. L. Alpert (Ed.), *Sexual abuse recalled: Treating trauma in the era of the recovered memory debate* (pp. 337–360). Northvale, NJ: Jason Aronson.

Chalk, R., & King, P. (1998). *Violence in families: Assessing prevention and treatment programs.* Washington, DC: National Academy Press.

Chesler, P. (1986). *Mothers on trial: The battle for children and custody.* New York: McGraw-Hill.

Cohen, M. A., & Miller, T. R. (1998). The cost of mental health care for victims of crime. *Journal of Interpersonal Violence, 13*, 93–110.

Commission on Gender Bias in the Judicial System. (1991). *Gender and justice in the courts: A report of the Supreme Court of Georgia.*

Dougher, M. J. (1995). Clinical assessment of sex offenders. In B. K. Schwartz & H. R. Cellini (Eds.), *The sex offender: Corrections treatment and legal practice* (vol. I, pp. 11-1–11-11). Kingston, NJ: Civic Research Institute.

Dutton, M. A. (1992). *Empowering and healing the battered woman: A model for assessment and intervention.* New York: Springer.

Dziech, B. W., & Schudson, C. B. (1991). *On trial: America's courts and their treatment of sexually abused children* (2nd ed.). Boston: Beacon Press.

Edleson, J. L., & Tolman, R. M. (1992). *Intervention for men who batter: An ecological approach.* Newbury Park, CA: Sage.

Felder, R., & Victor, B. (1996). *Getting away with murder: Weapons for the war against domestic violence.* New York: Simon & Schuster.

Feldman-Summers, S. (1996). Litigation pitfalls for the psychotherapist whose client "first remembers" childhood sexual abuse during therapy. *Women and Therapy, 19*, 109–122.

Finkelhor, D. (1986). Abusers: Special topics. In D. Finkelhor & Associates (Eds.), *Sourcebook on child sexual abuse* (pp. 119–142). Newbury Park, CA: Sage.

Freyd, J. J. (1996). *Betrayal trauma: The logic of forgetting childhood abuse.* Cambridge MA: Harvard University Press.

Gordon, L. (1988). *Heroes of their times: The politics and history of family violence.* New York: Viking.

Grand, S. (1995). Incest and the intersubjective politics of knowing history. In J. L. Alpert (Ed.), *Sexual abuse recalled: Treating trauma in the era of the recovered memory debate* (pp. 235–253). Northvale, NJ: Jason Aronson.

Greenfeld, L. A. (1997). *Sex offenses and offenders: An analysis of data on rape and sexual assault.* Washington, DC: U.S. Department of Justice, Bureau of Justice Statistics.

Harrell, A., Smith, B., & Newmark, L. (1993). *Court processing and the effects of restraining orders for domestic violence victims.* Washington, DC: Urban Institute.

Hartman, L. (1997). *Solutions: The women's crisis handbook.* Boston: Houghton Mifflin Co.

Hechler, D. (1988). *The battle and the backlash: The child sexual abuse war.* Lexington, MA: Lexington Books.

Herman, J. (1981). *Father-daughter incest.* Cambridge, MA: Harvard University Press.

Herman, J. (1989). Recognition and treatment of incestuous families. In L. J. Dickstein & C. C. Nadelson (Eds.), *Family violence: Emerging issues of a national crisis* (pp. 29–44). Washington, DC: American Psychiatric Press.

Hooper, C-A. (1997). Child sexual abuse and the regulation of women: Variations on a theme. In L. L. O'Toole & J. R. Schiffman (Eds.), *Gender violence: Interdisciplinary perspectives* (pp. 336–351). New York: New York University Press.

Johnson, J. T. (1992). *Mothers of incest survivors: Another side of the story.* Bloomington, IN: Indiana University Press.

Kelly, L., Burton, S., & Regan, L. (1992). And what happened to him?: Policy on sex offenders from the survivor's perspective. In *Beyond containment: The penal response to sex offenders* (pp. 14–27). London: Prison Reform Trust.

La Fontaine, J. (1990). *Child sexual abuse.* Cambridge, UK: Polity Press.

Leberg, E. (1997). *Understanding child molesters: Taking charge.* Thousand Oaks, CA: Sage .

Liss, M. B., & Stahly, G. B. (1993). Domestic violence and child custody. In M. Hansen & M. Harway (Eds.), *Battering and family therapy: A feminist perspective* (pp. 175–187). Newbury Park, CA: Sage.

McGraw, J. M., & Smith, H. A. (1992). Child sexual abuse allegations amidst divorce and custody proceedings: Refining the validation process, *Journal of Child Sexual Abuse, 1*(1), 49–62.

Miller, T. R., Cohen, M. A., & Wiersema, B. (1996). *Victim costs and consequences: A new look.* Washington, DC: National Institute of Justice.

Murphy, W. D. (1997, September/October). Massachusetts anti-SLAPP statute used to dismiss abusers' retaliatory litigation. *Sexual Asault Report,* p. 3.

Myers, J. E. B. (1997). *A mother's nightmare—Incest.* Newbury Park, CA: Sage.

Prendergast, W .E. (1991). *Treating sex offenders in correctional institutions and outpatient clinics: Guide to clinical practice.* Binghamton, NY: Haworth Press.

Prentky, R. A., Knight, R. A., & Lee, A. F. S. (1997). *Child sexual molestation: Research issues.* Washington, DC: National Institute of Justice.

Pope, K. S. (1996). Scientific research, recovered memory, and context: Seven surprising findings. *Women and Therapy, 19,* 123–140.

Pope, K. S., & Feldman-Summers, S. (1992). National survey of psychologists' sexual and physical abuse history and their evaluation of training and competence in these areas. *Professional Psychology, 23,* 353–361.

Schultz, R. (1997). Evaluating medical and mental health testimony in child sexual abuse cases. In *1997 Wiley Family Law Update* (pp. 167–200). New York: Wiley.

Smith, R., & Coukos, P. (1997, Fall). Fairness and accuracy in evaluations of domestic violence and child abuse in custody determinations. *The Judges' Journal, 36*(4), 40–56.

Stout-Miller, R., Miller, L. S., & Langenbrunner, M. R. (1997). Religiosity and child sexual abuse: A risk factor assessment. *Journal of Child Sexual Abuse, 6*(4), 15–34.

Taylor, G., Barnsley, J., & Goldsmith, P. (1996). *Women and children last: Custody disputes and the family "justice" system.* Vancouver, B.C.: Vancouver Custody and Access Support and Advocacy Association.

Thoennes, N., & Tjaden, P. G. (1990). The extent, nature, and validity of sexual abuse allegations in custody/visitation disputes. *Child Abuse and Neglect, 14,* 151–163.

Urbanic, J. C. (1993). Intrafamilial sexual abuse. In J. Campbell & J. Humphreys (Eds.), *Nursing care of survivors of family violence* (pp 132–155). St. Louis: Mosby.

Winner, K. (1996). *Divorced from justice: The abuse of women and children by divorce lawyers and judges.* New York: ReganBooks.

Wolf, S. C., Conte, J. R., & Engel-Meinig, M. (1988). Assessment and treatment of sex offenders in a community setting. In L. E. A. Walker (Ed.), *Handbook on sexual abuse of children* (pp. 365–383). New York: Springer.

Zorza, J. (1996a). Protecting the children in custody disputes when one parent abuses the other. *Clearinghouse Review, 29,* 1113–1127.

Zorza, J. (1996b). Retaliatory litigation. In S. Swihart (Ed.), *Florida domestic violence law* (pp. 22-1-2-3). Tallahassee: Florida Bar Association.

Zorza, J. (1997, June/July). Domestic violence seldom considered in psychologists' child custody recommendations. *Domestic Violence Report, 2*(5), 65.

Zorza, J. (1998, December/January). Our clients may affect us: Vicarious traumatization. *Domestic Violence Report, 3*(2), 21.

Part 7

Legal Issues

Due to the increasing number of questionable pubic policy responses to sex offenders, there has been increasing litigation challenging these policies. Two of the most controversial responses have been involuntary commitment of those individuals adjudged to be sexually violent predators and registration and public notification to communities in regard to the presence of sex offenders and, in some cases, sexually violent predators, in their midst.

As with almost all major changes in public policy regarding sex offenders, these policies were motivated by the violent attacks on, and in several cases murders of, young children. These crimes have always engendered outrage by the public, as well they should. Frustrated legislators attempt to respond to the outcry by doing something—anything. In the 1930s, states began passing Sexually Dangerous Person Acts, Mentally Disordered Sex Offender Acts, and Sexual Psychopath Laws in an attempt to confine for extended periods the most dangerous sex offenders. However, over the years these laws were gradually ignored or eliminated. But the 1990s have seen a rebirth of involuntary commitment and the institution of public notification.

Although these policies have numerous problems, including the difficulty in identifying which sex offenders are the most dangerous, financial concerns, and the policies' questionable ability to enhance public safety, this section concentrates on the legal challenges to these laws. In their analysis of the challenges to civil commitment, Elizabeth Rahmberg Walsh and Brian M. Flaherty point out that in the precedent-setting case, *Kansas v. Hendricks,* the main point was whether the Kansas law violated the ex post facto claim by imposing an enhanced punishment for a crime retroactively. On the same grounds, a double jeopardy issue was also raised. A critical issue was whether involuntarily committing an individual for treatment for a condition that could predispose him or her to committing sexually violent acts was a civil action or simply further punishment disguised as a civil action. The Supreme Court ruled that a state could confine someone merely because he was dangerous, but only when this the confinement is paired with a finding that the individual also has a "mental illness" or "mental disorder." The Court also ruled that the law was intended to be civil partially because it was not intended as a deterrent and did provide treatment. A number of cases involving a litigant named Linehan (*Linehan I, II, III, and IV*) have challenged the Minnesota law, but it has been upheld as the court has found that the purpose of the law is remedial.

The question whether policies related to sex offenders are punitive in nature is also a key to the controversy revolving around public notification. These laws have been mandated in order for states to collect certain funds under federal crime litigation. Walsh and Flaherty, in their chapter updating Megan's Law, explore the various challenges to this type of legislation. Although the laws have been challenged on a variety of constitutional issues, it has consistently been found that as long as these laws are not enacted as additional punishment, they do not violate the ex post facto, double jeopardy, cruel and unusual punishment, and bill of attainder clauses.

Walsh and Flaherty have also authored a chapter exploring the challenges to public notification on non-*Hendricks* related challenges involving sexually violent predators. Only a case in Ohio (*Ohio v. Cook*) has ruled that this legislation constitutes punishment according to that state's constitution. There have been many challenges to the manner of measuring risk. *Doe v. Pataki* has established the right of due process because the court ruled that the process did create an added stigma. Cases have also been brought regarding hearings, appeals, and notification of the offender.

Certainly there are a variety of ways in which society can choose to respond to sex offenders. Brian K. Holmgren of the American Prosecutors Research Institute presents a number of different suggestions based on cooperation between criminal justice system and sex offender treatment specialists. He bemoans the failure of society to take into account the knowledge of those who have expertise in sex offenders when constructing public policy. He suggests that assessments conducted by these professionals can be invaluable in prosecutions and sentencing proceedings. Prosecutors and treatment specialists should work together to overcome the impediments to gathering information and dealing with noncooperative offenders. Prosecutors must be careful not to settle for plea agreements with offenders whom treatment providers are reluctant to treat due to denial or other issues. Both groups of professionals need to lobby for more resources and training. Holmgren also urges treatment professionals to maintain their integrity by providing adequate disclaimers as to the efficacy of treatment, warn the criminal justice system about making unreasonable demands, and work to establish reasonable qualifications for therapists involved in this type of work.

While groups such as the Association for the Treatment of Sexual Abusers along with its state chapters and the Center for Sex Offender Management work diligently to educate policy makers about how to most safely manage sex offenders, ill-thought-out legislation continues to proliferate. A number of states have started involuntary commitment programs that will result in incredible expenses with questionable results. Other states are initiating "two strikes you're out" laws that are also incredibly costly, whereas long sentences such as a five- to seventy-year sentence for serious sex offenders would give systems the option of releasing individuals who are doing well while continuing to incarcerate those offenders who have done little to change.

In view of sentences that could span sixty to seventy years, it is interesting to speculate what will be learned about sex offenders in that time span. We may discover a physiological basis for some of this behavior. We may invent technology that makes monitoring and early intervention child's play. We may come up with an almost foolproof treatment, but none of these developments can help individuals sentenced to life sentences. Surely we should keep our options open in face of this rapidly changing world.

Chapter 34

Civil Commitment of Sexually Violent Predators

by Elizabeth R. Walsh, J.D., M.L.S.
and Brian M. Flaherty, M.L.S.

Overview

The U.S. Supreme Court has upheld civil commitment for sex offenders in *Kansas v. Hendricks* and *Linehan IV*. In this chapter the authors discuss the constitutional issues and relevant precedents addressed in these cases. They also discuss some of the issues being raised in related cases that are currently in the courts.

Introduction

Since Megan Kanka, a young New Jersey girl, was sexually abused and killed by her neighbor, a previously convicted sex offender, sex offender legislation has proliferated at both the state and federal levels.[1] In most instances state and federal legislation draws a clear distinction between sex offenders and sexually violent predators. A sex offender (SO) is described most commonly as a person who has been convicted of one of a number of sex offenses enumerated under the statute and who, upon release from custody, must register with local law enforcement and whose whereabouts may be reported to the community in which he or she resides.[2]

A sexually violent predator (SVP) is a person who has been designated by statute as either having committed or having been convicted of committing a sexual offense and has been diagnosed with a mental disease, mental disorder, mental abnormality, sexual disorder, or personality disorder that makes the person likely to engage in future predatory acts.[3] Legislation regarding an SVP can follow several paths: the SVP may be subject to civil commitment in lieu of criminal sanctions,[4] the SVP can be subject to civil commitment in addition to criminal sanctions (such as imprisonment),[5] the SVP may be subject only to registration and community notification provisions like his or her SO counterparts, except that the registration and community notification provisions are enhanced for sexually violent predators (the term for registration lasts longer, the SVP is required to report more frequently, the SVP is required to supply additional information to local law enforcement, etc.),[6] or the SVP may be subject to registration and/or community notification in addition to civil commitment.[7] In some instances, the SVP is subject to a mandatory term of life without parole[8] or his or her parole eligibility may be limited by his or her SVP status.[9] One state, Oklahoma, has enacted a statute for the specific purpose of studying the appropriate treatment for sexually violent predators.[10]

Challenges to Involuntary Commitment

This chapter discusses the recent case law that has addressed civil commitment of sexually violent predators. The chapter begins with a discussion of a U.S. Supreme Court case, *Kansas v. Hendricks*,[11] and then focuses on a line of Minnesota cases that address common state challenges to civil commitment of sexually violent predators or offenders, *In re Linehan*.[12] Chapter 36 discusses constitutional challenges to registration and/or community notification provisions raised by SVPs.

Kansas v. Hendricks

In the last few years, few criminal cases have been decided by the U.S. Supreme Court that provided either the impact or the surprise of *Kansas v. Hendricks*. Hendricks was convicted of a sexual offense in 1984 and admitted to sexual molestation and abuse of children as far back as 1955. His numerous attempts at rehabilitation were unsuccessful, and he was serving a sentence for taking indecent liberties with two young boys when he reached his conditional release date in September 1994. The Kansas state physician diagnosed him as a pedophile and found that he was not cured of this condition. Hendricks readily agreed with this assessment, as did the jury which found him to be a sexually violent predator and committed him under the Kansas Sexually Violent Predator Act (the "Act").[13]

The Act defined a sexually violent predator as "any person who has been convicted of, or charged with, a sexually violent offense and who suffers from a mental abnormality or personality disorder which makes the person likely to engage in predatory acts of sexual violence."[14] The state argued, and the jury concurred, that pedophilia constituted a "mental abnormality" under the Act. Hendricks appealed, claiming that applying the Act to him violated the United States Constitution's prohibitions against double jeopardy and ex post facto laws, and also that it violated his right to due process.

Hendricks' Claims. The substance of Hendricks' ex post facto claim was that the Act retroactively imposes additional punishment. In other words, the statute violated ex post facto prohibitions because it imposed an enhanced penalty for the crime after commission of the crime.[15] In addition, Hendricks claimed that it violated double jeopardy prohibitions because either it was a second prosecution for a single offense or it imposed a second punishment for the same offense.[16] Hendricks' substantive due process claim was based on the holding in *Foucha v. Louisiana*.[17] *Foucha* involved an insanity acquittee who had been civilly committed based on a diagnosis of antisocial personality. Foucha successfully argued that the statute required that he suffer from a mental illness to be civilly committed, that antisocial personality did not fulfill this requirement, and therefore he should be released. The Court in *Foucha* agreed. Hendricks argued that pedophilia did not constitute a mental illness. He further contended that civil confinement based on a finding of future dangerousness, together with his diagnosis as a pedophile, but without a finding that he suffered a mental illness, violated his substantive due process rights. He posited that confinement, absent a mental illness diagnosis, deprived him of his liberty, without just cause.

Substantive Due Process. *Foucha* seemingly set the stage for Hendricks' appeal. It was anticipated by many that the U.S. Supreme Court would uphold the Kansas Sexually Violent Predator Act. It was further anticipated that the debate would center around whether the Act violated substantive due process considerations because it allowed for civil commitment of persons who did not suffer from a mental illness but merely from a "mental abnormality" or "personality disorder."[18] Justice Thomas, writing for the majority, confirmed that a finding of dangerousness alone would be an insufficient basis for civil commitment but allowed that such a commitment is permitted where the finding of dangerousness is paired with a finding of " 'mental illness' or 'mental abnormality.' " The majority dismissed *Foucha's* seeming "requirement" that there be a finding of a mental illness by stating that "the term 'mental illness' is devoid of any talismanic significance," as not even psychiatrists agree on what mental conditions constitute a mental illness justifying civil confinement. As previously the Court has declined to adopt any particular terms of art to describe the mental conditions allowing for such confinement but has left it up to state legislatures to define their own terms when drafting such legislation, Thomas found that the state of Kansas was within its rights to prescribe a system of civil confinement for convicted sex offenders based on a finding of "mental abnormality" or "personality disorder," when coupled with a finding of dangerousness.

Ex Post Facto and Double Jeopardy. Hendricks' ex post facto and double jeopardy claims were decided based on the same threshold question: Did imposition of civil commitment after Hendricks had served a criminal sentence constitute punishment? Whether a statute imposes punishment is a critical determination, as elaborated in Chapter 35, "Megan's Law Update," which explains that to make this initial determination, courts would follow one of two lines of reasoning. However, the *Hendricks* Court followed neither the *Halper*[19] nor the *Hudson/Ward*[20] analyses but, rather, formulated its own unique analysis to answer this fundamental question, incorporating, "Chinese-menu" style, selected portions of the *Kennedy v. Mendoza-Martinez*[21] factors discussed in *Ward*.

To answer the fundamental question, "Does the order of civil commitment of an offender after he or she has served a term of incarceration constitute punishment?" the Court first considered whether the legislature intended the commitment to be a civil proceeding. The Court found that this indeed was the intent of the legislature, as it had placed the commitment proceeding, the Sexually Violent Predator Act, within the probate code and not the criminal code. In addition, nothing on the face of the legislation suggested that the commitment proceeding was intended to be other than civil. Specifically, the Court said:

> Where the State has "disavowed any punitive intent"; limited confinement to a small segment of particularly dangerous individuals; provided strict procedural safeguards; directed that confined persons be segregated from the general prison population and afforded the same status as others who have been civilly committed; recommended treatment if such is possible; and permitted immediate release upon a showing that the individual is no longer dangerous or mentally impaired, we cannot say that it acted with punitive intent.[22]

Although the Court recognized that simply applying a "civil" label was not dispositive of the issue, it placed a fairly heavy burden on Hendricks to challenge the legislative intent as civil. "[W]e will reject the legislature's manifest intent only where a party challenging the statute provides 'the clearest proof' that 'the statutory scheme [is] so punitive either in purpose or effect as to negate [the State's] intention' to deem it 'civil.'"[23] Not surprisingly, Hendricks failed to meet the burden.

Next, the Court looked at a selection of *Mendoza-Martinez* factors, particularly whether the behavior to which the statute applied was already a crime, that there was no required finding of scienter to commit an individual, that the legislature did not intend the statute to act as a deterrent or to be retributive, and that although the commitment proceeding did involve an affirmative restraint, detention alone did not constitute punishment.[24]

Finally, the Court weighed several factors that Hendricks claimed demonstrated Kansas' punitive intent: the potentially indefinite duration of the detention, the provision of criminal-like procedural safeguards for the potential committee, and the Act's failure to provide any legitimate treatment. The Court found that the term of detention is not indefinite but, rather, a one-year term, as the state must conduct an annual review of the commitment and, on each occasion, must show, beyond a reasonable doubt, that the person detained meets the same standards required for initial commitment. Hendricks' second claim here was summarily dismissed—the statute is not transformed from a civil to a criminal proceedings simply because the Kansas Legislature chose to provide additional procedural safeguards. Third, Hendricks had claimed that to declare him a sexually violent predator and to confine him without providing him any treatment was indicative of the Act's punitive intent. The Court posits that the Kansas Supreme Court's remarks on treatment could be interpreted in two different ways: that sexually violent predators are "not amenable to treatment," or that Hendricks' condition was treatable but that the concern for treatment was secondary to the Act's concern for incapacitation. Regarding the first interpretation, the

Hendricks Court found, however, that even if treatment were not possible, "incapacitation may be a legitimate end of the civil law."[25] If, as in this case, incapacitation is joined with the supplementary goal of providing treatment to offenders where possible, a punitive intent may not be inferred. The Court explained that to require treatment where no demonstrably acceptable treatment exists would be nonsensical, as would the release of certain individuals who are mentally ill and dangerous because they are not candidates for treatment. Regarding the second interpretation, the Court decided that because treatment is obligated in several other sections of the Act, the state, in essence, has agreed to provide treatment for persons committed under the Act.

To violate ex post facto principles, the Act must constitute punishment and be applied retroactively to the offender. Here, the Act does not violate ex post facto law because it neither constituted punishment nor was applied to Hendricks in a retroactive manner. First, the Act is not retroactive because it looks at future dangerousness, not past acts, and second, because the Court determined that the Act is civil and not criminal, it does not constitute punishment. In similar fashion, it does not violate the Double Jeopardy Clause, because being civil, it does not impose punishment at all and cannot, therefore, constitute a second punishment for a single crime. Finally, because the commitment proceedings are civil in nature, they do not constitute a second prosecution for a single offense.

In re Linehan

A large number of Minnesota cases address a litany of issues that are representative of those that arise in the context of civil confinement of sexually violent predators in many state and lower federal courts.[26] The Minnesota cases rely on the *Linehan* line of decisions (designated here as *Linehan I* through *Linehan V,* although most rely on the holding in *Linehan IV*), all of which deal with the civil commitment of Dennis Darol Linehan under either the Minnesota Psychopathic Personality Commitment Act[27] or the Sexually Dangerous Person statute.[28] *Linehan IV* was appealed to the U.S. Supreme Court (*Linehan V*), which remanded it for further hearing in the state court in light of the U.S. Supreme Court's decision in *Hendricks*. As of this writing the Minnesota Supreme Court has not yet heard *Linehan IV* on remand. Most of the Minnesota courts have stated that they have followed and will continue to follow the court's holdings in *Linehan I* through *Linehan IV* until such time as the Minnesota Supreme Court revisits these issues post-*Hendricks*.

Minnesota allows commitment of an offender as a sexually psychopathic personality (SPP) if the offender exhibited an "utter lack of power to control the person's sexual impulses and, as a result, is dangerous to other persons."[29] A sexually dangerous person (SDP) is one "who has engaged in a course of harmful sexual conduct . . . has manifested a sexual, personality, or other mental disorder or dysfunction . . . and as a result is likely to engage in acts of harmful sexual conduct.. . . For purpose of this section, it is not necessary to prove that the person has an inability to control the person's sexual impulses."[30] Challenges to these statutes are numerous and have been addressed by the *Linehan* line of cases and by *Kansas v. Hendricks,* as well.[31] The constitutional challenges to civil commitment discussed by *Linehan I* through *Linehan IV* include substantive due process, double jeopardy, equal protection, ex post facto, and failure by the state to meet its clear and convincing burden for commitment required under both Acts. Surprisingly, few Minnesota cases challenge commitment as an SDP or an SPP on a procedural due process basis. This topic is discussed outside the *Linehan* context.

Linehan I[32] held that the question whether the Minnesota Psychopathic Personality Commitment Act (MPPCA), now the SPP statute, violated substantive due process and equal protection principles had already been answered in the negative by *In re Blodgett*.[33] *Blodgett* held that the state has the burden to prove by clear and convincing evidence that there is "a habitual course of misconduct in sexual matters, an utter lack of power to control sexual impulses so that it is likely the person will attack or otherwise inflict injury, loss, pain, or other evil on the objects of their uncontrolled or uncontrollable desire."[34] *Linehan I* held that the state had failed to prove by clear and convincing evidence that the appellant exhibited an "utter lack of power to control his sexual impulses"and his commitment under the Act was reversed. The court stated that it was unnecessary to decide the second question, whether Linehan was likely to engage in future dangerous behavior, because in order to reach that question, the state had failed to prove the predicate finding, the offender's utter lack of power to control his sexual impulses. *Linehan II*[35] affirmed Linehan's initial commitment.

In *Linehan III*,[36] the Minnesota Supreme Court dealt with the scope of review and burden of proof at the sixty-day review hearing provided for under the SDP statute. The court affirmed Linehan's commitment under the SDP statute and held that Linehan had standing to appeal the district court's ruling on the scope of the review hearing; that the district court acted within its discretion in declining to credit the expert testimony that failed to reflect a change in his condition since the initial commitment hearing; and that sufficient evidence supported his commitment.

Linehan IV[37] determined that the Sexually Dangerous Persons Act[38] did not violate substantive due process, equal protection, ex post facto, and double jeopardy, and that the state had met its clear and convincing burden to show that Linehan was a sexually dangerous person as defined by the act. Under the SDP Act, unlike under the SPP statute, there is no requirement for the state to show that the offender was unable to control his or her sexual impulses; but, rather, the state is required to show only that the offender has engaged in a course of harmful sexual conduct and that he or she suffers from a sexual, personality, or other mental disorder, and as a result is likely to engage in serious or harmful sexual conduct in the future. This is similar to the Kansas civil commitment statute for sexual offenders upheld in *Hendricks*.

Linehan IV

Substantive Due Process. "[Substantive due process] may be broadly defined as the constitutional gurantee that no person shall be arbitrarily deprived of his life, liberty or property; the essence of substantive due process is protection from arbitrary and unreasonable action."[39] The majority in *Linehan IV* determined that freedom from physical restraint was a fundamental right and, therefore, subject to strict scrutiny, which means that the government would have to demonstrate that it had a compelling interest to justify the law, and that the statute was narrowly drawn to achieve that interest. The burden is on the government to demonstrate its compelling interest and that the statute is narrowly tailored.[40] Another test compares the magnitude of the liberty deprivation to the magnitude of the state's interests when determining the extent of the constitutional guarantee. The liberty deprivation here was the possible lifetime confinement of a sexually dangerous person. The state's proffered compelling interests were to protect the public from sexual assault and to care and treat the mentally disordered.

In its decision, the *Linehan IV* court cited *Foucha v. Louisiana,*[41] which held that prior to civilly committing an offender, the court must find him or her both mentally ill and dangerous. *Blodgett,* a Minnesota case, however, had held that there are three instances under which commitment can take place: Convicted criminals can be imprisoned for purposes of deterrence and retribution; mentally ill and dangerous persons can be civilly committed; and those who pose a danger to others may be subject to limited confinement in certain narrow circumstances, such as the pretrial detention of dangerous criminals.[42] No finding of mental illness is required, but some "mental health basis" plus a finding of future dangerousness is necessary for commitment. The court followed the reasoning in *Blodgett* and held that the SDP Act was sufficiently narrow to satisfy strict scrutiny.

In addition, Linehan asserted that because his diagnosis of antisocial personality disorder is little more than a definition of criminal behavior, it is an invalid basis for commitment. However, the court denied his claim. It deferred to the legislature to identify medically recognized mental disorders, and deferred to the fourth edition of the American Psychiatric Association's *Diagnostic and Statistical Manual of Mental Disorders* (1994) to define them.[43]

Ex Post Facto and Double Jeopardy. The Ex Post Facto Clause prohibits the government from applying a law retroactively that "inflicts a greater punishment, than the law annexed to the crime, when committed."[44] The Double Jeopardy Clause bans, among other things, "a second prosecution for the same offense after conviction . . . and multiple punishments for the same offense."[45] To determine whether a particular statute violates ex post facto or double jeopardy principles, the court must first determine whether the statute is intended to be remedial or punitive. The threshold question is, Does the statute impose punishment?[46]

In *Linehan IV*, to answer the threshold question, the court looked at the fact that the SDP Act provided for a treatment plan and found that the purpose of the legislation was remedial. Further, quoting *Ward*, it held that once the statute was determined to be remedial, Linehan had the burden to provide the "clearest proof that the Act was sufficiently punitive in purpose or effect to negate the civil label,"[47] and that he had failed to provide such proof. The court based its finding on the holdings of *In re Blodgett*[48] and *Call v. Gomez,*[49] which had previously found that the Act was not punitive for purposes of ex post facto and double jeopardy, respectively.

Equal Protection. The Equal Protection Clause provides that no state shall "deny to any person within its jurisdiction the equal protection of the laws."[50] Equal protection does not forbid all discrimination, only those distinctions that are arbitrary. This does not mean that "all persons must be treated alike, but, rather, that those similarly situated should be treated alike."[51] The analysis in an equal protection context will turn on whether the right at stake is a fundamental one or whether the person asserting the claim is a member of a suspect class. Here, the court found that although the interest involved was a fundamental liberty interest, the Act drew "genuine and substantial distinctions that define a class of dangerous and mentally disordered persons who victimize others in a particular manner."[52] and that the statute must survive not strict scrutiny but only heightened scrutiny, a form of intermediate scrutiny under the Minnesota Constitution. To pass constitutional muster under the intermediate scrutiny test, the state's "genuine and substantial distinctions" must be only "reasonably related to achieving the legitimate purpose, identify and treat sexual predators."[53] Following *Blodgett*, the court found that the statute's classification of offenders was justified and that there was a reasonable connection between the mental disorder defined by the statute and the state's stated interest to protect the public and treat the offender.

Sufficiency of the Evidence. The court held that there was sufficient evidence in the record that Linehan would commit future harm, and it cited the district court's participation in a multifactor analysis recommended in *Linehan I* to make that determination.[54] It also held that the court's findings did not lack specificity.

Impact of the *Linehan* and *Hendricks* Decisions

Linehan IV was decided prior to the U.S. Supreme Court's decision in *Hendricks*. Linehan appealed his case to the U.S. Supreme Court, which vacated the judgments and remanded the case to the Minnesota Supreme Court for further consideration in light of *Hendricks*. Because the Minnesota and the Kansas statutes are similar in their definition of sexually violent predator and the due process to which a potential civil committee is entitled, it is expected that the Minnesota Supreme Court will follow *Hendricks* and affirm Linehan's civil commitment under the SDP Act. The decision will affect not only *Linehan* but also many other Minnesota cases that have relied on the holdings in *Linehan I* through *Linehan IV*. In turn, because these issues are common in many states where civil commitment of SVPs or SOs is allowed, the *Linehan IV* decision could influence decisions in other states as well.

Procedural Due Process

As stated previously, *Linehan* does not raise a violation of due process principles as a basis for challenge to civil commitment. However, this is a claim made in several other state cases.[55] Three of the more interesting subissues raised under the due process umbrella have been the failure to provide a jury trial if requested by the offender prior to commitment as a sexual predator,[56] failure of the court to consider the least restrictive alternative prior to civil commitment,[57] and the type of hearing required on the petition for discharge from commitment.[58] The first issue, denial of a jury trial, is fairly intuitive under the Illinois statutory scheme. In *People v. Burk*,[59] the offender was subject to commitment to the Department of Corrections as an SDP. The court found that the due process concerns and the Act warrant certain protections to the offender who is subjected to loss of liberty, regardless of the finding that the Act was deemed to be civil.

Another due process issue raised in this context is the requirement that the court consider the least restrictive alternative prior to commitment. In Minnesota, this is required whether the offender is found to be an SDP or an SPP. The Act mandates that the proponent of commitment prove, by clear and convincing evidence, that there is no appropriate less restrictive alternative, although the court is not required to make findings of fact on this issue.[60]

The third due process concern is the type of hearing to which the SVP is entitled on a petition for discharge from commitment as an SVP. Upon a finding that the person is no longer an SVP, the Wisconsin statute requires a second hearing, at which the person is entitled to be present and receive the attendant due process rights. Because these due process rights are so clearly granted for the second hearing, and there is no mention of an evidentiary proceeding at the first hearing, the court presumes that due process is met by a "paper" hearing (based solely on review of the physician's report supplemented by oral argument).[61]

Conclusion

In *Hendricks*, the Court determined that civil commitment of sexually violent predators or offenders was constitutional. However, as can be seen from the number of cases discussed herein, those committed under sexually violent predator statutes refuse to go quietly. It is expected that this is not the last "noise" from this arena.

Footnotes

[1] See generally Chapter 35, in this volume; E. R. Walsh & F. Cohen, *Sex Offender Registration and Community Notification: A Megan's Law Sourcebook,* at 1-1, n. 2 (1998).

[2] See, e.g., Fla. Stat. Ann. §944.606.

[3] See, e.g., Fla. Stat. Ann. § 775.21.

[4] Illinois Sexually Dangerous Persons Act, Ill. Comp. Stat. Ann. ch. 116 (1938).

[5] Kan. Stat. Ann. §§ 59-29a01 et seq., as amended by 1998 Kan. Laws S.B. 171; Minn. Stat. Ann. Ch. 253B, as amended by 1998 Minn. Sess. Laws ch. 313 (S.F. 2373); N.J. Stat. Ann. § 30:4-27.24; Wash. Rev. Code Ann. §§ 71.09.02 et seq., as amended by 1998 Wash. Legis. Serv. ch. 146 (H.B. 2905); Wash. Rev. Code Ann. § 71.06.

[6] 42 U.S.C.A. §§ 14071 et seq.; 1997 Ark. Laws Act 989 (H.B. 1061); Colo. Rev. Stat. §§ 18-3-412.5 et seq., as amended by 1998 Colo. Legis. Serv. ch. 139 (H.B. 98-1177); 1997 D.C. Law §§ 24-1101 et seq.; Ga. Code Ann. §§ 42-1-12 et seq.; Burns Ind. Stat. §§ 5-2-12 et seq., as amended by 1998 Ind. Legis. Serv. P.L. 56-1998 (S.E.A. 429); Md. Code Ann. art. 27, § 792, as amended by 1997 Md. Laws ch. 754 (S.B. 705); Mont. Code Ann. §§ 46-23-501 et seq., as amended by 1997 Mont. Laws ch. 375 (H.B. 111); Neb. Stat. Ann. §§ 29-4001 et seq. and 29-4101 et seq.; N.Y. Correct. Law art. 6-C, §§ 168 et seq. (Proposed A. 1373 would provide for commitment of sexually violent predators); N.C. Gen. Stat. art. 27A, §§ 14-208.5 et seq., as amended by 1997 N.C. Sess. .Laws 1997-516 (S.B. 676); Or. Rev. Stat. §§ 181.585 et seq.; 42 Pa.Cons. Stat. Ann. §§ 9791 et seq.; R.I. Gen. Laws Ann. §§ 11-37.1-1 et seq.; 13 Vt. Stat. Ann. §§ 5401 et seq.; and W. Va. Code § 61-8F-1a, as amended by 1998 W. Va. Laws S.B. 158.

[7] Ariz. Rev. Stat. Ann. §§ 36-3701 et seq.; Cal. Welf. & Inst. Code §§ 6600 et seq., as amended by 1998 Cal. Legis. Serv. ch. 19 (S.B. 536); 1998 Fla. Sess. Law Serv. ch. 98-64 (C.S.H.B. 3327), creating Fla. Stat. Ann. § 916.30, the Jimmy Ryce Involuntary Civil Commitment for exually Violent Predators' Treatment and Care Act and Fla. Stat. Ann. § 775.21; 725 Ill. Comp. Stat. Ann. ch. 725 §§ 207/1 et seq., ch. 45 §§ 20/0.01 et seq., and ch. 725, Act 205; Iowa Code Ann. §§ 229A.1 et seq., 692A.1 et seq., as amended by 1998 Iowa Legis. Serv. S.F. 2292, § 901A, and 1998 Iowa Legis. Serv. S.F. 2410; N.D. Cent. Code §§ 12.1-32-15 and 25-03.3-01; Ohio Rev. Code Ann. §§ 2971.01 et seq., where the SVP is not civilly comitted but is subject to life without parole.

[8] Ohio Rev. Code Ann. §§ 2971.01 et seq.; 1998 Ohio Laws File 157 (S.B. 107), to amend §§ 2929.02, 2929.05, 2929.06, 2949.28, 2949.29, and 2949.31 and to repeal §§ 2949.30 and 2949.32.

[9] 1998 Idaho Laws ch. 327 (S.B. 1341), to amend Idaho Code § 20-223.

[10] 1997 Okla. Sess. Laws Serv. ch. 20 (H.B. 1636).

[11] 117 S. Ct. 2072 (1997).

[12] 518 N.W.2d 609 (Minn. 1994) (Linehan I); In re Linehan, 544 N.W.2d 308 (Minn. App. 1996) (Linehan II); In re Linehan, 557 N.W.2d 167 (Minn. 1996) (Linehan III); and In re Linehan, 557 N.W.2d 171 (Minn. 1996) (Linehan IV); *vacated and remanded*,118 S. Ct. 596 (1997) (Linehan V).

[13] Kan. Stat. Ann. §§ 59-29a01 et seq.

[14] Kansas v. Hendricks, 117 S. Ct. 2072, 2077 (quoting from Kan. Stat. Ann. § 59-29a02(b)).

[15] See Chapter 35, in this volume, at 35-3, n. 22.

[16] Id. at 35-3, n. 24.

[17] 504 U.S. 71 (1992).

[18] See Cohen, "Supreme Court Finds Sexually Violent Predator Law Constitutional," 1(3) *Offender Programs Report* 33, 33 (September/October 1997).

[19] United States v. Halper, 490 U.S. 435 (1989).

[20] Hudson v. United States, 118 S. Ct. 488 (1997); United States v. Ward, 448 U.S. 242 (1980).

[21] *Ward* used the seven-factor test set forth in Kennedy v. Mendoza-Martinez, 372 U.S. 144 (1963). Those factors are (1) whether the sanction involves an affirmative disability or restraint; (2) whether it has historically been regarded as punishment; (3) whether it comes into play only on a finding of scienter; (4) whether its operation will promote the traditional aims of punishment, retribution, and deterrence; (5) whether the behavior to which it applies is already a crime; (6) whether an alternative purpose to which it may be rationally be connected is assignable for it; and (7) whether it appears excessive in relation to the alternative purpose assigned. Id. at 168–169.

[22] 117 S. Ct. at 2085.

[23] Id. at 2082 (quoting from United States v. Ward, 448 U.S. 242, 248–249 (1980)).

[24] Id. at 2082–2083.

[25] Id. at 2084.

[26] Keith v. Sullivan, 956 F. Supp. 1478 (E.D. Wis. 1997); People v. Superior Ct. of San Francisco, 49 Cal. App. 4th 1164, 57 Cal. Rptr. 2d 296 (1st Dist. Div. 5 1997); People v. Hedge, 65 Cal. Rptr. 2d 693 (4th Dist. Div. 1 1997); Hubbart v. Superior Ct. of Santa Clara County, 58 Cal. Rptr. 2d 268 (previously published at 50 Cal. App. 4th 1155 1997)); People v. Putney, 67 Cal. Rptr. 2d 283 (previously published at 57 Cal. App. 4th 739 (1997)); In re Hay, 263 Kan. 822, 953 P.2d 666 (1998); People v. Williams, 1998 WL 112882 (Mich.App.); Washington v. Gaff, 954 P.2d 943 (Wash. App. Div. 1 1998); In re Clewley, 1998 WL 97222 (Wash. App. Div. 2); In re BeGay, 1997 WL 631546 (Wash. App. Div. 3) (unpublished opinion).

[27] Minn. Stat. §§ 526.09-10, since replaced by definition of a "sexual psychopathic personality" by § 253B.02, subd. (18b) (1994).

[28] In re Linehan, 518 N.W.2d 609 (Minn. 1994) (Linehan I); In re Linehan, 544 N.W.2d 308 (Minn. App. 1996) (Linehan II); In re Linehan, 557 N.W.2d 167 (Minn. 1996) (Linehan III); and In re Linehan, 557 N.W.2d 171 (Minn. 1996) (Linehan IV); *vacated and remanded,* 118 S. Ct. 596 (1997) (Linehan V).

[29] Minn. Stat. § 253B.02(18b), formerly Minnesota Psychopathic Personality Commitment Act (MPPCA), Minn. Stat. § 526.09-10.

[30] Minn. Stat. §§ 253.02(18c) (a) and (b).

[31] In re Anderson, 1998 WL 281914 (Minn. App.) (unpublished opinion); In re Anderson, 1997 WL 177698 (Minn. App.) (not reported in N.W.2d); In re Dunlavy, 1998 WL 2423 (Minn. App.) (unpublished opinion); In re Gleason, 1998 WL 218223 (Minn.App.) (unpublished opinion); In re J.L.D., 1998 WL 147859 (Minn. App.) (unpublished opinion); In re Kubec, 1998 WL 27295 (Minn. App.) (unpublished opinion); In re Larson, 1998 WL 236167 (Minn.App.) (unpublished opinion); In re Swan, 1998 WL 217190 (Minn. App.) (unpublished opinion); In re Ayers, 570 N.W.2d 21 (Minn. App. 1997); In re Beaulieu, 1997 WL 292316 (Minn.) (not reported in N.W.2d); In re Becker, 1997 WL 470170 (Minn. App.) (not reported in N.W.2d); In re Coleman, 1997 WL 585902 (Minn. App.) (not reported in N.W.2d); In re Creighton, 1997 WL 407802 (Minn. App.) (not reported in N.W.2d); In re Crocker, 1997 WL 471481 (Minn. App.) (not reported in N.W.2d);

In re Fries, 1997 WL 328022 (Minn. App.) (not reported in N.W.2d); In re Hall, 1997 WL 228971 (Minn. App.) (unpublished opinion); In re Hince, 1997 311662 (Minn. App.) (not reported in N.W.2d); In re Howard, 1997 WL 228989 (Minn. App.) (not reported in N.W.2d); In re Krueger, 1997 WL 206802 (Minn. App.) (unpublished opinion); In re Lindberg, 1997 WL 600584 (Minn. App.) (unpublished opinion); In re Muller, 1997 WL 600457 (Minn. App.) (unpublished opinion); In re Reb, 1997 WL 470154, (Minn. App.) (unpublished opinion); In re Shaw, 1997 WL 23454 (Minn. App.) (unpublished opinion); In re Schweninger, 1997 WL 613670 (Minn. App.) (unpublished opinion); In re Weiss, 1997 WL 666033 (Minn. App.) (unpublished opinion).

[32] 518 N.W.2d 609 (Minn. 1994).

[33] 510 N.W.2d 910 (Minn. 1994).

[34] 518 N.W.2d at 613 (Minn. 1994) (quoting elements first stated by the court in Minnesota *ex rel.* Pearson v. Probate Ct. of Ramsey County, 309 U.S. 270, 274 (1940), aff'g, 205 Minn. 545, 287 N.W. 297 (1939)).

[35] 544 N.W.2d 308 (Minn. 1996).

[36] 557 N.W.2d 167 (Minn. 1996).

[37] 557 N.W.2d 171 (Minn. 1996).

[38] Minn. Stat. § 253B.02, subds. 7a, 18c(a).

[39] Black's Law Dictionary 1281 (5th ed. 1979).

[40] 557 N.W. at 181.

[41] 504 U.S. 71 (1992).

[42] 510 N.W.2d 910, 914 (Minn. 1994). This is similar to the situation in United States v. Salerno, 481 U.S. 739 (1988), where Salerno was detained, pretrial, based solely on a finding of danger to the community.

[43] 557 N.W.2d at 184.

[44] Calder v. Bull, 3 U.S. (3 Dall.) 386, 390 (1798). An SVP claimant would argue that the commitment statute was enacted after the sex offender had committed his or her crime and that therefore, the statute would impose punishment, retroactively, on the offender.

[45] United States v. Halper, 490 U.S. 435, 440 (1989). SVP claimants would argue that because they have already completed their sentences, such as a jail or prison term or probation, the imposition of commitment imposes a second punishment for the same offense.

[46] For a thorough explanation of these principles, see Chapter 35, in this volume.

[47] 557 N.W.2d at 187 (quoting from United States v. Ward, 448 U.S. 242, 248–251 (1980)).

[48] 510 N.W.2d 910 (Minn. 1994)

[49] 535 N.W.2d 312 (Minn. 1995).

[50] U.S. Constitution amend. XIV, sec. 1.

[51] Doe v. Division of Probation and Correctional Alternatives, 171 Misc. 2d 210, 654 N.Y.S.2d 268, 271 (Dutchess County 1997); Artway v. New Jersey, 83 F.3d 594 (3d Cir. 1996) (petition for rehearing denied); Artway v. New Jersey, 81 F.3d 1235, 1267–1268 (3d Cir. 1996); Artway v. Attorney General of New Jersey, 876 F. Supp. 666 (D.N.J. 1995) (citing City of Cleburne, Tex. v. Cleburne Living Center, 473 U.S. 432, 439 (1985)).

[52] 557 N.W.2d at 186.

[53] Id.

[54] *Linehan I* allowed that after a finding of utter uncontrollability of sexual impulses, in predicting future dangerousness of a sexual offender the court should consider the following: the person's relevant demographic characteristics, such as age, education, etc.; the person's history of violent behavior; the base rate statistics for violent behavior among individuals of this person's background; the sources of stress in the environment; the similarity of the present or future context to contexts in which the person has used violence in the past; and the person's record with respect to sex therapy programs. 518 N.W.2d at 614.

[55] Garcetti v. Superior Ct., 57 Cal.Rptr. 420 (1996) (formerly reported at 49 Cal. App. 4th 1533); In re Parker, 60 Cal. App. 4th, 71 Cal. Rptr. 2d 167 (1998); In re Ahmen, 564 N.W.2d 223 (1997); Nicholaison v. Doth, 1998 WL 204495 (Minn. App.); In re Senty-Haugen, 1997 WL 328015

(Minn. App.); Osborn v. Psychiatric Security Review Bd., 325 Or. 135, 934 P.2d 391 (1996); Rios v. Psychiatric Review Bd., 325 Or. 151, 934 P.2d 399 (1997); Broer v. Washington, 957 P.2d 981 (Wash. App. Div. 1 1998); In re McClatchey, 133 Wash. 2d 1, 940 P.2d 646 (1997); Wisconsin v. Brunette, 212 Wis. 2d 139, 567 N.W.2d 647 (1997); Wisconsin v. Zanelli, 212 Wis. 2d 301, 569 N.W.2d 301 (1997); In re Paulick, 213 Wis. 2d 432, 570 N.W.2d 66 (1997); Wisconsin v. Keding, 214 Wis. 2d 450, 571 N.W.2d 450 (1997); Wisconsin v. Castillo, 213 Wis. 2d 488, 570 N.W.2d 44 (1997); Wisconsin v. Irish, 210 Wis. 2d 107, 565 N.W.2d 161 (1997).

[56] People v. Burk, 289 Ill. App. 3d 270, 682 N.E.2d 352 (1997), where the Illinois Sexually Dangerous Persons Act allows for commitment to the Department of Corrections upon the determination of the offender as a sexually dangerous person.

[57] In re Dunlavy, 1998 WL 2423 (Minn. App.) (unpublished opinion); In re Larson, 1998 WL 27295 (Minn. App.) (unpublished opinion); Nicholaison v. Doth, 1998 WL 204495 (Minn. App.) (unpublished opinion); In re Swan, 1998 WL 217190 (Minn. App.) (unpublished opinion); In re Ahmen, 564 N.W.2d 223 (1997); In re Ayers, 570 N.W.2d 21 (Minn. App. 1997); In re Senty-Haugen, 1997 WL 328015 (Minn. App.) (unpublished opinion); In re Becker, 1997 WL 470170 (Minn. App.) (unpublished opinion); In re Crocker, 1997 WL 471481 (Minn. App.) (not reported in N.W.2d); In re Hall, 1997 WL 228971 (Minn. App.) (unpublished opinion); In re Hince, 1997 WL 311662 (Minn. App.) (unpublished opinion); In re Howard, 1997 WL 228989 (Minn. App.) (unpublished opinion); In re Reb, 1997 WL 470154 (Minn. App.) (unpublished opinion); In re Weiss, 1997 WL 666033 (Minn. App.) (unpublished opinion);Washington v. Gaff, 964 P.2d 943 (Wash. App. Div. 1 1998).

[58] In re Paulick, 213 Wis.2d 432, 570 N.W.2d 66 (1997).

[59] 289 Ill. App. 3d 270, 682 N.E.2d 352 (1997).

[60] In re Senty-Haugen, 1997 WL 328015 (Minn. App.) (unpublished opinion).

[61] In re Paulick, 213 Wis.2d 432, 570 N.W.2d 66 (1997).

Chapter 35

Update on Megan's Law

by Elizabeth Rahmberg Walsh, J.D., M.L.S.
and Brian M. Flaherty, M.L.S.

Overview

Most states have enacted public notification laws for sex offenders that require these individuals to register and then allow for the dissemination of a varying amounts of personal information. Certainly these offenders view this process as an additional punishment that impairs their ability to find work and housing and maintain their privacy. Friends and relatives of sex offenders may agree that these laws certainly feel like punishment. However, advocates of this type of legislation argue that these laws protect the public. The authors discuss the legal definition of "punishment" as defined by a variety of precedent-setting cases.

Introduction

Numerous challenges have been made to sex offender registration and community notification statutes, known as "Megan's Laws."[1] These statutes require that an offender convicted of a statutorily designated sex offense must, upon release into the community, register with local law enforcement and provide certain personal information, such as name, home address, employment address, and social security number. In a number of states, this information is made available or made known to designated members of the public, such as those residing within a specific geographic area, or even to the public-at-large.[2] The bases of challenges to these laws have covered a broad range, from "punishment-related" challenges (e.g., ex post facto,[3] bill of attainder,[4] double jeopardy,[5] and cruel and unusual punishment[6]) to nonpunishment-related challenges (e.g., procedural due process,[7] substantive due process,[8] equal protection,[9] search and seizure,[10] void for vagueness,[11] and the Fifth and Sixth Amendments[12].

Megan's Law appellants have challenged the mandatory sex offender registration and/or community notification claiming that such requirements, applied after the appellants have already completed their sentence on the underlying offense, constitute an additional punishment and, as such, violate the principles of the Ex Post Facto, Double Jeopardy, and Bill of Attainder Clauses and the prohibition against cruel and unusual punishment found in the Eighth Amendment.

Punishment-Related Cases Challenge Intent of Laws

Although the latest challenges seem to echo those of the past, that is, focusing on the same issues as outlined earlier, there are differences in the disposition of these challenges. The most recent punishment-related cases have taken both *Kansas v. Hendricks*[13] and *Hudson v. United States*[14] into account in their holdings. In *Hendricks*, the U.S. Supreme Court held that a sex offender who had served a criminal sentence for a sexual offense, who was diagnosed with a current "mental disorder" or "personality disorder" and was deemed to be dangerous, could be civilly committed following his or her prison sentence without violating double jeopardy or ex post facto principles. The court reasoned that the Kansas sexual predator civil commitment statute did not impose punishment. Without punishment, there could be no ex post facto or double jeopardy violation. (This principle is discussed in more detail in the section, "Punishment as Defined in Megan's Laws.")

Hudson did not deal with a sex offender case but with penalties imposed in a banking case. The issue in *Hudson* was whether the imposition of civil penalties and, subsequently, criminal penalties, for the same offenses violated the Double Jeopardy Clause (discussed in more detail in the following section, "Punishment as Defined in Megan's Law"). In determining whether the statute in *Hudson* imposed criminal penalties, the court relied on several of the seven factors outlined in *Kennedy v. Mendoza-Martinez*,[15] a test which took into account not only the effect of the statute but also legislative intent. The *Hudson* court found that the statute was not punitive in nature and therefore there was no double jeopardy violation. Further, the *Hudson* Court denounced *United States v. Halper*,[16] which had held that double jeopardy "[c]an be identified only by assessing the character of the actual sanctions imposed on the individual"[17] (i.e., by looking at the actual effect of a statute). *Hudson* found that *Halper* had used an improper analysis to find that the statute there did not impose punishment for double jeopardy purposes and reinstated the holding of *United States v. Ward*,[18] which had relied on the *Mendoza-Martinez* test, as the proper reasoning to follow in this area of law.

Cases Defining Punishment

There are actually three cases, the *Halper/Austin/Kurth Ranch*[19] trilogy, which have served as the starting point for several courts when deciding whether a particular statute imposes punishment,[20] although *Halper* is more frequently cited. This is the second time that the Court has tempered the meaning and the impact of *Halper* and its progeny. The *Halper/Austin/Kurth Ranch* line of reasoning was previously modified by the U.S. Supreme Court in *United States v. Ursery*,[21] which followed the *Ward* rationale. It would seem that the Court is making a clear statement in *Hudson*: *Ward* is not only *an* appropriate line of reasoning, it is the *only* line of reasoning to be followed in this type of calculation.

Punishment as Defined in Megan's Laws

In Megan's Law jurisprudence, the underlying premise in punishment-related cases is that if the statute does not constitute punishment, the statute cannot violate the constitutional principles of ex post facto, double jeopardy, cruel and unusual punishment, and bill of attainder. This means that if a particular law or its application is appealed on a punishment-related basis, the sex offender registration or community notification law first must be deemed to have imposed punishment. Because a large number of challenges to Megan's Laws have been brought on punishment-related principles, the initial determination whether the statute imposes punishment is critical in this area of law.

The Ex Post Facto Clause prohibits the government from applying a law retroactively that "inflicts a greater punishment, than the law annexed to the crime, when committed."[22] The Bill of Attainder Clause forbids legislatures from engaging in "[l]egislative acts, no matter what their form, that apply either to named individuals or to easily ascertainable members of a group in such a way as to inflict punishment on them without judicial trial."[23] The Double Jeopardy Clause bans, among other things, "a second prosecution for the same offense after conviction . . . and multiple punishments for the same offense."[24] Finally, the Eighth Amendment prohibits, in part, the infliction of cruel and unusual punishments, which includes sentences that are disproportionate to the crime committed.[25] In each of these contexts, the point on which the determination turns is whether the statute requiring sex offender registration and/or community notification constitutes punishment.

With few exceptions, the courts have held that sex offender registration does not impose punishment.[26] There has been some division on whether community notification of the sex offender's whereabouts constitutes punishment. The majority of courts have found that community notification does not constitute punishment.[27] In the few cases that have found notification to be punitive, the holding has been narrow and the violation easily cured. For example, the Massachusetts Supreme Judicial Court found in *Doe v. Attorney General*[28] that two sections of the Massachusetts law allowed for dissemination of sex offender registry information, Sections 178I and 178J. However, where Section 178J contained a statement of remedial purpose, 178I did not; Section 178I could therefore be deemed to have a punitive purpose. Consequently, retroactive application of Section 178I could constitute punishment and, thus, an ex post facto violation.

What has happened to federal case law in this period that would affect the outcome of these cases in the future? Before we discuss the further significance of the holding in *Hudson v. United States*,[29] we must first lay the groundwork by deciphering *United States v. Ward*.[30]

Ward and Its Importance

Ward dealt with Section 311(b)(5) of the Federal Water Pollution Control Act (the Act), which imposed a duty on certain persons to report to the appropriate governmental agency any discharge of oil or hazardous substance into navigable waters. It provided for a fine of not more than $10,000 or imprisonment of not more than one year for failure to so notify. The Act also provided for "use immunity" for those who complied, which meant that those who provided such notification would not be prosecuted for any *criminal* offense other than perjury or giving a false statement.

Section 311(b)(6) provided for a *civil* penalty to be assessed against any owner who discharged such a hazardous substance in violation of the Act, with a penalty of up to $5,000 for each violation. Ward suffered an oil leak on his leased premises and notified the Environmental Protection Agency of the leak. He was assessed a $500 civil penalty under Section 311(b)(6). Administrative review of the civil penalty was denied Ward in accordance with Section 311(b)(5). He next sued in federal district court to enjoin the collection of the $500 civil penalty, claiming that the statutory scheme violated his Fifth Amendment right against self-incrimination. (He claimed that the statute required that he report his violation and then he was penalized for the self-reported violation, which abridged his right not to testify against himself.) The *Ward* Court determined that the seven factors set forth in *Mendoza-Martinez* were appropriate to make the determination whether the statute constituted punishment for Fifth Amendment compulsory self-incrimination purposes.[31]

The district court rejected *Ward's* argument that the reporting requirements violated his right against self-incrimination. The Tenth Circuit reversed and found that the *Mendoza-Martinez* factors demonstrated that the statute was sufficiently punitive to trigger Fifth Amendment protection. As a starting point, the Supreme Court found that the self-incrimination clause is limited to "any criminal case,"[32] which meant that if it found the statute to be civil, not criminal, the Fifth Amendment would, therefore, not apply. The Court first found that the legislature intended this statute to be civil; second, using the *Mendoza-Martinez* factors, it found that "the statutory scheme was not so punitive either in purpose or effect to negate that intent."[33]

Although the Court looked at all seven factors, it found only the fifth factor, "whether the behavior to which [the penalty] applies is already a crime," lent any support to Ward's contentions. In addition, the Court noted that "Congress may impose both a criminal and a civil sanction in respect to the same act or omission."[34] Therefore, the fact that both a civil and a criminal penalty were imposed did not automatically comprise a violation of constitutional proportions. The Court further noted that, "[T]he fact that the placement of criminal penalties in one statute and the placement of civil penalties in another statute enacted seventy years later tends to dilute the force of the fifth *Mendoza-Martinez* criterion in this case."[35] In other words, the seventy-year time lag between the enactment of the criminal penalty and the civil penalty suggests that the legislature did not expressly impose the civil penalty with the criminal sanction in mind.

The Court concluded that the *Mendoza-Martinez* factors, although neither exhaustive nor dispositive, were not sufficient in this case to make criminal what the legislature, in Section 311(b)(6) clearly intended to be civil. In addition, *Ward* failed to show the "clearest proof" that the penalty was punitive in purpose or effect, and therefore, the judgment of the court of appeals was reversed.[36]

What Did *Hudson* Say and What Did It Change?

Hudson dealt with the misapplication of bank funds by several bank officers. The Office of the Comptroller of the Currency (OCC) imposed civil fines and occupational disbarment against Hudson and others. Subsequently, Hudson and his fellow bank officers were indicted on criminal charges founded on the same misconduct as the civil penalties, and they moved to dismiss the charges on double jeopardy grounds. The U.S. Supreme Court affirmed the Tenth Circuit's decision to reinstate the indictments because, it said, the Double Jeopardy Clause protects against multiple punishments for the same offense only and that the OCC sanctions were civil, not criminal. Because the sanctions were civil, they did not constitute "punishment."

To reach this decision, the *Hudson* Court found *Ward*, not *Halper*, to be controlling. The Court first found that the legislature intended the statute to be civil. It then looked for the "clearest proof" that the legislative intent had been nullified and that the civil remedy had been transformed into a criminal sanction. It used the first five of the seven *Mendoza-Martinez* factors to make this decision, explaining that *Mendoza-Martinez* held that "these factors must be considered in relation to the statute on its face."[37]

The *Hudson* Court found that *Halper* had "bypassed the traditional threshold question whether the legislature intended the particular successive punishment to be 'civil' or 'criminal' in nature, focusing instead on whether the sanction was so grossly disproportionate to the harm caused as to constitute 'punishment.'"[38] It then pointed out that although *Mendoza-Martinez* had cautioned that no one factor should be controlling, *Halper* had singled out the last of the seven *Mendoza-Martinez* factors, whether the punishment appears excessive in relation to the alternative purpose assigned, and made that sole factor dispositive of the "punishment" question.[39]

The Court then explained that *Halper* had erred when it "assessed the character of the actual sanctions imposed, rather than, as *Kennedy* [*v. Mendoza-Martinez*] demanded, evaluating the 'statute on its face' to determine whether it provided for what amounted to a criminal sanction."[40] The Court found *Halper* to be clearly unworkable, as it forces the defendant to proceed through trial to judgment and then appeal the judgment on a double jeopardy argument.[41] Finally, the Court found that a double jeopardy argument is unnecessary in this context, as due process, equal protection, and the Eighth Amendment prohibition against excessive fines would provide the same protections to a defendant in this situation, without the legal contortions required by *Halper*.

Justice Stevens concurred in Chief Justice Rehnquist's opinion, making several important points. First, he asserted that the Court misread *Halper* altogether when it held previously that *Halper* permitted only successive sanctions that are "solely" remedial. Although there was language in *Halper* that seemed to suggest this, the holding was actually much narrower.[42] The Court clarified this point in *Ursery*, when it held that "yet nowhere in *Halper* does the Court purport to make such a sweeping change in the law, instead emphasizing repeatedly the narrow scope of its decision."[43] Rather, *Halper* said, "We . . . hold that under the Double Jeopardy Clause a defendant who has already been punished in a criminal prosecution may not be subjected to an additional civil sanction to the extent that the second sanction may not be fairly be characterized as remedial *but only* as a deterrent or retribution" (emphasis added).[44]

Justice Stevens' second point was also critical. He said that although the *Hudson* Court took great pains to repudiate *Halper*, it relied on a "multifactor" approach that was similar to the one used in *Mendoza-Martinez* to determine whether the sanction designated civil was actually criminal, and one that "look[ed] awfully similar to the reasoning in *Halper,* and while we are told that [these factors] are never by themselves dispositive, they should be capable of 'tipping the balance' in extreme cases."[45] In other words, Stevens asked whether the Court was really disavowing *Halper* or simply professing a preference with the form in which the determination was made? What Stevens seems to be saying is that there is a distinction in the way that *Ward* and *Halper* were decided, but it may be a distinction without a difference.

What Does It All Mean?

To reiterate, whether sex offender registration and/or community notification violates ex post facto, double jeopardy, cruel and unusual punishment, or bill of attainder principles will turn on whether the statute imposes punishment on the offender. Post-*Hudson*, when a punishment-related challenge arises in the Megan's Law context, it is highly likely that the court will use a *Ward* analysis, whereas pre-*Hudson* a court might have used a *Halper* analysis. Post-*Hudson* analysis will look first at whether the legislature intended to impose a civil or a criminal sanction. If a civil intent is found, the court then will use some combination of factors, such as those relied on in *Mendoza-Martinez,* to determine whether the purpose or effect of the statute is so punitive as to render the statute criminal, despite its civil intent. If the purpose or effect does not transform the statute from civil to criminal, then the appeal will fail, the sex offender will be required to register, and the community will be notified under the provisions of the state statute.

What has changed from the *Halper/Austin/Kurth Ranch* days? First, the *Hudson* decision will deter courts from relying on the confusing language in *Halper,* which implied that a statute is remedial *only if it has none other than a remedial purpose.* Later in the case the Court held that a second sanction may not be imposed (without violating ex post facto, double jeopardy, etc.) if the second sanction can be characterized *only as* a deterrent or as retribution, both punitive goals. *Halper's* initial statement implies that a statute with multiple purposes will be found punitive if *any* of the multiple purposes is punishment. The latter statement is clear that a statute may have multiple purposes, but that such statute will be determined punitive only where no remedial purpose can be found.

Second, *Hudson* will force the court to rely on *Ward. Ward* is perhaps merely a modified approach to the punishment question, albeit a more ordered one, with the factors delineated clearly by *Mendoza-Martinez.* Using a *Ward* analysis, courts will be required to consider more than simply whether the statute's purpose is punitive or remedial, à la *Halper,* but, rather, will be forced to conduct a more exhaustive analysis and consider "whether the sanction involves an affirmative disability or restraint; whether it has historically been regarded as punishment; whether it comes into play only on a finding of scienter; whether its operation will promote the traditional aims of punishment, retribution and deterrence; whether the behavior to which it applies is already a crime; whether an alternative purpose to which it may be rationally be connected is assignable for it; and whether it appears excessive in relation to the alternative purpose assigned."[46] Whether *Hudson* requires that the court consider all the factors delineated by *Mendoza-Martinez* is not clear, as *Hudson* itself failed to consider two of the seven factors.

Conclusion

What is clear, however, is that post-*Hudson*, determinations whether a statute imposes punishment and, therefore, violates ex post facto, bill of attainder, double jeopardy, and cruel and unusual punishment may be more involved and more interesting. What remains unclear is whether the results will differ at all. In other words, it remains to be seen whether under a *Hudson/Ward* analysis, statutes that require sex offenders to register and communities to be notified of sex offenders' presence will be found violative of ex post facto, bill of attainder, double jeopardy, and cruel and unusual punishment—the "punishment-based" challenges.

Footnotes

---

[1] These laws were named for Megan Kanka, a young girl from New Jersey who was sexually assaulted and strangled by her neighbor, a man who had been previously convicted and incarcerated for sex offenses.

[2] For a complete description of these statutes and their requirements, see Walsh, "Megan's Laws—Sex Offender Registration and Notification Statutes and Constitutional Challenges," in B. K. Schwartz & H. R. Cellini, *The Sex Offender: New Insights, Treatment Innovations and Legal Developments* (Vol. 2), at 24-1 through 24-6 (1997).

[3] See id. at 24-7 through 24-10; E. R. Walsh & F. Cohen, *Sex Offender Registration and Community Notification: A Megan's Law Sourcebook,* at 2-17 through 2-29. (1998).

[4] See Walsh, supra note 2, at 24-10; Walsh & Cohen, supra note 3, at 2-29 through 2-30.

[5] See Walsh, supra note 2, at 24-10; Walsh & Cohen, supra note 3, at 2-31 through 2-34.

[6] See Walsh, supra note 2, at 24-10; Walsh & Cohen, supra note 3, at 2-37 through 2-40.

[7] See Walsh, supra note 2, at 24-11 through 24-13; Walsh & Cohen, supra note 3, at 3-12 through 3-27.

[8] See Walsh, supra note 2, at 24-13 through 24-14; Walsh & Cohen, supra note 3, at 3-28 through 3-29.

[9] See Walsh, supra note 2, at 24-14; Walsh & Cohen,supra note 3, at 3-32 through 3-33.

[11] See Walsh, supra note 2, at 24-5 through 24-16; Walsh & Cohen, supra note 3, at 3-35 through 3-37.

[11] See Walsh, supra note 2, at 24-14 through 24-15; Walsh & Cohen, supra note 3, at 3-38 through 3-40.

[12] See Walsh & Cohen, supra note 3, at 3-40 through 3-41. Other challenges to state sex offender registration and community notification statutes have been based in the Administrative Procedure Act; the definition of the offense that triggered the registration; whether they apply to juveniles; the offender has failed to register; that the court or government agency lacks jurisdiction to order registration; an order of registration as a term of probation; the refusal to register as a basis of prison discipline; and other miscellaneous challenges.

[13] 117 S. Ct. 2072 (1997), which is discussed more fully in Chapter 34, in this volume.

[14] 118 S. Ct. 488 (1997).

[15] 372 U.S. 144 (1963).

[16] 490 U.S. 435 (1989).

[17] 490 U.S. 435 at 447.

[18] 448 U.S. 242 (1980), discussed in detail at pp. 35-3, 35-4, and Chapter 34, in this volume.

[19] United States v. Halper, 490 U.S. 435 (1989); Austin v. United States, 509 U.S. 602 (1993); Montana Department of Revenue v. Kurth Ranch, 114 S. Ct. 1937 (1994).

[20] Walsh & Cohen, supra note 3, at p. 2-8.

[21] 116 S. Ct. 2135 (1996).

[22] Calder v. Bull, 3 U.S. (3 Dall.) 386, 390 (1798). A Megan's Law claimant would argue that the Megan's Law statute was enacted after the sex offender had committed his or her crime and that therefore, the statute would impose punishment, retroactively, on the offender.

[23] United States v. Brown, 381 U.S. 437, 448-449 (1965). In a Megan's Law context, the group would be comprised of sex offenders, and the punishment without a trial would be the required registration and/or community notification without further judicial determination.

[24] United States v. Halper, 490 U.S. 435, 440 (1989). Megan's law claimants would argue that because they have already completed their sentence, such as a jail or prison term or probation, the imposition of registration and/or community notification imposes a second punishment for the same offense.

[25] Solem v. Helm, 463 U.S. 277, 284 (1983). In the Eighth Amendment context, the sex offender would argue that the imposition of registration and/or community notification, because of the wide-ranging consequences, is disproportionate to sex offense committed.

[26] The only cases that have found the retroactive application of the registration provision to be punitive are out of Louisiana: State v. Calhoun, 669 So. 2d 1359 (La. App. 1996), rev'd, State v. Calhoun, 694 So. 2d 909 (1997); State v. Payne, 633 So. 2d 701 (La. App. 1993), writ denied, 637 So. 2d 497; State v. Babin, 637 So. 2d 814 (La. App. 1994), writ denied, 644 So. 2d 649; State v. Bishop, 96-674 (La. App. Dec. 30, 1996), 686 So. 2d 1053 (La.App. Cir. 1996); State v. Linson, 654 So. 2d 440 (La. App. 1995).

[27] State v. Myers, 260 Kan. 669, 923 P.2d 1024 (1996), cert. denied, 117 So. 2d 2508 (1997); Doe v. Attorney General, 425 Mass. 217, 680 N.E.2d 97 (1997); Doe v. Gregoire, 960 F. Supp. 1478 (W.D. Wash. 1997); Rowe v. Burton, 884 F. Supp. 1372 (D. Alaska 1994), appeal dismissed, 85 F.3d 635 (1996); Roe v. Office of Adult Probation, 938 F. Supp. 1080 (D. Conn. 1996), rev'd, Roe v. Office of Adult Probation, 125 F.3d 47 (2d Cir. 1997) (the Second Circuit overturned the lower court's decision and found that notification did not constitute punishment); Doe v. Pataki, 940 F. Supp. 603 (S.D.N.Y. 1996), Doe v. Pataki, 919 F. Supp. 691 (S.D.N.Y. 1996), Doe v. Pataki, aff'd in part, rev'd in part, Doe v. Pataki, 120 F.3d 1263 (2d Cir. 1997) (the Second Circuit found notification was not punitive and overturned the lower court's decision); and Artway v. New Jersey, 83 F.3d 594 (3d Cir. 1996), petition for reh'g denied, Artway v. New Jersey, 81 F.3d 1235 (3d Cir. 1996), Artway v. Attorney General of New Jersey, 876 F.Supp. 666 (D.N.J. 1995).

[28] 425 Mass. 217, 680 N.E.2d 97 (1997).

[29] 118 S. Ct. 488 (1997).

[30] 448 U.S. 242 (1980).

[31] Those factors are: whether the sanction involves an affirmative disability or restraint; whether it has historically been regarded as punishment; whether it comes into play only on a finding of scienter; whether its operation will promote the traditional aims of punishment, retribution and deterrence; whether the behavior to which it applies is already a crime; whether an alternative purpose to which it may be rationally be connected is assignable for it; and whether it appears excessive in relation to the alternative purpose assigned. 372 U.S. 144, 168-169 (1963).

[32] United States v. Ward, 448 U.S. 242, 248 (1980).

[33] Id., at 248-149.

[34] 448 U.S. at 250.

[35] Id.

[36] The "clearest proof" standard was established by a group of cases: Flemming v. Nestor, 363 U.S. 603, 617 (1960); One Lot Emerald Cut Stones v. United States, 409 U.S. 232, 237 (1972); and Rex Trailer Co. V. United States, 350 U.S. 148, 154 (1956), id., at 248-249.

[37] 118 S. Ct. at 490 (quoting Kennedy v. Mendoza-Martinez, 372 U.S. 144, 169 (1963)).

[38] 118 S. Ct. at 490 (citations omitted).

[39] Id. at 494 (quoting Kennedy v. Mendoza-Martinez, 372 U.S. 144, 169 (1963)).

[40] Id. at 494.

[41] Stevens maintains that this would be an issue only where the civil proceeding follows a criminal one and is not an issue here, as the civil proceeding came first, followed by the criminal proceeding.

[42] Prior to stating its holding in Halper, the Court enunciated what looked like the rule of the case, but which was later referred to as dictum by the majority in United States v. Ursery, 518 U.S. 267, 286 (1996). The *Halper* Court said that a "civil sanction that cannot be fairly said *solely* to serve a remedial purpose, but rather can only be explained as also serving either retributive or deterrent purposes, is punishment" (emphasis added) 490 U.S. 435, 448 (1989). From the placement of the word "solely" in this sentence, it would seem that the Court was saying that unless the statute had none other but a civil purpose, it would be considered to be civil. If the statute imposed a sanction that might have additional purposes, one of could be criminal, such as retribution or deterrence, it would be considered punitive. Later in the case, the *Halper* Court limited its holding to a very specific type of case and stated that the it was "announcing the rule for the rare case . . . where a fixed penalty provision subjects a prolific but small-gauge offender to a sanction overwhelmingly disproportionate to the damages he has caused." 490 U.S. 435, 449-450 (1989). The Court in Halper then announced its holding, which allowed that an offender cannot be subjected to a second sanction where "the second sanction may not fairly be characterized as remedial, but only as a deterrent or retribution." 490 U.S. 435, 448 (1989).

[43] 518 U.S. 267, 286.

[44] 118 S. Ct. at 498 (quoting United States v. Halper, 490 U.S. 435, 448–449 (1989)).

[45] 118 S. Ct. at 499.

[46] Infra note 31.

Chapter 36

Non–*Hendricks*-Related Constitutional Challenges to Sexually Violent Predator Statutes

by Elizabeth R. Walsh, J.D., M.L.S. and Brian M. Flaherty, M.L.S.

Introduction

In this chapter, the author discusses the legal challenges to laws involving sexual predators, primarily in relation to the public notification laws. Sex offenders have challenged the law as representing an ex post facto application of punishment and as a violation of due process in a number of ways. The author reviews the court cases that have addressed these issues.

Overview

The U.S. Supreme Court ruled in *Kansas v. Hendricks*[1] that civil commitment of sexually violent predators (SVPs) after these offenders had served a term of incarceration was constitutional. This, decision, however, did not close the door on all challenges to SVP statutes. As discussed in Chapter 34, legislators in various states have devised myriad statutory schemes, in addition to civil commitment, that apply to SVPs.[2]

Ex Post Facto Challenges to SVP Registration and Community Notification Statutes

Although ex post facto challenges were discussed previously in Chapter 34,[3] this discussion was focused on such challenges in the context of civil commitment of SVPs and not in the context of registration and/or community notification requirements applied to SVPs. An ex post facto challenge, regardless of the framework, is resolved by determining, first, whether the statute constitutes punishment and second, whether the statute is applied retroactively. Whether or not the statute is applied retroactively, it must also constitute punishment to fail ex post facto scrutiny. Virtually every court that has been confronted with an ex post facto challenge to the registration requirement for a sex offender (those convicted of an offense under the sex offender statute) has held that such a statute does not violate ex post facto principles because it does not constitute punishment.[4] With few exceptions, courts have ruled in similar fashion that community notification provisions, as applied to sexual offenders, do not violate ex post facto law.[5] Not surprisingly, then, courts have ruled that laws requiring SVPs (those who, in most states, have been defined as someone who has been convicted of a sexually *violent* offense *and* who suffers from a mental abnormality or personality disorder[6] that makes it likely that he or she will engage in future sexual predatory acts) to register are not violative of ex post facto principles.

Three states—Florida, New York, and Ohio—are responsible for providing the bulk of the constitutional challenges to laws mandating registration of SVPs. One New York case which dealt with a sexually violent predator and raised an ex post facto challenge ruled that the matter had been previously and definitively determined by *Doe v. Pataki*.[7] *Ferrara v. Pataki*[8] held that retroactive application of New York's Sex Offender Registration Act did not violate the Ex Post Facto Clause because the Act, which required registration and authorized community notification, did not inflict punishment on the sex offender.

The lone recent Florida case on this issue held that although the Sexual Predators Act was applied to the offender retroactively, the requirement that the predator register and be subject to community notification did not violate the prohibition against ex post facto laws because it did not constitute punishment. Rather, the court, echoing most other courts confronted with these same issues, ruled that the "overriding purpose of the legislation designating certain individuals as 'sexual predators' and requiring these individuals to register themselves is to protect the public from repeat sex offenders, sex offenders who use violence, and those who prey on children."[9]

A series of cases from the state courts of Ohio not only have raised ex post facto challenges to registration and community notification of SVPs but also have challenged retroactive application of Sections 2950.01 et seq. of the Ohio Revised Code Annotated on the basis of Section 28, Article II of the Ohio Constitution, which prohibits retroactive laws. Sections 2950.01 et seq. define a sexual predator and require a person so designated to register as a sexual predator until determined in a court proceeding, by clear and convincing evidence, that he or she is no longer a sexually violent predator. It also subjects the predator to enhanced registration and community notification conditions.

The Ohio Retroactive Clause "provides generally that the general assembly has no power to pass retroactive laws."[10] Retroactive laws are those that "attach new legal consequences to events completed before its enactment"[11] or "take away or impair vested rights acquired under existing laws, or create a new obligation, impose a new duty, or attach a new disability, in respect to transactions or considerations already past."[12] In addition, "a statute purely remedial in it operation on pre-existing rights, obligations, duties and interests, is not within the mischiefs against which [Section 28, Article III] . . . was intended to guard, and is not, therefore, within a just construction of its terms."[13] The determination whether the statute violates Ohio's Retroactive Clause, then, does not differs significantly from the ex post facto determination; that is, Does the statute retroactively impose punishment? *Ohio v. Bartis*[14] announced the rule, and all but one Ohio case has followed its rationale and determined that Sections 2950.01 et seq. of the Ohio Revised Code Annotated violate neither the prohibition against ex post facto laws nor Ohio's Retroactive Clause.[15] The anomalous case, *Ohio v. Cook*, focused on the Ohio Retroactive Clause first. It found that the new statute was retroactive and that it also imposed new obligations that the former statute did not, in that it substantially broadened the notification provisions as they pertain to SVPs. Therefore, the court found that retroactive application of Section 2950.09 of the Ohio Revised Code Annotated to *Cook* violated the Ohio Retroactive Clause. Because the court found that it violated the Ohio Constitution, it found it unnecessary to address *Cook*'s federal ex post facto challenge.[16]

Ex post facto challenges to enhanced registration and community notification requirements, and their ilk, have been met with the same lack of success that challenges to registration and/or community notification requirements for sexual offenders have had. This is fairly intuitive. Courts have found that it does not constitute punishment to impose a registration requirement and then notify the community of a sex offender who has been convicted of a sexual offense. Therefore, it makes sense that it would not constitute punishment for a sexually violent predator to comply with the same provisions, because a sexually violent predator is someone who has been convicted of a sexually *violent* offense who *also has been found to have a mental abnormality or personality disorder which makes it likely that the offender will engage in future sexual predatory acts to register and have the community notified of his or her presence.* SVPs represent clearly represent a more dangerous threat to the community than do sex offenders.

Due Process Challenges to SVP Registration and Community Notification Statutes

An aspect that has generated, and will continue to generate, challenges to registration and community notification requirements for SVPs is the risk-level, or tier-level, determination. New York is but one state that creates a risk-level system. The New York system establishes three levels of risk, each level determined by the danger that the offender poses to the community. Level 1 constitutes low risk, level 2 is moderate risk, and level 3 designates high risk. The risk level is determined by the Department of Correctional Alternatives or by the Division of Parole, with assistance from the Board of Examiners of Sex Offenders (the Board). The risk assessment is made by assigning points under a formula that weights fifteen factors, which are then totaled to arrive at a score that indicates the likelihood that the offender will recidivate. The statute provides, in part:

> If the risk of repeat offense is high and there exists a threat to the public safety, such sex offender shall be deemed a *"sexually violent predator" and a level three designation shall be given to such sex offender*. In such case, the law enforcement agency having jurisdiction and the law enforcement agency having had jurisdiction at the time of his conviction shall be notified and may disseminate relevant information which may include the sex offender's exact address, a photograph of the offender, background information including the offender's crime of conviction, modus of operation, type of victim targeted, and the description of special conditions imposed on the offender to any entity with vulnerable populations related to the nature of the offense committed by such sex offender. Any entity receiving information on a sex offender may disclose or further disseminate such information at their discretion. In addition, in such case, the information described herein shall also be provided in the subdirectory established in this article and notwithstanding any other provision of law, such information shall, upon request, be made available to the public (emphasis added).[17]

In addition to being subject to enhanced registration provisions, such as creation of a sexually violent predator subdirectory,[18] verification of his or her address every ninety days rather than annually,[19] and registration until he or she is determined no longer a SVP, but for a minimum of ten years,[20] the determination of an offender as a sexually violent predator results in automatic designation as a level 3 offender, subjecting him or her to the most widespread community notification provisions. Therefore, the effect of being designated a sexually violent predator is of major consequence.

Due Process Analysis. The determination of whether the statute violates the offender's due process rights involves much more than a determination of whether the statute has "some effect." In a due process analysis, the first question is whether the interest affected involves a state of federally protected right. If the answer is yes, the second question is, How much process is due? *Doe v. Pataki*,[21] decided by the District Court for the Southern District of New York, in 1998, determined that the plaintiffs, some of whom were designated SVPs, had a protected liberty interest entitled to due process. The court found that a constitutional deprivation is established when the person suffers from "'stigma plus,' harm to reputation in addition to some other impediment."[22] Further, the court found that the community notification provisions that apply to level 3 offenders would not only harm their reputations but place a burden on the offender because the offender must register and provide personal information and update the information either annually or quarterly, and failure to comply is a crime. These provisions alter "the legal status of all convicted offenders subject to the Act [who may be subject to them] for a minimum of ten years and, for some, permanently."[23] This altered legal status comprises the "plus" in the "stigma plus" requirement for a due process violation. Finally, the court agreed with previous court decisions that found that "stigma plus" was fulfilled by harm to reputation in conjunction with infringement on the offenders right to privacy. Thus, the court held that the offenders subject to the Act are entitled to due process.[24]

But what process is due? To make this determination, the court weighed the private interests of the offenders in their liberty and reputation, the risk of erroneous assignment of a risk level or an erroneous classification as a sex offender, the state's compelling interest in the protection of its citizens from levels 2 and 3 offenders and its interest in maintaining a fair and accurate classification and notification system, and how to balance these interests. After weighing all of the above and considering what the New Jersey Supreme Court deemed appropriate under Megan's Law,[25] the New York court determined that sex offenders subject to the Act are entitled to a hearing before the court; notice of the classification proceeding; that the notice must contain a statement of the proceeding's purpose and the Board's recommend risk level; the opportunity to retain or have counsel appointed; an opportunity for prehearing discovery; that the state bears the burden of proof and that burden is by clear and convincing evidence; and the right to appeal.[26]

Risk Assessment—Instrument. Offenders were not so successful in challenging the numerical risk assessment method as arbitrary and capricious. In *People v. Nieves*,[27] the offender had been assessed a level 3 risk and claimed that the numerical risk methodology was an arbitrary and capricious procedure to calculate risk. However, the court found that the state had spent much time and energy to develop the risk criteria which were then reviewed by numerous experts in the field. In addition, the criteria were based on factors associated with past, present, and future criminal sexual conduct. The guidelines do not attempt to predict future conduct but, rather, recognize that certain factors are relevant regarding such conduct. The guidelines represent reasonable intrusions upon an individual's privacy for the protection of society and there is an objective and rational basis for the classification. Finally, the Board's determination is a recommendation to the sentencing court and not the final determination of risk level.[28]

Risk Assessment Instrument—Applied. The court in *New York v. Ayten*[29] found the risk-level determination to be arbitrary and capricious, based not on the risk assessment instrument itself but on how the instrument was applied to the offender. Although the Board had calculated Ayten's risk at a level 2 in accordance with his score, the Board recommended level 3 risk for Ayten to the trial court. The Board stated that was it appropriate to raise the level of risk because Ayten had committed two sexual offenses fairly soon after his arrival in this country, and because it could not obtain Ayten's criminal history from his native country of Turkey. At a hearing on the risk determination, the prosecution echoed the Board's arguments for raising the level and added that the facts of the crime were particularly heinous further supported a level 3 designation. However, the Supreme Court of Queens County determined that raising the risk level based on the inability to obtain criminal history information violated Ayten's due process rights. Also, it determined that the heinous facts of the crime were taken into account by the risk assessment instrument, and to do so a second time was unwarranted.[30]

In contrast, in *People v. Salaam*[31] the offender challenged his level 3 risk assessment. Salaam was one of the "Central Park Jogger" defendants.[32] The level 3 risk assessment was made on the basis of one of four possible overriding factors (that he inflicted serious injury on the victim) which resulted in an automatic level 3 assessment. The court here held that the Board and the sentencing court have the option of departing upward or downward from the calculated risk level, but only when the aggravating or mitigating factors were not taken into account in the calculation. The court found that the Board's recommendation is just that, a recommendation, and that the trial court is free to make its own determination. Here, the court found that there was clear and convincing evidence of the overriding factor on which the Board had relied and that there was less than clear and convincing evidence of any mitigating factors, and it upheld the upward departure to a level 3.[33]

Notice to Offender. It was settled by *Doe v. Pataki* that the sex offender/sexually violent predator is entitled to some due process prior to the risk-level determination. In *New York v. Jackson*,[34] the offender, who was assessed a level 3 risk, claimed that he was not provided adequate notice. However, the court found that when Jackson was released on parole the first time on April 19, 1996, and again prior to his rerelease on parole in October 25, 1996, he had given his address, but with different ZIP codes each time. He had then contacted the Department of Parole and had given them a third ZIP code. Notice of the hearing on his risk assessment was sent to the address with the last ZIP code Jackson had provided. It was not returned to the court, nor did Jackson appear. Later, Jackson filed an annual address verification that gave the same address but yet another ZIP code. Jackson claimed that the notice, sent to one of the previous ZIP codes he had provided, was insufficient. However, the court found that because the notice was sent to the address that Jackson himself had given to the court, it satisfied the due process requirement for notice and affirmed his level 3 risk.

Failure to Register—Due Process. Wayne Manson was charged with failure to register in a timely manner as a sexually violent predator. SVPs are required to register within ninety days of the initial release from, or commencement of, probation and then must verify the registration every ninety days for a minimum of ten years. The court in *New York v. Manson*[35] found that the information charging Manson with failure did not allege that Manson was classified as a sexually violent predator and it failed to identify the date from which the ninety-day period began to run. The court held that because the charging document was unclear, it raised the question whether the defendant had "knowingly and intentionally" failed to verify his registration. The court found that the statute provides, in part, that " a sex offender who fails or refuses to register is subject to the same penalties . . . .,"[36] and that therefore knowledge and intent are essential elements of the charge of failure to register. Thus, the notice to Manson was insufficient, and his motion to dismiss was granted.

Conclusion

When *Hendricks* was decided, it may have seemed as though most of the challenges to sexually violent predator statutes had been resolved. However, as seen by this brief look at sexually violent predator cases that deal not with civil commitment but with tier-level determination of risk, the challenges are far from over and the issues are far from resolved. It is expected that this area of law, risk level determination, will continue to generate turmoil in the state and federal courts. It remains to be seen what will occur regarding such determination and where the challenges will take us.

Footnotes

[1] 117 S. Ct. 2072 (1997).

[2] See Chapter 34, pp. 34-2, nn. 4–10.

[3] Id. at 34-3–34-5.

[4] See E. R. Walsh & F. Cohen, *Sex Offender Registration and Community Notification: A Megan's Law Sourcebook*, at 2-4 and 2-5, n. 29 (1998).

[5] Id. at 2-5, nn. 30 and 31.

[6] In some states the definition differs somewhat in that the person must suffer from a predatory disorder (Arkansas), may have a mental abnormality or personality disorder or attitude (Georgia), or a sexual disorder, a personality disorder, or other mental disorder or dysfunction (North Dakota), for example.

[7] 120 F.3d 1263 (2d. Cir. 1997); see also New York v. Ayten, 172 Misc. 2d 571, 575–578, 658 N.Y.S.2d 175, 178–180.

[8] 1997 WL 613249 (W.D.N.Y.) (not reported in F. Supp.).

[9] Fletcher v. Florida, 699 So. 2d 346 (Fla. App. 1997).

[10] Ohio v. Condron, 1998 WL 135817 (Ohio App. 2d Dist.) (unpublished opinion).

[11] Ohio v. Bartis, 1997 WL 771021 (Ohio App. 10th Dist.) (unpublished opinion).

[12] Ohio v. Cook, 1997 WL 452014, at *4 (Ohio App. 3d Dist.) (unpublished opinion) (citing Van Fossen v. Babcock & Wilcox Co., 36 Ohio St. 3d 100, 106, 522 N.E.2d 489, 496 (1988) (citations omitted)).

[13] Id. (citing Van Fossen, 522 N.E.2d at 107).

[14] 1997 WL 771021 (Ohio App. 10th Dist.) (unpublished opinion).

[15] Ohio v. Condron, 1998 WL 135817 (Ohio App. 2d Dist.) (unpublished opinion); Ohio v. Fugate, 1998 WL 42232 (Ohio App. 12th Dist.) (unpublished opinion); Ohio v. Glynn, 1998 WL 150359 (Ohio App. 9th Dist.) (unpublished opinion); Ohio v. Jones, 1998 WL 267914 (Ohio App. 4th Dist.) (unpublished opinion); Ohio v. Kline, 1997 WL 762940 (Ohio App. 2d Dist.) (unpublished opinion); Ohio v. Lance, 1998 WL 57359 (Ohio App. 1st Dist.) (unpublished opinion); Ohio v. Lyttle, 1997 WL 786216 (Ohio App. 12th Dist.) (unpublished opinion); Ohio v. Roberts, 1997 WL 799461 (Ohio App. 10th Dist.) (unpublished opinion), Ohio v. Russell, 1998 WL 151066 (Ohio App. 1st Dist.) (unpublished opinion); Ohio v. Williamson, 1997 WL 781998 (Ohio App. 10th Dist.) (unpublished opinion).

[16] 1997 WL 452014, at *4.

[17] McKinney's N.Y. Correct. art. 6-C, s. 168-l, subd. 6(c).

[18] McKinney's N.Y. Correct. art. 6-C, s. 168-b, subd. 6 and 168-q.

[19] McKinney's N.Y. Correct. art. 6-C, s. 168-f, subd. 3.

[20] McKinney's N.Y. Correct. art. 6-C, s. 168-h.

[21] 3 F. Supp. 2 (S.D.N.Y. 1998).

[22] Id. at *10.

[23] Id. at *12.

[24] Id.

[25] Doe v. Poritz, 142 N.J. 1, 662 A.2d 367 (N.J. 1995) and E.B. v. Verniero, 119 F.3d 1077 (3d Cir. 1997), *cert. denied*, 188 S. Ct. 1039 (1998), which provided for judicial review of tier levels, written notice to the offender, the right to counsel, prehearing discovery, the burden of persuasion on the state via clear and convincing evidence, and the right to seek a stay of notification.

[26] 1998 WL 230955, at *15–16; New York v. Stevens, 91 N.Y.2d 270, 692 N.E.2d 985, 669 N.Y.S.2d 962 (1998), decided prior to *Doe v. Pataki*, held that offender did not have the right to appeal a risk-level determination made under the Sex Offender and Registration Act (SORA) because appeal was not provided for in the statute. See also Ohio v. Soward, 1998 WL 134325 (Ohio App. 10th Dist.) (unpublished opinion), and Ohio v. Rhodes, 1998 WL 134322 (Ohio App. 10th Dist.) (unpublished opinion) (where it was found that the hearing for determination of SVP status must

be held prior to the offender's release from prison); Ohio v. Hardy, 1997 WL 638801 (Ohio App. 8th Dist.) (unpublished opinion) (holding that failure to notify the offender of the hearing on sexual predator status violates his due process rights).

[27] 172 Misc. 2d 346, 659 N.Y.S.2d 972 (1997).

[28] Id. at 975.

[29] 172 Misc. 2d 571, 658 N.Y.S.2d 175 (1997).

[30] Id. at 177–178.

[31] 174 Misc. 2d 722, 666 N.Y.S.2d 881 (Sup. Ct. N.Y. County 1997).

[32] A group of youths brutally beat and raped a jogger in Central Park, leaving her near death.

[33] 174 Misc. 2d 726, 732-736, 666 N.Y.S.2d 881, 886–889. The court declined to follow People v. Ross, 169 Misc. 2d 308, 312, 646 N.Y.S.2d 249, 252 (Sup. Ct. N.Y. County 1996), which had held that the court must uphold the Board's recommendation unless it is arbitrary and capricious.

[34] 176 Misc. 2d 476, 673 N.Y.S.2d 581 (Sup. Ct. Kings County 1998).

[35] 173 Misc. 2d 806, 661 N.Y.S.2d 773 (N.Y. County 1997).

[36] Id. at 777–778.

Chapter 37

Forging New Alliances— Proposals for Change in Managing Sex Offenders Within the Criminal Justice System

by Brian K. Holmgren, J.D.

Overview

Prosecuting attorneys and sex offender treatment professionals have been among the last people to forge a working alliance. They have often been on opposing sides of legal cases with the treatment professionals arguing for treatment and the prosecutors arguing for incarceration. However, these two alternatives are not necessarily mutually exclusive. In this chapter the author argues for a new spirit of cooperation with each group that brings their special insights together to mutually combat sexual abuse in the most responsible way.

Introduction

Over the past decade, the burgeoning number of sexual abuse cases referred for criminal prosecution have taxed the resources of the criminal justice system. Prosecutors, trial judges, treatment providers, and corrections, probation, and parole personnel struggle to manage ever-increasing numbers of offenders with limited and frequently inappropriate resources. Public attitudes toward these offenders have been influenced by recidivism data, and numerous multivictim and high-profile cases prompting calls for tougher responses. Legislators have catered to this demand by drafting criminal statutes with broader coverage and harsher penalties, federally mandated sex offender registration and public notification laws, and sexually violent predator statutes[1] that provide in limited instances for lifelong civil commitments following the criminal process. Although some of these legislative enactments have provided additional tools for managing offenders,[2] several measures have actually compounded the difficulties already present within the criminal justice response.[3]

Informed Professionals Are Underutilized

Professionals confronting these issues may rightfully ask when these problems will reach critical mass. Fortunately, research efforts and professional organizations have already contributed enormously to our growing knowledge base about offenders and to a heightened professional approach in many areas. Continued research and training programs will undoubtedly further this progress.

Unfortunately, numerous shortcomings remain endemic to the criminal justice response, frustrating current efforts with offenders and threatening future progress. This chapter proceeds from the perspective that the professionals who assess, manage, and treat sex offenders are a vastly underutilized and critical resource for informing the criminal justice response toward offenders. Traditionally, these professionals have not taken an active role in shaping these responses but, instead, have attempted to accommodate their services to the demands placed on them by the criminal justice system.

The success of future efforts necessitates that professionals appreciate the nature of the existing problems and work with those practitioners within the criminal justice system to address them. The paragraphs that follow identify several of these problems and suggest proposals to address them. These proposals are intended to be viewed as components of an overall scheme rather than as individual parts.

As this chapter demonstrates, the failure of one part of the system frequently results in the failure of others.

Alternative Proposals

Proposal 1: Appropriate Management of Sex Offenders Is Contingent Upon Proper Assessments of Offenders Before They Are Sentenced. As one commentator has suggested, the problem with sex offenders is that there are so many of them. These numbers are likely to continue to increase given greater public awareness of and media attention to these offenders, mandated reporting statutes, and improved investigative and prosecutorial responses. Offenders represent a highly diverse group, consisting of exhibitionists and voyeurs at one end of the spectrum to violent rapists and pedophiles at the other end. Criminal justice responses to these different types of offenders necessarily must vary considerably because the social harm and risks associated with these individuals is widely disparate. Informed decisions regarding the management of sex offenders requires an understanding of the factors that discriminate between offenders, their relative dangerousness, their likelihood of responding to different forms of intervention, and their risk of reoffense.[4]

Statistics dictate that existing correctional facilities can house only a small fraction of these offenders. Many professionals urge that some if not most offenders can be safely managed within the community.[5] However, because sex offenders often remain at risk for reoffense for most of their adult lives, they may remain under the supervision of the criminal justice system far longer than other types of criminals,[6] significantly increasing the number of offenders managed by the system at any given time.

Other offenders clearly require incarceration, many for periods well beyond the maximum penalties currently proscribed under existing statutes or the charge on which they are convicted.[7] This chapter does not examine the social policy arguments for or against increasing correctional facilities or the related arguments of incarcerating more or fewer offenders.[8] Rather, it proceeds from the position that correctional resources are likely to remain relatively fixed,[9] and accordingly, the key for appropriate management of offenders is to identify which offenders require which responses.

This identification can only be accomplished if those responsible for making critical decisions regarding the management of offenders, principally prosecutors and judges, have access to information that can inform this decision making. This information should be garnered through comprehensive assessments of offenders *before* sentencing.[10] This is not the current practice in the vast majority of jurisdictions. An unfortunate reality of the criminal justice system is that critical decisions during the plea negotiation and sentencing process of offenders are all too often made with little information,[11] which results from several systemic failures identified throughout this chapter. These failures include overburdened caseloads, inexperience from turnover and inadequate training, lack of vertical prosecution,[12] lack of knowledge of the scientific literature involving offenders, and legal impediments to obtaining information about the offender, which are discussed under Proposal 2.

Consequently, many prosecutors make improvident plea negotiation and sentencing recommendations. Courts similarly hand down inappropriate sentences because they do not have sufficient information about the offender to know whether he is an

appropriate candidate for community supervision or whether the offender should be
incarcerated and for how long he should be managed by the system. This process
could be significantly improved if information gathered from assessments of offenders informed such decisions.

Principally, there are two methods by which these assessments may be made prior
to sentencing. First, the prosecution may make such an assessment part of the plea
negotiation process, effectively offering some consideration by way of a sentencing
recommendation if the offender participates in the assessment.[13] Second, the assessment may be court ordered as part of the presentence investigation and report process,
following a conviction either by a plea or by a trial. Statutes in a few states specifically authorize such assessments and more laws of this type are needed across the
country.[14]

It is imperative that the criminal justice system have access to the professional's
knowledge regarding offenders before critical decisions are made. This can best be
accomplished by using highly skilled evaluators to conduct the assessments. These evaluators preferably should be appointed by the court or employed by state or local governmental agencies to help ensure neutrality and a lack of financial incentive regarding
the evaluation process.[15] The offender is similarly free to hire his own evaluator.

An in-depth discussion of the specific nature of the evaluation process is beyond
the scope of this chapter. However, this chapter does offer some general suggestions.
The evaluations should utilize a variety of assessment instruments including, where
appropriate, the Rapid Risk Assessment for Sex Offender Recidivism (RRASOR),
Violence Risk Appraisal Guide (VRAG), Hare Psychopathy Checklist—Revised
(PCL-R), Abel Screen, Minnesota Sex Offender Screening Tool (MnSOST and
MnSOST—Revised), plethysmography, Minnesota Multiphasic Personality Inventory
(MMPI), sexual abuse inventories, and polygraph validation.[16]

In general, the more knowledge we can obtain regarding the offender, the more
informed will be the decision-making process. Not all assessment instruments are
appropriate with all offenders. Clearly, a cost-benefit analysis must be considered with
each. The evaluation procedures currently being used to assess offenders under sexually violent predator laws and within the prison and parole system may serve as a blue-
print for the types of assessments that should be conducted prior to sentencing.

Unfortunately, several legal impediments compromise the ability to obtain this
information. These impediments are discussed in the next section.

**Proposal 2: The Legal System and Professionals Must Devise Strategies to
Overcome Legal Impediments to the Gathering of Information and to Deal With
Uncooperative Offenders.** The legal system creates its own impediments to the
acquisition of knowledge which might assist decision making. The offender's Fifth
Amendment protection against self-incrimination permit him to remain silent
throughout the criminal proceedings. Case law in some instances precludes consideration of that silence, including silence during the presentence investigation and at the
sentencing hearing, in determination of sentence.[17] Other case law suggests that harsher sentences cannot be provided for offenders who choose to exercise their right to
have a trial[18] or maintain their denial after trial,[19] although many judges routinely do
issue harsher sentences under such circumstances.[20]

Offender denial and minimization are also widely tolerated and encouraged by many of these protections. Offenders frequently use their attorneys as a spokesperson for their denials without ever testifying, confident that the attorney's words may not be used against them. Others push their cases up to and through the trial, only making grudging admissions of limited responsibility or a willingness to accept treatment when they perceive those admissions are necessary or likely to gain them some consideration.[21] Moreover, many offenders attempt to hide behind Fifth Amendment protections to prevent being revoked on probation for failure to make admissions in treatment.[22]

The attorney-client privilege and the therapist-patient privilege may similarly restrict the flow of information to decision makers during the various periods that professionals deal with offenders. For example, many offenders participate in pretrial treatment and evaluation programs with mental health providers, arranged through the defense attorney. If these mental health providers can offer favorable information that might benefit the offender during trial or sentencing, this information is certain to be brought forward. Conversely, if they have negative information to provide, that information will be suppressed and thus unavailable to the court or prosecutor. Often several evaluators are retained until a result favorable to the accused is obtained.

What can be done to overcome these hurdles? First, courts must be encouraged to adopt sentencing practices that reflect a philosophy that the most dangerous offender is the one about whom we know the least. Absent affirmative information from qualified evaluators indicating that the offender is capable of being safely managed within the community, the assumption should instead be that the offender should be incarcerated for a substantial amount of time. Community protection rather than rehabilitation should be the dominant sentencing consideration for the court. Unfortunately, many courts continue to place great faith in the belief that offenders can be "cured" or that treatment is a panacea for recidivism rather than the more realistic perspective that treatment is a method of risk reduction via relapse prevention and behavior modification.[23] This encouragement must come not only from prosecutors but also from professionals dealing with the treatment and management of offenders.

Second, prosecutorial practices in making plea negotiations and sentencing recommendations must also reflect this philosophy. Here, the guiding principle should be that offenders who do not make admissions acknowledging full responsibility, and who do not demonstrate their amenability to treatment, should not be afforded the opportunity for favorable dispositional recommendations, especially those countenancing some form of community supervision. Proposal 4 suggests further recommendations along this line.

Third, prosecutors must use the plea negotiation and sentencing process to obtain assessments of offenders which can inform dispositional determinations. Prosecutors exercise the greatest control over obtaining such assessments through the plea negotiation process because they can condition favorable recommendations on the defendant's willingness to participate in the evaluation process or, conversely, withhold such recommendations or favorable disposition of charges if the offender does not participate. An offender can voluntarily agree to waive his Fifth Amendment protections and cooperate with a presentence assessment. Offenders may be more willing to do so if they know it is the only way to obtain favorable consideration from the prosecutor.

The prosecutor must also request the court to order these assessments, educate the court on their importance, and provide information on which professionals in the community should conduct the assessment. Professionals can also assist prosecutors and the courts by making known their skills in this regard, and the types of resources they can provide to inform this decision-making process. Indeed professionals should insist on such assessments. Simply put, it is both wrong and dangerous to the community to saddle professionals with inappropriate obligations in the management of offenders, resulting from either ill-advised plea agreements or improper sentences, because prosecutors and judges failed to obtain needed assessment information prior to disposition.

Proposal 3: The Criminal Courts Must Be Willing to Deal Firmly With Offenders Who Do Not Cooperate With Predisposition Evaluations and Who Maintain Denial. The success of the previously stated proposals is contingent upon the courts' being willing to impose significant sentences on offenders who do not cooperate with the predisposition evaluation process and those who deny their offense. Many jurisdictions have specific sentencing guidelines for various sex offenses which may pose additional hurdles to this proposal. These guidelines are generally designed to control prison populations and to ensure similar sentences based on the offense rather than the type of offender, and they are not based on current research data involving sex offenders. Accordingly, such guidelines are poorly suited for a dispositional scheme premised on a risk-management approach to sex offenders. In addition, these guidelines fail to consider the risk that uncooperative and denying offenders pose to community safety.

The research data on offenders support the assumption that in the absence of evidence to the contrary, the court should assume the nonevaluated offender has other victims and is likely to reoffend. Indeed, the failure of the offender to cooperate with an evaluation suggests he is concealing information that would support both assumptions. Offenders again may be more willing to participate if they know this is the only way the courts will deal with them favorably.

Although the Constitution provides protections against self-incrimination and presumes every offender innocent until proven guilty, once that guilt is established by a conviction, the prosecution has no additional constitutional requirement to establish dangerousness to justify a particular penalty. The defendant is not entitled to a sentence of probation in lieu of incarceration; rather, probation is a matter of grace and judicial discretion.[24] Courts are free to sentence up to the maximum potential penalty for the convicted of offense. Nothing constitutionally precludes courts from adopting a sentencing philosophy with sex offenders that places the onus on the convicted offenders to demonstrate they are capable of being safely managed within the community.[25]

Unfortunately, the recent U.S. Supreme Court decision in *Mitchell v. United States* (discussed at note 17) makes this proposal potentially more problematic. The *Mitchell* decision could be interpreted by future courts to imply that (1) defendants have an absolute right to remain silent throughout the presentence investigation and sentencing phase of the criminal proceeding, and (2) sentencing judges can draw no adverse inferences from this silence, or impose a harsher sentence in consequence of the defendant's silence and lack of cooperation. The dissenting opinion, however, seems to suggest a more narrow interpretation of the Court's holding and points out the absurdity of prohibiting judges from considering the defendant's silence or cooperation in assessing his character, remorse, and prospects for rehabilitation. Unfortunately, this issue is particularly salient in the context of sex offenders because it is precisely these considerations that should weigh heavily on the court's determination of how to manage these individuals.

The *Mitchell* dissent also notes that courts cannot realistically make constitutional distinctions between "enhancing" punishment for offenders who are silent or denying them the "leniency" they claim would be appropriate if they had cooperated. Indeed, such distinctions on appeal would often turn on the skill with which the court articulated its sentencing rationale or concealed its own agenda and philosophy by offering other justifications for the sentence imposed in order to avoid constitutional scrutiny. It is doubtful, however, that in response to *Mitchell*, courts will abdicate their traditional practice of punishing offenders who are uncooperative, maintain denial and display no remorse and conversely of rewarding offenders who throw themselves on the mercy of the court. Nor is it clear how the *Mitchell* decision will influence future application of earlier precedent that supported these practices.

Several court decisions support the position that effective treatment and safe management of offenders outside the correctional setting cannot occur with offenders who are in denial,[26] and that successful completion of treatment can be conditioned on admissions.[27] Other decisions similarly support the position that an offender's acceptance of responsibility and demonstrations of remorse are an appropriate consideration in mitigation of sentence and evidence the offender's likely prospects of rehabilitation, whereas withholding mitigation in the absence of such factors does not amount to impermissible punishment.[28]

If courts fail to take this position, there will be no incentive for offenders to participate in the evaluation process or to admit their conduct, which will result in the offender's denial and pathology becoming even more entrenched.[29] Moreover, giving lenient treatment to denying and uncooperative defendants is against public policy concerns for community safety and victim restitution.

Unfortunately, such results may be mandated if the *Mitchell* holding is interpreted as broadly as suggested previously. Sex offenders could seek to have their no-contest pleas accepted by the courts and thereafter maintain denial through their silence during the presentence and sentencing phase, hoping that they will receive a sentence involving community supervision or a less severe period of incarceration, especially when such sentences may be called for by sentencing guidelines, statute, or court practice. Their attorneys would also marshal arguments for more lenient dispositions because the defendant has accepted the consequences of his actions, thrown himself on the court's mercy, spared the victim from testifying, and saved the court's time and the public expense of a trial. Indeed, courts might be inclined to offer more lenient sentences to such defendant's precisely because they fear that any articulation of harsher penalties based on the defendant's failure to make greater acknowledgments of responsibility (besides entry of a plea) will be challenged as a violation of the defendant's self-incrimination privilege.

In addition, a defendant who testifies falsely at trial in denying the offense will have no constitutional basis for challenging the court's use of the perjured testimony as a factor in aggravation of sentence, whereas a defendant who enters a no-contest plea but maintains that same denial through silence up through the sentence may be constitutionally protected. Ideally, future appellate decisions will clarify application of the *Mitchell* holding to the unique sentencing issues involving sex offenders in such a way that judges will not be frustrated in their ability to fashion appropriate decisions in consideration of the offender's self-professed or unprofessed attitude toward the offense.

Proposal 4: Prosecutors Need to Maintain Integrity in Charging Decisions, Plea Negotiations, and Sentencing Recommendations. Inexperienced prosecutors routinely offer denying offenders opportunities to plea to charges contingent upon a sentencing recommendation of probation. When these recommendations are sanctioned by the courts, probation agents find themselves managing resistive offenders, and mental health providers are ordered to provide treatment to an individual who denies he has a problem. Similarly, an offender charged inappropriately or given a plea bargain to reduced charges or a lenient sentencing recommendation may be under the supervision of the correctional system for too short a period to adequately protect the community. The end result is that the offender will likely be managed in an inappropriate fashion by other professionals through no fault of their own.

Most professionals have mixed responses to the plea bargaining process based on their personal experiences with it. Many recognize it as a "necessary evil" in light of the high volume of sex offender cases that must be dealt with and the number of difficulties associated with trials of these offenses. Experienced prosecutors, while acknowledging its limitations, recognize plea bargaining as an important tool to effect justice. One of the principle weaknesses with the plea negotiation process is that too often the agreement is reached under circumstances in which prosecutors have inadequate knowledge regarding the offender to make an informed decision regarding the case.

When inappropriate decisions regarding management are made, they are often difficult to rectify. This results again from the legal system's rules and procedures. In recent years, a number of court cases have examined the issue of whether an offender's probation can be revoked for failure to acknowledge responsibility for the offense.[30] The appellate courts have divided, with many of the decisions turning on the issue of whether the defendant was convicted based on a plea or trial,[31] the type of plea entered by the defendant (guilty, no-contest, *Alford*[32]), and the defendant's subjective awareness at the time of his plea or sentence that an admission would ultimately be required.[33] Litigation of this issue can be avoided by making an admission an explicit part of the plea negotiation process and the court's orders at the time of acceptance of the plea and sentencing. Similar issues may arise during parole hearings and litigation surrounding mandatory sex offender treatment programs in the prison system.[34]

In addition, many offenders on probation may not be revoked for noncriminal violations due to administrative regulations imposed as a result of prison overcrowding. Incarcerated offenders may likewise be released at their earliest parole eligibility date for similar reasons, regardless of their participation or cooperation in correctional treatment programs.

The advent of sexual predator statutes may actually increase the likelihood that prosecutors and judges will make inappropriate decisions. The possibility that an offender may later be eligible for civil commitment under these statutes at the expiration of his sentence may encourage judges to defer giving lengthy sentences, believing that if the offender is truly that dangerous he will be committed under these laws.

Prosecutors may be disinclined to take a firmer position in plea negotiations and to push for lengthy sentences for similar reasons.[35] The relatively small number of offenders who would qualify for consideration under these statutes make such decisions by judges and prosecutors ill advised.[36] Moreover, offenders in jurisdictions that have passed these statutes have evidenced less willingness to enter pleas and to participate in treatment programs or assessment procedures. These factors may similarly prompt prosecutors to take more expedient, less appropriate measures to resolve difficult cases.

Prosecutors need to maintain integrity in their charging decisions, plea negotiations, and sentencing recommnedations by pursuing convictions and dispositions that reflect the seriousness of the offense(s) and the dangerousness of the offender.[37] The repeat offender, and offenders who are clearly identified as likely to reoffend, should be dealt with as aggressivley as possible. Enhanced penalties under "repeater" and "multiple strikes" provisions should be used to provide the greatest protection for the public. Unless there is a compelling reason for a reduction in charges or a favorable dispositional recommendation, prosecutors should reserve the benefits of plea offers to offenders who acknowledge responsibility for their conduct through "guilty" pleas and demonstrate a willingness to participate in the assessment process and treatment programs. Those who do not should be afforded their right to a trial or the opportunity to plead without an agreement.

Plea agreements and sentencing recommendations should also specify the need for complete admissions in order to successfully complete any treatment programs. These admissions may encompass not only the charged conduct or the offense(s) pled to but also uncharged "other acts" including offenses against other known and unknown victims. These admissions may also potentially implicate Fifth Amendment protections[38] or place offenders at greater risk for civil commitment under sexually violent predator statutes. Consequently, the offender may be disinclined to make these admissions in the context of treatment. These issues are best dealt with up front at the plea negotiation and sentencing stage rather than being litigated at postconviction or probation revocation hearings. Verification of the accuracy of these admissions is frequently made by comparing them to the victim's account of the offense(s) and through polygraph examination.[39]

Similarly, the prosecutor must work with professionals who will be responsible for managing the offender to identify the expectations and requirements these professionals will have for the offender following disposition. These expectations and requirements should be outlined by the prosecutor for the court and the offender and incorporated into the plea process and sentencing recommendations. Professionals must also include these requirement in their reports and recommendations to the courts. Early recognition of these issues by offenders and the courts can help avoid subsequent litigation challenging these requirements when they are imposed by the court or by professionals.

Proposal 5: Criminal Justice System Needs to Pay Greater Attention to the Scientific Research and Data on Offenders and Seek Expertise of Those With Knowledge of Such Data Throughout Stages of the Criminal Proces. By and large, prosecutors and judges remain relatively unaware of the scientific literature on offenders. Despite the fact that research has been out for several years documenting important characteristics regarding offenders which should inform the decision-making process, this information is infrequently accessed. This information includes data on multiple types of deviant behavior engaged in by offenders,[40] multiple offense histories the majority of which are undetected,[41] and high rates of nonsexual crimes committed by sex offenders.[42] Although courts and prosecutors are generally aware of high rates of recidivism, few understand the factors that increase this risk or appreciate that offender recidivism is also high for nonsexual offenses.

The assessment devices routinely used in correctional settings to make predictions of dangerousness for purposes of parole release, community notification or registration, and/or civil commitments are rarely used prior to sentencing. Although many assessment devices may have little utility for making guilt-innocence determinations, they can provide useful information in structuring responses for the management of offenders.[43] Most prosecutors and courts are unfamiliar with these techniques and consequently do not request or order their use to assist in the sentencing process. The importance of this research and these assessment tools clearly needs to be communicated to prosecutors and judges by professionals who do have this knowledge.

Ironically, these types of assessment devices are most commonly used with incarcerated offenders, and frequently with offenders ordered by the courts to participate in treatment programs. This of course begs the question of how many offenders may have been sentenced and managed differently if this information were made available earlier, and how many are never appropriately evaluated in the first place. The reality of the current system is that the best data we might have to make an informed decision are rarely available at the time those decisions are made.

Professionals with knowledge of such data should be participants in the criminal case at various points in time. As noted earlier, these professionals should be used to conduct offender evaluations prior to disposition. Moreover, professionals may be involved as expert witnesses and evaluators during multiple stages of the criminal case. These include participation in determinations of whether juvenile offenders should be waived into adult court, whether offenders should be released from or revoked on probation or parole, their classification on probation and parole in terms of community notification and sexual predator statutes, and whether offenders are eligible for commitment pursuant to sexual predator statutes. Sentencing memoranda which reference relevant research can also be used to educate the court. Professionals can assist prosecutors both in the preparation of these memoranda and by forwarding relevant research articles which can be attached to documents provided to the court.

Proposal 6: Resources, Options, and Expertise Must Be Increased Across the Board. Predisposition assessments of offenders would significantly increase the efficiency of decisions on the appropriate management of offenders using existing resources. However, they will not address the problem of insufficient resources. In addition, such assessments themselves necessitate an increase in the number of skilled professionals who can conduct them. As we increase our knowledge of offenders and do a better job in assessing them, we are likely to find these offenders more dangerous than existing beliefs reflect. This, in turn, increases the likelihood that more offenders will need to be incarcerated, and more will need to be managed more intensively and for longer periods.[44]

Shortages of skilled and knowledgeable professionals within the criminal justice system result in the mismanagement of large numbers of offenders. This problem is particularly acute in the area of inexperienced prosecutors and uninformed judges, but shortages of skilled mental health professionals and correctional personnel also contribute. Although legislators have been quick to pass laws increasing workloads for system professionals, they have been slow to appropriate financial resources to increase the number and longevity of these professionals or to improve their skills through training. Turnover[45] within these professions and among professionals who conduct investigations of sex offenses remains high, further inhibiting efforts at improved professionalism.

Inexperienced prosecutors and uninformed judges are particularly problematic because the decisions these individuals make tend to significantly influence how other professionals interface with the offender. Of course, there are no guarantees that even if the prosecutor makes the right judgments and recommendations, the judge sentencing the offender will also make the right decisions.[46] Judges are often poorly informed regarding offenders, resulting from a variety of factors including their lack of specialized knowledge and professional training and the failure of litigants and experts to provide appropriate and professionally competent information that might assist judges in making more informed decisions. A judge's personal philosophies on sentencing also influence both the likelihood of incarceration and its length. Litigants' knowledge of these proclivities in turn influences the plea negotiation process.

Several things can be done to address these concerns. First, continued training programs need to be offered for all practitioners dealing with offenders. Judicial training is particularly critical. One way of increasing judicial involvement in training efforts is to ask judges to participate as speakers in local training programs. In addition, practitioners can share conference notebooks from professional trainings with judges and forward relevant articles to further this educational process. Professional organizations such as the Association for the Treatment of Sexual Abusers (ATSA), the National District Attorney's Association (NDAA), and the American Professional Society on the Abuse of Children (APSAC) should also endeavor to promote training by their members at judicial conferences.

Incentives must also be created for professionals dealing with sex offenders to remain in their practices and to encourage others to take up such work.[47] These incentives may include faster promotional opportunities and higher pay, increased training opportunities, and more vacation time. Political leaders in communities must likewise recognize the need for these increased resources and appropriate sufficient funds to make these resources available. These leaders must be encouraged to take a long-term macroeconomic approach to such issues, focusing on the cost savings to victims and community safety from preventative measures using skilled and dedicated professionals.[48]

Finally, legislators must provide greater options to the criminal justice system and professionals for managing offenders. Jurisdictions that have inadequate laws must address this issue and leaders within the criminal justice system and other professionals need to bring these issues to their attention. Increased penalties, multiple-strikes legislation, and lifetime probation statutes are important resources for managing offenders for a sufficient amount of time to protect the public. Sexually violent predator statutes provide some additional options, although they are clearly not as applicable as these other options for the great majority of offenders, and predator statutes are extremely expensive to implement.[49]

In addition, significant resources must be expended to increase both correctional and outpatient treatment programs and to provide adequate systems to monitor compliance with treatment and other conditions of community release. Because a substantial portion of offenders must be managed within the community, community protection and treatment efficacy will be directly tied to the availability of treatment programs and sufficient external monitors to ensure compliance by offenders.[50] Management without sufficient resources is destined for failure, especially given the manipulative and deceitful nature of sex offenders.[51] Similarly, incarcerated offenders in most instances will be released back into the community. Failure to provide adequate and early treatment opportunities will only make these offenders more dangerous.[52]

Proposal 7: Professionals Must Maintain Integrity in Their Management of Offenders. Professional integrity in the management of offenders encompasses three principle considerations. First, professionals must provide appropriate disclaimers regarding the limitations of their abilities to manage offenders and the accuracy of their opinions and recommendations for the courts. Second, professionals must advise the criminal justice system regarding the inappropriateness of dispositions that impose directives on professionals which they cannot fulfill. Third, professionals must ensure high standards for qualifications of those who assess and manage offenders.

Although we have learned much through research on offenders over the last several decades, much still remains unknown. The limitations of this research must be clearly articulated in order for courts to make informed decisions and to ensure that judges remain confident in the opinions they receive from professionals. As one commentator has noted, "[a]lthough many practitioners may be reluctant to make predictions because of problems with prediction accuracy and ethics, they are constantly under pressure to do so by formal systems, other professionals, clients and client's families."[54] Professionals must be sensitive to these dynamics, especially when courts issue directives that conflict with the abilities of professionals to satisfy them. Ethical standards for many of these professionals also necessitate that disclaimers be provided through reports to the court and during expert testimony.

For example, an expert may believe that an offender can be safely managed within the community but only under stringent conditions of supervision. The expert's recommendation should clearly identify these conditions and suggest that the offender should not receive supervision if the court does not order all these conditions or community resources cannot provide them. Similarly, many courts continue to order denying offenders into treatment programs. Treatment providers must disclose to the courts the inappropriateness of such dispositions and the inability to work with the offender under these circumstances rather than simply accepting the court's order for treatment without challenge.

An expert's ethical duties of impartiality toward and candor with the court, however, has far-reaching implications. For example, an expert's philosophical beliefs on the propriety of treatment may cause some to favor alternatives to incarceration, offer unrealistic prospects for behavior modification, and be less conservative regarding issues of public safety. Conversely, those holding a dim view toward offender treatment may correspondingly advocate greater use of incarceration for offenders who may be safely managed in the community. In both instances, the philosophical bias of the evaluator arguably should be disclosed if he or she is making recommendations to the court.

Similar issues may be present involving predictions of the future risk of reoffense in sexually violent predator cases and for purposes of criminal sentences. Many professionals have strong philosophical opposition to predator laws which may color their objectivity in making risk predictions. Beyond those sentiments, however, risk prediction itself contemplates an implicit value judgment by the expert. Although actuarial data may offer some framework for offering these opinions,[55] and statutory criteria and case law may establish legal definitions of risk,[56] the interpretation of these standards depends largely on the expert's own perspectives. For example, an expert who places a higher value on avoiding false negative predictions may be less likely to predict future dangerousness than an expert who values community safety and is more willing to accept the risk of false positives.

If treatment programs and community supervision are to be efficacious, they must carry with them the ability and willingness of professionals to terminate the offender's participation when the offender is noncompliant or maintains denial. Denying offenders should no more be continued in treatment because there is a hope of future admissions or a desire for revenue from treatment than should probation revocation proceedings be thwarted because there is no bed space in the prison. Professionals should have a zero tolerance for noncompliant offenders and the criminal justice system must back them up.[57]

Both the criminal justice system and professionals should insist on high standards of qualification and competency for those managing offenders, especially those doing offender evaluations and treatment. Insistence that professionals comport with certification standards and training programs devised by professional organizations such as ATSA is one means of doing this. Some legislative initiatives have also been undertaken in this regard.[58]

Perhaps more important, professionals must monitor others in the field to ensure that best practices are being followed. Where they are not, such information must be directed to the courts, and where appropriate to professional boards authorized to deal with unprofessional conduct. Unprofessional and unethical behavior by those offering expert opinion testimony or reports to the court inevitably leads to a loss of confidence in the integrity of experts as a whole, and a lack of willingness by courts to use experts in the future. The need for professionals to share their expertise with the criminal justice system is vital; their value to all cannot be compromised by the irresponsible conduct of a few.[59]

Conclusion

The criminal justice system has much to gain by opening a dialogue by those mental health professionals who specialize in treating sexual abusers. These individuals are able to assist with wise decision making at a variety of junctions. Careful assessment can help in sorting out which offenders present the most risk to the public. They can suggest which offenders can benefit from community treatment and which ones may require incarceration. In addition, treatment providers can continue to advise supervising officers as to the progress or lack thereof when offenders are given community-based sanctions. If this partnership is to work to the maximum benefit of all, there needs to be an open flow of communication with sharing of relevant information. Therefore both groups need to stay abreast of current research in order to enhance their decisions.

Footnotes

[1] See, e.g., Ariz. Rev. Stat. Ann. § 13-4601-4613 (1995); Cal. Welf. & Inst. Code §§ 6600–6608 (West 1996); Fla. Stat. Ann. § 916.32 (1998); § 725 Ill. Comp. Stat. Ann. 207/1 (1997); § 229a Iowa Code Ann. (1998); Kan. Stat. Ann. § 59-29a01 (1994); Minn. Stat. Ann. §§ 253B.02, 253B.185 (West 1996); Rev. Stat. Mo. § 589.400–589.425 (1998); N.D. Cent. Code § 25-03.3–25-01 (1997); S.C. Code § 44-48-30 (1998); Wash. Rev. Code § 71.09.010 (1990); Wis. Stat. Ann. §§ 980.01–980.12 (1996). New Jersey had provided for commitment of sexually violent predators through its civil mental health commitment statute. See N.J. Stat. § 30:4-82.4 (West 1994). However, New Jersey recently enacted a postincarceration commitment statute similar to those listed above. See 1998 N.J. ALS 71 (1998). In addition, North Carolina and North Dakota recently enacted special procedures for the classification and registration of sexually violent predators, although the statutes do not provide for postincarceration civil commitments of these offenders. See N.C. Gen. Stat. § 14-208.20 (1997); N.D. Cent. Code § 12.1-32-15 (1997).

[2] Throughout the course of this chapter, the term "management" of offenders is applied generically to the range of criminal justice responses following conviction and sentence, including but not limited to probation and parole supervision, court-ordered treatment programs, incarceration, and civil commitment of offenders under recently enacted sexually violent predator laws.

[3] See, e.g., R. A. Prentky, R. A. Knight, & A. F. S. Lee, *Child Sexual Molestation: Research Issues*, at 8 (1997), commenting that community notification laws may compound the difficulties of reintegrating offenders within the community and increase stressors that may lead to recidivism. Notification and registration programs can also significantly increase law enforcement workloads. See also Holmgren, "Sexually Violent Predator Statutes—Implications for Prosecutors and Their Communities," 32(3) *The Prosecutor* 20–41 (1998), discussing the impacts of these statutes on existing community resources.

[4] Prentky, Knight, & Lee, supra note 3; Becker & Murphy, "What We Know and Don't Know About Assessing and Treating Sex Offenders," 4(1–2) *Psychology, Public Policy and Law* (forthcoming).

[5] Berliner, Schram, Miller, & Milloy, "A Sentencing Alternative for Sex Offenders: A Study of Decision Making and Recidivism," 10(4) *Journal of Interpersonal Violence* 487–502 (1995).

[6] See, e.g., Ariz. Rev. Stat. 13-902 (providing lifetime probation for sex offenders); Wis. Stat. Ann. § 973.09(2) (providing for probationary period up to maximum potential sentence of forty years for first-degree sexual assaults). These probationary periods may also be run consecutive to a prison sentence. Research also suggests significant rates of recidivism in later years following release from prison, suggesting the need for extended periods of parole or probation consecutive to prison release. See Prentky, Knight, & Lee, supra note 3, at 13–14; Hanson, Scott, & Steffy, "A Comparison of Child Molesters and Nonsexual Criminals: Risk Predictors of Long-Term Recidivism," 32 *Journal of Research in Crime and Delinquency* 325–337 (1995); Soothill & Gibbens, "Recidivism of Sex Offenders: A Reappraisal," 18 *British Journal of Criminology* 267–276 (1978).

[7] For example, a study of sixty-one incarcerated sex offenders in Washington who were not considered eligible for a sexually violent predator petition revealed that on average they had 2.6 sex convictions and 95% were alleged to have other known offenses for which they had not been convicted, yet these offenders spent an average of only 5.1 years in prison for their index offense. See D. D. Schram, & C. D. Milloy, *Sexually Violent Predators and Civil Commitment: A Study of the Characteristics and Recidivism of Sex Offenders Considered for Civil Commitment But for Whom Proceedings Were Declined* (1998).

[8] Compelling arguments can be raised for approaching the disposition of sex offenders from a purely deterrent-punitive perspective rather than the current focus of most courts, which looks at the

offender's amenability to treatment and risk to the community. Because the risk-management approach is the dominant philosophy of the current criminal justice response, the proposals herein are designed to improve that response. For a philosophical discussion of this approach focused on the most dangerous sex offenders see R. Lieb, V. Quinsey, & L. Berliner, "Sexual Predators and Social Policy," in *Crime and Justice: A Review of Research* (M. Tonrey, ed., 1998). Neither does the article discuss the importance of meeting the victim's sense of justice in the management of sex offenders. For example, the victim's sense of an appropriate resolution to the case and desires regarding the offender's accountability, punishment, supervision, and treatment are critical considerations in any plea negotiation and sentencing process. For a thorough discussion of these issues, see American Prosecutors Research Institute, "Charging, Plea Negotiation and Sentencing," in *Investigation and Prosecution of Child Abuse* (2d ed. 1993). Alexandria, VA: National Center for Prosecution of Child Abuse.

[9] Statistical data reveal that between 1930 and 1995, the number of sentenced sex offenders admitted to state prisons has increased only slightly in comparison to the increase for all convicted offenders in prison. See Bureau of Justice Statistics, *Correctional Populations in the United States, 1995* (1997).

[10] See generally Becker & Murphy, supra note 4. Becker and Murphy point out there are a wide variety of assessment procedures and capabilities that vary in their utility and reliability depending on the stage at which they are conducted (pretrial, predisposition, posttreatment) and their purpose (diagnosis, risk assessment, guide for treatment program, release determination). This chapter refers to assessments principally in terms of a predispositional risk assessment tool for determining how offenders should be managed through the criminal justice and correctional systems. Elsewhere, Murphy suggests that professionals conducting assessments and evaluations for the court should not make specific recommendations regarding disposition but merely provide the criminal justice system with information that will assist this determination. See Murphy & Smith, "Sex Offenders Against Children: Empirical and Clinical Issues," in *The APSAC Handbook on Child Maltreatment* (J. Briere, L. Berliner, J. A. Bulkley, C. Jenny, & T. Reid, eds., 1996).

[11] Difficulties with the criminal justice response are not restricted to the plea negotiation and sentencing process, although inaccurate decisions at this point significantly contribute to other errors in system responses. A recent National Institute of Justice Report notes that "rigorous programs to enhance the accuracy of predictive decisions involving [child] sexual offenders are of fairly recent origin," and before the criminal justice community can effectively combat this problem, it must first understand it. See Prentky, Knight & Lee, supra note 4.

[12] Vertical prosecution refers to the process of having a single prosecutor follow the case from charging all the way through trial and sentencing. This practice is widely favored for several reasons, including maintaining continuity and rapport between a single prosecutor and the victim and more efficient case management by ensuring that important information regarding the case is not lost in the transfer from one prosecutor to the next. See generally American Prosecutors Research Institute, *Investigation and Prosecution of Child Abuse,* supra note 8.

[13] For example, the prosecutor might offer a recommendation of probation if the assessment suggests that the offender is an appropriate candidate for probation and treatment. Alternatively, the prosecutor may agree not to make a specific sentencing recommendation (e.g. incarceration for a specified time) in the event the assessment is not favorable. In addition, the prosecutor may adopt a no-bargain position if the offender refuses to participate in an assessment or advocate harsher sentences in the absence of information that might mitigate against a lengthy period of incarceration.

[14] See, e.g., Wash. Rev. Code § 9.94A.120(8), which provides for a court-ordered assessment to be conducted to determine whether the offender is appropriate for a community-based treatment program in lieu of incarceration. See also Ariz. R. Crim. Proc. 26.5, providing that "[a]ny time before sentence is pronounced the court may order the defendant to undergo mental health examination or diagnostic evaluation"; and N.C. Gen. Stat. § 14-208.20, providing for an evaluation of the defendant by a panel of sex offender experts prior to sentencing if the prosecution has sought to classify the defendant as a "sexually violent predator" by its charging document. This procedure is not designed to be used, however, with the vast majority of defendants charged with sex offenses in North Carolina. This classification of a "sexually violent predator" is also distinct from the types of postconviction civil commitment statutes, referenced supra note 1.

[15] For example, in many communities which lack a large number of professional evaluators, evaluations are conducted by treatment providers. These evaluations are potentially subject to challenge because the evaluator may have a financial stake in recommending dispositions that involve their treatment program.

[16] See also Loza & Dhaliwal, "Psychometric Evaluation of the Risk Appraisal Guide (RAG): A Tool for Assessing Violent Recidivism," 12(6) *Journal of Interpersonal Violence* 779–793 (1997), discussing various risk assessment devices currently used with incarcerated offenders. Arizona's evaluation process includes a listing of more than forty tools used to assess offenders.

[17] See generally Soeffing, "Annotation: Plea of Guilty or Conviction as Resulting in Loss of Privilege Against Self-Incrimination as to Crime in Question," 9 *A.L.R.3d* 990 (1996). The issue of the defendant's continuing right to assert a Fifth Amendment privilege often turns on whether the defendant has entered a plea or whether the defendant has been convicted by way of a trial. Compare, e.g., Boykin v. Alabama, 395 U.S. 238 (1969) (plea of guilty waives privilege against self-incrimination), and Neal v. Shimoda, 131 F.3d 818 (9th Cir. 1997) (plea agreement to dismiss sexual assault charges removes jeopardy and creates no potential for self-incrimination for treatment program requirement that defendant acknowledge sexual conduct), with Mills v. United States, 281 F.2d 736 (1960) and Thomas v. United States, 386 F.2d 941 (5th Cir. 1966) and Taylor v. Best, 746 F.2d 220, 222 (4th Cir. 1984) (privilege against self-incrimination remains where the defendant has not been sentenced and the time for appeal has not run), and Bankes v. Simmons, 963 P.2d 412 (Kan. 1998), and Lile v. McKune, 24 F. Supp. 1152 (D. Kan. 1998) (privilege remains where admissions might contradict defendant's trial testimony denying offense, thereby subjecting him to possible perjury charges). The U.S. Supreme Court recently decided that a defendant's failure to testify at a sentencing hearing cannot be used by the sentencing judge to draw negative inferences against the defendant which may increase his punishment. See Mitchell v. United States, 1999 U.S. LEXIS 2348. The Court also ruled that the defendant's entry of a guilty plea, which encompasses a waiver of the right to remain silent, did not abdicate the defendant's rights to reassert the privilege during the sentencing phase of the proceedings. Although *Mitchell* is a drug case sentenced under the federal sentencing guidelines, it has potentially significant implications for sentencing sex offenders. Arguably, the Court's Fifth Amendment analysis could be interpreted to preclude the sentencing judge from drawing adverse considerations or sentencing a sex offender more harshly if the offender fails to cooperate with a presentence investigation or psychosexual assessment or discuss the offense based on his self-asserted privilege against self-incrimination. If part of the assessment involves disclosure of other uncharged sexual offenses, this implicates Fifth Amendment considerations as well. See, e.g., Mace v. Amestoy, 765 F. Supp. 847 (D. Vt. 1991) (defendant could not be compelled to admit to uncharged offenses in treatment absent grant of immunity). Compare State v. Carrizales, 528 N.W.2d 29 (Wis. Ct. App. 1995) (conviction removes threat of additional prosecution for admissions made involving offense that is subject of conviction).

[18] See, e.g., United States v. Tateo, 214 F. Supp. 560 (S.D.N.Y. 1963) (defendant's constitutional right to a trial requiring government to establish guilt cannot be overshadowed by threat that if he is found guilty he will receive maximum sentence but if he pleads he will receive substantially reduced term, "such alternatives amount to coercion as a matter of law.")

[19] See, e.g., *Thomas*, supra note 17 (improper for court to punish defendant for his failure to "come clean" at sentencing where defendant had denied offense in testimony at trial and still had appeal rights available); Scales v. State, 219 N.W.2d 286 (Wis. 1974) (refusal to admit guilt cannot alone be used to justify incarceration rather than probation); State v. Imlay, 813 P.2d 979 (Mont. 1991) (cannot augment sentence because of refusal to admit crime or exercise of privilege). But see State v. Noyes, 596 A.2d 340 (Vt. 1991) (Fifth Amendment is not implicated by presentence comments on defendant's refusal to acknowledge guilt where defendant testified at trial and jury's verdict rejected testimony as false); State v. Baldwin, 304 N.W.2d 742 (Wis. 1981) (distinguishing *Scales* and *Thomas* in holding defendant's lack of remorse is an appropriate factor to consider at sentencing); United States v. Trujillo, 906 F.2d 1456 (10th Cir. 1990) (failure to cooperate with presentence report and accept responsibility justifies denying defendant credit toward reduction of sentence under federal sentencing guidelines). But see United States v. Mitchell, supra note 17 (Court does not decide whether assertion of silence is appropriate factor to consider regarding downward departure under guidelines).

[20] These sentences are often based on considerations that the impact to the victim has been increased by the necessity of the victim's testifying at trial, the offender's lack of demonstrated remorse by maintaining his denial through trial, or the offender's false testimony in support of a defense the jury rejected at trial. Other judges simply impose harder sentences following trial as a means of controlling their caseload, encouraging criminal defendants to avoid time-consuming trials by affording them lighter sentences following a plea. See, e.g., United States v. Grayson, 438 U.S. 41 (1978) (defendant's truthfulness or mendacity while testifying has been deemed probative of his prospects for rehabilitation and hence relevant to sentencing); *Noyes*, supra note 19 (court may take defendant's false testimony inconsistent with verdict into account); Coleman v. State, 409 N.E.2d 647 (Ind. App. 1980) (lack of remorse appropriate consideration in determining need for corrective treatment as opposed to probation); State v. Loveland, 684 A.2d 272 (Vt. 1996) (same); *Baldwin*, supra note 19.

[21] See, e.g., State v. Loveland, 684 A.2d 272 (Vt. 1996).

[22] See, e.g., Carrizales, supra note 17; Mace v. Amestoy, supra note 17; and cases cited infra notes 30–34.

[23] See generally Pithers & Cummings, "Relapse Prevention: A Method for Enhancing Behavioral Self-Management and External Supervision of the Sexual Aggressor," in B. K. Schwartz & H. R. Cellini, *The Sex Offender:Corrections, Treatment and Legal Practice* (Vol. I), Ch. 20 (1995); Pithers, "Relapse Prevention With Sexual Aggressors," in *Handbook of Sexual Assault: Issues, Theories, and Treatment of the Offender* (W. Marshall, D. Laws, & H. Barbaree eds., 1990).

[24] See, e.g., Gilfillen v. State, 582 N.E.2d 821 (Ind. 1991); Carrizales, supra note 17; Wisconsin *ex rel.* Warren v. Schwartz, 579 N.W.2d 698 (Wis. 1998); People v. Birdsong, 958 P.2d 1124 (Colo. 1998); People v. Ickler, 877 P.2d 863 (Colo. 1994) (probation is a privilege not a right).

[25] Loveland, supra note 21 ("If defendant can find a method of convincing the court that community safety can be assured with a probationary sentence, the court must be open to that possibility. Where he presents no realistic alternative, beyond an illusory commitment to participate in treatment programs as directed, the court is free to consider the prospect of rehabilitation, and the safety of the community, in fashioning a sentence.").

[26] See *Grayson,* supra note 20; *Coleman*, supra note 20; Carrizales, supra note 17; State v. Gleason, 576 A.2d 1246 (Vt. 1990).

[27] See, e.g., Gleason, supra note 26; Loveland, supra note 21; Russell v. Eaves, 722 F. Supp. 558 (E.D. Mo. 1989) (parole eligibility determined by completion of inmate treatment program requiring admissions upheld). But see Gilfillen, supra note 24 (reasonable condition of probation does not include insisting on admissions in treatment where defendant convicted at trail and denied guilt, but denial can be considered to determine appropriateness of probation). For an extensive discussion of the propriety of requiring admissions as a prerequisite to effective treatment, see J. E. B. Myers, Brief of Amicus Curiae American Professional Society on the Abuse of Children Supporting Neither Party, Montana v. Imlay, No. 91-687, April 10, 1992, on writ of certiorari to the Montana Supreme Court.

[28] See, e.g., State v. Sims, 608 A.2d 1149 (Vt. 1991) ("We are unprepared to equate the possibility of leniency with impermissible punishment"; "If we were to characterize the denial of a reduction as a penalty, it would be to say that defendants who express genuine remorse for their actions can never be rewarded at sentencing. This the Constitution does not require."); Mitchell, supra note 17 (dissenting opinion). See also United States v. Parker, 903 F.2d 91 (2d Cir. 1990); United States v. Henry, 883 F.2d 1010 (11th Cir. 1989); Brady v. United States, 379 U.S. 742 (1970) (not unconstitutional to extend a benefit to a defendant who demonstrates a willingness to accept rehabilitation); *Myers*, supra note 27.

[29] See, e.g., *Gilfillen*, supra note 24 (thought control through compelled admissions in treatment are not a reasonable condition of probation and cannot be a basis for revocation where defendant's deny the offense and are convicted following a trial); Morstad v. State, 518 N.W.2d 191 (N.D. 1994) (dissenting opinion) (criticizing appropriateness of trial court determination that denying offender is not likely to repeat behavior). These decisions highlight the importance of not affording denying offenders the privilege of probation because of the difficulties with managing the offender and revoking probation for failure to make admissions in treatment.

[30] See, e.g., State v. Imlay, 813 P.2d 979 (Mont. 1991), *cert. dismissed*, Montana v. Imlay, 113 S. Ct. 444 (1992); *Gilfillen*, supra note 24; *Gleason*, supra note 26; *Birdsong*, supra note 24; Henderson v. State, 543 So. 2d 344 (Fla. Dist. Ct. App. 1989); Archer v. State, 604 So. 2d 561 (Fla. Dist. Ct. App. 1992); Diaz v. State, 629 So. 2d 261 (Fla. Dist. Ct. App. 1993); Bell v. State, 643 So. 2d 674 (Fla. Dist. Ct. App. 1994); Bennett v. State, 684 So. 2d 242 (Fla. Dist. Ct. App. 1996); People v. Walters, 164 Misc. 2d 986, 627 N.Y.S.2d 289 (1995); Wisconsin *ex rel.* Warren v. Schwartz, *supra* note 24. Compare People v. Prusak, 558 N.E.2d 696 (Ill. App. 3d 1990) (court's decision revoking defendant's probation for failure to make admissions in treatment and discharge from treatment program was against the manifest weight of the evidence; because denial is "almost universal" among sex offenders, it is paradoxical to classify the defendant as a sex offender, place him on probation, and then revoke his probation because he exhibits behavior commonly displayed by sex offenders).

[31] Compare, e.g., *Imlay*, supra note 19; *Gilfillen*, supra note 24 (no revocation where defendant had trial and denied) with State v. Butler, 900 P.2d 908 (Mont. 1995) and Lind v. State, 550 N.E.2d 823 (Ind. 1990) (revocation upheld; defendant waives right against self-incrimination by entering plea); State v. Jones, 926 P.2d 1318 (Idaho App. 1996) (same)

[32] North Carolina v. Alford, 400 U.S. 25 (1970). *Alford* pleas involve the entry of a guilty plea by the offender coupled with a denial of the offense. Because of the legal fiction involved with this type of plea, it is widely disfavored for use in sex crimes prosecutions and acceptance of the plea is usually conditioned on both the court and prosecution's acquiescence.

[33] See, e.g., *Butler*, supra note 31, and *Jones*, supra note 31 (defendant aware of necessity for admission); *Birdsong*, supra note 24 (defendant aware); *Diaz*, supra note 30, *Bennett*, supra note 30, and *Walters*, supra note 30 (defendant unaware); Morstad v. State, 518 N.W.2d 191 (N.D. 1994) (court's ambiguous comments at sentencing did not specifically advise defendant failure to admit would constitute probation violation); *Bell*, supra note 30 (court did not specify admission as part of probation conditions and imposition of this condition by probation agent was improper upward modification of court's conditions); *Mace*, supra note 17 (sufficient notice provided by probation agent's rules despite failure of court to address issue at plea or sentencing).

[34] See Russell v. Eaves, 722 F. Supp. 558 (E.D. Mo. 1989); *Shimoda,* supra note 17; and *Simmons*, supra note 17. Compare *McKune*, supra note 17.

[35] The U.S. Supreme Court itself warned against using these statutes as a backstop for poor plea negotiations and dispositions. See Kansas v. Hendricks, 117 S. Ct. 2072, 138 L. Ed. 2d 501, 1997 U.S. Lexis 3999 (Kennedy, J., concurring), "If the civil system is used simply to impose punishment after the State makes an improvident plea bargain on the criminal side, then it is not performing its proper function." See also Foucha v. Louisiana, 504 U.S. 71, 82 (1992) (charge, conviction, and heightened penalties for recidivists are "the normal means of dealing with persistent criminal conduct").

[36] Most predator statutes apply only to offenders who are incarcerated, excluding those currently on probation, and less than 15% of incarcerated offenders are actually petitioned against. See Holmgren, supra note 3.

[37] See generally American Prosecutors Research Institute, "Charging, Plea Negotiation and Sentencing," in *Investigation and Prosecution of Child Abuse,* supra note 8. See also Lieb, Quinsey & Berliner, supra note 8, "The imposition of appropriate criminal sanctions requires accurate charging decisions to ensure that offenders are convicted of serious crimes that carry lengthy penalties. Pressures to resolve cases by plea bargains to less serious, nonsexual or nonviolent crimes create the conditions that lead to sensational failures and public outcry." Id. at 98.

[38] See, e.g., cases cited supra note 17.

[39] See, e.g., Blasingame, "Suggested Clinical Use of Polygraphy in Community-Based Sexual Offender Treatment Programs," 10(1) *Sexual Abuse: A Journal of Research and Treatment* 37–45 (1998); O'Connell, "Using Polygraph Testing to Assess Deviant Sexual History of Sex Offenders," 58(8-A) *Dissertation Abstracts International* 3023 (Feb. 1998). See also State v. Dods, 941 P.2d 1116 (Wash. App. 1997) (sex offender in the course of undergoing polygraph tests as condition of sentence revealed sexual abuse of minor); State v. Riles, 957 P.2d 655 (Wash. 1998) (polygraph

may enhance assessment, treatment and monitoring process); *Bankes,* supra note 17; and *McKune,* supra note 17.

[40] See, e.g., Abel, Becker, Mittelman, Cunningham-Rathner, Roleau, & Murphy, "Self-Reported Sex Crimes of Non-Incarcerated Paraphiliacs," 2 *Journal of Interpersonal Violence* 3–25 (1987).

[41] Id.; Groth, Longo, & McFadin, "Undetected Recidivism in Rapists and Child Molesters," 28 *Crime and Delinquency* 450–458 (1982); R. E. Freeman-Longo, *Incidence of Self-Reported Sex Crimes Among Incarcerated Rapists and Child Molesters.* Unpublished manuscript, Correctional Treatment Program, Oregon State Hospital (1999); Weinrott & Saylor, "Self-Report of Crimes Committed by Sex Offenders," 6(3) *Journal of Interpersonal Violence* 286–300 (1991); O'Connell, supra note 38. In addition, Weinrott and Saylor found that offenders self-reported a high degree of crossover in offense types with rapists also offending against children and incest offenders also offending outside the home. O'Connell similarly found that polygraph testing caused offenders to reveal previously undisclosed crossover offenses with incest offenders admitting offenses outside the home, and child molesters disclosing they had engaged in forced sex offenses and offenses against both boys and girls.

[42] Weinrott & Saylor, supra note 41.

[43] See generally Becker & Quinsey, "Assessing Suspected Child Molesters," 17 *Child Abuse and Neglect* 169–174 (1993). For example, the MMPI and the plethysmograph do not have predictive value for determining whether an offender engaged in the alleged conduct, but these instruments are nevertheless widely recognized for their utility in assessing offenders, structuring treatment programs, and assessing the viability of treatment regimens.

[44] See, e.g., Prentky, Knight & Lee, supra note 3, noting that appropriate management of offenders necessitates that caseloads for probation and parole supervision must be low, and there must be sufficient treatment programs; P. Green & B. Franklin, "The Sex Offender, the Polygraph, and Community Corrections," Chapter 13, in this volume, noting the need for extensive supervision and aftercare for offenders because of their risk of reoffense throughout their lifetime.

[45] Turnover can result both from individuals leaving their current positions or professions, and from the failure to allocate sufficient resources enabling an individual to remain with a particular case for its entirety. Similar problems may arise from an offender being managed by multiple probation agents.

[46] The cases cited in notes 17–35 reflect numerous instances in which courts have made inappropriate decisions regarding management of offenders.

[47] The District Attorneys Offices in Tucson, Arizona and West Palm Beach, Florida currently have such progressive programs and numerous law enforcement agencies also promote this type of specialization through similar incentives. Specialization has also occurred with probation officers. See Green & Franklin, supra note 44.

[48] Recent efforts have been made to examine these costs. See generally T. Miller, M. Cohen, & B. Wiersema, *Victim Costs and Consequences: A New Look* (1996); U.S. Department of Justice, *Sourcebook of Criminal Justice Statistics—1994* (1994). From a more simplistic standpoint, if a jury trial costs a community several thousand dollars each day, it makes sense to have experienced prosecutors conducting those trials and ensuring a higher likelihood of conviction, even if it costs more in salaries to retain experienced prosecutors. The increases in salaries will be more than offset by the cost savings to the community and the victims.

[49] See Holmgren, supra note 3; Becker & Murphy, supra note 4.

[50] *Myers,* supra note 26, noting the important role the courts play in providing incentives for treatment through the threat of punitive sanctions, and referencing B. Smith, S. Hillenbrand, & S. Goretsky, *The Probation Response to Child Sexual Abuse Offenders: How Is It Working?* (1990), wherein the authors noted the importance of close monitoring of offenders and coordination between treatment providers and probation officers to ensure offender compliance and public safety; Pithers & Cummings, supra note 23. See also Abel et al., "Predicting Child Molesters' Response to Treatment," 528 *Annals of N.Y. Academy of Sciences* 223 (1988), noting high dropout rate from treatment when offenders suffered no adverse consequences from withdrawal.

[51] See Becker & Murphy, supra note 4; Hildebran & Pithers, "Relapse Prevention: Application and

Outcome," in *The Sexual Abuse of Children: Clinical Issues* (vol. 2) (W. O'Donohue & H. H. Greer eds., 1992), reporting low rates of recidivism in a statewide program with extensive treatment services, after-care programs and skilled probation and parole agents.

[52] See Becker & Murphy, supra note 4, noting that lack of treatment options and the failure to provide early treatment intervention to incarcerated offenders increases their dangerousness by allowing entrenchment of their denial and reinforcement of their deviant behavior thereby making their condition more chronic.

[53] Milner & Campbell, "Prediction Issues for Practitioners," in *Assessing Dangerousness: Violence by Sexual Offenders, Batterers, and Child Abusers* (J. C. Campbell ed., 1995).

[54] See, e.g., American Psychological Association, *Ethical Principles of Psychologists and Code of Conduct* (1992). See also American Psychiatric Association, *Task Force Report on Sexually Dangerous Offenders* (in press). Washington, DC: Author. This report suggests that psychiatrists should vigorously oppose involuntary civil commitment of sex offenders under current sexual predator statutes. Accordingly, psychiatrists involved in such proceedings may be obligated to disclose this type of policy statement by the APA because it may affect the opinions rendered in legal proceedings.

[55] Compare, e.g., Janus & Meehl, "Assessing the Legal Standard for Predictions of Dangerousness in Sex Offender Commitment Proceedings," 3(1) *Psychology, Public Policy and Law* 33–64 (1997), urging a conservative approach to actuarial prediction, with Doren, "Recidivism Base Rates, Predictions of Sex Offender Recidivism, and the 'Sexual Predator' Commitment Laws," 16(1) *Behavioral Sciences and the Law* 97–114 (1998), suggesting actuarial methods underpredict dangerousness. See also Becker, supra note 4, "Whether the concern is false positives or false negatives also has social policy implications. Do we minimize false positives for protection of individual freedom, or do we try to minimize false negatives for protection of society? That question will not be answered by the data alone."

[56] See, e.g., In re Linehan, 544 N.W.2d 308 (Minn. Ct. App. 1996), *aff'd*, 577 N.W.2d 171 (Minn. 1996), and In re Young, 857 P.2d 989 (Wash. 1993), setting higher standards for predictions of future dangerousness than those actually required by the statutory scheme.

[57] One example of this approach is the Dallas Police Department's Sexual Offender Apprehension Project (SOAP). The SOAP unit is designed to be a proactive law enforcement system promoting public safety by monitoring offenders to ensure compliance with probation conditions and community notification laws. The unit has been widely successful in arresting noncompliant offenders who then face revocation proceedings. Other offenders can then be deterred from such violations through their awareness of this monitoring and the likelihood of being caught.

[58] Arizona has proposed legislation setting forth extensive qualifications for competency of professionals. Other laws dealing with sexual predators frequently set forth some minimal qualifications for evaluators and experts who can participate in this area.

[59] Regrettably, unprofessional conduct seems endemic to our legal process. As one court has noted, "[t]here is hardly anything not palpably absurd on its face which cannot now be proved by some so-called expert." Chaulk v. Volkswagen of America Inc., 808 F.2d 639, 644 (7th Cir. 1986). For example, several "so-called" experts continue to attempt to offer expert testimony on "profiles" of offenders in support of factual determinations of the defendant's guilt or innocence. See, e.g., Kavanagh v. Berge, 73 F.3d 733 (7th Cir. 1996); Hulbert v. State, 529 N.W.2d 632 (Iowa Ct. App. 1995); State v. Michaels, 642 A.2d 1372 (N.J. 1993) (holding testimony scientifically unreliable); United States v. Powers, 59 F.3d 1460 (4th Cir. 1995) (profile based on defendant's performance on penile plethysmograph not scientifically reliable). Extensive professional commentary indicates the inappropriateness of this conduct and its lack of scientific validity. See Peters & Murphy, "Profiling Child Sexual Abusers: Legal Considerations," 19(1) *Criminal Justice and Behavior* 38–53 (1992); Murphy & Peters, "Profiling Child Sexual Abusers: Psychological Considerations," 19(1) *Criminal Justice and Behavior* 24–37 (1992); Marshall & Hull, "The Value of the MMPI in Deciding Forensic Issues in Accused Sex Offenders," 7 *Sexual Abuse: A Journal of Research and Treatment* 205 (1995).

Appendix A

Bibliography

Abel, G. G. (1995). *Abel Assessment for Sexual Interest™: Therapists' product information.* Atlanta, GA: Abel Screening, Inc.

Abel, G. G., Becker, J. V., & Cunningham-Rathner, J. (1984). Complications, consent, and cognitions in sex between children and adults. *International Journal of Law and Psychiatry, 7,* 89–103.

Abel, G. G., Becker, J. V., Mittelman, M., Cunningham-Rathner, J., Roleau, J. L., & Murphy, W. D. (1987). Self-reported sex crimes of non-incarcerated paraphiliacs. *Journal of Interpersonal Violence, 2,* 3–25.

Abel, G. G., & Blanchard, E. B. (1974). The role of fantasy in the treatment of sexual deviations. *Archives of General Psychiatry, 30,* 467–475.

Abel, G. G., Blanchard, E. B., Becker, J. V., & Djenderedjian, A. (1978). Differentiating sexual aggressives with penile measures. *Criminal Justice and Behavior, 5,* 315–332.

Abel, G. G., Gore, D. K., Holland, C. L., Camp, N., Becker, J. V., & Rathner, J. (1989). The measurement of the cognitive distortions of child molesters. *Annals of Sex Research, 2,* 135–152.

Abel, G. G., Huffman, J., Warberg, B., & Holland, C. L. (1998). Visual reaction time and plethysmography as measures of sexual interest in child molesters. *Sexual Abuse: A Journal of Research and Treatment, 10*(2), 81–95.

Abel, G. G., Lawry, S. S. Karlstrom, E., Osborn, C. A., & Gillelspie, C. F. (1994). Screening tests for pedophilia. *Criminal Justice and Behavior 21*(1), 115–131.

Abel, G. G., Mittelman, M., Becker, J. V., Rathner, J., & Rouleau, J. (1988). Predicting child molesters' response to treatment. *Annals of N.Y. Academy of Sciences, 528,* 223.

Abel, G. G., Mittelman, M., & Becker, J. (1985). Sex offenders: Results of assessment and recommendations for treatment. In J. Ben-Aron, S. Hucker, & C. Webster (Eds.), *Clinical criminology: Current concepts* (pp. 127–155). Toronto: M & M Graphics.

Abel, G. G., Mittelman, M., Becker, J., Rathner, J., & Roulear, J. (1988). Predicting child molesters' response to treatment. In R. A. Prentky & V. L. Quinsey (Eds.), *Human sexual aggression: Current perspectives* (pp. 223–234). New York: New York Academy of Science.

Abel, G. G., & Rouleau, J. L. (1990). Male sex offenders. In M. E. Thase, B. A. Edelstein, & M. Hersen (Eds.), *Handbook of outpatient treatment of adults* (pp. 271–290). New York: Plenum Press.

Abrams, R. I., & Greaney, J. M. (1989). *Report of the gender bias study of the Supreme Judicial Court.*

Abrams, S., & Abrams, J. (1993). *Polygraph testing of the pedophile.* Portland, OR: Ryan Gwinner Press.

Abruzzi, W. (1975). Severe personality disorders in an institutional setting. *American Journal of Psychoanalysis, 35*(3), 269–277.

Ackerman, M. J., & Ackerman, M. C. (1996). Child custody evaluation practices: A 1996 survey of psychologists, *Family Law Quarterly 30*(3), 565–586.

American Prosecutors Research Institute. (1993). Charging, plea negotiation and sentencing. In *Investigation and prosecution of child abuse* (2d ed.). Alexandria, VA: National Center for Prosecution of Child Abuse.

American Psychiatric Association. (1987). *Diagnostic and statistical manual of mental disorders* (rev. 3rd ed.). Washington, DC: Author.

American Psychiatric Association. (1994). *Diagnostic and statistical manual of mental disorders* (4th ed.). Washington, DC: Author.

American Psychiatric Association. (in press). *Task force report on sexually dangerous offenders.* Washington, DC: Author.

American Psychological Association. (1992). *Ethical principles of psychologists and code of conduct.* Washington, DC: Author.

American Psychological Association. (1996). *Violence and the family: Report of the American Psychological Association Presidential Task Force on Violence and the Family.* Washington, DC: Author.

Anderson, D., Fernandez, Y. M., & Marshall, W. L. (1997). *Integrating treatment components in sexual offender therapy: Toward a more cost-effective approach.* Paper presented at the meeting of the Association for the Treatment of Sexual Abusers, Arlington, VA.

Anderson, H., & Goolishian, H. A. (1988). Human systems as linguistic systems: Preliminary and evolving ideas about the implications for clinical theory. *Family Process, 27,* 371–393.

Anderson, J., Williams, S., McGee, R., & Silva, P. (1987). DSM-III disorders in preadolescent children. *Archives of General Psychiatry, 44,* 69–76.

Anderson, R. D., Gibeau, D., & D'Amora, D. A. (1995). The sex offender treatment rating scale: Initial reliability data. *Sexual Abuse: A Journal of Research and Treatment, 7,* 221–227.

Andrews, D. A., & Bonta, J. L. (1994). *The psychology of criminal conduct.* Cincinnati, OH: Anderson.

Andrews, D. A., & Kiessling, J. J. (1980). Program structure and effective correctional practices: A summary of the CaVIC research. In R.R. Ross & P. Gendreau, (Eds.), *Effective correctional treatment* (pp. 441–463). Toronto: Butterworths.

Andrews, D. A., Zinger, I., Hoge, R. D., Bonta, J. L., Gendreau, P., & Cullen, F. T. (1990). Does correctional treatment work? A psychologically informed meta-analysis. *Criminology, 28,* 369–404.

Armentrout, J., & Hauer, A. (1978). MMPIs of rapists of children and non-rapist sex offenders. *Journal of Clinical Psychology 34*(2), 330–332.

Armstrong, L. (1994). *Rocking the cradle of sexual politics: What happened when women said incest.* New York: Addison-Wesley.

Arther, R. O., & Caputo, R. R. (1959). *Interrogation for investigators.* New York: William C. Copp & Associates.

Ascher, L. (1980). Paradoxical intention. In A. Goldstein & E. B. Foa (Eds.), *Handbook of behavioral interventions: A clinical guide* (pp. 261–321). New York:Wiley.

Association for the Treatment of Sexual Abusers. (1993). *Auditory stimuli for penile plethysmograph.* Beaverton, OR: Author.

Association for the Treatment of Sexual Abusers. (1997). *Ethical standards and principles for the management of sexual abusers.* Beaverton, OR: Author.

Aubut, J., Proulx, J., Lamoureux, B., & McKibben, A. (1998). Sexual offenders' treatment program of the Philippe-Pinel Institute of Montreal. In W. L. Marshall, Y. M., Fernandez, S. M. Hudson, & T. Ward (Eds.), *Sourcebook of treatment programs for sexual offenders* (pp. 221–233). New York: Plenum Press.

Austin, J. T., & Vancouver, J. B. (1996). Goal constructs in psychology: Structure, process, and content. *Psychological Bulletin, 120,* 338–375.

Awad, G. A., & Saunders, E. B. (1991) Male adolescent sexual assaulters: Clinical observations. *Journal of Interpersonal Violence, 2,* 3–25.

Awad, G., Saunders, E., & Levene, J. (1984). A clinical study of male adolescent sexual offenders. *International Journal of Offender Therapy and Comparative Criminology, 28,* 105–115.

Bancroft, J., Jones, H. G., & Pullan, B. R. (1966). A simple transducer for measuring penile erection with comments on its use in the treatment of sexual disorders. *Behaviour Research and Therapy, 4,* 239–241.

Bandura, A. (1973). *Aggression: A social learning analysis.* Englewood Cliffs, NJ: Prentice-Hall.

Bandura, A. (1977). *Social learning theory.* Englewood Cliffs, NJ: Prentice-Hall.

Bandura, A. (1997). Self-efficacy. *Harvard Mental Health Letter, 13*(9), 4–6.

Barbaree, H. E. (1990). Stimulus control of sexual arousal: Its role in sexual assault. In W. L. Marshall, D. R. Laws,

& H. E. Barbaree (Eds.), *Handbook of sexual assault: Issues, theories and treatment of the offender* (pp. 115–142). New York: Plenum Press.

Barbaree, H. E. (1991). Denial and minimization among sex offenders: Assessment and treatment outcome. *Forum on Corrections Research, 3,* 300–333.

Barbaree, H. E. (1997). Evaluating treatment efficacy with sexual offenders: the sensitivity of recidivism studies to treatment effect. *Sexual Abuse: A Journal of Research and Treatment, 9,* 111–128.

Barbaree, H. E., & Marshall, W. (1988). Deviant sexual arousal, offense history and demographic variables as predictors of reoffense among child molesters. *Behavioral Sciences and the Law, 6,* 267–280.

Barbaree, H. E., & Marshall, W. L. (1991). The role of male sexual arousal in rape: Six models. *Journal of Consulting and Clinical Psychology, 59,* 621–630.

Barbaree, H. E., Marshall, W. L, & Hudson, S. M. (1993). *The juvenile sex offender.* New York: Guilford Press.

Barefoot, J. K. (Ed.). (1974). *The polygraph story.* Anniston, AL: American Polygraph Association.

Barkley, R. A. (1994). Impaired delayed responding: A unified theory of attention-deficit hyperactivity disorder. In D. K. Routh (Ed.), *Disruptive behavior disorders in childhood: Essays honoring Herbert C. Quay* (pp. 11–57). New York: Plenum Press.

Barnard, G. W., Robbins, L., Newman, G., & Hutchinson, D. (1985).

Differences found between rapists and child molesters. *Psychiatric News, 20,* 34–35.

Barrett, K. C. (1995). A functionalist approach to shame and guilt. In J. P. Tangney & K. W. Fischer (Eds.), *Self-conscious emotions: Shame, guilt, embarrassment, and pride* (pp. 25–63). New York: Guilford Press.

Bartholomew, K. (1993). Understanding the inner nature of low self-esteem: Uncertain, fragile, protective, and conflicted. In R. F. Baumeister (Ed.), *Self-esteem: The puzzle of low self-regard* (pp. 201–218). New York: Plenum Press.

Baumeister, R. F. (1989). Masochism as escape from self. *Journal of Sex Research, 25,* 28–59.

Baumeister, R. F. (1990). Suicide as escape from self. *Psychological Review, 97,* 90–113.

Baumeister, R. F. (1991). *Escaping the self.* New York: Basic Books.

Baumeister, R. F. (1993). Understanding the inner nature of low self-esteem: Uncertain, fragile, protective, and conflicted. In R. Baumeister (Ed.), *Self-esteem: The puzzle of low self-regard* (pp. 201–218). New York: Plenum Press.

Baumeister, R. F., & Heatherton, T. F. (1996). Self-regulation failure: An overview. *Psychological Inquiry, 7,* 1–15.

Baumeister, R. F., Tice, D., & Hutton, D. (1989). Self-presentational motivations and personality differences in self-esteem. *Journal of Personality, 57,* 547–579.

Bays, L., & Freeman-Longo, R. (1989).

Why did I do it again? Brandon, VT: Safer Society Press.

Bays, L., & Freeman-Longo, R. (1990). *How can I stop?* Brandon, VT: Safer Society Press.

Beck, A. J., & Shipley, B. E. (1987). *Recidivism of young parolees.* Washington, DC: U.S. Department of Justice, Bureau of Justice Statistics.

Beck, A. T., Ward, C. H., Mendelson, M., Mock, J., & Erbaugh, J. (1961). An inventory for measuring depression. *Archives of General Psychiatry, 14,* 561–571.

Becker, J. V. (1990). Treating adolescent sexual offenders. *Professional Psychology: Research and Practice, 21,* 362–365.

Becker, J. V. (1994). Offenders: Characteristics and treatment. *Sexual Abuse of Children, 4,* 176–197.

Becker, J. V., & Coleman, E. M. (1988). Incest. In V. B. Van Hasselt et al. (Eds.), *Handbook of family violence* (pp. 187–205). New York: Plenum Press.

Becker, J. V., & Hunter, J. A. (1992). Evaluation of treatment outcome for adult perpetrators of child sexual abuse. *Criminal Justice and Behavior, 19,* 74–92.

Becker, J. V., & Hunter, J. A. (1993). Aggressive sex offenders. *Child and Adolescent Psychiatric Clinics of North America, 2*(2), 477–487.

Becker, J. V., Kaplan, M., Cunningham-Rathner, J., & Kavoussi, R. (1986). Characteristics of adolescent incest perpetrators: Preliminary findings. *Journal of Family Violence, 1,* 85–97.

Becker, J. V., Kaplan, M., Tenke, C., & Tartaglini, A. (1991). The incidence of depressive symptomatology in juvenile sex offenders. *Child Abuse and Neglect, 15,* 531–536.

Becker, J. V., & Murphy, W. D. (in press). What we know and don't know about assessing and treating sex offenders. *Psychology, Public Policy and Law, 4*(1–2).

Becker, J. V., & Quinsey, V. L. (1993). Assessing suspected child molesters. *Child Abuse and Neglect, 17,* 169–174.

Becker, J. V., & Stein, R. V. (1991). Is sexual erotica associated with sexual deviance in adolescent males? *International Journal of Law and Psychiatry, 14*(1–2), 85–95.

Beckett, R., Beech, A., Fisher, D., & Fordham, A. S. (1994). *Community-based treatment of sex offenders: An evaluation of seven treatment programmes.* Home Office Occasional Paper. London: Home Office.

Bench, L. L., Kramer, S. P., & Erickson, S. (1997). A discriminant analysis of predictive factors in sex offender recidivism. In B. K. Schwartz & H. R. Cellini (Eds.), *The sex offender: New insights, treatment innovations and legal developments* (vol. II, pp. 15-1–15-14). Kingston, NJ: Civic Research Institute.

Berger, D., & Berger, L. (1991). *We heard the angels of madness.* New York: William Morrow.

Berlin, F. S., & Krout, E. (1986). Pedophilia: Diagnostic concepts, treatment, and ethical considerations. *American Journal of Forensic Psychiatry, 7*(1), 13–30.

Berlin, F. S., & Meinecke, C. F. (1981). Treatment of sex offenders with antiandrogenic medication: Conceptualization, review of treatment modalities, and preliminary findings. *American Journal of Psychiatry, 138,* 601–607.

Berliner, L., & Conte, J. (1993). Sexual abuse evaluations: Conceptual and empirical obstacles. *Child Abuse and Neglect, 17,* 111–129.

Berliner, L. Schram, D., Miller, L. L., & Milloy, C. D. (1995). A sentencing alternative for sex offenders: A study of decision making and recidivism. *Journal of Interpersonal Violence, 10*(4), 487–502.

Berry, J. (1992). *Lead us not into temptation: Catholic priests and the sexual abuse of children.* New York: Doubleday.

Biederman, J., Farone, S. J., Spencer, T., Wilens, T., Norman, D., Lapey, K. A., Mick, E., Lehman, B. K., & Doyle, A. (1993). Patterns of psychiatric comorbidity, cognition, and psychosocial functioning in adults with attention-deficit disorder. *American Journal of Psychiatry, 150*(12), 1792–1798.

Biederman, J., Newcorn, J., & Sprichs, M. (1991). Comorbidity of attention deficit hyperactivity with conduct, depressive, anxiety and other disorders. *American Journal of Psychiatry, 148,* 564–577.

Blader, J. C., & Marshall, W. L. (1989). Is assessment of sexual arousal in rapists worthwhile? A critique of current methods and the development of a response compatibility approach. *Clinical Psychology Review, 9,* 569–587.

Blaine, B., & Crocker, J. (1993). Self-esteem and self-serving biases in reaction to positive and negative events: An integrative review. In R. F. Baumeister

(Ed.), *Self-esteem: The puzzle of low self-regard* (pp. 55–58). New York: Plenum Press.

Blasingame, G. D. (1998). Suggested clinical use of polygraphy in community-based sexual offender treatment programs. *Sexual Abuse: A Journal of Research and Treatment, 10*(1), 37–45.

Blaske, D., Borduin, C. M., Henggeler, S. W., & Mann, B. J. (1989). Individual, family and peer characteristics of adolescent sex offenders and assaultive offenders. *Developmental Psychology, 25,* 846–855.

Blume, S. (1989). Dual diagnosis: Psychoactive substance dependence and the personality disorders. *Journal of Psychoactive Drugs, 21*(2), 139–144.

Boer, D. P., Wilson, R. J., Gauthier, C. M., & Hart, S. D. (1997). Assessing risk of sexual violence: Guidelines for clinical practice. In C. D. Webster & M. A. Jackson (Eds.), *Impulsivity: Theory, assessment and treatment* (pp. 326–342). New York: Guilford Press.

Borduin, C. M., Henggeler, S. W., Blaske, D. M., & Stein, R. J. (1990). Multisystemic treatment of adolescent sexual offenders. *International Journal of Offender Therapy and Comparative Criminology, 34,* 105–113.

Boudouris, J. (1983). *The recidivism of releasees from the Iowa State Penitentiary at Fort Madison, IA.* Fort Madison: Iowa Department of Corrections, Bureau of Data, Research and Planning.

Bowlby, J. (1969). *Attachment and loss: Attachment* (Vol. 1). New York: Basic Books.

Bradford, J. M. W., Boulet, J., & Pawlak, A. (1992, March). The paraphilias: A multiplicity of deviant behaviors. *Canadian Journal of Psychiatry, 37,* 104–108.

Bradley, G. W. (1978). Self-serving biases in the attribution processes: A reexamination of the fact or fiction question. *Journal of Personality and Social Psychology, 36,* 56–71.

Braithwaite, J. (1989) *Crime, shame and reintegration.* Melbourne, Australia: Oxford University Press.

Braithwaite, J. (1992) Reducing the crime problem: A not so dismal criminology. *Australian and New Zealand Journal of Criminology,* 25.

Braithwaite, J. (1993). Shame and modernity. *British Journal of Criminology, 33*(1), 1–18.

Braithwaite, J., & Daly, K. (1994) Masculinities, violence and communitarian control. In T. Newburn & E. Starks (Eds.), *Just boys doing business?* London:Routledge.

Brannon, J. M., & Troyer, R. (1991). Peer group counseling: A normalized residential alternative to the specialized treatment of adolescent sex offenders. *International Journal of Offender Therapy and Comparative Criminology, 35*(3), 225–234.

Brantlinger, E. (1983). Measuring variation and change in attitudes of residential care staff towards the sexuality of mentally retarded persons. *Mental Retardation, 21*(1), 17–22.

Bratter, B., Bratter, T., Radda, H., &

Steiner, K. (1993). The residential therapeutic caring community. *Psychotherapy, 30*(2), 299–304.

Breer, W. (1987). *The adolescent molester.* Springfield, IL: Charles C. Thomas.

Bremer, J. F. (1992). Serious juvenile sex offenders: Treatment and long-term follow-up. *Psychiatric Annals, 22*(6), 326–332.

Brendtro, L. (1985a). Making caring fashionable: Philosophy and procedures of service learning. *Child Care Quarterly, 14*(1), 4–13.

Brendtro, L. (1985b). Synergistic relationships: The powerful "SR" of reeducation. *Milieu Therapy, 4*(1), 3–12.

Brier, N. (1989). The relationship between learning disability and delinquency: A review and reappraisal. *Journal of Learning Disabilities, 22*(9), 546–553.

Briere, J., & Runtz, M. (1989). University males' sexual interest in children: Predicting potential indices of "pedophilia" in a non-forensic sample. *Child Abuse and Neglect, 13,* 65–75.

Brooker, B. H., & Cyr, J. J. (1986). Tables for clinicians to use to convert WAIS-R short forms. *Journal of Clinical Psychology, 42,* 983.

Brown, E. J., Flanagan, T. J., & McLeod, M. (1984). *Sourcebook of criminal justice statistics—1983.* Washington, DC: Bureau of Justice Statistics.

Brown, L. S. (1995). The therapy client as plaintiff: Clinical and legal issues for the treating therapist. In J. L. Alpert

(Ed.), *Sexual abuse recalled: Treating trauma in the era of the recovered memory debate* (pp. 337–360). Northvale, NJ: Aronson.

Brown, T. E. (in press). *Brown Attention Deficit Disorders Scales.* San Antonio, TX: Psychological Corporation.

Bumby, K. (1994, November). *Cognitive distortions of child molesters and rapists.* Paper presented at the Thirteenth Annual Research and Treatment Conference of the Association for the Treatment of Sexual Abusers, San Francisco.

Bumby, K. M. (1996). Assessing cognitive distortions of child molesters and rapists: Development and validation of the MOLEST and RAPE scales. *Sexual Abuse: A Journal of Research and Treatment, 2*(1), 37–54.

Bumby, K. M., & Hansen, D.J. (1997. Intimacy deficits, fear of intimacy, and emotional loneliness among sexual offenders. *Criminal Justice and Behavior, 24,* 315–331.

Bumby, K. M., Levine, H., & Cunningham, D. (1996). *Empathy deficits, shame, guilt, and self-consciousness.* Paper presented at Fifteenth Annual Association for the Treatment of Sexual Abusers, Chicago.

Bureau of Justice Statistics. (1997). *Correctional populations in the United States, 1995.* Washington, DC: Author.

Burgess, A. W., Hartman, C. R., Ressler, R. K., Douglas, J. E., & McCormack, A. (1986). Sexual homicide: A motivational model. *Journal of Interpersonal Violence, 1*(3), 251–272.

Burggraf, S. A., & Tangney, J.P. (1989). *The Self-Conscious Affect and Attribution Inventory for Children (SCAAI-C).* Bryn Mawr, PA: Bryn Mawr.College.

Burke, A. (1980). A cross cultural study of delinquency among West Indian boys. *International Journal of Social Psychiatry, 26*(2), 81–87.

Burt, M. R. (1980). Cultural myths and support for rape. *Journal of Personality and Social Psychology, 38,* 217–230.

Calsyn, D., Fleming, C., Wells, E., & Saxon, A. (1996). Personality disorder subtypes among opiate addicts in methadone maintenance. *Psychology of Addictive Behaviors, 10*(1), 3–8.

Calsyn, D., & Saxon, A. (1990). Personality disorder subtypes among cocaine and opiod addicts using the Millon Clinical Multiaxial Inventory. *International Journal of the Addictions, 25,* 1037–1049.

Cambone, J. (1995). Rethinking how we think about troubled children. *Journal of Emotional and Behavioral Problems, 3*(4),12–14.

Camp, B. H., & Thyer, B. A. (1993). Treatment of adolescent sex offenders: A review of empirical research. *Journal of Applied Social Sciences, 17*(2), 191–206.

Candeon, M. K., & Nutter, D. E. (1988). A preliminary examination of the pornography experience of sex offenders, paraphiliacs, sexual dysfunction patients, and controls based on Meese Commission recommendations. *Journal of Sex and Marital Therapy, 14,* 285–298.

Caparulo, F., Comte, M., Gafgen, J., Haaven, J., Kaufman, K., Kempton, W., Sissala, L., Whitaker, J. M., & Wilson, R. (1988, March). *A summary of selected notes.* Presented at working sessions of the first national training conference on the assessment and treatment of intellectually disabled juvenile and adult sex offenders, Columbus, OH.

Card, R. D., & Dribble, A. (1995). Predictive value of the Card/Farrall stimuli in discriminating between gynephilic and pedophilic sex offenders. *Sexual Abuse: A Journal of Research and Treatment, 7*(2), 129–142.

Card, R. D., & Olsen, S. E. (1996). Visual plethysmograph stimuli involving children: Rethinking some quasi-legal issues. *Sexual Abuse, 8*(4), 267–271.

Carnes, P. (1983). *Out of the shadows: Understanding sexual addiction.* New York: Norton.

Carnes, P. (1991). *Don't call it love; recovery from sexual addiction.* New York: Bantam Books.

Carter, D. L., Prentky, R. A., Knight, R. A., Vanderveer, P. L., & Boucher, R. J. (1987). Use of pornography in the criminal and developmental histories of sexual offenders. *Journal of Interpersonal Violence, 2,* 196–211.

Cashwell, C. S., & Carusso, M. E. (1997). Adolescent sex offenders: Identification and intervention strategies. *Journal of Mental Health Counseling, 19*(4), 336–348.

Castonguary, L. G., Proulx, J., Aubut, J., McKibben, A., & Campbell, M. (1993).

Sexual preference assessment of sexual aggressors: Predictors of penile response magnitude. *Archives of Sexual Behavior, 22,* 325–334.

Cesnik, J., & Coleman, E. (1989). Use of lithium carbonate in the treatment of autoerotic asphyxia. *American Journal of Psychotherapy, 43,* 277–286.

Chalk, R., & King, P. (1998). *Violence in families: Assessing prevention and treatment programs.* Washington, DC: National Academy Press.

Chesler, P. (1986). *Mothers on trial: The battle for children and custody.* New York: McGraw-Hill.

Child, I. L., Frank, K. F., & Storm, T. (1956). Self-ratings and TAT; their relation to behavior. *Journal of Personality, 25,* 96–114.

Clark, S. H., & Crum, L. (1985). *Returns to prison in North Carolina.* Chapel Hill: Institute of Government, University of North Carolina.

Cohen, F. (1995). Therapeutic uses of sexually explicit material and the plethysmograph. In B. K. Schwartz & H. R. Cellini (Eds.), *The sex offender: Corrections, treatment and legal practice* (vol. I, pp. 29-1–29-10). Kingston, NJ: Civic Research Institute.

Cohen, F. (1997, September/October). Supreme Court finds sexually violent predator law constitutional. *Offender Programs Report, 1*(3), 33.

Cohen, J. (1992). A power primer. *Psychological Bulletin, 112,* 155–159.

Cohen, M. A., & Miller, T. R. (1998).

The cost of mental health care for victims of crime. *Journal of Interpersonal Violence, 13,* 93–110.

Coleman, E. (1990). The obsessive-compulsive model for describing compulsive sexual behavior. *American Journal of Preventative Psychiatry and Neurology, 2,* 9–13.

Coleman, E. (1991). Compulsive sexual behavior: *New Concepts and Treatments. Journal of Psychology and Human Sexuality, 4*(2), 37–52.

Commission on Gender Bias in the Judicial System. (1991). *Gender and justice in the courts: A report of the Supreme Court of Georgia.*

Condelli, W., & Hubbard, R. (1994). Client outcomes from therapeutic communities. In F. Tims, G. DeLeon & N Jainchill (Eds.), *Therapeutic community: Advances in research and application* (pp. 80–98) (NIDA Research Monograph 144, NIH Publication No. 94-3633). Rockville, MD: National Institute on Drug Abuse.

Connors, C. K. (1989). *Connors Rating Scale manual.* Toronto: Multi-Health Systems.

Connors, C. K. (1994). *Attention deficit hyperactivity disorder: Assessment and treatment for children and adolescents.* Toronto: Multi-Health Systems.

Cooke, D. J., & Michie, C. (1997). An item response theory analysis of the HARE Psychopathy checklist—revised. *Psychological Assessment, 9,* 3–14.

Cooper, A. J. (1987). Medroxyprogesterone acetate (MPA) treatment of sexually act-

ing out in men suffering from dementia. *Journal of Clinical Psychiatry, 48,* 368–370.

Coopersmith, S. (1967). *The antecedents of self-esteem.* San Francisco: Freeman.

Cornick, M. (Producer). (1996, October 18). Sentences of public humiliation as punishment. *20/20.* New York: ABC News.

Correctional Service of Canada. (1997). *Basic facts about corrections in Canada: 1997 edition.* Ottawa, Canada: Ministry of Supply and Services.

Count-Van Manen, G. (1991). Drama-imagery processes as socialization: An interdisciplinary perspective. Imagery and sociology [Special issue: Imagery and sociology]. *Journal of Mental Imagery, 15*(1–2), 243–293.

Craig, R. J., & Olson, R. E. (1990). MCMI comparisons of cocaine and heroin addicts. *Journal of Clinical Psychology, 15*(1–2), 231–237.

Crelinstein, R. D. (Ed.). (1977). *Dimensions of victimization in the context of terrorist acts.* Montreal, Canada: International Centre for Comparative Criminology.

Crepault, C., & Courture, M. (1980). Men's erotic fantasies. *Archives of Sexual Behavior, 9,* 565–582.

Crime statistics report. (1996). Washington, DC: Bureau of Justice Statistics.

Cronbach, L. J. & Meehl, P. F. (1955). Construct validity and psychological tests. *Psychological Bulletin, 52,* 281–302.

Cunningham, T. (1986). *King baby.* Center City, MN: Hazelden.

Curry, S., Marlatt, G A., & Gordon, J. (1987). Abstinence violation effect: Validation of an attributional construct with smoking cessation. *Journal of Consulting & Clinical Psychology, 55*(2), 145–149.

Davis, G. E., & Leitenberg, H. (1987). Adolescent sex offenders. *Psychological Bulletin, 101,* 417–427.

Davis, M. H. (1983). Measuring individual differences in empathy: Evidence for a multidimensional approach. *Journal of Consulting Psychology, 24,* 349–354.

Davidson, P. R. (1984). *Behavioral treatment for incarcerated sex offenders: Post-treatment outcome.* Unpublished manuscript. Kingston, Ontario: Regional Treatment Center.

Deitz, S. R., Blackwell, K. T., Daley, P. C., & Bently, B. J. (1982). Measurement of empathy toward rape victims and rapists. *Journal of Personality and Social Psychology, 43,* 372–384.

Deitz, S. R. Littman, M., & Bentley, B. J., (1984). Attribution of responsibility for rape: The influence of observer empathy, victim resistance, and victim attractiveness, *Sex Roles, 10,* 261–280.

Delaware Executive Committee. (1984). *Recidivism in Delaware after release from incarceration.* Dover: Delaware Executive Department Statistical Analysis Center.

DeLeon, G. (1984). The therapeutic community: Study of effectiveness (NIDA Research Monograph, DHHS Publication No. ADM 84-1286).

Washington, DC: U.S. Government Printing Office.

DeLeon, G. (1985). The therapeutic community: Status and evolution. *International Journal of the Addictions, 20*(6–7), 823–844.

DeLeon, G. (1987). Alcohol use among drug abusers: Treatment outcomes in a therapeutic community. *Alcoholism, Clinical and Experimental Research, 11*(5), 430–436.

DeLeon, G. (1988). *The therapeutic community and behavioral science* (NIDA Research Monograph 84). Rockville MD: National Institute on Drug Abuse.

DeLeon, G. (1989). Psychopathology and substance abuse: What is being learned from research in therapeutic communities. *Journal of Psychoactive Drugs, 21*(2), 177–187.

DeLeon, G. (1990–1991). The therapeutic community and behavioral science [Special issue: Substance user treatment for research, practice, and policy]. *International Journal of the Addictions, 25*(12A), 1537–1557.

De Leon, G. (1995, January–March). Residential therapeutic communities in the mainstream: Diversity and issues. *Journal of Psychoactive Drugs, 27*(1), 3–15.

DeLeon, G. (1995). Therapeutic communities for addictions: A theoretical framework. *International Journal of the Addictions, 30*(12), 1603–1545.

Dell, P. F. (1985). Understanding Bateson and Maturana: Toward a biological foundation. *Journal of Marital and Family Therapy, 11,* 1- 20.

DiGiorgio-Miller, J. (1994). Clinical techniques in the treatment of juvenile sex offenders. *Journal of Offender Rehabilitation, 21*(1–2), 117–126.

Donnenberg, D. (1978). Art therapy in a drug community. *Confinia Psychiatrica, 21*(1–3), 37–44.

Doren, D. (1998). Recidivism base rates, predictions of sex offender recidivism, and the "sexual predator" commitment laws. *Behavioral Sciences and the Law, 16*(1), 97–114.

Dougher, M. J. (1995). Clinical assessment of sex offenders. In B. K. Schwartz & H. R. Cellini (Eds.), *The sex offender: Corrections, treatment and legal practice* (vol. I, pp. 11-1–1-11). Kingston, NJ: Civic Research Institute.

Dutta, T. (1979). Education for problem children [Special issue]. *Indian Psychological Review, 18*(1–4), 31–34.

Dutton, M. A. (1992). *Empowering and healing the battered woman: A model for assessment and intervention.* New York: Springer.

Dutton, D., van Ginkel, C., & Starzomski, A. (1995). The role of shame and guilt in the intergenerational transmission of abusiveness. *Violence and Victims, 10*(2), 121–131.

Dwyer, M., & Amberson, J. I. (1985). Sex offender treatment program: A follow up study. *American Journal of Social Psychiatry, 4,* 56–60.

Dwyer, S. M., & Rosser, B. R. S. (1992). Treatment outcome research: Cross referencing a six month to ten year followup study on sex offenders. *Annals of Sex Research, 5,* 87–97.

Dziech, B. W., & Schudson, C. B. (1991, 1989). *On trial: America's courts and their treatment of sexually abused children* (2nd ed.). Boston: Beacon Press.

Earls, C. M., & Proulx, J. (1986). The differentiation of francophone rapists and nonrapists using penile circumferential measures. *Criminal Justice and Behavior, 13,* 419–429.

Eckstein, M. (1995). Foster family clusters: Continuum advocate home network. In L. Combrinck-Graham, (Ed.), *Children in families at risk: Maintaining the connection* (pp. 275–298). New York: Guilford Press.

Edleson, J. L., & Tolman, R. M. (1992). *Intervention for men who batter: An ecological approach.* Newbury Park, CA: Sage.

Egan, G. (1973). *Face to face.* Monterey, CA: Brooks/Cole.

Eisenberg, M. (1985). *Factors associated with recidivism.* Austin: Texas Board of Pardons and Parole.

Ellis, H. (1933). *Psychology of sex.* London: Heinemann.

English, K., Pullen, S., & Jones, L. (1996). *Managing adult sex offenders: A containment approach.* Colorado Division of Criminal Justice & American Probation and Parole Association.

Epperson, D. L., Kaul, J. D., & Huot, S. J. (1995, October). *Predicting risk for recidivism for incarcerated sex offenders: Updated development for the Sex Offender Screening Tool (SOST).* Poster session presented at the annual conference of the Association for the Treatment of Sexual Abusers. New Orleans, LA.

Ericson, R., & Carriere, K. (1994) The fragmentation of criminology. In D. Nelson (Ed.), *The futures of criminology*. Thousand Oaks, CA: Sage.

Ericson, W., Luxenberg, M., Walbek, N., & Seely, R. (1987). Frequency of MMPI two-point code types among sex offenders. *Journal of Consulting and Clinical Psychology, 55*(4), 566–570.

Fagan, J., & Wexler, S. (1988). Explanations of sexual assault among violent delinquents. *Journal of Adolescent Research, 3,* 363–385.

Farnsworth, M. G., Seely, R. K., & Walbek, N. H. (1996). *Evolution of sexual psychopath laws and design of a sex offender program in Minnesota.* St. Peter: Minnesota Security Hospital.

Faux, E., & Dixon, D. (1967) Children in the therapeutic community. *Diseases of the Nervous System, 28*(3), 170–177.

Fedoroff, J. P., Wisner-Carlson, R., Dean, S., & Berlin, F. S. (1992). Medroxy-Progesterone Acetate in the treatment of paraphiliac sexual disorders. *Journal of Offender Rehabilitation, 18*(3/4), 109–123.

Fehrenbach, P. A., & Monastersky, C. (1988). Characteristics of female adolescent sexual offenders. *American Journal of Orthopsychiatry, 58,* 148–151.

Fehrenbach, P. A., Smith, W., Monastersky, C., & Deisher, R. W. (1986). Adolescent sexual offenders:

Offender and offense characteristics. *American Journal of Orthopsychiatry, 56,* 225–233.

Feixas, G. (1990). Personal construct theory and systemic therapies: Parallel or convergent trends? *Journal of Marital and Family Therapy, 16,* 1-20.

Felder, R., & Victor, B. (1996). *Getting away with murder: Weapons for the war against domestic violence.* New York: Simon & Schuster.

Feldman-Summers, S. (1996). Litigation pitfalls for the psychotherapist whose client "first remembers" childhood sexual abuse during therapy. *Women and Therapy, 19,* 109–122.

Ferguson, E., & Haaven, J. (1990). On the design of motivating learning environments for intellectually disabled offenders. *Journal of Correctional Education, 41*(1), 33.

Fernandez, Y. M., & Marshall, W. L. (1998). *The Rapist Empathy Measure.* Manuscript submitted for publication.

Fernandez, Y. M., Marshall, W. L., O'Sullivan, C., & Lightbody, S. (1997). *The Child Molester Empathy Measure: Description and examination of its reliability and validity.* Manuscript submitted for publication.

Feshbach, N., & Feshbach, S. (1982). Empathy training and the relation of aggression: Potentialities and limitations. *Academic Psychology Bulletin, 4,* 399–413.

Figia, N. A., Lang, R. A., Plutchik, R., & Holden, R. (1987). Personality differences between sex and violent offenders.

International Journal of Offender Therapy and Comparative Criminology, 31, 211–226.

Finkelhor, D. (1984). *Child sexual abuse.* New York: Free Press.

Finkelhor, D. (1986). Abusers: Special topics. In D. Finkelhor & Associates (Eds.), *Sourcebook on child sexual abuse* (pp. 119-142). Newbury Park, CA: Sage.

Finkelhor, D. (1988). The trauma of sexual abuse: Two models. In G. Wyatt & G. Powell (Eds.), *Lasting effects of child sexual abuse* (pp. 61–82). Newbury Park, CA: Sage.

Fitch, J. (1962). Men convicted of sexual offenses against children: A descriptive follow-up study. *British Journal of Criminology, 3,* 18–37.

Ford, M E., & Linney, J. A. (1995). Comparative analysis of juvenile sexual offenders, violent nonsexual offenders, and status offenders. *Journal of Interpersonal Violence, 10*(1), 56–70.

Freeman-Longo, R. E. (1985). The adolescent sexual offender: Background and research perspectives. In E. M. Otey & G. D. Ryan (Eds.), *Adolescent sex offenders: Issues in research and treatment* (pp. 130–146). Rockville, MD: Department of Health and Human Services.

Freeman-Longo, R. E. (1999). *Incidence of self-reported sex crimes among incarcerated rapists and child molesters.* Unpublished manuscript, Correctional Treatment Program, Oregon State Hospital.

Freeman-Longo, R., & Bays, L. (1988). *A guided workbook for clients in evaluation and beginning treatment.* Brandon, VT: Safer Society Press.

Freeman-Longo, R. E., Bird, S., Stevenson, W. F., & Fiske, J. A. (1995). *1994 nationwide survey of treatment programs and models serving abuse-reactive children and adolescent and adult sex offenders.* Brandon, VT: Safer Society Press.

Freeman-Longo, R. E., & Knopp, F. H. (1992). State-of-the-art sex offender treatment outcome and issues. *Annals of Sex Research, 5,* 141–160.

Freud, S. (1953). Three essays on the theory of sexuality. In J. Strachey (Ed. and Trans.), *The standard edition of the complete works of Sigmund Freud* (Vol. 7, pp. 225–243). London: Hogarth Press.

Freud, S. (1962). Creative writers and daydreaming. In J. Strachey (Ed. and Trans.), *The standard edition of the complete works of Sigmund Freud* (Vol. 9). London: Hogarth Press.

Freund, K. (1987). Courtship disorder: Is this hypothesis valid. *Annals of the New York Academy of Sciences, 528,* 172–182.

Freund, K., & Blanchard, R. (1989). Phallometric diagnosis of pedophilia. *Journal of Consulting and Clinical Psychology, 57*(1), 100–105.

Freund, K., Scher, H., & Hucker, S. (1983). The courtship disorders. *Archives of Sexual Behavior, 12,* 369–379.

Freyd, J. J. (1996). *Betrayal trauma: The logic of forgetting childhood abuse.*

Cambridge MA: Harvard University Press.

Fried, E. R. (1986, May). *A multimodal treatment of developmentally disabled sex offenders.* Paper presented to the Fourth National Conference on the Sexual Victimization of Children, New Orleans.

Friedrich,W. (1993). Foreword. In E. Gil & T. Johnson (Eds.). *Sexualized children: Assessment and treatment of sexualized children who molest* (pp. x–xii). Rockville, MD: Launch Press.

Friedrich, W. N. (1994, August 12). *Psychological assessment of sexually abused children: The case for abuse-specific measures.* Paper presented at the annual convention of the American Psychological Association, Los Angeles.

Frisbie, L. V., & Dondis, E. H. (1965). *Recidivism among sex offenders.* California Mental Health Research Monogram No. 5. Sacramento: California Department of Mental Hygiene.

Furby, L., Weinrott, M. R., & Blackshaw, L. (1989). Sex offender recidivism: A review. *Psychological Bulletin, 105,* 3–30.

Furr, K. D. (1993). Prediction of sexual or violent recidivism among sexual offenders: A comparison of prediction instruments. *Annals of Sex Research, 6,* 271–286.

Gacono, C. B., & Hutton, H. E. (1994). Suggestions for the clinical and forensic use of the HARE Psychopathology checklist—revised. *International Journal of Law and Psychiatry, 17,* 303–317.

Gacono, C. B. (n.d.). Suggestions for the institutional implementation and use of the Psychopath Checklist.

Gafgen, J. (1988, October). [Taped interview by F. H. Knopp].

Galanter, M., Egelko, S., DeLeon, G., & Rohrs, C. (1993). A general hospital day program combining peer-led and professional treatment of cocaine abusers. *Hospital Community Psychiatry, 44,* 644–649.

Graham, J. (1977). *The MMPI: A practical guide.* New York: Oxford University Press.

Gardner, H. (1983). *Frames of mind: Theory of multiple intelligences.* New York: Basic Books.

Gendreau, P., Little, T., & Goggin, C. (1996). A meta-analysis of the predictors of adult offender recidivism: What works! *Criminology, 34*(4), 575–607.

Gerber, J. (1994). The use of art therapy in juvenile sex offender specific treatment. *Arts in Psychotherapy, 21*(5), 367–374.

Gerhard, R., & Dorgan, R. (1970). A catchment milieu training-service model for the mental retardation sector: A documented proposal. *International Journal of Social Psychiatry, 16*(3), 221–227.

Gerritsen, M. (1995). Art therapy: The real art is the process. *Therapeutic Communities: International Journal for Therapeutic and Supportive Organizations, 16*(1), 25–35.

Gilligan, J. (1996). *Violence: Our deadly epidemic and its causes.* New York: G.P. Putnam's Sons.

Goldstein, S. (1987). *The sexual exploitation of children.* CRC Press.

Goleman, D. (1995) *Emotional intelligence: Why it can matter more than IQ.* New York:Bantam Books.

Goocher, B. E., (1994). Some comments of the residential treatment of juvenile sex offenders. *Child and Youth Care Forum, 23*(4), 243–250.

Gordon, L. (1988). Heroes of their times: The politics and history of family violence. New York: Viking.

Gorzalka, B., Mendelson, S., & Watson, N. (1990). Serotonin receptor subtypes and sexual behavior. *Annals of the New York Academy of Sciences, 600,* 435–446.

Graham, J. (1977). *The MMPI: A practical guide.* New York: Oxford University Press.

Grand, S. (1995). Incest and the intersubjective politics of knowing history. In J. L. Alpert (Ed.). *Sexual abuse recalled: Treating trauma in the era of the recovered memory debate* (pp. 235–253). Northvale, NJ: Aronson.

Grasmick, H., Bursick, R., & Kinsey, K. (1991). Shame and embarrasment as deterents to noncompliance with the law. *Environment and Behavior, 23,* 233–251.

Gray, A. S., & Pithers, W. D. (1993). Relapse prevention with sexually aggressive adolescents. In H. E. Barbaree, W. L. Marshall, & S. M. Hudson (Eds.), *The juvenile sex offender* (pp. 289–320). New York: Guilford Press.

Greenfield, L. A. (1985). *Examining recidivism.* Washington, DC: U.S.

Department of Justice, Bureau of Justice Statistics.

Greenfeld, L. A. (1997). *Sex offenses and offenders: An analysis of data on rape and sexual assault.* Washington, DC: U.S. Department of Justice, Bureau of Justice Statistics.

Griffiths, D., Hinsburger, D., & Christian, R. (1985). Treating developmentally handicapped sexual offenders: The York behavior management services treatment program. *Psychiatric Aspects of Mental Retardation Reviews, 4,* 49–54.

Griffiths, D. M., Quinsey, V. L., & Hingsburger, D. (1989). *Changing inappropriate sexual behavior: A community-based approach for persons with developmental disabilities.* Baltimore: Paul H. Brookes.

Grossman, H. (1983). *Manual on terminology and classification in mental retardation.* Washington, DC: American Association on Mental Deficiency.

Groth, A. N. (1977). The adolescent sexual offender and his prey. *International Journal of Offender Therapy and Comparative Criminology, 21,* 249–254.

Groth, A. N. (1979). Sexual trauma in the life histories of rapists and child molesters. *Victimology: An International Journal, 4,* 10–16.

Groth, A. N. (1982) The incest offender. In S. M. Sgroi (Ed.), *Handbook of clinical intervention in child sexual abuse* (pp. 215–239). Lexington, MA: Heath.

Groth, A., Longo, A., & McFadin, J. (1982). Undetected recidivism among rapists and child molesters. *Crime and Delinquency, 28,* 450–458.

Groth, N. (1979). *Men who rape.* New York: Plenum Press.

Groth, Longo, & McFadin, (1982). Undetected recidivism in rapists and child molesters. *Crime and Delinquency, 28,* 450–458.

Groth, N., & Loredo, C. M. (1981). Juvenile sex offenders: Guidelines for assessment. *Journal of Offender Therapy and Comparative Criminology, 25,* 31–39.

Grubin, D., & Wingate, S. (1996). Sexual offense recidivism: Prediction versus understanding. *Criminal Behavior and Mental Health, 6,* 349–359.

Grunfeld, B., & Noreik, K. (1986). Recidivism among sex offenders: A follow-up study of 541 Norwegian sex offenders. *International Journal of Law and Psychiatry, 9,* 95–102.

Gudjonsson, G. H. (1990). Cognitive distortions and blame attribution among paedophiles. *Sexual and Marital Therapy, 5*(2), 183–185.

Gunther, J., & Hawkins, F. (1997). *Total quality management in human service organizations.* New York: Springer.

Gusfield, J. (1981). *The culture of public problems: Drinking, driving and the symbolic order.* Chicago: University of Chicago Press.

Guttmacher, M. (1951). *Sex offenses. The problem, causes and prevention.* New York: Norton.

Haag, A., Schorsch, E., Galedary, G., &

Hauch, M. (1985) Sexual perversions as diagnostic clues. *Nervenarzt, 56*(7), 373–378.

Haaven, J., Little, R., & Petre-Miller, D. (1990). *Treating the intellectually disabled sex offender: A model residential program.* Orwell,VT: Safer Society Press.

Haley, J. (1984). *Ordeal therapy.* San Francisco: Jossey-Bass.

Hall G. C. N. (1990). Prediction of sexual aggression. *Clinical Psychology Review, 10,* 229–245.

Hall, G. C. N. (1995). Sexual offender recidivism revisited: A meta-analysis of recent treatment studies. *Journal of Consulting and Clinical Psychology, 63*(5), 802–809.

Hall, G. C. N., & Barongan, C. (1997). Prevention of sexual aggression: Sociocultural risk and protective factors. *American Psychologist, 52*(1), 5–14.

Hall, G. C. N., & Hirschman, R. (1991). Towards a theory of sexual aggression: A quadripartite model. *Journal of Consulting and Clinical Psychology, 59,* 662–669.

Hall, G. C. N., Shondrick, D., & Hirschman, R. (1993). The role of sexual arousal in sexually aggressive behavior: A meta-analysis. *Journal of Consulting and Clinical Psychology, 61,* 1091–1095.

Hall, K. S., Binik, Y., & DiTomasso, E. (1985). Concordance between physiological and subjective measures of sexual arousal. *Behaviour Research and Therapy, 23,* 297–303.

Hallowell, E. M., & Ratey, J. J. (1994). *Driven to distraction: Recognizing and coping with attention-deficit disorder from childhood through adulthood.* New York: Simon & Schuster.

Hanson, K. R. (1996). Evaluating the contribution of relapse prevention theory to the treatment of sexual offenders. *Sexual Abuse: A Journal of Research and Treatment, 8*(3), 201–208.

Hanson, R. K. (1997). How to know what works with sexual offenders. *Sexual Abuse: A Journal of Research and Treatment, 9,* 129–145.

Hanson, R. K. (in press). Assessing sexual offenders' capacity for empathy. *Psychology, Crime and Law.*

Hanson, R. K., & Bussière, M. T. (1996). *Predictors of sexual offender recidivism: A meta-analysis.* (User Report No. 1996-04). Ottawa: Corrections Branch, Ministry of the Solicitor General of Canada.

Hanson, R. K., & Bussière, M. T. (1998). Predicting relapse: A meta-analysis of sexual offender recidivism studies. *Journal of Consulting and Clinical Psychology, 66,* 348–362.

Hanson, R. K., & Harris, A. J. R. (1997). *Dynamic predictors of sexual reoffense project 1997.* Presentation at the annual conference of the Association for the Treatment of Sexual Aggressor. Arlington, VA.

Hanson, R. K., & Scott, H. (1995). Assessing perspective taking among sexual offenders, nonsexual criminals and nonoffenders. *Sexual Abuse: A Journal of Research and Treatment, 7*(4), 259–277.

Hanson, R. K., Scott, H., & Steffy, R. A. (1995). A comparison of child molesters and nonsexual criminals: Risk predictors and long-term recidivism. *Journal of Research in Crime and Delinquency, 32*(3), 325–337.

Hanson, R. K., Steffy, R. A., & Gauthier, R., (1993). Long-term recidivism of child molesters, *Journal of Consulting and Clinical Psychology, 61,* 646–652.

Hare, R. D. (1991). *The Hare PCL-R.* North Tonawanda, NY: Multi-Health Systems.

Hare, R. D. (1991). *Manual for the Revised Psychopathy Checklist.* North Tonawanda, NY: Multi-Health Systems.

Hare, R. D., McPherson, L. M., & Forth, A. E. (1988). Male psychopaths and their criminal career. *Journal of Consulting and Clinical Psychology, 56,* 710–714.

Harpur, T. J., Hakstian, R., & Hare, R. D. (1988). Factor structure of the psychopathy checklist. *Journal of Consulting and Clinical Psychology, 56,* 741–747.

Harrell, A., Smith, B., & Newmark, L. (1993). *Court processing and the effects of restraining orders for domestic violence victims.* Washington, DC: Urban Institute.

Harris, G. T., & Rice, M. E. (1996). The science in phallometric measurement of male sexual interest. *Current Directions in Psychological Science, 5,* 156–160.

Harris, G. T., Rice, M. E., & Cormier, C. A. (1989, April). *Violent recidivism among psychopaths and nonpsychopaths treated in a therapeutic community.* Research report from the

Penetanguishene Mental Health Centre VI(1), Penetanguishene, Ontario.

Harris, G. T., Rice, M. E., & Cormier, C. A. (1991). Psychopathy and violent recidivism. *Law and Human Behavior, 15,* 625–637.

Harris, G. T., Rice, M. E., Quinsey, V. L., & Chaplin, T. C. (1996). Viewing time as a measure of sexual interest among child molesters and normal heterosexual men. *Behaviour Research and Therapy, 34,* 389–394.

Harris, G. T., Rice, M. E., Quinsey, V. L., Chaplin, T. C., & Earls, C. (1992). Maximizing the discriminant validity of phallometric assessment data. *Psychological Assessment, 4*(4), 502–511.

Harry, B., Pierson, T. R., & Kuznetsov, A. (1993). Correlates of sex offender and offense traits by victim age. *Journal of Forensic Sciences, 38*(5), 1068–1074.

Hart, S. D., Cox, D. N., & Hare, R. D. (1995). *Manual for the Psychopathy Checklist: Screening Version (PCL-SV).* Toronto: Multi-Health Systems.

Hart, S. D., Kropp, P. R., & Hare, R. D. (1988). Performance of male psychopaths following conditional release from prison. *Journal of Consulting and Clinical Psychology, 56,* 227–232.

Hartley, C. C. (1998). How incest offenders overcome internal inhibitions through the use of cognitions and cognitive distortions. *Journal of Interpersonal Violence, 13*(1), 25–39.

Hartman, L. (1997). *Solutions: The women's crisis handbook.* Boston: Houghton Mifflin.

Hawk, G. L., Rosenfeld, B. D., & Warren, J. I. (1993). Prevalence of sexual offenses among mentally retarded criminal defendants. *Hospital and Community Psychiatry, 44*(8), 784–786.

Hayashino, D. S., Wurtele, S. K., & Klebe, K. J. (1995). Child molesters: An examination of cognitive factors. *Journal of Interpersonal Violence, 10*(1), 106–116.

Hayashino, D. S., Wurtele, S. K., & Klebe, K. J. (1995). Long-term recidivism of child molesters. *Journal of Consulting and Clinical Psychology, 61,* 646–652.

Haywood, T. W., Grossman, L. S., & Cavanaugh, J. L. Jr. (1990). Subjective versus objective measurements of deviant sexual arousal in clinical evaluations of alleged child molesters. *Psychological Assessment, 2,* 269–275.

Henry, L. (1992, October). Should rapists ever be set free? *Glamour,* pp. 275, 294–297.

Hechler, D. (1988). *The battle and the backlash: The child sexual abuse war.* Lexington, MA: Lexington Books.

Herman, J. I. (1992). *Trauma and recovery.* New York: Basic Books.

Herman, J. (1981). *Father-daughter incest.* Cambridge, MA: Harvard University Press.

Herman, J. (1989). Recognition and treatment of incestuous families. In L. J. Dickstein & C. C. Nadelson (Eds.), *Family violence: Emerging issues of a national crisis* (pp. 29–44). Washington, DC: American Psychiatric Press.

Hildebran, D. D., & Pithers, W. D. (1992). Relapse prevention: Application and outcome. In W. O'Donohue, & J. H. Geer (Eds.), *The sexual abuse of children: clinical issues* (vol. 2, pp. 365–393), Hillsdale, NJ: Erlbaum.

Hilton, Z. (1993). Childhood sexual victimization and lack of empathy in child molesters: Explanation or excuse? *International Journal of Offender Therapy and Comparative Criminology, 37*(4), 287–296.

Hinshaw, S. P. (1987) On the distinction between attention deficits/hyperactivity and conduct problems/aggression in child psychopathology. *Psychological Bulletin, 101,* 443–463.

Hinshaw, S. P. (1994). Conduct disorder in childhood: Conceptualization, diagnosis, comorbidity, and risk status for anti-social functioning in adulthood. In D. Fowles, P. Sutker, & S. Goodman (Eds.), *Psychopathy and antisocial personality: A developmental perspective* (pp. 3–44). New York: Springer.

Hinshaw, S. P., Heller, T., & McHale, J. P. (1992). Covert antisocial behavior in boys with attention-deficit hyperactivity disorder: External validation and effects of methylphenidate. *Journal of Consulting and Clinical Psychology, 57,* 636–643.

Hinshaw, S. P., Henker, B., Whalen, C. K., Erhardt, D., & Dunnington, R. E. (1989). Aggressive, prosocial, and nonsocial behavior in hyperactive boys: Dose effects of methylphenidate in naturalistic settings. *Journal of Consulting and Clinical Psychology, 57*(5), 636–643.

Hinshaw, S. P., & Melnick, S. (in press). Peer relationships in children with attention-deficit hyperactivity disorder with and without comorbid aggression. *Development and Psychopathology.*

Hinshaw, S. P., Simmel, C., & Heller, T. L. (1995). Multimethod assessment of covert antisocial behavior in children: Laboratory observations, adult ratings, and child self-report. *Psychological Assessment, 7,* 209–219.

Hirshfield, M. (1948). *Sexual anomalies and perversions.* London: Francis Alder.

Hobson, W. F., Boland, C., & Jamieson, D. (1985). Dangerous sexual offenders. *Medical Aspects of Human Sexuality, 19*(2), 104–123.

Hogan, R. (1969). Development of an empathy scale. *Journal of Consulting and Clinical Psychology, 33,* 307–316.

Hoge, R., & Andrews, D. A. (1996). *The Youth Level of Service/Case Management Inventory (YLS/CMI): Intake manual and item scoring key.* Carleton University, Ottowa, Canada.

Holmgren, B. (1998). Sexually violent predator statutes—Implications for prosecutors and their communities. *The Prosecutor, 32*(3), 20–41.

Hooper, C-A. (1997). Child sexual abuse and the regulation of women: Variations on a theme. In L. L.O'Toole & J. R.Schiffman (Eds.), *Gender violence: Interdisciplinary perspectives* (pp. 336–351). New York: New York University Press.

Hope and recovery: A twelve step guide

for healing from compulsive sexual behavior. (1987). Minneapolis, MN: CompCare.

Houts, S. (1995). Explaining alcoholism treatment efficacy with the theory of reintegrative shaming. *Alcoholism Treatment Quarterly, 13*(4), 25–38, 1995.

Howe, R. J. (1995). A survey of plethysmographic assessment in North America. *Sexual Abuse, 7*(1), 9–24.

Huba, G. J., Singer, J. L., Aneshensel, C. S., & Antrobus, J. S. (1984). *The short Imaginal Processes Inventory.* Port Huron, MI:Research Psychologists Press.

Hucker, S. J. (1997) Sexual sadism: Psychopathology and theory. In D. R. Laws & W. O'Donohue (Eds.), *Sexual deviance: Theory, assessment and theory* (pp. 194–209) New York: Guilford Press.

Hudson, S. M., Marshall, W. L., Wales, D., McDonald, E., Bakker, L., & McLean, A. (1993). Emotional recognition in sex offenders. *Annals of Sex Research, 6,* 199–211.

Hunter, J. A., & Becker, J. V. (1994). The role of deviant sexual arousal in juvenile sexual offending: Etiology, evaluation, and treatment. *Criminal Justice and Behavior, 21*(1), 132–149.

Hutchens, L. (1989). *Restitution, treatment and training. R.T.A.T. manual* (available from RTAT Inc., P.O. Box 800, Ontario, OR 97914).

Hutton, D. G. (1991). *Self-esteem and memory for social interaction.* Unpublished dissertation, Case Western Reserve University, Ohio.

Jablonski, J. R. (1992). *Implementing TQM.* San Diego: Pfeiffer.

Jainchill, N. (1994). Co-morbidity and therapeutic community treatment. In F. Tims, G. DeLeon, & N Jainchill (Eds.), *Therapeutic community: Advances in research and application* (pp. 209–231) (NIDA Monograph No. 144, NIH Publication No. 94-3633). Rockville, MD: National Institute on Drug Abuse.

James, A. C., & Neil, P. (1996). Juvenile sexual offending: One-year period prevalence study within Oxfordshire. *Child Abuse and Neglect, 20*(6), 477–485.

Janus, E. S., & Meehl, P. E. (1997). Assessing the legal standard for predictions of dangerousness in sex offender commitment proceedings. *Psychology, Public Policy and Law, 3*(1), 33–66.

Jenicke, M. (1989). Obsessive-compulsive and related disorders. *New England Journal of Medicine, 321,* 539–541.

Jenicke, M, Baer, L., & Minichiello, W. (1990). *Obsessive-compulsive disorders, theory and management.* Chicago: Year Book Medical Publishers.

Jenkins, A. (1994). *Invitations to responsibility.* Adelaide, Australia: Dulwich Centre Publications.

Jenkins, A. (1998). Invitations to responsibility: Engaging adolescent and young men who have sexually abused. In W. L. Marshall, Y. M. Fernandez, S. M. Hudson, & T. Ward (Eds.), *Sourcebook of treatment programs for sexual offenders* (pp. 163–189). New York: Plenum Press.

Jenkins-Hall, K. D., & Marlatt, G. A. (1989). Apparently irrelevant decisions in the relapse process. In D. R. Laws (Ed.), *Relapse prevention with sex offenders* (pp. 47–55). New York: Guilford Press.

Johnson, J. T. (1992). *Mothers of incest survivors: Another side of the story.* Bloomington: Indiana University Press.

Johnston, L., & Ward, T. (1996). Social cognition and sexual offending: A theoretical framework. *Sexual Abuse: A Journal of Research and Treatment, 8,* 55–80.

Johnston, L., Ward, T., & Hudson, S. M. (1997). Suppressing sex: Mental control and the treatment of sexual offenders. *Journal of Sex Research, 34,* 121–130.

Jones, E. (1953). *Sigmund Freud: Life and work.* London: Hogarth Press.

Jones, J. C., & Barlow, D. H. (1990). Self-reported frequency of sexual urges, fantasies, and masturbatory fantasies in heterosexual males and females. *Archives of Sexual Behavior, 19*(3), 269–279.

Kafka, M. (1991). Successful antidepressant treatment of nonparaphilic sexual addictions and paraphilias in men. *Journal of Clinical Psychiatry, 52,* 60–65.

Kafka, M., & Prentky, R. (1992). A comparative study of nonparaphilic sexual addictions and paraphilias in men. *Journal of Clinical Psychiatry, 53*(10), 345–349.

Kahn, T. J., & Chambers, H. J. (1991). Assessing reoffense risk with juvenile sexual offenders. *Child Welfare, 70,* 333–345.

Kalliopuska, M. (1987). Relation of empathy and self-esteem to active participation in Finnish baseball. *Perceptual and Motor Skills, 65,* 107–113.

Karpman, B. (1926). The psychopathology of exhibitionism. *Psychoanalytic Review, 13,* 64–97.

Kashkin, K. (1990). *Sex offenders treated with flouxetine: Preliminary results.* Poster presentation at the annual meeting of the American Psychiatric Association. Washington, DC: American Psychiatric Association.

Katz, R. (1990). Psychological adjustment in adolescent child molesters. *Child Abuse and Neglect, 14,* 567–575.

Kaufman, G. (1985). *Shame: The power of caring* (rev. ed.). Cambridge, MA Schenkman Books.

Kavoussi, R. J., Kaplan, M., & Becker, J. V. (1988). Psychiatric diagnoses in adolescent sex offenders. *Journal of the American Academy of Child and Adolescent Psychiatry, 27*(2), 241–243.

Kelley, S. (1986). Learned helplessness in the sexually abused child. *Issues in Comprehensive Pediatric Nursing, 9*(3), 193–207.

Kelly, L., Burton, S., & Regan, L. (1992). "And what happened to him?": Policy on sex offenders from the survivor's perspective. In *Beyond containment: The penal response to sex offenders* (pp. 14–27). London: Prison Reform Trust.

Kelly, R. J. (1982). Behavioral reorientation of pedophiliacs: Can it be done? *Clinical Psychology Review, 2,* 387–408.

Kenny, V., & Gardner, G. (1988). Constructions of self-organizing systems. *The Irish Journal of Psychology, 9,* 1-24.

Kernis, M. (1993). The roles of stability and level of self-esteem in psychological functioning. In R. F. Baumeister, *Self-esteem: The puzzle of low self-regard* (pp. 76–85). New York: Plenum Press.

Kimball, W., Nelson, W. M., & Politano, P. (1990). The role of developmental variables in cognitive behavioral interventions with children. In A. J. Finch, W. M. Nelson III, & E. Ott (Eds.), *Cognitive behavioral procedures with children and adolescents: A practical guide* (pp. 20–35). Boston: Allyn & Bacon.

Kinsey, A. C. (1948). *Sexual behavior in the human male.* Philadelphia: Saunders.

Klein, R., & Manuzza, S. (1991). Long-term outcome of hyperactive children: A review. *Journal of the American Academy of Child and Adolescent Psychiatry, 30,* 1120–1134.

Knafo, D., & Jaffe, Y. (1984). Sexual fantasizing in males and females. *Journal of Research in Personality, 18,* 451–462.

Knight, R. A., & Prentky, R. A. (1990). Classifying sexual offenders: The development and corroboration of taxonomic models. In W. L. Marshall, D. R. Laws, & H. E. Barbaree (Eds.), *Handbook of sexual assault: Issues, theories and treatment of the offender* (pp. 23–52). New York: Plenum Press.

Knopp, F. (1982). *Remedial intervention in adolescent sex offenses: Nine program descriptions.* Syracuse, NY: Safer Society Press.

Knopp, F. H. (1984). *Retraining adult sex offenders: Methods and models.* Syracuse, NY: Safer Society Press.

Knopp, F. H. (1990). Introduction. In J. Haaven, R. Little, & D. Petre-Miller (Eds.), *Treating intellectually disabled sex offenders: A model residential program.* (pp. 2–9). Orwell, VT: The Safer Society Press.

Knopp, F. H., Rosenburg, J., & Stevenson, W. (1986). *Reports on nationwide survey of juvenile and adult sex-offender treatment programs and providers.* Syracuse, NY: Safer Society Press.

Knopp, F. H., & Stevenson, W. F. (1989). *A nationwide survey of juvenile and adult sex-offender treatment programs and models, 1988.* Orwell, VT: Safer Society Press.

Kohut, H. (1987). *The restoration of the self.* New York: International Universities Press.

Krafft-Ebing, R. (1912). *Psychopathis sexualis* (12th ed.). New York: Rebman.

Kutschinski, W. (1977). Milieu therapy under the primary caretaker system at the University of Michigan's Children's Psychiatric Hospital. *Child Psychiatry and Human Development, 8*(1), 31–42.

Lab, S. P., Shields, G., & Schondel, C. (1993). Research note: An evaluation of juvenile sexual offender treatment. *Crime and Delinquency, 39,* 543–553.

La Fontaine, J. (1990). *Child sexual abuse.* Cambridge, England: Polity Press.

Lahey, B., Loeber, R., Hart, E., Frick, P., & Applegate, B. (1995). Four-year longitudinal study of conduct disorder in boys: Patterns and predictors of persistence. *Journal of Abnormal Psychology, 104*(1), 83–93.

Lakey, J. F. (1995). Myth information and bizarre beliefs of male juvenile sex offenders. *Journal of Addictions and Offender Counseling, 13*(1), 2–10.

Lakey, J. F. (1996, November). *Creative therapy for low-functioning adolescent sex offenders.* Paper presented to the Association for the Treatment of Sexual Abusers (ATSA), Chicago.

Lalumière, M. L., & Quinsey, V. L. (1994). The discriminability of rapists from non-sex offenders using phallometric measures: A meta-analysis. *Criminal Justice and Behavior, 21*(1), 150–175.

Lang, R., Langevin, R., Checkley, K., & Pugh, G. (1987). Genital exhibitionism: Courtship disorder or narcissism? *Canadian Journal of Behavioural Science, 19*(2), 216–232.

Langevin, R. (Ed.). (1985). *Erotic preference, gender identity, and aggression in men: New research studies.* Hillsdale, NJ: Erlbaum.

Langevin, R. (1991). A note on the problem of response set in measuring cognitive distortions. *Annals of Sex Research, 4,* 287–292.

Langevin, R., Paitich, D., Freeman, R., Mann, K., & Handy, L. (1978). Personality characteristics and sexual anomolies in males. *Candian Journal of Behavioral Science, 10,* 222–238.

Langevin, R., Paitech, D., Ramsay, G., Anderson, C., Kamrad, J., Pope, S., Geller, G., Pearl, L., & Newman, S. (1979). Experimental studies of the etiology of genital exhibitionism. *Sexual Behavior, 8*(44), 307–331.

Langevin, R., Wright, P., & Handy, L. (1989). Characteristics of sex offenders who were sexually victimized as children. *Annals of Sex Research, 2,* 227–253.

Lanyon, R.I. (1991). Theories of sexual offending. In C. R. Hollin & K. Howells (Eds.), *Clinical approaches to sex offenders and their victims* (pp. 35–54). Chichester: Wiley.

Lawler, E. J. (1992). Affective attachments to nested groups: A choice-process theory. *American Sociological Review, 57,* 327–339.

Laws, D. R. (1989). *Relapse prevention with sex offenders.* New York: Guilford Press.

Laws, D. R. (1993, April). The president's column. *ATSA Newsletter, 5*(2), 2–4.

Laws, D. R. (1995). Verbal satiation: Notes on procedure, with speculations on its mechanism of effect. *Sexual Abuse: Journal of Research and Treatment, 7*(2), 155–166.

Laws, D. R. (1996). Marching into the past: A critique of Card and Olsen. *Sexual Abuse, 8*(4), 273–278.

Laws, D. R., Gulayets, M. J., & Frenzel, R. R. (1995). Assessment of sex offenders using standardized slide stimuli and procedures: A multisite study. *Sexual Abuse, 7*(1), 45–66.

Laws, D. R., & Marshall, W. L. (1990). A conditioning theory of the etiology and maintenance of deviant sexual preference and behavior. In W. L. Marshall, D. R. Laws, & H. E. Barbaree (Eds.), *Handbook of sexual assault: Issues, theories and treatment of the offender* (pp. 209–229). New York: Plenum Press.

Leberg, E. (1997). *Understanding child molesters: Taking charge.* Thousand Oaks, CA: Sage.

LeClair D. P. (1985). *The effect of community reintegration on rates of recidivism: A statistical overview of data for the years 1971–1982.* Boston: Massachusetts Department of Corrections.

Lee, D. G., & Olender, M. B. (1992). Working with juvenile sex offenders in foster care. *Community Alternatives: International Journal of Family Care, 4*(2), 63–75.

Lewis, D. O., Shankok, S., & Balla, D. (1979). Perinatal difficulties, head and face trauma, and child abuse in the medical histories of seriously delinquent children. *American Journal of Psychiatry, 136*(4-A), 419–423.

Lewis, D. O., Shankok, S., & Pincus, J. (1979). Juvenile male sexual assaulters. *American Journal of Psychiatry, 136,* 1194–1196.

Lewis, H. B. (1971). *Shame and guilt in neurosis.* New York: International Universities Press.

Lewis, H. B. (1987). Shame and the narcissistic personality. In D. L. Nathanson (Ed.), *The many faces of shame* (pp. 93–132). New York: Guilford Press.

Lewis, H. B. (1991). Self-conscious emotions and the development of self. In T. Shapiro & R. Emde (Eds.), New perspectives on affect and emotion in psychoanalysis. *Journal of the American Psychoanalytic Association, 39*(Suppl.), 45–73.

Lieb, R., Quinsey, V. , & Berliner, L. (1998). Sexual predators and social policy. In M. Tonrey (Ed.), *Crime and justice: A review of research* (pp. 43–114). Chicago: University of Chicago Press.

Lilly, J., Cullen, F., & Ball, R. (1995). *Criminological theory.* Thousand Oaks, CA: Sage.

Linehan, M. M. (1993). *Skills training manual for treating borderline personality disorder.* New York: Guilford Press.

Lipton, D. N., McDonel, E. C., & McFall, R. M. (1987). Heterosexual perception in rapists. *Journal of Consulting and Clinical Psychology, 55,* 17–21.

Liss, M. B., & Stahly, G. B. (1993). Domestic violence and child custody. In M. Hansen & M. Harway (Eds.), Battering and family therapy: A feminist perspective (pp. 175–187). Newbury Park, CA: Sage.

Little, R. (1992, November). *Assessment and treatment of intellectually disabled sex offenders.* ACTION Group, Burlington, VT.

Loftus, E. F. (1993). The reality of repressed memory. *American Psychologist, 48,* 518-537.

Loney, J. (1987). Hyperactivity and aggression in the diagnosis of attention deficit disorder. In B. B. Lahey & A. E. Kazdin (Eds.), *Advances in clinical child psychology* (Vol. 10, pp. 99–135). New York: Plenum Press.

Looman, J. (1995). Sexual fantasies of child molesters. *Canadian Journal of Behavioral Sciences, 27,* 321–332.

Lopez, M., Forness, S., MacMillan, D., Bocian, K., & Gresham, F. (1996). Children with attention deficit hyperactivity disorder and emotional or behavioral disorders in primary grades: Inappropriate placement in the learning disorder category. *Education and Treatment of Children, 19*(3), 286–299.

Losada-Paisey, G., & Paisey, T. J. H. (1988). Program evaluation of a comprehensive treatment package for mentally retarded offenders. *Behavioral Residential Treatment, 3*(4), 247–265.

Loza, W., & Dhaliwal, G. K. (1997). Psychometric evaluation of the Risk Appraisal Guide (RAG): A tool for assessing violent recidivism. *Journal of Interpersonal Violence, 12*(6), 779–793.

Lowenstein, L. (1982). The treatment of aggressive behaviour in maladjusted children. *National Council for Educational Standards Bulletin. No. 5,* pp. 15–20.

Luft, J. (1970). *Group processes: An introduction to group dynamics.* Palo Alto, CA: Mayfield.

Lund, D. (1995). Matrilineal descent and juvenile offender counseling. *International Journal of Offender Therapy and Comparative Criminology, 39*(1), 43–46.

Lynam, D. R. (1996). Early identifica-tion of chronic offenders: Who is the fledgling psychopath? *Psychological Bulletin, 120*(2), 209–234.

MacCulloch, M. J., Snowden, P. R., Wood, P. J. W., & Mill, H. E. (1983). Sadistic fantasy, sadistic behavior and offending. *British Journal of Psychiatry, 143,* 20–29.

Malamuth, N. M., Heavey, C. L., & Linz, D. (1993). Predicting men's antiso-cial behavior against women: The inter-action model of sexual aggression. In G. C. N. Hall, R. Hirschman, J. R. Grahaj, & M. S. Zaragoza (Eds.), *Sexual aggres-sion: Issues in etiology, assessment and treatment* (pp. 63–97). Washington, DC: Taylor & Francis.

Maletzky, B. M. (1991). Aversive respondent conditioning techniques. In B. M. Maletzky, *Treating the sexual offender* (pp. 67–95). Newbury Park, CA: Sage.

Maletzky, B. M. (1991). *Treating the sexual offender.* Newbury Park, CA: Sage.

Maletzky, B. M. (1993). Factors associ-ated with success and failure in the behavioral and cognitive treatment of sexual offenders. *Annals of Sex Research, 6,* 241–258.

Maletzky, B. M. (1994). Exhibitionism. In C. Last & M. Hersen (Eds.), *Adult behavior therapy handbook* (pp. 235–257). New York: Plenum Press.

Mander, A. M., Atrops, M. E., Barnes, A. R., & Munafo, R. (1996). *Sex Offender Treatment Program: Initial recidivism study.* Anchorage: Alaska Justice Statistical Analysis Unit, Justice Center University of Alaska.

Margolis, R. B., Taylor, J. M., & Greenlief, C. C. (1986). A cross-validation of two short forms of the WAIS-R in a geriatric sample suspected of dementia. *Journal of Clinical Psychology, 42,* 145–146.

Marlatt, G. A. (1989). Feeding the PIG: The problem of immediate gratification. In D. R. Laws (Ed.), *Relapse prevention with sex offenders* (pp. 56–62). New York: Guilford Press.

Marlatt, G. A. (1990). Cue exposure and relapse prevention in the treatment of addictive behaviors. *Addictive Behaviors, 15*(4), 395–399.

Marlatt, G. A. (1996). Section I. Theoretical perspectives on relapse: Taxonomy of high-risk situations for alcohol relapse: Evolution and development of a cognitive-behavioral model. *Addiction, 91*(Suppl.), S37–S49.

Marlatt, G. A., & Gordon, J. R. (Eds.). (1985). *Relapse prevention: Maintenance strategies in the treatment of addictive behaviors.* New York: Guilford Press.

Marques, J. K., Day, D. M., Nelson, C., Miner, M. H., & West, M. A. (1991). *The sex offender treatment and evaluation project: Report to the legislature.* Sacramento: California Department of Mental Health.

Marques, J. K., Day, D. M., Nelson, C., & West, M. A. (1994). Effects of cognitive-behavioral treatment on sex offender recidivism: Preliminary results of a longitudinal study. *Criminal Justice and Behavior, 21,* 28–54.

Marshall, W. I. (1983). The classification of sexual aggressives and their associated demographic, social, developmental, and psychological features. In S. N. Verdun-Jones & A. A. Keltner (Eds.), *Sexual aggression and the law* (pp. 3–13). Vancouver, BC: Criminology Research Center, Simon Frasier University.

Marshall, W. L. (1979). Satiation therapy: A procedure for reducing deviant sexual arousal. *Journal of Applied Behavior Analysis, 12*(3), 377–389.

Marshall, W. L. (1989). Intimacy, loneliness, & sexual offenders. *Behavior Research and Therapy, 27,* 491–503.

Marshall, W. L. (1996). Assessment, treatment, and theorizing about sex offenders: Developments during the past twenty years and future directions. *Criminal Justice and Behavior, 23,* 162–199.

Marshall, W. L. (1996). The sexual offender: Monster, victim, or everyman? *Sexual Abuse: A Journal of Research and Treatment, 8,* 317–335.

Marshall, W. L. (1997, June 20). *Treating sex offenders.* Presentation to the Wisconsin Sex Offender Treatment Network, Madison, WI.

Marshall, W. L. (1997, August 22). *Assessment and treatment of the adult sexual offender: The state of the science. Sexual offenders: Assessment, risk management and treatment: A gathering of leading experts.* San Diego, CA.

Marshall, W. L., Anderson, D., & Champagne, F. (1997). Self-esteem and its relationship to sexual offending. *Psychology, Crime and Law, 3,* 161–186.

Marshall, W. L., & Barbaree, H. E. (1988). The long-term evaluation of a behavioral treatment program for child molesters. *Behaviour Research and Therapy, 26,* 499–511.

Marshall, W. L., & Barbaree, H. E. (1990). An integrated theory of the etiology of sexual offending. In W. L. Marshall, D. R. Laws, & H. E. Barbaree (Eds.), *Handbook of sexual assault: Issues, theories and treatment of the offender* (pp. 257–275). New York: Plenum Press.

Marshall, W., & Barbaree, H. E. (1990). Outcome of comprehensive cognitive-behavioral treatment program. In W. L. Marshall, D. R. Laws, & H. E. Barbaree (Eds.), *Handbook of sexual assault: Issues, theories, and treatment of offenders* (pp. 363–385). New York: Plenum Press.

Marshall, W. L., Barbaree, H. E., & Eccles, A. (1991). Early onset and deviant sexuality in child molesters. *Journal of Interpersonal Violence, 6,* 323–336.

Marshall, W. L., Barbaree, H. E., & Fernandex, Y. M. (1995). Some aspects of social competence in sexual offenders. *Sexual Abuse: A Journal of Research and Treatment, 7,* 113–127.

Marshall, W. L., Champagne, F., Brown, C., & Miller, S. (1995). *Empathy, intimacy, loneliness, and self-esteem in nonfamilial child molesters.* Unpublished manuscript.

Marshall, W. L., Champagne, F., Sturgeon, C., & Bryce, P. (1997). Increasing the self-esteem of child molesters. *Sexual Abuse: A Journal of Research and Treatment, 9,* 321–333.

Marshall, W. L., & Eccles, A. (1993). Pavlovian conditioning processes in adolescent sex offenders. In H. E. Barbaree, W. L. Marshall, & S. Hudson (Eds.), *The juvenile sex offender* (pp. 118–142). New York: Guilford Press.

Marshall, W. L., Hudson, S. M., Jones, R., & Fernandez, Y. M. (1995). Empathy in sex offenders. *Clinical Psychology Review, 15,* 99–113.

Marshall, W. L., & Hull, G. (1995). The value of the MMPI in deciding forensic issues in accused sex offenders. *Sexual Abuse: A Journal of Research and Treatment, 7,* 205.

Marshall, W. L., Jones, R., Ward, T., Johnston, P., & Barbaree, H. E. (1991). Treatment outcome with sex offenders. *Clinical Psychology Review, 11,* 465–485.

Marshall, W. L., & Mazzucco, A. (1995). Self-esteem and parental attachments in child molesters. *Sexual Abuse: A Journal of Research and Treatment, 7,* 279–285.

Marshall, W. L., Payne, K., Barbaree, H. E., & Eccles, A. (1991). Exhibitionists: Sexual preferences for exposing. *Behavioral Research and Therapy, 29*(l), 37–40.

Marshall, W. L., & Pithers, W. D. (1994). A reconsideration of treatment outcome with sex offenders. *Criminal Justice and Behavior, 21,* 10–27.

Massachusetts Association for the Treatment of Sex Abusers. (1997). *No more victims: A master plan for addressing the problem of sexual assault in the Commonwealth of Massachusetts.*

McCarty, L. M. (1986). Characteristics of the offender. *Child Welfare, 65,* 447–458.

McConaghy, N. (1993). *Sexual behavior: Problems and management.* New York: Plenum Press.

McConaghy, N., Blaszczynski, A., Armstrong, M. S., & Kidson, W. (1989). Resistance to treatment of adolescent sex offenders. *Archives of Sexual Behavior, 18*(2), 97–107.

McDonel, E. C., & McFall, R. M. (1991). Construct validity of two heterosexual perception skill measures for assessing rape proclivity. *Violence and Victims, 6,* 17–30.

McGovern, K., & Peters, J. (1988). Guidelines for assessing sex offenders. In L.A. Walker (Ed.), *Handbook on the sexual abuse of children* (pp. 216–246). New York: Springer.

McGrath, M., Cann, S., & Konopasky, R. (1998). New measures of defensiveness, empathy and cognitive distortions for sexual offenders against children. *Sexual Abuse: A Journal of Research and Treatment, 10*(1), 25–36.

McGrath, R. (1991). Sex-offender risk assessment and disposition planning: A review of empirical and clinical findings. *International Journal of Offender Therapy and Comparative Criminology, 35,* 328–350.

McGraw, J. M., & Smith, H. A. (1992). Child sexual abuse allegations amidst divorce and custody proceedings: Refining the validation process. *Journal of Child Sexual Abuse, 1*(1), 49–62.

McKibben, A. Proulx, J., & Lusignan, R. (1994). Relationships between conflict, affect and deviant sexual behaviors in rapists and pedophiles. *Behavior Research and Therapy, 32,* 571–575.

Mehrabian, A., & Epstein, N. (1972). A measure of emotional empathy. *Journal of Personality, 40,* 525-543.

Mehta, S. N. (1996, May 24). Treating sex offenders becomes an industry, but does it work? *Wall Street Journal,* pp. 1, A6.

Merton, R. (1968). *Social theory and social structure.* New York: Free Press.

Messina, N., Wish, E., & Nemes, S. (1997, November). *The efficacy of therapeutic community treatment for substance abusers with co-occuring antisocial personality disorder.* American Society of Criminology Annual Conference, San Diego, CA.

Metropolitan Community Mental Health Center. (1996, March 6–7). *Strategies for community-based treatment of sex offenders with special needs.* Workshop, Eveleth, MN.

Meyers, L. C., & Romero, J. J. (1980). *A ten-year follow-up of sex offender recidivism.* Philadelphia: J. J. Peters Institute.

Miller, D. T., & Ross, M. (1975). Self-serving biases in attribution of causality: Fact or fiction? *Psychological Bulletin, 82,* 213–225.

Miller, J. G. (1992). On mitigating professional arrogance in the treatment of sex offenders. *International Journal of Medicine and Law, 11,* 485-491.

Miller, R. S., & Lefcourt, H. M. (1982). The assessment of intimacy.

Journal of Personality Assessment, 66, 514–518.

Miller, T. R., Cohen, M. A., & Wiersema, B. (1996). *Victim costs and consequences: A new look.* Washington, DC: National Institute of Criminal Justice.

Miller, W. R. (Ed.). (1980). *The addictive behaviors.* Oxford, UK: Pergamon Press.

Millich, R., & Dodge, K. A. (1984). Social information processing in child psychiatry populations. *Journal of Abnormal Child Psychology, 12,* 471–489.

Millon, T. (1994). *Millon Clinical Multiaxial Inventory—III manual.* Minneapolis, MN: National Computer Systems.

Milner, J. S., & Campbell, J. C. (1995). Prediction issues for practitioners. In J. C. Campbell (Ed.), *Assessing dangerousness: Violence by sexual offenders, batterers, and child abusers.* Thousand Oaks, CA: Sage.

Miner, M. H. (1997). How can we conduct treatment outcome research. *Sexual Abuse: A Journal of Research and Treatment, 9,* 95–110.

Miner, M. H., & Dwyer, S. M. (1995). Analysis of dropouts from outpatient sex offender treatment. *Journal of Psychology and Human Sexuality, 7,* 77–93.

Miner, M. H., Marques, J. K., Day, D. M., & Nelson, C. (1990). Impact of relapse prevention in treating sex offenders: Preliminary findings. *Annals of Sex Research, 3,* 165–185.

Moffitt, T. E. (1990). Juvenile delinquency and attention deficit disorder: Boys' developmental trajectories from age 3 to age 15. *Child Development, 61,* 893–910.

Mohr, J., Turner, R., & Jerry, M. (1964). *Pedophilia and exhibitionism.* University of Toronto Press: Toronto, Canada.

Monastersky, C., & Smith, W. (1985). Juvenile sexual offenders: A family systems paradigm. In E. M. Otey & G. D. Ryan (Eds.), *Adolescent sex offenders: Issues in research and treatment* (pp. 130–146). Rockville, MD: Department of Health and Human Services.

Money, J. (1972). The therapeutic use of androgen-depleting hormone. *International Psychiatry Clinics, 8,* 165–174.

Money, J. (1981). Paraphilia and abuse-martyrdom: Exhibitionism as a paradigm for reciprocal couple counseling combined with antiandrogen. *Journal of Sex and Marital Therapy, 7*(2), 115–123.

Morenz, B, & Becker, J. V. (1995). The treatment of youthful sexual offenders. *Applied and Preventive Psychology, 4,* 247–256.

Morgenstern, M. (1973). Community attitudes toward sexuality of the mentally retarded. In F. F. de la Cruz & G. D. LaVeck (Eds.), *Human sexuality and the mentally retarded* (pp. 157–163). New York: Brunner/Mazel.

Morrison, T., Erooga, M., & Beckett, R. (1994). *Sexual offending against children: Assessment and treatment of male abusers.* London and New York: Routledge.

Morrison, W. (1994). Criminology, modernity, and the "truths" of the human condition: Reflections on the melancholy of postmodernism. In D. Nelson (Ed.), *The futures of criminology*. Thousand Oaks, CA: Sage.

Murphy, W. D. (1990). Assessment and modification of cognitive distortions in sex offenders. In W. L. Marshall, D. R. Laws, & H. E. Barbaree (Eds.), *Handbook of sexual assault: Issues, theories, and treatment of the offender* (pp. 331–342). New York: Plenum Press.

Murphy, W. D. (1997, September/October). Massachusetts anti-SLAPP statute used to dismiss abusers' retaliatory litigation. *Sexual Asault Report*, p. 3.

Murphy, W. D., & Barbaree. H. E. (1994). *Assessments of sex offenders by measures of erectile response: Psychometric properties and decision making* (rev. and updated). Brandon, VT: Safer Society Press.

Murphy, W. D., Coleman, E. M., & Abel, G. G. (1983). Human sexuality in the mentally retarded. In J. L. Matson & F. Andrasik (Eds.), *Treatment issues and innovations in mental retardation* (pp. 581–644). New York: Plenum Press.

Murphy, W. D., Coleman, E. M., & Haynes, M. R. (1983). Treatment and evaluation issues with the mentally retarded sex offender. In J. G. Greer & I. R. Stuart (Eds.), *The sexual aggressor: Current perspectives on treatment* (pp. 22–41). New York: Van Nostrand Reinhold.

Murphy, W. D., Coleman, E. M., & Haynes, M. R. (1986). Factors related to coercive sexual behavior in a nonclinical sample of males. *Violence and Victims, 1*, 255–278.

Murphy, W. D., Haynes, M. R., & Worley, P. J. (1991). Assessment of adult sexual interest. In C. R. Hollin & K. Howells (Eds.), *Clinical approaches to sex offenders and their victims* (pp. 77–92). New York: Wiley.

Murphy, W. D., & Peters, J. M. (1992, March). Profiling child sexual abusers: Psychological considerations. *Criminal Justice and Behavior 19*(1), 24–37.

Murphy, W. D., & Smith, T. A. (1996). Sex offenders against children: Empirical and clinical issues. In J. Briere,L. Berliner, J. A. Bulkley, C. Jenny, & T. Reid, (Eds.), *The APSAC Handbook on Child Maltreatment*. Thousand Oaks, CA: Sage.

Murphy, W. D., & Stalgaitis, S. J. (1987). Assessment and treatment considerations for sexual offenders against children: Behavioral and social learning approaches. In J. R. McNamara & M. A. Appel (Eds.), *Critical issues, developments and trends in professional psychology* (vol. 3, pp. 177–210). New York: Praeger.

Myers, J. E. B. (1997). *A mother's nightmare—Incest*. Newbury Park, CA: Sage.

Nadar, K., & Pynoos, R. (1991). Play drawing techniques as tools for interviewing traumatized children. In C. Schaefer, K. Gitlin, & A. Sandgrund (Eds.), *Play diagnosis and assessment* (pp. 375–389). New York: Wiley.

National Seminars, Inc. (1992). *Total quality management: A supervisor's* handbook. Bethesda, MD: National Press Publications.

National Task Force on Adolescent Sexual Offending. (1988). Preliminary Report 1988. *Juvenile and Family Court Journal, 39,* 1–21.

Needham, J. P. (1977). Neutralization of prison hostage situations. *Criminal Justice Monograph, 8*(1).

Nezu, C. M., Nezu, A. M., & Gill-Weiss, M. J. (1992). *Psychopathology in persons with mental retardation: Clinical guidelines for assessment and treatment.* New York: Guilford Press.

Nicholaichuk, T. (1997). *Does participation in treatment reduce recidivism.* Paper presented at the National Conference: Community notification and other techniques for managing high-risk and dangerous offenders. Winnipeg, Canada.

Nichols, H. R., & Molinder, I. (1984). *Multiphasic Sex Inventory manual: A test to assess the psychosexual characteristics of the sexual offender.* Tacoma, WA: Nichols & Molinder.

Nielsen, A., & Scarpitti, F. (1995). Argot use in a therapeutic community. *Deviant Behavior: An Interdisciplinary Journal, 16,* 245–267.

Northey, W. F. Jr. (1995). *The use of presumptive realities in the treatment of incarcerated juveniles adjudicated on sexual offenses: A grounded theory study.* Unpublished doctoral dissertation, Kansas State University.

Novaco, R. W. (1975). *Anger control.* Lexington, MA: Lexington Press.

O'Connell, M. A. (1998, February). Using polygraph testing to assess deviant sexual history of sex offender. *Dissertation Abstracts International, 58*(8-A), 3023.

O'Donohue, W., & Leterneau, E. (1992). The psychometric properties of the penile tumescence assessment of child molesters. *Journal of Psychopathology and Behavioral Assessment, 14,* 123–174.

Oregon Crime Analysis Center. (1984). *Recidivism of releases from Oregon corrections institutions.* Salem: Author.

Palmer, P. (1986). *The company of strangers.* New York: Cross Road.

Patrick, C. J., & Iacono, W .G. (1989). Psychopathy, threat, and polygraph test accuracy. *Journal of Applied Psychology, 74,* 347–355.

Patterson, G. R. Reid, J. B., & Dishion, T. J. (1992). *Antisocial boys.* Eugene, OR: Castalia.

Pearson, D., Norton, A., & Farwell, E. (1997). Attention-deficit hyperactivity disorder in mental retardation: Nature of attention deficits. In J. Burack & J. Enns (Eds.), *Attention, development, and psychopathology* (pp. 205–221). New York: Guilford Press.

Pearson, H. (1990). Paraphilias, impulse control and serotonin. *Journal of Clinical Psychopharmacology, 10*(3), 233.

Pendergast, W. (1991). *Treating sex offenders in correctional institutions and outpatient clinics.* New York: Hawthorn Press.

Persky, R. (1972). In W. Wolfensburger (Ed.), *The principle of normalization in human services.* Toronto, Canada: National Institute on Mental Retardation.

Peters, J. J., & Roether, H. A. (1971). *Success and failure of sex offenders.* Philadelphia: American Association for the Advancement of Science.

Peters, J. M., & Murphy, W. D. (1992). Profiling child sexual abusers: Legal considerations. *Criminal Justice and Behavior, 19*(1), 38–53.

Petersen, K., et al. (1982). EEG antecedents of thievery. *Acta Psychiatrica Scandinavica, 65*(5), 331–338.

Petrovich, M., & Templer, D. I. (1984). Heterosexual molestation of children who later become rapists. *Psychological Reports, 54,* 810.

Pierce, L. H., & Pierce, R. L. (1987). Incestuous victimization by juvenile sexual offenders. *Journal of Family Violence, 2,* 351–364.

Pithers, W. D. (1982). *The Vermont Treatment Program for Sexual Aggressors: A program description.* Waterbury: Vermont Department of Corrections.

Pithers, W. D. (1990). Relapse prevention with sexual aggressors. In W. L. Marshall, D. R. Laws, & H. E. Barbaree (Eds.), *Handbook of sexual assault* (pp. 343–361). New York: Plenum Press.

Pithers, W. D. (1994). Process evaluation of a group therapy component designed to enhance sex offenders' empathy for sexual abuse survivors. *Behavior Research and Therapy, 32,* 565–570.

Pithers, W. D., Beal, L. S., Armstrong, J., & Petty, J. (1989). Identification of risk factors through clinical interviews and analysis of records. In D. R. Laws (Ed.), *Relapse prevention with sex offenders* (pp. 63–72). New York: Guilford Press.

Pithers, W. D., & Cummings, G. F. (1995). Relapse prevention: A method for enhancing behavioral self-management and external supervision of the sexual aggressor. In B. K. Schwartz & H. R. Cellini, (Eds.), *The sex offender: Corrections, treatment and practice* (vol. I, pp. 20-1–20-32). Kingston, NJ: Civic Research Institute.

Pithers, W., Cumming, G., Beal, L., Young, W., & Turner, R. (1988). Relapse prevention. In B. K. Schwartz (Ed.), *A practitioner's guide to treating the incarcerated male sex offender—breaking through the cycle of abuse* (pp. 123–140) Washington, DC: U.S. Department of Justice, National Institute of Corrections.

Pithers, W. D., & D. R. Laws. (1995). Phallometric assessment. In B. K. Schwartz & H. R. Cellini (Eds.), *The sex offender: Corrections, treatment and legal practice* (vol. I, pp. 12-1–121-18). Kingston, NJ: Civic Research Institute.

Pithers, W. D., Marques, J. K. Gibat, C. C., & Marlatt, G. A. (1983). Relapse prevention with sexual aggressives: A self-control model of treatment and maintenance of change. In J. G. Greer & I. R. Stuart (Eds.), *The sexual aggressor: Current perspectives on treatment* (pp.

214–234). New York: Van Nostrand Reinhold.

Plassman, R. (1987). Supportive treatment of exhibitionism: A psychoanalytic approach. *Psyche-Zeitschrift-fur-Psychoanalyse und ihre-Anwendungen, 41*(2), 140–147.

Pollack, N. L., & Hasmall, J. M. (1991). The excuses of child molesters. *Behavioral Sciences and the Law, 9,* 53–59.

Pompi, K. (1994). Adolescents in therapeutic communities: Retention and post-treatment outcome. In F. Tims, G. DeLeon, & N. Jainchill (Eds.), *Therapeutic community: Advances in research and application* (pp. 128–161) (NIDA Research Monograph 144, NIH Publication No. 94-3633). Rockville, MD: National Institute on Drug Abuse.

Pope, K. S. (1996). Scientific research, recovered memory, and context: Seven surprising findings. *Women and Therapy, 19,* 123–140.

Pope, K. S., & Feldman-Summers, S. (1992). National survey of psychologists' sexual and physical abuse history and their evaluation of training and competence in these areas. *Professional Psychology, 23,* 353–361.

Potter-Efron, R. (1993). Three models of shame and their relation to the addictive process. *Alcoholism Treatment Quarterly, 10*(1–2), 23–48.

Prendergast, W. E. (1991). *Treating sex offenders in correctional institutions and outpatient clinics: Guide to clinical practice.* Binghamton, NY: Haworth Press.

Prentky, R. (1990). *Sexual violence: A review.* Paper presented at the Ninth Annual Clinical and Research Conference on the Assessment and Treatment of Sexual Abusers, Their Families and Victims, Toronto, Canada.

Prentky, R., & Burgess, A. W. (1990). Rehabilitation of child molesters: A cost benefit analysis. *American Journal of Orthopsychiatry, 60*(1), 250–261.

Prentky, R., & Edmunds, S. (Eds.). (1997). *Assessing sexual abuse: A resource guide for practitioners.* Brandon, VT: Safer Society Press.

Prentky, R., & Knight, R. (1988). *Antisocial personality disorder and Hare assessments of psychopathy among sexual offenders.* Unpublished manuscript.

Prentky, R. A., Knight, R. A., & Lee, A. F. S. (1997). *Child sexual molestation: Research issues.* Washington, DC: National Institute of Justice.

Prentky, R. A., Knight, R. A., & Lee, A. F. S. (1997). Risk factors associated with recidivism among extrafamilial child molesters. *Journal of Consulting and Clinical Psychology, 65*(1), 141–149.

Prentky, R. A., Knight, R. A., Sims-Knight, J. E., Strauss, H., Rokous, F., & Cerce, D. (1989). Developmental antecedents of sexual aggression. *Development and Psychopathology, 1,* 153–169.

Prentky, R. A., Lee, A. F. S., Knight, R. A., & Cerce, D. (1995). Predictive validity of lifestyle impulsivity for rapists. *Criminal Justice and Behavior, 32*(2), 106–128.

Prentky, R. A., Lee, A. F. S., Knight, R. A., & Cerce, D. (1997). Recidivism rates among child molesters and rapists: A methodological analysis. *Law and Human Behavior, 21*(6), 635–659.

Program Evaluation Division. (1994). *Sex offender treatment programs.* St. Paul, MN: Office of the Legislative Auditor.

Proulx, J. (1989). Sexual preference assessment of sexual aggressors. *International Journal of Law and Psychiatry, 12,* 275–280.

Proulx, J., Aubut, J., McKibben, A., & Côté, M. (1994). Penile responses of rapists and non rapists to rape stimuli involving physical violence or humiliation. *Archives of Sexual Behavior, 23,* 295–310.

Proulx, J., Côté, G., & Achille, P. A. (1993). Prevention of voluntary control of penile response in homosexual pedophiles during phallometric testing. *Journal of Sex Research, 30,* 140–147.

Proulx, J., McKibben, A., & Lusignan, R. (1996). Relationships between affective components and sexual behaviors in sexual aggressors. *Sexual Abuse: A Journal of Research and Treatment, 8*(4), 279–290.

Proulx, J., Pellerin, B., Paradis, Y., McKibben, A., Aubut, J., & Ouimet, M. (1997). Static and dynamic predictors of recidivism in sexual aggressors. *Sexual Abuse: A Journal of Research and Treatment, 9,* 7–27.

Pullis, M. (1991). Practical considerations of excluding conduct disordered students: An empirical analysis. *Behavioral Disorders, 17*(1), 9–22.

Pynoos, R. S., & Nader, K. (1988). Children who witness the sexual assaults of their mothers. *Journal of the American Academy of Child and Adolescent Psychiatry, 27,* 567–572.

Quinsey, V. (1977). The assessment of treatment of child molesters: A review. *Canadian Psychological Review, 18,* 204–220.

Quinsey, V. L. (1980). The base rate problem and prediction of dangerousness: A reappraisal. *Journal of Psychiatry and Law, 8,* 329–340.

Quinsey, V. L. (1992, March). Presentation at Risk Prediction Workshop. Ontario Regional Psychologists, Correction Service Canada.

Quinsey, V. L., & Chaplin, T. C. (1988). Penile responses of child molesters and normals to descriptions of encounters with children involving sex and violence. *Journal of Interpersonal Violence, 3,* 259–274.

Quinsey, V., Chaplin, T., & Carrigan, W. (1980). Biofeedback and signaled punishment in the modification of sexual age preference. *Behavior Therapy, 11,* 567–576.

Quinsey, V. L., Harris, G. T., Rice, M. E., & Lalumière, M. L. (1993). Assessing treatment efficacity in outcome studies of sex offenders. *Journal of Interpersonal Violence, 8,* 512–523.

Quinsey, V., & Lalumière, M. (1996).

Assessment of sexual offenders against children. Thousand Oaks, CA: Sage.

Quinsey, V. L., Lalumière, M. L., Rice, M. E., & Harris, G. T. (1995). Predicting sexual offenses. In J. C. Campbell (Ed.), *Assessing dangerousness: Violence by sexual offenders, batterers, and child abusers.* Thousand Oaks, CA: Sage.

Quinsey, V. L., Rice, M. E., & Harris, G. T. (1995). Actuarial prediction of sexual recidivism. *Journal of Interpersonal Violence, 10*(1),85–105.

Rada, R. (1976). Alcoholism and the child molester. *Annals of New York Academy of Science, 273,* 492–498.

Radar, C. (1977). MMPI profile types of exposers, rapists and assaulters in a court services population. *Journal of Consulting and Clinical Psychology, 45*(1), 61–69.

Rapoport, J. (1989). The biology of obsessive-compulsive disorders. *Scientific American, 260,* 83–89.

Reebye, P., Moretti, M., & Lessard, J. (1995). Conduct disorder and substance use disorder: Comorbidity in a clinical sample of preadolescents and adolescents [Special issue on child and adolescent psychiatry]. *Canadian Journal of Psychiatry, 40*(6), 313–319.

Reiss, A. (1951). Delinquency as the failure of personal and social controls. *American Sociological Review, 16,* 196–207.

Rice, M. E., Chaplin, T. E., Harris, G. E., & Coutts, J. (1994). Empathy for the victim and sexual arousal among rapists and nonrapists. *Journal of Interpersonal Violence, 9*(4), 435–449.

Rice, M. E., & Harris, G. T. (1997). Cross-validation and extension of the Violence Risk Appraisal Guide for child molesters. *Law and Human Behavior, 21*(2), 223–241.

Rice, M. E., Harris, G. T., & Quinsey, V. L. (1993). Evaluating treatment programs for child molesters. In J. Hudson & I. V. Roberts (Eds.), *Evaluation research in canadian justice programs.* Calgary: University of Calgary Press.

Rice, M. E., Quinsey, V. L., & Harris, G. T. (1991). Sexual recidivism among child molesters released from a maximum security psychiatric institution. *Journal of Consulting and Clinical Psychology, 59,* 381–386.

Rickles, N. (1950). *Exhibitionism.* Philadelphia: J. B. Lippincott.

Rider, D. M. (1994). *Overview of sexual boundaries in ministry: Ethical, clinical and liability considerations.* New York: Episcopal Church Pension Fund.

Ritchie-Matsumoto, P. (1997). Quality improvement for a demanding correctional environment. *Offender Programs Report, 1*(1), 5–13.

Roberts, M., & Bushaw, E. (1978). Food for thought: Participation of kitchen staff in milieu treatment. *Child Care Quarterly, 7*(3), 242–249.

Rokach, A. (1990). Content analysis of sexual fantasies of males and females. *Journal of Psychology, 124*(4), 427–436.

Romero, J., & Williams, L. (1985). Recidivism among convicted sex offenders: A 10-year follow-up study. *Federal Probation, 49,* 58–64.

Rosellini, G. (1985). Stinking thinking. Center City, MN: Hazelden.

Rosen, R., & Beck, J. G. (1988). *Patterns of sexual arousal: Psychophysiological processes and clinical applications.* New York: Guilford Press.

Roundtree, G. A., Edwards, D. W., & Parker, J. B. (1984). A study of personal characteristics of probationers as related to recidivism. *Journal of Offender Counseling, 8,* 53–61.

Rubinstein, M., Yeager, C. A. Goodstein, C., & Lewis, D. O. (1993). Sexually assaultive male juveniles: A follow-up. *American Journal of Psychiatry, 150,* 262–265.

Russell, K., Sturgeon, V. H., Miner, M. H., & Nelson, C. (1989). Determinants of the abstinence violation effect in sexual fantasies. In D. R. Laws (Ed.), *Relapse prevention with sex offenders* (pp. 63–72). New York: Guilford Press.

Ryan, G. (1995). *Resistance versus temperament: Characteristics which will not change.* Paper presented at the meeting of the National Adolescent Perpetrator Network, St. Louis, MO.

Ryan, G., Miyoshi, T. J., Metzner, J. L., Krugman, R. D., & Fryer, G. E. (1996). Trends in a national sample of sexually abusive youths. *Journal of the American Academy of Child and Adolescent Psychiatry, 35*(1), 17–25.

Ryan, G. D. (1991). Incidence and prevalence of sexual offenses committed by juveniles. In G. D. Ryan & S. Lane. (Eds.), *Juvenile sexual offending: Causes, consequences, and correction* (pp. 9–19). Lexington, MA: Lexington Books.

Ryan, G. D., & Lane, S. (Eds.). (1991). *Juvenile sexual offending: Causes, consequences, and corrections.* Lexington, MA: Lexington Books.

Safer Society Program. (1988, March 25–27). *A summary of selected notes from the working sessions of the first national training conference on the assessment and treatment of intellectually disabled juvenile and adult sexual offenders.* Presented under the auspices of Ohio Youth Services Network, Safer Society Program, and other related Ohio agencie, Columbus, OH.

Salekin, R. T., Rogers, R., & Sewel, K. W. (1996). A review and meta-analysis of the Psychopathy Checklist and Psychopathy Checklist—Revised: Predictive validity of dangerousness. *Clinical Psychology: Science and Practice, 3,* 203–215.

Salter, A. (1988). *Treating child sex offenders and victims.* Newbury Park, CA: Sage.

Samenow, S. E. (1984). *Inside the criminal mind.* New York: Times Books.

Sandberg, S., Weiselberg, M., & Shaffer, D. (1980). Hyperkinetic and conduct problem children in primary school population: Some epidemiological considerations. *Journal of Child Psychology and Psychiatry, 21,* 293–311.

Sapp, A. D., & Vaughn, M. S. (1990). Juvenile sex offender treatment at state-operated correctional institutions. *International Journal of Offender Therapy and Comparative Criminology, 34*(2), 131–146.

Sattler, J. M. (1992). *Assessment of children* (3rd ed.). San Diego, CA: Author.

Schewe, P. A., & O'Donohue, W. (1993). Sexual abuse prevention with high-risk males: The roles of victim empathy and rape myths. *Violence and Victims, 8,* 339–351.

Schilling, R. F., & Schinke, S. P. (1989). Mentally retarded sex offenders: Fact, fiction, and treatment. *Journal of Social Work and Human Sexuality, 7*(2), 33–48.

Schlank, A., & Bumby, K. (1997, October). *Issues in the assessment of sexual offenders' cognitive distortions.* Paper presented at the Sixteenth Annual Research and Treatment Conference of the Association for the Treatment of Sexual Abusers, Arlington, VA.

Schlank, A. M., & Shaw, T. (1997). Treating sexual offenders who deny: A review. In B. K. Schwartz, & H. R. Cellini (Eds.), *The sex offender: Corrections, treatment and legal practice* (vol. I, pp. 6-1–6-7). Kingston, NJ: Civic Research Institute.

Schoen, J., & Hoover, J. H. (1990). Mentally retarded sex offenders. *Journal of Offender Rehabilitation, 16*(1/2), 81–91.

Schram, D. D., & Milloy, C. D. (1998). *Sexually violent predators and civil commitment: A study of the characteristics and recidivism of sex offenders considered for civil commitment but for whom proceedings were declined.* From the Washington State Institute for Public Policy, Evergreen State College, Olympia, WA.

Schram, D. D., Milloy, C. D., & Rowe, W. E. (1991). *Juvenile sex offenders: A follow-up study of reoffense behavior.* From the Washington State Institute for Public Policy.

Schultz, R. (1997). Evaluating medical and mental health testimony in child sexual abuse cases. In Wiley Editorial Staff (Eds.), *1997 Wiley family law update* (pp. 167–200). New York: Wiley.

Schwartz B. K. (1977). *Factors associated with response to treatment in aggressive sex offenders.* Doctoral dissertation, University of New Mexico.

Schwartz, B. (1995). Decision making with incarcerated sex offenders. In B. K. Schwartz & H. R. Cellini (Eds.), *The sex offender: Corrections, treatment and legal practice* (vol. I, pp. 8-3–8-5). Kingston: NJ: Civic Research Institute.

Schwartz, B. K. (1995). Introduction to the integrative approach. In B. K. Schwartz & , H. R. Cellini (Eds.), *The sex offender: Corrections, treatment and practice* (vol. I, pp. 1-1–1-13). Kingston, NJ: Civic Research Institute.

Schwartz, B. K., & Canfield, G. M. S. (1996). *Facing the shadow.* Kingston, NJ: Civic Research Institute.

Schwartz, B. K., & Cellini, H. R. (Eds.). (1995). *The sex offender: Corrections, treatment and legal practice.* Kingston, NJ: Civic Research Institute.

Schwartz, I. M. (1989). *Justice for juveniles: Rethinking the best interests of the child.* Lexington, MA: Lexington Books.

Schwartz, M. F., Galperin, L. D., & Masters, W. H. (1995, October). *Post-traumatic stress, sexual trauma and dissociative disorders: Issues related to intimacy and sexuality.* Paper presented at the Annual Conference of the Association for the Treatment of Sexual Abusers, New Orleans.

Scully, D. (1988). Convicted rapists' perceptions of self and victim: Role taking and emotions. *Gender and Society, 2,* 200–213.

Segal, S. (1973). Retarded readers and anti-social young people: An English study. *International Journal of Offender Therapy & Comparative Criminology, 17*(3), 297–302.

Segal, Z. V., & Stermac, L. E. (1990). The role of cognition in sexual assaults. In W. L. Marshall, D. R. Laws, & H. E. Barbaree (Eds.), *Handbook of sexual assault: Issues, theories, and treatment of the offender* (pp. 161–174). New York: Plenum Press.

Segalowitz, S., & Brown, D. (1991). Mild head injury as a source of developmental disabilities. *Journal of Learning Disabilities, 24*(9), 551–559.

Seghorn, T. K., Prentky, R. A., & Boucher, R. A. (1987). Childhood sexual abuse in the lives of sexual offenders. *Journal of the American Academy of Child and Adolescent Psychiatry, 26,* 262–267.

Seidman, B. T., Marshall, W. L., Hudson, S. M., & Robertson, P. J. (1994). An examination of intimacy and loneliness in sex offenders. *Journal of Interpersonal Violence, 9,* 3–11.

Seidman, B. T., & Williams, S. M. (1997, August). *Hostage-Takings of Correctional Service of Canada (CSC) Staff: Psychological Impact and Institutional Management.* Internal publication.

Seligman, M. E. P. (1996). Long term psychotherapy is highly effective: The Consumer Reports study. *Harvard Mental Health Letter, 13*(1).

Serber, M. (1970). Shame aversion therapy. *Journal of Behavior Therapy and Experimental Psychiatry, 1,* 217–226.

Serber, M., & Wolpe, J. (1966). *Behavior therapy techniques.* New York: Pergamon Press.

Serber, M., & Wolpe, J. (1972). Behavior therapy techniques. In H. L. P. Resnick & M. E. Wolfgang (Eds.), *Sexual behaviors* (pp. 239–254). Boston: Little, Brown.

Serin, R. C. (1996). Violent recidivism in criminal psychopaths. *Law and Human Behavior, 20*(2), 207–217.

Serin, R. C., Malcolm, P. B., Khanna, A., & Barbaree, H. (1994). Psychopathy and deviant sexual arousal in incarcerated sexual offenders. *Journal of Interpersonal Violence, 9*(1), 3–11.

Seto, M. (1992). *Victim blame, empathy and disinhibition of sexual arousal to rape in community males and incarcerated rapists.* Unpublished master's thesis, Queen's University, Kingston, Ohio.

Sgroi, S. (1982). *Handbook of clinical*

intervention in child sexual abuse. Lexington, MA: Lexington Books.

Shaw, T. A, Herkov, M. J., & Green, R. A. (1995). Examination of treatment completion and predicted outcome among incarcerated sex offenders. *Bulletin of the American Academy of Psychiatry and Law, 23*(1), 35–41.

Shoor, M., Speed, M., & Bartelt, C. (1966). Syndrome of the adolescent child molester. *American Journal of Psychiatry, 122,* 783–789.

Short, A., & Halvorson, D. (1991, November 10–12). Free to rape. *Star-Tribune,* p. 1.

Simkins, L., Ward, W., Bowman, S., & Rinck, C. (1989). The Multiphasic Sex Inventory: Diagnosis and prediction of treatment response in child sexual abusers. *Annals of Sex Research, 2,* 205–226.

Simkins, L., Ward, W., Bowman, S., & Rinck, C. M. (1990). Characteristics predictive of child sex abusers' response to treatment: An exploratory study. *Journal of Psychology and Human Sexuality, 3*(1), 19–55.

Simon, W. T., & Schouten, P. G. W. (1991). Plethysmography in the assessment and treatment of sexual deviance: An overview. *Archives of Sexual Behavior, 20,* 75–91.

Simon, W. T., & Schouten, P. G. W. (1992). Problems in sexual preference testing in child sexual abuse cases: a legal and community perspective. *Journal of Interpersonal Violence, 7*(4), 503–516.

Singer, J. L. (1975). *The inner world of daydreaming.* New York: Harper & Row.

Singer, J. L. (1978). Experimental studies of daydreaming and the stream of thought. In K. S. Pope & J. L. Singer (Eds.), *The stream of consciousness* (pp. 187–223). New York: Plenum Press.

Sipe, A. W. R. (1990). *A secret world: Sexuality and the search for celibacy.* New York: Brunner/Mazel.

Sipe, A. W. R. (1995). *Sex, priests, and power. Anatomy of a crisis.* New York: Brunner/Mazel.

Smith, B., Hillenbrand, S., & Goretsky, S. (1990). *The probation response to child sexual abuse offenders: How is it working?* Washington, DC: American Bar Association.

Smith, H., & Israel, E. (1987). Sibling incest: A study of the dynamics of 25 cases. *Child Abuse and Neglect, 11*(2), 325–341.

Smith, R. (1995). Sex offender program planning and implementation. In B. K. Schwartz & H. R. Cellini (Eds.), *The sex offender. Corrections, treatment and legal practice* (vol. I, pp. 7-1–7-13) . Kingston, NJ: Civic Research Institute.

Smith, R., & Coukos, P. (1997, Fall). Fairness and accuracy in evaluations of domestic violence and child abuse in custody determinations. *The Judges' Journal, 36*(4), 40–56.

Smith, T., & Wolfe, R. (1988). A treatment model for sexual aggression [Special issue: The sexually unusual: Guide to understanding and helping].

Journal of Social Work and Human Sexuality, 7(1), 149–164.

Smith, W. R. (1988). Delinquency and abuse among juvenile sexual offenders. *Journal of Interpersonal Violence, 3,* 400–413.

Smith, W. R., & Monastersky, C. (1986). Assessing juvenile sexual offenders' risk for reoffending. *Criminal Justice and Behavior, 13,* 115–140.

Smith, W. R., Monastersky, C., & Deisher, R. M. (1987). MMPI-based personality types among juvenile sexual offenders. *Journal of Clinical Psychology, 43,* 422–430.

Snowdon, R. (1984). Working with incest offenders: Excuses, excuses, excuses. *Aegis, 35,* 56–63.

Soeffing, E. R. (1996). Annotation: Plea of guilty or conviction as resulting in loss of privilege against self-incrimination as to crime in question. 9 *American Law Reports 3d, 9,* 990.

Soothill, K., & Gibbens, T. (1978). Recidivism of sex offenders: A reappraisal. *British Journal of Criminology, 18,* 267–276.

Spencer, S. J., Josephs, R. A., & Steele, C. M. (1993). Low self-esteem: The uphill struggle for self-integrity. In R. F. Baumeister (Ed.), *Self-esteem: The puzzle of low self-regard* (pp. 21–36). New York: Plenum Press.

Spielberger, C. G., Gorsuch, R. L., & Lushene, R. D. (1970). *Manual for the State–Trait Anxiety Inventory (self-evaluation questionnaire).* Palo Alto, CA: Consulting Psychologist Press.

Spohn, R. B. (1993). Social desirability correlates for acceptance of rape myth. *Psychological Reports, 73,* 12–18.

Stanfield, J. (1992). *Be Cool: Coping with difficult people.* Santa Barbara, CA: Author.

Steele, N. (1995). Cost-effectiveness of treatment. In B. K. Schwartz, & H. R. Cellini (Eds.), *The sex offender: Corrections, treatment and legal practice* (vol. I, pp. 4.1–4.15). Kingston, NJ: Civic Research Institute.

Steffenhagen, R. A. (1990). *Self-esteem therapy.* New York: Praeger.

Stein, D., Hollander, E., Anthony, D., Schneir, F., Fallon, B., Liebowitz, M., & Klein, D. (1992). Serotonergic medications for sexual obsessions, sexual addictions, and paraphilias. *Journal of Clinical Psychiatry, 53,* 267–271.

Stermac, L. E., & Segal, Z. V. (1989). Adult sexual contact with children: An examination of cognitive factors. *Behavior Therapy, 20,* 573–584.

Stermac, L. E., Segal, Z. V,. & Gillis, R. (1990). Social and cultural factors in sexual assault. In W. L. Marshall, D. R. Laws, & H. E. Barbaree (Eds.), *Handbook of sexual assault: Issues, theories, and treatment of the offender* (pp. 143–159). New York: Plenum Press.

Stevenson, H. E., & Wormith, J. S. (1987). *Psychopathy and the level of supervision inventory.* Report No. 1987-25. Ottawa, Ontario, Canada: Ministry of the Solicitor-General of Canada.

Stout-Miller, R., Miller, L. S., & Langenbrunner, M. R. (1997).

Religiosity and child sexual abuse: A risk factor assessment. *Journal of Child Sexual Abuse, 6*(4), 15-34.

Sullivan, H. S. (1953). *The interpersonal theory of psychiatry.* New York: Norton. Swanson, C. K., & Garwick, G. B. (1990). Treatment for low-functioning sex offenders: Group therapy and interagency coordination. *Mental Retardation, 3,* 155–161.

Tangney, J. P. (1990). Assessing individual differences in proneness to shame and guilt: Development of the Self-Conscious Affect and Attribution Inventory. *Journal of Personality and Social Psychology, 59,* 102–111.

Tangney, J. P. (1991). Moral affect: The good, the bad, and the ugly. *Journal of Personality and Social Psychology, 61,* 598–607.

Tangney, J. P. (1995). Shame and guilt in interpersonal relationships. In J. P. Tangney & K. W. Fischer (Eds.), *Self-conscious emotions: Shame, guilt, embarrassment, and pride* (pp. 14–139). New York: Guilford Press.

Tangney, J. P,. & Fischer, K. W. (1995). *Self-conscious emotions: Shame, guilt, embarrassment, and pride.* New York: Guilford Press.

Tangney, J. P., Wagner, P. E., Fletcher, C., & Gramzow, R. (1992). Shamed into anger? The relation of shame and guilt to anger and self-reported aggression. *Journal of Personality and Social Psychology, 62,* 669–675.

Tarter, R. E., Hegedus, A. M., Alterman, A. I., & Katzgaar, L. (1983). Cognitive capacities of juvenile violent, non-violent, and sexual offenders. *Journal of Nervous and Mental Diseases, 171,* 564–567.

Task Force on Juvenile Sexual Offenders and Their Victims. (1996). *Juvenile sexual offenders and their victims.* Tallahassee, FL: Author.

Taylor, G., Barnsley, J., & Goldsmith, P. (1996). *Women and children last: Custody disputes and the family "justice" system.* Vancouver, BC: Vancouver Custody and Access Support and Advocacy Association.

Templer, D., Kasiraj, J.,Trent, N., Trent, A., Hughey, B., Keller, W., Orling, R., & Thomas-Dobson, S. (1992). Exploration of head injury without medical attention. *Perceptual and Motor Skills, 75*(1), 195–202.

Tennen, H., & Herzberger, S. (1987). Depression, self-esteem, and the absence of self-protective attributional biases. *Journal of Personality and Social Psychology, 52,* 72–80.

Therapeutic Communities of America. (1994). *Paradigms: Past, present and future.* Proceedings of the Therapeutic Communities of America 1992 planning conference, Chantilly, VA.

Thoennes, N., & Tjaden, P. G. (1990). The extent, nature, and validity of sexual abuse allegations in custody/visitation disputes. *Child Abuse and Neglect, 14,* 151–163.

Thomas, H. (1995). Experiencing a shame response as a precursor to violence. *Bulletin of the American Academy of Psychiatry and the Law, 23*(4), 587–593.

Thompson, J. S. (1988, August). *Comparison of mentally retarded and non-retarded defendants referred for competency*. Paper presented at the annual meeting of the American Psychological Association, Atlanta, GA.

Tibbetts, S. (1997). Shame and rational choice in offending decisions. *Criminal Justice and Behavior, 24*(2), 234–255.

Travin, S., Bluestone, H., Coleman, E., Culler, K., & Melella, J. (1985). Pedophilia: An update on theory and practice. *Psychiatric Quarterly, 57*(2), 89–101.

Travin, S., Cullen, K., & Melella, J. (1988). The use and abuse of erection measurements: A forensic perspective. *Bulletin of the American Academy of Psychiatry and the Law, 16*(3), 289–299.

Trepper, T., & Barrett, M.J (1989). *Systemic treatment of incest: A therapeutic handbook*. New York: Brunner/Mazel..

Truax, C., & Carkhuff, R. (1967). *Toward effective counseling and psychotherapy*. Chicago: Aldine.

U.S. General Accounting Office. (1996). *Sex offender treatment: Results inconclusive about what works to reduce recidivism*. Washington, DC: Author.

University of Hawaii-Manoa. (1984). *Recidivism of 1979 adult probation, Third Circuit Court*. Honolulu, HI: Youth Development and Research Center.

Urbanic, J. C. (1993). Intrafamilial sexual abuse. In J. Campbell & J. Humphreys (Eds.), *Nursing care of survivors of family violence* (pp 132–155). St. Louis: Mosby.

Van Eys, P. (1997). Group treatment for prepubescent boys with sexually aggressive behavior: Clinical considerations and proposed treatment techniques. *Cognitive and Behavioral Practice, 4,* 349–382.

Van Ness, S. R. (1984). Rape as instrumental violence: A study of youth offenders. *Journal of Offender Counseling Services and Rehabilitation, 9,* 161–170.

Wallerstadt, J. F. (1984). *Returning to prison*. Washington, DC: Bureau of Justice Statistics.

Walsh, E. R. (1997). Megan's Laws—Sex Offender Registration and Notification Statutes and Constitutional Challenges. In B. K. Schwartz & H. R. Cellini, *The sex offender: New insights, treatment innovations and legal developments* (vol. II, pp. 24-1-4-6).

Walsh, E. R., & Cohen, F. (1998). *Sex Offender Registration and Community Notification: A Megan's Law Sourcebook*. Kingston, NJ: Civic Research Institute.

Ward, K. M., Heffern, S. J., Wilcox, D. A., McElwee, D., Dowrick, P., Brown, T. D., Jones, M. J., & Johnson, C. L. (1992). *Managing inappropriate sexual behaviors: Supporting individuals with developmental disabilities in the community*. Anchorage: Alaska Specialized Education and Training Services.

Ward, T., Fon, C., Hudson, S. M., &

McCormach, J. (1998). A descriptive model of dysfunctional cognitions in child molesters. *Journal of Interpersonal Violence, 13*(1), 129–155.

Ward T., & Hudson, S. M. (1996). Relapse prevention: A critical analysis. *Sexual Abuse: A Journal of Research and Treatment, 8*(3), 177–200.

Ward, T., & Hudson, S. M. (in press). A self-regulation model of relapse prevention. In D. R. Laws, S. M. Hudson, & T. Ward (Eds.), *Remaking relapse prevention with sex offenders: A Sourcebook* (2nd ed.). Thousand Oaks, CA: Sage.

Ward, T. , Hudson, S. M., Johnston, L., & Marshall, W. L. (1997). Cognitive distortions in sex offenders: An integrative review. *Clinical Psychology Review, 17*(5), 479–507.

Ward, T., Hudson, S. M., & Marshall, W. L. (1994). The abstinence violation effect in child molesters. *Behaviour Research and Therapy, 32,* 431–437.

Ward, T., Hudson, S. M., & Marshall, W. L. (1995). Cognitive distortions and affective deficits in sex offenders: A cognitive deconstructionist interpretation. *Sexual Abuse: A Journal of Research and Treatment, 7,* 67–83.

Ward, T. Hudson, S. M., & Marshall, W. L. (1996). Attachment style in sex offenders: A preliminary study. *Journal of Sex Research, 33,* 17–26.

Ward, T., Hudson, S. M., Marshall, W. L., & Siegert, R. (1995). Attachment style and intimacy deficits in sexual offenders: A theoretical framework. *Sexual Abuse: A Journal of Research and Treatment, 7,* 317–335.

Ward, T., Hudson, S. M., & Siegert, R. J. (1995). A critical comment on Pithers's relapse prevention model. *Sexual Abuse: A Journal of Research and Treatment, 7,* 167–175.

Ward, T., Louden, K., Hudson, S. M., & Marshall, W. L. (1995). A descriptive model of the offense chain for child molesters. *Journal of Interpersonal Violence, 10,* 453–473.

Ward, T., McCormack, J., & Hudson, S. M. (1997). Sexual offenders' perceptions of their intimate relationships. *Sexual Abuse: A Journal of Research and Treatment, 9,* 57–74.

Warren, J. I., Fitch, W. L., & Deitz, P. E. (1991). Criminal offense, psychiatric diagnosis and psycholegal opinion: an analysis of 894 pre-trial referrals. *Bulletin of the American Academy of Psychiatry and the Law, 21,* 63–69.

Wechsler, D. (1981). *Wechsler Adult Intelligence Scale—Revised.* San Antonio, TX: Psychological Corporation.

Wegner, D. M. (1994). Ironic processes of mental control. *Psychological Bulletin, 101,* 34–52.

Weinrott, M., & Saylor, M. (1991). Self-report of crimes committed by sex offenders. *Journal of Interpersonal Violence, 6*(3), 286–300.

Weisburd, D., Petrosino, A., & Mason, G. (1993). Design sensitivity in criminal justice experiments. In M. Tonry (Ed.), *Crime and justice: A review of research* (vol. 17, pp. 337–378). Chicago: Chicago University Press.

Wexler, H., & Love, C. (1994). Therapeutic communities in prison. In F.

Tims, G. DeLeon, & N Jainchill (Eds.), *Therapeutic community: Advances in research and application* (pp. 181–208). (NIDA Monograph No. 144, NIH Publication No. 94-3633). Rockville, MD: National Institute on Drug Abuse.

White, J. L., Moffitt, T. E., Caspi, A., Bartusch, D., Needles, D., & Stouthamer-Loeber, M. (1994). Measuring impulsivity and examining its relationship to delinquency. *Journal of Abnormal Psychology, 103,* 192–205.

Wickramasekera, I. (1976). Aversive behavior rehearsal for sexual exhibitionism. *Behavior Therapy, 7*(2), 167–176.

Widon, C. S. (1995, March). V*ictims of childhood sexual abuse—Later criminal consequences. Research in brief.* Washington, DC: U.S. Department of Justice.

Wiener, R. L., Wiener, A. T., & Grisso, T. (1989). Empathy and biased assimilation of testimonies in cases of alleged rape. *Law and Human Behavior, 13,* 343–355.

Williams, S. M. (1995, August). *Review of sexual assaults and forcible confinements.* Internal publication.

Willis, V. (1980, July). Design considerations for mental health facilities. *Hospital and Community Psychiatry, 31*(7), 483–490.

Wills, T. A. (1981). Downward comparison principles in social psychology. *Psychological Bulletin, 90,* 245–271.

Wilson, D. G. (1985). *Persistent felony offenders in Kentucky: A profile in the institutional population.* Louisville: Kentucky Criminal Justice Statistical Analysis Center.

Wilson, G. D., & Lang, R. J. (1981). Sex differences in sexual fantasy patterns. *Journal of Personality and Treatment, 7,* 317–335.

Winner, K. (1996). *Divorced from justice: The abuse of women and children by divorce lawyers and judges.* New York: ReganBooks.

Wolf, S. C., Conte, J. R., & Engel-Meinig, M. (1988). Assessment and treatment of sex offenders in a community setting. In L. E. A. Walker (Ed.), *Handbook on sexual abuse of children* (pp. 365–383). New York: Springer.

Wolfe, J., & Baker, V. (1980). Characteristics of imprisoned rapists and circumstances of the rape. In C. Warner (Ed.), *Rape and sexual assault* (pp. 265–278). Rockville, MD: Aspen Systems.

Wong, S. (1984). *The criminal and institutional behaviors of psychopaths.* (User Report No. 1984-87). Ottawa: Ministry of the Solicitor General of Canada.

Wurtele, S., Marrs, S., & Miller-Perrin, C. (1987). Practice makes perfect? The role of participant modeling in sexual abuse prevention programs. *Journal of Consulting and Clinical Psychology, 55*(4), 599–602.

Yablonsky, L. (1969). *Synanon: The tunnel back.* Baltimore: Pelican Books.

Yalom, I. D. (1985). *The theory and practice of group psychotherapy* (3rd. ed.). New York: Basic Books.

Yochelson, S., & Samenow, S. (1977). *The criminal personality, Vol. 1: A profile for change.* New York: Jason Aronson.

Yokley, J. (1996, March). *The development of abuse in youth sex offenders: A conceptual model with treatment implications.* Twelfth Annual Conference of the National Adolescent Perpetrator Network, Minneapolis.

Yokley, J., & Laraway, C. (1996, November). *The use of therapeutic community learning experiences in the treatment of youth sex offenders: An outpatient clinical trial.* Fifteenth Annual Research and Treatment Conference of the Association for the Treatment of Sexual Abusers, Chicago.

Yokley, J., Laraway, C., & Clough, A. (1997, November). *Behavior therapy and criminal justice: The controversy over boot camp treatments.* Thirty-first Annual Convention of the Association for the Advancement of Behavior Therapy, Miami Beach, FL.

Zagar, R., Arbit, J., Hughes, J., Busell, R., & Busch, K. (1989). Developmental and disruptive behavior disorders among delinquents. *Journal of the American Academy of Child and Adolescent Psychiatry, 28*(3), 437–440.

Zahn-Waxler, C., & Radke-Yarrow, M. (1990). The origins of empathic concern. *Motivation and Emotion, 14,* 107–130.

Zametkin, A. J., Liebenauer, L. L., Fitzgerald, G. A., & King, A. C. (1993). Metabolism in teenagers with attention-deficit hyperactivity disorder. *Archives of General Psychiatry, 50*(5), 333–340.

Zametkin, A. J., Nordahl, T. E., Gross, M., & King, A. C. (1990). Metabolism in adults with hyperactivity with child-hood onset. *New England Journal of Medicine, 323*(20), 1361–1366.

Zavolta, H., & Rogoff, S. (1990). An overview of the vocational rehabilitation process in a long-term drug rehabilitation program [Special issue]. *Journal of Applied Rehabilitation Counseling, 21*(3), 40–44.

Zehr, H. (1990). *Changes lenses.* Scottsdale, AZ: Herald Press.

Zelin, M. L. Bernstein, S. B., Heijin, C., Jampel, R. M., Myerson, P. G., Adler, G., Buie, D. H., & Rizzuto, A. M. (1983). The Sustaining Fantasy Questionnaire: Measurement of sustaining functions of fantasies in psychiatric inpatients. *Journal of Personality Assessment, 47,* 427–439.

Zorza, J. (1996). Protecting the children in custody disputes when one parent abuses the other. *Clearinghouse Review, 29,* 1113–1127.

Zorza, J. (1996). Retaliatory litigation. In S. Swihart (Ed.), *Florida domestic violence law* (pp. 22-1–2-3). Tallahassee: Florida Bar Association.

Zorza, J. (1997, June/July). Domestic violence seldom considered in psychologists' child custody recommendations. *Domestic Violence Report, 2*(5), 65

Zorza, J. (1998, December/January). Our clients may affect us: Vicarious traumatization. *Domestic Violence Report, 3*(2), 21.

Zuckerman, M. (1979). Attribution of success and failure revisited, or the motivational bias is alive and well in attribution theory. *Journal of Personality, 47,* 245–287.

Appendix B

Table of Figures and Tables

Appendix C

Table of Cases

Index

[References are to pages.]

[References are to pages.]

[References are to pages.]

[References are to pages.]

[References are to pages.]

[References are to pages.]

[References are to pages.]

[References are to pages.]